# The Human Factor

# The Human Factor

## *The Demography of the Roman Province of Hispania Citerior/Tarraconensis*

ALEJANDRO G. SINNER
CÈSAR CARRERAS
PIETER HOUTEN

OXFORD
UNIVERSITY PRESS

OXFORD
UNIVERSITY PRESS

Great Clarendon Street, Oxford, OX2 6DP,
United Kingdom

Oxford University Press is a department of the University of Oxford.
It furthers the University's objective of excellence in research, scholarship,
and education by publishing worldwide. Oxford is a registered trade mark of
Oxford University Press in the UK and in certain other countries



Published in the United States of America by Oxford University Press
198 Madison Avenue, New York, NY 10016, United States of America

British Library Cataloguing in Publication Data
Data available

Library of Congress Control Number: 2023944716

ISBN 9780192848598

DOI: 10.1093/9780191943881.001.0001

Printed and bound by
CPI Group (UK) Ltd, Croydon, CR0 4YY

# Contents

# List of Illustrations

# List of Tables

# 1
# Introduction

In recent years, demography in antiquity has become a frequent subject of consideration among scholars conducting research on the economy of the Graeco-Roman world. Indeed, it is a fundamental question for anyone studying agricultural or industrial production as well as trade, urbanization, and settlement patterns. However, all those who work in this field agree about the inherent uncertainty of numbers when calculating large-scale demographic estimates such as the overall population of the Roman Empire in the mid-second century CE, which nowadays is considered to have been between 55 and 75 million inhabitants (Bowman and Wilson, 2011: 2).

In the past, such a wide range made ancient demographic estimates appear unreliable. However, recent works have searched for more accurate data in the field of archaeology since it provides physical evidence even though this is normally fragmentary in nature. Remains of cities, settlements, houses, public buildings, and cemeteries have provided a basic body of archaeological material that can be used to construct population estimates. Nevertheless, there can be no straightforward demographic calculations on the basis of archaeological structures, and complex methodologies need to be applied in order to employ such data in a suitable way that allows for valid demographic discussion. Furthermore, archaeological data are still only one part of the evidence available for ancient populations, and they can be complemented, in some cases, with literary sources and other written documentation (e.g. papyri, epigraphy).

Most of the recent ancient demographic studies can trace their roots to the work carried out to estimate the population of Egypt, where local census records on papyri were compared with archaeological and literary sources (Bagnall and Frier, 1994; Scheidel, 1996). However, Egypt is a somewhat special Roman province, shaped by peculiar population dynamics, as the population distribution was concentrated along the Nile and around a few oases with suitable conditions for agricultural production. In contrast, records for the desert regions reflect a very low population density. Due to the province's specific characteristics, the demography of Roman Egypt does not appear to be a model that can be extrapolated to other provinces, but it provides useful insights about life expectancy, gender, and urban populations. For instance, the average population densities for the Roman provinces in the *Cambridge Economic History* are all below 50 inhabitants per km$^2$, except the case of Egypt, which reports between 167 and 200 inhabitants per km$^2$ (Scheidel et al., 2007).

Traditional demographic studies have analysed the Roman Empire using a large-scale approach, considering provinces or large cities as basic units (Corvisier and Suder, 2000). Therefore, population estimates could vary according to calculation methods or datasets that could affect the results when applied to the Empire as a whole. Contemporary scholars believe that this so-called 'shotgun approach' conveys a general view of ancient demography and provides some basic trends (Hansen, 2006), although datasets are always prone to error when they are analysed at a smaller scale. The recent work by Hanson (2016) adopts this 'big data' approach, which, of course, provides interesting demographic pictures, but also reveals its weakness at the provincial and especially regional and local levels. Without rejecting such a holistic method, precise studies, targeting specific provinces and regions, with all their social and cultural specifics, are required to generate solid demographic estimates that can later be compared with other areas and historical periods.

At the provincial and regional level, apart from the research on Roman Egypt (Bagnall and Frier, 1994), other demographic studies have focused on Rome, Pompeii, and Italy (Morley, 1996; Storey, 1997; De Ligt, 2012; Flohr, 2017). Italy, as one of the most urbanized areas, and Rome, as the largest city in antiquity, deserve such attention but they are still quite unique case studies when compared with what we see in other regions of the Empire. Besides, ancient sources and fieldwork supply high quality data for demographic research on Roman Italy that does not exist, or not yet, elsewhere.

The pioneering demographic study on Roman Italy by Hin (2013) is the most suitable model to follow in the study of the western Roman provinces, since it combines the use of literary sources together with urban, architectural, and archaeological evidence and survey data. One of Hin's main contributions is the dynamic approach to population changes over time and in relation to historical events. That is why regional and provincial studies on population are significant; they can detect how the Roman conquest, for example, affected regular local demographic growth and urbanism. In order to do so, however, detailed knowledge of the previous Iron Age populations is a key element to understand the process of conquest and the subsequent acculturation and integration in the frameworks of Empire (i.e. adaptive evolution).

## 1.1 Why Hispania Citerior/Tarraconensis

The increasing number of demographic studies of the Roman world and the need for provincial and regional studies, are only two of the many reasons why a book specifically devoted to the demography of Hispania Citerior (Tarraconensis after 27 BCE) is necessary.

In the late third century BCE, the Romans arrived in a territory occupied by complex societies—sometimes defined as proto-states—such as those of the

Iberians, Vacceans, Vettones, and Celtiberians, among other native groups, together with some Greek and Phoenician colonies. These peoples were characterized by considerable cultural, ethnic, and social diversity. Such diversity is recorded in the sources by ancient Greek and Roman historians and geographers, as well as by a rich epigraphic corpus of pre-Roman inscriptions, of which over 3,000 are preserved. No fewer than four writing systems—in addition to Phoenician, Greek, and Latin—were used between the fifth century BCE and the first century CE to write the local languages of the Iberian peninsula (Sinner and Velaza, 2018; 2019 with bibliography). The gradual conquest of Iberia resulted in one of the longest and most complex occupation processes known in the Roman world. This process took place over two centuries and included the arrival of newcomers from Italy and elsewhere.

With such a complex political, social, and cultural panorama, the analysis of the population of the largest province of the Hispaniae is a conundrum that deserves attention for several reasons. The classical sources are not very explicit about the inhabitants of the peninsula and, in many cases, only vaguely describe the geographical distribution of the different *civitates* or groups, as well as the location of some of its main urban or proto-urban centres. References to population numbers, life expectancy, pathologies, and other fundamental demographic characteristics of the population are almost non-existent for Hispania Citerior/Tarraconensis in the sources, defining a qualitative image of the ethnic location of populations than a quantitative one of their number or of their most outstanding characteristics. Another issue that has prevented in-depth demographic study of the Iberian peninsula is the fact that different cultures and periods have historically been studied in isolation, without any comparison between them or of their population dynamics being made (Gracia Alonso et al., 1996). This last point alone calls for a study that uses a different and more integrated approach.

Making demographic calculations of Iron Age populations presents even greater difficulties than in the case of the Roman world. One of the main problems is that there are no censuses. Moreover, Graeco-Roman authors did not manifest particular interest in evaluating these groups in demographic terms, only estimating casualties during battles and conflicts, which alone is insufficient to carry out credible demographic calculations. In the archaeological studies conducted to date, estimates of population size include wide variability margins. The Iberian peninsula, however, thanks to a strong historic tradition of academics interested in the study of the Iron Age, is a good case study to define and test methodologies that allow diachronic comparisons between these two periods and the cultures that characterize them. Additionally, the introduction of non-intrusive/destructive methods of archaeological exploration—such as ground penetrating radar, LIDAR, and magnetometry to name a few, fundamental in providing reliable images of settlement location and size without the need to undertake large excavations—is rapidly increasing the quantity and quality of data available for this period as well as for the Roman one. Therefore, an up-to-date, state-of-the-art compilation and interpretation of all these new datasets is much needed (see Appendices I–III for data; discussion in Chapters 4 and 5).

If we focus now on the Roman period, over two decades ago, one of us undertook an initial study on the demography of Hispania (Carreras, 1996), with the aim of calculating the approximate total population of the Iberian peninsula during the Early Empire. As happens in many Roman provinces, the Hispaniae have not provided us with either censuses (Kron, 2005; 2017) or ancient texts from which population numbers can be inferred (Hin, 2013). Without these resources, knowledge of ancient demography in the Iberian peninsula has to be investigated using alternative documentary sources to complete this fragmentary picture. Analysing the abundant archaeological evidence is therefore core to reconstructing the demography of the period. When this examination of the demography of Roman Spain was started (Carreras, 1996), the study enabled differences in regional distribution, both urban and rural, based on city dimensions and field surveys, to be observed. However, some of those dimensions and surveys have already been superseded by recent works (Carreras, 2014; Houten, 2021), and they continue to experience constant change, making necessary a volume that can update and interpret them.

Since the 1990s, some published estimates of population in Hispania have defined values between 7 and 9 million inhabitants, with an increase from the Republican period to the mid-second century CE, and a later decrease in the Late Roman period (Frier, 2000: 814, table 6; Scheidel, 2007). However, these values are not supported by an in-depth analysis of archaeological and/or historical evidence, and provide densities of 12 to 15 inhabitants per km$^2$, which are not even recorded in fifteenth-century censuses (*fuegos, fogatges*) (Iglesias, 1979; 1981). Therefore, it is necessary to critically revise these estimates and provide new ones that are supported with a robust interdisciplinary analysis of the existing historical, anthropological, and archaeological data available.

In the last couple of decades, complementary information has been obtained on epigraphic grounds, allowing us to slowly improve our comprehension of these complex demographic materials. One of the pioneering works was that of García Merino (1976), who began a study of the population of the *conventus* Cluniensis (central northern Spain) based on its epigraphy, including more than 410 individual records. Although the epigraphic data are partial and present numerous biases (Hopkins, 1966: 246–7; MacMullen, 1982: 239–40; Saller and Shaw, 1984: 130; Shaw, 1991: 33–41; Morris, 1992: 157–66; Parkin, 1992: 7–19; see also Chapter 2), they can provide meaningful qualitative information about population characteristics. Nowadays, there is a large number of inscriptions from Hispania Tarraconensis that can be employed to generate statistics about life expectancy, age of death, and other social patterns. A recent work by Alonso (2018) illustrates the potential of the material when treated in a suitably critical way and has provided new valuable information for studying the demography of

Hispania. Similarly, thanks to the excellent work done by the LatinNow project, the epigraphic corpus available for the province under study has increased and now numbers 18,500 inscriptions (Beltrán, 2023: 39). The introduction of this large body of newly complied epigraphic data as a qualitative proxy combined with other categories of information, such as anthropological studies, and making it easily comparable with data from other nearby provinces, is also a strong argument for the value of a study focusing on the demography of Hispania Citerior/Tarraconensis.

Lastly, the increase in mitochondrial DNA (mtDNA) and genomic studies and biochemical methods over the past decade has led to significant advancements in our understanding of ancient populations. Recent studies, such as those conducted in Rome by Killgrove and Montgomery (2016), have demonstrated the potential for large-scale population data collection, as well as the ability to identify family relationships, phenotype, ancestry, and pathologies. The palaeogenomics data available for Hispania Citerior/Tarraconensis are relatively modest, but provide valuable information—although from very few case studies. On the other hand, substantial data from the Bronze and Iron Ages periods exist from this region, allowing for diachronic comparison of the material over time. Also important, there are genomic data for Etruscan populations (Posth et al., 2021) and Iron Age groups near Rome in Italy. A study compiling and examining the genetic evidence available in Hispania from the Iron Age to the Late Roman period and highlighting the critical milestones that must be achieved to gain a comprehensive understanding of the genetic history of Hispania is certainly needed.

In sum, this volume is the first study to compile the new epigraphic, archaeological, and genetic data, and study them paying attention to the cultural and social diversity of the territory under investigation. The diachronic integration and comparison of two periods that are otherwise studied in isolation has never been attempted either, resulting in a volume that provides a deeper understanding of forms of historical and archaeological demographic analysis over time (population characteristics, numbers, and movements). It also succeeds in evaluating their explanatory potential in order to comprehend and interpret the processes of cultural, economic, and social change that individuals and groups made to the developments associated with the conquest and the subsequent colonial process. Engaging in constructive dialogues and sharing and integrating datasets, geneticists, archaeologists, historians and anthropologists can build a more complete picture of the ancient populations of Hispania and their demographics. This integrated approach is a cornerstone of this book.

The volume provides novel and more accurate methodologies to estimate population numbers, and offers insight into the rich, newly compiled datasets that exist for this province but which have received scant, if any, scholarly attention to date, especially in English-language publications. It also sheds new light on how settlement patterns, urbanism, and urbanization rates developed and changed over time. The fulfilment of the aforementioned goals, together with a discussion of a large number of case studies of diverse demographic aspects and from different perspectives covering most—if not all—the territories that once comprised Hispania Citerior/Tarraconensis, has resulted in a book with strong argumentative and methodological chapters examining the demographic patterns and characteristic of this Roman province.

By integrating different periods instead of treating them in isolation, the book avoids the perspective of a history of a province differentiated in two stages separated by the Cantabrian Wars: a first phase—Hispania Citerior—represented by the two last centuries of the Republic, in which cultural and demographic change is viewed as a result of a necessary adaptation to the violence of the conquest; followed by a second phase—Hispania Tarraconensis—of stability in which the Roman social and administrative model, based on a more or less widespread urbanization process, would experience only minor readjustments until the so-called third-century crisis. In estimating population numbers and reconstructing settlement patterns from the Late Iron Age period down to the Late Roman one—urban and rural—as a core objective and an innovative aspect of this volume (Chapters 4–6), we demonstrate the falsity of such polarized, rigid, and generic interpretations for the evolution of the province and its inhabitants.

The diachronic approach, however, raises some terminological and spatial/geographical issues that must be addressed. First, the territories that once comprised Hispania Citerior/Tarraconensis were never identical, although roughly similar in extension and therefore comparable (see Fig. 1.1) to those populated by the different ethnic Iron Age groups discussed in this book. Because we are imposing a later administrative structure onto a previous system, to a certain extent, we must be flexible with boundaries, avoiding excluding core settlements that may be key to the organization and understanding of settlement patterns—and their hierarchies—of some Iron Age groups, which could be excluded otherwise if a strict boundary is employed. Second, during the Roman period, these territories—now a province—changed name on several occasions, being known as Hispania Citerior since 197 BCE, Hispania Tarraconensis after 27 BCE, and were finally divided in three—Tarraconensis, Carthaginensis, and Gallaecia—by the emperor Diocletian in 298 CE. On the other hand, the epigraphic record shows inscriptions of *flamines* (and others) referring to P(rouincia) H(ispania) C(iterior) up to the third century CE. Thereafter P(rouincia) H(ispania) TARR(aconensis) becomes more common, showing that epigraphic mentions to Citerior did last for a long time. For clarity and with the aim to simplify this terminological issue, in this book we will use the term Citerior when the discussion is focused on the period before 27 BCE and we will change to Tarraconensis after that date and for all the Imperial period. Where the discussion is more general and may include both periods, we will employ Hispania Citerior/Tarraconensis.

The authors' wish is that a wide range of readers are able to benefit from and engage with the chapters in this volume. While some chapters may have a strong methodological component that requires more specialized knowledge, all

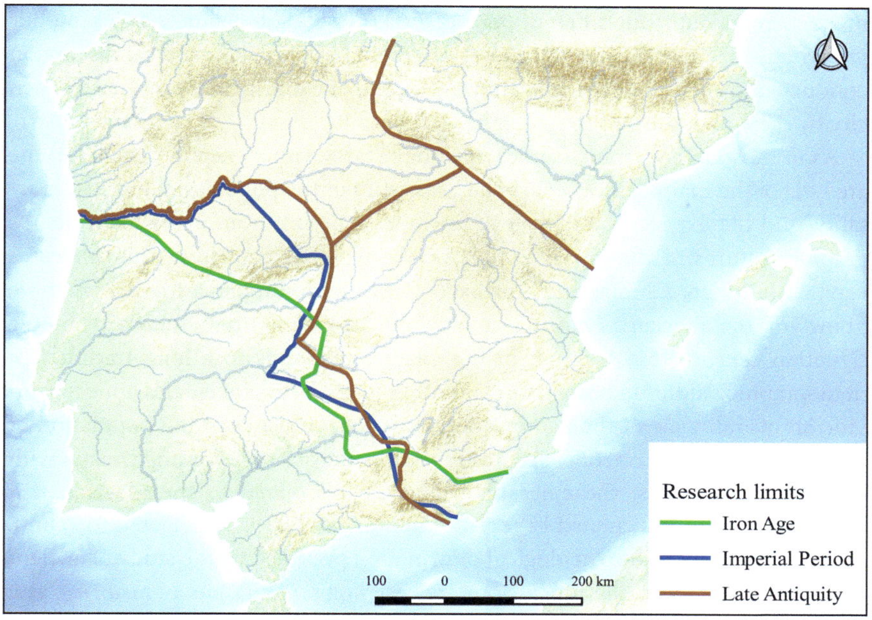


**Fig. 1.1** Research limits to the south for the Iron Age, imperial period, and late antiquity

chapters include sections discussing and interpreting the data. All discussions aim to be accessible to a general scholarly audience but also to advanced undergraduate and graduate students. In terms of academic disciplines, the contents in this volume straddle the fields of archaeology, anthropology, demography, classical studies, ancient history, and philology. We hope that advanced students as well as academics in these areas—and many others—will find the contents in this book interesting and stimulating, since a rich array of archaeological, epigraphic, architectonic and, to a much lesser extent, osteological and genetic evidence is presented and discussed for the first time.

## 1.2 Book Structure and Contents

With these historical, methodological, and theoretical frameworks in mind, the authors have put together a volume comprising seven main chapters in addition to this introduction (Chapter 1) and a concluding chapter that draws the main ideas, results and limitations together (Chapter 9). These chapters, sometimes individually, but also functioning as part of a larger block (especially Chapters 3–6), aim to systematically examine core and interconnected aspects of the demography of the territory under study over time. Some of the most important cities of the province (e.g. Tarraco, Carthago Nova, Clunia, etc.) are discussed in most chapters but from different perspectives (population characteristics, mobility, urbanism, etc.). The idea is to integrate them in the specific topical discussion conducted in each chapter while building a complete diachronic overview of each city by the end of the book.

As in most demographic studies, the book starts with a chapter devoted to the analysis of the main demographic characteristics of the population: fertility, mortality, and life expectancy. Chapter 2 includes a description of the main demographic features of the province based on epigraphic data from the *conventus* capitals (Tarraco, Clunia, and Carthago Nova) and compares it with what we know for the Iberian peninsula as a whole and with the evidence from the Egyptian census. The structure of the chapter responds to a long tradition of demographic studies in both Spain and other Roman provinces, and aims to provide an overall view of the composition and characteristics of the population of Hispania Citerior/Tarraconensis. To minimize the issue of working mostly with funerary inscriptions, the epigraphic data are compared to the ideal ancient demographic models created in recent years (Séguy, 2019; Verhagen, 2019) and, when possible, with the osteological information provided by the study of ancient cemeteries. Therefore, the conclusions are based on several types of historical and archaeological evidence and do not rely merely on epigraphic grounds. As concerns fertility, the use of selected case studies together with comparisons and anthropological models has provided us with suitable data to undertake this study.

Most demographic studies when used as a proxy for economic analysis require populations to be quantified and described as numerical estimates that evolve over the course of time. Therefore, a focus of this book has been to transform the qualitative data from different sources into robust quantitative data. To do so, we first undertake a reflection on the existing methodologies employed to quantify ancient populations (Chapter 3). Later, in Chapters 4–6, a rural and urban diachronic study of the population numbers of the province and its urbanization takes place. To allow for credible comparisons between periods, three large territories are distinguished and compared over time (Mediterranean coast, inland Mesetas, and the Atlantic-Cantabric regions). As a result, a time series of population estimates and urbanization rates for the Late Iron Age (Chapter 4) and Early Empire (Chapter 5) are obtained and debated.

As discussed earlier, if the raw data for population estimates in Hispania and elsewhere are undergoing constant amendment, methods of calculation should always be under discussion and in constant evolution. Population studies in archaeology are based on several methodological approaches, such as the study of architectural remains and cemeteries to reconstruct the populations numbers of past societies and their evolution over time. Chapter 3 is a methodological chapter that discusses in detail all the different methods, formulae, and variables that have been used in the past to carry out this type of calculation in the rural and urban areas, and explores their limitations and possibilities.

Many methods have been applied to urban settlements in which the length of the perimeter wall is recorded together with suburban areas, or where public buildings such as amphitheatres or circus are well defined (Hanson, 2016). In fact, city wall perimeters seem to be the most popular calculation method despite potential errors, as Wilson (2011: 170) has pointed out: 'the method remains the least bad one available, and it is the *only* method for which there exist sufficiently abundant data for large numbers of cities'.

Nevertheless, in Chapter 3 an attempt is made to follow a bottom-up approach discussing the concept of 'living space' as the minimum needed space for a single person in a dwelling, together with the number of residential houses and their average area and the standard number of members in a Roman family (Sinner and Carreras, 2019). All those single values allow us to differentiate the residential and public areas of both Iron Age and Roman centres, and their potential population. The chapter shows how a range of densities per hectare can be determined at each type of site and for each region, which permits a straightforward calculation based on urban extent over time according to diverse categories. Iron Age scholars in France have used such methods of calculation during recent decades (Py, 1996; Isoardi, 2012) when analysing Iron Age *oppida* with relatively small public areas and large residential units. They have also realized that individual or family living space can vary from site to site and in different regions, perhaps as a result of obvious elements such as climate, culture, or living standards. Therefore, a more regional approach to the calculation of population densities may model the reality of antiquity in a more suitable way.

When the ancient sources remain silent, the only way to calculate ancient rural densities is derived from archaeological field surveys and these are therefore also discussed in Chapter 3—and applied to Chapters 5 and 6—since they record scatters of potsherds that identify either productive or residential spaces. Although the scatters of potsherds and structures may cover a considerable area, different methods can help to define a contour and the extent of ancient productive and residential structures. By applying the values of living space per person, a potential estimate of population can be calculated from any of those scatters. The chapter will discuss how studies of data from field surveys in the Iberian peninsula can provide an average value expressed in inhabited points per km$^2$, numbers that can later be converted to an average of inhabitants per km$^2$—and compared with the densities obtained from Pliny's statements about the north-west (Plin. *NH* III.4.28).

Hin (2013) provides an excellent comparison to the arguments discussed in Chapter 3, by offering field survey data obtained in Italy over the course of time, which can be placed alongside those for Hispania Citerior/Tarraconensis. At both the large-scale level and in more restricted case studies, the data from Hin's survey offer an alternative view of the rural populations, which range from 90% to 75% of the total estimates of any population study. Some initial estimates of population densities in the Roman Iberian peninsula ranged from 12 to 20 inhabitants per km$^2$ including cities (Pounds, 1973: 116), but without any archaeological support. It is difficult to accept such values if it is considered that the 1787 Floridablanca census in Spain provided a density of 20.7 inh./km$^2$ including cities. Even though some estimates of population evolution in the Iberian peninsula suggest an increase of 50% from 14 CE to 164 CE, there is no solid evidence for such claims (Frier, 2000). Therefore, Chapter 3 seeks to justify these developments and densities using archaeological and historical evidence. Past censuses of the Iberian peninsula from other historical periods, especially medieval and early modern ones, are used as a control tool to avoid extreme estimates. There are useful fourteenth- and fifteenth-century censuses from Spain that provide an interesting picture of urban and rural territories, whose values may not have differed radically from the ones in Roman times.

In Chapter 4, we lay out a thorough and systematic methodological approach to conduct population estimates based on the palaeodemographic study of each *oppidum* individually, as well as of different types of sites in terms of size, culture, and urban layout. The chapter also address the important issues we face while working in the Iron Age period, such as not knowing the total sample of cities (*oppida*) that once existed, as well as the problem of what type of *oppida* should be understood as cities/urban (or proto-urban), secondary agglomerations, or rural sites. In the case of the Early Empire, the count carried out by Pliny the Elder (*NH* III.3.7–17; IV.4.18–30; IV.35.113–18) facilitates this task, and number of cities that may have existed in Hispania Tarraconensis by the first century CE (Houten, 2021) can be inferred. Because no similar source exists for the Iron Age, in Chapter 4 a detailed list of settlements is compiled using archaeological publications (see Appendix I) and conforming the main datasets to look at population estimates, urbanization ratios, and settlement patterns. When interpreting this information, Chapter 4 shows how many features of the Late Iron Age urban population and its demographic characteristics (e.g. population numbers and settlement patterns) in Hispania were firmly established prior to the Roman arrival and deeply conditioned the demographics of the later Roman periods.

One last core aspect of the study undertaken in Chapter 4—also later applied to Chapter 5—is the employment of rank-size analysis. With this method, the chapter evaluates whether city sizes showed some kind of regularities that indicate a hierarchy that can be related with forms of territorial and/or political control. There have already been several attempts at applying this approach to the Iberian peninsula (Marzano, 2011; Carreras, 2014; Houten, 2021), but never using such a large sample of sites or looking at each Iron Age group individually, which provides a novel picture highlighting both similarities and differences between some of these groups and their systems.

If the estimation of population numbers from Iron Age archaeological remains is still very complex, almost utopic, the situation does not improve much when looking at the Roman period. With that in mind, the application of new technologies and lately geophysics in archaeology (Keay and Earl, 2011) has provided further information about the extent of ancient urban centres. These variations in size regarding past estimates are significant, and Chapters 5 and 6 present a review of urban areas of cities in the province of Hispania Citerior/Tarraconensis, together with a more dynamic and diachronic approach to urbanization changes. Even with the many limitations of the archaeological data for the later Roman period, it is feasible and very revealing to monitor relative changes over time in a specific territory. Studies conducted on Roman Italy are a good example, showing how during the middle and late Republic, the population increased, reaching a peak in the first century BCE and/or the first century CE, and declining thereafter.

Chapter 5 offers an in-depth study of the urban and rural population of Hispania Tarraconensis in the first century CE together with a comparison with other provinces of the Empire, as well as with earlier and later periods. Therefore, the chapter is always in a constant dialogue with Chapters 4 and 6 and will present the reader with a nuanced diachronic evolution of the population and urbanization in the province of Hispania Citerior/Tarraconensis over the course of time. This novel approach allows us to study demography as a continuum and not as an isolated feature characteristic of a specific historical period. This chapter aims at giving a comprehensive overview of the urban centres of the Iberian peninsula and understanding the urbanization rate in the Early Empire by looking at case studies of well-researched rural populations.

Chapter 5 also discusses the difficulty of establishing an accurate analysis of the population of Hispania Tarraconensis because the classical literary sources are not very explicit about the inhabitants of the province. The ancient sources only describe the distribution of the local *civitates* or tribes, as well as the location of the main urban or proto-urban centres. Pliny (*NH* III.18) states that there were 179 *oppida* in 293 *civitates* and 114 places that were *civitates* without an *oppidum* (dispersed *civitates*) (Houten, 2021: 94–104), but Ptolemy (II.4–6) lists only 282 *poleis*. A general qualitative picture is inferred from those descriptions, one that defines the location of ethnic groups rather than their numbers or compositions. However, the ancient sources do provide some useful evidence about population distribution in the Iberian peninsula during the Early Empire, which was not homogeneous and tended to be concentrated in specific regions.

Furthermore, Pliny (*NH* III.4.28) states that the free inhabitants of the *conventus* Bracarum numbered 285,000, while there were 240,000 in the *conventus* Asturum, and, finally, the number for the *conventus* Lucensis only reached 166,000. Taking into account those values and the extent of each *conventus*, population densities including urban and rural sites are estimated in Chapter 5. The results are significant since they are not far from the densities calculated from eighteenth-century censuses in this region (the Campoflorido census in 1717 or the so-called census of Ensenada carried out in 1752).

Chapter 5 not only helps the reader to understand the urban fabric characteristic of the Early Empire, population densities included, but it also highlights the importance of the road network and navigable rivers for the settlement and population patterns of Hispania Citerior/Tarraconensis. This network will also be central to understand how people moved in the province, a topic that is the focus of Chapter 7 (see below). However, above all, the comparison between the Iron Age and the Roman periods shows that the settlement pattern in the Early Empire can be explained in terms of the pre-existing urban framework that is known to have already been in place in the third century BCE (see Chapter 4). Furthermore, Chapter 5 also looks into the urbanism in the province. Looking at several case studies across the province clearly shows that urbanism was quite diverse, in terms of its development and population—especially in the main cities. In many cases an interesting combination of foreign and local traditions and populations is clearly detected, in others, however, foundations *ex novo* were established in areas without previous Iron Age settlement to settle Italian veterans, coming to existence as legionary camps prior to becoming permanent elements of the urban network of the province.

Methodology is also core to the chapter. After seeing that the range rule—which consists of calculating the natural logarithm of the dimensions of the cities based on the range they belong to—is difficult to standardize, a step further is taken by employing a rank-size analysis. This type of graph does not require arbitrary ranges and allows for assessment between completely different settlements systems making feasible the comparison between the Iron Age (Chapter 4) and the Roman periods.

Size does not only allow ranks and hierarchies between cities to be established, but also most scholars still use it to debate what characterizes a city. Many consider that an ancient city must have a minimum population of between 1,000 and 5,000 inhabitants (between 5 and 25 ha). According to this definition, only between 10% and 12% of the population in the Roman Empire lived in an urban settlement (Scheidel, 2007: 78; Hanson, 2016: 95). Therefore, some small agglomerations included in our urban lists do not fulfil those conditions because they measure below the cut-off point of 4 ha, as do many of the Iron Age settlement (see Appendices I and II), and should be considered as rural agglomerations. This wide variety of 'small towns' has become one of the distinctive settlement typologies present in the province of Hispania Tarraconensis (Fernández Ochoa et al., 2014; Houten, 2021), and is given a special and detailed treatment in Chapter 5 by looking at the case studies of Portus Ilicitanus, Segobriga, Aquae Querquernae (Galicia), and Iturissa.

Chapter 6 continues our diachronic journey and leads the reader into the 'crisis' or perhaps better said, evolution, of the Late Roman city in the Iberian peninsula. This has been a popular subject in recent years since some abandonments and decreases in city size can be dated earlier than expected, at least from the late second century CE (Brassous and Quevedo, 2015; Andreu, 2017). Chapter 6 offers an overview of urban change and population dynamics in this period, as well as the city–countryside relationship. These topics have again become a phenomenon of interest and deserve a full explanation, since opposing patterns can be observed in the countryside, where luxurious *villae* were built in the same period, revealing a dynamic territory in constant evolution rather than one in decline or crisis.

This chapter therefore tackles the question of whether what can be seen is an overall urban decline in the Iberian peninsula or rather a shift from urban to rural, with a change in the level of urbanization in the peninsula. One of the major challenges is to quantify the 'decline' of an urban community since it is difficult to detect expansion and contraction in urban archaeology. There are still only a few Late Roman cities whose perimeter wall or urban occupation have been calculated, and in general, they are reduced in size—although exceptions exist. However, a more complete set of Late Roman urban data is required to see regional variations and general trends, making it impossible to employ the same rigorous calculations to estimate population numbers and urbanization rates by area as used in Chapters 4 and 5, nor can we apply the rank-size analysis to our sample. However, thanks to the use of detailed archaeological reports of well-researched case studies such as Tarraco, Clunia, or Valentia, Chapter 6 provides valuable insights into the development of the population and urbanism of the late antique city.

As Chapters 4–6 show, the population in the province of Hispania Citerior/Tarraconensis was never stable nor did it show a natural constant growth, but the settlement patterns established over time do seem to reflect—to a certain extent—the existing transportation network (roads, rivers, and sea) available at the time. This hypothesis is explored in Chapter 7, where movement within the province and from outside is investigated over time (conquest, colonization, and invasion) as well as what infrastructure existed to facilitate those movements and how it conditioned them. Population movement, whether seasonal, temporal, or permanent, has always been an economic strategy in the Iberian peninsula that kept an equilibrium in the province and between territories.

For a long time, the impression that the Roman conquest of Hispania involved a substantial transfer of Italic people to this territory has been widely, but incorrectly, accepted (Wilson, 1966: 9–12; Gabba, 1973; Marín Díaz, 1986; 1988: 47–109; Brunt, 1971). Perhaps the idea behind such mass Italian migration comes from an imperialist concept of colonization comparable to other colonialist periods in which Spain and Portugal were the main actors. Chapter 7 indicates the opposite by a thorough examination of the archaeological evidence. As some scholars have already started to point out (Le Roux, 1995; Cadiou, 2008: 627–61), urban sites were always close to areas occupied by indigenous *oppida*, and population densities remained close to those in the Iron Age period. Some early foundations of urban settlements have only produced graffiti written in epichoric alphabets, or at least mainly such written texts, which confirms that most of the population was of local origin (Pera, 2005; Torra, 2009; Sinner and Ferrer, 2016; 2018). It is true that there must have been some degree of Italic immigration in Hispania Citerior (Díaz Ariño, 2008; Orejas and Beltrán, 2010; Stefanile, 2017), but this was related to particular places, such as mining districts and major harbours, and periods, and never took place in great numbers. Following Haley's study on the immigration to the Hispanic provinces (1991) during the Empire, which revealed that immigrants represented fewer than 5% of the total population attested in the epigraphic record, Chapter 7 discusses how a large degree of long-distance mobility has traditionally been inferred when, in reality, what can be seen is a limited amount of permanent mobility that sustained a high degree of connectivity (Sinner, 2024). If Chapter 7 shows that large migratory fluxes did not seem to take place in the province under study, it also shows that what did change over time is the origin—mainly Italy, Gaul, and Africa—and the reasons—commercial, military, administrative, etc.—that triggered those migrants' movements. In any case, all the many and diverse types of mobility discussed in the chapter were only possible thanks to the existence of an efficient transportation network. How this infrastructure evolved over time is fundamental to consider and appreciate how population movements and the supply of cities took place and at what cost.

The last chapter of the book (Chapter 8) is an invited contribution that aims to show how new methods and datasets such as ancient DNA (aDNA) and palaeoanthropological studies will play a key role in the study of ancient demography in the future. Although those studies are well established in other European countries, they are still quite young in Spain and Portugal. Therefore, while a few remarkable case studies exist, there are not enough data to generate an overall well-documented picture for the whole province over time. It is expected that these fields will develop in the near future providing alternative data that may challenge and/or complement our present views.

Chapter 7 shows how migratory flows may have been a factor of limited significance in Hispania Citerior/Tarraconensis, but studying them can still provide important data. However, these migrants are hard to detect archaeologically, even when stable isotope analysis is applied to determine the origin of buried individuals. Chapter 8 undertakes this task by using a genetic approach. It is often difficult to separate the biological and cultural influences, but genetic studies using ancient material have shed some light on this still obscure panorama. The increase in and improvement of mtDNA and genomic studies and biochemical methods have been considerable in the last ten years, enabling us to begin to identify ancient migratory processes, as has recently been achieved for the city of Rome (Killgrove and Montgomery, 2016). The possibility of obtaining large numbers of informative positions, and even complete genomes, can provide population data, as well as details of family relationships or information about individuals (phenotype, ancestry, pathology), to understand the past and its people. Chapter 8 engages with the question of whether Iron Age genetic substrata were modified in Hispania, and whether admixture or replacement occurred, and if so, where it took place and when.

Similarly, the study of health, pathologies, and pandemics are traditionally treated as separate fields. However, areas such as the study of ancient demography, analysis of human remains, and medical history have recently started to collaborate and, in some cases, even to merge. This is crucial because understanding population shifts involves not only investigating their demography in terms of age and sex distribution, but also understanding the health and diseases of the different communities in existence. In other words, osteoarchaeological studies may provide an alternative view about general demographic characteristics of the province that so far is mostly obtained from texts and epigraphic materials (Chapter 2). Unfortunately, there are few osteoarchaeological studies of Roman populations in the Iberian peninsula, and they are based on small samples; in many cases, only specific cases of a particular pathology are reported, without extensive and integrated studies. Thus, currently, very little is known about how Iron Age and Roman populations lived and died. With the intention of filling this gap, or better said, starting the discussion, Chapter 8 provides an overview of life, health, and disease during the Iron Age and the Roman periods by integrating palaeodemographic, anthropometric, palaeopathological, and palaeodietary data from numerous burials and some necropolis in the province under study. The chapter considers funerary archaeology in order to investigate societal changes, evaluates the limitations in the available data and the current methodology, and suggests possibilities for future work.

To conclude, this book should lay the foundations and suggest future directions for this promising field of study for Hispania, as it is currently in its infancy. However, it would also be a good case study for other Roman provinces and periods. Population studies can be technical and, in many cases, require comparative and interdisciplinary approaches in order to reach a satisfactory outcome. For this reason, this book has been designed in a multidisciplinary manner, by assembling a team that includes historians, archaeologists, and anthropologists capable of creating a comprehensive volume that includes the latest cutting-edge research and methodological innovations in the study of areas as diverse as those described above. The goal is simple: to provide the first comprehensive state-of-the-art analysis of the Iron Age and Roman demography of Hispania Citerior/Tarraconensis and to compare it with other territories and provinces, especially Italy. This work seeks to advance the field by defining methodologies that will allow diachronic comparisons between different periods and cultures, comparing the demography of the previous Iron Age communities (fourth and third centuries BCE) in order to evaluate Roman immigration into the province (first century BCE to first century CE), and subsequent Imperial society and its transition into the Late Roman period (third to fourth centuries CE).

This volume promotes the understanding of many other historical, social, cultural, and economic factors that affect the Roman archaeology of the Iberian peninsula and the western Mediterranean. Demographic patterns are a key element to understand any modern or ancient society and its change over time. As Scheidel (2007) has pointed out, in the societies that preceded the Industrial Revolution, population size was the main indicator of economic growth and performance, and the distribution of people between town and country was instrumental in the negotiation of collective identities. Additionally, human mobility of all kinds mediated information and technological flows and promoted cultural change. Finally, it should be noted that any state has three elements: (1) the ability to raise revenue; (2) a monopoly of violence, through an army and police force that fight external threats, maintain internal order, and enforce policy; and (3) administrative competence, the ability to develop policy, deliver public goods, and regulate markets. Whether ancient Rome can be considered a strong state, a weak one, or a state at all, throughout most of its history is beyond the scope of this book, but these three elements were certainly present and closely related to its demographic numbers. It is therefore necessary to continue advancing in the study of this complex and fascinating field of study. This book does so for the largest province of the Hispaniae.

## 1.3 Acknowledgements

We would like to express our gratitude to those who have made this book possible with their help: of course, Assumpció Malgosa, Núria Armentano, Laura Castells, and Cristina Santos for accepting our invitation to write Chapter 8. Thanks to them, the volume includes new datasets and perspectives that will be core to the future of demographic studies. We are also grateful to them for their flexibility and for kindly engaging in a constant dialogue and exchange of ideas with the authors; to the reviewers for their detailed and thoughtful comments on earlier versions of this book, which have helped to improve significantly the final text; to the scholars, institutions, museums, and collections that have allowed the reproduction of a number of illustrations; to Philip Banks and OUP copy editor Jo North, who have ensured the linguistic correctness of the text; and Oxford University Press, in particular Cathryn Steele and Charlotte Loveridge, who have been of extraordinary assistance in producing an attractive design. This project would have never been possible without the financial support of the University of Victoria (Book Subvention Fund) and especially of the Social Science and Research Council of Canada, the University Autonomous of Barcelona, the Spanish Ministry of Science and Innovation (PID2019-104120GB-I00), and Generalitat de Catalunya, which have funded the projects Beyond Contacts: Tracing Identities and Cultural Change in the Roman West (A. G. Sinner) and The Forum of Iulia Libica (C. Carreras), in addition the ERC funded project LatinNow (no. 715626) and ANR-DFG project ATLAS (ANR-20-FRAL-009 and DFG ref. 449592738) (P. H. A. Houten). Lastly, but no less important, we must mention our families and beloved ones. Their support has been fundamental for ensuring that the book reached completion.

*The Human Factor: The Demography of the Roman Province of Hispania Citerior/Tarraconensis.* Alejandro G. Sinner, Cèsar Carreras, and Pieter Houten, Oxford University Press. 
DOI: 10.1093/9780191943881.003.0001

# 2

# Population Characteristics

## Fertility, Mortality, and Life Expectancy

The first modern demographic study of Hispania Tarraconensis was the work by García Merino (1976).[1] It was quite an innovative approach for the Iberian peninsula, which applied epigraphy as a support for analysing fertility, mortality, and migration in the *conventus iuridici* Cluniensis. This Roman *conventus* was located in the centre of the province, present-day northern Spain, in a region that was densely populated during the Iron Age and under the Early Empire (see Chapters 4 and 5). Her research included only 410 inscriptions that combined data about the gender, age of death, and origin of the deceased.

This epigraphic study revealed the lack of information on newborn deaths, a bias towards the presence of male inscriptions, as well as an irregular pattern of age at death, as ages tended to finish in I, V, X, L, or C. This abnormal distribution was also present in the epigraphy of other provinces, which was interpreted as a sign of ignorance about one's own age (Henry, 1959; Duncan-Jones, 1977). Such distortions are a good example of why many scholars are extremely critical about the use of epigraphy for the study of demography among ancient populations (Fig. 2.1).

Additionally, the treatment of this type of epigraphic data is only applicable to Roman times. While tombstones are estimated to represent approximately three-quarters of the entire available corpus of Roman inscriptions (Saller and Shaw, 1984: 124), the practice of inscribing epitaphs was not adopted by many of the pre-Roman populations of the Iberian peninsula until well after the Roman conquest (Velaza, 2017; 2018). All the above issues greatly condition the calculations and estimates that can be obtained from epitaphs by shifting the results upwards or downwards, based on various factors such as wealth, gender, age, etc. (Shaw, 1991; Saller, 1994: 35–40). The number of epigraphic monuments in the peninsula will have varied considerably during the periods studied in this chapter, being non-existent at the textual level in pre-Roman times, rare during the late Republic (second-first centuries BCE), very common under the Early Empire, and much less frequent throughout the Late Roman period (Andreu, 2009). Based on

[1] Two early works by García-Bellido (1954) and Balil (1955) were the pioneer studies in this subject in the Iberian peninsula, but García Merino's work (1976) became a model for later ones.

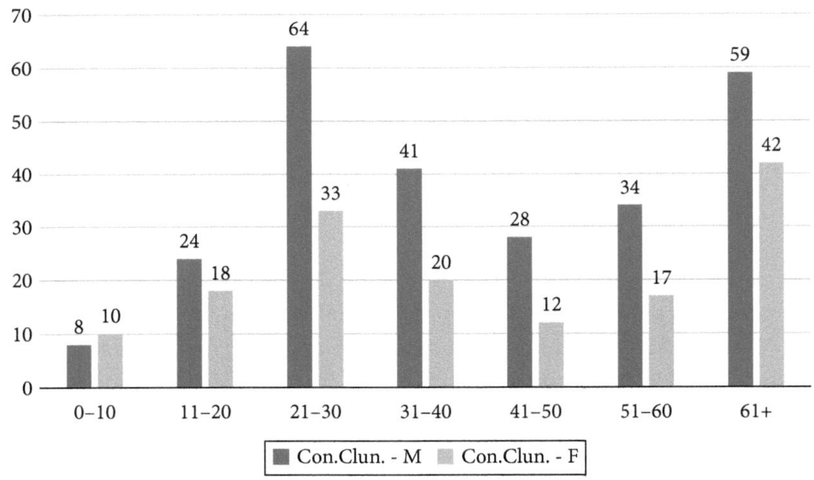


**Fig. 2.1** Age distribution from *conventus* Cluniensis (after García Merino, 1976)

all the aforementioned arguments, many scholars have insisted on the impossibility of using epitaphs to identify absolute demographic patterns for the Roman period (Hopkins, 1966: 246–7; 2017; MacMullen, 1982: 239–40; Saller and Shaw, 1984: 130; Shaw, 1991: 33–41; Morris, 1992: 157–66; Parkin, 1992: 7–19; Scheidel, 2017). However, currently, the only sources for calculating Roman populations are epigraphy, historical data (e.g. censuses, papyri archives, literary sources), archaeological (structures and environment), and palaeoanthropology (human remains) (Séguy, 2019: 24). Therefore, epigraphy is still a basic source that can shed light on general trends treated as relative data to document commemorative practices and draw tentative conclusions by comparing them with the known data from censuses and the study of human remains found in cemeteries of the same period and region, which is what it is aimed to do in this chapter.

## 2.1 Mortality and Life Expectancy

According to the Clauss-Slaby database EDCS (2016), there are at least 8,076 Roman funerary inscriptions from the Iberian peninsula, although only 3,327 of these record ages (Alonso, 2018). With an updated dataset from the LatinNow project, we have been able to extend this to 10,676 funerary inscriptions, out of a total of 29,449 inscriptions. The distribution of inscriptions (see Fig. 2.2) records the highest concentrations at Gades (569 insc.), Emerita Augusta (460), Corduba (397), and Tarraco (398). Furthermore, the map reveals a distinctive pattern for epigraphic practices, associated not only with

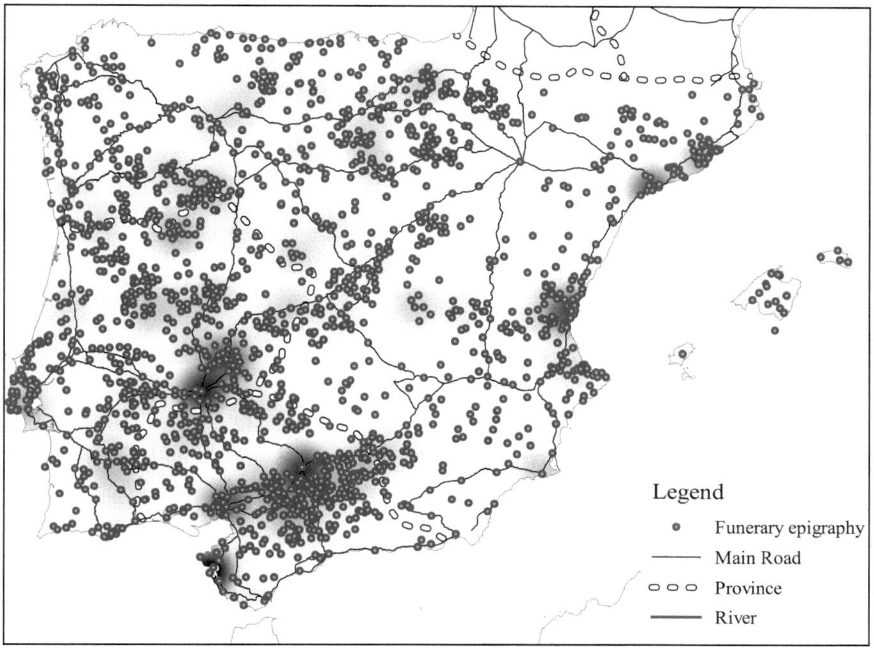


**Fig. 2.2** Distribution of funerary epigraphy on the Iberian peninsula; the darker colour indicates high concentrations

high population densities (see Chapter 5), but also with the extent to which the epigraphic funerary culture was adopted.

It is clear that Fig. 2.2 shows a lack of inscriptions and therefore of an epigraphic habit in the northern mountains (Picos de Europa and Pyrenees) and the regions inhabited by the Celtiberian tribes of the Titti, Belli, and Lusones on the Meseta (central plateau) and the Oretani and Olcades in the south-eastern part of the province. Some of these areas were less densely populated even in the Iron Age (see Chapter 4) and therefore display a lower degree of urbanization and adaptation to Roman culture in later periods. The higher concentrations indicated by the darker areas are found near the abovementioned cities and along the eastern coast.

Returning to the epigraphic data, it can be observed that the percentages of inscriptions stating the deceased's age reflect a divergence between males and females. Of the 3,327 funerary inscriptions, 57.4% were dedicated to males, whereas only 42.59% record females. It is evident that these proportions did not represent the percentage of population for the genders in the Iberian peninsula, but instead reflect a commemorative custom that focused on memorializing men.

Second, Alonso (2018) analyses the 1,933 male inscriptions that provide evidence for age in a frequency histogram (see Fig. 2.4). Apart from male life expectancy, the histogram also detects the anomaly that led to more ages finishing in 0 or 5, which clearly suggests that ages were rounded up or down (Duncan-Jones, 2010: 79–92). This abnormal distribution is less evident for young people, but it becomes clear from the age of 30 onwards, a detail that has also been detected in the city of Rome, where the epigraphic record underreports the loss of life at very young ages and vastly neglects death in old age (Fig. 2.3) (Paine and Storey, 2006: 72).

As scholars have explained, these values are not statistically reliable (Henry, 1959; Séguy, 2019: 28) because, on the one hand, they reflect an epigraphic age-rounding practice rather than real ages, and on the other, they overrepresented death at an age when it might have been less expected if life expectancy tables are considered. Fig. 2.4 illustrates the frequency of male death age in the Iberian peninsula with an evident age rounding from the 20s onwards. Below the highest peaks, there is a general bell-shaped curve with high values of age at death between the 20s and 30s. This bell-shaped curve is certainly much closer to being representative of the male life expectancy of those commemorated in the inscriptions—not the whole population—except for perinatal death, which is hardly recorded at all. It is also remarkable that some epitaphs registered ages at death that reached 90 and even 110 years. Such ages are also recorded in a myriad of literary sources and, once again, they are the exception rather than the norm, especially if we compare them with the data derived from the palaeodemographic study of necropoleis (see Fig. 2.14).

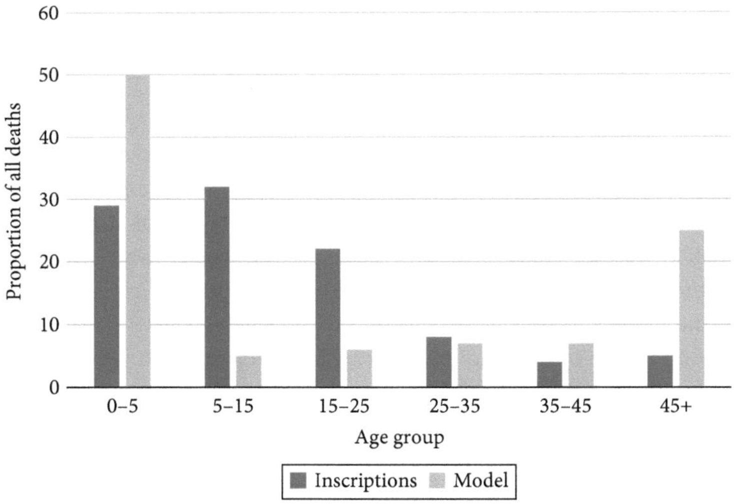


**Fig. 2.3** Age-at-death distribution in funerary inscriptions from the city of Rome and in a plausible model life table (after Paine and Storey, 2006: 72)

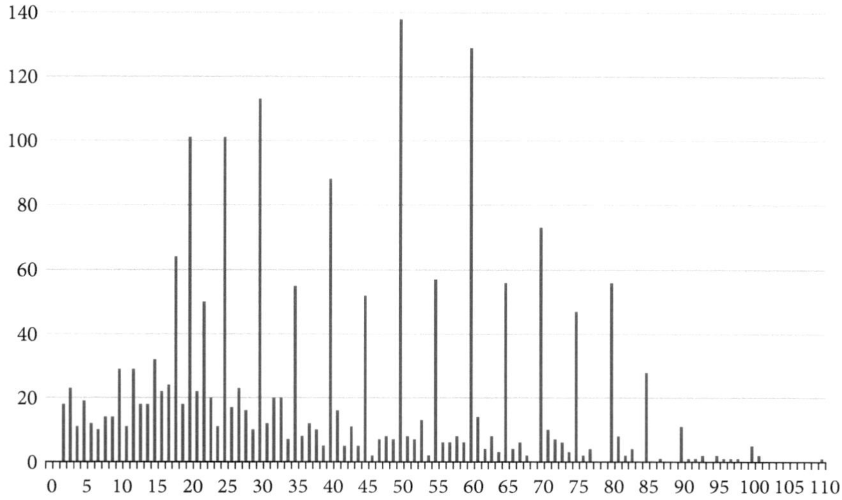


**Fig. 2.4** Frequency of male age deaths in the Iberian peninsula in the Roman period (redrawn after Alonso, 2018)

The age distribution is also irregular in the 1,488 female inscriptions recorded in the Iberian peninsula. Again, ages finishing in 0 or 5 became more common from the 20s onwards (see Fig. 2.5). The bell-shaped curve appears later with the highest rates between the ages of 15 and 30 years.

Combining the life expectancy of both genders, the main differences appear in the peak period of fertility—around 15–30 years old—when females faced the risk of dying in childbirth. After this age, the life expectancies of both genders were similar from the age of 40 onwards. Scholars agree that a value between 20 and 30 years is the life expectancy that can be calculated for the Roman Empire as a whole (Hin, 2013: 170), although the few censuses preserved for Roman Egypt (Bagnall and Frier, 1994: 103) suggest that the rate could be higher—around 32–35 years. According to this general picture, only 7% of the population reached an age that was above 70. Besides, the group of *senes* over the age of 60 largely consisted of males rather than females. The life expectancy given by the censuses as well as the low percentage of individuals that reached 60+ years also emerge in some of the osteological data from the necropoleis studied in the province (see Fig. 2.14 and Table 2.1).

According to the funerary inscriptions from the Iberian peninsula, the average life expectancy was 33.29 years for males and 32.03 for females, numbers that are close to those in the Egyptian censuses. The life expectancy graph in Fig. 2.6 summarizes the data from the 3,327 recorded ages in the Clauss-Slaby database according to gender (Alonso, 2018).

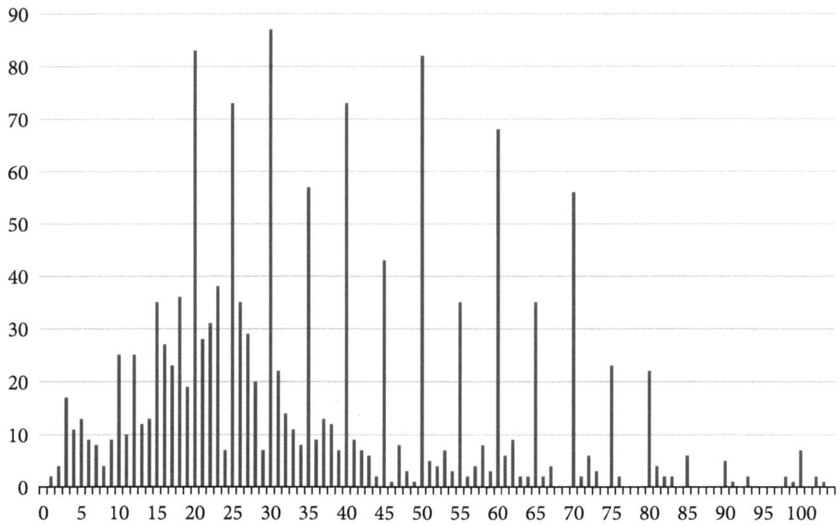


**Fig. 2.5** Frequency of female age deaths in the Iberian peninsula in the Roman period (redrawn after Alonso, 2018)

However, as mentioned above, epigraphy does not record most of the perinatal or newborn mortalities, which, according to Baxarias (2002), may have been as many as one third of the children born.

The ancient sources provide good evidence for how frequently the loss of infants occurred. In 165 CE, M. Cornelius Fronto, after losing his grandson, wrote a letter expressing his pain. Fronto's correspondence provides a good example of high infant mortality:

> Indeed, I have lost five of my children under the most wretched circumstances possible, for I lost all five one at a time, each an only child. Thus I endured this series of losses, never having a child born to me except when I had lost another. So I always lost children without any remaining as a consolation, and I sired others weighed down by fresh grief. *De Nepote Amisso* 2

The chances of survival must have been even lower when twins or triplets were born. As Hug (2014: 140) has pointed out, twin or triplet births where one or more of the babies died were probably quite common and therefore not worth recording. A similar idea can be extracted from a quote from Pliny:

> When twins are born it is rare for either the mother or for more than one of the children to live, but if twins are born that are of different sex it is even rarer that either survives. Pliny the Elder, *NH* VII.37

**Table 2.1** Demographic composition by age from nine necropoleis in Hispania Citerior/Tarraconensis

| Necropolis | Chronology | 0–12 | 13–19 | 20–40 | 41–59 | 60+ | Indet. | TOTAL |
|---|---|---|---|---|---|---|---|---|
| Sotaterra | 2nd–3rd c. CE | – | – | 10 | 3 | – | – | 13 |
| Guissona | 1st–3rd c. CE | 2 | – | 4 | 1 | – | – | 7 |
| Tarragona | 3rd–5th c. CE | 5 | – | 137 | 38 | 9 | – | 189 |
| Barcino (Vila de Madrid) | 1st–3rd c. CE | 28 | 6 | 21 | 3 | – | 21 | 79 |
| Empúries | 3rd–8th c. CE | 1 | – | 17 | 10 | – | – | 28 |
| Valentia | 2nd–1st c. BCE | 7 | 8 | 36 | 12 | – | 12 | 75 |
| Pollentia (Can Reiners) | 7th c. CE | 14 | 6 | 28 | 15 | 4 | – | 67 |
| Pintia (Valladolid)* | 5th c. BCE–2nd c. CE | 2 | 1 | 17 | 62 | – | 8 | 90 |
| A Lanzada (Galicia) | 2nd–6th c. CE | 13 | – | 43 | 17 | 4 | 8 | 85 |
| El Vergel (Ávila) | 4th c. CE | 3 | – | 5 | 3 | – | – | 11 |
| Iuliobriga (Cantabria) | 6th c. CE | 2 | – | 3 | 4 | 1 | – | 10 |
| La Magdalena III–IV (Alcalá de Henares) | 3rd–5th c. CE | 38 | 5 | 54 | 29 | 11 | 21 | 158 |
| Villa of Almenara (Valladolid) | 5th–6th c. CE | 1 | 2 | 6 | – | – | – | 9 |
| **TOTAL** | | **116** | **28** | **381** | **197** | **29** | **70** | **821** |

* This is a cremation necropolis; the remaining ones are all inhumations.

*Source*: Data from Pérez-Pérez and Lazuela, 1992; Polo-Cerdá et al., 2004; Jordana and Malgosa, 2007; Cardona, 2009; Moreda et al., 2010–11; López Costas, 2012: 111–13; Heras and Galera, 2016: figs. 16–17; Carnicero, 2017: Tabla—III; García Merino and Sánchez-Simón, 2020: fig. 4.

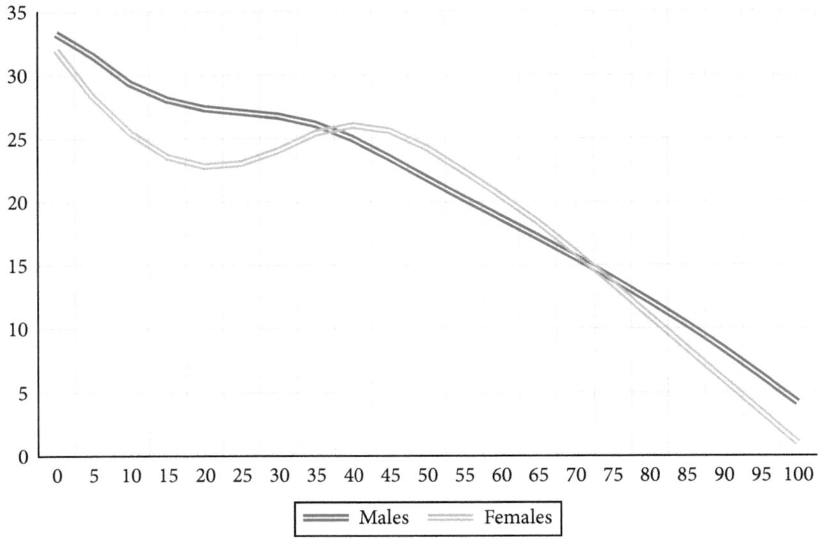


**Fig. 2.6** Life expectancy in the Iberian peninsula in the Roman period (adapted from Alonso, 2018)

Normally, perinatal deaths did not lead to any proper mourning or commemoration, and infants were buried in private as Ulpian stated:

> A child less than a year receives neither formal mourning nor marginal mourning. Ulpian, *FIRA* 2.536

Many infants lived for barely a week, while a further substantial percentage died during the first year of life. The majority were never buried in Roman cemeteries,[2] but rather under houses or in gardens, so their burial never left any epigraphic record, but was an archaeological disposal of their remains instead.

> They that complain thus allow that if a young child dies, the survivors ought to bear his loss with equanimity; that if an infant in the cradle dies, they ought not even to utter a complaint. Cicero, *Tusculan Disputations* 1.39

According to some scholars, such perinatal deaths could have reached levels of between 30% and 40% (Golden, 1988; Garnsey, 1991: 51–2), and some even

[2] Italy: at Gubio, infants less than 1 year = 1.6–2.2% of the burials; at Via Lucrezia Romana, infants less than 1 = 5.8% of the burials; at Via Aldini, infants less than 1 = 8% of the total burials; at Via Basiliano, infants less than 1 = 11% of the total burials; at Viale Serenissima, infants less than 1 = 12.5% of the total burials; at Isola Sacra (Portus), infants less than 1 = *c.*10% of the total burials (Carroll, 2011). Etruria: in Musarna no children under the age of 1 were found. France: at St-Paul-Trois-Châteaux, infant burials = 3% of the burials; at Marseille (Ste. Barbe), infant burials = 8% of the burials; at Argenton, infant burials = 26% of the burials.

calculate a loss of half the total number of children before the age of 10. The most useful dataset to evaluate these hypotheses is necropolis II at Kellis (Egypt), where 25% of the children buried were under the age of 12 months and 15% were not even born (Tocheri et al., 2005; Cope, 2008). Likewise, the data from burials in the suburbs of Rome confirm this assessment (Catalano et al., 2006). That said, we must bear in mind that there was not universal treatment of infant burial, but different regional traditions all over the Roman Empire as the evidence in Britain and other provinces suggests (Pearce, 2008; Pearce et al., 2015). In the Iberian peninsula, for example, the tradition of burying foetuses and newborn children under the floors of houses dates back to at least the Bronze Age. During the Iron Age, these burials appear both in Iberia and in the Celtic and Indo-European zones. By the second and first centuries BCE, the tradition is recorded in both rural settlements and cities and continues to be found in later domestic contexts.[3]

Among the 16,000 inscriptions from Rome and Italy recording age at death, only 1.3% were of children less than one year old (Hopkins, 1983: 225). It is clear that the epigraphic record in this respect is not a reliable source.

The study of necropoleis can shed some light on this issue of epigraphic reliability for Hispania Tarraconensis, but estimating infant mortality remains problematic. In the first place, it is clear that, in most cases, infant burials are rarely found in the cemeteries of Tarraconensis (14.13%). This reinforces the hypothesis that children were not usually buried following the same ritual or in the same spaces as adults (Table 2.1 and Fig. 2.7). On the other hand, the presence of infants in almost all the necropoleis analysed is a clear indicator that certain categories of infants did find their final resting place in cemeteries. Unfortunately, with the current data, it is impossible to explain the criteria or reasons behind this phenomenon. However, the necropolis of Vila de Madrid in Barcino and that of La Magdalena III–IV (Alcalá de Henares) are exceptions and deserve special attention. In the former, 38 infants were recorded (24%). In the latter, 28 children (35%) between the ages of 0 and 12 were documented, thus showing in both cases a pattern that differs from the rest. This is especially interesting for two reasons. First, because it provides archaeological examples from Tarraconensis where infants were frequently buried in a necropolis together with adults, enabling more realistic percentages of infant mortality to be seen. Second, in the case of Vila de Madrid, it might be noted that to date, the only example of a cemetery where infants represent a majority of the burials is that of the Mercat de Sant Antoni, also in Barcino (see section 2.3). This makes Barcino an interesting case study to support the hypothesis that practices regarding the burial of the youngest were not universal and might have varied inside the province, something that Table 2.1 also suggests.

[3] In general, they are individual burials, without accompanying grave goods. Most could reflect specific rites for stillborn and newborn infants, but they have also been interpreted as foundational, purification, or propitiatory offerings (see Pérez Ruiz, 2022: 111–13).

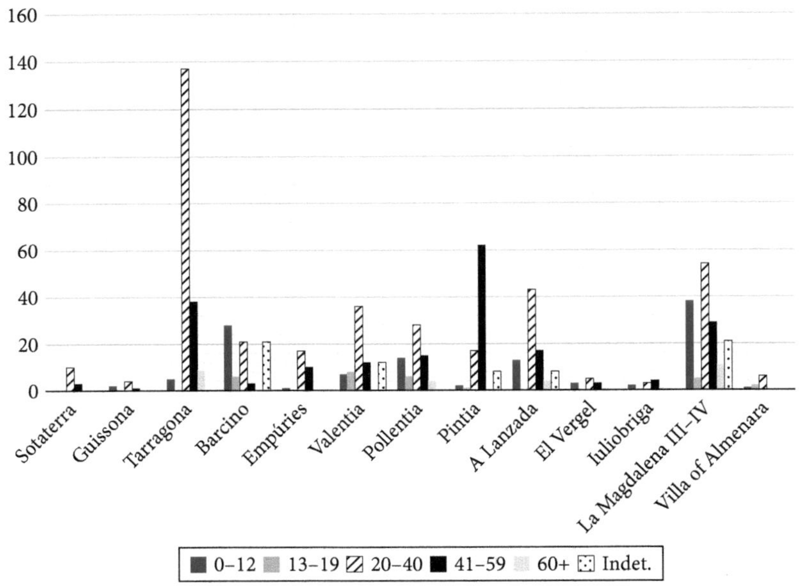


**Fig. 2.7** Demographic composition by age from the 13 necropoleis in Table 2.1

Consequently, modern life expectancy models have been used to complete these missing values from ancient censuses, inscriptions, and necropoleis (Parkin, 1992; Bagnall and Frier, 1994: 33). One of the most frequently used sets are the Coale-Demeny model life tables (Coale and Demeny, 1983), which were initially employed by the United Nations to identify trends in modern-day populations. Scholars studying populations in Graeco-Roman times (Parkin, 1992; Bagnall and Frier, 1994; Akrigg, 2019) normally applied the West model: levels 2 to 4 in the Coale-Demeny tables, which fit quite well with these partial data recorded for ancient populations. Perhaps the West model: level 3 is the table that best fits the epigraphic data from the Iberian peninsula for both genders (Alonso, 2018).[4] The main difference comparing the two graphs (Fig. 2.8) is the lower life expectancy of children in the first year of life, which is not recorded in either the epigraphic record of the Iberian peninsula or in most of the cemeteries.

The data described so far seem to reflect the situation in the three provinces in the Iberian peninsula; however, a separate study of each province reveals some minor variations.[5] Perhaps the most remarkable distinction in the epigraphic

[4] Most scholars employ different levels of the West model tables of Coale and Demeny (1983) for each gender. For instance, level 2 is more suited for female data in Roman Egypt or ancient Athens and level 4 for male populations (Akrigg, 2019: 30).

[5] The inscriptions employed for this detailed analysis come from the *CIL* database of Heidelberg (https://edh-www.adw.uni-heidelberg.de/home) consulted on 20 February 2019. The Heidelberg database is a more detailed and robust archive, and despite including fewer inscriptions it offers more reliable information.

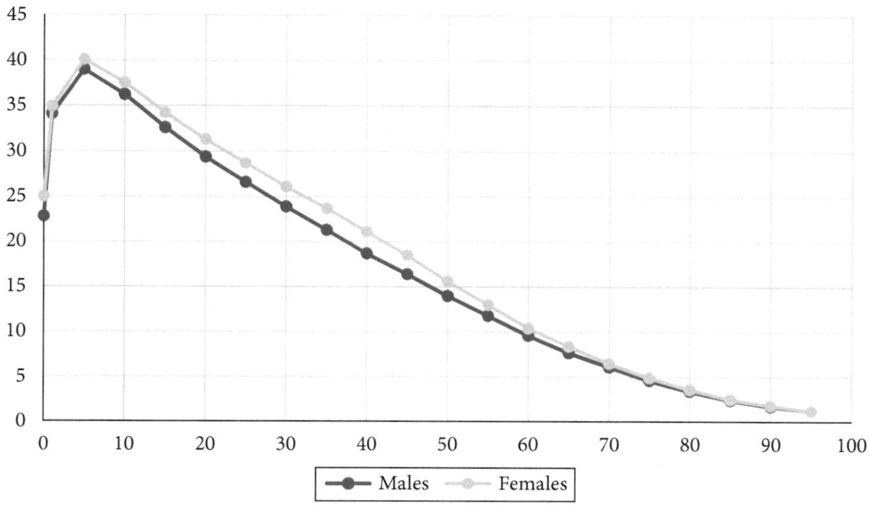


**Fig. 2.8** Life-expectancy of West model: level 3

habit is the higher number of inscriptions with ages from Hispania Tarraconensis (870 insc. including age) than the other two provinces. This may have been a consequence of the large size of the province, compared to the relatively medium size of Lusitania (433 insc.) and Baetica (681 insc.). Despite the fact that the province of Baetica registered the highest density of population during the Roman period (see Chapter 5), it has not produced the largest number of inscriptions. Therefore, the general picture observed for the Iberian peninsula based on epigraphy largely depends on the population of the province of Hispania Tarraconensis.

Returning to Fig. 2.2, we can observe the distribution of epigraphy in the province according to the LatinNow database. The map records an irregular pattern with high distributions of funerary inscriptions in the Mediterranean coastal regions, with 636 funerary inscriptions in the north-eastern region, around Tarraco and Barcino, and 652 funerary inscriptions in the east, the Valentia region. In other words, the *conventus* Tarraconensis has the highest number of inscriptions. The second highest number of inscriptions comes from the *conventus* of Carthaginensis, with a substantial number from the coastal area around Carthago Nova (150 insc.), and also a noteworthy presence can be detected in the inland region of Carpetania (322 insc.), around the cities of Complutum, Valeria, and Segobriga.

The third *conventus* as regards the number of inscriptions was Cluniensis (452 insc.), which also had a high density of urban population (see Chapter 5). In contrast, the *conventus* Caesaraugustanus in the middle Ebro valley provides a relatively low number of inscriptions (209 insc.) with the main exception of the capital Caesaraugusta. Finally, the three *conventus* in the north-west, where the Roman presence left far fewer traces, have produced a relatively low number of inscriptions: Asturum (290 insc.), Lucensis (112 insc.), and Bracarum (157 insc.). To a certain extent it seems as if the epigraphic habit reflects a key aspect of Roman culture, in other words how the provincials adopted the Roman way of commemorating their deaths.

A comparison of the three Iberian provinces shows that the gender proportion is similar in Baetica and Lusitania, whereas Hispania Tarraconensis has produced an asymmetrical number of male records. On the one hand, the evidence from the provinces of Baetica and Lusitania reveals a slight predominance of male inscriptions over female ones; in marked contrast, however, in Hispania Tarraconensis, the number of male inscriptions is double that of female ones. Such imbalance in the epigraphic practice between genders may identify also a difference in status between men and women in military districts (Haynes, 2013: 49–50). In this context, the importance of the epigraphic practice among the military and administrative personnel ascribed to the north-western district and the capital of the province, Tarraco, should be borne in mind (see Chapter 7).

After the Cantabrian and Asturian wars (29–19 BCE), the military units in Hispania Tarraconensis were gathered in eight military camps (see Table 2.2), which obviously created the most important concentration of military inscriptions in the province. Some of them died at an early age—around their 30s—probably during service, but there were also epitaphs of veterans who retired in places like Asturica Augusta (Moralejo, 2018: 270) after more than 25 years of military service (*aerorum/stipendium*).

Two examples from Petavonium (Rosinos de Vidriales) depict the specific male life expectancy in military regions; for instance, Lucius Herennius Callicus (*AE* 1928: 0180) died at the age of 29 after nine years' service, whereas Marcus Cornelius (*AE* 1990: 00558) lived only to the age of 22, having served for three years (Moralejo, 2018). These military camps with a predominantly male

**Table 2.2** Location of the main military units in Hispania Tarraconensis in the Early Empire

| Site | Military camp | Unit | No. inscriptions |
|---|---|---|---|
| Legio (León) | Legionary | Legio VI/VII | 24 |
| Petavonium (Rosinos) | Legionary | Legio X. Ala II Flavia. Ala Parthorum | 17 |
| Pisoraca (Herrera Pisuerga) | Legionary | Legio III. Coh. I Gallica | 2 |
| Asturica Augusta (Astorga) | Legionary | Legio X | 18 |
| Lucus Augusti (Lugo) | Legionary | Legio VI? | 6 |
| Aquae Querquernae (Baños de Bande) | Auxiliary | Unknown | x |
| Citadela (Monte Cildá) | Auxiliary | Coh. III Celtiberorum | 3 |

population also included females as either partners or wives (Allison, 2006; 2013a; 2013b; 2015), although Roman law did not always allow and recognize such relationships.[6] There are some military inscriptions dedicated to wives (*uxores*) and their children (Green, 2015). Military districts were special demographic areas with a predominance of males, who married or cohabited later in their service life (Séguy, 2019: 34), with fewer children being born than in mainly civilian regions (Verhagen, 2019).

Another particular feature of military districts is the obviously high presence of an immigrant population (see Chapter 7), since most legionaries and auxiliaries came from and went to different provinces and parts of the Empire (Meyer, 2013). By way of example, the first generation of legionaries of the *Legio X Gemina* based at Asturica Augusta (Astorga) who died when on active service indicated their *origo*, which was principally in Gallia Narbonensis or Italy (Moralejo, 2018: 252 et seq.).

The study of the human remains from several cemeteries in Hispania Tarraconensis can cast some light on the gender proportion in the province. A predominantly male population can be detected in five of the necropoleis (Table 2.3 and Fig. 2.9); female burials are higher in number in three cemeteries, and the numbers are almost identical for both genders in another five burial places. If we look at those necropoleis with a higher number of individuals recorded, the cemetery of the plaça de la Vila de Madrid in Barcino had a total of 51 individuals over 12 years old. Among those, 28 were male (55%), 13 female (25.5%), and 10 (19.5%) undetermined, showing that men received burial in this cemetery more often than women did, at least in the area that was excavated. In A Lanzada (Galicia), among a sample of 85 individuals, 36 (42.3%) were male, 28 (33%) female, and 21 (24.7%) undetermined. A similar case is documented in Valentia (the calle Quart necropolis), but for an earlier period than in Barcelona and A Lanzada. There, of 75 individuals belonging to the republican levels of the city (second–first centuries BCE), 44% were male, 26.7% were female, and the remaining 29.3% were undetermined. However, Tarraco, the provincial capital and the largest city in the province, with a clear predominance of male funerary inscriptions (see below), seems to be the exception. In Tarragona, female burials (54.3%) predominate over male ones (41.8%). Women also seem to be more present (although the difference is small) in the Vacceo-Roman cremation cemetery of Pintia. The remaining burial grounds in Table 2.3, although in many cases with smaller samples, have an almost identical number of male and female burials, as in the case of Pollentia, Empúries, and Sotaterra. Especially significant is the cemetery of La Magdalena III–IV, where 39 females and 38 males found their

[6] On the ban on marriage for ordinary soldiers in active service during the early imperial period see Watson (1969: 134) and Wells (1998) among others.

**Table 2.3** Demographic composition by gender from nine necropoleis in Hispania Citerior/Tarraconensis

| Necropolis | Chronology | Female | Male | Indet. | TOTAL |
|---|---|---|---|---|---|
| Sotaterra | 2nd–3rd c. CE | 4 | 4 | 5 | **13** |
| Guissona | 1st–3rd c. CE | 1 | 3 | 1 | **5** |
| Tarragona | 3rd–5th c. CE | 100 | 77 | 7 | **184** |
| Vila de Madrid (Barcelona) | 1st–3rd c. CE | 13 | 28 | 38 | **79** |
| Empúries | 3rd–8th c. CE | 10 | 11 | 6 | **27** |
| Valentia | 2nd–1st c. BCE | 20 | 33 | 22 | **75** |
| Pollentia (Can Reiniers) | 7th c. CE | 26 | 26 | 15 | **67** |
| Pintia (Valladolid)* | 5th c. BCE–2nd c. CE | 24 | 19 | 42 | **85** |
| A Lanzada (Galicia) | 2nd–6th c. CE | 28 | 36 | 21 | **85** |
| El Vergel (Ávila) | 4th c. CE | 4 | 4 | 4 | **12** |
| Iuliobriga (Cantabria) | 6th c. CE | 2 | 7 | 0 | **9** |
| La Magdalena III–IV (Alcalá de Henares) | 3rd–5th c. CE | 39 | 38 | 81 | **158** |
| Villa of Almenara (Valladolid) | 5th–6th c. CE | 4 | 2 | 33 | **9** |
| TOTAL | | **275** | **288** | **245** | **808** |

* This is a cremation necropolis; the remaining ones are all inhumations.

*Source*: Data from Pérez-Pérez and Lazuela, 1992; Polo-Cerdá et al., 2004; Jordana and Malgosa, 2007; Cardona, 2009; Moreda et al., 2010–11; López Costas, 2012: 111–13; Heras and Galera, 2016: figs. 16–17; Carnicero, 2017: Tabla—III; García Merino and Sánchez-Simón, 2020: fig. 4.

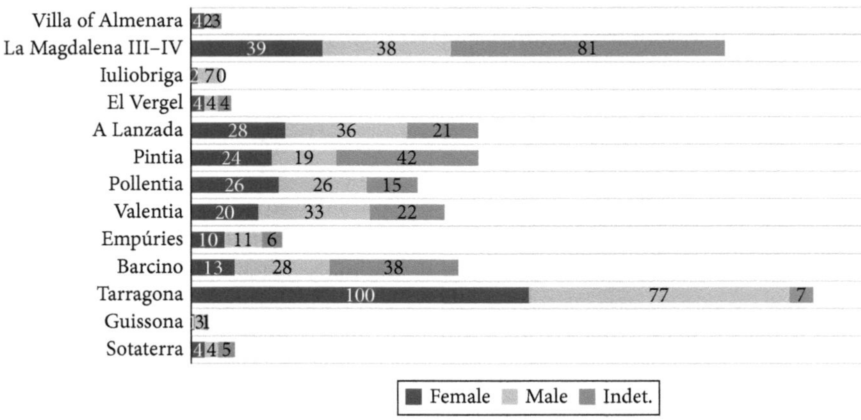


**Fig. 2.9** Demographic composition by gender from the 13 necropoleis in Table 2.3

last resting place. In sum, the study of 13 cemeteries in Hispania Citerior/Tarraconensis with dates ranging from the second century BCE to the seventh century CE indicates that the presence of each gender seems to vary from case to case (Table 2.3). This should not surprise us. Cemeteries are always partially preserved and sometimes only partly excavated, thereby always providing a fragmentary type of evidence. That said, if the overall picture is considered, of 808 individuals documented in these necropoleis, 275 (34.1%) were female, 288 (35.6%) were male, and 245 (30.3%) were of undetermined gender, the proportion between males and females being much closer in the necropoleis than is reflected in the epigraphic evidence from the province.

Returning to the gender variation in life expectancy in the province from an epigraphic perspective, a close look at the age at death in the province according to gender (Fig. 2.10) shows a slight difference between male and female frequencies, with the exception of those individuals over 60 years old. It seems that this age group reveals a greater difference in the epigraphic habit between males and females, perhaps because military and administrative honours were mainly granted to the elderly male population. For instance, a closer look at the inscriptions from Tarraco shows a predominance of males (80%) in the only 23 inscriptions that include age. Besides, the inscriptions included 30% with an age range between 1 and 20, while 40% were from 21 to 40, and once again, 30% above 41 years old.

Comparing the male age of death of the three provinces in the Iberian peninsula (see Fig. 2.11), the highest peak corresponds to the decade between the ages of 20 and 30, although Hispania Tarraconensis peaks earlier in the decade between

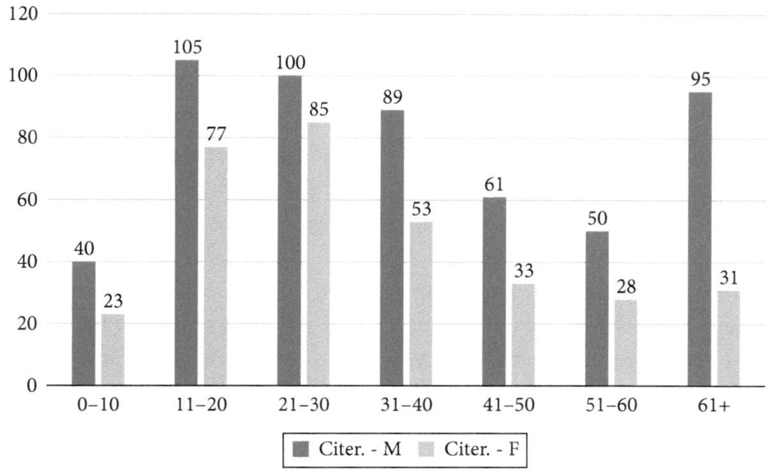


**Fig. 2.10** Frequency of death ages in the inscriptions of Hispania Citerior/Tarraconensis

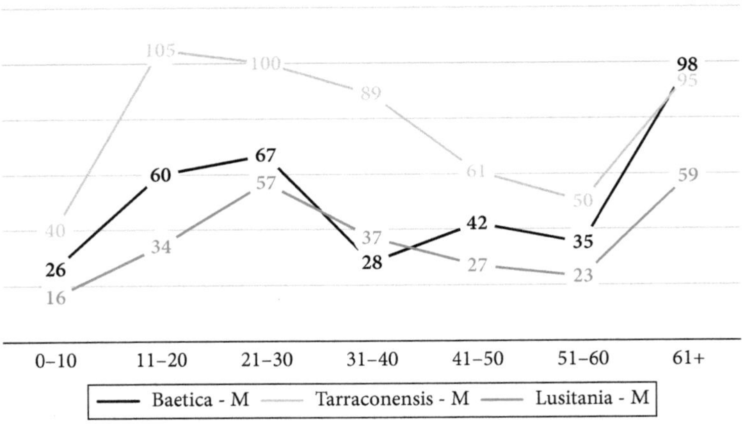


**Fig. 2.11** Frequency of death ages in male funerary inscriptions according to provinces

10 and 20 years old. No clear explanation can be put forward to justify this earlier peak in the province, although for the Roman Empire as a whole, Frier (2000: 790) establishes the average life expectancy at 20.4 years. Another interesting feature of the three provinces is the longevity of many citizens. There are many elderly individuals over the age of 60, and a few of them even reached their 90s and 100 years old according to the inscriptions. As Hippocrates said:

> Old men generally have less illnesses than young men; but such complaints as become chronic in old men generally last until death.
>
> Hippocrates, *Aphorisms* 2.39

In Hispania Tarraconensis, at least three funerary inscriptions of persons dying after the age of 100 years old are known: Caius Caronis at 100 (Méntrida: *AE* 1986: 0432), Aurelius Talavi at 100 (Sao Sebastao: *AE* 2002: 0773), and Victorinus at 120 years (Tines: *AE* 1992: 0999). Notwithstanding the exception of those longer lives, ancient writers such as L. Anneo Seneca, who was himself from Baetica, recorded in his *Brevitae vitae* that longer lives were not so rare:

> And so I should like to lay hold upon someone from the company of older men and say: "I see that you have reached the farthest limit of human life, you are pressing hard upon your hundredth year, or are even beyond it; come now, recall your life and make a reckoning. Consider how much of your time was taken up with a moneylender, how much with a mistress, how much with a patron, how much with a client, how much in wrangling with your wife, how much in punishing your slaves, how much in rushing about the city on social duties. Add the

> diseases which we have caused by our own acts, add, too, the time that has lain idle and unused; you will see that you have fewer years to your credit than you count. Look back in memory and consider when you ever had a fixed plan, how few days have passed as you had intended, when you were ever at your own disposal, when your face ever wore its natural expression, when your mind was ever unperturbed, what work you have achieved in so long a life, how many have robbed you of life when you were not aware of what you were losing, how much was taken up in useless sorrow, in foolish joy, in greedy desire, in the allurements of society, how little of yourself was left to you; you will perceive that you are dying before your season!" Seneca, *Brev. Vitae* III.2

Life expectancy in the province is quite consistent with the values provided by Frier (2000: 790) as an average of 20.4 for males and 22.5 for females. The calculations of average ages were obtained from what is known as Ulpian's life table.[7] Although some scholars consider the table to be schematic (Saller, 1987) or only to refer to slave and freedman populations (Duncan-Jones, 2010: 99–101), it is similar to the Coale-Demeny West model: level 2 and pre-modern societies. Besides, the almost 300 censuses recovered from papyri in Roman Egypt supply a similar picture with an average life expectancy of 25 years for males and 22 for females (Bagnall and Frier, 1994: 75–100).

Concerning female life expectancy, the three Iberian provinces reveal similar trends (see Fig. 2.11) with a peak of deaths in the decade from 20 to 30 years of age. The only difference is recorded among the elderly, where Baetica and Lusitania still record a substantial number of females over the age of 60, whereas there is a clear decline in Hispania Tarraconensis. As expected, the highest rate of female mortality identifies the age of childbearing (20–35 years), when women faced the risks of childbirth in especially unhealthy conditions (Hopkins, 2017). The ancient demographic regime had a low life expectancy in childbirth. It required four to six children per woman (one third might die) to preserve replacement levels for a society, which means at least two children per couple in each generation. Therefore, four or six births per woman supposed an increasing risk.

These were the conditions that existed until the end of the eighteenth century CE, when there was a demographic transition with an increased life expectancy of females and children (Séguy, 2019: 24).[8] There is at least one inscription in the province, which documents a young, 25-year-old *serva* called Gemina, who died when giving birth:

[7] The information appears from a comment by Aemmilus Macer (*c.*230 CE) (*Dig.* XXXV.2.68) on Ulpian's schedule for calculating tax for *alimenta* and usufructs (*lex Iulia XX hereditatum*—6 CE).

[8] The ancient demographic regime was defined by high fertility and mortality, whereas the present-day regime is characterized by low fertility and mortality, and therefore longevity.

> *Gemina D(ecimi) Pu/blici Subici ser(va) an(norum) / XXV h(ic) s(ita) e(st) obit in / partu C(aius) Aerariu[s l(ibertus)] / posui[t ci]ppum PA[-]/[---]S mihi si qu[a] / inferi sapent ut m[e] / abducaeres si me amasti fac abdu/cas s(it) t(ibi) t(erra) l(evis)*[9] Cortijo del Chantre (Úbeda): *AE* 1991: 1076

The minimum age for marriage was 12 years old for females and 14 for males, although according to the Egyptian censuses and epigraphy, most marriages took place between the ages of 18 and 25 for women and between 20 and 25 years of age for men (Bagnall and Frier, 1994: 113–17). In fact, around 80% of women were married before the age of 20, and 15% as young as the age of 12 (Frier, 2000: 798–9). There was an average of 7.5 years of difference between males and females in married couples according to those same censuses.

Fig. 2.12 portrays the death age frequency in female inscriptions in the Iberian peninsula, which exhibits similar trends to those recorded elsewhere. There was a high percentage of female deaths in the fertile age, although inscriptions did not record the cause of death. The life expectancy of Roman females fits better with the Coale-Demeny model West: level 2 or Weiss (Bagnall and Frier, 1994: 33), which is normally applied to a female population in ancient and medieval societies.

Turning to the data from necropoleis (Table 2.1), once again the difference between the epigraphic record and the study of human remains is clear. The study

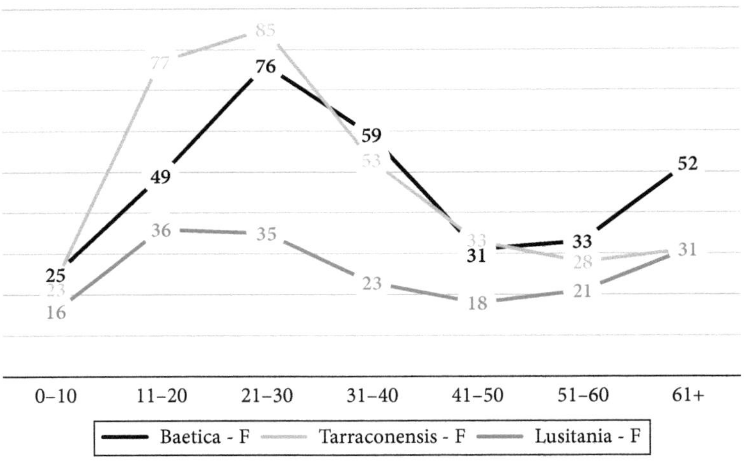


**Fig. 2.12** Frequency of death ages in female funerary inscriptions according to provinces

[9] Translation: 'Gemina slave of Decimus Publicus Subicus who was 25. She lies here after dying in childbirth. Caius Aerarius freedman set this tombstone up PA…S to me if any in the underworld should be wise carry me away if you loved me rescue me. Let the earth be mild.'

of necropoleis shows that the cases of individuals reaching old age were minimal (3.5% of the total), probably presenting a scenario for Tarraconensis in which we see a pattern of commemoration that favours this age range, overemphasizing their real presence (Table 2.1). If we consider the age of death, only 3.4% of deaths corresponded to juveniles (ages 13–19), showing that those individuals that survived childhood would usually reach adulthood. The highest frequency for the age of death recorded in the cemeteries studied pertains to adulthood. Up to 46.4% of the individuals documented are young adults (20–40 years) and 24% can be defined as mature adults (41–59 years) (Table 2.1, Fig. 2.13). The substantial peak of inscriptions commemorating individuals who passed away between the ages of 11 and 20 years (Figs. 2.11 and 2.12) is not paralleled in the study of the necropoleis of Hispania Citerior/Tarraconensis. In ten cemeteries young adults have the highest frequency of death and in another two the highest mortality rate occurs among mature adults. Therefore, the high number of epitaphs commemorating those lost between the ages of 11 and 20 may well be the result of frequently commemorating an unexpected loss. Furthermore, the epigraphic and osteological evidence agree that the most common age at death in the province is between 20 and 40 years old (Fig. 2.13).

The study of human remains also makes it clear that life expectancy may vary significantly between the genders from site to site depending on the specific nature of the population buried in the cemetery. Missing data can also be a major problem since it is difficult to know what percentages of the total population buried in the necropolis have come down to us while it should also be recalled

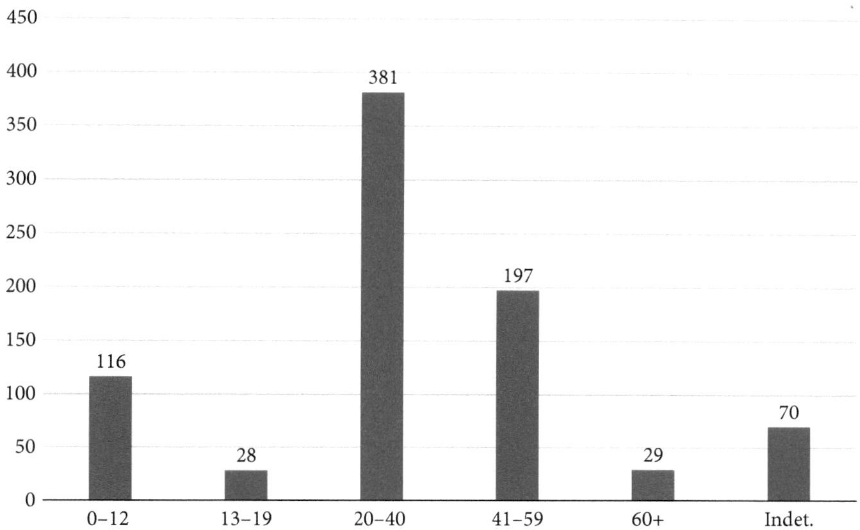


**Fig. 2.13** Age frequency in the necropoleis of Citerior/Tarraconensis in Table 2.1

that some of the cemeteries were in use for several centuries. Besides, perhaps only a minority of the population in Roman times received formal burial in necropoleis, as the evidence from Britain seems to suggest (Pearce, 2008). We must also consider that there is a difference between receiving formal burial (if any) and putting up an epitaph.

It should be expected that the living conditions of a population may have changed over such a long period of time and this was certainly the case, depending on its geographical location and the social group that was buried in it. Bearing all these limitations in mind, it is worth pointing out that in Barcino, the female mortality rate between the ages of 15 and 40 is higher than that observed for the male population, with the rate subsequently balancing out among those individuals over 40 years old. This trend, common in pre-industrial societies, is reflected in the lower life expectancy of women, which is 32 years after overcoming childhood (Jordana and Malgosa, 2007: 71). For men it is 36 years. In Valentia, on the other hand, we see the opposite dynamic, since during the second century BCE, the mortality rate among young adults was higher among the male population, becoming equal for both sexes after reaching the age of 40. The comparison between republican Valentia and imperial Barcino shows how local realities as well as chronology, geography, and sample preservation among many other variables can affect the data provided by the cemetery evidence. In general, however, life expectancy at birth based on the study of necropoleis usually seems to reach the 30s. In the case of women, as happens in Pollentia, their lower life expectancy tends to correspond with the reproductive period (Iscan and Kennedy, 1989). It must be highlighted, however, that as happens in the epigraphic record, infants are underrepresented in the necropoleis, positively impacting life expectancy estimates at birth. In the few cases where infants are noticeably present, such as in the case of Vila de Madrid in Barcelona, the life expectancy of a newborn was just 21 years for both genders (Fig. 2.14). A good example of to what extent infant mortality modifies life expectancy at birth can also be seen from A Lanzada (Galicia). This necropolis can be divided into two periods of use. The first one broadly matches the Roman period while the subsequent one can be described as Late Roman. In the earlier phase, infant burials are not recorded, raising life expectancy at birth to 38 years. On the other hand, the 13 infants buried at A Lanzada (15.3% of the total) belong to the Late Roman period and represent 33.3% of the total sample documented in this later phase of the cemetery, lowering the life expectancy at birth to 25.5 years. Interestingly, if we examine life expectancy after surviving childhood, both phases display very similar figures (23 and 25 years respectively). The combined examples of Vila de Madrid (Barcino) and A Lanzada (Galicia) clearly highlight the effect that the underrepresentation of infant mortality can have in estimating life expectancy.

A similar picture seems to emerge from the necropoleis in the other provincial capitals. In Augusta Emerita (Lusitania) for example, a recent palaeodemographic

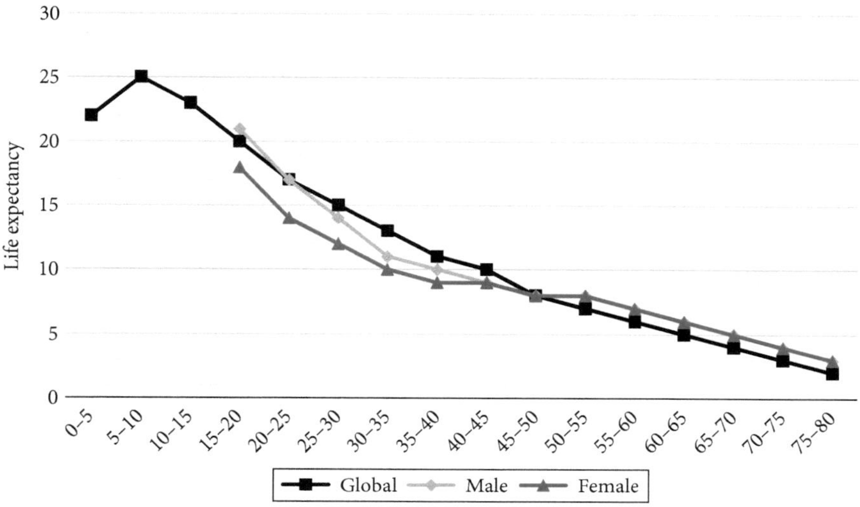


**Fig. 2.14** Life expectancy of the population buried in the Vila de Madrid necropolis (after Jordana and Malagosa, 2007: fig. 6)

study conducted on 33 female individuals has estimated the adult age at death of this group as lying between the ages of 25 and 39 (Vázquez Espinar, 2017: 588–9). Interestingly, this same study compared these figures with those obtained from the corpus of inscriptions published for the city (not the provincial one as in Fig. 2.13), which established the average age of death at 37 years (83 epitaphs were used) (Vázquez Espinar, 2017: 613–14). The results show a certain concordance between the two datasets. In Corduba (Baetica) a sample of 89 individuals (fourth–eighth centuries CE) from the Cortijo Coracho necropolis (Lucena, Córdoba) has been studied. The palaeodemographic results show a life expectancy at birth of 34 years (Diéguez Ramírez et al., 2010: 247). The authors of the study also point out that this number is very similar to the data from the cemeteries of Cortijo Nuevo (Lucena) and El Ochavillo (de Hornachuelos), both in the vicinity of modern Córdoba (Diéguez Ramírez et al., 2010: 247). At Cortijo Coracho, however, infants were underrepresented, only 12 individuals being under the age of 20. As can be seen, the picture from Baetica and Lusitania does not seem to be very different from the one obtained for our study of Tarraconensis, making life expectancy for the Roman period quite uniform, palaeodemographically speaking, but also higher (30s) than what was probably the true situation (20s) due to the underrepresentation of infants in most samples.

Returning to the epigraphic data, apart from the gender differences in life expectancy, epigraphy may help to distinguish spatial variation in different parts of the province. It was decided to compare the death ages of the seven capitals of *conventus iuridici* in the province as well as the main legionary camp at

Legio (León). Fig. 2.15 shows the location of the *conventus iuridici* and their capitals in Hispania Tarraconensis.

Although the number of funerary inscriptions with ages in each *conventus* capital is not especially significant,[10] there is a coincidence between the capital Tarraco and the north-western *conventus* capitals with a meaningful number of inscriptions with adult ages at death (between 21 and 40), a situation that is also recorded at Clunia Sulpicia. In contrast, epitaphs of younger people (between 1 and 20) are only reported in considerable numbers at Carthago Nova and Clunia Sulpicia with relative low values in the other *conventus* capitals (Fig. 2.16).

Finally, the eldest group above 40 years of age is mainly recorded at Tarraco, Bracara Augusta, and Asturica Augusta. Most of these are honorific inscriptions to patrons, military or administrative personnel ascribed to the office of military detachments or of the province governor. These cities (see Chapter 7), especially Tarraco as the provincial capital, may have exercised a greater power of attraction for men taking up administrative positions. Part of the explanation of the higher concentrations in the north-western cities could be the veterans from Legio settling in nearby cities. The lower number in Lucus Augusti could simply be the result of a slightly lower number of inscriptions. This bias in the epigraphic record

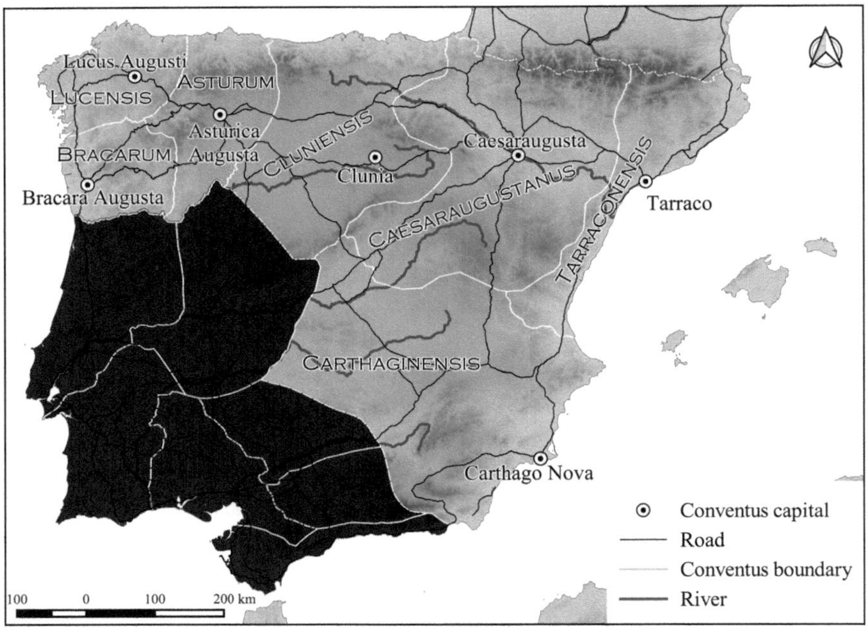


**Fig. 2.15** *Conventus iuridici* in Hispania Tarraconensis

[10] Data obtained from the *CIL* Heidelberg database (April 2020).

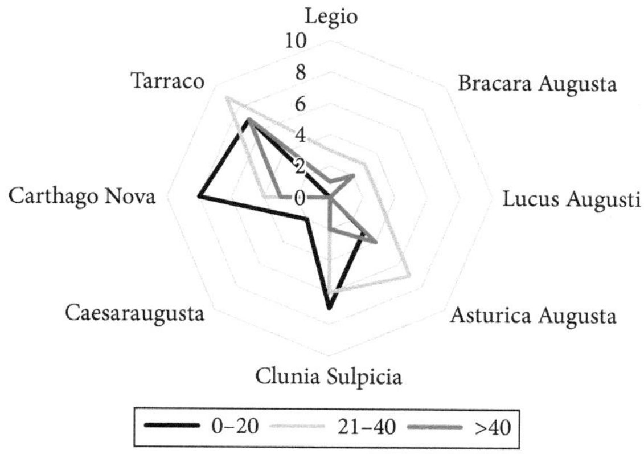


**Fig. 2.16** Comparison of death ages between *conventus* capitals and the main legionary camp

certainly explains the apparent absence of men in Caesaraugusta, which has a very limited number of inscriptions.

## 2.2 Fertility and Maternity

All free females married at least once in their lives, whereas only 70% of males married according to the data of the Egyptian censuses. Romans hardly ever wedded close kin, since in only 10% of epitaphs do the *nomina* of husbands and wives coincide. And even in those cases, the *nomina* were so common that they may not indicate that they were relatives or, alternatively, they may have been cousins, uncles/aunts, or nephews/nieces (Shaw and Saller, 1984).

Among the Romans, reproduction was considered the primary function of marriage, and one of the most important, if not the main, duty of women was to produce children:

> Since women are married for the sake of bearing children and heirs, and not for pleasure and enjoyment, it is totally absurd to inquire about the quality or rank of their family line or about the abundance of their wealth, but not to inquire about their ability to conceive children. Soranus, *Gynecology* 1.34.1

Following Aulus Gellius (*NA* 18.6), *matrona*, the word used to define a married Roman woman, was thought to derive from *mater* ('mother'). Cicero mentions how a 'wise man should desire... in order that he might live in accordance with nature, to marry a wife and to want to have children by her' (*Fin.* 3.20.68). Similarly, Ulpian (*Dig.* 1.1.1.3) says that the joining of male and female, 'which we call marriage', is to continue the procreation of children. As Hug (2014: 13) has pointed out, Sp. Ligustinus, his fertile wife, and their six sons and two daughters represented the perfect Roman family, but he also emphasizes the importance of female fertility (for the idea of *fecunditas* as a virtue see Hug, 2014: 87–100) and the creation of offspring as key elements in a proper Roman marriage and its legitimation.

> When I first came of age, my father gave to me his brother's daughter as a wife, who brought with her nothing other than her free birth and her sexual virtue and, along with these things, a fertility such that it would be enough even for a wealthy home. We have six sons, and two daughters, and both of our girls are already married. Four of our sons wear a man's toga; two still wear the one for boys. Livy 42.34.3–4

Both ancient sources and inscriptions provide testimonies of the importance of fecundity and children in Roman society at all levels. Triplets—the Horatii from Rome and the Curiatii from Alba—are central to the foundational myths of Rome (Liv. 1.24–6; Dion. Hal. *Ant. Rom.* 3.12–22). In one of his letters (8.10), Pliny the Younger also highlights the importance of children among elite families: 'you could not desire great-grandchildren more fervently than I desire children. I think that political careers will be easy for them . . .'. Similarly, Cicero expressed his joy in his letters to Atticus (1.2.1) after Terentia was blessed with a son, commenting that she was doing well after having given birth. Inscriptions from houses in Pompeii announcing the birth of children are also good evidence that the pride and happiness that parents felt after a successful birth was not exclusive to the elites in Rome (*CIL* IV 294, 8149).

Direct evidence for fertility, however, is scarce in texts, censuses, and epigraphy, but bearing in mind that a third of children died in their early years, Hopkins (1983) proposed six children as an average Total Fertility Rate (TFR). However, Hin (2013) diminished this TFR to a range of four to six children in women's period of fertility from the age of 15 to 45. The estimate has been calculated at an even lower figure, an average of 3.3 TFR, by means of using calculations of female pelvis remains by Riddle (1991: 14 et seq.; Caldwell, 2006). Due to the high perinatal mortality, the ratio between mothers and daughters should have reached 2.8 (Gross Reproduction Rate), which allowed Roman society to maintain the population constant in each generation.

One unique inscription from Aquincum is normally used by scholars (Curchin, 2000–1) to confirm this high fertility rate:

> *Hic sita sum matrona genus nomen/que Veturia Fortunati coniux de patre Vetu/ rio nata ter novenos misera et nupta bis octo / per annos unicuba uniiuga quae*

*post / sex partus uno superstite obii / T(itus) Iulius Fortunatus |(centurio) leg(ionis) II ad(iutricis) p(iae) f(idelis) / coniugi incomparabili et insigni in se pietate*[11]

*Aquincum* (*CIL* III 3572) - 201–250 CE

The epitaph acknowledged that Veturia Fortunati gave birth to six children—the average TFR according to Hopkins (1983)—and lived for 27 years, therefore dying relatively young. She was married for 16 years, thus at the age of 11, and only one of her children survived her. In this case, she was unable to reach the minimum Gross Reproduction Rate that guaranteed the maintenance of population figures. Unfortunately, epigraphy did not normally record either fertility or survival data, so the only alternative data come from legislative and literary sources.

Textual sources also present several cases in which women reached and even surpassed the TFR suggested by Hopkins (1983). Valerius Maximus reports the story of an individual named Terentius who raised eight sons to *adulescentia* and then gave one away in adoption (Val. Max. 7.7.5). Pliny the Elder (*NH* VII.33) records a case in the Peloponnese of a woman who not only gave birth four times to quintuplets, but that in each birth, most of the children survived.[12] Egypt was viewed as an especially fertile region by Roman sources. Pliny the Elder (*NH* VII.33) comments how giving birth to more than triplets was portentous 'except in Egypt, where the River Nile causes fecundity in those who drink from it'. Similarly, Strabo states that 'Egyptian women sometimes actually bear four children'. The *Digest* (5.4.3 (Paul)) also acknowledges Egyptian fertility. In a section commenting on the rarity of births producing more than three offspring, it goes on to say that 'many women in Egypt have produced seven children at one birth'. However, most of the accounts (a collection in Hug, 2014: 120–40) either stress the high financial cost to the family as a consequence of extreme reproductive success, describe how the children in question brought pride or infamy upon their family, or note rare cases of multiple births—certainly the exception rather than the norm—but never attempt to provide a real picture of the fertility rate. Be that as it may, the few and incomplete sources we have been able to find make Hin's (2013) TFR (a range of 4 to 6) more plausible than the one (6 children) proposed by Hopkins (1983).

The three laws enacted during the Augustan period may also allow it to be suggested that the TFR was not reached among the upper classes, since this

[11] Translation: 'Here I lie, Veturia my name and descent, a married woman. I was Fortunatus' wife, my father was Veturius. Sadly, I lived for thrice nine years, and was married for twice eight. I slept with one man; I was married to one man. I died after having borne six children; one of them survives me. Titus Iulius Fortunatus, centurion of the Second Legion Adiutrix, set this up to his incomparable and exceptionally respectful wife.'

[12] Pliny's version probably comes from Aristotle, who in his *History of Animals* explains that one woman had given birth to twenty children in four births and bearing five infants each time (*Hist. an.* 7.4.584b).

legislation favoured and encouraged fertility. The *lex Iulia Maritandis Ordinibus* (18 BCE) (*Dig.* 38 tit. 11; *Dig.* 23 tit. 2) favoured the fertility of married couples, whereas it limited inheritances for single individuals and couples without children. It was complemented with a moralistic family law known as the *lex Iulia de Adulteriis Coercendis* (17 BCE), which punished adultery, made divorces difficult, and considered it an offence to remain single or without children. Finally, the *lex Papia Poppaea* (9 CE) completed the regulations promoting marriage and limiting inheritances. For instance, unfertile widows should wed before two years had elapsed, whereas divorced women had eighteen months to remarry.

The best candidates for marriage in the *lex Papia Poppaea* were widows and divorced citizens who had already borne children (Tac. *Ann.* XV.19; Plin. *Ep.* VII.16). There were also some benefits for freedwomen with a certain number of living children, who were free from *operarum obligatione* (*Dig.* 38. Tit. 1), and in the case of those women with four children they were released from their patron's *tutela* (Ulp. Frag. tit. 29). Besides, freedwomen with three children alive in Rome, four children alive in Italia, or five children in the provinces were excused from the office of *tutor* and *curator* (*Inst.* 1.25; *Dig.* 27.1). Although there is no direct evidence for fertility in censuses, epigraphy, or literary sources for Hispania Tarraconensis, it is likely to have been higher than that expected in Rome and Italy, as can be inferred from the previous legal reference.

Ancient sources portrayed different attitudes towards fertility between the upper and lower classes. Whereas upper-class women could be sterilized or take abortion drugs, poor women had to accept all the risks of childbirth. Juvenal drew a clear distinction between those two social groups among women:

> [Y]et these [poor women] at least endure the dangers of child birth, and all the troubles of nursing which their fate urges them: how often do gilded-beds witness a lying-in when we have so many sure-fire drugs for inducing sterility or killing an embryo child? Our skilled abortionists know all the answers. So, cheer up, my poor friend, and give her the stuff to drink whatever it shall be. Things might be worse – just suppose she wanted to get big and torture her womb with bouncing boys; you might become the father of an Ethiopian, and soon you will find that a dark-coloured heir whom you would rather not meet by daylight, shall fill up your wills. Juvenal, *Satirae* 6.592–601

In *De Sterilitate* (*On Barrenness*, *c.* fourth century BCE), it is written that the fertility of a woman could be tested by giving her the milk of a nursing mother and butter. If eructing occurs after eating these products, the woman will get pregnant (3.214).

Oral contraceptives such as *silphium* or *artemisia* were well-known in Graeco-Roman societies (Riddle and Estes, 1992; Nelson, 2009) as a way to prevent pregnancy or produce abortions. From Hippocrates to Galen, ancient texts record different plants and contraceptives, which were even described by a gynaecologist such as Soranus (second century CE). As happened in other historical periods, contraception was employed in particular social contexts, but not as a common structural means of birth control.

Despite the high proportion of miscarriages and the risk to women's lives in childbirth, special care was taken of the children that survived (Laes, 2011). Cicero's daughter Tullia is a good example of child survival, because she had only one child after three marriages and many miscarriages. Normally, the birth interval was extended by a long lactation period, which was presumed to be the healthiest feeding for a newborn child. High-class families could employ a wet nurse (*nutrix*). For lower-class families, this was rarely an option. Moreover, breastfeeding could bring about malnutrition for the mother. As a result, this would lead to a higher age difference between children. Even so, epitaphs of lower-class families seldom record more than two children that survived infancy (Rawson, 1986: 9).

Malnutrition is still difficult to prove from skeletal remains (see Chapter 8); however, there are indications that point towards it, a good example being discussed below in the study of the Sant Antoni necropolis (Barcelona). The nutritional intake in the Vila de Madrid necropolis in Barcino was not sufficient either. A high frequency of hypoplasia, possibly due to a nutritional deficiency and various problems during the transition from breastfeeding to the consumption of solid foods, has been recorded in the growth of subadult individuals (Jordana and Malgosa, 2007: 78). Additionally, the results from the Prat de la Riba necropolis at Tarraco (Baxarias, 2002) show that the average height of males was 1.57 m and of females was 1.52 m, thus providing evidence that the population of Hispania Tarraconensis was somewhat shorter since malnutrition in the mother or at a young age affects the growth of individuals. Actually, the general trend in the Roman Empire was a lower biological standard of living than in the late Iron Age and medieval periods (Harper, 2019: 102; Jongman et al., 2019: 149).

Apart from that, among the upper classes, the milk of a wet nurse was considered healthier than the mother's own milk (Garnsey, 1991: 60–1). Bradley (1991: 220) has suggested than in some cases, the use of a wet nurse among upper-class women may have taken place in order to limit emotional bonding and attachment with the child due to the high infant mortality.

Therefore, some slaves, freedwomen, and lower-class freeborn women were employed as wet nurses (*nutrices*). Soranus provides us with the characteristics that wet nurses should have:

> One should choose a wet nurse not younger than twenty or older than forty years, who has already given birth twice or thrice, who is healthy, of good habitus, of large frame and of a good colour. Her breasts should be of medium size, lax, soft and unwrinkled, the nipples neither big nor too small and neither too compact nor too porous and discharging milk over abundantly. She should be self-controlled, sympathetic and not ill-tempered, a Greek, and tidy.
>
> Soranus, *Gynaeciorum* II.19

In the case of Rome, Bradley (1986: 203) has concluded that nearly half of the funerary inscriptions set up for *nutrices* belong to the senatorial or equestrian order, but the practice is not limited to the elites and a significant number of epitaphs including wet nurses mention that they are of servile condition. In the Iberian peninsula, seven inscriptions of *nutrices* are recorded from the Early Empire (second–third centuries CE) basically in urban areas (Alfaro, 2010). Only two are documented in the cities of Hispania Tarraconensis, namely Fabia Tertulla from Barcino:

> *D(iis) M(anibus)/ Fabiae Tertullae/ nutrici*
>
> (*AE* 1966: 197; *IRC* IV. no. 165)

and Pontiena Novella from Valeria (Cuenca):

> *[Pont]iena/ Novel[l]a/ [D]omiti nutrix.*
>
> (*CIL* II 3190)

We might add a third possible inscription from Mentesa Oretanorum (Alcaraz):

> *[Aelia ? L]asciva / nu[trix ind]ulgentis(s)uma(!) / an(norum) LVII[II pr]o merit[i]s / suis L(ucius) Ae[li]us Celer / Ingenu(u)s praestitit / impensam fu[ne]ris lo/cum sepultur[ae] monu(mentum) / [ordo decrevit?] / hic [sita est - - -]*
>
> (*AE* 1990: 606)

Furthermore, Egyptian papyri have even revealed the prices of wet nurses, who received between 7 and 10 drachmas/month in the first century CE to 16 to 20 drachmas in the second century CE (Alfaro, 2010).[13] Therefore, social attitudes may have generated a distinction in fertility between the lower and upper classes in Roman society. The high fertility of the poor classes was a consequence of the fact that they considered children as economic assets (Caldwell, 1982; Hin, 2007: 2) not as a burden. It should be borne in mind that children could work at the age of 10, so the family's investment in bringing them up was minimal and was soon paid back since they received all the earnings from their children's first jobs (Bradley, 1985).

Besides, it was well regarded in Roman society to have large number of offspring as:

> a man who has many children is honoured in the city, (...) he has the respect of his neighbours. (...) he has more influence than his equals if they are not equally blessed with children. I need not argue that a man with many friends is more powerful than one who has no friends, and so a man who has many children is

[13] On the wet nursing contracts from Roman Egypt see Pudsey (2013: 489); Bradley (1986: 202).

more powerful than one without any or with only a few children, or rather much more so, since a son is closer than a friend. *Musonius Rufus* XV

In contrast, upper-class males may have had fewer children because they could enjoy sexual intercourse with slaves and concubines apart from their legal wives. Besides, for upper-class families the cost of raising many children could be a burden, as in the case of Terentius discussed above (Val. Max. 7.7.5). The result of such behaviour was a lower Gross Reproduction Rate among the upper classes, which ended in the decline and downfall of some important families and *cognomina* (Hin, 2007: 9). Moreover, late male marriage minimized the risk of property division among future heirs, which was a sensible economic strategy.

The cult of Fortuna Muliebris may enable us to gain some insight into mentalities among upper-class females (Bailón, 2012). The cult defended the adult feminine values of the social group of *matronae uniuirae*. The term *matrona* identifies a woman with at least one child alive, whereas *materfamilias* reflects a woman with at least two (the basic Gross Reproduction Rate). Such an ideal was complemented with the adjective *uniuirae*, in other words a woman married only once, which would have been the model of *pudicitia* (modesty). Therefore, this cult, together with the cult of Mater Matuta and Pudicitia, promoted feminine fertility and the protection of children.

The regeneration of the Roman population became successful when children reached adulthood. As happens today, any teenage deaths were considered a terrible fate for the family, which explains why there were many elaborate epitaphs dedicated to children who died at an early age, such as the case of the poet Sulpicius Maximus (Goldsmith and Graziosi, 2018). One example in Tarraconensis was the inscription recorded at Iesso (Guissona) dedicated by Servillia Praepusa to her daughter Lesbia, who died at the age of eleven (Fig. 2.17):

*Servilla Praepusa / filiae suae Lesbiae / a(nnorum) XI m(ensium) X hic sepul(tae) s(it) l(evis) t(erra) / quid sibi fata velint bellissima quaeque / creari edita laeti(ti)ae commoda si rapiu/{u}nt sed quae fatorum legi serva[r]e necesse est / perverso lacrimas fundimus officio haec bis sex / annos vix bene transierat ill<a> suas la[c]rimas nondum emiserat / omnes et poterat semper flebilis esse suis parcite enim vobis tristes / sine fine parentes parcius et manes sollicitare meos ponimus hunc / titulum luctus solacia nostri qui legit ut dicat sit tibi terra levis*[14]

Guissona (*AE* 1968: 0236; *IRC* II76)

[14] Translation: 'Servilia Praepusa to her daughter Lesbia, who was eleven years and ten months old. Here she is buried. Why have the fates created such beautiful things, if they took from us what was made for our bliss? Since we have to respect the fates' rules, we shed tears for a duty that should not be ours. She had hardly reached twice six years, she had not shed yet all the tears she had inside and could be lamented by her relatives. Save yourselves from being sad for ever, my parents, and let my Manes rest. We set this inscription up, as a consolation to our pain. Whoever reads this say aloud: May the earth lie lightly upon you.'

**Fig. 2.17** Inscription of Servilia Praepusa to Lesbia (Guissona: *AE* 1968: 0236; *IRC* II76)

Finally, in terms of health, most physicians were men except when it came to women's pregnancies, in which midwives played an important role. There are few inscriptions referring to doctors from Hispania Citerior/Tarraconensis, two of the best-known coming from Tarraco. The Greek doctor Antonius Musa took care of Augustus in 23 BCE, and Tiberius Claudius Apolicenius also practised as a doctor at Tarraco. In the same city a female doctor is recorded in an anonymous inscription (*CIL* II 43114, 26–7) (Alfaro, 2010).

## 2.3 The Mercat de Sant Antoni: Anthropological Analysis of an Early Imperial Burial Site in Tarraconensis Linked to Maternity?

As mentioned above, Barcino, thanks to its well-studied necropolis, is an excellent case study to approach some demographic aspects of its inhabitants. We have already discussed the data from the cemetery at Vila de Madrid (see Tables 2.1 and 2.3) and, in the following lines, we will conduct a detailed analysis of the necropolis located in the Mercat de Sant Antoni, since it offers excellent data to study infant burials and perhaps to suggest a link between the cemetery and maternity. The foundation of the colony in 15–10 BCE coincided with the reorganization and reform of land transport routes in Hispania (see Chapter 7). It was in this context that a road fork that connected the main road parallel to the coast, the Via Augusta, with the coastal towns as well as Barcino (Barcelona) was built. At the archaeological site of the Mercat de Sant Antoni in Barcelona a 50-metre-long section of this original road has been unearthed. This section, located over a kilometre from the south-western gate of the Roman walls, is a western extension of the *Cardo Maximus*. Between the mid-first century and the beginning of the second century, cemeteries were laid on either side of this road and would have welcomed anyone arriving in the Roman town of Colonia Iulia Augusta Faventia Paterna Barcino. The necropolis found during the excavations in the Mercat de Sant Antoni is one of those cemeteries that had been laid out alongside this main road (Hinojo and Miró, 2017).

The Mercat de Sant Antoni cemetery contained a minimum number of 27 burials, 13 of which consisted of primary burial inhumations in single graves, and the remaining 14 of cremations. The methods used to undertake the analysis have been adapted to each type of burial (Fig. 2.18 A and B), since cremated human remains will not provide the same type of bioarchaeological data as the inhumed ones (see Chapter 8).

### 2.3.1 Cremated Human Remains

The demographic profile provided by the cremated human remains is of 14 adult individuals found at the Mercat de Sant Antoni and was carried out using the

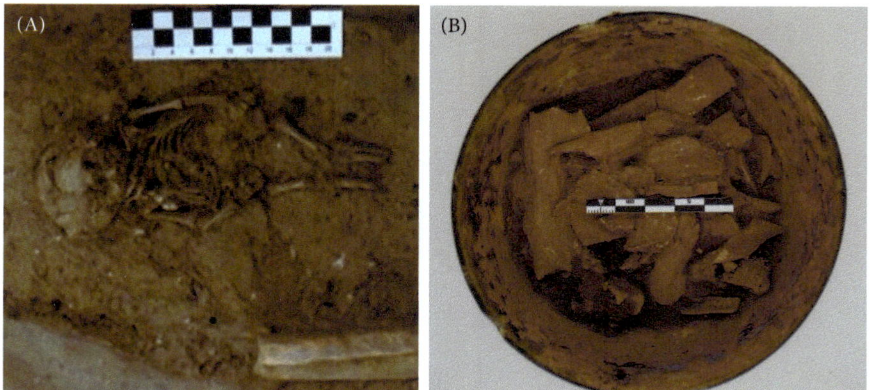


**Fig. 2.18** (A) Inhumed remains of a non-adult individual in a single grave (Mercat de Sant Antoni, UF7), (B) Cremated remains of an adult individual found in a cremation urn (Photograph: Emiliano Hinojo)

standard methodological methods for cremated remains (Gómez-Bellard, 1996; Polo-Cerdá et al., 2005; Wells, 1960). Among the cremated human remains, different types of burial rites have been identified in the form of primary and secondary deposits. Primary deposits are those where the cremation took place at the same place as the final burial, and which are represented by *bustum* structures. In contrast, secondary deposits are those that represent the final resting place of the remains after the cremation had taken place somewhere else (i.e. an *ustrinum*). Secondary deposits are represented by structures such as *loculi*, *cupae structiles*, and cremation urns (Fig. 2.19).

The cremated remains analysed exhibit medium-sized fragmentation (between 1 and 1.5 cm), although, in a few cases, the size of the fragments was smaller. The cremated bone recovered is completely fragmentary and, in many cases, also reveals deformation. The bone fragmentation observed in this set of remains is in the form of curved or transverse fractures, which is the characteristic pattern of fragmentation associated with the exposure of living bone to very high temperatures (Etxeberria, 1994; Ubelaker, 2009). The increasing firing temperature causes the heating and boiling of the water and fat contained in the living bone, and results in internal bone pressure and the subsequent fragmentation of the bone (Trellisó, 2001; Trancho, 2010). The areas of transverse fractures thus represent the weaker points in the bone and are clearly different from the burn patterns that dry, and therefore non-elastic, bone would exhibit (Correira, 1997).

**Fig. 2.19** (A) Bustum. (B) Loculus. (C) Ustrinum

The weight of the cremation remains varies between 12.66 and 1025.69 g. The weight of the cremations in the *bustum* structures corresponds with what would be expected from the cremation of a complete adult individual (970–2630 g) (Le Goff, 2002). In total, 45% of the cremated fragments can be classified as long bone fragments; thus, this anatomical area is the main one represented; 28% of the fragments were unidentifiable, and 15% were classified as cranial fragments. Less than 1% of the fragments of cremated remains recovered were from the mandible and teeth, and these were thus the least represented parts of the skeleton. The high representation of long bone fragments is common in cremated remains; however, the extremely low representation of teeth is not common and could suggest a loss of remains associated with the secondary deposition of the cremations (Armentano and Malgosa, 2002).

In terms of bone colouration, most of the bone fragments are white (suggesting the bone was completely oxidized), although there are fragments bearing black, grey, and, less often, ochre stains. This variation in the colour of the cremated bone suggests that either the pyre had more than one focus of fire and/or that the temperature at which the body was cremated did not remain constant throughout the ritual (Susini et al., 1988).

### 2.3.2 Inhumed Human Remains

The demographic profile provided by the 13 inhumations found at the Mercat de Sant Antoni was carried out using the standard methods in anthropological analysis (Ferembach et al., 1980; Scheuer et al., 1980; Walker et al., 1988; Ubelaker, 1989; Scheuer and Black, 2000; Chapter 8). Osteological analysis shows a high presence of very young infants with nine (70%) individuals with an estimated age of less than two years at the time of death. Of these, there were four perinates (aged between 24 weeks and seven postnatal days), two neonates (aged between birth and one month), two infants (aged between birth and one year), and one foetus (aged between 8 weeks and birth) (Lewis, 2007: 2). Only four adult individuals were found at this site, three of which were assessed as female (Table 2.4). This demographic profile is very unusual (see Tables 2.1 and 2.3), and it clearly does not represent the entire population as no adult male individuals, old adult individuals, and other juvenile age ranges were recovered. However, it should be taken into account that this site was not completely excavated, and these other segments of the society could have been buried in other areas of the same burial site.

Most of the inhumations were found in simple graves with or without a lid while the three youngest infants were buried in amphorae (Fig. 2.20). All but two of the individuals were laid in supine position with the upper and lower extremities either extended or semi-flexed, regardless of their type of burial; the remaining two individuals were laid in a prone position (UF8 and UF21; Fig. 2.21).

**Table 2.4** Characterization of the inhumed skeletal remains found at the Mercat de Sant Antoni necropolis in Barcino

| Funerary unit | Age at death | Sex | Grave style | Body position |
|---|---|---|---|---|
| UF1 | 4–6 months | Indeterminate | Simple burial with lid | Supine |
| UF2 | Adult | Prob. female | Simple burial without lid | Supine |
| UF3 | Adult | Prob. female | Simple burial without lid | Supine |
| UF4 | Perinate (indet.) | Indeterminate | Amphora | Supine |
| UF5 | <1 month | Indeterminate | Simple burial without lid | Supine |
| UF6 | 38–40 weeks *in utero* | Indeterminate | Amphora | Supine |
| UF7 | 34–36 weeks *in utero* | Indeterminate | Simple burial with lid | Supine |
| UF8 | 30–35 years | Prob. female | Simple burial without lid | Prone |
| UF9 | <1 month | Indeterminate | Simple burial without lid | Supine |
| UF10 | 2–3 months | Indeterminate | Amphora | Supine |
| UF11 | 38–40 weeks *in utero* | Indeterminate | Simple burial without lid | Supine |
| UF12 | Perinate (indet.) | Indeterminate | Simple burial without lid | Supine |
| UF21 | Adult | Indeterminate | Simple burial without lid | Prone |

**Fig. 2.20** Amphora burial of a non-adult individual. In this period, this burial rite is common for very young infants (Photograph: Emiliano Hinojo)

**Fig. 2.21** Skeletal remains found in UF8. Primary burial of an individual in prone position with complete flexion of the upper extremities. It is not a common burial position in this necropolis (Photograph: Emiliano Hinojo)

While none of the perinatal individuals were buried in a prone position at this site, it is common to find perinatal human remains laid in a lateral or prone position. In fact, this position is coherent with the foetal position that neonates preferably adopt during their first weeks of life, and it reproduces their tucked-in presentation position in the womb (Fig. 2.22). However, it is uncommon to find adult individuals laid in a prone position in the Roman period (Philpott, 1991: 71). In the Mercat de Sant Antoni cemetery, there are two individuals, a young female and an indeterminate adult individual, who were buried in this position.

As mentioned above, in Roman society, according to Juvenal and Pliny the Elder, until infants had teethed, usually after the second half of the first year, they were not considered to be separate individuals and thus could not be given the same burial rites as the rest of society (Millett and Gowland, 2015). Therefore, the combination of high numbers of neonate and perinatal individuals with the two

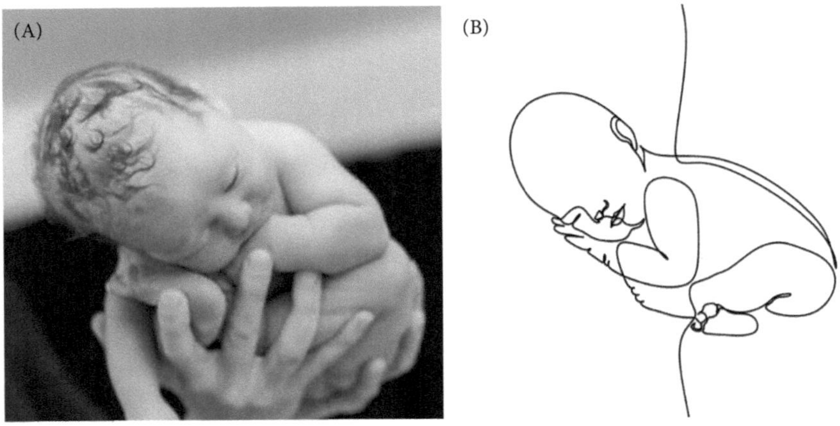


**Fig. 2.22** (A) Folded-in position of the extremities typical of neonates in their first three months of life. (B) Drawing of folded-in position (Photographs: Images available online)

adult individuals laid in a prone position, at least one them a female, found in this area of the cemetery could suggest that this burial site was reserved for such individuals (Polo and García-Prósper, 2001). Furthermore, the demography of the area in this cemetery could suggest this burial site may have been linked to maternity and could shed light on the quality of life of pregnant women as well as the causes of death associated with childbirth and motherhood.

There is a wealth of funerary texts that refer to the death of women during pregnancy, childbirth, and the postpartum period (Fig. 2.23). In the third volume of Soranus' *On Midwifery and the Diseases of Women—Gynaikeia*—there are references to childbirth and how to take care of mothers and neonates. It is thanks to this treatise that we know that, in this period, the main tool midwives had was the birthing chair. This special chair had a back, arms, and a seat with an opening that allowed the neonate to pass and be caught by the midwife. The dilatation was carried out on the bed, and the pregnant woman sat on the chair just before the birth happened. The midwife was usually assisted by three people, two at either side and the last one behind the chair.

Caesarean sections, also known as C-sections, only took place if the mother had already died. This is because the haemorrhages and infections associated with this type of surgery posed a very high risk to living women. Documentary references suggest that the *Lex Regia* or the Law of the Kings promulgated by the Roman king Numa Pompilius between 715 and 673 BCE prohibited the burial of a pregnant woman before the child had been extracted from the womb. During the Empire, Pompilius' *Lex Regia* became the *Lex Caesarea*. The law further stated that whoever violated it was deemed to have destroyed the child's expectancy along with the mother (Lurie, 2005: 282).

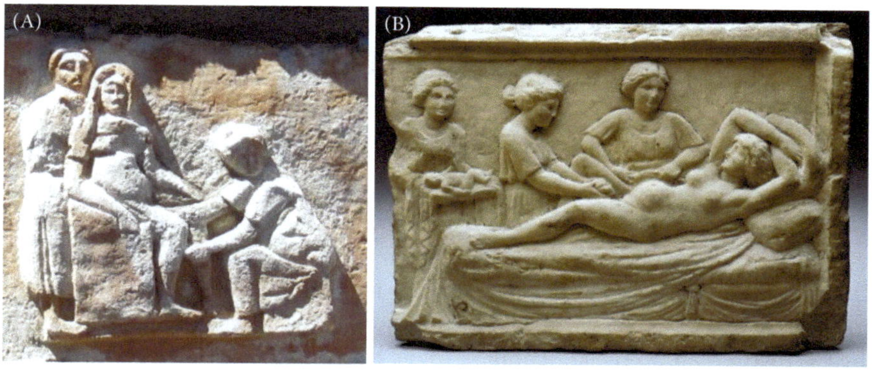


**Fig. 2.23** Examples of Roman reliefs showing childbirth. (A) Terracotta gravestone from Isola Sacra (Ostia). (B) Fragment of a marble bas-relief from a funerary monument (Ostia Antica)

As already discussed, the neonatal mortality rate (the number of stillbirths and neonates that died within the first seven days of life per 1,000 live births a year) was around 300/1,000 (WHO, 2020). This is a very high rate compared with the modern global neonatal mortality rate which is 13.9/1,000. Therefore, in the Roman period, between 30% and 40% of infants died in their first year, and a third of the child population died before the age of 10 (Montanini, 2009; Vázquez Espinar, 2017).

This extremely high mortality was associated with malnutrition, poor hygiene where childbirth took place, and the high virulence of the infectious diseases affecting the Roman population, especially those affecting the youngest members of society (Lalueza and García, 1994; Baxarias, 2002). Furthermore, practices such as infanticides and the abandonment of infants were not uncommon (Harris, 1994; Dasen, 2013; Grubbs, 2013). Contemporary written sources suggest that both practices were accepted given specific circumstances such as infants with physical disabilities, illegitimate children, and those born into already large families who could not afford more members. Therefore, these two practices would have been a way to control the increase in the child population while avoiding other high-risk practices such as abortion (Gowland et al., 2014; Watts, 1973).

Anthropological analysis of the archaeological human remains recovered has allowed us to investigate the palaeodemographic profile of this early imperial burial site. With regards to the inhumed remains, the Mercat de Sant Antoni necropolis is unique as it could shed light on the perception and treatment of pregnant women and infants in early imperial Roman society in Hispania Tarraconensis. When the information obtained from the cremated and the inhumed human remains is combined with the archaeological study of the site itself and the data from the Vila de Madrid cemetery, the analysis shows that Roman Barcino was inhabited by a diverse population in terms of age groups and social strata, which included members from the elite as well as the poorest people living in this Roman city. This diversity observed in death is considered to be a reflection of the diversity of the living. This societal diversity in life is reflected in Roman burial sites and can be documented thanks to palaeoanthropological studies as we will see in Chapter 8.

## 2.4 Slaves and Former Slaves

The lowest social stratum in Roman society was the servile group, made up by slaves and freedmen/women. However, their conditions could vary widely according to their activity (e.g. mining, agricultural, trade, household) and economic income. According to the Clauss-Slaby database–EDCS, the life expectancy of this group for the Iberian peninsula was slightly different from the rest of the population. It seems that life expectancy for slaves was an average of 41.64 years in the Iberian peninsula, whereas for former slaves it was 46.51 years, in other words higher than the rest of the population (Alonso, 2018: 35). Of course, the epigraphic habit may have been very unusual among mining and rural slave communities, so the lack of reliable homogeneous data for the servile group as a whole clearly affects these values. The fact that the difference in life expectancy compared with free-born people is striking supports the idea that the epigraphic evidence alone is not directly useful for demographic calculations.

By way of comparison, the skeletal remains from the Prat de la Riba cemetery (Tarraco) (Baxarias, 2002) showed that the adult population (40–50 years) engaged in strenuous physical activity that resulted in arthrosis (almost 25%). Some examples of slaves' tombs with signs of shackles have been recorded at Valentia, Ilipa, and Gades (García-Prósper et al., 2009). In Roman times, slaves and the destitute were buried in large trenches and wells, together with rubbish deposits, which are known as *puticuli* (Varro, *LL* 5.25) as Horace well described:

> Once slaves paid to have the corpses of their fellows,
> Cast from their narrow cells, brought here in a cheap box.
> This was the common cemetery for a mass of paupers,
> Like that joker Pantolabus, and the wastrel Nomentanus.
> Here a pillar marked a width of a thousand feet for graves,
> Three hundred deep, ground 'not to be passed to the heirs'!
> Now you can live on a healthier Esquiline and stroll
> On the sunny Rampart, where sadly you used to gaze
> At a grim landscape covered with whitened bones.
>
> Horace, *Sat.* I, 8, 8–16

The only *puticuli* documented so far in the Iberian peninsula were close to the Cuartel de Artilleria necropolis in Augusta Emerita. It is described as a huge trench of 43 by 30/14 metres wide and 4.5 metres deep, which included 64 individuals of different ages—including unborn babies—and genders that seem to have been thrown away (Márquez Pérez and Pérez Maestro, 2005). Unfortunately, these mass graves have not yielded any epigraphic evidence but the disposal of the skeletons, some literally thrown away, while others had been carefully placed, as well as the fact that some contained grave goods, seems to indicate the existence of different treatments among those buried in the *puticuli* (Márquez Pérez and Pérez Maestro, 2005: 541–2).

However, one interesting observation that can be made from servile inscriptions is the variation between patterns of slaves' and freedmen/women's death ages (see Fig. 2.24). The average age of slaves at death is lower than that of freedmen and freedwomen. However, it should be borne in mind that slaves might have been freed (manumission) or been able to buy their own freedom. Clearly these events would take place at a greater age; it logically follows that on average freedmen/women were older at death.

From the 1,037 inscriptions of members of the servile population with ages, a high percentage of elderly people is recorded as over 50 years old. Regarding their gender, the age at death appears to be identical for males and females (see Fig. 2.25), which is a variation from the pattern recorded for the overall population of Hispania.

Although the epigraphic sample of the slave and ex-slave population in Hispania Tarraconensis is limited in number, it presents some particular patterns that deserve detailed explanation. First of all, the distribution of the servile

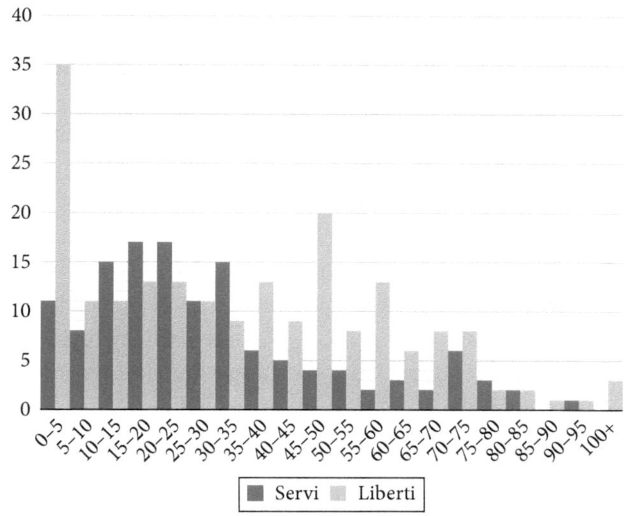


**Fig. 2.24** Comparison of death ages between slaves and freedmen/women in the Iberian peninsula (after Alonso, 2018)

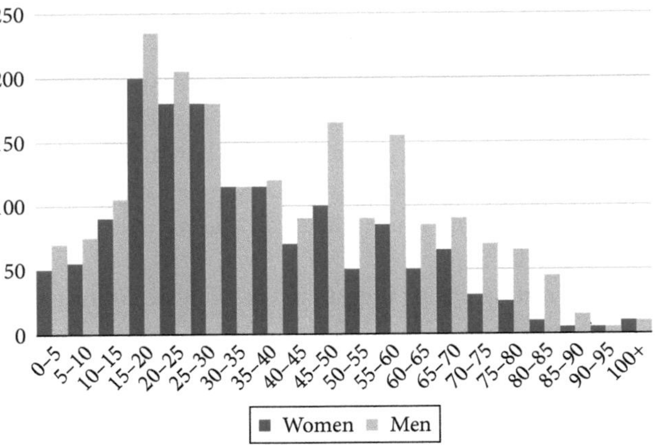


**Fig. 2.25** Servile population death age for genders in the Iberian peninsula (after Alonso, 2018)

population. According to the epigraphic evidence, in a large province such as Tarraconensis the slave and former slave population appears to be a Mediterranean phenomenon, contrasting with the total distribution of inscriptions for the province as depicted in Fig. 2.2. It is worth noting than the province covered a very wide area that stretched as far as the Atlantic coast (see Fig. 2.26). The figure is derived from 387 inscriptions from the LatinNow database, which include the terms 'servus/a' (slave) or 'libertus/a' (freedman/woman), clearly revealing a concentration of slaves and ex-slaves on the Mediterranean coast from Laeetania to the regions around Saguntum (37) and Carthago Nova (102). Another remarkable feature is that the focal point for the largest number of inscriptions naming slaves and freedmen/women was not the capital of the province, Tarraco (47).

In terms of regions, the eastern coastal region has the greatest concentration of slave and ex-slave inscriptions with high densities in urban centres such as Saguntum (37 insc.), Valentia (7 insc.), Edeta Lliria (9 insc.), or Oliva (5 insc.), but also at the nearby rural sites around them. Presumably, maritime and commercial activity may justify this special pattern of distribution. At the local level, the city of Carthago Nova has the greatest concentration of such inscriptions: 102 freedmen/women and 13 slaves (Fig. 2.27). These can also be divided between the republican (28 freedmen/women and 10 slaves) and the imperial period (70 freedmen/women and 3 slaves) (De la Escosura Balbás, 2021: 33–4). Probably most of this segment of the population was involved in mining, agricultural, or commercial activities (see Chapter 7). A good argument to justify this statement is that of the 122 individuals recorded in inscriptions in the republican period, only 11 (9%) are women. This pattern of commemoration aligns well with the prominent place that commercial and honorific epigraphy occupied in the city during this period (De la Escosura Balbás, 2021: 36) (Fig. 2.28).

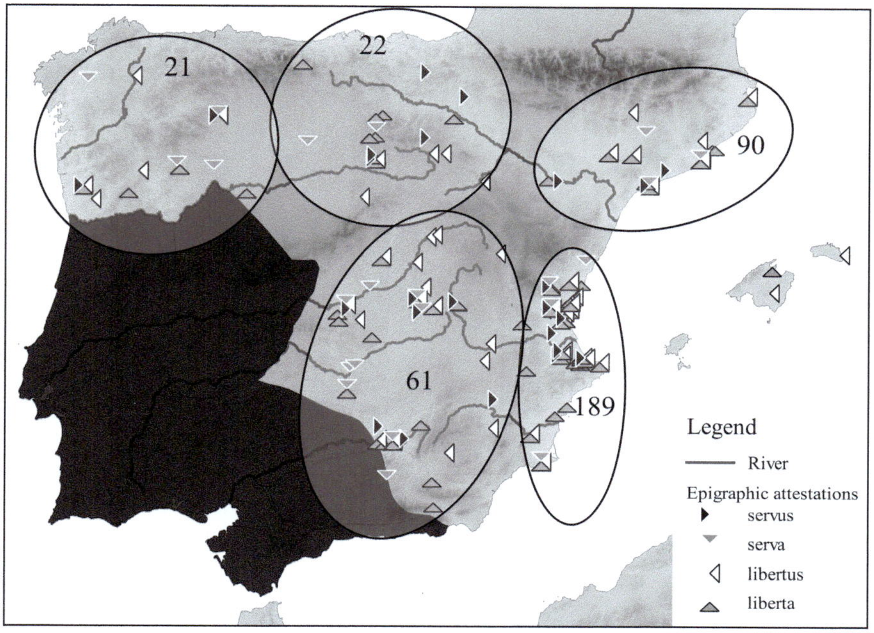


**Fig. 2.26** Distribution of slave and ex-slave population in Hispania Tarraconensis (after LatinNow data, April 2022)

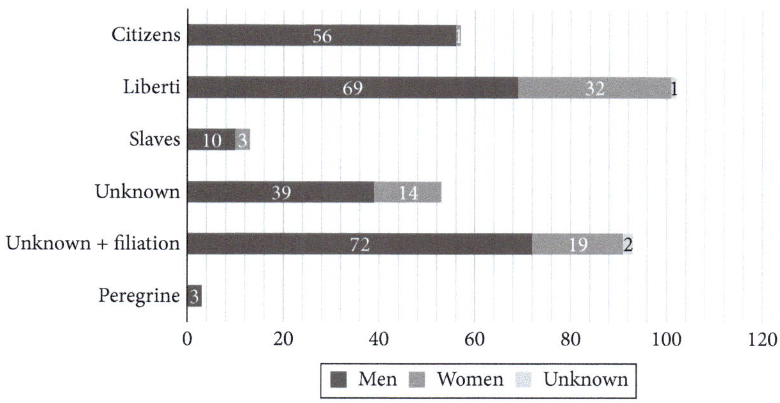


**Fig. 2.27** Population in Carthago Nova divided by their juridical category and status (after De la Escosura, 2021: fig. 2.1)

During the Empire, on the other hand, a shift towards funerary epigraphy as opposed to commercial and honorific inscriptions can be observed (Fig. 2.28). This change enabled freedmen and women to be much more visible in the epigraphic record than in the republican period (De la Escosura Balbás, 2021: 74) (Fig. 2.28).

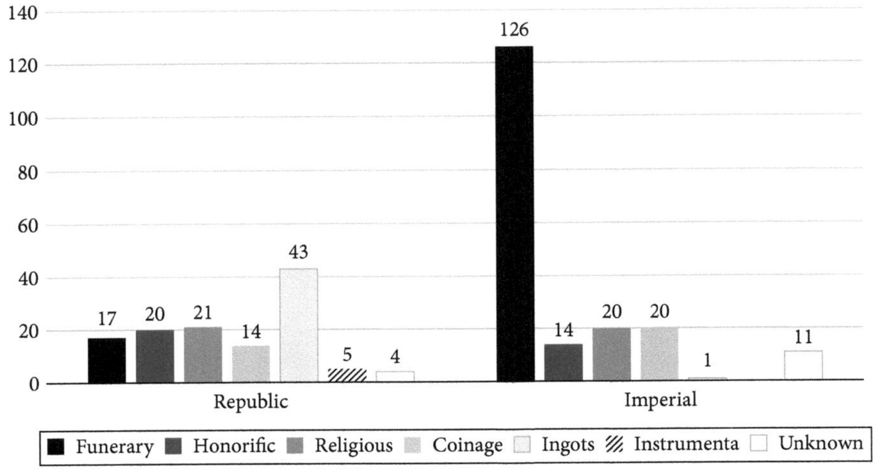


**Fig. 2.28** Population in Carthago Nova divided by period and the type of inscription in which the individuals were commemorated (after De la Escosura, 2021: figs. 4 and 6)

A second concentration of inscriptions referring to slaves and ex-slaves is found in the north-eastern region in the small city of Barcino (24 insc.), which has the highest number of texts; this is quite curious especially if compared to the numbers recorded in the capital Tarraco (8 *servi/servae* and 38 *liberti/libertae*) or Emporiae (7 *liberti/libertae*).

In the inland territories of the province, inscriptions recording slaves and ex-slaves were less frequent, except for a relatively noticeable presence in the Carpetanian area (*conventus* Carthaginensis) with Segobriga (9 *servi/servae* and 4 *liberti/libertae*) as the main focus, while in the *conventus* Cluniensis, Clunia has the largest number of epitaphs (1 *serva* and 4 *liberti/libertae*). In spite of these two concentrations, an even lower presence of slaves and freedmen/women can be detected in the remaining *conventus*, the two Atlantic ones, Bracarensis and Lucensis, being the ones with hardly any. Some of the slaves in the north-west of Hispania were public, so they belonged to the city or other public institutions (Maroto Rodríguez, 2018).

With regards to the slaves' life expectancy according to gender, there are only minor differences in the groups aged over 40, in which males were predominant in the epigraphic record (see Fig. 2.29). In the light of the perinatal mortality rate, women are likely to have died at a younger age. However, it is unlikely that no women lived beyond the age of 40, especially when compared with the data obtained from the study of the cemeteries (Tables 2.1 and 2.3). Commemorative practices tend to focus on males as can be seen in their predominance in the record as a whole.

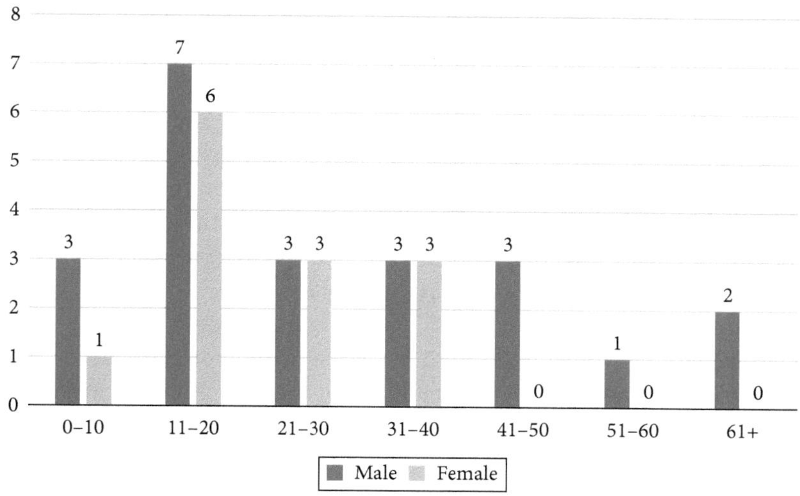


**Fig. 2.29** Life expectancy of slave population according to gender in Hispania Citerior/Tarraconensis

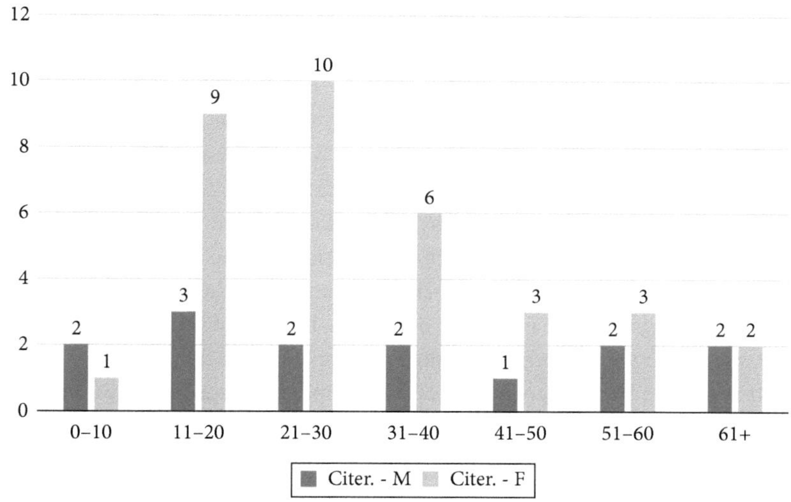


**Fig. 2.30** Life expectancy of freedmen and freedwomen according to gender in Hispania Citerior/Tarraconensis

However, the main differences occur in the group made up by former slaves (Fig. 2.30), in which freedwomen were predominant in almost all the age groups from 11 to 60 years old. There is no clear explanation for this phenomenon, which might be a reflection of a particular epigraphic practice amongst the collective of freedmen and women.

## 2.5 Tarraco: The Case Study of the Capital

Perhaps a closer examination of the capital of Hispania Citerior/Tarraconensis may help to gain an insight into some specific aspects of the population of the province. It must be borne in mind that a capital had a different social composition than the rest of the cities and settlements in the province, with a greater concentration of military and administrative staff. However, a thorough examination of Tarraco's funerary epigraphy can illustrate some clear contradictions. This set contains 326 inscriptions recognized as funerary in nature.

One of the distinctive features of Tarraco was the variation in epigraphic custom depending on gender. Of 23 inscriptions including gender and age, around 80% were males and 20% females. In an analysis of the 155 inscriptions from Tarraco, the basic proportions of the two genders remain largely unmodified, with a total of 116 males (*c.*75%) and 39 females (*c.*25%). Such a high proportion of male inscriptions is unusual in the province, and as has been pointed out (see above) it may be due to the preponderance of honorific inscriptions related to military and administrative personnel. Besides, the preponderance of priesthoods in the religious capital of the province may also explain such bias to some extent. Comparison with the data from the study of the cemeteries is extremely instructive and reinforces this hypothesis, especially if it is remembered that the cemeteries of Tarraco provided a total of 100 women as opposed to 77 men (Table 2.4).

For instance, 16% of the people quoted in the body of inscriptions were soldiers attached to the governor's office. They were, of course, all male and can be identified as belonging to different military ranks (25 insc.) from *miles* from the *Legio VII* (11 insc.) to *legati* (2 insc.), *tribuni militum* (2 insc.), *centuriones* (3 insc.), *beneficiarii* (3 insc.), and others. Furthermore, the administrative personnel only include a couple of inscriptions of *procuratores* and one of a *quaestor*. Some of the military staff formed part of this provincial administration led by the *legatus augustus pro praetore*, the provincial governor of Tarraconensis.

With regard to the age groups, the 23 inscriptions recording ages among the citizens of Tarraco to some extent identify the general trend in the province (Fig. 2.11). The highest levels of death are recorded for individuals in their 20s, and there was a considerable number of inscriptions of individuals that lived beyond the age of 40, but only two who reached what might be considered old age (60+) (see Fig. 2.31).

Another interesting feature of Tarraco is the presence of inhabitants of different origins. At least 7% of inscriptions refer to immigrants, indicating the person's place of origin (see Chapter 7). Most of them came from other parts of the province, such as the *conventus* Lucensis, Bracarensis, Caesaraugustanus, or Clunienses. Only three cases revealed that they could trace their origins to neighbouring provinces

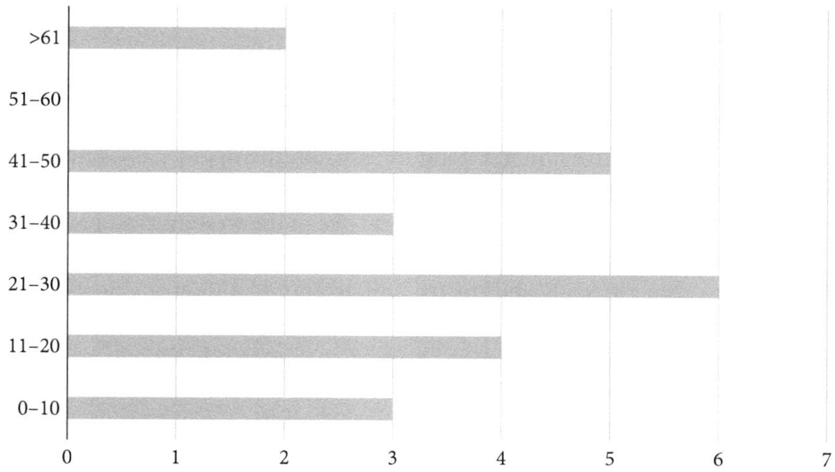


**Fig. 2.31** Life expectancy of the population in Tarraco

such as Aquitania and Narbonensis, and in only one case did the immigrant come from a distant province, namely the city of Tarsus in Cilicia.

## 2.6 Conclusion

Life expectancy, mortality, and fertility are among the most complicated areas of ancient demography to address. The main sources to study them at our disposal, namely epigraphic data, censuses, ancient sources, life tables, and osteological analysis of human remains from necropoleis, are all problematic and present serious limitations.

The epigraphic record lacks information on newborn and infant deaths, and heavily favours the presence of male inscriptions, as well as inscriptions referring to certain social groups such as former slaves. Such inscriptions also tend to round off the age at death in numbers finishing in I, V, X, L, or C, making demographic estimates on the basis of this data in isolation impossible. Be that as it may, the epigraphic corpus offers a large sample and, in many cases, provides valuable information concerning aspects such as the gender, or social and juridical status of the individual. To a certain extent, censuses and life tables represent the other side of the coin. While their data are much more realistic than those supplied by epigraphic evidence, the former, while contemporary to the period under study, have the drawback of being geographically very restricted, since in most cases they originate in Egypt. The latter are valid for a much larger part of the globe but have the disadvantage of offering information that is obtained by studying societies that are chronologically distant from the Roman period. In both cases, their data are very informative but cannot be directly extrapolated to the reality of the province under study in the Roman period. Textual sources, when discussing concepts such as mortality or fertility, did not look at them from a demographic perspective and also tend to focus on the upper classes in Rome from an urban male standpoint. They may be a good complement to other data sources, but they are never sufficient to analyse one of the westernmost provinces of the Empire. Palaeodemographic estimates, on the other hand, are an excellent source of data directly applicable to the inhabitants of the area under study. However, they also suffer from serious limitations. In the first place, the number of anthropological studies that allow comparison with each other is at present still modest—although increasing exponentially. Second, when working with cemetery evidence, it is almost impossible to know what percentage of the total original burial area has survived; moreover, sometimes the whole cemetery is not excavated but rather only one section of it. Third, infants are underrepresented in the majority of cemeteries. Lastly, in many cases cemeteries were in use for long periods of time, with the result that the sample under study covers several centuries in which living standards may have been quite different. In the case of necropoleis, in many cases it is also difficult to be certain of the social and juridical status of those who were buried in them.

In sum, on their own none of the tools that we have to gain a clearer idea of ancient demography is reliable enough or sufficient to obtain a true understanding of life expectancy, mortality, and fertility. For this reason, in this chapter, an attempt has been made to apply an innovative methodological approach: to work with all the above datasets, combining and comparing their results and using their strengths to balance their respective limitations.

On the basis of the epigraphic evidence, the average life expectancy in the Iberian peninsula was 33.29 years for males and 32.03 for females. If these figures are broken down by gender, life expectancy as illustrated by inscriptions reveals a marked difference in the peak period of fertility—around 15–30 years old—when females ran the greatest risk of dying in childbirth. After this fertile stage of life, life expectancy for both genders was comparable from their 40s onwards. The study of thirteen cemeteries in Citerior/Tarraconensis shows that life expectancy reached the 30s in many cases for both genders—although a margin of difference applies from site to site—meaning that these two datasets were not radically different from each other, but were equally problematic if taken at face value, since infants are underrepresented in both cemeteries and epitaphs, thereby substantially increasing life expectancy estimates at birth. In the few cases where infants are present in the expected numbers (30–50%, since perinatal deaths can be estimated to have reached between 30% and 40% according to Golden, 1988: 152–63; Garnsey, 1991: 51–2), such as in the case of Vila de Madrid and A Lanzada (later Roman phase), the life expectancy of a newborn was just 21 and 25.5 years respectively.

The almost 300 censuses known from Roman Egypt provide an average life expectancy of 25 years for males and 22 for females (Bagnall and Frier, 1994: 75–100), thus revealing similar figures to those calculated on the basis of the necropoleis in the province under study where infant mortality is not heavily underrepresented. Similarly, broader studies focusing on the Empire as a whole concur that a value of 25 years (between 20 and 30 years) of life expectancy is plausible (Hin, 2013: 170), while Frier (2000: 790) establishes the average life expectancy at 20.4 years. Model tables, normally the West model: levels 2 to 4 in the Coale-Demeny tables (Coale and Demeny, 1983), also fit quite well with these partial data recorded for ancient populations. West model: level 3 gives a life expectancy at birth of 23 and 25 years for females and males respectively.

When considering life expectancy combining all the datasets, it seems quite feasible to suggest that life expectancy at birth in Hispania Citerior/Tarraconensis might have been somewhere in the mid-20s with a margin of two to three years' error upwards or downwards.

Moving to mortality rates, comparison of the epigraphic data of male age of death in the three provinces of Hispania revealed a peak that corresponds to the decade between the ages of 20 and 30 in Baetica and Lusitania. However, in Hispania Tarraconensis, mortality was most frequent in the decade between the ages of 10 and 20. This earlier peak in the province seems inexplicable. It also suggests, as some sources do, that some individuals reached ages of over 60, and a few of them even reached their 90s and the age of 100. Palaeodemographic data can filter these results. In the thirteen necropoleis studied, only 3.4% of deaths corresponded to juveniles (ages 13–19), while the highest age frequency of death (46.4%) corresponds to young adults (20–40 years) and 24% to mature adults (41–59 years). Individuals reaching ages above 60 numbered very few (3.5% of the total). The data from the necropoleis align well with the expected frequency of death from life tables such as the West model: level 3 and, therefore, should be taken as the valid dataset when it differs markedly from the epigraphic evidence. The ages at death in the epigraphic corpus that are overrepresented seem to commemorate exceptional cases, the unusual, such as unexpected losses, young individuals (13–19) who had survived birth and childhood, together with those who had enjoyed a very long life (+60).

Thanks to the combined study of mortality and life expectancy, approximately one third of children are known to have died in their early years in the province under study. Based on this high infant mortality rate, a high TFR was necessary so as not to jeopardize the demographic balance of the population. Unfortunately, direct testimonies on fertility are rare and fragmentary in texts, censuses, and epigraphy, and almost non-existent for the province under study. Based on the combined study of all our sources, it seems feasible to follow Hin's (2013) proposal for Citerior/Tarraconensis of a TFR range of between 4 and 6 children. Due to the high perinatal mortality, the ratio between mothers and daughters must have reached 2.8 (Gross Reproduction Rate), thereby enabling Roman society to keep population numbers steady in each generation.

Based on the combination of the high number of neonate and perinatal individuals with the two adult individuals laid in a prone position in the Mercat de Sant Antoni cemetery, we have suggested that this burial site was used for those individuals who were not yet considered full members of Roman society. Furthermore, the demography of the area in this cemetery could suggest that this burial site may have been linked to maternity, thus being a unique case that in the future may shed light on the quality of life of pregnant women in the province as well as the causes of death associated with childbirth and motherhood.

*The Human Factor: The Demography of the Roman Province of Hispania Citerior/Tarraconensis.* Alejandro G. Sinner, Cèsar Carreras, and Pieter Houten, Oxford University Press. 
DOI: 10.1093/9780191943881.003.0002

# 3

# Population Estimates

## Formulae, Methods, Variables, and Limitations

At present, there are many different methods that use archaeological, anthropological, and historical evidence to estimate population numbers in both qualitative and quantitative ways. Not all of them, however, are equally reliable and most of them—if not all—suffer from a serious degree of variability due to the nature of the data. The aim of this chapter is to present and review the most important methods and formulae used by historians and archaeologists to make demographic calculations, as well as to consider their strong points and limitations.

It is essential to mention that, while many of the formulae or mechanisms that will be discussed here are useful when carrying out relative estimates, such as of population increases or decreases, there are few that can approximate to numerical figures whose margins of error are low enough to be acceptable and, in many cases, when that happens these must be restricted to a certain regional or even local framework.

There is another kind of approach that prefers rough estimates without precision because they can generate patterns that are useful for historical or archaeological discussion. This is the so called 'shotgun' approach (Hansen, 2006; Hanson, 2016), which generates big data, but can contain inherent bias when estimating the size of sites leading to systematic errors. This approach bases population numbers on a multitude of methods resulting in an average. As there will always be lacunae in our data, the unknowns can be resolved by extrapolating the known data. The assumption of the 'shotgun' approach is that each method has its flaws, but that the combination of the different approaches will lead to a value close enough to identify patterns.

However, working in a limited territory such as the Roman province of Hispania Citerior/Tarraconensis, we should attempt to obtain the most accurate data possible that will allow for a more nuanced picture of population evolution over the course of time as well as regional variations. Of course, this aim cannot always be fulfilled because of the quality of the data, but systematic errors should be avoided as far as possible.

## 3.1 Summed Calibrated Date Probability Distributions (SCDPD)

In prehistoric periods, in which both funerary and architectural archaeological remains are scarce and poorly preserved, the technique known as Summed Calibrated Date Probability Distributions (henceforth SCDPD) of radiocarbon dates (Shennan et al., 2013) has recently been used with interesting results in Britain (Collard et al., 2010) and the Iberian peninsula (Balsera et al., 2015). This method can be applied to estimate relative changes in the size of prehistoric populations (e.g., and without being exhaustive, Shennan and Edinborough, 2007; Collard et al., 2010; Shennan et al., 2013). Part of the hypothesis or premise is that the number of dates/chronologies estimated from radiocarbon studies can serve as a proxy to quantify the size of a given population (Balsera et al., 2015).

The basic premise is that the more people there were, the more organic remains were generated and therefore the more likely we are to date them (Balsera et al., 2015: 208). The value of this approach is that, to a greater or lesser extent, a standardized proxy of measurement can be established, by which regional trends can be successfully compared (Shennan et al., 2013). Recently, these types of studies have been considerably refined, incorporating adjustments that correct some of the problems associated with the applications of SCDPD methods (Balsera et al., 2015: 209), such as the effects of the calibration curve (Michczyński and Michczyńska, 2006), the sample size used/required (Michczyńska et al., 2007), or taphonomic loss, a concept that denotes the tendency for younger things to be overrepresented in comparison with older ones in the archaeological record (Surovell et al., 2009), among many others that escape the scope of our study.

While the validity of SCDPD as a demographic proxy has been reinforced with a comparison between the largest analysis of European cemeteries and the SCDPD obtained from archaeological sites (Downey et al., 2014), it must be noted that the Iberian peninsula was poorly represented in this study, with only four cemeteries and without SCDPD dates; indeed, the method still generates controversy today and is the subject of intense debate among the academic community (e.g. Contreras and Meadows, 2014). While the SCDPD starts from the presumption that a proportional relationship exists between the size of a specific population and its production, recovery, preservation, and, more importantly the analysis of $^{14}C$-datable samples, it is certainly an interesting possibility to contemplate when the archaeological record does not offer any of the other possibilities that will be discussed in this chapter. However, the method also has limitations, such as the level of archaeological research/excavations conducted in different regions. This can lead to research foci being generated (see Fig. 3.1), from which larger or smaller amounts of data arise, which are subsequently interpreted as population densities. In these cases, interpolation—and a clear description of how this process has been performed—of the areas where less research has

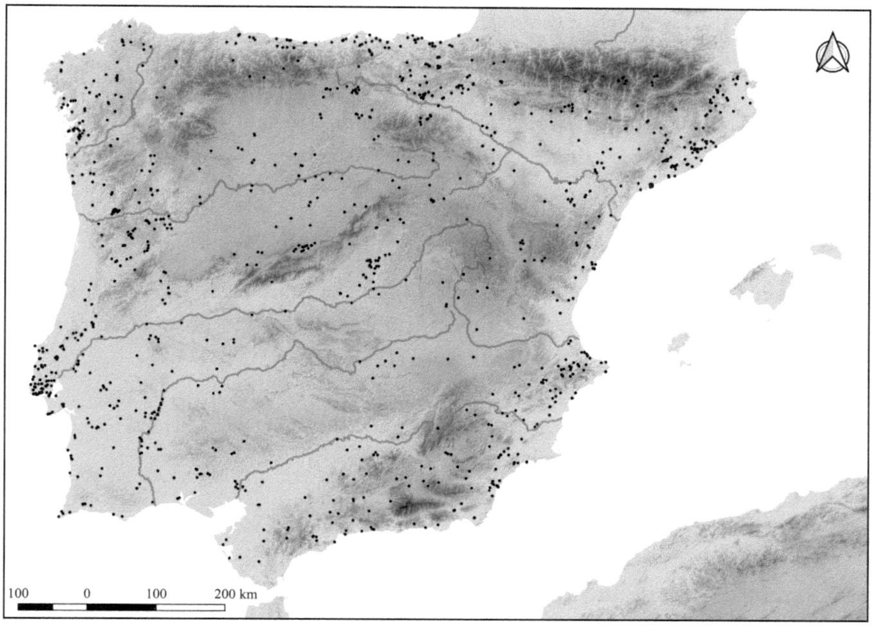


**Fig. 3.1** Distribution of dated sites from Iberia included in the SCDPD study of Balsera et al. (2015: fig. 1)

taken place will be important to avoid skewing the data. As far as is known, this method has not been considered in historical periods when we possess higher quality data.

## 3.2 Epigraphy and Cemeteries

We have already discussed many of the limitations that data from epigraphy and necropoleis pose to conducting demographic studies in Chapter 2. Therefore, here we will only focus on their pros and cons to specifically conduct populations' estimates. In the case of cemeteries, one should be aware that they usually only provide us with partial or fragmentary information since the whole population universe remains unknown. This is sometimes due to the fact that the necropolis areas have not been fully excavated; because even when fully excavated only part of them has been preserved; or because in some cases, as happens with cremation, the funeral rite chosen creates problems, in the same way that the use of this methodology complicates the fact that the evidence for life expectancy or mortality rates among ancient populations is complex and fragmentary, to the extent that many scholars agree that it is useless for establishing demographic patterns (Scheidel, 2001 with bibliography) (see Chapters 1 and 2).

All the obstacles described above have not prevented a number of formulae having been developed over time in order to calculate population estimates by combining information from cemeteries or areas of necropoleis with the number of known dwellings in the associated settlement/s, mortality rates, and evidence of age. Good examples of these types of formulae, as well as their complexity are those found in Buikstra (1976), Neustupny (1983), and Wells (1984):

- Formula 1: $D+ = R \times Pr \times d \times Px$
  Where: D+ (number of burials) = (R) (number of households) × Pr (average size of the household group) × d (mortality rates) × Px (proportion of individuals over a specific age of reference) (Neustupny, 1983).
- Formula 2: $P = D \times e/t$
  Where: P (population numbers) = D (number of burials) × e (life expectancy)/t (time) (Wells, 1984).
- Formula 3: $P = S \times n \times A/m^2 \times t$
  Where: P (density of population by square mile) = S (minimum number of skeletons per mortuary unit) × n (number of tumuli in a specific region) × A (average age at death)/$m^2$ (square miles of the area under study) × t (temporal amplitude) (Buikstra, 1976).

McIntyre (2015) calculated the population of Roman York (Eboracum) by using both settlement sizes and burial data. The second method involved recording the number of burials (in relation to the potential burial ground), site occupation length, and an estimate of life expectancy (32.36) years.

If one can assume that a large sample of a given population in the classical world will have received a proper burial, which does not necessarily imply having a tombstone, the representativeness of the sample is perhaps the main issue when dealing with funerary epigraphy. As already discussed, most scholars generally agree that the data we can work with are only representative of a part/segment of the total existing population, those who could afford to pay for a gravestone. Freedmen, for example, were extremely prone to commemorating their life achievements on tombstones (see Chapter 2 for Citerior/Tarraconensis, the case of Emerita Augusta for Lusitania (Edmondson et al., 2001: 80–4, 93–4), or the city of Rome in Italy (Taylor, 1961)). Similarly, men are usually far more frequently represented than women (Gozalbes Cravioto, 2001; 2003), and some age groups more than others (Table 3.1).

As we have seen in Chapter 2, the use of this type of epigraphy is only applicable to Roman times. While tombstones are estimated to represent approximately three-quarters of the entire available corpus of Roman inscriptions (Saller and Shaw, 1984: 124), the practice of inscribing epitaphs was not adopted by many of the pre-Roman populations of the Iberian peninsula until well after the Roman

**Table 3.1** Proportion of male vs. female tombstones in different territories of the Roman Empire

| Territory | Ratio: male vs. female |
|---|---|
| Hispania | 126:100 |
| Italy | 140:100 |
| Egypt | 139:100 |
| Africa Proconsularis | 140–146:100 |

*Source*: Gozalbes Cravioto (2001; 2003).

conquest (Velaza, 2017; 2018). All the above issues greatly condition the calculations and estimates that can be obtained from epitaphs by breaking down the results, based on various factors such as wealth, gender, age, etc. (Shaw, 1991; Saller, 1994: 35–40). The number of epigraphic monuments in the peninsula will have varied considerably during the periods studied in this chapter, having been non-existent at the textual level in pre-Roman times, rare during the late Republic (second–first centuries BCE), very common during the Principate and the Early Empire, and much less frequent throughout the Late Roman period (Andreu, 2009). Based on all the above, many scholars have insisted on the impossibility of using epitaphs to achieve absolute demographic patterns for the Roman period (Hopkins, 1966: 246–7; MacMullen, 1982: 239–40; Saller and Shaw, 1984: 130; Shaw, 1987: 33–41; Morris, 1992: 157–66; Parkin, 1992: 7–19; Scheidel, 2007).

On the other hand, in some rare cases, the epigraphic record can provide exceptional information—although not free of problems—either directly or indirectly, to estimate demographic numbers for the classical period. The cases of Pompeii, Ostia, and Apamea are excellent examples. For the last city, we have an inscription (*ILS* 2683) on the tombstone of a soldier who died in Syria in the year 6 CE. The inscription reminds us that following Quirinius' orders, he (the soldier honoured in the text) took the census at the *civitas* of Apamea and recorded 117,000 citizen people. As Price (2011: 18) and others have suggested, the use of 'citizen people' is problematic, but it is quite feasible that it refers to the entire free population (male, female, and children) of the *civitas*, which probably means the city as a whole, including its territory. Even more interesting, due to the exceptional preservation of the vestiges that allow comparison between the epigraphic and the architectural remains, but no less problematic in their interpretation, are the cases of Pompeii and Ostia.

In the inscription of one of the leading men in Ostia during the mid-first century BCE, P. Lucilius Gamala the Elder, one passage relating to feeding his fellow citizens at 217 *triclinia* is of particular interest (*CIL* XIV 375 = *CIL* I2 3031a = *ILS* 6147).

The assumption of scholars is that at Ostia only adult male citizens (the *coloni*) were able to participate (D'Arms, 2000: 197; Lo Cascio, 2004: 87). Assuming that there were nine participants at each *triclinium*, the number of *coloni* would have come to 1,953. The demographic significance of these figures is important since, based on this inscription, the total population of Ostia in about the 40s BCE can be estimated to have been in the range of 10,000–14,000 (including slaves) (Zevi, 1973: 579–80, n.1; D'Arms, 2000: 197, n.31; Bodel et al., 2019: 157). On the other hand, these estimates need to be revised in the light of the evidence produced by the joint project conducted by the Deutsches Archäologisches Institut and the American Academy in Rome (Heinzelmann et al., 1997; 2000; Heinzelmann, 1998a; 1998b; Heinzelmann and Granino Cecere, 2001; Heinzelmann and Martin, 2002) and the work conducted by Keay et al. (2020). Over 70 hectares of the city were analysed by means of magnetometry (which proved very successful) as well as electroresistivity (in selected zones). These studies have demonstrated that the extent of the city today is larger than that known when Zevi and D'Arms were publishing their results.

The case of Pompeii is much more complex. The recently discovered anonymous *eulogia* (Osanna, 2018; Bodel et al., 2019; Flohr and Hunink, 2019, Maiuro, 2019; Wallace-Hadrill, 2019) is a good illustration of how complicated and open to interpretation calculating demographic estimates from the epigraphic record can be. Osanna (2018: 316) has correctly suggested that the new inscription brings to the table relevant information on Pompeii's population size; the question is which information? From the specification that fifteen people were reclining on each of the 456 *triclinia* (for a different interpretation see Flohr and Hunink, 2019: 27) laid out during the banquet he gave on the day that he assumed the toga *virilis*, Osanna calculated that a total of 6,840 members of the *populous* participated in the event. If, as he has suggested, this number represents the total adult male population, which means about 27–30% of Pompeii's population, Osanna's figures (later accepted by Maiuro, 2019) give rise to, at the very least (see Bodel et al., 2019: 156), a total population of about 30,000 inhabitants. Such numbers are two to three times larger than any other demographic estimate ever attempted for the Vesuvian city, numbers which usually range between 7,500 and 15,000 inhabitants (see below) (Wilson, 2011: 172; Flohr, 2017). Many factors complicate this reading: what does *populo Pompeiano* mean? The inscription does not specify the status or gender of the 6,840 guests; the term *homines* could refer to 'persons' in general; should women and even minors also be included here as Bodel et al. (2019: 158) have suggested? If we believe in the veracity of the numbers (456 *triclinia* occupied by fifteen people each), as Osanna did, but we understand that the participants constituted all the free adult populace, and we add to these numbers an extra 30% (3,000 individuals) for the slave population (following Scheidel, 2005: 66–7), a total of approximately 10,000 inhabitants is reached (Bodel et al., 2019: 158–9). Without entering a complex debate that escapes the nature of this chapter, the epigraphic record is usually open to interpretation, due to its fragmentary nature in some cases and to the subjectivity of the text in many others, therefore allowing wide margins when calculations are feasible. In extreme cases, as in Pompeii, values of at least 30,000 or in the region of 10,000 people are reached from reading the same text.

## 3.3 Public Buildings and Infrastructure

Another methodology employed starts from the premise that an approximation regarding the population of a specific urban centre can be put forward based on estimating the capacities of certain public buildings, especially amphitheatres and/or theatres (see Table 3.2). As happens when dealing with funerary epigraphy, in the case of the Iberian peninsula, we have a formula that is only useful for carrying out population calculations from early imperial times onwards and in those cities where these types of buildings were built and have survived. In addition, this method has a serious limitation in the fact that, on most occasions, the capacity of these public infrastructures exceeds the total population of a city or municipality, as they offered entertainment to the citizens of rural areas and

**Table 3.2** Comparison between populations calculated from areas of public buildings in cities of northern Italy

| City | Population area × density per ha | Amphitheatre capacity |
|---|---|---|
| Mediolanum | 12,000 | 31,634 |
| Verona | 7,500 | 30,451 |
| Aquileia | 10,500 | 26,384 |
| Parma | 4,500 | 16,152 |
| Ariminum | 6,150 | 13,918 |
| Forum Livii | 4,500 | 13,848 |
| Forum Iulii | 1,875 | 13,848 |
| Forum Cornelii | 4,800 | 11,970 |
| Aosta | 6,255 | 9,765 |
| Eporedia | 4,500 | 8,042 |
| Patavanium | 19,500 | 7,220 |
| Libarna | 3,450 | 5,397 |
| Segusium | 2,250 | 3,014 |

*Source*: De Ligt (2012).

other nearby cities as well, sometimes even from across the *conventus* or province. Tacitus (*Ann.* 14.16) attests to this fact when he tells us about the famous altercation that took place in 59 BCE in the Roman city of Pompeii, and in the course of which the inhabitants of that city brutally clashed with those of the neighbouring city, Nuceria, who also attended the event in substantial numbers.

The comparison between population size, according to the extent of the intramural area and the capacity of the amphitheatres in northern Italy, shows the difficulties involved in using this method in order to estimate the number of residents inhabiting a specific city (De Ligt, 2012) (see Table 3.2). Although it does not necessarily fully discredit the method as a proxy to evaluate population hypotheses in a broader sense, which may include the *ager* of the city and neighbouring territories, scholars studying Roman Spain have recently realized that civic urbanism went far beyond the requirements of some cities (e.g. public buildings), which can be explained as a kind of competition among cities in the Julio-Claudian period (Brassous and Quevedo, 2015; Andreu, 2017; see Chapter 5). Some of those cities entered a recession in the second century CE, because they could not afford to maintain those services for a dwindling urban population (see Chapter 6). The possibility of galleries having been added by using wooden constructions increases their problematic nature.

Other possibilities of this method include studying the number of people available and necessary to carry out collective works of this nature (Nougier, 1959: 277–8; Diamond, 2006: 114–15), though military help cannot be disregarded.

In Hispania Tarraconensis (see Chapter 5 for a more detailed analysis), the Roman city of Segobriga (Cuenca) is an illustrative example of how buildings for entertainment may indicate more about the wealth of a town or its territory than really about the total population. The city's intramural extent covers 10.5 ha, so if a density of 225–250 inhabitants per ha is applied (see below), the total population of Segobriga may have reached between 2,363 and 2,625 citizens. However, this wealthy city, which supplied *lapis specularis* all around the western Mediterranean, built a theatre for 2,000 spectators (55 cm seat) and an amphitheatre for between 5,500 and 7,383 spectators (40–55 cm seat). Therefore, those buildings for public spectacles were designed to cover the demand arising from the territory as well.

Besides, calculations of populations based on other public infrastructures, such as water supply, are even more complicated since most water in ancient towns may have been used for other requirements, such as bathing or industry (Vitr. 8.6.1–2; Frontin. *De Aquaed. Urb. Rom.* 1.23). In addition, we must not exclude the possibility of conspicuous consumption of water in some urban centres. These limitations, however, have not been an impediment for this method being used to calculate the population of ancient cities both outside (Lloyd and Lewis, 1976–7; against Duncan-Jones, 1977–8: 51) and within the Iberian peninsula (Uxama Argaela: García Merino, 2007).

The use of an artificial water supply is also employed for estimating the population, but this approach is very problematic (Wilson, 2011: 170). The first obvious caveat is that this will only be a limitation for population in places where artificial water supply or water containment is absolutely needed. The urban centres of the Iberian peninsula tend to be located in regions with sufficient rainfall to support agriculture irrigated by rainfall (Houten, 2021). However, in dry seasons, when natural access to water through springs or wells might dwindle or even dry up, an artificial supply was certainly needed. In Mediterranean cities the containment of runoff water in cisterns is a widely established custom in the public and domestic sphere. In addition, we find the most obvious artificial water supply: the aqueduct. On the one hand, the construction of aqueducts has been seen as a way to guarantee a continuous supply of water and needed in times of drought in particular. On the other, aqueducts are taken to reflect conspicuous consumption, since they would be the means to supply luxurious baths and fountains (Martínez Jiménez, 2019).

Based on the account of Vitruvius (5.1.2), the forum size seems to be a good indicator of population. He stated that the size of the forum must be such that the population could fit within it, and that it should not appear too large (*vastum forum videatur*). However, calculating population from the size of the forum is again a rather complicated matter (see Chapter 5 for examples). First, there is no clear method to calculate the population from the size of the forum. Moreover, some of the fora might have been used for a second purpose (e.g. as a location for games), which could have led to a larger forum. Lastly, some of the fora might have served a larger area than the *civitas* they belonged to. *Conventus* capitals do not have a second forum whereas provincial capitals tend to have one. As a result, *conventus* capital fora are significantly larger than those of other *civitates*.

## 3.4 Population Density Coefficients

The most frequent method used to estimate population numbers is the one known as the 'density per area' or 'people per area' method, due to its relative simplicity. The method consists of the calculation of populations from settlement extent, on most occasions interpreting or assuming, which in itself already entails a margin of error that must be borne in mind, that this coincides with the perimeter of the walls or even including extramural quarters, and subsequently multiplying this figure by a density per hectare. Especially during the Roman period, there are cities with a large number of *insulae* of more than one floor, such as the cases of Rome or Ostia in Italy, but probably also Tarraco in Spain. In addition, as part of the urbanism that defines the Roman city, many settlements devoted a larger area for public buildings (e.g. roads, temples, fora, etc.) than they did in previous periods. Therefore, this method—with various methodological variations (Sinner and Carreras, 2019)—also presents many limitations that alter the reliability of this simple calculation, but, on the other hand, in our opinion it remains the most suitable one. The formula for the calculation of urban populations is as follows:

- Formula: $P = k \times A$
  Where: P (population) = k (density of population per unit) × A (area occupied by the settlement).

As Wilson (2011) has pointed out, the method of density per area is far from perfect, but it does allow—at least to a certain extent—to minimize the existing bias towards those more extensively excavated sites or those better represented in literary sources and for which there is sufficient evidence that enables us to explore general patterns and trends to be corrected. In his words, 'this method remains as the least bad one available, and it is the only method for which there exist sufficiently abundant data for large numbers of cities' (Wilson, 2011: 170).

However, there is no standard density value for Roman cities as Hanson points out (2016: 53). The largest cities in the Roman period recorded high densities, for instance Rome (471–561 inhabitants/ha), Alexandria (514 inh./ha), or Antioch (501 inh./ha) (Hanson, 2016: 53), but one must bear in mind that these numbers are always based on estimations. Most scholars in the field of Roman demography assume population densities between 100 and 400 inhabitants/ha. In order to make a study of a particular province such as Hispania Citerior/Tarraconensis consistent, one should choose a single k value (density of population per unit), and justify any exception to the rule (e.g. large cities) (see Chapters 4 and 5).

In recent work, Hanson and Ortman (2017: 306) have reinforced the validity of this method by proposing that the relationship between the area and the population of a settlement can be expressed by a single mathematical equation since they appear to be consistent enough to model mathematically. This allows the formulation of a model that predicts the general rate at which settlements will increase their density. To do so, the authors start from the basis that the population of the settlements and their infrastructure (public spaces, buildings, roads, water, etc.) are related in a sublinear manner (the larger the city, the fewer kilometres of roads per capita). Additionally, larger cities not only have higher population densities than smaller towns, but also much higher levels of wealth and poverty, crime, pollution, and disease (Hanson and Ortman, 2017: 305).

## 3.5 Housing Unit Method

This method establishes total population estimates by multiplying an ethnographic or historical value—the number of inhabitants per household or dwelling unit—by an archaeological variable—the number of households at a specific archaeological site. The advantage of this method is that it can provide far more accurate estimates for a specific case study than just using a predetermined population density coefficient (k), since it adapts to the specific features of each site studied.

The versatility of this method offers great possibilities to undertake diachronic comparison (see Sinner and Carreras, 2019 and Chapter 4).

The housing unit method can be a useful source of data for the population density coefficient method (see above) since it will ultimately provide all the necessary data to reach an adequate density of population per unit (k) that can later be used to estimate the population numbers in settlements with similar characteristics, but a much worse state of preservation. However, as we have suggested in the past (Sinner and Carreras, 2019), and will see in Chapters 4 and 5, achieving an adequate value for k implies working with several case studies that are similar socially, culturally, chronologically, typologically, and in terms of size and urbanism to our case study and for which certain variables (such as the number of households, living space, and people per dwelling) are known or can be adequately estimated.

However, several methodological issues can also be identified in connection with this method, the most noteworthy one being the difficulty in defining the 'household' and the development of a standard empirical figure for household size (Birch-Chapman et al., 2017: 5). The archaeological record is affected by a series of post-depositional processes that noticeably mark the condition in which we find it (Schiffer, 1996). Therefore, it is sometimes difficult to recognize, especially during the Iron Age and earlier periods, which architectural remains correspond to archaeological structures that can be identifiable as residential spaces rather than stores or working spaces. Even when living spaces are identified, when estimating population numbers, the term 'household' commonly employed in archaeological studies is interpreted as equivalent to the total number of people living within a single dwelling, perhaps a notion more successfully defined by the term 'domestic group' (Wilk and Rathje, 1981: 620). This number, as well as the layout or plan of the household, can vary significantly, based on the type of family structure—nuclear or extended families—(Grau, 2015) and, as has been suggested for the case of the Celtiberian peoples, it might have changed over time from the Iron Age to the Roman period (Bermejo, 2014).

### 3.5.1 People or Inhabitants per Dwelling

With the above in mind, a fundamental aspect in order to carry out population estimates in any society in the ancient world is the calculation of the number of inhabitants per domestic unit. This method, used since the beginning of the twentieth century (Nelson, 1909), consists of estimating the total of a specific population by multiplying a specific number of people, normally obtained from historical or ethnographic evidence, by the number of households documented in the field or study area. This variable, the only one that cannot be calculated from the archaeological record, is therefore essential for any approach that aims to obtain an estimate of the number of inhabitants for a specific settlement and requires consideration of two basic aspects: (a) the composition of the dwelling unit: an individual, a couple, a nuclear or extended family, or a non-related group; (b) the number of people typically thought to have comprised that particular dwelling unit.

There have been several proposals made over time, so it seems necessary to provide a synthetic review of the numbers suggested by other scholars working on the same topic. It is clear that the studies that work in pre-Roman Spain or in pre-Roman Gaul are of special interest, but so are those that deal with the same area of study in more recent periods (Roman, medieval, and early modern times), and even those that deal with areas and cultures far from those that concern us here, but which might share similar family structures.

For the Iberian peninsula in the Iron Age, the proposals made have been diverse. Almagro-Gorbea (2001: 52–3) suggested a figure of 5 or 6 inhabitants per household when calculating the number of inhabitants in Celtiberian *oppida*. More contradictory are the figures offered by Gracia Alonso et al. (1996: 181) in a study that covered similar chronologies but devoted to Iberian settlements. Initially, the authors defend figures of 6 or 7 inhabitants per domestic unit for those households that have only one floor, but then these figures are reduced to 4 or 5 while estimating the total number of inhabitants per settlement (Gracia Alonso et al., 1996: 183), values that Maluquer de Motes (1983) also adopted in his study of the Iberian settlement of La Ferradura (Ulldecona). Only two years later, Gracia Alonso (1998: 108), took Appian's numbers (*Iber*. 19–20) as his starting point to consider a figure of 5 individuals per household as the most appropriate for the Iberian communities in the north-east of the peninsula. This method for calculation has recently been dubbed Late-Iberian estimation (Nión-Álvarez, 2023: 4) and has been further developed by Sinner and Carreras (2019). As can be seen above, the average number of inhabitants per house can see small variations based on available data and cultural factors.

Further north, in pre-Roman Gaul, Py (1996: 251), in a substantial synthesis dedicated to urban planning and habitat spaces of the Lattara *oppidum* (Lattes, Hérault), states that 93% of the structures had an area of less than 66 m$^2$, and therefore it is difficult to imagine anything more than a nuclear family of 4 to 6 individuals (including children) per household. Isoardi (2009: 71–2), although she was reluctant to estimate the number of inhabitants of the *oppida* of pre-Roman southern Gaul and basing her figures on previous studies by Dedet (1987: 172, 205–6; 1999: 313–14) and Py himself (1996: 251), estimated that the most plausible number of inhabitants per household was 5. Hansen (2006: 59) argues that the size of a family varied during its lifetime from 3 to 7 persons, and the average was 5.

If we move forward diachronically, and now focus on the Roman period, it can be seen that the estimates are calculated on the basis of more reliable data since we have the first information provided by censuses. One of the best supported estimates is that made by Kennedy (2006). This scholar starts from the study of 167 family censuses in Egypt to suggest an average of 4.3 inhabitants per household. Bagnall and Frier (1994: 55), in their important work dedicated to the demography of Roman Egypt, propose a number of 5.3 inhabitants per household for the city of *Hermopolis*, which they justify on the basis of 177 census statements preserved (Bagnall and Frier, 1994: 67). They also distinguished between a family average of 4 in the metropolis, whereas on rural sites this figure reached 4.5 inhabitants.

Based on this work, Carreras (1996) suggests an average of 4 people per household or family unit, instead of the 5.3 employed by the above mentioned authors. This estimate is obtained from the data contained in the 136 complete censuses recovered so far and does not quantify the remaining 41 censuses that are partially preserved. From papyrological evidence, Alston (2002: 70) estimates that the houses were inhabited by just under 8 people on average. Without leaving the Roman era, but now moving to Pompeii, Flohr recovers Wallace-Hadrill's idea (1994) that different families and domestic spaces very possibly housed somewhat more disparate numbers of individuals, depending not only on their surface but also on the type of family structure and number of slaves. The author suggests a figure of 3 to 4 individuals in taverns and between 2 and 5 for second-floor apartments (Flohr, 2017: 63), numbers that fit well with those between 3 and 5 individuals that Storey (1997: 972) had already suggested in the past for such structures. To assess the number of inhabitants who occupied the houses, Flohr takes Alton's data (*c.* 8 individuals) as a starting point and proposes a figure of between 7 and 12 individuals (Flohr, 2017: 64–5). In this estimation, Flohr's numbers are conservative if we compare them with those of Storey, who suggested that the size of the Roman nuclear family should be between 3 and 5 individuals, to later add between 10 and 12 additional persons to cover slaves and other dependants, reaching figures between 13 and 17 people (Storey, 1997: 972–3). At this point and after seeing how the debate about the number of individuals is profusely more complex in Roman times—perhaps because the historical and archaeological evidence is richer—we must add Wallace-Hadrill's interesting observation (1994: 213–14, 225–7) that larger domestic units do not always have to house a greater number of people. Finally, to determine the populations of a large number of cities throughout the Roman world, including the main cities of Hispania, Hanson and Ortman (2017: 308) use a standard figure and suggest that the size of each household ranged between 3 and 7 people, accepting an average of 5 individuals per household.

Under the label 'Roman' we encompass a significant number of peoples and cultures that stretch across a wide area, and who were organized inside and outside the domestic unit in very different ways. Therefore, although significant, the estimates just discussed cannot be extrapolated to Roman Hispania. Before deciding what the most reasonable number per domestic unit for the Hispanic case seems to be, it is necessary to assess what information is available for this territory in later times for which we have reliable census information.

The preserved medieval and modern censuses provide data of great interest. In 920 CE, in the town of Baén (Catalonia, Spain), 80 inhabitants could be counted in 18 families, which gives us a total of 4.4 people per family unit (Salrach, 1982: 209–10). In 1378 the population of the city of Barcelona (Catalonia, Spain) was 34,447 individuals belonging to 7,655 households. Therefore, it is clear that the number of inhabitants per household in Barcelona during the fourteenth century was 4.49 (Iglesias, 1981; 1991). Pérez Puchal (1972: 4), when estimating the population of Valencia in 1418, uses a proportion of 4 to 4.5 inhabitants per household (based on hearth-tax—*foc* or *fogatge*—figures). In the 1631 census of the city of Girona (Catalonia, Spain), 4,900 people were counted in a total of 1,292 households, which gives us a total of (3.79) 4 inhabitants per household (Alberch and Castells, 1985). It is interesting to note that the above areas in NE and E Mediterranean Spain were among the most densely populated in 1787 (see Fig. 3.2).

The Haggadot or Passover prayer books produced in Barcelona in the first half of the fourteenth century can also shed light on the household's number of inhabitants, since families are depicted in dining scenes. In most of these works we can see a family of five or six individuals (Fig. 3.3). In fact, a family size of five

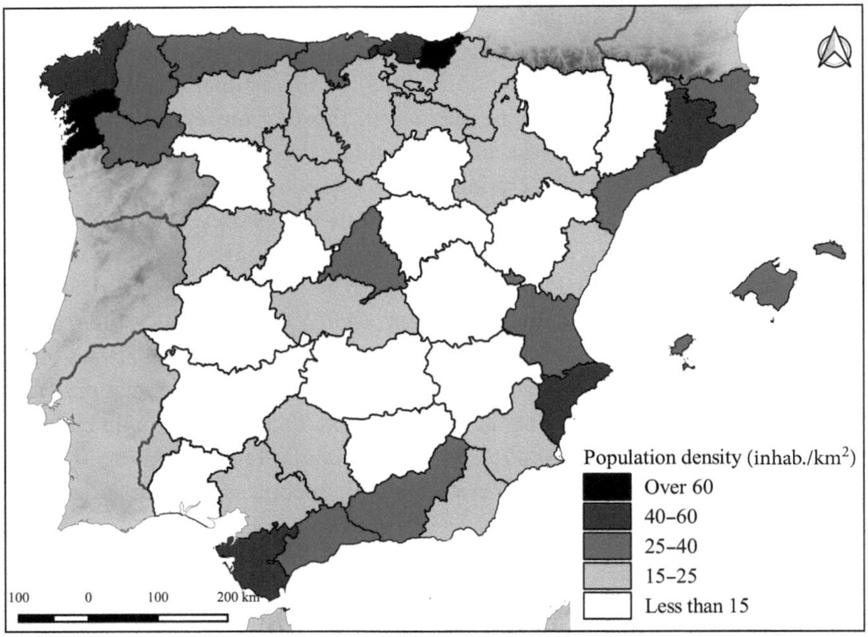


**Fig. 3.2** Map with the distribution of the population in Spain in 1787

**Fig. 3.3** Four representations of families in the Haggadot or Passover prayer books from fourteenth century Catalonia: (A) British Library fol. 28v. (B) The Barcelona Haggadah fol. 19v. (C–D) The Sarajevo Haggadah

members has been used in studies discussing the Jewish population of Barcelona in the year 1079 CE (Banks, 1981: 831).

If we now focus our attention again on Egypt, widely used as a comparator before, but in this case in modern times, we see that the average size of the family unit has decreased slightly compared with that of the Roman era, the 3.5 members registered in rural cities in Egypt being a good example of this (Zorn, 1994).

Family size has been and continues to be one of the fundamental issues to consider in any demographic study, regardless of region or study period. Therefore, the list of estimates that could be cited here is very long, almost endless if we start to consider studies—on the other hand, very interesting ones—that deal with other cultures that are not Graeco-Roman or if we incorporate the extant medieval and modern censuses throughout the European continent into our study. However, for the purpose of this work, we think that we have presented a sufficiently complete sample that allows us to visualize a number of trends, which will now be summarized.

When dealing with pre-industrial societies, the most acceptable proportion of inhabitants/households seems to range between 4 and 6 people per household

(Hanson and Ortman, 2017: 305). These figures seem to be quite homogeneous throughout the pre-Roman period at the level of the Iberian peninsula and in southern France. This does not mean that they are free of controversy or universally accepted, as Isoardi (2012: 43) has made clear: 'Indeed, during our research, it has become apparent that the figure of 4–6 individuals per dwelling usually proposed for this civilization rests, insofar as it has support, on weak arguments. . .'.

Estimates suffer from greater variability in Roman times ranging from 4 to 12 individuals per household (up to 17 if Storey's proposal is accepted). This is basically due to two fundamental interrelated factors that are very difficult to assess generically since they can vary considerably, depending on the area under study: (1) the proliferation of habitat structures of a much larger size than those we can find in the pre-Roman period; (2) the presence of slaves and other dependants within the family unit and about which there is a far-reaching debate as regards how they should be quantified (Scheidel, 2005). However, it should be noted that when studies of a broader nature have been carried out—either at the provincial level (Carreras, 1996; 2014) or throughout the Empire (Hanson and Ortman, 2017)—surveys that do not focus exclusively on a single case study, it seems that the most widely accepted figures do not experience major modifications and are maintained around a family unit of between 4 and 6 individuals (see Table 3.3).

**Table 3.3** Summary of different estimates put forward to determine the number of inhabitants per household

| *Oppidum*/City/Territory | Household members | Reference |
|---|---|---|
| Pre-Roman Gaul (Languedoc) | 5 | Isoardi, 2009: 71–2 |
| Lattara (Lattes, France) | 4–6 | Py, 1996: 251 |
| **Pre-Roman NE Spain (Iberian *oppida*)** | 6–7 | Gracia Alonso et al., 1996: 181 |
| **Pre-Roman NE Spain (Iberian *oppida*)** | 4–5 | Gracia Alonso et al., 1996: 183 |
| **Pre-Roman NE Spain (Iberian *oppida*)** | 5 | Gracia Alonso, 1998: 108 |
| La Ferradura (Iberian *oppidum*) | 4–4.5 | Maluquer de Motes, 1983 |
| Pre-Roman Spain (Celtiberian *oppida*) | 5–6 | Almagro-Gorbea, 2001: 52–3 |
| Hermopolis (Roman Egypt) | 5.3 | Bagnall and Frier, 1994: 55 |
| Roman Spain in the Early Empire | 4 | Carreras, 1996 |
| Baén in 920 CE (Lleida, Spain) | 4.4 | Salrach, 1982: 209–10 |
| Barcelona in the 14th century | 4.5 | Iglesias, 1962 |
| Valencia in 1418 | 4–4.5 | Pérez Puchal, 1972: 4 |
| Girona in 1631 | 4 | Alberch and Castells, 1985 |

| | | |
|---|---|---|
| Early modern Spain in 1755 | 4–5 | Iglesias, 1979 |
| Native American Communities | 4–5 | Hassan, 1981: 73 |
| Broken K Pueblo | 6.1 | Hill, 1970 |
| Western Pueblo People | 5.5 | Turner and Lofgren, 1966 |
| Pueblo People | 5.03 | Steward, 1937: 87–104 |

Finally, these numbers are reinforced with the appearance of census information in the Iberian peninsula. As we have seen above, the data from several medieval and modern censuses in different parts of the Iberian peninsula seem to show that family units maintain a ratio of between 4 and 6 individuals per household throughout much of a long historical period. The application of this method normally generates wide ranges of population estimation, except when the existence of large family units can be excluded because the inhabitable area recommends it. As this method incorporates by default the nuclear family unit as the standard, it is necessary to bear in mind that population estimates will be inflated for those communities in which there are homes with single or two-person occupation without dependants of any kind (Birch-Chapman et al., 2017: 5). A 'control' mechanism that can be used in these cases is the use of the minimum living space variable that can regulate the maximum number of inhabitants that can coexist in a given space.

### 3.5.2 Residential Area Density Coefficient Method or Living Space

There can be no doubt that a family unit could occupy a space of greater or lesser area depending on its social status and wealth, but there is no doubt either that, anthropologically, an individual needs a minimum basic space in which to subsist. Numerically defining this space is of great interest when carrying out demographic estimates since minimum living space and the size of the family unit are two variables that are constantly interrelated in this type of calculation. In many cases, the first of these variables can be used to calculate the second and vice versa.

The residential area density coefficient or living space is a measure that quantifies the average space occupied or needed by an individual within the domestic unit. Through this method, the estimated total area of a dwelling is divided by a predetermined figure that is obtained as a result of ethnographic and archaeological research. Naroll (1962) tried to establish a universal value for the minimum living space that a person requires by examining ethnographic data from the study of eighteen nomadic and sedentary societies. The author proposed a standard constant of 10 $m^2$ of roofed area per person, a proposal accepted by Leblanc (1971), but which other authors such as Summer (1979), Hill (1970), or

Kramer (1979) reduced to a figure of 5 $m^2$, compared to the criteria of Cook and Heizer (1968), who introduced a mixed criterion by assigning a minimum surface area of 2.325 $m^2$ for the first six people and 9.3 $m^2$ for the remaining ones. Other research conducted in south-west Asian villages and comparable villages elsewhere has produced a wide range of personal space estimates from around 1.86 $m^2$ to 13.2 $m^2$ per person (Birch-Chapman et al., 2017: 3 with bibliography). The latter authors note that the most significant cause of inconsistency is due to the different definitions of 'space'. 'Space' can refer to the total roofed floor area, although alternatively it can refer to total household area, total built area, and the total area in which people lived and slept. When estimates were based on this last definition, the differences between density coefficient areas were reduced considerably to between 2 and 5 $m^2$ (Hill, 1970: 75; Clarke, 1974: 286; Hayden et al., 1996: 152, 159).

When estimating density coefficients in the classical period, two different methodologies are used. The first is to omit those spaces that are not considered as living areas, although in many cases they are part of the dwelling under study (Hill, 1970; Kramer, 1979; Hayden et al., 1996; Birch-Chapman, 2017: 5). Good examples are courtyards, storage areas, production spaces, stairs, walls, etc. This method is problematic insofar as it requires an excellent archaeological record that allows the function of each space to be identified with certainty and raises issues. Additionally, for the Iron Age Iberian peninsula, and especially for the early Roman period, the principles of 'form equals function' and 'style equals users' need not be true. The same space, particularly one inside a domestic unit, may have had a number of different uses and users during its existence (Van Oyen, 2015; Sinner, 2015). Slaves are a good example since, in the Roman world, they do not seem to have had specific sleeping quarters, although there is ample debate on this topic (Joshel, 2010; DuBois, 2019), and they might have slept in different spaces within the house. The type of family structure—nuclear or extended—once again is fundamental in this debate and requires the inhabitants of the household to be identified. This can be very problematic in an area, Hispania, where cohabitation between colonizers and natives over several centuries is involved. The inhabitants of different households could have been of different cultural substrata, and therefore different family structures might have occupied similar physical spaces (see Chapter 7). The domestic spaces that have been excavated at several sites in the Iberian and Celtiberian regions (Cortés, 2014; Uribe, 2015) are good examples of this issue. They include houses of very different sizes, shapes, complexity, and styles. On the other hand, it is advantageous to focus only on living areas or even sleeping areas, if feasible, since this approach estimates the resident population, differentiating other spaces that, for example, in the Roman world are frequent in aristocratic houses, but which are known to have satisfied social needs (Vitr. 6.5.1–2; Wallace-Hadrill, 1988; 1994), and which need not have been directly related to the number of individuals resident. The second option, to a large extent, simply includes the covered areas or the entire surface of the house as part of the available space.

Py's (1996) consideration of a family unit of 4 to 5 members, would represent an individual living space of around 10 to 12 $m^2$ for the inhabitants of Lattes (Gaul), figures that are quite close to those already commented on by Naroll (1962: 588). In the case of the pre-Roman towns in the north-east of the Iberian peninsula, the domestic space, as a general rule, presents substantial differences, which means that considering the vital space variable is a key factor in order to calculate the number of individuals that inhabited the smaller- and larger-than-average structures (between 10 and 15 $m^2$) (Belarte, 2010: 114). In these exceptional cases, the application of the figures given by Naroll would mean that spaces inhabited by a single individual or couple must have existed. However, if we accept Summer's numbers, these spaces could have housed a family unit consisting of four individuals. Using a slightly different approach, since its calculations are based on sleeping instead of on living space, Hemsley (2008: 131) working on Neolithic populations of the Levant such as Jericho, estimated the minimum sleeping space requirements necessary of 1.24 $m^2$ and 1.77 $m^2$ based on modern human measurements of 1.65 m and 1.83 m, respectively. In her estimates she also added the need to avoid hearths and other surrounding activity zones, access, and three different degrees of personal annual residential storage space. She estimated that smaller, single-roomed structures of $\leq$ 10 $m^2$, therefore relevant to the numbers we have been considering here, may have accommodated up to four people.

Whatever the case, such small spaces represent a minority, and in most Iberian settlements for which open-area excavations have been undertaken, simple houses, with surfaces ranging between 20 and 40–50 $m^2$, coexist with complex residences, which usually exceed 50 $m^2$ and often 100 $m^2$ (with exceptions that reach 1,000 $m^2$), and have multiple rooms (Belarte, 2010: 114; Chapter 4).

In Roman times, archaeology records different sizes for households, which are understood to have been inhabited by different family sizes. In Pompeii, Wallace-Hadrill (1994: 91–117) distinguished between large houses occupied by large families (7 to 10 members) or small and medium-sized houses for nuclear families (4 to 5 members). These calculations, combined with those carried out by Storey (1997: 973–4) for the city of Rome, have led to the conclusion that each person occupied an average space of 35 $m^2$, much higher than all the numbers discussed above and showing how important it is to contextualize our numbers culturally, geographically, and chronologically. Apart from the aforementioned estimates, Storey (1997: 969–73) also calculated the North African population for the city of Sabratha. This city covers an area of 31 ha, of which only 25.4 ha were considered residential (81% of the total area). Bearing in mind that the average surface area of each identified residential structure occupied approximately 100 $m^2$, the personal life space available to each individual can be estimated at around 20 $m^2$ (for a five-member nuclear family, see below). This space could be reduced by half (10 $m^2$) for those with larger family units (ten members). Another study of interest for the Roman period is that of Hermopolis (Egypt). The exceptional

**Table 3.4** Estimate of minimum living space per person in Roman cities

| City | Area | Minimum living space per person | Reference |
|---|---|---|---|
| Pompeii | 64–7 ha | 35 $m^2$ | Wallace-Hadrill (1994: 91–117) |
| Sabratha | 31 ha | 10–20 $m^2$ | Storey (1997: 969–73) |
| Timgad | 9.96 ha | +20 $m^2$ | Storey (1997: 969–73) |
| Hermopolis | 120 ha | 19 $m^2$ | Bagnall and Frier (1994: 55) |
| Lattes | 3.5 ha | 10–12 $m^2$ | Py (1996: 251) |

conservation of this 120-hectare Egyptian city (Bagnall and Frier, 1994: 55) has allowed two of its four quarters to be revealed. In the known sectors, 4,200 households (*oikiai*) are documented according to the SPP V.101 papyrus. From these figures, Bagnall and Frier calculated that the four quarters of the city could have contained a minimum of 7,000 houses. Taking into account that only 60% of the city was occupied by households (72 ha), the average size of the homes was 102 $m^2$. As the authors also studied the city census and the average family had 5.3 members, the living space of each inhabitant can be estimated at around 19 $m^2$. Another case study provided by Storey (1997: 969–73) refers to the city of Timgad, which covers an area of 9.96 ha, with 109 identified households. The average size of these units is 100 $m^2$, so each member of a nuclear family would have enjoyed at least 20 $m^2$ (see Table 3.4).

Beyond the figure one decides to apply, what is fundamental is to recognize that the minimum space requirements that a given person needs are conditioned by several factors, not only economic, but also climatic and cultural ones. If we are aiming to establish diachronic comparisons, before adopting any of the previously proposed figures, it is necessary to take into account variables such as the space available in the settlement, notions of privacy, type of family structure, and shape and size of the household, since many of these factors changed considerably in the Iberian peninsula between the fourth–third centuries BCE and the Late Roman period.

## 3.6 Storage Provision Formulae

This very specific method, which has not been applied so far to the classical period, was developed by Hemsley (2008) to study Pre-Pottery Neolithic (PPNA and PPNB) built environments in the Near East for her PhD thesis and has later been applied to a case study in the north-west of the Iberian peninsula (Punta de Muros) during the Iron Age (Nión-Álvarez, 2023). Hemsley attempted to calculate the number of persons sleeping inside a structure by creating a formula that includes a complex number of variables such as access routes, hearths, activity zones, and up to three degrees of personal annual storage provisions (zero provisions; moderate: 0.46 $m^3$; maximum: 0.92 $m^3$).

From this data, different formulae where 'P' is the average number of sleeping occupants and 'A' is the estimated residential floor area were constructed by correlating the maximum number of sleeping occupants to the available residential floor area:

- no personal storage (P = 0.3944A – 0.375);
- a moderate degree of personal storage (0.46 cum: P = 0. 2477A + 0.0339); and
- a high degree of personal storage (0.92 cum: P = 0.1903A + 0.3976).

In a later study, 'Estimating population size, density and dynamics of Pre-Pottery Neolithic villages in the central and southern Levant' (Birch-Chapman et al., 2017: 6), this method was applied in two different ways: first by assigning the total residential floor area estimates functioning contiguously as 'A' to estimate the total population numbers ('P'); second, by assigning to 'A' the mean residential floor area of complete dwellings in order to estimate the average number of inhabitants per domestic unit ('P'). The resultant value was later multiplied by the number of contemporaneous dwellings.

Interestingly, in a study that considered several of the methods described in this chapter, the authors concluded that the storage provisions formula was the most valid method. The argument behind this belief is that it 'is based almost exclusively on archaeological evidence and empirically-derived values for human sleeping space. It does not incorporate assumptions regarding dwelling unit size, the constitution of the dwelling unit or perceptions relating to space preference' (Birch-Chapman et al., 2017: 6).

Because this method has the advantage that it does not rely on employing ethnographically derived coefficients from settlements and periods that may not be directly comparable with the specific case studies under consideration, it may therefore be of interest as a standard of comparison for the study of Iron Age and pre-Roman populations. However, the main advantage of such a universal approach is significantly reduced when we can differentiate using cultural factors (Nión-Álvarez, 2023: 6). This applies especially for the Roman period, thanks to the existence of extremely well-preserved case studies such as Hermopolis, Ostia, and Pompeii, which combine excellent archaeological, epigraphic, and even census evidence, compared with the evidence provided by census of the latter periods, and seem to result in data that are close enough to the reality of our case studies to prioritize the use of other methods described above, more specifically the housing unit method and the residential area density coefficient method.

Interestingly, as shown in Table 3.5, with exceptions, the difference in the estimates between the three methods is not large enough to radically change total

**Table 3.5** Summary estimates for people per dwelling comparing different methodologies

| **Method used to estimate people × dwelling** | **Subphase A1** | **Subphase A2** | **Subphase B2** | **Subphase C2** |
|---|---|---|---|---|
| Housing unit method | 3–8 | 3 | 3 | 3–8 |
| Residential area density coefficient method | 1.9–5.5 | 1.3–3.7 | 1.1–3.2 | 2.8–7.8 |
| Storage provision formula 1 | 2.4–4.2 | 1.6–2.5 | 1.4–2.2 | 3.4–6.4 |
| Storage provision formula 2 | 2.9–4.2 | 1.8–2.5 | 1.7–2.1 | 4.3–6.4 |

*Source*: Birch-Chapman et al. (2017: table 4).

population estimates, especially if we consider those in Phase C, where the architecture is defined by Byrd (2005: 28) as agglomerated, rectilinear, and often including two-storey structures of predominantly masonry construction (between 3 and 8 or 4 and 6 occupants using the storage provision formula), and therefore more similar in terms of urban layout and architecture—although still very distant from—to what can be seen in our case studies (Table 3.3).

## 3.7 Formulae and the Rural World

As Witcher (2011: 46) underlines, the main sources of information for ancient populations are historical texts, comparative data from other later periods, and archaeological evidence. In the case of rural populations of Hispania Tarraconensis, for which only a few texts provide indirect rural censuses, medieval and modern data are an excellent comparative source while field survey data are in an early stage.

With regard to estimates of rural populations, the censuses quoted by Pliny the Elder (*NH* III.3.28) for the three *conventus* of north-western Tarraconensis produce a range of densities for inhabitants per km$^2$ (Asturum: 5.1; Lucensis: 6.3; Bracarum: 12.2). The average of these three values would be a density of 7.87 persons per km$^2$, which may have been an appropriate value for the whole Iberian peninsula, which can be later discussed. Likewise, Hin (2013: 303–5) records similar differences in rural densities in regions of Roman Italy, which she believes were due to variations in the living conditions and the resources of each territory.

Most studies that provide estimates of 6 million inhabitants for the Iberian peninsula, such as Corvisier and Suder (2000), were based on rural densities of 10.1 inhabitants/km$^2$ (Aüsbuttel, 1998), with no special argument to justify this

**Table 3.6** Density of population in the northern Spanish kingdoms in 1490

| Territory | Population | Extent | Density |
|---|---|---|---|
| Castile | 4,300,000 | 355,000 | 12.11 |
| Kingdom of Aragón | 250,000 | 47,720 | 5.23 |
| Principate of Catalonia | 300,000 | 32,108 | 9.34 |
| Kingdom of Valencia | 255,000 | 23,25 | 10.96 |
| Kingdom of Mallorca | 50,000 | 4,992 | 10.01 |
| Kingdom of Navarre | 120,000 | 11,700 | 10.25 |

*Source*: After Ladero Quesada (2014).

figure. However, other similar provinces have been assigned lower densities Gallia (7.7 persons/km$^2$), Greece (7.5 persons/km$^2$), or Africa (7.5 persons/km$^2$), closer to the average estimate obtained from Pliny's figures.

The second source of information—modern comparative data—reveals its usefulness because it defines a range of feasibly densities per km$^2$ that can be compared to the data obtained in ancient sources and archaeological evidence. The first extant census in north-eastern Spain (1497) recorded an average density of population of 12 inhabitants per km$^2$ (Iglesias, 1979), of whom a quarter were urban inhabitants. Therefore, the average rural density was around 9 to 10 inhabitants per km$^2$, in other words two hearths ('focs' in Catalan—each of four or five family members). This figure is not far from the 7.87 inhabitants per km$^2$ obtained in Roman times. A recent study by Ladero Quesada (2014) reveals a density of 10.9 inhabitants per km$^2$ in 1490, including cities for the Iberian peninsula as a whole, so the rural values would have been around 8 or 9 inhabitants per km$^2$. If the medieval kingdoms that occupied the former Hispania Tarraconensis alone are taken into account, they offer the densities listed in Table 3.6.

Apart from ancient texts and comparisons with other historical periods, rural populations can only be inferred from archaeological survey data. Field survey methodologies have improved in recent years by considering the intensity of survey, visibility, and material dispersal (Millett, 1991; Barker and Mattingly, 1999–2000; Banning, 2002) as well as comparing results from different Mediterranean regions (Alcock and Cherry, 2004; Johnson and Millett, 2013).

Perhaps, the Ager Tarraconensis survey (1985–90) (Carreté et al., 1995) is one of the best early methodological models in the Iberian peninsula. It surveyed a series of transects using individual fields as sample units for mapping distributions, which were measured in numbers of basic squares to obtain densities. Quantities of pottery collected for each of four periods defined (Iberian, Republican, Principate, and Late Roman) were divided according to extensions of individual fields (i.e. densities per hectare). Since those densities did not show any Normal Distribution, all the 'abnormal densities above background scatters' (adabs) were considered potential sites based on the chronological evidence (Carreté et al., 1995: 60). Of course, it was not possible to evaluate those potential sites with sample excavations or geophysical surveys.

Since the mid-1990s, demographic studies in Roman Italy (Witcher, 2008a; Fentress, 2009; Launaro, 2011; Hin, 2013: 298–341) have taken archaeological survey data into account, though the methods of their interpretation remain open to contention.

Calculations of rural populations based on archaeological surveys depend on:

(a) **Site size**: this normally refers to the extent of material scatter, which may have been affected by many post-depositional processes. Alluviation and intensive modern agriculture have blurred the remains of ancient settlement pattern (Haselgrove, 1985). In some cases, those processes hide the ancient rural site limits, and in other cases, they extend the area covered by scatter. With regard to size, different ways to correct the 'haloes' or excessive extension of the site scatter have recently been introduced (Witcher, 2008a; 2008b; 2011). Modern methods employing GPS enable concentrations in material scatters to be defined (see Grau, 2014), and therefore more accurate limits of the site can be ascertained.

(b) **Recovery rates**: this refers to the total number of sites identified in the survey in relation to the ones that existed in the past.[1] Cambi (1999) suggested a general recovery rate of 33% of the total number of past sites, which involved adding 66% of 'invisible' missing sites to the survey data. Employing such correction value, Fentress (2009) added about 26% of sites to the Albegna valley survey, which supposed 8,000 persons more and densities around 21 persons/$km^2$. Relating those values to the population assumed for a particular territory, there are two different approaches: the low and the high count.[2] There is an average view that establishes a normal rate of 50% (Hin, 2013: 312). However, Witcher (2011: 54) distinguishes between three types of site (nucleated villages; large villas; small farms), which have different rates of recovery because of their size. He assigns a recovery rate of 80% for nucleated sites, 60% for large villas, and 30% for small farms. Therefore, the weighted values only affect the small farms.

[1] Sites are counted by period, but if the period is long there is a chance that people moved from one to another dwelling. Dewar (1991) detected such practices and warned about the risk of 'double counting', in other words, the same human group dwelling on two different sites.

[2] The two approaches are related to the calculation of population in Roman Italy. Scholars who defend the low count calculate a population of 7 million, whereas high count supporters suggest between 12 and 14 million inhabitants (Witcher, 2011: 49).

(c) **Number of inhabitants per unit**: this refers to the different categories of sites, depending on their physical extent, and the particular number of dwellers associated with the same. If a 50% recovery rate is accepted, the key issue is to evaluate the pattern of material scatters that identify particular types of rural sites. Some surveyors have defined rural site categories without reducing the 'halo' effects produced by post-depositional processes. For instance, Fentress (2009) uses data from her Djerba and also the Albegna valley surveys (Perkins, 1999) to establish the following categories according to scatter dimensions:

- Large *vicus* – 80 people (800 $m^2$) – 10 $m^2$ per person
- Large villa – 50 people (500 $m^2$) – 10 $m^2$ per person
- Small *vicus* – 40 people (400 $m^2$) – 10 $m^2$ per person
- Small villa – 30 people (300 $m^2$) – 10 $m^2$ per person
- Large farm – 10 people (100 $m^2$) – 10 $m^2$ per person
- Small farm – 5 people (60 $m^2$) – 12 $m^2$ per person

However, archaeological surveys may record even smaller scatters, whose potential inhabitants can be obtained by using the figure of 10 or 20 $m^2$ per individual. Here again, the living space matters since our urban data established a median value of 20 $m^2$ in the Roman period. In appraising these values, it seems somewhat strange that the minimum human living space on rural sites should be taken as identical to the minimum defined for urban sites (see Table 3.2, 10–12 $m^2$), given that rural sites include production areas such as warehouses, workshops, barns, seasonal shelters, or presses (Osborne, 1992).

Some field survey projects in the Alcoi valley (Alacant, Spain) (Grau, 2014) illustrate how difficult it can be to relate material scatters to archaeological settlements. One of the surveys, at El Carrascalet, covered an area of 18.5 ha, which was field-surveyed by transects to record material concentrations. The highest density of pottery was concentrated in a space of 1.1 ha, which was later surveyed by geophysics (resistivity), registering some minor anomalies. These areas were later excavated, but no signs of architectural remains were revealed, despite the presence of ancient materials, mostly ceramics. Another survey at Torre Redona revealed three pottery concentrations for different chronological periods (Iberian and Roman). The Roman concentration covered an extent of almost 0.5 ha, which was surveyed by geophysics (resistivity), with anomalies only being traced in one area of 900 $m^2$. Later archaeological exploration yielded two buildings, one covering around 200 $m^2$, which was probably the dwelling, and the other of 100 $m^2$, with a possible agricultural function. Therefore, only a small area of scatter may identify the living space of a group of people.

The values defined above are the ones employed by Witcher (2005) in his study of Rome's suburbs (up to 50 km around the city) and are based on different surface surveys. From the 323 km$^2$ surveyed, he identified an average of one villa and two farms per km$^2$, thus providing a total number of 18,100 theoretical settlements (with a 1:2 ratio between *villae* and farms) in the 50 km zone around the city of Rome (Morley, 1996). Multiplying those theoretical settlements by their potential dwellers, he concluded that the hinterland of Rome supported a density of 60 inhabitants/km$^2$, although most scholars previously accepted a rural density of no more than 24 inhabitants per km$^2$.

With similar site categories and inhabitant numbers for each category, Fentress (2009) established an average density of 30 inhabitants per km$^2$ for her survey of the island of Djerba (Tunisia), without differentiating the urban sites; this is quite a high value. Similarly, the demographic analysis of the Albegna survey by Perkins (1999) provided a value of 19 inhabitants per km$^2$ in the countryside. Finally, another interesting example is Antium (Latium) (Attema and De Haas, 2011), where a recent survey carried out by Groningen University registered a density of 17.5 inhabitants per km$^2$, considering that the territory includes coastal *villae*, which may have been seasonal summer residences. Table 3.7 summarizes the values of the different surveys and the one census. Other calculations for the hinterland of Neapolis or Pompeii, as well as the Nile riverside, reached values of 50 to 150 people per km$^2$ (De Simone, 2017), which are also high.[3]

As Attema and De Haas (2012) pointed out, there is also wide variability in the density of rural populations in the same territory depending on the period(s) being analysed (Antium survey), from 3.4 persons/km$^2$ in the republican period (350–250 BCE) to 13.1 persons/km$^2$ in the Augustan period. Some surveys have detected a lack of sites around urban centres, which has been justified by the fact that urban-dwelling citizens may have been the farmers of the surrounding land, in what are called agro-towns (Lo Cascio, 2009).

**Table 3.7** Density of population in rural archaeological Mediterranean surveys

| Surveys | Density | Literature |
|---|---|---|
| Rome's suburbia | 60 persons/km$^2$ | Witcher (2005) |
| Djerba (Tunis) | 30 persons/km$^2$ | Fentress (2009) |
| Albegna (Etruria) | 19 persons/km$^2$ | Perkins (1999) |
| Antium (Latium) | 17.5 persons/km$^2$ | Attema and De Hass (2012) |
| Kasserine (Tunis) | 36 persons/km$^2$ | Mattingly (2011) |
| UNESCO Libyan | 32,5 persons/km$^2$ | Mattingly (2011) |
| Wadi Fayan (Jordan) | 48 persons/km$^2$ | Mattingly (2011) |

[3] In contrast, some surveys such as Biferno valley (Wilson, 2008) provide very low densities that are not so distant from the historical densities of medieval Spain (Table 3.6).

If we bear in mind, as we have seen in the cases of the Alcoi valley and El Carrascalet, that the scatter dimensions of dwelling units tend to be considerably overestimated in survey demographics, and that a ratio of 20–30 $m^2$ per person is probably more accurate, then many of the values discussed here should be revised, and data compared with the numbers provided by historical censuses.

Such methodological difficulties in assigning categories and values to the survey data have been resolved by Launaro (2011) and Hin (2013: 298–341) by using relative values. They compare the number of the same categories of site (similar scatters) for different periods in each *regio* of Roman Italy without attempting to calculate the number of inhabitants. Thereby, as a general trend they conclude that the number of farms increased from the Republic to the Principate by around 34% and the *villae* by almost 68%. Of course, this trend in Roman Italy may not have been matched in other provinces.

A final discussion that arises from those field surveys is the relative proportions of rural and urban populations, which in general have been established as having been only 15% for the urban population, on the basis of some case studies, such as Kyaneai (Price, 2011: 22; Witcher, 2011: 62). Other case studies, however, such as the Laconian survey, proposed higher percentages of urban population, reaching as many as 29–35%. Again, comparison with historical data from the same region is a way to balance those extreme positions.

## 3.8 Conclusions

While different methods that use archaeological, anthropological, and historical evidence to estimate population numbers in both qualitative and quantitative ways have been presented in this chapter, it is quite clear that none of them can be employed alone to perform accurate demographic calculations. All of them suffer from a large degree of variability, broad uncertainty, and considerable margins of error due to the fragmentary nature of the data and the subjectivity involved in interpreting them.

It is almost impossible to quantify populations using data from cemeteries, since the population universe is unknown. This can sometimes be a direct consequence of the fact that some funerary areas have not been fully excavated or because in those cases when cemeteries are excavated in their totality, only a part of the original burial area may have come down to us. Similarly, depending on the funerary and burial rite used (e.g. cremation), which depends on economic, social, and cultural factors, the survival of the remains may be better or worse as well as more or less representative of the total. In sum, only by comparing these archaeological data with censuses such as those from Roman Egypt (Karanis, Tebytnis), may one be able to relate the data to universal populations.

Epigraphic evidence, on the other hand, can provide excellent demographic data in very specific cases (e.g. Ostia, Apamea, and Pompeii), but also suffers from interpretative issues as the case of Pompeii clearly highlights. Additionally, when studying the Iberian peninsula, not only is it specific to the Roman period, and therefore diachronic analysis is not possible, but there is also a clear bias towards some specific categories of the population (see Chapter 2), depending on factors such as wealth, gender, age, etc. (Shaw, 1991; Saller, 1994: 35–40). It is also open to interpretation due to the fragmentary and decontextualized nature of the texts themselves.

Public buildings, fora, and other public urban infrastructures, including water supply, do not perform any better than the previous categories. While estimating the capacities of certain public buildings, especially amphitheatres and/or theatres, may provide some valuable information, the capacity of these public buildings tends to surpass the total population of a city, as they were also meant to accommodate the inhabitants of rural areas and nearby cities belonging to the same *conventus* or province. Additionally, the construction of monumental public spaces in the Roman world went far beyond the requirements of the town's inhabitants and was used as a means of propaganda, resulting in competitive euergetism on the part of the local and provincial elites (see Chapter 5). Similar issues arise when demographic estimates are calculated on the basis of water supply, since water in ancient towns may have been used for many purposes other than drinking (e.g. bathing or specialized industrial purposes) and therefore the need for/consumption of water may not correlate at all with population numbers.

Much more relevant for the chronological periods and the type of populations that we are aiming to study in the following three chapters are the methods discussed in sections 3.4–3.7. The most popular method used to carry out population estimates is the 'density per area' or 'people per area' method. This method has the advantage of being quite simple since it only requires the size of the site under study to be multiplied by a density per hectare. Therefore, it can be applied to a large number of archaeological sites that have been not yet been excavated or that are poorly preserved. On the other hand, the method has huge limitations since it tends to fail to take into account the possibility of vertical constructions (much more densely populated) and, more importantly, there is no standard density value for Roman cities that can simply be applied to all case studies, but a range of values. In brief, as a method, it requires data to be extrapolated from other case studies that share similar social, cultural and urban characteristics in order to be of value.

Much more reliable when the archaeological data are extremely well preserved—more the exception rather than the rule—is the housing unit method, considered to be the 'less inaccurate' method of all methods under scrutiny for other scholars working in the Iron Age Iberian peninsula (Nión-Álvarez, 2023: 9). Multiplying the number of inhabitants per household or dwelling unit by the number of households at a specific archaeological site can seem straightforward and quite accurate. This method can be used to estimate the population numbers and density per hectare in settlements that are well preserved, allowing us to later extrapolate that density to sites of the same chronology, size, culture, layout, and urban design, but with a much worse state of preservation, contextualizing and minimizing the error in the calculations made using the 'density per area' method (see Chapter 4).

Unfortunately, this method is also problematic and suffers from methodological issues. In the first place, it can be quite difficult in archaeological terms to define what a 'household' is and to calculate a standard empirical figure for household size. The area, layout and plan, and number of inhabitants of a household can vary significantly, based on the type of family structure—nuclear or extended families—and in the case of Citerior/Tarraconensis it has been suggested that, in some cases, it might have changed from the Iron Age into the Roman period. More importantly, two core variables to apply the housing unit method are also far from clear and objective. Even if the exact number of households on a specific site is known, it is impossible to estimate the total number of inhabitants if we do not know how many people were living in each domestic unit, so again an average value is used. Unfortunately, this variable is archaeologically invisible and cannot be calculated from the archaeological record, so we must employ historical and ethnographical data in order to reach credible numbers. Obviously, such data do not exist for the area and periods that will be studied in Chapters 4–6. Therefore the best way to proceed is by looking at later censuses in the same territory, existing censuses in other areas but chronologically contemporary with our case studies, and considering ethnographic parallels belonging to other groups that lived in similar built spaces. Only by comparing all these results is it feasible to visualize a pattern and to establish a credible range of inhabitants per household.

Other methods, such as the storage provision formulae, present the advantage that they do not depend on employing ethnographically derived coefficients from periods and sites that may not be directly comparable with our case studies and have the advantage of being approaches almost exclusively based on archaeological evidence. However, one cannot ignore the issue that they have not yet been applied to the classical period, making it impossible to compare results with other case studies. More importantly, the methods rely on identifying and quantifying functional categories such as personal storage in archaeological terms, which is by no means easy or straightforward when examining hundreds of sites. While such methods may be an excellent choice for a small number of case studies, they do not seem appropriate for the study of a whole province, especially considering that, on the occasions when they have been tested against the housing unit method and the residential area density coefficient method, the results are quite similar, as shown in Table 3.5.

After reviewing all the existing formulae and methods, as well as their limitations, it is clear that there is no perfect formula or method that enables accurate ancient population estimates to be proposed. On the other hand, it is worth bearing in mind that we are working in a period for which extremely well-preserved case studies such as Hermopolis, Ostia, and Pompeii, which combine excellent archaeological, epigraphic, and even census evidence, exist. It is also important to note that we can compare these data with the evidence provided by censuses of later periods in the area under study. This provides numbers that are likely to be close enough to the reality of our case studies, by means of making use of the housing unit method and the residential area density coefficient method which are the ones preferred for the purposes of this book.

Finally, we should not exaggerate the value of the specific numbers provided by these types of calculations (see Chapters 4–6), since they may lead to a false sense of precision. Instead, we should use them as guidelines and merely indicative tools. This, however, should not prevent us from seeing the potential value in them. The fact that there is a consensus among researchers working in the same period concerning which methods should be used to perform the calculations, allows comparisons to be made in a relatively reliable manner. That is, beyond the resemblance that numerical figures have with the real ones—since they are always to a greater or lesser extent approximations—they offer an actual relative comparison, because the error in the aforementioned calculations will be similar for all the estimates put forward in this study, something that enables them to be compared with each other in relative terms.

By way of conclusion, the effort of creating demographic figures for any population or settlement is complex, but is also worthwhile since it provides us a proxy that has hitherto been ignored and complements and expands our view of past societies.

*The Human Factor: The Demography of the Roman Province of Hispania Citerior/Tarraconensis.* Alejandro G. Sinner, Cèsar Carreras, and Pieter Houten, Oxford University Press. 
DOI: 10.1093/9780191943881.003.0003

# 4
# Population, Urbanization, and Settlement Patterns in the Late Iron Age

## 4.1 Urban Characteristics, Methods, and Densities

Producing demographic estimates of pre-Roman populations presents even greater difficulties than in the case of the Roman period (see Chapter 5). One of the main issues is that censuses, which can serve as a point of reference in later historical periods, do not exist for the Iron Age. Additionally, Graeco-Roman authors did not show special interest in evaluating the demography of the different groups that inhabited the territories that later constituted the province of Hispania Citerior. The only references in existence are estimates of casualties and the size of armies during battles and conflicts (e.g. Liv. *Per.* 55.9; Flor. 1.34; Oros. 5.7; App. *Iber.* 76; *Iber.* 97 for Numantia; App. *Iber.* 45 for the coalition of Belli, Titti, and Arevaci; App. *Iber.* 100 for the Celtiberian revolt subjugated by Valerius Flaccus). These data alone, although of great value when combined with the archaeological evidence (see below), are insufficient to provide credible demographic estimates since, in many cases, the numbers given are exaggerated and clearly biased.

In the archaeological studies conducted to date, wide margins of variability have been suggested to estimate the population of the diverse pre-Roman groups, ranging from 200 inhabitants per hectare to figures above 1,750 (Sinner and Carreras, 2019 with bibliography) when discussing the Iberians, Celtiberians, Carpetanians, and Vacceans and as low as *c.* 20 inhabitants per hectare when discussing the particular case of the Vettones. These figures, in some cases hard to believe, especially at the very high and low ends of the spectrum, are the result of a wide diversity of formulae (see Chapter 3) and the lack of a uniform methodology that can be applied to each case study as well as to the diverse settlement patterns and traditions that are characteristic of each cultural group. Sometimes the numbers are based on calculations carried out by using the information compiled by the ancient sources, while, in other cases, they are the result of very generic methodological approaches (Gracía et al., 1996: 182–4), which establish the same size for all domestic units in *oppida* of similar dimensions and date, and located in adjoining territories (Table 4.1).

**Table 4.1** Examples of population densities of Iron Age settlements in Spain

| Settlement | Density/ha | Reference |
|---|---|---|
| Numantia & Las Cogotas | 208 | Álvarez Sanchís and Ruiz Zapatero, 2001 |
| Torre dels Encantats | 400 | Garcès, 2013: 14–15 |
| Asturian castros | 200–250 | Sánchez Palencia and Fernández Posse, 1986: 378 |
| Celtiberian *oppida* | 300–720 | Almagro-Gorbea, 2001: 54 |
| Moleta del Remei | 772 | Gracia Alonso et al., 1996 |
| Puig de la Nao | 1,530 | Gracia Alonso et al., 1996 |
| Coll de Moro | 1,718 | Gracia Alonso et al., 1996 |
| Ulaca | *c.* 20 | Ruiz Zapatero et al., 2020: 135 |

In order to overcome some of these problems, two of us recently conducted a study in which we proposed a methodology that would allow more realistic estimates to be made for the case of the Iberian *oppida* in the north-east of the peninsula (Sinner and Carreras, 2019). The aim was to study the palaeodemography of each *oppidum* individually, when possible, prior to extrapolating the lowest figure (426 inhabitants/hectare) to those cases in which the archaeological record does not allow for individual calculations. This methodological approach will be expanded and improved in this chapter in order to fit the needs of a larger area of study that includes different types of sites in terms of size and layout. We aim to offer a more developed approach by proposing a range (not just the lowest figure) that will be previously established from a series of individual case studies encompassing examples of each type of *oppida* as well as the specific pre-Roman culture to which they belong (see Fig. 4.1). The peoples inhabiting the lands that became Hispania Citerior after 197 BCE were many and diverse. This diversity does not allow the numbers for the Iberian groups of north-eastern Spain, obtained by Sinner and Carreras (2019), to be applied directly to calculate the population density of other groups such as the Celtiberians, Vacceans, Carpetanians, Vettones, or the Callaecians, among others.

While the uncertainties, even after improving the existing methodology, remain numerous and the margin of error wide, the use of a single method applicable to all *oppida*, expressed in inhabitants per hectare, allows for a study of the distribution of the pre-Roman population comparable with those conducted for the Roman period (Chapter 5) to be put forward for the first time.

Other problems faced when estimating the demography of the peninsula in the fourth and third centuries BCE, is the total sample of cities (*oppida*) with which we work. In the case of the Early Empire, the count carried out by Pliny the Elder (*NH* III.3.7–17; IV.4.18–30; IV.35.113–18) (see Chapter 5), included a total

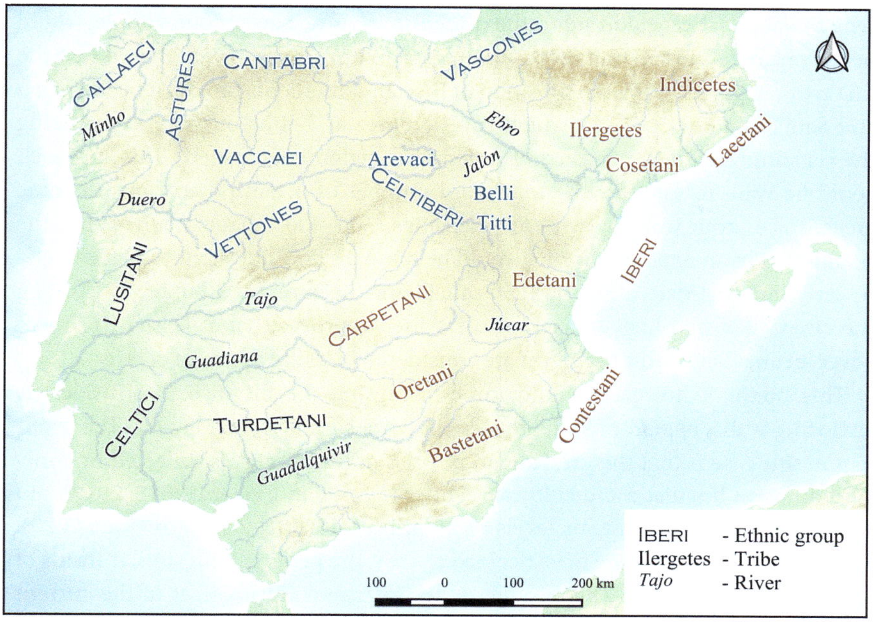


**Fig. 4.1** Pre-Roman peoples considered in section 4.2. The Iberian groups in brown and the north-western group in blue

of 399 urban entities (*civitates* and *populi*), providing an approximately realistic number of cities that are known to have been scattered across the Hispaniae by the first century CE (Houten, 2021). Thanks to this, it is possible to reliably estimate—or at least approximate—what percentage of the total number of Roman cities in existence have been included in our calculations. Unfortunately, there is no similar documentation for the Iron Age. Therefore, all we can do is compile a detailed list of settlements from the archaeological record (see Appendix I). The problem is obvious: there is no way to know what percentage of the total *oppida* in existence our sample represents. Additionally, when working with archaeological materials, it is impossible to specify chronologies as precisely as Pliny (72–4 CE) does, so there is always the risk that some sites, although archaeologically contemporary (fourth–third centuries BCE), were not coetaneous.

Lastly, what we should understand/count as cities/urban (or proto-urban) sites when dealing with archaeological remains of *oppida* is also a problem. The emergence of a hierarchy of settlements of different categories and functions is well known to have been one of the main characteristics of the Iberian and Celtiberian systems, and perhaps of other pre-Roman groups that populated Iberia. However, as we shall see, this does not mean that the existing different categories always functioned or were organized equally, which makes generalizing risky.

One possibility, bearing in mind the dimensions of the sites in our sample, would be to consider as urban and proto-urban centres only those *oppida* that fit into the first two categories of the classification of Iberian settlements provided by Sanmartí and Santacana (2005: 60–6), which cover an area of 3–4 ha or more, considering the remaining settlements as rural, secondary agglomerations, etc. This approach could be valid to estimate the minimum number of urban populations in some areas, since, even working with low densities (300–400 inhabitants/hectare), the population in an *oppidum* of 3 ha would be more or less equivalent to that of a city of early imperial date of 6.5 ha (250 inhabitants/hectare, see Chapter 5). Among the cities cited by Pliny, archaeological evidence proves that at least 74 of them cover an area below this figure yet are considered by Pliny as urban centres.

This method, however, would imply accepting the premise that inside the enclosing walls, *oppida* of similar sizes shared a similar urban layout. The problem in this case is that the pre-Roman peoples of the peninsula reflected not only very different linguistic and cultural realities (Sinner and Velaza, 2018; 2019), but also displayed heterogeneous levels of urbanization (Ruiz Zapatero et al., 2020). To overcome this issue, we have decided to treat the peoples with similar forms of urbanism as one group. This is often in accordance with practices in the current literature. As such we consider all the Iberian Levantine coast as one group, the Iberians, even though we are aware that differences in urban layout between these peoples existed, especially in the south-east. Similarly, we deal with the Atlantic coastal area as another large group named the north-western group. Both these areas are characterized by groups organized in relatively densely occupied smaller settlement types. Moreover, these peoples are found in the same geographical areas (Houten, 2021: 20). However, we deviate from the geographical approach with inland groups that are analysed separately. There are two reasons for this. First, their urban system is clearly different between them and when compared with what we see in the Iberian and north-western areas. Second, these groups are often considered as separate peoples in the ancient literature.

Another approach to solve the problem of defining what is rural and what is 'urban' is to simply include all the settlements in our sample and not to calculate the urban and rural population separately, but just the total population. This option would involve expanding the theoretical proposal of Arturo Ruiz (1994) on Iberian urbanism to all the pre-Roman groups under discussion and therefore accepting two main premises. First, pre-Roman urbanism differs from that of the Greek and the Roman periods and, therefore, cannot be interpreted in the same way. The categories rural and urban do not necessarily need to define the *oppida* system. Instead, it should be considered as being closer to clientele networks than political practices and citizenship. Second, the territory and the countryside are realities that are inseparable from the urban space (*oppidum*), and while different models of occupation may coexist—polynuclear with a concentrated population (Alto Guadalquivir); hierarchical settlement patterns (east of Iberia);

micronuclear with medium/small centres with a scattered population as in the north-east—these are all variants of the same system and types of relationships within a larger *oppida* system (Ruiz Zapatero et al., 2020: 130).

If this strategy is chosen, it must be borne in mind that a significant number of small fortified and almost all the unfortified isolated farms and rural settlements will escape our count (for rural estimates in the Roman period see Chapter 5). Additionally, while larger *oppida* are more visible in the archaeological record and tend to be better known, those less than 3 ha in area, and especially under 1 ha, are much less visible. This phenomenon means that the areas that have been studied in greater depth in archaeological terms, better surveyed, and that are covered by specific research projects devoted to recording settlement patterns and urban plan, will have a larger number of smaller *oppida* than others (Fig. 4.26). Good examples of this phenomenon can be seen in the north-west (modern Galicia) and north-east (Catalonia) of the Iberian peninsula.

In sum, on the basis of size alone, it is currently very difficult to establish a common figure for all these groups that enables us to differentiate which towns can be considered urban and which not with some degree of credibility. Needless to say, in many cases the size of these settlements is poorly known and in others the numbers given by different scholars may differ significantly.

One method that we can employ to compare different urban systems is rank-size analysis (RSA). This enables us to obtain an idea of the hierarchy and spread of settlement sizes. The sizes are ranked from largest, at position one, to the smallest and plotted onto a log-log graph to obtain a view of the spread. In general, there are four possible shapes for these graphs (see Fig. 4.2): (1) a straight line, also referred to as Zipf's law, which is supposed to indicate an ideal hierarchical spread of the settlements that are part of one fully integrated system. The line following Zipf's law is indicated on our graphs to aid reading. (2) A convex or primate shape; in this case we find that one settlement is significantly larger than the rest of the settlement system. This is understood as a clearly hierarchical system. (3) A concave spread, where there is a higher number of large settlements; this can indicate either the pooling of multiple settlement systems in one graph, or a settlement system without a clear hierarchy. (4) A primo-concave spread, which is similar to the concave system; however, there is one settlement clearly standing out as the primary settlement, whereas the lower order settlements follow a more heterarchical spread (Houten, 2021: 209).

Plotting the Iron Age settlements of 3 ha and more gives us an insight into the spread of the settlements (see Fig. 4.2b). We can clearly see that the graph is concave, or possibly primo-concave. To verify our first observation of the graph we must turn to the two formulae in the graph related to the trend line it contains. The first value is $R^2$, which gives us the fit of the trend line. With a $R^2$ of 0.9316 there is a good fit, and the $q$-value can be used to understand the graph; this is the value found in the y-equation. This value gives us the slope of the trend line and

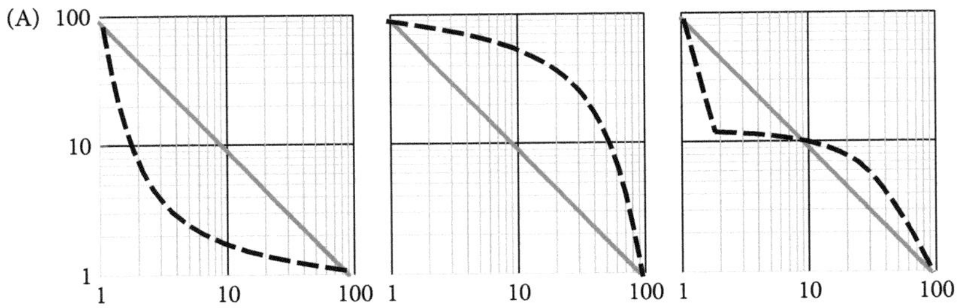


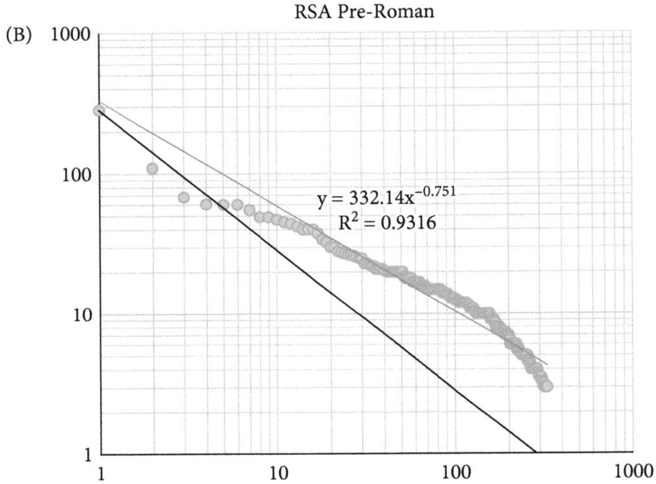


**Fig. 4.2** (A) Examples of shapes for RSA graphs left to right: primate or convex, concave and primo-concave graphs (Houten, 2021: fig. 6.1 209). (B) RSA data of pre-Roman settlements covering 3 ha or more (n = 332)

helps us to understand whether there is a strongly hierarchical system, recognized by a slope above–1. In this case the q-value is lower than–1, and it can thus be stated that the settlement system is not strongly hierarchical. In this case we can see that the *q*-value indicating the slope of the trend line of our graph is–0.751, thus indicating that the settlement system under consideration is less hierarchical than might be expected at first glance. The few highest-ranking settlements are larger and more widely spread than those at the lower end of the scale. However, as the majority of the settlements are found in the middle section, the trend line is visibly slightly flattened. Starting to understand the graph using the knowledge obtained so far on the pre-Roman settlement systems, it must be admitted that the current concave distribution could well be the result of 'pooling', the combining of different settlement systems. To see whether it is, in fact, a question of pooling, we will turn to the individual ethnic organizations and create the RSA and population estimates for each of these groups.

Even with all the aforementioned limitations—which are many—and although it seems difficult to estimate the total population in the Late Iron Age for the territories that were later to make up Hispania Citerior, it does seem feasible to suggest a minimum number of inhabitants concentrated in urban and proto-urban centres. Even though it is difficult to accept these calculations are being strictly accurate, the exercise is interesting and both the distribution map of the sites included in this work (Fig. 4.26) and the minimum number of inhabitants that we have calculated provide novel and valuable information—as well as highly hypothetical data in the latter case—in order to understand the impact that Rome had on the urban network and demography of the peninsula.

With all the above in mind, in order to decide which density per hectare is most suitable for each of the *oppida* in the area under study, separate calculations that adapt as well as possible to the cultural, social, and urban characteristics of each of the main pre-Roman groups that inhabited the lands of what later became Hispania Citerior need to be undertaken.

## 4.2 Iberian *Oppida*

The emergence of a hierarchy of settlements of different categories and functions is one of the main characteristics attributed to the Iberian system (Sanmartí and Belarte, 2001). As can be seen in Appendix I, the term *oppidum* reflects a wide variety of realities and sizes. However, if it is understood as a well-fortified settlement located in a dominating position and, most importantly, one of an urban nature, we should probably include only those settlements of 3 ha or more (much larger examples, over 50 ha, are known in southern Iberia but fall outside the geographical scope of this book). Iberian *oppida* with the above characteristics have been considered to be political and economic centres of archaic proto-states. From the fourth century BCE onwards, the large *oppida* controlled rational and well-organized territories including their rural population, often comprising farms and subordinate settlements of less than 3 ha. These generic characteristics are valid for the Iberian settlements in the territory under study—or at least of the vast majority—especially those located in the eastern and north-eastern areas of the province (Bonet Rosado et al., 2008). Additionally, scholars have suggested that as part of these hierarchical settlement systems, at least three subcategories among the smallest sites below 3 ha can be noted: (1) villages/fortified villages, such as Castellet de Bernabé (Llíria, Valencia) (0.1 ha), which are understood as the residence of an aristocratic family and their dependants (Guérin, 2003); (2) hamlets or houses with rural installations, such as L'Alt del Punxó; and (3) farms and small huts such as those at L'Hort de la Torre (Grau, 2014). These sites are of diverse types, and it has been suggested that they were households occupied by nuclear families. Of course, the last two categories, for the most part, remain

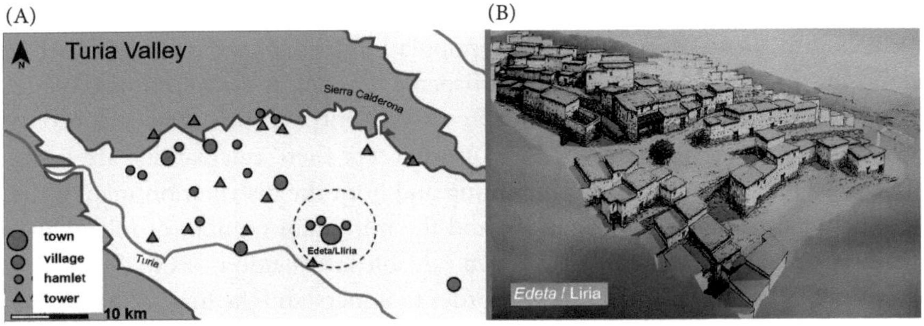


**Fig. 4.3** (A) Settlement pattern of the Turia valley in the Iberian period. (B) Reconstruction of part of the town of Edeta/Llíria (after Bonet Rosado and Vives-Ferrándiz, 2011)

invisible in studies such as the one undertaken here. Based on their size and definition, it seems plausible to consider these sites as rural (Fig. 4.3).

From an urban point of view, the layout of the larger *oppida* can vary as well, but they tend to display important common characteristics, such as the presence of elite residences, public/communal spaces, in most cases devoted to storage and production, and sometimes sanctuaries or some sort of religious space, and parallel streets (Quesada, 2017: 534), the latter being more common among the Iberian groups in the east and the south of Iberia than among those in the north-east.

One of the main issues to obtain population estimates for the Iberian settlements is that, in general, archaeological preservation and excavation favours the largest—and usually fortified—sites. We also find this focus on larger fortified sites in the range of the smallest sites described above (0.1–3 ha). Due to their fortifications, smaller sites, which should probably be considered as agricultural or rural settlements, are included in the 'urban' range. At the lowest end of the range, the sites are often hard to identify; farms tend to be too small and built with perishable materials and do not survive well in the archaeological record. In addition, their very limited size makes it hard to identify them. At the higher end (over 3 ha), larger *oppida* are seldom well known, and very few examples exist that are well preserved and have been the object of large open-area excavations that allow for some interpretation of their urban layout. These issues were reflected by Sinner and Carreras (2019), in which they conducted customized calculations for a substantial number of small *oppida* (Table 4.2) but did not address the case of the larger settlements.

In addition to the population estimates and a much more homogeneous density per hectare than previously thought (400–750 inhab./ha), the use of the customized methodology for the very well preserved sites of Castellet de Bernabé and Els Estinclells (Sinner and Carreras, 2019) allowed the validity—among this

**Table 4.2** Estimated density calculated by Sinner and Carreras (2019) of several *oppida* in pre-Roman Spain

| Iberian *oppida* | Average house | Size in ha | Density per ha |
|---|---|---|---|
| Puig Castellar | 21.5 $m^2$ | 0.35 ha | 1108 (SE 87.19) |
| Els Estinclells | 42.4 $m^2$ | 0.2 ha | 580 (SE 39.6) |
| Bolvir | 50.3 $m^2$ | 0.6 ha | 426 (SE 78.33) |
| Moleta del Remei | 30.7 $m^2$ | 0.5 ha | 784 (SE 46.32) |
| Molí d'Espigol | 40 $m^2$ | 0.8 ha | 775 (SE 150) |
| Font de la Canya | 38.4 $m^2$ | 0.07 ha | 629 (SE 60.9) |
| Castellvell | 31.4 $m^2$ | 0.49 ha | 759 (SE 138) |
| Sant Julià de Ramis | 40.9 $m^2$ | 0.7 ha | 582 (SE 75.77) |

category of sites—of certain assumptions that are of some significance when the archaeological remains are not perfectly preserved to be tested, more specifically the relationship between household surface and communal surface. In both cases the hypothesis supporting an approximate proportion of *c*. 60% of household surface as opposed to *c*. 40% of communal surface seemed quite realistic, although never exact.

Finally, due to the partial preservation of the archaeological remains, any methodological approach will always imply a certain margin of error (Sinner and Carreras, 2019). In fact, the larger the area of uncertainty—the worse the state of preservation of the site—or the larger the difference between the surface area of the known houses, the greater the margin of error the methodology will accumulate. In order to make the accuracy of the estimates for each case study displayed in Table 4.2 accessible to the reader, the authors applied a standard error (SE) to each of their calculations (number of houses, inhabitants per house, and density per ha ), as is the case in this chapter as well. The SE is a measurement of the statistical accuracy of an estimate, equal to the standard deviation of the theoretical distribution of a large population of such estimates (Devore, 2012). In this case, it will enable us to know how great might be the possibility of missing houses or individuals, or of the density having been miscalculated.

### 4.2.1 Oppida over 3 Ha: Case studies

If we seek to gain an idea of reliable numbers for all the Iberian territories in what later became the province of Citerior, we cannot avoid producing estimates for the largest *oppida*—something that was not done in previous studies (Sinner and Carreras, 2019). These are especially important because they are likely to have concentrated most of the population and were the main nodes of the urban network. Unfortunately, very few of these settlements are well preserved and have been object of large open-area excavation, Castellet de Banyoles and La Bastida de les Alcuses being two exceptions.

It is true that the layouts of most of the Iberian settlements of similar characteristics to Castellet de Banyoles are almost unknown, but the existence of an elite that inhabited large houses—a situation that has been documented at Castellet de Banyoles (Asensio et al., 2012: 176–84) and Ullastret (Belarte, 2010: 114)—must be expected on those sites with a surface of more than 3 ha. The existence of these large structures, which at Castellet de Banyoles can sometimes attain surfaces of over 200 and 300 $m^2$, and even 1,000 $m^2$ at Ullastret, could potentially reduce the total density if we continue to apply a figure of 4–5 individuals per household (see Chapter 3). In addition, the urban layout of these much larger sites seems more complex than the proportion of 60% of household surface versus 40% of communal space used for the lower size category, which thus needs to be tested before using it in our estimates.

To do so, three different case studies (two excavated and one based on a ground-penetrating radar survey) for which the urban layouts, including houses, streets, and public spaces are well known to an extent that allows for reasonable extrapolations are used here.

On the basis of the published archaeological plans (Figs. 4.4–4.6), the surface of the areas excavated and/or interpreted as having been occupied by streets, squares, and open spaces was measured. Once a surface area was obtained, the percentage of household surface vs. communal surface was estimated. The numbers obtained in each case study can be seen in Table 4.3. It is important to highlight some limitations. First of all, there is a certain degree of subjectivity in deciding where to close certain spaces. In the case of La Bastida de les Alcuses, perhaps the best-known Iberian site covering more than 3 ha, approximately only 50% of the total site could be used to conduct our estimates (Fig. 4.4). Therefore, our numbers in Table 4.3 rely on the assumption that substantial differences did not exist in the urban layout between the central section of the site and its two extremes. At Banyeres del Penedès, on the other hand, the limitations are different. We worked with a plan of 1.5 ha of a site that is estimated to have a total area of 3.5 ha. More importantly, the urban layout was documented by means of a geophysical survey, ground-penetrating radar (GPR), and has not been fully confirmed by archaeological excavation. That said, recent excavations at specific points of the site do seem to confirm most of the geophysical anomalies previously recorded. Nonetheless, we believe that this exercise is meaningful since the percentages are quite close from site to site; communal surface always occupies *c.* 20–25% of the total surface studied and, therefore, may be taken as indicative. Obviously, not all the built structures can be understood as households. In fact, in the well preserved and excavated sites of Castellet de Bernabé and Els Estinclells, several buildings were interpreted after excavation as workshops, production,

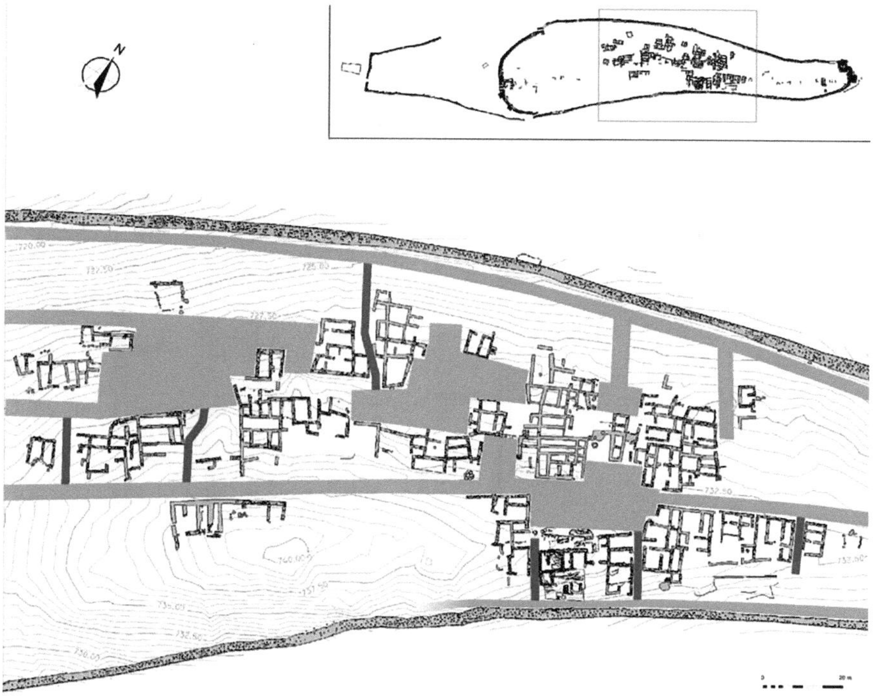

Fig. 4.4 Plan of La Bastida de les Alcuses with the known streets and open spaces marked in light and dark gray (after Bonet Rosado and Vives-Ferrándiz, 2011: 88, fig. 29)

**Table 4.3** Total surface, communal surface, and percentage of communal surface known for the Iberian *oppida* of La Bastida de les Alcuses, Alorda Park, and Banyeres del Penedès

| Site | Total site surface | Surface studied/ known | Total CS of the surface studied | % of CS |
|---|---|---|---|---|
| La Bastida de les Alcuses | 4.2 ha | 20,965.7949 m² | 4,585.0189 m² | 22 |
| Alorda Park | 0.4 ha | 1,838.1928 m² | 372.8019 m² | 20 |
| Banyeres del Penedès | 3.5 ha | 1.5 ha | 3,163.9452 m² | 21 |

storage, and agricultural spaces (Fig. 4.7). Based on all the above, when considering the largest Iberian sites, it seems impossible to assume a total communal space lower than 30% of the total surface of the site, making the ratio of 60% of household surface as opposed to 40% of communal surface already used for those *oppida* of smaller size quite realistic and unlikely to be much higher or lower. In brief, when there is no archaeological evidence available, the surface devoted to

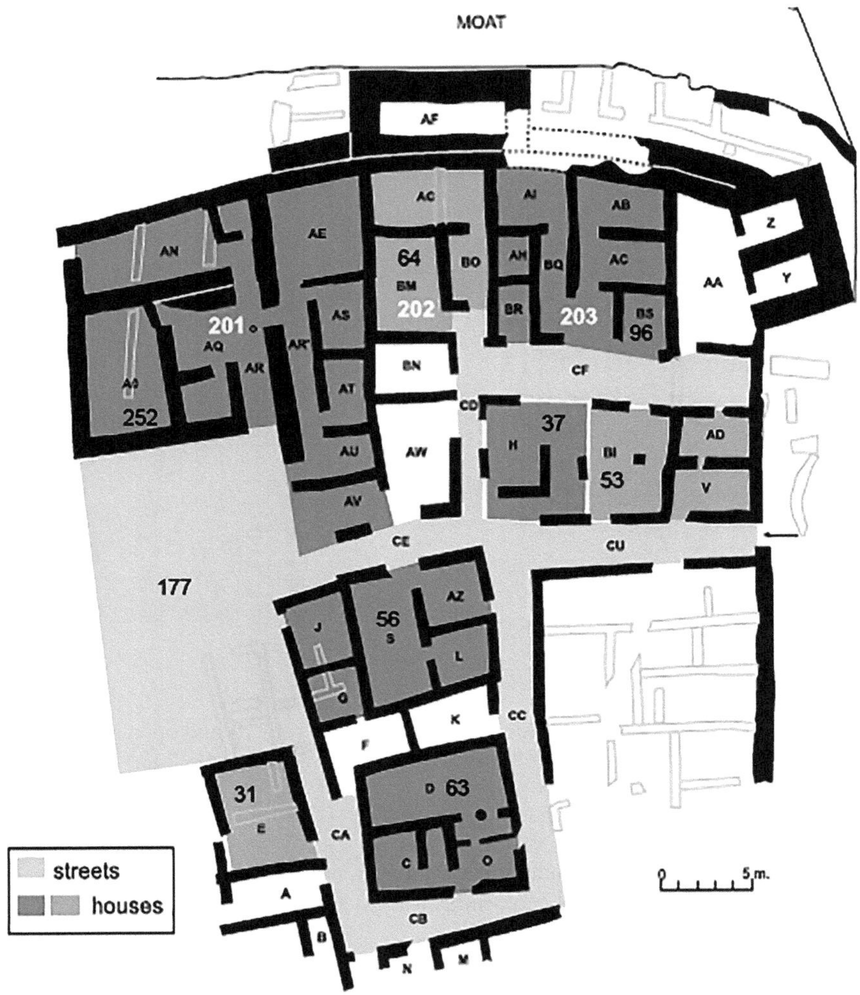


**Fig. 4.5** Plan of Alorda Park (Asensio et al., 2005: 613 fig. 4b)

communal use in the Iberian *oppida* should be considered to have occupied between 30% and 40% of the total surface.

With this information in mind and following the methodology described in Sinner and Carreras (2019) and the methodological adaptations discussed above, we have conducted demographic estimates for the two best preserved large Iberian *oppida* (more than 3 ha): Castellet de Banyoles (4.5 ha) and La Bastida de les Alcuses (4.2 ha), with the aim of achieving a credible ratio of inhabitants per hectare that can later be used to calculate the population for those *oppida* with similar characteristics whose poor preservation does not allow for customized studies.

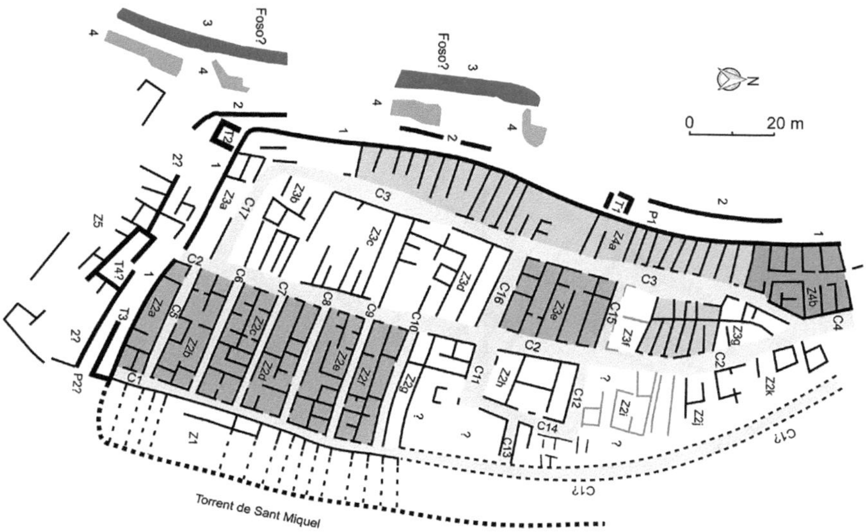

**Fig. 4.6** Plan of the *oppidum* of Banyeres del Penedès with streets and open spaces marked in light grey (Noguera and Olcina, 2020)

For Castellet de Banyoles, thanks to the work of Asensio et al. (2012), the total surface of 11 fully excavated buildings that have been interpreted as households is known. The structures are of different sizes, ranging between 34 and 360 $m^2$. However, most of them can be grouped in two categories: 30–60 $m^2$ (5 houses) and 100–360 $m^2$ (6 houses). The average house in the sample is 137.6 $m^2$. The case of La Bastida is similar. Six houses have a surface area between 25 and 85 $m^2$ while the other five have sizes between 110 and 150 $m^2$. Only one building, the interpretation of which as a house is debated, measures 300 $m^2$. Due to the uncertainties surrounding this building, our calculations have been carried out with and without including this structure (see Table 4.4). As can be seen in Table 4.4, the results of both estimates—always using 4 inhabitants per household—are not far from each other and, therefore, can be used to suggest some valid ranges for this type of settlement . However, the density obtained for La Bastida seems more realistic since more structures are known and a larger area of the site has been excavated. Therefore, the houses employed for our calculations seem to be more representative of the average inhabited space than in the case of Castellet de Banyoles. In the latter, our estimates rely on the excavated areas, which occupy a smaller part of the site and, to date (Fig. 4.8), a similar number of large (+100 $m^2$) and smaller houses (30–60 $m^2$) have been identified. It seems likely that this proportion will change as excavations uncover new sectors of the site with a higher number of small houses, thereby increasing the density.

In addition to these two case studies, when attempts to estimate the density of inhabitants per ha for one of the first category *oppida* were made, in the case of

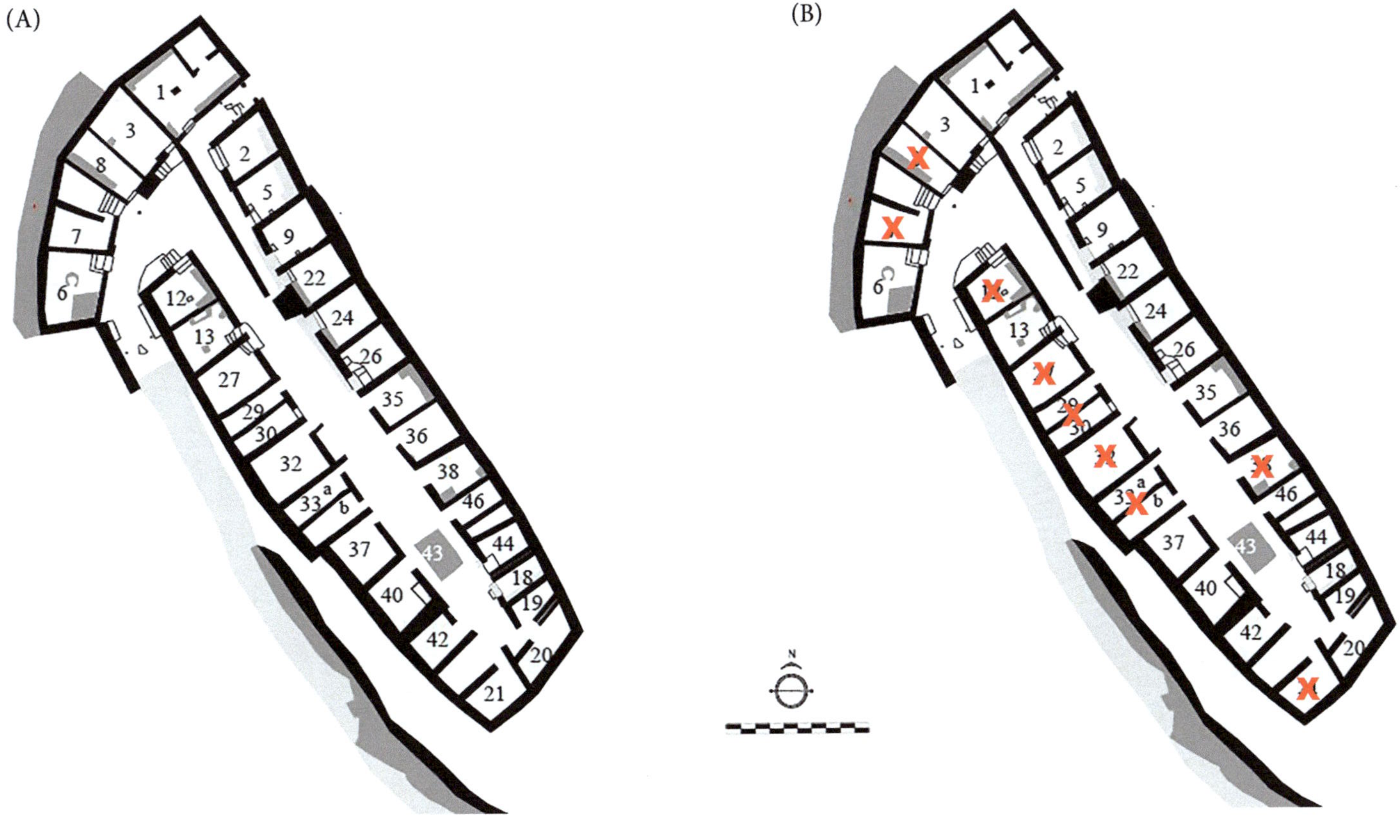


**Fig. 4.7** (A) Plan of Castellet de Bernabé (Guerin, 2003: 160, fig. 244). (B) Plan of Castellet de Bernabé showing the rooms that cannot be interpreted as households (Guerin, 2003: 160, fig. 244, modified by the authors)

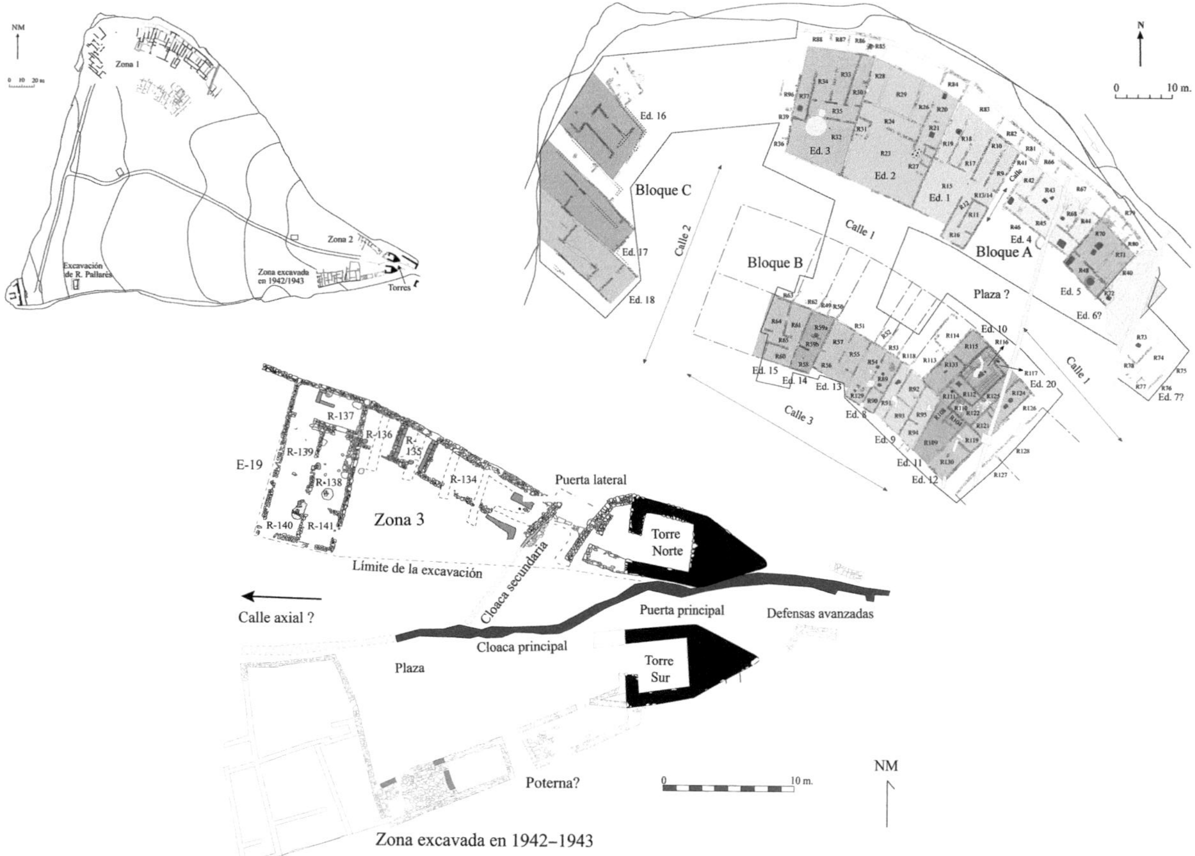


**Fig. 4.8** Plan of the excavated areas at Castellet de Banyoles (after Asensio et al., 2012)

**Table 4.4** Results of the density per hectare estimates for the Iberian sites of more than 3 ha

| Iberian *oppida* | Average house | Size in ha | Density per ha |
|---|---|---|---|
| La Bastida de les Alcuses | 95.5 $m^2$ | 4.2 ha | 251.41 (SE 53.66) |
| La Bastida de les Alcuses* | 70.5 $m^2$ | 4.2 ha | 340.42 (SE 55.58) |
| Castellet de Banyoles | 137.64 $m^2$ | 4.5 ha | 174.44 (SE 42.47) |

* Excluding the house of 300 $m^2$ from the estimates.

Ullastret (9 ha), values of 400 inhab./ha were established (Sanmartí and Belarte, 2001: 167). Based on the above and bearing in mind that the standard error seems to be *c.*50 inhab./ha in all cases, we suggest that a density range of 250–400 inhab./ha should be applied for the larger Iberian *oppida* (over 3 ha, see Table 4.4), and a higher one of 450–650 inhab./ha for those sites with a surface under 3 ha when the archaeological data are poor and populations are to be calculated just by dividing the total surface of the settlement by a specific density obtained from other case studies.

Once each *oppidum* has been considered as an independent case study, following the same methodological approach, it is clear that the densities of these settlements are higher, in general, than those estimated for the Roman period (see Chapter 5). However, the variability of the density between sites is not as heterogeneous as believed in the past (see Tables 4.2 and 4.4). The only clear outlier is Puig Castellar, but this case was already addressed by Sinner and Carreras in a previous article (2019: 313), together with other corrections applied to the cases of Moleta del Remei and Castellvell. It is important to highlight that, when the variable of minimum living space is taken into account (see Chapter 3), the lowest estimates displayed in Table 4.2 seem more realistic than the highest.

### 4.2.2 Demographic Analysis

As Sanmartí (2001; 2004, fig. 4) has remarked, the main Iberian groups settling in the coastal territories of the north-east of the peninsula occupied territories of similar extensions: 2,775 $km^2$ for the Indicetia, 2,000 $km^2$ for the Laeetani, and 2,800 $km^2$ for the Cossetani. He suggested a population density of 15 inhabitants per $km^2$, which is equivalent to a population of 41,625, 30,000, and 42,000 inhabitants, respectively. Similarly, Sanmartí puts forward an area of 9,500 $km^2$ and a

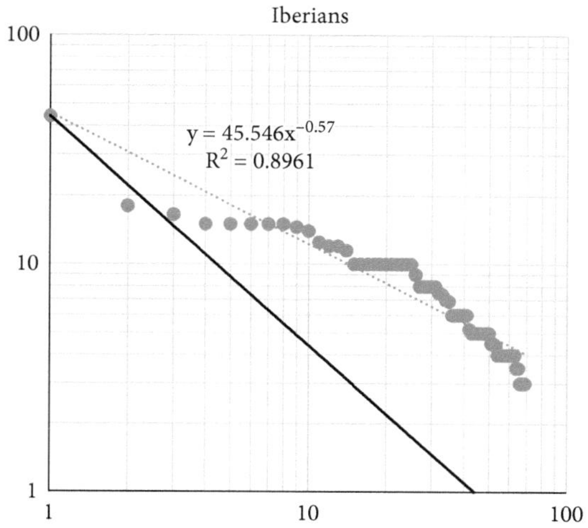


**Fig. 4.9** RSA data of the Iberian sites over 3 ha (n = 69)

density of less than 14.3, for the Ilergetan territory, giving a total population of 136,000 inhabitants, similar to the population in the sixteenth century for that same region.

The demographic study carried out by Valor and Garibo (2002) on the population of 21 Iberian settlements documented in the region of Requena-Utiel, in the territory of Kelín (Mata et al., 2001), makes them suggest a total of 12,151/12,447 inhabitants, which in an area of approximate 3,000 m² translates to a density of 4.05/4.15 inhabitants per km². This would be the territory of the Edetani peoples, where we find a much lower density than the above mentioned areas. It is to be expected that the vast and culturally diverse area of the Iberians would hold different densities.

Before turning to the population of the Iberian area, we should look at the RSA of this group (Fig. 4.9). At first glance, we can see that the primo-concave graph deviates quite a bit from Zipf's law. The *q*-value is 0.57, indicating that the slope of the graph is not very steep, and there is no strong hierarchy in the settlement system. The fit of the trend line, the $R^2$ value, of 0.8961 indicates a relatively low fit. Unfortunately, the data contain several sites with a size estimation, or rounded to the nearest number, leading to levelling at the round numbers and enhancing the low fit. Nonetheless, even with the exact sizes, these settlements would be around their estimated numbers and the settlement system would still be rather unhierarchical. The first settlement we have to explain is the primary settlement of 44 ha, outnumbering the second settlement quite a bit. The largest site is Castulo, which we find at the boundary of the later to be created provinces of Hispania Citerior and Ulterior. The city is considered to be the capital of the Oretani, and it is worth noting that the second settlement in the Iberian graph, Alarcos with

**Table 4.5** Results using different urbanization rates for the southern Iberian groups

| | 'Urban' | 30% | 25% | 20% |
|---|---|---|---|---|
| Low count | 85,890 | 286,300 | 343,560 | 429,450 |
| High count | 137,424 | 458,080 | 925,536 | 1,156,920 |

18 ha, also belongs the Oretani. The settlements of this group are larger than those of the remaining Iberian groups. Their settlement system follows the already mentioned southern pattern of larger *oppida* up to 50 ha. This brings us to the explanation for this concave graph with little hierarchy and levelling at a certain size: pooling of multiple systems. Therefore, the urban system of the Iberians should be divided into multiple systems. One of the major groups is that of the Oretani, controlling a large area in the basin of the Guadiana in the Southern Submeseta. This large group has a strongly hierarchical settlement system, with Castulo as its primary centre (see Fig. 4.10).

Table 4.5 shows population estimates based on the urbanization rate. To the left we see the low and high count of 'urban' population using the *oppida* we have been able to locate with a size above 3 ha. We avoid calculations with smaller settlements as these are less representative as they are chance finds due to their small size. To establish the numbers of inhabitants we have multiplied the sizes in hectares with the densities presented above: 250 as the low count number and 400 for the high count. The columns to the right in the table, give us the low and the high count total population if we assume the above stated percentage for the urbanization rate. With this urbanization rate we can then calculate the possible total populations. With the 14.3 inhabitants per square kilometre in mind given by Sanmartí (2001) and a rough size of the area (80,000 km$^2$) we can calculate which urbanization rate would be needed to meet his numbers. The urbanization rate of 25% and the high count would lead to a density of 14 inhabitants per square kilometre.

On the contrary, we find that northern Iberian settlement systems consist of relatively small but numerous settlements. This region is the same as that treated by Sanmartí (2001), and it is interesting to see if our calculations reach similar densities. In contrast to the southern Iberians, the areas occupied by the groups in the north are much smaller and each has a primary *oppidum* of roughly 10 ha, with lower order fortified and non-fortified rural settlements. As our graph only shows settlements of 3 ha and over, the lower order settlements are left out, thereby creating the picture of a heterarchical system of cities of similar size. Due to the relatively small size of the northern Iberian *oppida*, the cut-off point at 3 ha excludes quite a large proportion of the settlement system. However, due to the small nature of these settlements many of them are most likely missed in

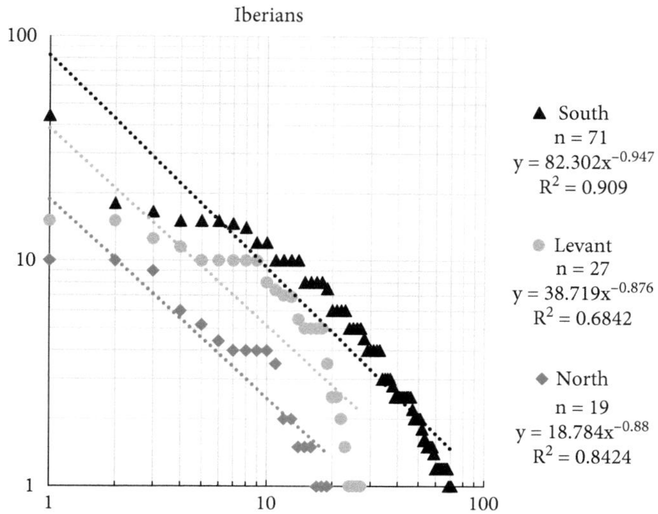


**Fig. 4.10** RSA data of the Iberian sites over 1 ha for the three main Iberian regions

archaeological surveys. Unsurprisingly, when we graph specifically for the northern Iberians (see fig. 4.10), those above the Ebro, including the settlements as small as 1 hectare, we get a different picture.

The second RSA graph for the Iberians is divided in three regions (north, levant and south), including much smaller settlements from 1 hectare and larger (Fig. 4.10). However, there are a few issues that we have to address. Admittedly, for the northern region with only twenty sites it is hard to draw any conclusions on general patterns. Nonetheless, we can observe some interesting things. One of the observations we can make is that there seem to be different layers of settlements. This is the result of two interlocking effects: first and foremost, the already mentioned pooling of sizes around round numbers. We see clearly that the smaller sites are 1, 1.5, and 2 ha. Second, the northern region is known for the multiple smaller settlement systems, for instance amongst others the Ilergeti, Cossetani, and Laietani (see Fig. 4.1), which means we are still polling multiple smaller systems. The settlement system in the levantine regions follow a hierarchical system with primary centres, secondary settlements, and numerous smaller rural settlements (Houten, 2021: 36), whereas the north had a more heterarchical system with numerous small oppida.

Table 4.6 gives us the population numbers with several urbanization rates for the northern Iberian settlement system. In the case of the northern Iberians we find that with the low count and an urbanization rate of 30% the total population for the Iberian region would be just under 65,000 inhabitants, and the high count gets us just over 105,000 inhabitants for the whole region. The region comprises roughly that of the modern provinces of Girona, Barcelona, Lleida, and Tarragona,

**Table 4.6** Results using different urbanization rates for the northern Iberian groups

| | 'Urban' | 30% | 25% | 20% |
|---|---|---|---|---|
| Low count | 19,340 | 64,467 | 77,360 | 96,700 |
| High count | 31,734 | 105,780 | 126,936 | 158,670 |

**Table 4.7** Results using a lower range of urbanization rates for the northern Iberians

| | 'Urban' | 15% | 12 .5% | 10% |
|---|---|---|---|---|
| Low count | 19,340 | 128,933 | 154,720 | 193,400 |
| High count | 31,734 | 211,560 | 253,872 | 317,340 |

which is about 25,000 km$^2$. This brings us to a density of only 4 people per square kilometre, which is much below the estimation of 14.3 given by Sanmartí (2001). We must conclude that if the estimation by Sanmartí is right, the urbanization rate would have been a lot lower. Moreover, as already stated, it is likely that the cut-off point at 3 ha has excluded quite a few urban Iberian settlements. Therefore, a much lower urbanization rate is to be expected when using 3 ha as the cut-off point.

When returning to the density estimation made by Sanmartí for a density of 14.3 inhab./km$^2$ we would have to use the high count of 10% urbanization rate (Table 4.7). These low urbanization rates indicate that the area has a relatively small and dispersed population. We must conclude that in the northern Iberian area people tended to live in rural settlements and the overall population density was rather low, especially if we compare it with the population calculations for the Celtiberian area (see below), which is slightly larger than the northern Iberian region. It seems likely that when considering urbanism in the northern Iberian system, *oppida* between 1 and 3 ha should be considered as urban.

## 4.3 Celtiberian *Oppida*

Uxama, Termantia, Arekoratas, Segontia, Clunia, and Contrebia Leukade, among others, are some of the most important Celtiberian urban centres (Lorrio, 1997; Burillo Mozota, 2008). In this study a list of as many as 65 sites that can be attributed to the Celtiberians has been compiled, of which 39 are over 3 ha in area. Most of the Celtiberian *oppida* are of modest dimensions, but, on average, they are certainly larger than the Iberian ones, many of them covering areas that range between 7 and 15 ha (see Fig. 4.12 RSA).

Surrounded by strong defensive walls, their internal layout tends to be orthogonal and in many cases a network of intersecting streets has been identified. A type of settlement with influences from the Iberian model, in which public and monumental architecture is rare and intramural occupation patterns are dense. Living spaces usually occupied a larger surface than communal and/or public spaces (Ruiz Zapatero, 2011). The Celtiberian model, previously defined as a city-state model (Ruiz Zapatero et al., 2020: 144), can be defined in the words of Ruiz Zapatero et al. (2020: 132)—building on Burillo Mozota (2011)—as 'characterized by an intricate network of fortified villages and minor rural entities that accommodated the majority of the population and the urban aristocracies'.

Based on the plans of some of the preserved settlements and the aforementioned description, and the sizes recorded for the Celtiberian *oppida* listed in this book (see Appendix I), we find *oppida* of a similar type to those just discussed for the Iberian territory. The main difference seems to reside in the fact that *oppida* over 3 ha in area are much more numerous among the Celtiberians while the smallest ones of less than 1 ha are much less frequent.

### 4.3.1 Numantia: The Celtiberian Case Study Par Excellence

Many ancient and modern estimates exist for what is perhaps the most famous Celtiberian city of all: Numantia (Fig. 4.11). The demographic estimates, however, are far from uniform but, in combination with the well-preserved archaeological remains of the settlement, they make it an excellent case study to gain an idea of the demography of the Celtiberians. The Roman author Florus (1.34) indicates that 4,000 Celtiberians resisted the Roman forces for eleven years, a figure that is also repeated by Livy (*Per.* 55). Appian (*Iber.* 76; 97), on the other hand, points out that the number of Numantine men did not exceed 8,000 in times of peace. It is important to highlight that the number of men in the classical texts would have included those from the territory pertaining to the *oppidum*, not just the *oppidum* itself.

On the basis of the numbers provided by the sources, Schulten (1914; 1945) suggested the number of 2,000 warriors or 8,000 inhabitants for the entire Numantine region in times of peace, calculating the ratio of one to four members in each family. Taracena (1941: 71) considered that these figures were acceptable for a settlement of 22 ha and houses of around 100 m$^2$. Caro Baroja (1976: 156) also believed this latter extent of the *oppidum* feasible and proposed 2,000 houses with between 6,000 and 8,000 inhabitants.

**Fig. 4.11** Plan of Numantia (Ortego y Frias, 1967)

Using Numantia as his main case study, Almagro-Gorbea (2001: 53 et seq.) suggested that a multiplying factor of 5–6 people per household should be applied (see Chapter 3) and that only 60% of the total surface of the settlement would have been occupied by dwellings and have been of a residential nature, a calculation that is also accepted for Numantia by Jimeno Martínez and Tabernero Galán (1996: 427). Moreover, it reinforces the data obtained in our estimates of communal surface and household surface for the Iberian *oppida*.

However, the best study available to estimate the population of Numantia is that of Jimeno Martínez and Tabernero Galán (1996) since it is based on a study of the existing archaeological remains. Of the three overlapping cities that make up the stratigraphy of Numantia, they pointed out an area of 10.7 ha for the Roman imperial city. Of that, only 6.48 ha would have been inhabited, the remaining space being occupied by streets and other open spaces. These figures allowed the authors to suggest a total of 648 houses of 100 m$^2$, which at four occupants per house, would represent just over 2,500 inhabitants in the imperial period. Taking into account other spaces not intended for housing, such as public buildings, they estimate that the figure would not have been much higher than 2,000 inhabitants.

When discussing the surface of the remains of the city besieged by Nobilior in 133 BCE, Jimeno Martínez and Tabernero Galán put forward a built surface of 7.2 ha of which only 4.35 ha were occupied by residential spaces, the average house occupying 80 m$^2$, a surface not far from that estimated for the Iberian settlement of La Bastida de les Alcuses (Table 4.4). On the basis of these data, the authors estimated a total population around 1,500 or 2,000 individuals and a density of 208–278 inhab./ha). If we apply all their data to our methodology, we obtain the following estimates:

Household surface = 4.35 ha = 43,500 m$^2$ (of houses).
43,500 m$^2$ (surface occupied by houses) / 80 (average of a house) = 544 houses.
Estimated number of inhabitants: 544 (houses) × 4 (hab./house) = 2,176 persons.
Density: 2,176 inhab./7.2 ha. = 302 inhab./ha.

Other scholars have also estimated densities for the main Celtiberian *oppida*. Quesada (2006: 153) has suggested values of around 400 and 500 inhab./ha for the densely urbanized Celtiberian *oppida*. Finally, Almagro's estimates for Celtiberian *oppida* proposed densities of around 600/720 inhab./ha, but his numbers do not seem reliable since he used an average house size of about 50 m$^2$, figures that have already been shown to be far from the average house size established for all the previous sites discussed of more than 3 ha in area and where the archaeological evidence is relatively well preserved.

In short, based on the results of our estimates as well as those proposed by other scholars, it seems feasible to suggest a narrower range (300–400 inhab./ha) for the density of the Celtiberian *oppida* when the archaeological data are not enough to carry out individualized calculations and populations are estimated by multiplying the total surface of the settlement by a specific density.

### 4.3.2 Demographic Analysis

Almagro-Gorbea (2001: 47) also attempted to estimate the rural population of Celtiberia. To do so and since survey data are too scarce to provide reliable estimates for the pre-Roman period, showing once more how common is the lack of evidence to conduct rural estimates, he undertook an ethnographic comparison between the ancient and some recent populations who, in his view, inhabited landscapes and had living conditions that made this comparison feasible. Almagro-Gorbea (2001: 50) concluded that population densities would have ranged between 5 and 13 inhab./km$^2$. In his opinion, a density of about 10 inhab./km$^2$ would instead be acceptable in areas such as the middle valley of the Ebro or the River Jalón basin, since they are lower than those provided by Pliny for the early imperial period in the north-west of the peninsula (see Chapter 5).

In brief, following Almagro-Gorbea's figures, Celtiberia (45,000 km$^2$) would have had a total population between 225,000 and 585,000 inhabitants. Quesada (2006: 154) narrows down this huge gap between the lowest and the highest

**Table 4.8** Total population estimates for Celtiberia based on the numbers of troops provided by Appian for 153 BCE and different estimates of the percentage of the total population serving in the army

| Celtiberian troops | Total population (8%) | Total population (15%) | Total population (22%) |
|---|---|---|---|
| 4,000 men | 50,000 | 26,000 | 18,000 |
| 8,000 men | 100,000 | 53,000 | 36,000 |
| 25,000 men | 312,000 | 167,000 | 113,000 |

*Source*: Quesada (2006: table 1).

possible population estimates suggesting numbers based on the number of troops discussed by Appian during the campaigns of 153 BCE. Following Quesada, the army formed by the Belli, Titti, and Arevaci probably did not exceed 8% of the total population (or 16% of the male population), and therefore a total population of about 312,000 people for the Celtiberian territory (31,250 $km^2$) (Table 4.8), numbers that could be expressed as a density (10 inhab./$km^2$) very close to that suggested by Almagro.

For the Celtiberian area we have been able to obtain dimensions for 65 different settlements, of which 39 are over 3 ha in area and are included in the graph (Fig. 4.12). In much the same way as the Iberian graphs, a primo-concave graph, with a slight slope, can be observed. Three settlements stand out over the concave section: Segontia Lanca (60 ha), Augustobriga (49 ha), and Uxama Argaela (30 ha). These are followed by a number of settlements of around 20 ha, from which point the concave shape can be observed. The Celtiberian settlement system certainly consisted of larger *oppida* than that of its eastern neighbours, the Iberians. The large *oppida* were further apart than the Iberian ones, as the territories of the different Celtiberian groups or cities were larger.

In section 4.3.1 we reached an estimate of 300 to 400 inhab./ha for the density of the Celtiberian *oppida*. With the 39 *oppida* over 3 ha, we have a total of 579.8 ha of 'urban' settlement. Multiplying this number by the lower density of 300 inhabitants per hectare, we obtain a population of 173,940 'urban' Celtiberians, whereas the high count provides a total of 231,920 'urban' Celtiberians. As this number represents just under two-thirds of the total located settlements, 39 of 65, it could be assumed that this includes approximately 60% of the total population. Admittedly this is a very high number for the urbanization rate; effectively, larger and fortified sites are likely to be overrepresented in research as these tend to be found more easily. However, it should be borne in mind that we are looking at communities that used to live in fortified sites. Moreover, our cut-off point is rather low, as we decided to include all settlements of 3 ha and above. This low cut-off point certainly includes non-urban fortified sites. Nonetheless, we can

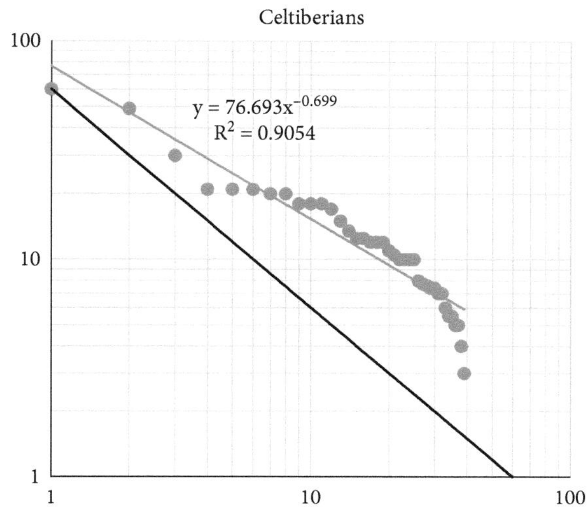


**Fig. 4.12** RSA graph of Celtiberian sites (n = 39)

**Table 4.9** Results using different urbanization rates for the Celtiberians

| | 'Urban' | 60% | 50% | 40% |
|---|---|---|---|---|
| Low count | 173,940 | 289,900 | 347,880 | 434,850 |
| High count | 231,920 | 386,533 | 463,840 | 579,800 |

turn to three different scenarios for urbanization rates to calculate the total population of the Celtiberian area (see Table 4.9).

Interestingly our range between the extremes, 289,000 to 579,000 Celtiberians, does not deviate much from the 225,000 to 585,000 given by Almagro-Gorbea. However, as we believe that the evidence indicates that the Celtiberian *oppida* were rather large—most of the sites we have found are between 7.5 and 15 ha—so the cut-off point of 3 ha is likely to have included a certain number of 'rural' sites, thus revealing interesting differences to what has been seen for the Iberian case and highlighting why looking at each group separately is extremely important. As a result of this low cut-off point, the 'urbanization' level is high. Using the calculations with the high urbanization rate of 60% we reach a number fairly close to the estimates given by Quesada. With a population between 289,900 and 386,533, a density between 9 and 12 inhabitants per km$^2$ can be established. It is of interest to note that this high urbanization rate might be the result of the development of a city-state like organization with agro-towns as the centres (Burillo Mozota, 2008: 260).

## 4.4 The *Carpetani*

In a survey conducted in 1997 on Carpetanian urbanism in the middle section of the River Tagus, in an area known as La Mesa de Ocaña, Urbina Martínez revealed the existence of two clearly differentiated types of settlement. The first kind were located on the plain, without any appreciable defences and frequently overlying pre-existing settlements dating from the First Iron Age. The second kind, on the other hand, were characterized by their fortifications (walls and often surrounded by a moat) and location on hills. Urbina Martínez interpreted that the settlements on the plain were usually larger (8–10 ha) and belonged to Late First/Early Second Iron Age (fifth to late third century BCE), whereas the fortified settlements corresponded to a later period of occupation that cannot be dated earlier than the second half of the fourth century BCE (Urbina Martínez, 1997: 549). This pattern could also be extrapolated to the territories of what is the modern-day Autonomous Community of Madrid (Morín de Pablos and Urbina Martínez, 2005: 109). The latter category of sites displayed a greater variability in size. In the Tagus valley, for example, the average extent of the settlements is 6–7 ha, but in some cases, the surface does not exceed 2–3 ha. In the Cedrón-Melgar valley, the average is around 1 ha, with only a few cases surpassing this surface area.

Following Urbina Martínez (2000), it seems that the populations inhabiting the settlements on the plain of La Mesa de Ocaña eventually moved to the fortified *oppida*, which was to be the most characteristic settlement in the area at the time of the Roman conquest. One issue in working with the Carpetani is the lack of excavations; consequently, it remains unclear whether some of these settlements (on the plain and hillforts) were occupied simultaneously, as has been suggested in some cases. With that in mind, a close look at the number of settlements known to date in the area, seems to suggest that there are not enough fortified vs. unfortified settlements to support the hypothesis that the populations inhabiting the settlements on the plain of La Mesa de Ocaña eventually moved to the fortified *oppida*, or at least not in all cases and areas (Fig. 4.13). Succinctly, there seems to be a particular concentration of fortified towns in the valley of the River Tagus and at its confluence with the River Jarama. In this case, the previous settlement system appears to have been completely replaced. However, in other valleys in the area of Carpetania it seems that the settlements on the plain and on the high ground could have coexisted in the fourth to third centuries BCE.

### 4.4.1 El Llano de la Horca

The urban layout of Carpetanian *oppida* is generally poorly understood; for this reason, our knowledge of the internal organization of the settlements and their development over time is limited (Dávila, 2007: 25; Ruiz Zapatero, 2009: 191).

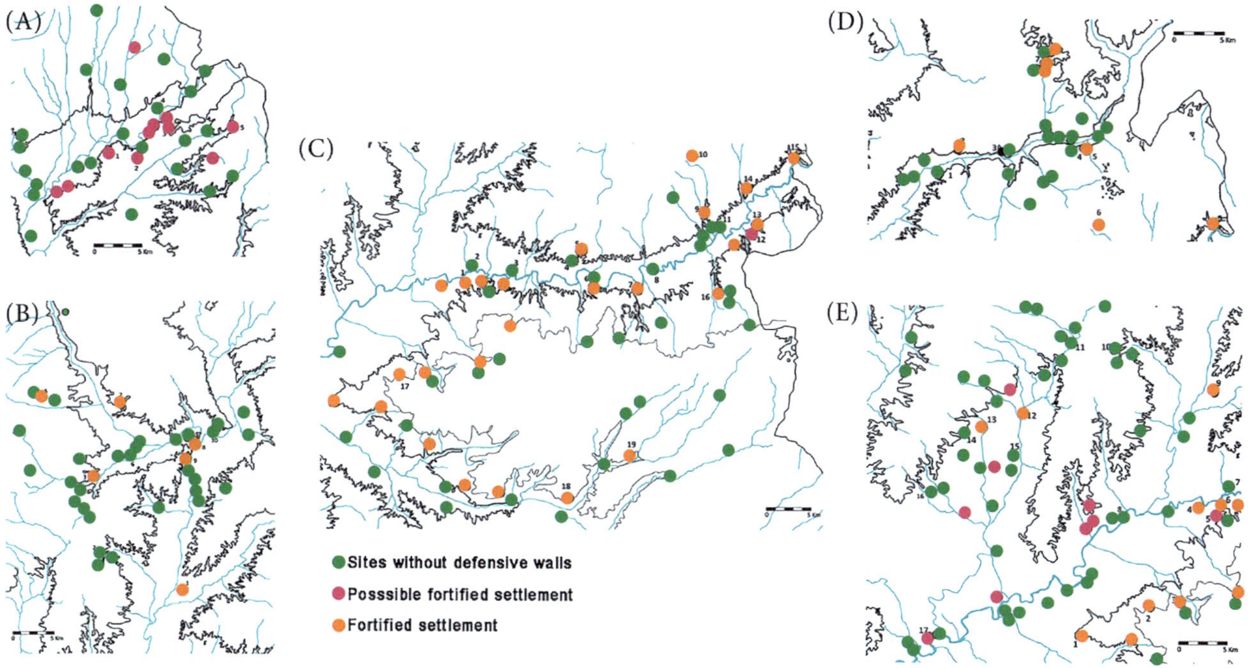


**Fig. 4.13** Settlement distribution in several areas of Carpetania (after Torres Rodríguez, 2012: 442–6): (A) River Henares. (B) Lower and Mid Jarama. (C) La Mesa de Ocaña. (D) Tajuña valley. (E) Confluence between the Rivers Tagus and Jarama and the Guatén stream

Therefore, the excavation and geophysical and magnetic survey work carried out at El Llano de la Horca are fundamental to identify the organization of the different spaces in the settlement during its most important phase of occupation (mid-third century BCE to mid-first century BCE) (Baquedano Pérez et al., 2007: 380). There can be no doubt that, during this period, the settlement reached the urban configuration of an authentic *oppidum*, and it is therefore useful to improve our understanding of the possible appearance of these settlements in the territory of the Carpetani.

The urban model recorded at El Llano de la Horca is quite regular. It occupies most of the intramural surface of the settlement and reflects a clear differentiation between areas on the basis of functional criteria. A complex urban plan with blocks of houses can clearly be seen (Fig. 4.14). A densely populated radial layout of the streets converges on a large central open space. This large square is directly connected with the main entrance of the *oppidum* by means of the largest streets recorded so far (Contreras et al., 2014: 117).

(A)

(B)

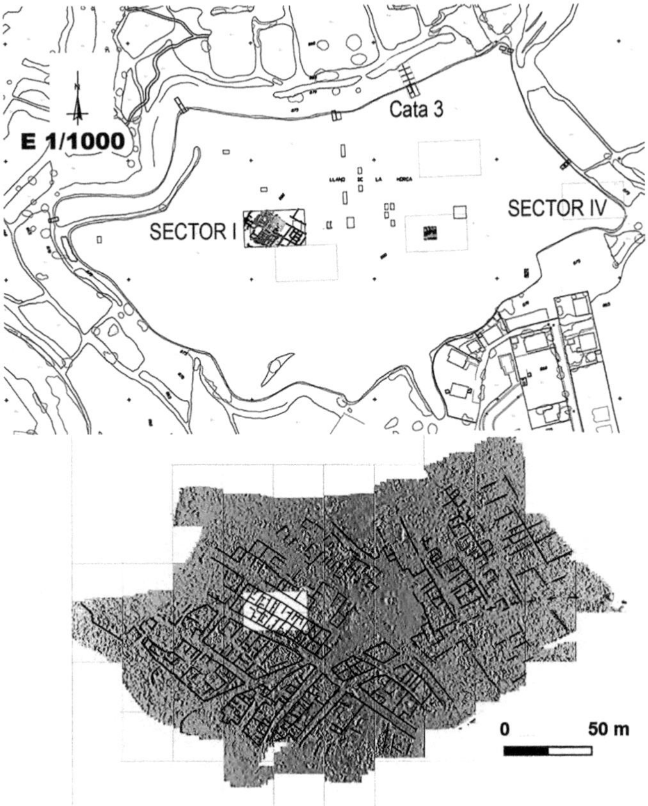


**Fig. 4.14** Plan with the areas at El Llano de la Horca: (A) excavated. (B) surveyed by ground-penetrating radar (after Contreras et al., 2014: fig. 6)

Using the plan in Fig. 4.14, we have measured the surface occupied by the streets and other open spaces. As a result, a total area of 6,786.79 m$^2$, which represents slightly more than 23% of the total surface measured in Fig. 4.14 (29,231.79 m$^2$) has been obtained. This enables us to suggest a very similar ratio of communal surface and household surface to that documented for Iberian and Celtiberian sites (Table 4.3). Based on these calculations and counting the specialization of some built areas detected at the sites, it seems reasonable to suggest that only 60% of the total surface inside the walls was occupied by residential quarters.

Another scenario could be presented if the ethnoarchaeological study conducted by Kramer (1979) on traditional rural societies on the Iranian plateau is taken into account. There, the built surface was estimated to occupy 60% of the village (in this case a settlement of 29 ha), as at El Llano, but only 53% of these constructions were roofed structures (about one- third of the total). In our measurements, about 77% of the intramural space seems to have been constructed. Therefore, even if we use numbers closer to Kramer's estimates, communal surface must have been around 30–40%. Below estimates will be calculated on the basis of both values.

While only a very few houses have been excavated at El Llano, two types of residential structures seem to be repeatedly detected (Fig. 4.15). The first type, rectangular in plan, is divided into three main spaces and always matches houses of about 70 m$^2$. The largest structures, around 100 m$^2$ (such as the so-called 'house of the columns') are of square layout. Based on these numbers, the average house at the site can confidently be estimated to have been around 80–85 m$^2$, once again quite close to the numbers that have been seen in previous case

**Fig. 4.15** Aerial view of the houses excavated in Sector I at El Llano de la Horca. Inside the black square the Casa Sur (Contreras et al., 2014: fig. 3)

studies, such as Numantia (80 $m^2$) and not far from those recorded in La Bastida de les Alcuses (97 $m^2$).

If we apply all the above data to our methodology using a communal surface of 40%, it would be possible to estimate the following number of inhabitants and densities for El Llano de la Horca:

Household surface = 10 ha– 40% of communal surface = 60,000 $m^2$ (of houses).
60,000 $m^2$ (surface occupied by houses) / 80 (average of a house) = 750 houses.
Estimate of inhabitants: 750 (houses) × 4 (hab./house) = 3,000 persons.
Density: 3,000 inhab./10 ha. = 300 inhab./ha.

If, on the other hand, we were to apply a communal surface of 60%, the result would be as follows:

40,000 $m^2$ (surface occupied by houses) / 85 (average of a house) = 470 houses.
Estimation of inhabitants: 470 (houses) × 4 (hab./house) = 1,882 persons.
Density: 1,882 inhab./10 ha. = 188 inhab./ha.

Urbina Martínez also proposed demographic estimates based on the data from later periods (Table 4.10). Based on these numbers, he estimated a density of 113 inhab./ha, a figure that he later applied to the Iron Age settlements in La Mesa de Ocaña. With regard to Urbina Martínez's estimates, two factors must be taken into account: in the first place, it is important to say that, by the end of the seventeenth century in La Mesa de Ocaña the average house was about 500 $m^2$ and 1,215 $m^2$ in 1984. Therefore, they were much larger than the ones recorded by archaeology during the Iron Age (Urbina Martínez, 2000: 144–5). Similarly, the average number of inhab./household was not much higher in the seventeenth and

**Table 4.10** Demographic estimates in La Mesa de Ocaña from the fifteenth century onwards

| Period | Inhab./ha | Inhab./$km^2$ |
|---|---|---|
| 16th century | – | 23 |
| 17th century | 113.7 | – |
| 18th century | 62.8 | 19.3 |
| Ciruelos | 156.7 | – |
| Dosbarrios | | – |
| 1984 | 52.3 | 22 |

*Source*: Urbina Martínez (2000: 14–15).

eighteenth centuries (5.8). Considering the size of the houses at El Llano de la Horca and other Iron Age settlements studied in this chapter, it makes sense to obtain densities that are higher than those estimated by Urbina Martínez, especially after analysing the urban layout of El Llano de la Horca in detail.

Taking into account the similarities between some of the Carpetanian *oppida* and those of the Celtiberians and the Iberians, a point already noted by Urbina Martínez (2000: 236, fig. 81), together with the fact that the size of the houses is also quite similar, it seems quite reasonable to suggest at least a range of 200–300 inhab./ha for the larger Carpetanian *oppida* and a slightly larger one (300–400), similar to the case of the Iberian ones, for those under 3 ha, although it has proved impossible to conduct estimates on well-preserved sites of the later type.

### 4.4.2 Demographic Analysis

The research carried out in the past two decades allows us to start reconstructing the population numbers of the Carpetani and their *oppida*. It has been possible to establish the size of 53 pre-Roman *oppida*, which have been analysed by means of a rank-size graph (Fig. 4.16).

The urban system of the Carpetani seems to have been hierarchical, with a *q*-value of 0.818. The $R^2$ value indicates there is a reasonable fit, but when we turn to the graph, the settlement pattern can be observed. The largest settlements are slightly under the trend line of the graph, indicating that the upper echelons do

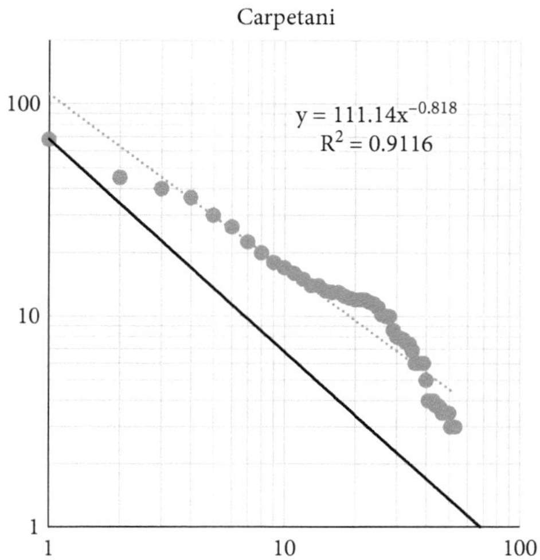


**Fig. 4.16** RSA graph for the Carpetanian sites (n = 53)

**Table 4.11** Results using different urbanization rates for the Carpetanians

| | 'Urban' | 60% | 50% | 40% |
|---|---|---|---|---|
| Low count | 137,500 | 229,167 | 275,000 | 343,750 |
| High count | 206,250 | 343,750 | 412,500 | 515,625 |

not follow a clear hierarchy. One *oppidum* can be seen to stand out, namely Complutum, covering an area of 68 ha. This distribution could indicate that Complutum was the primary centre of the Carpetani, followed by a second tier created by three *oppida* of a similar category of size: Contrebia Carbica (45 ha), Toletum (40 ha), and Vilora (36.3 ha).

Turning to the population numbers, we have used the established densities of between 200 and 300 per hectare for the *oppida* over 3 ha. With these calculations, the outcome is a rather high number. The total 'urban' population, considering all the *oppida* covering more than 3 ha as 'urban', would reach 137,500 people using the low count and 206,250 with the high count. These numbers are similar to those for the Celtiberians, so we might expect the urbanization rate to be high (Table 4.11).

Assuming the high urbanization rate, as applied to the Celtiberian area, a total of 229,167 to 343,750 Carpetanians living in the region is obtained. With a rough estimate of their area being 25,000 km$^2$, this would lead to a slightly higher density than that of the Celtiberians: between 9 and 14 people per square kilometre.

## 4.5 The Vettones

On the basis of the evidence derived from our sample of fourteen settlements belonging to this pre-Roman group, their main *oppida* can be stated to have covered areas of between 5 and 15 ha, at least from the fourth century BCE onwards, good examples being Las Cogotas (Cardeñosa), Yecla (Yecla de Yeltes), Castillejo de la Orden (Alcántara), and Villasviejas (Botija). During the following century, some settlements of the Vettones came to occupy much larger areas: El Raso (20 ha), Cerro de San Vicente (20 ha), and Ulaca, which reached 60 ha (Ruiz Zapatero, 2005) (Fig. 4.17). These large settlements were strongly fortified by means of defensive towers at the gates and monumental stone walls between 4 and 8 m thick (Ruiz Zapatero et al., 2020: 134).

Their large size, however, did not reflect a dense urban layout. Public buildings are quite unusual, and most people continued to live in rural settlements of small dimensions (Ruiz Zapatero et al., 2020: 135). Only a small part of the population

**Fig. 4.17** The *oppidum* of El Raso (Candeleda) showing the remains of a dozen towers, houses, and stone walls. Photograph and map by Jesús Álvarez-Sanchís (Ruiz Zapatero et al., 2020: fig. 8.2)

lived within the walls of the *oppida* and even in the case of the largest settlements, scholars have argued that the population numbers would not have surpassed 1,500 inhabitants (Álvarez Sanchís and Ruiz Zapatero, 2001), although these figures may be somewhat conservative in some cases (see below).

The organization of these *oppida* was defined by the topography (Ruiz Zapatero and Álvarez Sanchís, 1995; Ruiz Zapatero, 2018), and the excavated households do not follow a preconceived urban layout. The dimensions of the rectangular or square houses tend to range between 50 $m^2$ and 250 $m^2$ (Ruiz Zapatero et al., 2020: 135). The *oppida* included substantial intramural areas that were not built up, but used as pastures, a type of organization that is of great significance in order to put forward demographic estimates. An argument that seems to reinforce the presence of such intramural green areas is the existence of houses outside the walls. It has been argued that in times of conflict or uncertainty, those living outside the walls would have been able to seek refuge inside the fortified *oppidum*, which means that space to accommodate them must have existed (Ruiz Zapatero et al., 2020: 134).

In brief, this is a group characterized by a very different urban structure to those described so far. They may have built extensive fortified *oppida*, but these had the specific characteristic that they were largely unoccupied and lacked a standardized urban layout (Ruiz Zapatero et al., 2020: 133). When discussing the *oppida* of the Vettones, some have put forward the idea of a low-density pattern of urbanism (Moore, 2017)—for Ulaca approximately 20 individuals per hectare—a suggestion that needs to be taken into account and tested against the archaeological evidence available. Needless to say, this is a very important element since, if we attribute the same densities as suggested for the Iberian, Celtiberian, and Vaccean ones—even at the low end—to the *oppida* of the Vettones, their population numbers will be greatly overestimated.

### 4.5.1 Estimating the Demography of El Raso

El Raso seems to have been inhabited between the late third century BCE and 50 BCE, thus having a life span of little more than 150 years. The urban layout of El Raso was likely to have been created without a preconceived plan or urban project, and the existence of isolated houses is well documented (Fernández Gómez, 1986: 392). However, there are certain criteria applicable to all those who wish to live together or grouped in clusters of houses. The streets are not regular or homogeneous. On the contrary, very variable spaces can be detected when they are compared. They can sometimes be interpreted as proper streets while in other cases they look much more like simple, narrow, tortuous alleys, more probably designed for drainage purposes or for the removal of water rather than with any urban layout in mind (Fernández Gómez, 1986: 389).

In his first study on the demography of El Raso, Fernández Gómez (1986: 950) estimated that the *oppidum* could have had about 600 houses with an average area of 125 m$^2$, estimating that only 50% of the total intramural surface (150,000–180,000 m$^2$) was built up.

These early numbers have been updated in a subsequent publication that included the excavation of an additional surface of 4,000 m$^2$ and 27 new buildings. Of those, 20 were interpreted as living spaces providing the interesting detail that approximately 25% of the structures were not inhabited. In this second demographic study, Fernández Gómez (2011: 395) provides us with valuable information, since from the newly excavated area of 4,000 m$^2$ only 1,761 m$^2$ were built up, providing a ratio of *c.* 44% of communal surface. If we add the *c.* 25% of built space that was not inhabited, the conclusion can be reached that a total of 70% of the intramural surface was not employed as residential space. Extending these numbers to all the excavated houses (29) at El Raso, Fernández Gómez estimates a total of 112 inhabitants (116 if we accept 4 inhab./household). If this number is multiplied by the total surface of the site (20 ha), it provides a total population of approximately 2,400 persons (Fernández Gómez, 2011: 395) and a density of 120 inhab./ha. On the other hand, it is important to highlight the fact that other scholars have estimated the population of El Raso to have numbered no more than 500 (Ruiz Zapatero and Álvarez Sanchís, 1995: 232), which would mean that it supported a density of no more than 25 inhab./ha, reflecting the dichotomy that exists as regards how to estimate the population of the towns of the Vettones. This substantial difference in calculations arises from the acceptance of the presence of large open spaces inside the walls.

Our own estimates for El Raso have, in the first place, reconsidered the average household area. After measuring the area of the published plan of each house (Fig. 4.18) and even without taking into account those under 20 m$^2$, which may well have served other purposes (see Chapter 3), the average area barely reached 60–70 m$^2$, with only a few houses slightly over 100 m$^2$. These numbers seem much more realistic if they are compared to the other case studies discussed, where the average house area rarely surpasses 70–80 m$^2$. In the few cases where the surface areas are over that number, one or more houses (in samples that comprise 10–12 domestic units) are over 300 m$^2$. According to the evidence of the published plans, there are no houses at El Raso close to those dimensions, and therefore an average of 125 m$^2$ seems somewhat high. It seems to be more realistic, at least judging from the limited archaeological evidence available, to suppose that only about 40% of the space was built up. However, as has been seen above and in previous cases, not all the intramural buildings can be considered residential and, therefore, this number needs to be lowered to a maximum of 30%. In sum, based on what we know and, we must stress that it is very little, about the intramural layout of the settlements of the Vettones, no more than 20–30% of the total intramural surface can be interpreted as residential spaces at sites like El Raso. With values of 20% of household surface, our estimates would provide a total number of *c.* 666 houses and 2,667 inhabitants, resulting in a density of 133 inhab./ha (SE 29.27), numbers very close to those estimated by Fernández Gómez (2011: 395).

Other estimates produced for towns of the Vettones include those for the settlement of La Hoya (Alava), which covers just under 3 ha (28,000 m$^2$). Llanos (1990 145) estimated that around 560 houses existed, housing a total population of about 2,240. This estimate produces a density per hectare of 800 inhabitants, which is much higher than those discussed for El Raso or for any of the scenarios already mentioned. In our opinion, this deviation of the density for La Hoya from the other figures put forward makes it hard to support.

Similarly, and also in the light of the archaeological evidence of El Raso, it seems difficult to accept the very low densities that have been suggested for some of the major towns of the Vettones including 200 inhabitants at Las Cogotas (15 inhab./ha), 300 for Mesa de la Miranda (Chamartín de la Sierra) (Ruiz Zapatero and Álvarez Sanchís, 1995: 232; Álvarez Sanchís, 1999: 306), and between 1,000 and 1,500 for Ulaca (20 inhab./ha) (Álvarez Sanchís et al., 2008: 347), the largest *oppidum* of the Vettones, which covered 60 ha.

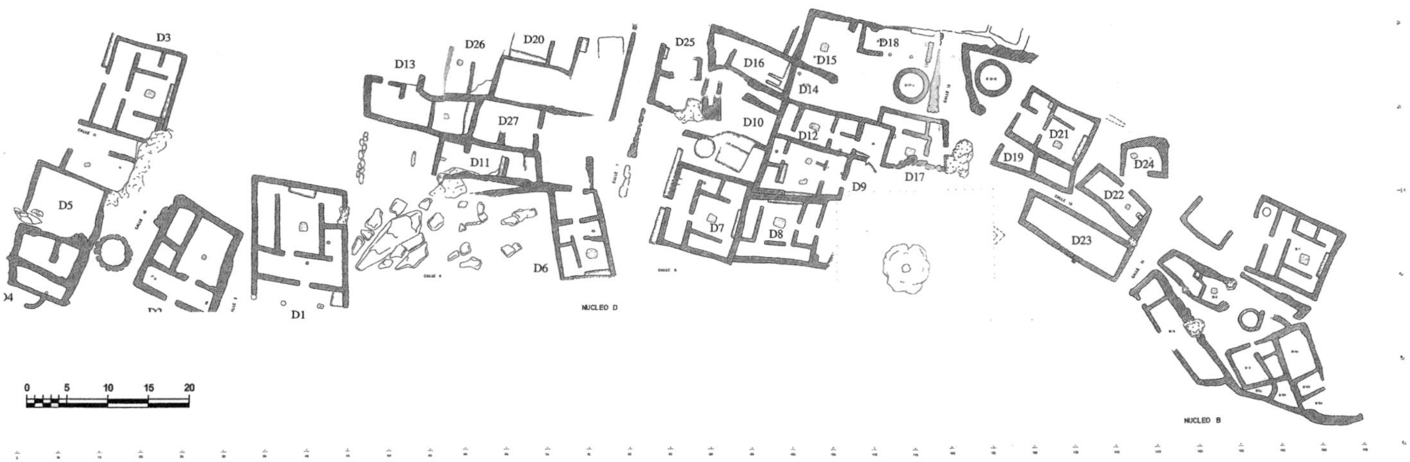


Fig. 4.18 Plan of one of the excavated sectors at El Raso (after Fernández Gómez, 2011)

### 4.5.2 Reconsidering the Density of Ulaca

The disparity between some of the estimates discussed above makes it necessary to ascertain the relationship between household surface and communal spaces in order to confirm whether the very low densities suggested are realistic or too pessimistic. Due to its considerable extent as well as the fact that it is a well-known archaeological site, Ulaca provides a good case study.

In past studies, over 250 houses, with areas ranging between 50 and 150 m², have been identified inside the walls of Ulaca (Álvarez Sanchís et al., 2008: 343). Were we to apply an average of four individuals per house, which would immediately lead to a population of over 1,000 inhabitants, the numbers would exceed 1,250 with an average of five inhabitants per house. If one accepts a total population for Ulaca of between 1,000 and 1,500 inhabitants (*c.* 15–20 inhab./ha), these numbers will mean that almost all the houses in a 60 ha *oppidum* have been preserved and recorded. This is a difficult assumption since, as has been seen in many of our case studies, even on much smaller sites, a large number of the structures have not survived the passage of time.

When the plan of Ulaca (Fig. 4.19a) is examined, there is no doubt that the site had large open spaces inside the walls, but it is also true that some areas seem to be have been relatively built up. Unfortunately, with the data currently at our disposal, it seems impossible to gain an idea of the relationship between communal surface and household surface for the site as a whole, but an approximate figure for this ratio can be calculated for a specific section of the town (Fig. 4.19b). If the

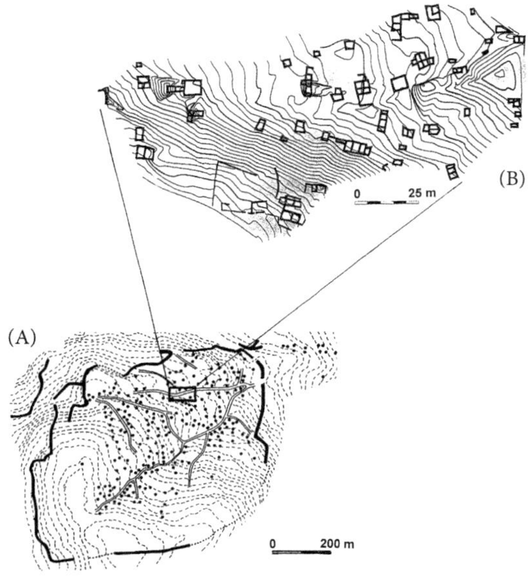


**Fig. 4.19** (A) Plan of Ulaca with all the structures recorded. (B) Detail of the urban layout in one of the sectors of Ulaca (Álvarez Sanchís et al., 2008)

total surface of the sector in question is measured, as well as that occupied by each structure—and considerable caution must be exercised with the results obtained when working with published plans—it can be seen that the area occupied by the houses seems to cover approximately 10% of the total. If, as has been seen at El Raso, of this built-up space, around 25% was not used for human habitation, the final figure for residential space is a total of 7.5%. If we extrapolate this ratio to the remaining areas of Ulaca, estimating that the average house size is *c.* 70 $m^2$ (based on the numbers discussed in previous case studies and the fact that known houses range between 50 and 150 $m^2$), that would increase the number of houses to about 875 and the population to numbers close to 3,000 inhabitants (42.8 inhab./ha). In this scenario, while it is still clear that we are discussing densities much lower than in any other of the pre-Roman *oppida* studied, it is also true that this figure would be double the numbers previously suggested.

To summarize, while it is true that certain variables, such as the ratio of household surface versus community surface and the densities of inhabitants per hectare must be reconsidered and significantly lowered with respect to the other Iron Age groups and sites discussed in this chapter, on the basis of the existing archaeological evidence for El Raso, densities under 100 inhab./ha seem hard to support at the sites of the Vettones covering intramural areas between 5 and 20 ha. On the other hand, if we follow the data obtained while considering the case of Ulaca, the densities of the larger *oppida* should be halved (40–50 inhab./ha). Although we are fully aware of the limitations of this proposal and accept that there is much room for improvement, it seems clear that, as happened in the case of the Iberian settlements, using the same densities/ha for the *oppida* of the Vettones of very different sizes does not seem to be a good approach. Based on all the above, in this chapter a density of 80–100 inhab./ha for the *oppida* of the Vettones between 5 and 20 ha and 50 inhab./ha for those with an intramural area of over 20 ha will be used.

### 4.5.3 Demographic Analysis

Even though the urban system of the Vettones is located at the limit of our research area, we have decided to include these sites to be able to consider all the urban systems of the Northern Submeseta so as to understand the relationships between them. The area of the Vettones is known for its large *oppida* controlling extensive territories. This has an effect on the urbanization rate, which will have to be applied later in our analysis. First, however, the settlement system will be examined in a RSA graph (Fig. 4.20).

The RSA graph of the Vettones follows the concave shape with an $R^2$ of −0.863, although its plateau is seemingly odd. It is clear that their *oppida* are, in general, large settlements, the largest being Ulaca (60 ha), Mesas de Miranda (37.5 ha),

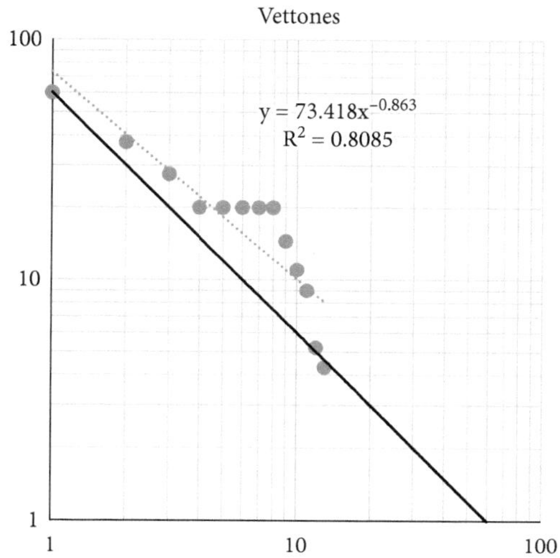


**Fig. 4.20** RSA graph for the sites of the Vettones (n = 14)

and Sanchorreja (27.5 ha), before the plateau of 20 ha *oppida* is reached. Even though this is clearly a consequence of levelling around a round number, the *oppida* can be assumed to have covered about 20 ha, and this plateau therefore reflects a genuine reality. From that point, a relatively steep drop can be traced. The system of the Vettones poses a considerable number of questions. How should we interpret the upper tier settlements? Are the three largest *oppida* of greater importance? They are located fairly close to each other, which means that it is illogical that only these three would have fulfilled the role of regional centres. For the significantly larger *oppidum* of Ulaca, it has been argued that it could have acted as the religious centre (Álvarez Sanchís, 2011: 154). The other *oppida* should probably be understood as equal parts in the settlement system. The other two would certainly have been located within their own region, where they would have acted as central places where people could find refuge, in line with the existence of 'pastures' inside the walled areas. However, within the settlement system of the Vettones as a whole, we could envisage a heterarchical system, with no clear hierarchy. In comparison with the other settlement systems discussed so far, we must conclude that all the *oppida* of the Vettones are large. However, as discussed above, at the same time we should focus on the low densities of occupation within the *oppida* themselves.

The established literature uses densities of about 15 to 20 inhabitants per hectare, calculated from the estimates given by scholars (see above in section 4.5.1). In this case our estimates are less conservative, as we have recalculated the densities for the *oppida* based on the case studies on El Raso and Ulaca. In the case of the *oppida* under 20 ha, a density of 80 to 100 inhabitants per hectare will be used

**Table 4.12** Estimates of large *oppida* compared

| Oppidum | Hectares | Traditional | New |
|---|---|---|---|
| Ulaca | 60 | 1,000–1,500* | 2,400–3,000 |
| Mesas de Miranda | 37.5 | 300–400* | 1,500–1,875 |
| Sanchorreja | 27.5 | 413–550 | 1,100–1,375 |
| Arroyo Manzanas | 20 | 300–400 | 800–1,000 |
| El Raso | 20 | 300–400 | 800–1,000 |
| Segovia | 20 | 300–400 | 800–1,000 |
| Salmantica | 20 | 300–400 | 800–1,000 |
| Albocela | 20 | 300–400 | 800–1,000 |
| Las Cogotas | 14.5 | 200* | 1,160–1,450 |
| Ledesma (Bletisama) | 11 | 165–220 | 880–1,100 |
| Irueña | 9 | 135–180 | 720–900 |
| Las Merchanas | 5.2 | 78–104 | 416–520 |
| Yecla de Yeltes | 4.3 | 65–86 | 344–430 |

*Note*: Figures indicated with * are provided by other scholars.

**Table 4.13** Results using different urbanization rates for the population of the Vettones

| | 'Urban' | 30% | 20% | 10% |
|---|---|---|---|---|
| Low count | 12,520 | 41,733 | 62,600 | 125,200 |
| High count | 15,650 | 52,167 | 78,250 | 156,500 |

(Table 4.12). Those of 20 ha and more are interpreted as having had a lower density, approximately half the figure proposed for the small *oppida*.

Continuing with our lower estimates, we obtain a total urban population of 12,520 for the Vettones; a high count would lead to a total of 15,650 urban inhabitants (Table 4.13). As mentioned above, the *oppida* are few and far apart. A relatively high proportion of the people might be expected to have lived outside the *oppida* in smaller rural settlements that are below our cut-off point. As a result, a relatively low urbanization rate for the Vettonian system might be expected to be necessary.

Even with an urbanization rate of 10%, which would indicate that we expect that our sample includes only 10% of the population, a relatively low number of Vettones is obtained. The area assigned to this people is approximately 40,000 km$^2$. Using our most optimistic number of 156,500 inhabitants in the area they occupied would result in a density of less than 4 inhab./km$^2$. It is evident that this area had few inhabitants and was sparsely occupied.

## 4.6 The Vacceans

The Vaccean *oppida* of the middle Duero valley shared a particular settlement pattern, characterized by large towns (from 5–20 ha to more than 40 ha) that were built at some distance from each other (Sacristán de Lama, 2011). The Vaccean settlement system contains the largest *oppidum* known in the Iberian peninsula: Peña Ulaña covering a total of 586 ha, with an acropolis of 285 ha (Cisneros, 2004: 90; Torres Martínez, 2011: 269). This settlement not only stands out because of its massive size, but also due to its less structured urban layout, although more research is needed to fully understand it. The other *oppida* must have had a well-planned urban layout and controlled modular territories of 400–500 km$^2$ (Ruiz Zapatero et al., 2020: 132). The numbers occasionally provided by ancient sources, such as the 23,000 victims that perished at Lucullus' hands (App. *Iber.* 50), or the 20,000 foot-soldiers and 2,000 horsemen who met at Intercatia shortly after this event (App. *Iber.* 53) (Sacristán de Lama, 2011), cannot be relied on to estimate the population of the Vaccean towns.

However, a reasonable approximation is feasible if, as Sacristán de Lama (2011: 198) suggested, most of the *oppida* present similar urban layouts characterized by occupation of most of the space inside the walls (Fig. 4.21). Archaeological evidence, especially from the *oppida* of Pintia (Padilla de Duero), Tiedra, and Cauca (Coca), indicates that their intramural areas comprised a regular organization with complex layouts of roads, blocks of rectangular houses built of adobe with shared rear areas, and doors and gates opening onto two streets (Sanz Mínguez and Velasco Vázquez, 2003; Blanco, 2018).

In his study of Vaccean urban design, Sacristán de Lama (2011: 198) assumes that houses occupied 70% of the total built space, therefore leaving the remaining 30% for the communal surface. In our opinion, and considering the calculations conducted above for the Iberian and Celtiberian *oppida*, as well as estimating the ratio between household surface and communal spaces in the Carpetanian town of Caraca (Fig. 4.22), where the well-defined streets and public spaces already occupy 18.5% of the total surface, these values seem quite feasible. Sacristán de Lama (2011: 198) suggested a reasonable 100 m$^2$ (including space for animals) for the average house, also close to the areas obtained for the cases of Numantia and La Bastida de les Alcuses, as well as an estimate of four individuals per home. If we follow those values, when estimating the population numbers of most of the Vaccean *oppida*, a total of 70% of household surface and 280 residents per hectare (four residents per household) should apply. These numbers seem quite reasonable and are in line with the estimates that have been carried out for Numantia and other Celtiberian towns and with our estimates on the largest (more than 3 ha)

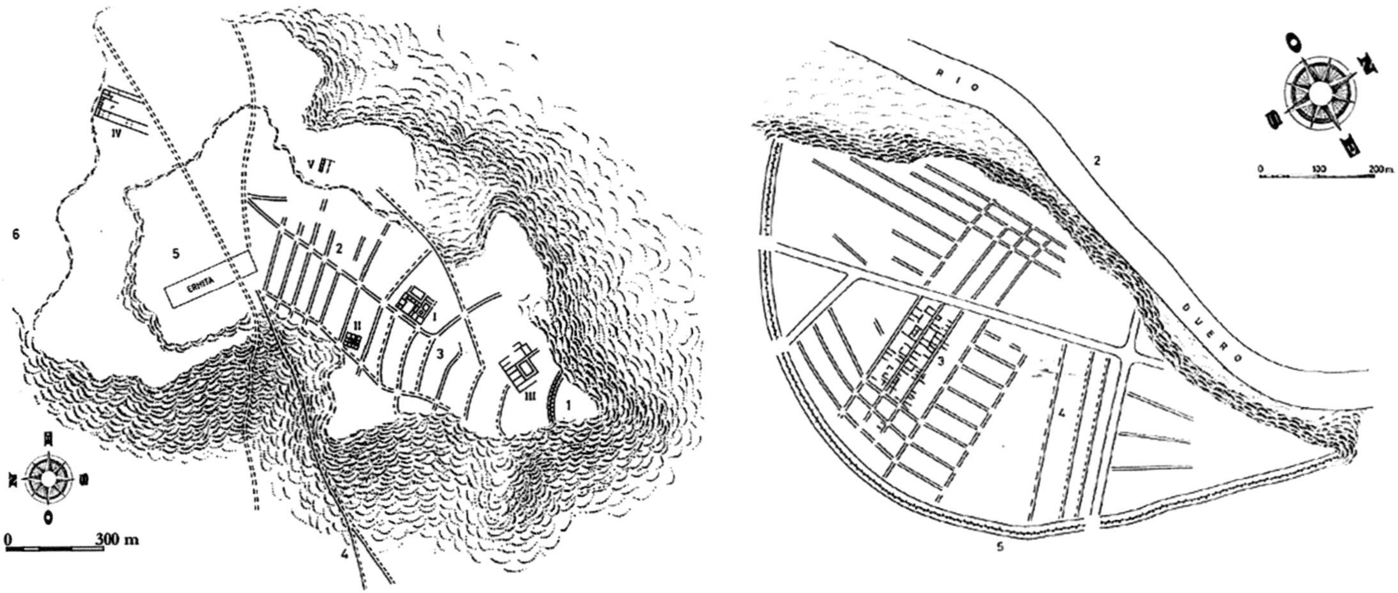


**Fig. 4.21** Plans of the Vaccean *oppida* of Tiedra (left) and Pintia (right) showing their urban layout organized from a longitudinal road that articulates multiple perpendicular streets

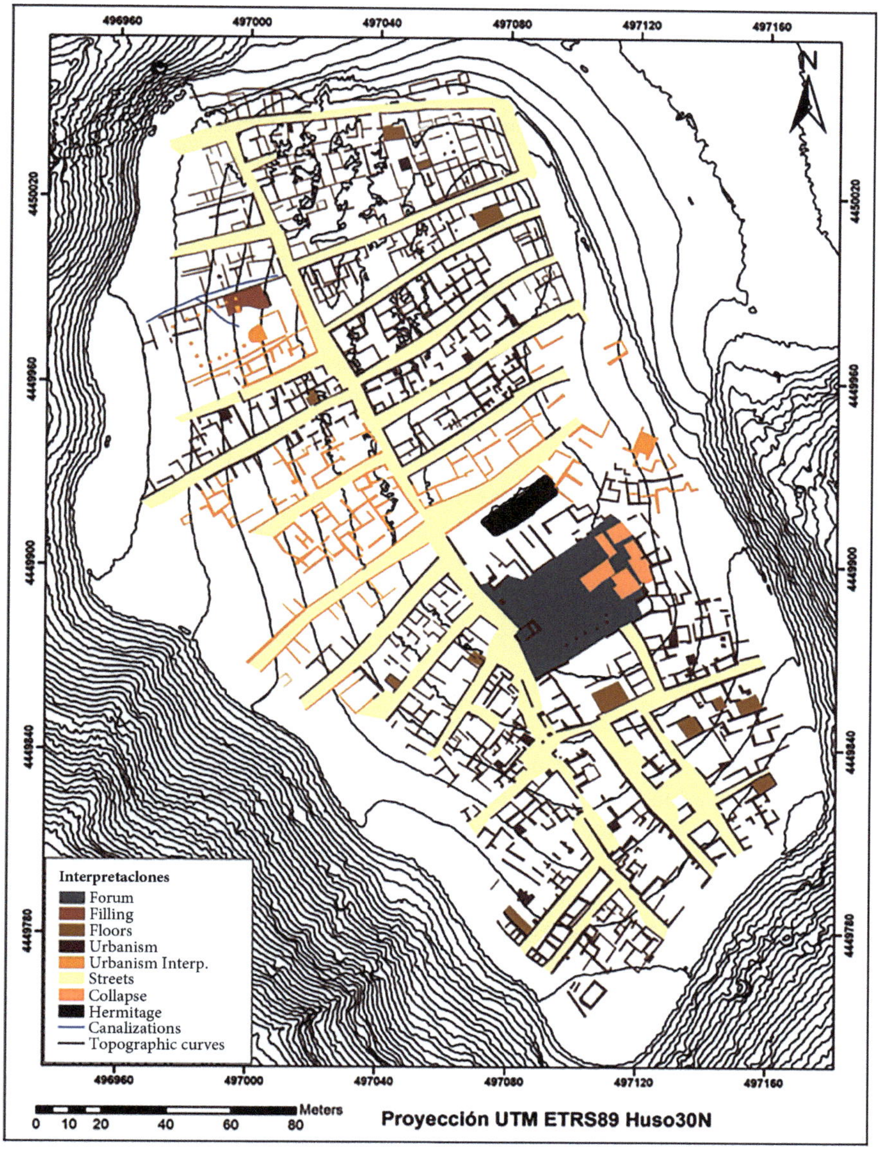


**Fig. 4.22** Plan of Caraca with the street layout in marked in yellow after the georadar campaigns (CAI of Archaeometry and Archaeological Analysis of the UCM) (Gamo and Fernández Ortea, 2019: 60, fig. 9)

Iberian *oppida* (see above). If one accepts those densities, the Vaccean *oppida* listed in Appendix I with 3+ ha. could have housed between 560 (3.2 ha) and 5,950 (34 ha) inhabitants (Ruiz Zapatero et al., 2020: 133, estimate numbers between 1,500 and 5,000) and the largest ones, La Peña, Intercatia, and Pallantia, with 49, 55, and 110 ha respectively, would have reached populations of around 8,000, 9,500, and 17,500 inhabitants (estimates using 250 inhab./ha). Of course, these numbers, especially in the latter case, must be taken as mere estimates since we know almost nothing about the urban plan of these sites.

Unfortunately, these densities are much harder to test for the very large *oppida* (over 20 ha), since their urban layout is not well known and could have differed significantly from those described above. Nonetheless, a range between 250 and 350 inhab./ha for the residential areas seems reasonable. When estimating the population of the Vaccean *oppida* merely based on the area enclosed by their walls, we have to account for the 30% non-residential area. This includes the 18.5% mentioned above for clearly defined streets. In addition to these, we need to account for other public and non-residential areas (e.g. workshops, stables, etc. See also the Castellet de Bernabé (Fig. 4.7 )). This leads to densities of 175 to 245 inhabitants per hectare.

## 4.6.1 Demographic Analysis

Previous analyses of the Vaccean form of settlement have tended to assume a low density of population in the wider territory as a whole, always below its potential capacity. This type of model of isolated large cities without tributary villages imposes a maximum limit of between 5,000 and 10,000 for the number of inhabitants that each city can support, after which it would have been necessary to establish secondary settlements to absorb the excess population (Sacristán de Lama, 2011: 217).

Some estimates have been put forward in the past to calculate the total population of the Vaccean lands approximately. Sacristán de Lama (2011: 198) has suggested that an average town with a surface of 10 ha would have housed 2,800 inhabitants. Based on those estimates and bearing in mind that most of the Vaccean *oppida* covered more than 5 ha (and half of them over 10 ha), the author reaches numbers ranging between 1,500 and 5,000 inhabitants. Consequently, following Sacristán de Lama (2011: 198), an *oppidum* like Pintia (25 ha), if one assumes that it was fully built up, would have had a total of 7,000 inhabitants.

With all the above thoughts underpinning the previous estimates of the Vaccean population, even in a scenario in which an average number of 2,500 inhabitants per *oppidum* applies, in the 32,000 km$^2$—the whole territory—the

Vacceans would barely have reached a total of 160,000 inhabitants, with a density of 5 inhab./km$^2$ (Sacristán de Lama, 2011: 198).

The RSA of the Vaccean *oppida* shows a highly hierarchical settlement system; the $q$-value is–1.318 and the $R^2$ is 0.9662, indicating a hierarchy (Fig. 4.23). This may be the result of an overrepresentation of large *oppida*, which could make sense, since all the sites in Appendix I except one are indeed over 3 ha. The set even includes the two largest *oppida* in our research area: Peña de Ulaña (285 ha) and Pallantia (110 ha). Moreover, we can observe levelling around several sizes. This levelling is something that can be detected in most graphs as the exact size frequently cannot be established, and scholars decide to give the next ten or five as the approximate size. As a result, we tend to see a levelling effect in the RSA graphs around such numbers. However, in the Vaccean graph levelling takes place around 25, 15, and 7. Turning to the analysis of the settlement system by Sacristán de Lama in order to understand the situation more thoroughly, in fact a hierarchical system in which *oppida* can be divided in different tiers can be detected (Table 4.14).

Sacristán de Lama (2011: 187) states that approximately 24 of the *oppida* for which he calculated a size are between 10 and 20 ha, although he states that some are over 20 ha. He then mentions those over 20 ha: Olmillos de Sasamón, Villavieja de Muñó, Valoria, and Padilla de Duero as covering about 25 ha, and Tardajos and Montalegre de Campos over 40 ha. This leads us to a number of 17 *oppida* between 10 and 20 ha. Unfortunately, we do not have all the exact

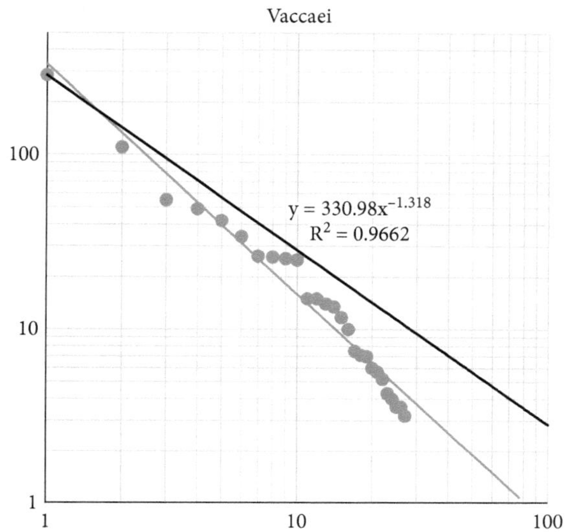


**Fig. 4.23** RSA graph for the Vaccean sites (n = 27)

**Table 4.14** Comparison of the tiers proposed by Sacristán de Lama and our data for the Vacceans

| | Size in hectares | RSA | Sacristán de Lama |
|---|---|---|---|
| Large urban *oppida* | >30 | 6 | 2 |
| Urban *oppida* | Between 15 and 30 | 4 | 4 |
| Small urban *oppida* | Between 10 and 20 | 6 | 17 |
| Large subordinate settlements | Between 5 and 10 | 6 | 13 |
| Small subordinate settlements | Under 5 | 5 | 11 |

**Table 4.15** Calculated population for the Vacceans based on different urbanization rates

| | 'Urban' | 60% | 50% | 40% |
|---|---|---|---|---|
| Low count | 92,500 | 154,167 | 185,000 | 231,250 |
| High count | 129,500 | 215,833 | 259,000 | 323,750 |

figures of Sacristán de Lama's publication and therefore cannot combine the numbers we have.

If, however, we turn to the numbers we do have, the sum of the 27 Vaccean *oppida* with an area of more than 3 ha is 529.2 ha. This number excludes the 285 of Peña de Ulaña, on which more research needs to be carried out in order to understand its urban plan. As argued above, we can assume that about 70% (Sacristán de Lama, 2011: 198) of the total area of these *oppida* is residential, with a density of 250 and 350 inhab./ha. The sum of the residential areas of the Vaccean *oppida* would therefore be about 370 ha, leading to the numbers shown in Table 4.15.

With the low count, we have 92,500 'urban' inhabitants and with the high count 129,500 'urban' inhabitants. As with the Celtiberians, the *oppida* of 3 ha and more have been included, thereby incorporating subordinate settlements. As a result, we expect the 'urbanization rate' to be rather high. For the Vacceans, it can be observed that if *oppida* over 3 ha are included and the density proposed by Sacristán de Lama of just under 160,000 inhabitants in total is respected, an urbanization rate of between 50% and 60% is to be expected. Obviously, this number still excludes the massive *oppidum* of Peña de Ulaña, which, if we include accepting its current size, would add 25,000 to 35,000 to the urban population. Measured approximately, the whole Vaccean area is just under 25,000 km$^2$; thus, maintaining the 160,000 inhabitants estimated by Sacristán de Lama, we would see a density of 6.4 inhab./km$^2$ in the Vaccean area.

## 4.7 The North-Western Groups

The north-western region has a different form of proto-urbanism often referred to as the Castro Culture to reflect the main type of settlement, the castro. A castro can be considered as a hillfort type settlement with visual control over one of the many valleys found in the north-west of the Iberian peninsula. Most of the castros in this region feature circular buildings housing families and massive defensive walls located on easily defendable locations with control over their immediate surroundings and territory (Almagro-Gorbea, 1994: 15; Coelho Ferreira da Silva, 2007: 99; Lemos et al., 2011: 189). The spatial distribution of most castros follows the pattern of a 5–10 km inter-distance, often within sight of each other, creating an intricate pattern of settlements with visual control over large areas covering several valleys.

The term 'Castro Culture' refers to a diversity of settlement types (Coelho Ferreira da Silva, 2007: 99; Lemos et al., 2011: 189). First, it should be borne in mind that the Castro Culture is found in a large and geographically diverse region. The image of hillforts controlling valleys does not include the *castros maritimas*, forts along the coast overlooking the rugged seaboard of the north-west. Second, castros have a long history, which started in the late Bronze Age and continued well into the Late Roman period (Hipólito Correia, 2001: 214). As this settlement type continued for over a millennium, these sites tend to vary considerably. Nonetheless, the terminology has been used for the whole period, leading to different phases being grouped together. Moreover, many of these castros have only been recognized by their ramparts or standing walls through using remote sensing techniques, lacking archaeological excavations to date them. Lastly, not only their geography and chronology differentiate the castros, the hierarchy of castros is also a factor to bear in mind. In general, on the one hand, castros are seen as a hierarchical settlement system that can be reconstructed by taking size variation into account (Cruz, 2015: 408). This approach fits the evidence seen so far in other regions. However, on the other hand, there is an on going debate regarding the Castro Culture as a heterarchical system (Perreira Menaut, 1982: 255; Sastre Prats, 2008: 1022).

To understand the demography of the castros and their change over time, several well-known case studies will be considered: the Citânia de Briteiros in Callaecia and Chao Samartín in Asturias. Occupation at these castros started in the Iron Age and continued well into the Roman period, allowing us to appreciate the demographic changes of these settlements and their wider regions.

### 4.7.1 Chao Samartín

The castro of Chao Samartín (Grandas de Salime, Asturias) was located in a central point between Lucus Augusti and Lucus Asturum, and lies in the eastern part of the region of the Castro Culture in the Asturian Massif. This castro, first occupied in the eighth century BCE, is considered a type-site for understanding the castros of the Asturian region (Villa Valdés, 2007a: 28). One of the main elements for its fame is irrelevant for our inquiry into pre-Roman demography, namely the Roman *domus*. Going back to the earliest evidence for activity on the site, the acropolis (2,400 m$^2$) was the first part to be occupied, in the eighth and seventh centuries BCE. After what seems to have been a fire, the acropolis was abandoned as a domestic area and acquired a religious or sacred function (Montes Lopéz et al., 2012: 204). After this event, the castro was extended to the lower plateau (see Fig. 4.24).

The earliest occupation layer at Chao Samartín has been dated to the late ninth or early eighth century BCE, in other words the Late Bronze Age (González Ruibal, 2006: 87; Villa Valdés, 2007a: 28). This occupation was concentrated in the acropolis, or *croa*, of the settlement. In this area the remains of a rectangular house

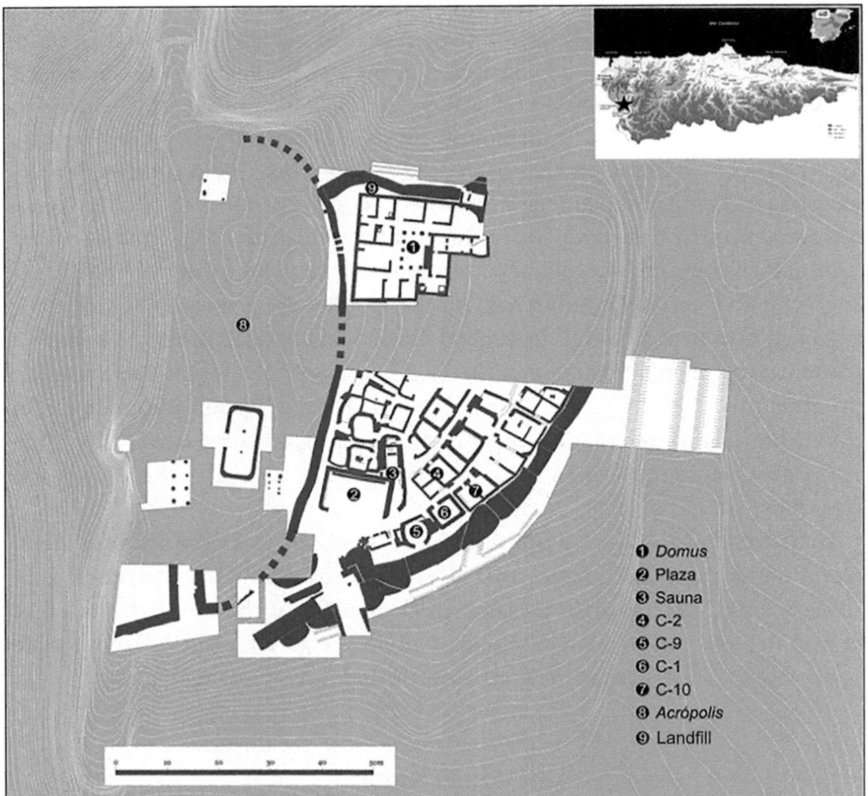


**Fig. 4.24** Internal divisions, public areas, and houses at Chao Samartín (Montes Lopéz et al., 2012: 214)

have been found, the finds from which consisted of ceramics and metal objects unrelated to the domestic sphere. In view of these non-domestic finds, the function of the building is thought to have been ceremonial. This is comparable with finds from other castros, where the acropolis acquired a ceremonial function after the extension of the castro.

The extension of the fortification and its inhabited areas can be dated to the Iron Age (Villa Valdés, 2007b: 202; 2009: 9). The newly enclosed area includes several buildings of a public nature. In the southern area, a large enclosure, building or square, was found, which is significantly larger than other buildings within the settlement. Alongside this large enclosure is a clearly public building: the sauna of the settlement (Villa Valdés, 2000: 110). Interestingly these two structures are located at the main entrance to the site. The castro of Chao Samartín must be regarded as an important settlement in the region as it has a relatively large public area, combining a sauna with what could be a house or square for assembly purposes.

Nearby, only 4.5 km from Chao Samartín, we find the smaller (0.3 ha) mining castro of Monte Castrelo de Pelou (Grandas de Salime), which reached its peak in the fourth and third centuries BCE (Montes Lopéz et al., 2009: 313). The latest test pits have indicated that this small castro had a similar layout to the castro of Chao Samartín in the Iron Age and contained the traditional circular or oblong houses and a sauna (Montes Lopéz et al., 2010: 19).

Turning to the well-researched northern sector of the Castro de Coaña in Asturias, it can be confirmed that the site was densely inhabited. This northern part of the site was excavated in the late nineteenth century and has long been one of the most iconic Asturian castros, especially due to the reconstruction drawing provided by García y Bellido in 1942. The layout of the castro follows a familiar pattern: there is an acropolis, which is considered to be the area of the earliest occupation. Unfortunately, the acropolis is less well known. It is considered to be the sacred area of the castro as it contains two saunas and the rectangular structure numbered 81, known as the Casa Grande (Menéndez Granda and Villa Valdés, 2013: 197). Our interest focuses on the 'extramural' or northern district of the castro dated to the fourth or third century BCE, consisting of eighty circular or oblong buildings similar to those at Chao Samartín (see Fig. 4.25) (Villa Valdés, 2013: 151). However, not each building can be considered as a separate house. In these castros, the small circular buildings often open up onto 'inner' courtyards, leading to the interpretation of shared space, or a house composed of multiple buildings. Villa Valdés has turned to the evidence of quern stones to establish the number of households at about fifteen (Villa Valdés, 2013: 151). This leads to a population of about 60 to 75 inhabitants for the area. Villa Valdés states that this figure might lie at the low end of the possible range, but that it would not be much higher than a hundred people. Since the northern district is roughly half a hectare, this would lead to a density of about 200 inhab./ha in the lower area.

**Fig. 4.25** The distribution of quern stones and the interpretation of buildings forming households in the Castro de Coaña (Villa Valdés, 2013: 159)

### 4.7.2 Citânia de Briteiros

With its 24 ha, the castro of Citânia de Briteiros is among the largest castros although so far only 7 ha have been excavated (Almagro-Gorbea, 1994: 65; Lemos et al., 2011: 194). Despite its extraordinary size, it is seen as a type-site for Callaecian castros. The defence consists of multiple rings of ramparts, the largest enclosing 24 ha. The largest extension of the ramparts has been dated to the second century BCE. The archaeological remains found inside the castro testify to occupation of the site until the first century CE (Alarcão, 1988: 1/243; Coelho Ferreira da Silva, 1995a: 517).

The three rings of ramparts divide the castro into three sections (see Fig. 4.26). The acropolis, the oldest inhabited area, is an oval-shaped area of 3.75 ha (150 m × 250 m). The archaeological excavations have focused on this area, which is divided into four sectors by the two perpendicular main streets (Alarcão, 1988: 1/243; Almagro-Gorbea, 1994: 65). From these main roads some minor streets branch out and further divide the quarters into smaller sections.

The main type of building in the castro is the circular houses typical of the region. In addition, a number of public buildings can be observed. As in the case of Chao Samartín, we find a large sanctuary on the acropolis. This sanctuary is

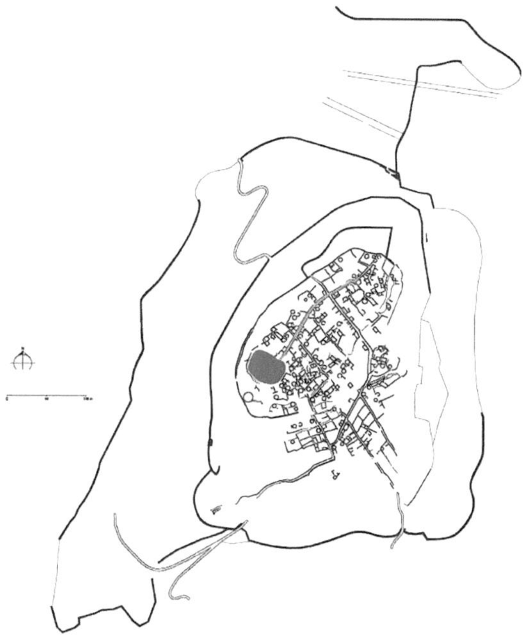

**Fig. 4.26** Citânia de Briteiros with the 'sanctuary' in grey (Cruz, 2015: fig. 7, p. 425)

located at the highest point of the castro, its identification as a religious area being based on the presence of votive statues and ceramics related to banqueting (Cruz, 2015: 410). Unfortunately, the continuous use and reorganization of the area, up to the construction of a chapel, has destroyed most of the archaeological remains related to the pre-Roman period. In addition to this sanctuary, two saunas typical of the area have been recorded (Str. III 3.6; Coelho Ferreira da Silva, 1995b: 283). Lastly, there is a larger circular building of 11 m in diameter with benches along the walls. This building has been identified as a probable meeting place for local leaders or even a council (Coelho Ferreira da Silva, 1995b: 283; Cruz, 2015: 410).

The excavated area of 7 ha contains 104 family compounds (Lemos, 2007: 88). If the proposed figure of four people per household is maintained, there would have been some 416 inhabitants in this area, the density of which was thus about 60 inhabitants per hectare. If we were to consider the number of six inhabitants per house, as proposed by Lemos, we would obtain a figure quite similar to the number proposed for Chao Samartín (above). However, as we see no reason to deviate from the family unit of four people, a maximum of 1,200 inhabitants, when using the 20 ha of possibly inhabitable area in the castro, is obtained. The real number would have been slightly lower, as we have to account for possible public areas in the unexcavated parts of the castro. The number of 1,500 inhabitants given by Lemos (2007: 88) seems high but feasible to us.

As for the development of a territory, in the direct vicinity of Citânia de Briteiros there are two other castros: Castro de Santa Iria and Castro de Sabroso. These castros are located along the River Ave within 3 km of Citânia de Briteiros. A GIS analysis of the visual control of these three settlements shows that Citânia de Briteiros is clearly the dominant settlement (Fonte et al., 2011: 362). This leads to the hypothesis that these other two castros formed an integral part of the territory of Citânia de Briteiros, but were abandoned in favour of the latter settlement in the Roman period.

For the Castro Culture we must come to the conclusion that the density is rather low and should be estimated as having been between 75 and 100 inhabitants per hectare. The number is significantly lower than that of other regions and much more similar to that suggested for the case of the Vettones. Other studies, however, have come to the same conclusion (Fernández Acebo et al., 2010b: 620). Therefore, in this chapter we will use 75 inhabitants as the lower end of the range in combination with 100 as the higher end of the range when estimating the population of the castros.

### 4.7.3 Demographic Analysis

The north-western part of the Iberian peninsula saw a dense settlement pattern of small castros controlling the valleys and rias. The castros pose a considerable problem. Thanks to satellite imagery, a multitude of such sites can be recognized.

Although for many of them their precise date remains uncertain, as the Castro Culture started in the late Bronze Age and continued well into the Roman period, the castros need research on the ground to establish their chronology and whether they were continuously occupied. Nonetheless, only those castros that were occupied in the third and fourth centuries BCE and for which we have an indication of their probable size in this period are included.

The RSA of the north-west can be taken as a combination of all three regions and peoples or differentiated by grouping (Fig. 4.27). We should ideally turn to the different peoples so as to understand their different forms of urban organization. However, as can be seen, the total number of identified sites is at times very low, especially for the Asturians, for whom we only have eleven sites. From this number it is impossible to draw firm conclusions. Nonetheless, it can be observed that the largest city of the Astures was Lancia, twice the size of the next settlement. Cassius Dio mentioned that Lancia was the capital of the Asturians (53.25.8), which supports the idea of a more hierarchical community.

Following this line of thought, Monte Bernorio would be expected to have played a similar role for the Cantabrians, as it is three times larger than the next Cantabrian settlement. Furthermore, the overall shape of the RSA for the Cantabrians could be described as primo-concave, which would indicate a rather

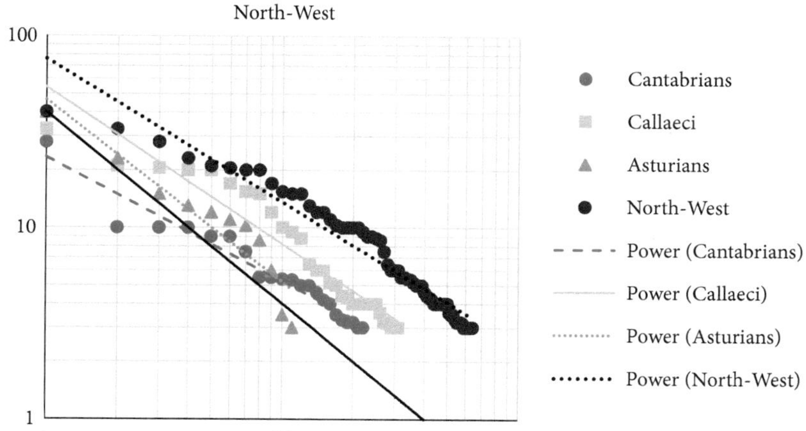


| Asturians | Callaeci | Cantabrians | Combined |
|---|---|---|---|
| $y = 46.522x^{-0.95}$ | $y = 23.38x^{-0.647}$ | $y = 54.19x^{-0.818}$ | $y = 75.86x^{-0.749}$ |
| $R^2 = 0.8767$ | $R^2 = 0.9438$ | $R^2 = 0.9186$ | $R^2 = 0.9445$ |
| n = 11 | n = 31 | n = 22 | n = 64 |

**Fig. 4.27** RSA graph of the combined north-west and the major peoples separated

heterogeneous settlement system with one large outlier, which could be the capital. In the case of Monte Bernorio, this settlement is unlikely to have been a capital per se, but more of a key site to control access to the lands of the Cantabri.

The combined analysis has the advantage of illustrating the Castro Culture as a whole and providing an analysis with slightly higher numbers. The combined graphs show more clearly the effect of levelling around numbers, especially around 20, 10, and interestingly 4. These sizes were most likely slightly smaller, filling the gaps following the levelling. Turning to the specific details of the combined graph a number of observations can be made. The *q*-value of −0.749 indicates we are not dealing with a strongly hierarchical structure, and the $R^2$ value indicates a good fit. This observation can be confirmed by noticing how the line as a whole deviates from the Zipf line. However, it must be admitted that the $R^2$ of the combined set provides a better fit for the lower order settlements. The higher order settlements deviate considerably from the best fit. This supports the idea of the less hierarchical settlement system of the Castro Culture (Pereira Menaut, 1982: 255). Admittedly, the impact of pooling multiple systems must be acknowledged here. This leads to a levelling of the higher order settlements and the illusion of a more hierarchical system. It is clear from the separate graphs that the Cantabrian and Asturian systems seem to be hierarchical, as each of them has a clear primary centre.

As stated above, the population densities of these castros are rather low. As has been pointed out, households often appear to consist of several circular buildings

**Table 4.16** Population numbers for the north-west based on urbanization rates

| | Urban | 30% | 20% | 10% |
|---|---|---|---|---|
| Low count | 43,098 | 143,660 | 215,490 | 430,980 |
| High count | 57,464 | 191,547 | 287,320 | 574,640 |

that open up onto a central courtyard or, alternatively, might include a number of private open spaces lying between the circular houses proper. Moreover, most castros have public areas with a religious significance, mostly located in the *croa* or acropolis, the highest and oldest part of the castro. A density of 75 to 100 inhabitants per hectare for the whole walled castro has therefore been decided on. The sum of the size of the 64 castros covering more than 3 ha is 574.64 ha (Table 4.16).

As the north-western area is a relatively densely occupied region with a multitude of very small castros, we should contemplate a low urbanization rate. Moreover, with the census numbers of the early imperial period given by Pliny for the three north-western *conventus* in mind, we can estimate approximately the range that might be taken into consideration. Pliny states figures of 240,000 for Asturum (32,000 km$^2$), 166,000 for Lucensis (24,500 km$^2$), and 285,000 for Bracarum (21,000 km$^2$), which excludes the Cantabrian region (12,500 km$^2$), which belonged to another *conventus*. Consequently, some 691,000 inhabitants are known to have been present in a region of about 77,500 km$^2$ in Roman times, from which a density of almost nine inhabitants per square kilometre in Roman times can be obtained. With a low urbanization rate of 10%, densities of between five and six inhabitants per square kilometre might be proposed for the region during the pre-Roman period/three or four centuries beforehand.

## 4.8 Population Estimates for the Late Iron Age

Of the total of 651 pre-Roman settlements included in our sample (see Appendix I), 370 sites have a surface area of less than 3 ha, which would mean that, broadly speaking, half of the sample could not be included within the category of urban centres if the above mentioned criteria are applied. Admittedly, it must be acknowledged that our selection of the urban settlements is only a representation of the current *status quaestionis* and will change as more studies of the settlement patterns during the late Iron Age in the region take place. Nonetheless, the patterns observed from this study present a reality for the period and regions.

It has been noted that the central regions had the largest *oppida*, whereas the littoral regions, both the Atlantic and Mediterranean, reveal a more dispersed

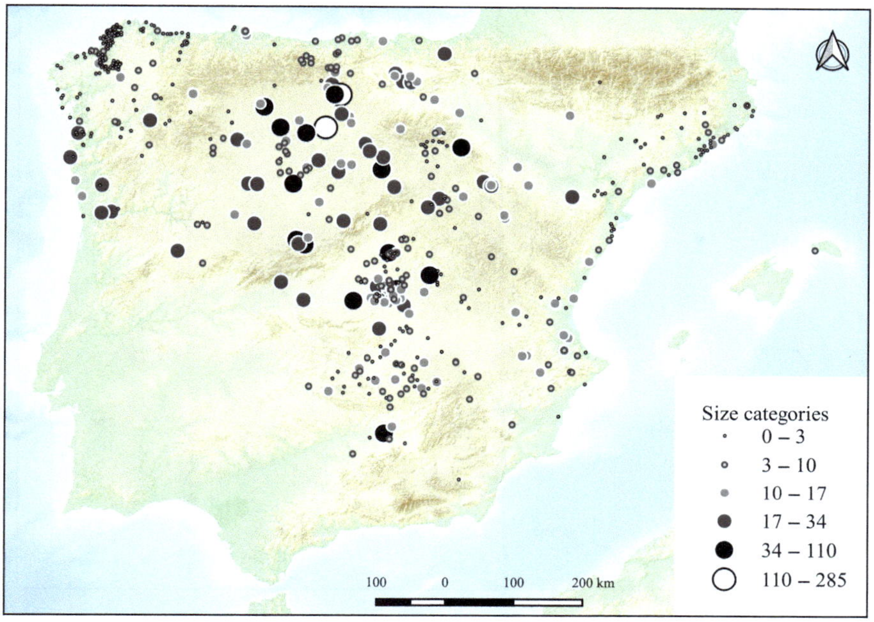


**Fig. 4.28** Distribution map of the *oppida* in the territory under study during Late Iron Age

settlement pattern with smaller settlements (see Fig. 4.26). Due to the dispersed nature and small size of the settlements in the littoral areas, it can be noted that they had a lower urbanization rate, but not necessarily a lower density of population. With the population numbers that it has proved possible to calculate, we attain a total urban population of 565,000 when the low count is applied. The total low count population would be 2,000,000 for the area under study—equivalent to the later Hispania Citerior—with an overall urbanization rate of 28%. This is a relatively high urbanization rate but, as already stated, for some of the areas (Celtiberians, Carpetani, and Vacceans) the final figure presented suggests a rather high rate, as settlements that should be considered to have been rural, because of the large size of the *oppida*, are very likely to have been included. On the other hand, the cut- off of the Iberian hillforts at 3 ha seems to exclude smaller urban realities as rural showing that there is not a perfect cut- off point that works for all the regions under study.

As can be seen from the distribution map (Fig. 4.28), our research is far from conclusive. For several regions (the central Ebro valley, the Pyrenees, and the lower Duero valley) more research needs to be undertaken to establish the nature of the settlement system in these regions. Combining this distribution map with the heat map weighted by size showing the 651 pre-Roman settlements (see Appendix I), the areas of high and low concentration can readily be observed

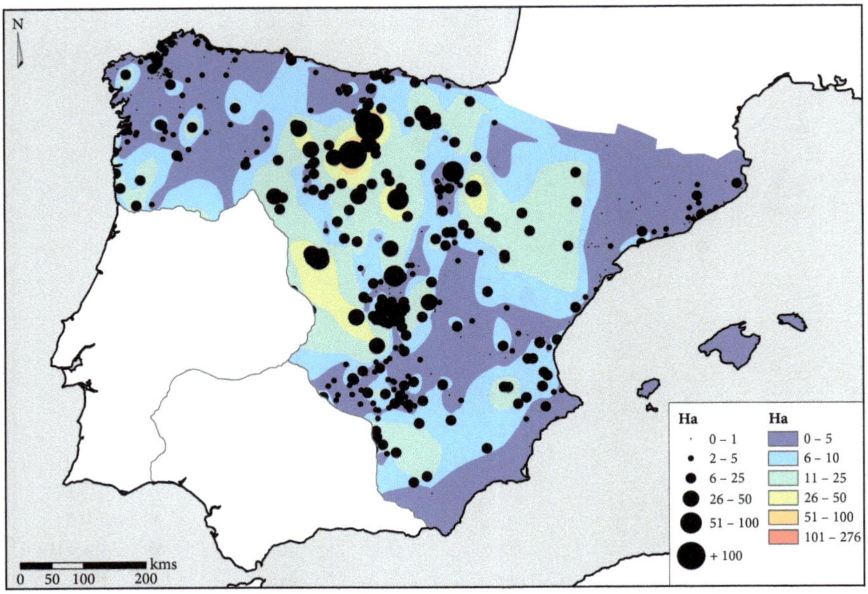


**Fig. 4.29** Heatmap of Iron Age population in the territories that later became Hispania Citerior according to *oppida* sizes

(Fig. 4.29). Obviously, the data presented here correspond to the *oppida* that formed part of the territories of what subsequently came to constitute the province of Hispania Citerior. This obliges us to impose a later administrative organization onto the previous pre-Roman urban system.

In the first place, our attention is swiftly drawn to the existence of a pattern of high densities in the inland areas of the peninsula, while the densities in the littoral areas are extremely low even when in some areas, such as the east and the north-east, a large number of *oppida* are known. There is a clear concentration of urban population in the middle and upper valley of the River Ebro and on the northern plateau, a phenomenon already recorded in the past, which reflects the well-established settlement patterns of important pre-Roman population groups, such as the Celtiberians, Vacceans, and the Carpetani (Álvarez Sanchís and Ruiz Zapatero, 2001; Romero Carnicero and Sanz Mínguez, 2010; De Soto and Carreras, 2002). Of the 36 *oppida* over 20 ha in our sample, eleven in Vaccean territory, seven among the Carpetani, six are assigned to the Celtiberians. Interestingly, eight of the remaining large *oppida* belong to the north-western groups. Only one oppidum over 20 ha can be assigned to the Iberians, namely Castulo, the supposed capital of the Oretani in the south.

The distribution of the 36 largest urban centres explains the high densities visible in Fig. 4.29 perfectly, regardless of the number of inhabitants per hectare that is used when carrying out population calculations. Perhaps it should not surprise us that these three groups were the ones that were to offer the greatest resistance to the Roman conquest. The Celtiberians in particular are famed for their resistance against Rome in the three Celtiberian Wars. Based on the data presented here, it can be hypothesized that these three groups alone accounted for approximately two-thirds of the pre-Roman urban population by the third century BCE (430,980 inhabitants with the low count), when the Roman forces arrived in the peninsula, so that, apart from their martial skills, it is logical that these inland areas represented one of the main focuses of resistance during the conquest. They had both the numbers and the large centres to resist the Roman conquest.

The north-western area contained a large number of small castros. These are so numerous that most have not yet been studied in depth. As a result, we cannot include many of them as they are not yet measured or dated. Nonetheless, the general pattern reveals that the castros were relatively small and large *oppida* were few in number. It must be considered that these few *oppida* played central roles in the settlement systems of the north-west. Nevertheless, the general pattern of many castros of limited size controlling small valleys in this mountainous region seems to indicate that the castros were organized in a relatively heterarchical manner.

Finally, in the southern and the eastern Mediterranean areas, an interesting phenomenon can be detected, one that certainly seems to suggest a restricted exploitation of marine resources by the pre-Roman peoples who occupied these coastal regions, as do the faunal studies, in which the exploitation of marine resources is minimal compared with what is recorded in Roman times. This pattern perhaps helps to explain the relative ease with which the Phoenicians and Greeks were able to establish their emporia. Large *oppida* are scarce; there are only ten urban centres with areas of between 10 and 15 ha, corresponding to the capitals of the abovementioned archaic Iberian proto-states, such as Burriac, Kese, Arse, and Saitabi. In general, in the east and north-east of the peninsula, the urban phenomenon follows a model in which small settlements predominate and do not make a significant demographic contribution to the peninsula as a whole. To the contrary of what happened for the Celtiberian case, the low population numbers and densities along the north-east coast of the peninsula may help to explain, among other things, the fast process of conquest that the area suffered during the Second Punic War and later in 197 BCE when Cato intervenes with his consular army (App. *Iber.* 41).

In sum, our demographic analysis in this chapter seems to overlap quite well with the overall review of urbanism in the Iberian peninsula during the Late Iron Age conducted by Ruiz Zapatero et al. (2020). We also observe three different demographic and urbanization trends in the different regions: the Iberian territories in the Mediterranean coast; the so-called 'Celtic' territories in the central peninsula, and, finally, the north-western territories and the Cantabrian region (Fig. 4.30).

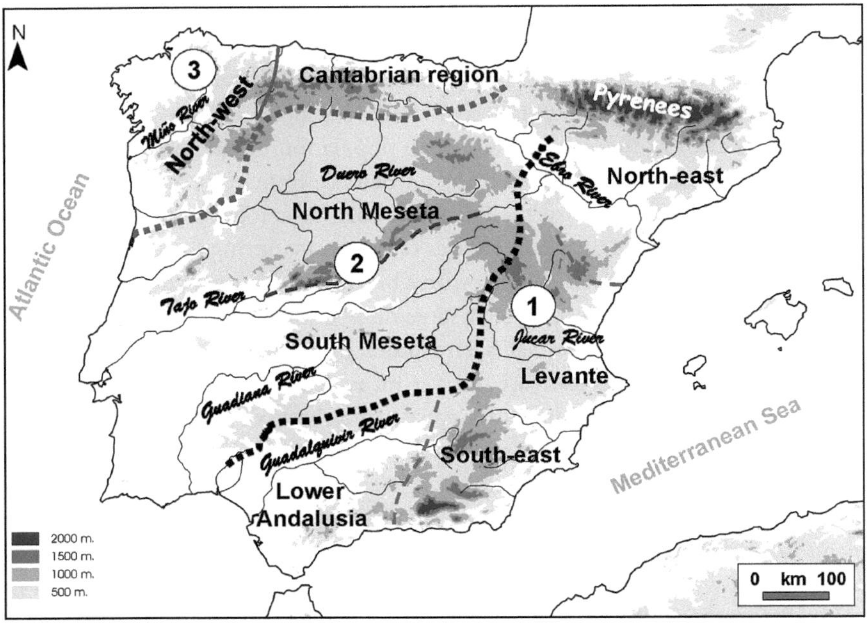


**Fig. 4.30** Map of the Iberian Peninsula with main regions, rivers, and the three cultural areas described by Ruiz Zapatero et al. (2020: fig. 8.1): (1) Mediterranean. (2) inland (Meseta). (3) north-west/north

## 4.9 Conclusions

In this chapter we have aimed to improve the existent methodological apparatus to conduct more credible demographic calculations, establish urbanization rates, and to interpret and compare different urban systems in order to obtain the hierarchy and spread of settlement sizes for the different ethnic and political realities that populated the Iberian peninsula during the fourth and third centuries BCE. While doing so, interesting results have been obtained, and will hopefully set the basis for future research in the field.

As a whole, the urban network of the Late Iron Age, including its population concentrations, and beyond the reliability of the calculations that estimate population figures, seems to be satisfactorily explained on the basis of its mineral wealth (Polyb. 10.2.20; 34.9.8; App. *Iber.* 19, 23; Liv. 23.45.9, 24.41.7) and of the accessibility and vitality that the main navigable rivers conferred to the territories through which they flowed (Str. 3.1.9), the preferred axes being the Guadalquivir, the Ebro valley, and the 'Ruta de la Plata' (Figs. 4.28 and 4.29).

Also in general terms, and while some important variables needed to conduct reliable demographic estimates seem to apply well to some of the pre-Roman groups discussed in this chapter, our analysis proves that is necessary to customize our methods and values on a case-by-case basis if we want to successfully achieve reliable (or at least credible) populations numbers for the Late Iron Age in the peninsula. We have demonstrated that extrapolating a specific density/hectare number to all the *oppida* in the area under study is not an option, nor is applying the same density/hectare to all the *oppida* belonging to a specific group. The very diverse sizes, intramural built up densities, urban configurations, and ways of living, require approaches that can respond to all these realities.

With the above in mind, and after studying each case separately—when possible—our research shows that some of the main variables needed to work on population estimates (see Chapter 3) seem to find close values for several of the Iron Age groups discussed in this chapter. In first place, when assessing the function of the built spaces in *oppida*, especially the largest ones (over 3 ha), it seems that ratios of 30–40% of communal/not residential space vs. 60–70% of household space seem to be the norm among the Iberian, Celtiberian, Carpetani, and Vacceans settlements. However, even in this case, extrapolating can be dangerous since a very different reality arises when looking at the Vettones and the north-west territories.

Similarly, household architecture may be very diverse typologically and have broad size ranges inside the same *oppidum* as well as from site to site, and group to group. When the average size house can be calculated from a large enough sample, the numbers do not seem to be that far apart. We see numbers between 75–125 $m^2$ for the large Iberian *oppida* (+3 ha), 80 $m^2$ in Numantia (Celtiberia), 80–85 $m^2$ for the Carpetanian cases, a range between 70 and 100 $m^2$ in the Vettones *oppida*, and 100 $m^2$ for the Vaccean example. Therefore it seems plausible to argue that a household average between 70 and 100 $m^2$ seems to be the norm in most of the large Iron Age *oppida* discussed in this chapter. Perhaps this reflects that the necessity of a minimum living space per person may have not been so different from group to group (see discussion in Chapter 3). If we agree on a ratio of four or five inhabitants per household, 15–20 $m^2$ of basic living space would very well justify these preferred household sizes. Nevertheless, we cannot forget that even in this case, customized calculations must always be conducted. Not only because it is not the same to have an average size house of 70 $m^2$ compared to one of 100 $m^2$, but also because we see how the average size in some of the smaller Iberian *oppida* is much smaller and seems to be between 30 and 50 $m^2$. Similarly, the size for the north-west cases would also differ and it adds the complexity that not every building can be considered as a separate household, since there are examples of several circular buildings that are articulated around courtyards, something similar to what we see in some of the large Iberian houses where an inner courtyard articulates the space, and that can be interpreted as a shared space, or a house composed of multiple buildings adding an additional layer of uncertainty into how to estimate the actual size.

Similar issues are found when using the sizes in hectares of the settlements. First of all we observe quite considerable differences in the average size and distribution of the different groups under scrutiny.

Even within groups we can divide the settlement systems as we saw with the Iberians. The geographical spread of the *oppida* already indicated that we had to differentiate between the Northern Iberians with relatively small but numerous *oppida* and the Oretani in the south, with larger *oppida*. In addition to the difference in size, the rank- size analysis indicates that the hierarchy of both settlement systems are different. The Oretani have a hierarchical system with Castulo (at 44 ha) as the primary centre. Using the estimations by Sanmartí (2001) for the total population of the region we would find an urbanization rate of roughly 25%. In contrast, the Northern Iberians are in a more heterarchical system. One explanation for this heterarchical system might be found in the multitude of groups mentioned by the classical sources for this region. Since the classical sources mention several groups acting independently from each other we might have to consider these as separate groups. Nonetheless, their settlement systems are very similar with relatively small settlements, the largest just reaching 10 ha. As a result the 3 ha cut-off point for 'urban' sites might have been too large for this group. The resulting urbanization rate of 10% could be representing the exclusion of 'urban' sites. Were we to include sites with a smaller size as urban we would reach a higher urbanization rate.

Relatively similar to southern Iberians we can see the inland groups: the Celtiberians, Carpetanians, Vettones, and Vacceans. All these groups have relatively large settlements and are organized in a hierarchical manner. We see that the Carpetanian and Celtiberian groups have a rather similar settlement system and hierarchy. The western inland groups both stand out for different reasons. The Vaccean *oppida* stand out to all the others with their extremely large sites of Peña de Ulaña (285 ha) and Pallantia (110 ha). These large primary centres automatically lead to a strongly hierarchical system. It must be noted that for these sites it is likely that not the whole area would have been occupied. However, even if they had been half their size we would find it to be a hierarchical system. Admittedly, the Vettones with only 14 *oppida* with sizes over 3 ha need more research. A RSA with such a small number changes easily with a few more data points. In addition, we find the strange case of Mesas de Miranda in this set: an *oppidum* with an enclosed area without any sign of occupation. More research, geophysical survey and excavation are needed to establish the exact built-up size of the *oppida*. Interestingly we find relatively high urbanization rates for most of these communities. It is likely that the communities were organized following the city-state model, where most of the population lives in what have been defined as 'agro-towns'.

In conclusion we observe that the coastal areas hold settlement systems with many smaller settlements. As a result, both the northern Iberian and the north-west settlement systems have a low urbanization rate and heterarchical settlement system. Admittedly, we do observe that the groups that were conquered the last, the Cantabrians and Asturians, did have some larger primary centres. It is very likely that this development is the result of the Roman policy to concentrate peoples in order to more easily conquer their territories. Attacking sites like Monte Bernorio and Lancia, where peoples concentrate to make a last stand, is easier than conquering each hilltop one by one. As we will see in the next chapter, the Roman state did prefer an urban system for control, explaining well why the different territories discussed in this chapter evolved differently—demographically and urbanistically speaking—under Roman rule.

*The Human Factor: The Demography of the Roman Province of Hispania Citerior/Tarraconensis.* Alejandro G. Sinner, Cèsar Carreras, and Pieter Houten, Oxford University Press. 
DOI: 10.1093/9780191943881.003.0004

# 5

# Population, Urbanization, and Settlement Patterns in the Early Empire

Most population estimates for the Iberian peninsula in Roman times are part of general demographic calculations for the Roman Empire as a whole during the Early Empire. The first proposal was put forward by Beloch (1909), who established a minimum population of 6 million and a maximum of 9 million inhabitants. Other calculations provided lower values for Roman Spain, such as the 4 million inhabitants (Russell, 1958) based on the words of Pliny the Elder (*NH* III.18) (Taracena, 1949: 428) and comparisons with later historical periods that preserve reliable censuses.

The currently accepted estimates come from Frier (2000), whose values are adapted from the calculations by Beloch (1909), and a more recent publication by McEvedy and Jones (1978), who charted the evolution of population from antiquity to modern times by country (see Fig. 5.1).

According to McEvedy and Jones (1978), the population of Roman Spain in 1 CE was 4.5 million and that of Portugal was 0.5 million. They recorded estimates for every 200 years with oscillations which were not explained. If we look at Frier's estimates (2000: 812, table 5; 814, table 6) for the Iberian peninsula, he provides data for 14 CE and 164 CE as shown in Table 5.1.

The 14 CE value comes from the addition of the population of Portugal and Spain from McEvedy and Jones (1978), while the 164 CE estimate is reached by a schematic assumption of a mean annual growth rate of 0.15% from 14 CE onwards. In other words, all the values are theoretical estimates combined with an expected regular growth that is neither recorded in any ancient documents nor demonstrated by archaeological evidence. Our only textual reference is Pliny the Elder (*NH* III.3.7–17; IV.4.18–30; IV.35.113–18), who listed the number of 399 *civitates* and 114 *populi* in a manuscript written in the mid-70s CE (see Fig. 5.2 and Table 5.2) although the *populi* were most likely non-urban (Houten, 2021: 96–7 and 109).

Pliny the Elder (*NH* III.3.7–17) refers to the province of Baetica in the following terms:

> Baetica, so called from the river which divides it in the middle, excels all the other provinces in the richness of its cultivation and the peculiar fertility and

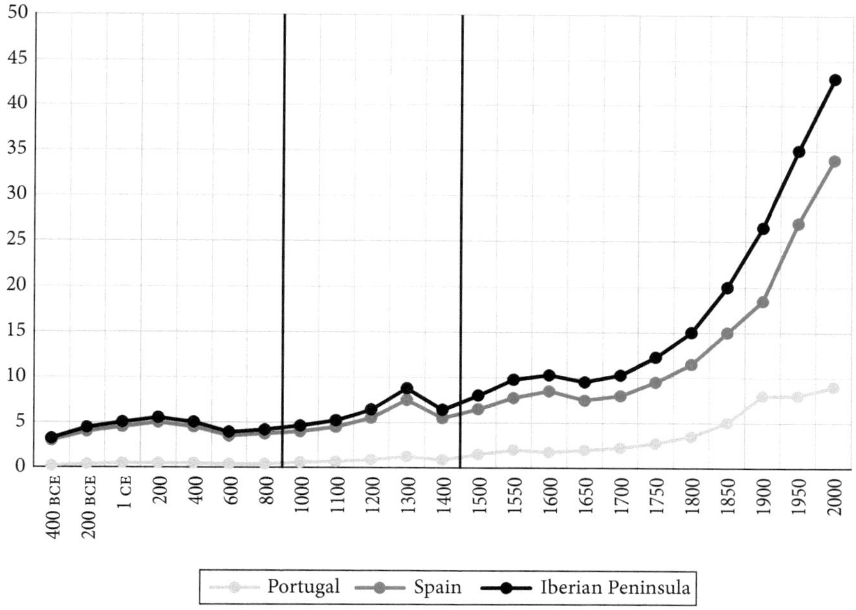


**Fig. 5.1** Graph with the population of Spain and Portugal (after McEvedy and Jones, 1978: 103–5)

> beauty of its vegetation. It consists of four jurisdictions, those of Gades, of Corduba, of Astigi, and of Hispalis. The total number of its towns is 175; of these nine are colonies, and eight municipal towns; twenty-nine have been long since presented with the old Latin rights; six are free towns, three federate, and 120 tributaries.

However, Lusitania was the last and smallest province to be created in the Iberian peninsula, after crossing the River Durius (present-day Douro), which Pliny the Elder (*NH* IV.35.113–18) outlines as follows:

> The whole of this province is divided into three jurisdictions, those of Emerita, Pax, and Scallabis. It contains in all forty-five peoples, among whom there are five colonies, one municipal town of Roman citizens, three with the ancient Latin rights, and thirty-six that are tributaries.

Finally, Pliny the Elder (*NH* IV.4.18–30) describes the urban network of Hispania Tarraconensis as follows:

> The whole province is now divided into seven jurisdictions, those of Carthage, of Tarraco, of Cæsar Augusta, of Clunia, of Asturica, of Lucus, and of the Bracari.

**Table 5.1** Estimates of populations during the Empire

| Region | Area (1,000 km$^2$) | 14 CE Population (millions) | 14 CE Density (per km$^2$) | 164 CE Population (millions) | 164 CE Density (per km$^2$) | Population increase (%) |
|---|---|---|---|---|---|---|
| Greece | 267 | 2.8 | 10.5 | 3.0 | 11.2 | 7.1 |
| Anatolia | 547 | 8.2 | 15.0 | 9.2 | 16.8 | 12.2 |
| Greater Syria | 109 | 4.3 | 39.4 | 4.8 | 44.0 | 11.6 |
| Cyprus | 9.5 | 0.2 | 21.2 | 0.2 | 21.1 | – |
| Egypt | 28 | 4.5 | 160.7 | 5.0 | 178.6 | 11.1 |
| Libya | 15 | 0.4 | 26.7 | 0.6 | 40.0 | 50.0 |
| *Greek East* | 975.5 | 20.4 | 20.9 | 22.9 | 23.5 | 12.3 |
| *Annexations* | | | | 0.2 | | |
| *Greek East (with annexations)* | | | | 23.1 | | |
| Italy | 250 | 7.0 | 28.0 | 7.6 | 30.4 | 8.6 |
| Sicily | 26 | 0.6 | 23.1 | 0.6 | 23.1 | – |
| Sardinia and Corsica | 33 | 0.5 | 15.2 | 0.5 | 15.2 | – |
| Maghreb | 400 | 3.5 | 8.8 | 6.5 | 16.3 | 85.7 |
| Iberia | 590 | 5.0 | 8.5 | 7.5 | 12.7 | 50.0 |
| Gaul and Germany | 635 | 5.8 | 9.1 | 9.0 | 14.2 | 55.2 |
| Danube Region | 430 | 2.7 | 6.3 | 4.0 | 9.3 | 48.1 |
| *Latin West* | 2,364 | 25.1 | 10.6 | 35.7 | 15.1 | 42.2 |
| *Annexations* | | | | 2.5 | | |
| *Latin West (with annexations)* | | | | 38.2 | | |
| *Roman Empire* | 3,339.5 | 45.5 | 13.6 | 61.4 | 15.9 | 34.9 |

*Source*: After Frier (2000: 812, table 5 and 814, table 6).

**Table 5.2** Roman city categories according to Pliny the Elder (*NH* III.3.7–17; IV.4.18–30; IV.35.113–18)

| | Lusitania | Baetica | Tarraconensis | Total |
|---|---|---|---|---|
| Roman colonies | 5 | 9 | 12 | 26 |
| Roman *municipia* | 1 | 8 | 13 | 24 |
| Latin *municipia* | 3 | 27 | 18 | 48 |
| *Civitas foederata* | 0 | 3 | 1 | 4 |
| *Civitas amicitia* | 0 | 6 | 0 | 6 |
| *Civitas stipendiaria* | 36 | 120 | 135 | 291 |
| **Total** | **45** | **175** | **179** | **399** |

> To these are to be added the islands, which will be described on another occasion, the province has 293 states, besides those dependent on others; 179 towns of these, twelve are colonies, thirteen towns with the rights of Roman citizens, eighteen with the old Latin rights, one confederate, and 135 tributaries.

The 43 colonies and *municipia* in Hispania Tarraconensis were basically concentrated on the Mediterranean coast, in the mid- and upper-Ebro valley, and on the central Meseta. In contrast, the north-western sector only had three main urban centres, which coincided with the *conventus* capitals (see Fig. 5.3).

Therefore, the first contradiction arises in the chronology of the population estimate by Frier (2000), because the ancient census data by Pliny refer to the late first century CE—neither 14 CE nor 164 CE. Pliny probably used the Augustan census, but the data published were those he accessed as *procurator metallorum* in the Hispania Tarraconensis in 73 CE. The second contradiction refers to the population figures recorded by Pliny (*NH* III.4.28) for the three north-western *conventus* of Hispania Tarraconensis, which allow us to generate real densities of 6.8 inhab./km$^2$ (Asturum), 7.59 inhab./km$^2$ (Lucensis), and 13.2 inhab./km$^2$ (Bracarum), whose average of 7.4 inhab./km$^2$, is slightly below the 14 CE density of 8.5 inhab./km$^2$ proposed by Frier (2000: 812, table 5; 814, table 6). Historical censuses in the Iberian peninsula confirm such densities (see Chapter 3), for instance in north-eastern Catalonia in 1553 with an average density of 9–10 inhab./km$^2$.

The population densities of the medieval kingdoms in the Iberian peninsula in the fifteenth century vary only slightly from this value, ranging from 7.72 inhab./km$^2$ (Aragon) to 11.83 inhab./km$^2$ (Castile) (Table 5.3).

The first of these censuses was carried out by the Count of Aranda (1768–9), who registered a population of 9.3 million in Spain; this figure totalled 10.4 million in the census of Floridablanca (1787). For earlier historical periods, the

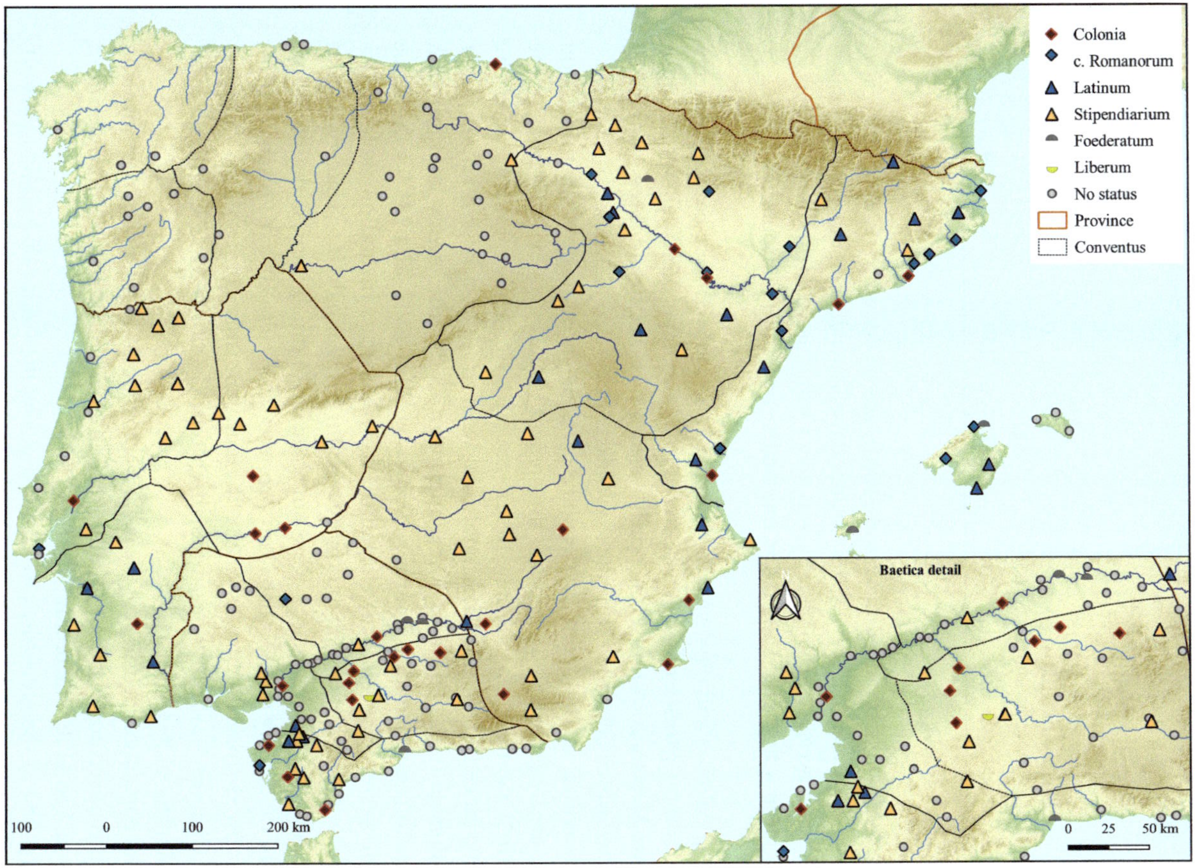


**Fig. 5.2** Cities in the Iberian peninsula according to the privileges listed by Pliny the Elder

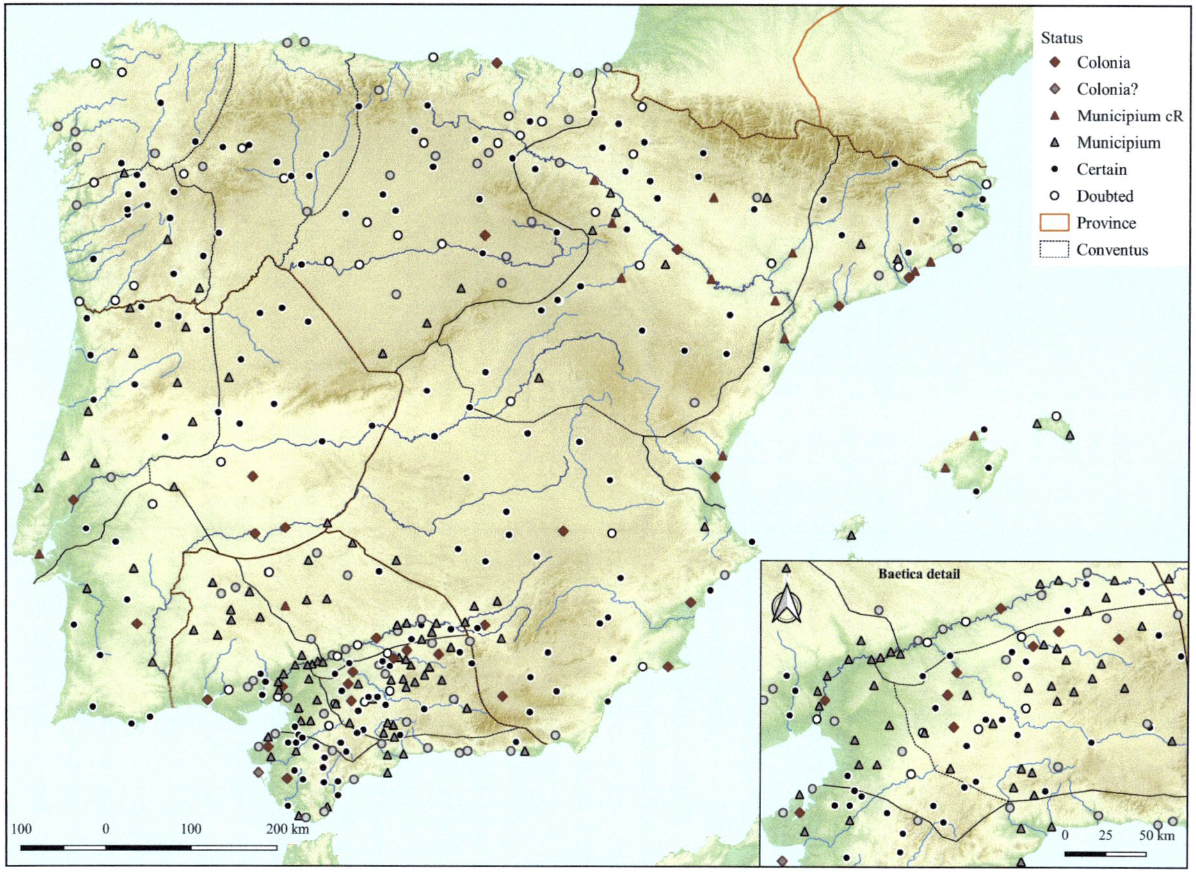


Fig. 5.3 Juridical status of self-governing communities in Hispania

**Table 5.3** Population densities in the fifteenth-century kingdoms of the Iberian peninsula

| Medieval kingdoms | Area ($km^2$) | Inhabitants | Densities |
|---|---|---|---|
| Navarre | 11,700 | 120,000 | 10.9 |
| Granada | 30,000 | 300,000 | 10 |
| Portugal | 88,000 | 1,000,000 | 11.36 |
| Aragon | 110,000 | 850,000 | 7.72 |
| Castile | 355,000 | 4,200,000 | 11.83 |

*Source*: Pérez (2010).

sources do not offer minimum guarantees although there are some approximate estimates, among which the ones by Domínguez (1963) and Nadal (1984) stand out. The latter estimate is the most widely accepted one. This scholar proposed a population of nearly 4.6 million inhabitants in the late fifteenth century, which reached 6.7 million in the late sixteenth century, and 7.5 million in 1717.

In 1996, Carreras published a study devoted considering the demography of Roman Hispania. Its main objective was to undertake an approximate calculation of the total population of the Iberian peninsula, as well as to observe its territorial distribution, both urban, based on the dimensions of its cities, and rural, by using the data available from the existing archaeological surveys. This work was followed by a second study (Carreras, 2014) in which some methodological aspects were clarified, and in which the sample of cities was expanded considerably, increasing from 106 to 209 cities. Due to the type of archaeological evidence available for Hispania, the method considered most suitable for calculating these estimates in both studies, partly because of its relative simplicity, was the population density coefficient by settlement (see Chapter 3).

This method, used in the majority of existing demographic estimates, starts from the assumption that there is a direct correlation between the dimensions of the settlement, the size of its population, and its density. As already mentioned, there are several estimates made for the early imperial period in other parts of the Empire where the exceptional preservation of the remains allows them to be used as a proxy. Thanks to these extraordinary cases, which will be briefly summarized below, the most appropriate density that should be used in our calculations can be extrapolated when the archaeological record is not rich enough to make individual calculations—the majority of cases.

According to the works of Wallace-Hadrill (1994: 91–117) and Storey (1997: 973–4), the total population of Pompeii reached between 11,000 and 11,500 inhabitants, with a density of 166 to 175 citizens per hectare, while Flohr (2017) estimated a minimum of 7,250 and a maximum of 11,750 inhabitants. Similarly, the city of Sabratha could have attained an estimated population of between 5,148 and 19,989 inhabitants, with a density of 166 to 414 inhabitants per hectare, while Timgad could have had between 2,844 and 3,555 inhabitants, with a density of 286 to 357 inhabitants per hectare (Storey, 1997: 969–73). Finally, the Egyptian city of Hermopolis, from the information obtained from the study of preserved censuses, offers a possible total population of 37,000 inhabitants with a density of 309 people per hectare (Bagnall and Frier, 1994: 55) (Table 5.4).

It is interesting to observe how the urban population densities for Roman cities obtained from archaeological evidence and census data do not differ substantially, perhaps with the exception of the highest possible estimate for Sabratha. Additionally, these data fit well with the information offered by the ancient sources (Table 5.5) when they discuss the cases of some colonial foundations in northern Italy in the years immediately after their construction. In these cases, we have the literary evidence for the number of settlers, which must match the archaeological evidence of the original city wall circuit. The numbers again show considerable variability, but remain relatively uniform between certain figures, in

**Table 5.4** Estimated density per ha in Roman cities

| City | Population | Density/ha | Reference |
|---|---|---|---|
| Pompeii | 11,000–11,500 | 166–175 | Wallace-Hadrill (1994: 91–117) |
| Sabratha | 12,000 | 166–414 | Storey (1997: 969–73) |
| Timgad | 12,000 | 286–357 | Storey (1997: 969–73) |
| Hermopolis | 37,000 | 309 | Bagnall and Frier (1994: 55) |

**Table 5.5** Population densities of some of the Roman colonies founded during the second–first centuries BCE

| Colony | Area (ha) | Population | Density/ha | Date |
|---|---|---|---|---|
| Augusta Praetoria | 42 | 12,000 | 288 | 25 BCE |
| Bononia | 50 | 12,000 | 240 | 189 BCE |
| Comum | 25 | 12,000 | 482 | 89 BCE |
| Aquileia | 41 | 13,440 | 328 | 181 BCE |
| Concordia | 40 | 12,000 | 300 | 42 BCE |

*Source*: Kron (2017: 76, fig. 6).

most cases ranging between 250 and 350 inhabitants per hectare, with Comum being the exception. Finally, Hanson and Ortman (2017), based on a sample of 885 Roman cities, have defined a series of urban densities elicited from archaeologically identified residential areas, which reach similar values—although they have a greater degree of variability. Their numbers range between 100 and 500 inhabitants per hectare. In our opinion, some densities below 100, several of them proposed when discussing Roman cities in Hispania, seem too low and should be reconsidered.

For the case of Hispania, in 1996 Carreras assigned two different generic values: 326 inhabitants per hectare to the main centres and 233 inhabitants per hectare in the case of secondary centres. In contrast, in his second study, he decided to apply a single figure to all the settlements studied, whether they were primary or secondary centres (Carreras, 2014). The calculations were carried out on the basis of three different proposals: 250 inhab./ha, 233 inhab./ha, and 200 inhab./ha. Finally, in a recent study (Sinner and Carreras, 2019), two of us decided to use the number of 250 inhab./ha as the highest feasible figure when estimating the population of Roman cities in the area under study (north-eastern Spain) and comparing them with the pre-Roman ones. To do so, we rely on the fact that this figure seems to adapt well to the numbers that are known for later periods.

An excellent case study is the city of Barcelona (Banks, 2005). The city was to experience rapid growth in terms of extent and population during the medieval period, a population of 1,500 inhabitants (12 ha) being estimated in the year 1000 CE (125 inhab./ha), and 4,000–5,000 inhabitants and 30 ha at the end of the eleventh century CE (166.66 inhab./ha). Only during the twelfth and thirteenth centuries would the city grow rapidly (60 and 120 ha respectively), reaching an estimated total population between 10,000 and 12,000 inhabitants (200 inhab./ha) in the twelfth century and around 30,000 in the following century (250 inhab./ha).

The number of Jewish families in Barcelona in the year 1079 CE can provide another interesting parallel. It seems to have been about 54 families (Banks, 1981: 831), if the list presented in a document of that year is complete. Given that this corresponds to the period soon after the definition of the Call (Jewish quarter), it is a valuable piece of information. The Call covered an area of approximately 1.8 ha, and if it is accepted that the majority of these families lived within its limits, and allowing for five or six members for each family (see Chapter 3), a total of 270 to 325 is reached, that is between 150 and 180 inhab./ha. Moreover, this number fits well within the likely progression in size of the Jewish community, for that of Gerona had 24 families in the later tenth century and was qualified as 'small' by Benjamin of Tudela (1167). At the end of the life of the Call (1391), there were about 95 properties (excluding synagogues) in the Call, so the population could have been around 500 (about 260–316 inhab./ha). Other parts of the city were more densely populated; in the case of nearby city blocks for which we have

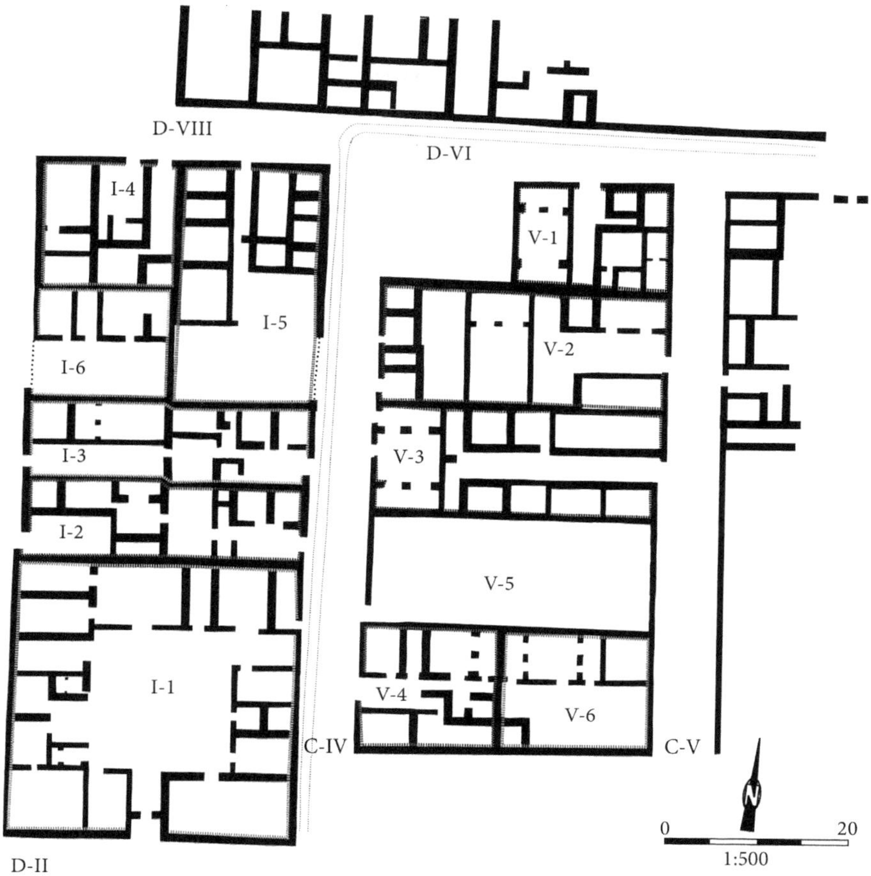


**Fig. 5.4** Plan of La Caridad (Uribe, 2015: fig. 135; after Ezquerra, 2005)

*fogatges* (hearth-tax records), a block behind the cathedral had 25 residences in 1378 in about 0.25 ha, so possibly as many as 500 inhab./ha.[1]

There are not many archaeological examples with enough preserved and well excavated houses that allow us to conduct estimates similar to those in Chapter 4. That said, the case studies of Celsa (Velilla de Ebro, Zaragoza) and La Caridad (Caminreal, Teruel) can be quite revealing.

La Caridad is a 12.5 ha settlement located in the Jiloca river. The town was built *ex novo* with a clear orthogonal plan (Fig. 5.4) in the Late Republican period (*c.* 120 BCE) and was destroyed during the Sertorian War (80–71 BCE ), leaving

[1] We would like to thank Philip Banks for his invaluable comments on the demographics of medieval Barcelona.

**Table 5.6** Population densities for La Caridad when applying the number of inhabitants per house used in Pompeii by Flohr (2017: 64–5)

| Flohr's estimates (Pompeii) | No. of inhab./house | Total inhab. | Density/ha |
|---|---|---|---|
| Low | 7 | 2,058 | 164.4 |
| Intermediate | 9.5 | 2,793 | 226.4 |
| High | 12 | 3,528 | 282.2 |

behind a well preserved settlement with probably a single period of occupation. A total of 11 architectonic units have been fully excavated and studied (Ezquerra, 2005; Uribe, 2015: 312–31). With the exception of the so-called Likine house (915 $m^2$), which has been interpreted as a *collegium* or *statio* (Beltrán Lloris, 2011: 145–8) and, as a result, will be excluded from our housing estimates, all the other households in La Caridad have surfaces between 177.33 $m^2$ and 389.69 $m^2$, providing an average household area of 255 $m^2$.

If we replicate the proportions between household space and public/communal spaces discussed in Chapter 4, we can determine that a total of 75,000 $m^2$ of residential space were occupied by a 294 houses that would have sheltered 1,176 inhabitants (four individuals per house). This will provide a total density of 94.08 inhabitants per hectare, 117.6 if we apply an average of five inhabitants per house.

These numbers, while not impossible, are certainly in the lowest end of the spectrum of what is credible, and are not considering the social complexity of some Roman domestic spaces that may include the presence of slaves among the inhabitants of the household (see Chapter 3). If we apply Flohr's suggested figures of between 7 and 12 individuals (Flohr, 2017: 64–5) for the houses in Pompeii, the resulting densities at La Caridad will range between 164.4 and 282.2 inhabitants per hectare (Table 5.6). These numbers seem to align well with the evidence we have obtained in the case studies discussed above.

The case of the Colonia Victrix Iulia Lepida/Celsa—the Iberian Kelse—is even more complex, but it also reveals some of the possibilities and limitations that the archaeological record as well as the social complexity pose during the Roman period for this type of study. In Celsa (Fig. 5.5), a city estimated to be 44 ha in size, we know the total surface of nine households thanks to the work conducted by Uribe (2015: 268–94).

However, differently to what happens in La Caridad, the houses in Celsa seem to have a much wider range of sizes, the smallest unit being only 45.15 $m^2$ and the largest 1,374.96 $m^2$. It should be noted, however, that five of the nine households in Celsa have areas measuring between 135 $m^2$ and 300 $m^2$. The remaining three, on the other hand, are quite diverse (578.19, 723.8, and 1,374.96) and therefore much harder to group. With such a large difference between surface areas, it

**Fig. 5.5** Plan of Celsa (Uribe, 2015: fig. 135; after Beltrán, 1987)

seems problematic to establish a single average house size for the site of Celsa, since the minority but very large households are likely to provide an overestimation for the average surface of houses in the town. With that problem in mind, and being fully aware of the limitations that it entails, since we still grouping houses of significantly diverse size, we have divided the sample into two different groups. The first one (45–300 $m^2$) comprises two-thirds of the sample and provides an average house of 205.2 $m^2$. The second (578–1,375 $m^2$), represents one-third of the known sample and leaves us with an average house of 892.3 $m^2$. With these two groups in place, we can adapt the methodology used in La Caridad to Celsa in order to conduct demographic estimates.

If we subtract the area estimated to be occupied by communal and public spaces/buildings at Celsa, we are left with a residential space of 264,000 $m^2$. If we subdivide this area extrapolating the two groups of houses discussed above, we can suggest that 175,824 $m^2$ (two-thirds of the total residential space) were occupied by a total of 858 houses (205 $m^2$ in average), while the remaining 88,176 $m^2$ (one-third of the residential space) included 99 houses with an average size of 892.3 $m^2$. When adding these two groups together we get a total estimate of 957

**Table 5.7** Population densities for Celsa when applying the number of inhabitants per house used in Pompeii by Flohr (2017: 64–5)

| Flohr's estimates (Pompeii) | No. of inhab./house | Total inhab. | Density/ha |
|---|---|---|---|
| Low | 7 | 6,699 | 152.2 |
| Intermediate | 9.5 | 9,091 | 206.6 |
| High | 12 | 11,484 | 261 |

houses. Once again, if we use the lowest possible estimate of four individuals per house—which seems certainly unlikely considering the size of some of the households at Celsa—we reach a total estimated population of 3,828 individuals and 87 inhabitants per hectare (108.75 inhab./ha if using five individuals per household). Is worth noting the similitudes with the results in La Caridad, which may suggest that densities below 100 inhabitants per hectare cannot be suggested for Hispania during the Roman period.

If we apply the same range of estimates to Celsa that we have employed in La Caridad, and that seem to adapt better to the complex social composition of the wealthy and larger Roman domestic units, the densities range between 150 inhabitants per hectare in the low end and 260 inhabitants per hectare with the highest estimates (Table 5.7). Once again, these results are almost identical to the estimates calculated for La Caridad.

Only future excavations and research will provide new case studies to test the reliability of these estimates. However, while we acknowledge that the methodology can and must be improved and tested in future studies, the uniformity of the results obtained does seem to point out what are the estimates that we can accept as possible in the Roman period.

On the basis of the evidence presented so far, which includes a combination of literary sources, diverse archaeological estimates, and census data from different periods, it seems reasonable to carry out calculations for the case of Hispania Tarraconensis, always bearing in mind that a substantial variety that surely existed is being homogenized, based on figures between 150–200 and 250–300 inhabitants per hectare.

If the sample that has been employed is analysed, it should be remarked that Pliny the Elder recorded a total of 399 urban entities, *oppida*, in Hispania. From these lists, most of the main urban centres belonging to the province of Tarraconensis (179 urban *civitates/oppida*; 114 *civitates/populi* without an *oppidum*, making a total of 293 *civitates*) are included in our study (see Appendix II). To write this chapter, we have worked with the area covered by 177 urban centres, so only a total of 115 centres would be missing from Pliny's list—most probably those with an area of under 10 ha.

For the calculation of the Iberian peninsula as a whole, approximate values have been assigned to these settlements (93 centres of 7 ha on average and 99 of 3 ha) as was done in previous works (Carreras, 2014). In this study, the same criteria will be followed, with the only difference that a value of 5 ha will be assigned to those that in 2014 were given a figure of 3 ha. This change is justified probabilistically from the study of the sample listed in Appendix II. If the number of settlements with a surface area under 10 ha is examined, there are only 7 cities with values between 2.0 and 3.75 ha, while there are 26 between 5 and 5.6 ha. Therefore, it is statistically more feasible than the missing settlements conform to the latter size, since it is the most frequently recorded. This interpolation leaves us with a total of 50 settlements of 7 ha on average and 59 with a value of 5 ha.

Despite the changes in settlement size and the density per hectare used, in addition to having a larger sample, the total urban population for all Hispania (1,372,415), is not far from the one obtained in 1996, which was 1,002,000, and that for the province of Tarraconensis could be estimated as having been between 576,532 (200 inhab./ha) and 721,815 (250 inhab./ha) in the first century CE. Obviously, it is very important to bear in mind that this population calculation must be located at a very specific moment in time, such as the Early Empire, and more exactly at the moment when Pliny the Elder recorded the *civitates* and *populi* of the Iberian peninsula during his stay in Asturica Augusta as *procurator metallorum* in the years 72–4 CE. Today, these demographic patterns for the Roman cities in the Iberian peninsula are only well documented in very specific case studies (Carreras, 2014: 56–7), it being impossible to undertake demographic estimates at regular time intervals (e.g. every 25–50 years), which would undoubtedly be of great interest to understand the evolution of the province in terms of its population.

In addition to this temporal limitation, we have to bear in mind that our estimates are only for those cities that have been located and studied in such a manner that an approximation of their size can be put forward. Based on the idea that these cities roughly follow the general distribution within the region, and that their sizes can be taken as representative of the larger cities in the area, while also noting that smaller cities are very likely to be missing from this list, we could generate a heat map to represent the probable urban density based on city size (see Fig. 5.6).

Since we are working with a sample that incorporates a large number of Roman cities and their intramural extent, the so-called range rule can be applied in accordance with the size. The range rule basically consists of calculating the natural logarithm of the dimensions of the cities based on the range they belong to, resulting in a linear function of decreasing type. The first person to apply this method to Roman urbanism was Morley (1996), who carried out an interesting study of the relationship of Rome to the other cities of the Italian peninsula. To carry out his calculations, the author used a density of 300 inhabitants per hectare and concluded that 40% of the population of the peninsula lived in cities:

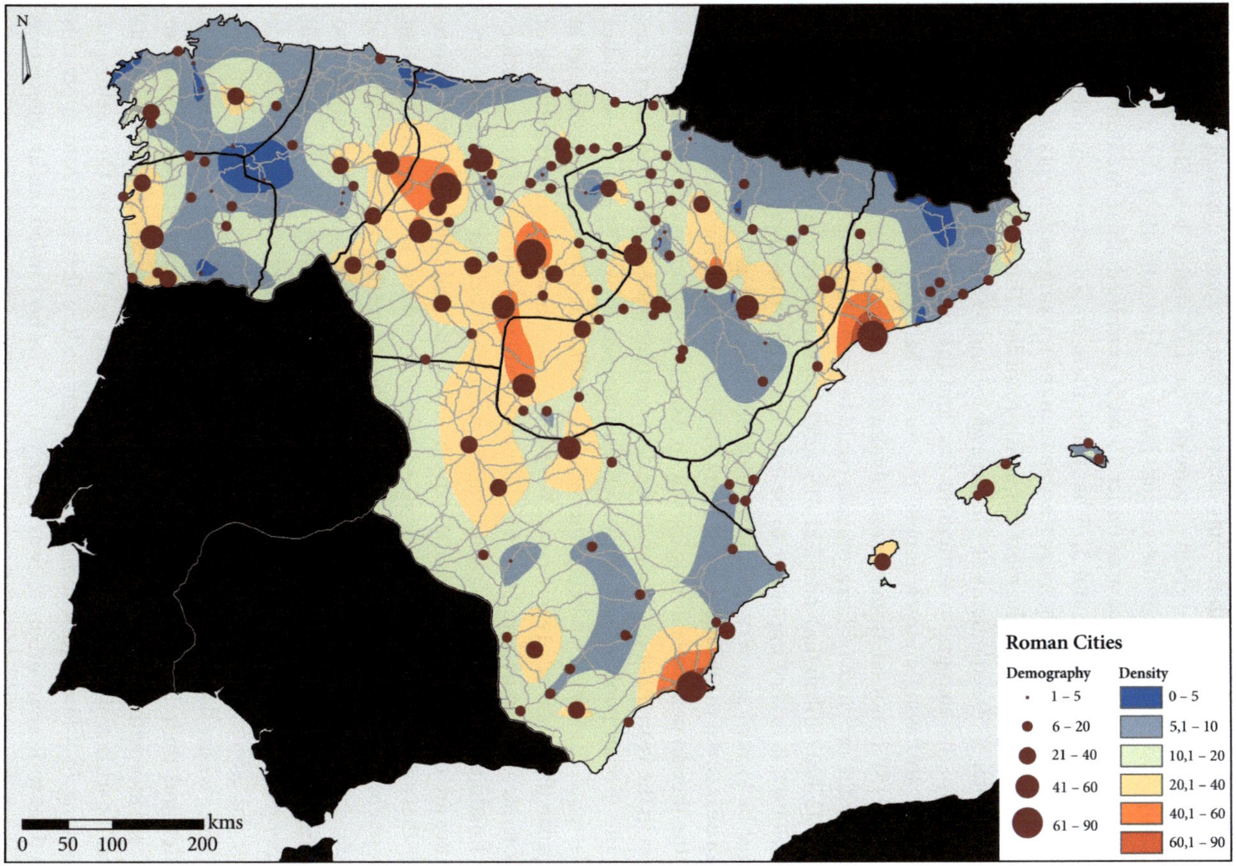


**Fig. 5.6** Urban population density for the Iberian peninsula in the Early Empire (De Soto and Carreras, 2022)

1. Range—Rome (1–1.5 million)
2. Range—Ostia and Puteoli (+ 100 ha) (30,000 inhabitants)
3. Range—Mediolanum, Patavium, and *Capua* 83–133 ha (25,000–40,000 inhabitants)
4. Range—25 cities between 16 and 83 ha (5,000–25,000 inhabitants)
5. Range—400 cities between 3 and 16 ha (1,000–5,000 inhabitants)

Turning to the range rule for the province under study we note that the cities do not cover more than 100 ha:

1. Range: none
2. Range: none
3. Range: Tarraco (90 ha)
4. Range: 66 cities between 16.5 and 80 ha
5. Range: 110 cities between 1 and 16 ha.

Clearly this method of comparison is difficult to standardize: should we reorganize the ranges so we have five classes, or should we follow the ranges as presented by Morley? A step further than the range rule is a rank-size analysis. RSA graphs do not require arbitrary ranges and allow for comparison between completely different settlement systems. By turning to deviations from Zipf's law as such, De Ligt has analysed the Italian peninsula; the dimensions of the cities were not adapted to the decreasing linear logarithmic function (Zipf's law), but to a concave curve (De Ligt, 2016).

Zipf's law postulates that random processes will create a distribution that follows a slope of −1 in a logarithmic rank-size graph (Zipf, 1949). It has been argued that well integrated urban systems would follow Zipf's law. However, in most pre-modern societies a deviation from Zipf's law has been observed. These deviations are often explained as the result of incomplete data or a combination of multiple data sets. There are three possible deviations (see Fig. 4.2). Rather than going into complex interpretations of these curves, on which no agreement has been reached so far, they can be used as a method to compare different systems. In order to do so, a few standard elements are needed: first, a trend line with a slope of −1 indicating Zipf's law; in this way the deviation from Zipf's law can be observed; second, the trend line and equation of fit for the data under scrutiny. The equation gives us two important values: the $q$-value, which is the exponent in the y equation, indicates the slope of the graph; and the $R^2$ to indicate the degree of fit of the trend line. Only if both the $q$-value and $R^2$ approach 1 can we consider it to satisfy Zipf's law.

The RSA graph with the known sizes of the cities in Hispania Tarraconensis includes a total of 155 sites of 5 ha and over (see Fig. 5.7). However, the lower order settlements are certainly incomplete. According to Hanson (2016: 95),

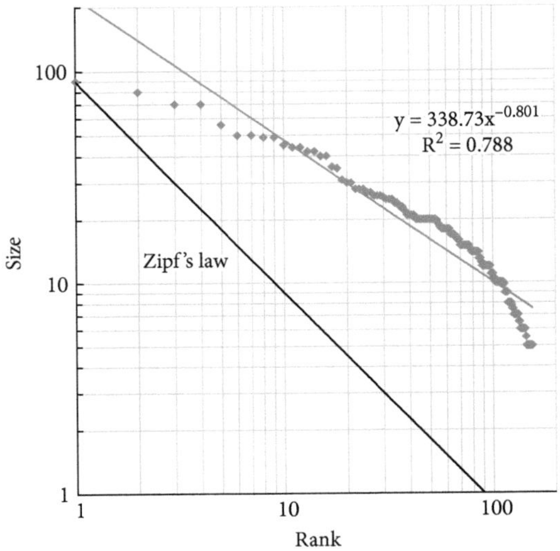


**Fig. 5.7** RSA for Hispania Tarraconensis (n = 155)

those agglomerations should not be considered as cities, since most scholars define a classical city as one with a minimum of 5 to 25 ha, in other words 1,000 to 5,000 inhabitants. It is difficult to admit that such agglomerations are city-like despite their size, since they act as administrative, commercial, political, and religious centres of the whole territory. They should be identified as secondary agglomerations acting as urban centres, and therefore part of the urban population. If this argument is accepted, the proportion between urban and rural population would be closer to 25–75% rather than the most widely accepted ratio of 10–90%.

Despite the inclusion of smaller places as urban settlements, the steep drop at the end of a complete RSA graph does not aid in understanding the whole settlement system. Therefore, it is standard practice to create a cut-off point, which we have set at 5 ha and below. The effect of the exclusion of the lower order creates a minimal levelling of the curve (Houten, 2021).

The graph gives us a $q$-value of 0.801 and an $R^2$ of 0.788. From the $q$-value we can derive that the urban system is not very hierarchical. However, the fit of the trend line must be considered low. Indeed, we observe a levelling at the highest order settlements. The four largest settlements are Tarraco (90 ha), Carthago Nova (80 ha), Clunia (70 ha), and Lacobriga (70 ha). The first three are, as is to be expected, the provincial capital and two *conventus* capitals. However, the other *conventus* capitals, namely Caesaraugusta (56 ha), Bracara Augusta (42 ha), Lucus Augusti (35 ha), and Asturica Augusta (27 ha), are not among the largest in the province, although they are relatively large within their own regions. Lacobriga is a surprisingly large city as it has no specific role in the Roman imperial structure. The explanation for its size must be sought in an earlier, pre-Roman period.

The graph can clearly be described as concave. It clearly departs from the Zipf law trend line and will return there, as the drop at the lower end indicates. The majority of the settlements cluster between 10 and 30 ha. At the lower end we observe the onset of the steep drop of the small agglomerations. The concave distribution with a concentration in medium-sized cities can be interpreted as a less integrated system. In this system, cities can be expected to operate in a regional field rather than the 'global' Empire. If the pyramidal Roman Empire were a reality, with Rome as the apex and the provincial capitals as the next layer, we would expect either a hierarchical or primate distribution.

In order to understand the settlement system, we should turn to the Iron Age template and its system. For the collection of these data, we have to turn to different publications by Almagro-Gorbea (1988 and 2001) among other scholars (e.g. Moret, 1996; Grau, 2015) (see Chapter 4 and Appendix I). Obviously, the data for Hispania Tarraconensis will be compared with approximately the same area in earlier times (see Fig. 1.1). This obliges us to impose a later administrative organization onto the Late Iron Age urban system. Clearly this will lead to combining the data of different settlement systems together. However, as Almagro-Gorbea (1988) already pointed out, and as we have recently suggested for the case of the north-east of the peninsula (Sinner and Carreras, 2019), it is very possible that much of the urban demographic pattern of the Roman era directly reflects the occupation patterns of the territory in pre-Roman times (Álvarez and Ruiz Zapatero, 2001).

Adding the data of the Iron Age settlement system to the graph (see Fig. 5.8), it can be observed that from the *q*-value of 1.118 this could be considered a primate system. The slope of the graph is steeper than −1. Because of the similar $R^2$ value to the Roman data set, we know the fit is not significant. The high *q*-value must be sought in the rather large high-rank settlements. In particular, the settlements of the Vettones and Vaccaei are quite large. However, it must be realized that these are the walled areas of the few, widely separated *oppida*. In addition, these *oppida* often used the topography of the region to aid the protection of the community, the walled area enclosing the whole hilltop. Lastly, as discussed in Chapter 4, these communities were pastoral and may have used part of the *oppidum* to protect their cattle. The slightly smaller high-rank settlements are most likely to have been a result of the concentration of the urban population although we should not rule out the possibility of better understood settlement patterns for the Roman period for which we can include the built-up area instead of the walled area. In the case of Roman Clunia the walled area also measured 130 ha, whereas the built-up area only covered 70 ha.

Despite these possibly larger high-rank settlements, it can be seen that the middle and lower-order settlements are quite similar to the Roman settlement system. The majority of settlements lie between 10 and 20 ha, slightly smaller than the Roman ones, leading to the steeper slope. It can therefore be stated that

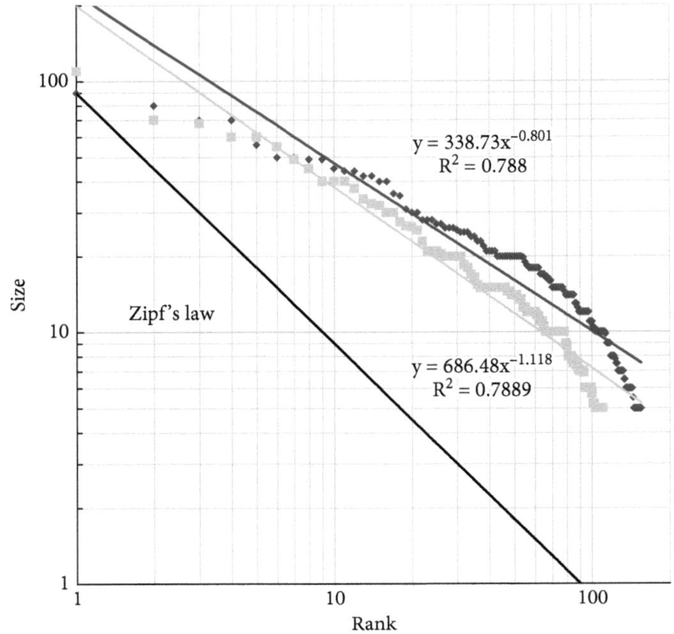


**Fig. 5.8** Comparison between the RSA of the pre-Roman settlements (n = 110 light) vs. the Roman cities of the Early Empire (n = 155 dark) over 5 ha

the demographic shift from the Iron Age to the Roman system is one of simple demographic growth (see below).

## 5.1 The Population of Hispania Tarraconensis

The urban phenomenon in the province is clearly visible from Fig. 5.9 (hectares map), created from the perimeters of the 177 sites, concentrated in specific areas that surely reflect or fossilize the urban or proto-urban world formed during the Iron Age (see Fig. 4.28). There is a clear concentration of urban population in the middle and upper Ebro valley and on the northern plateau (Meseta), a phenomenon already recorded in the study by Carreras carried out in 2014 and which, as we can see in Fig. 5.10, reflects the solidly established Celtiberian settlement pattern (of the Suessetani, Celtiberii, Arevaci, Vaccaei, Turmogi, Berones, and Pelendones) prior to the Roman conquest.

The total urban population of Hispania Tarraconensis from those 177 cities (density of 250 inhabitants per ha) was 579,803 citizens, almost 42.2% of the total town dwellers in the Iberian peninsula. Calculating the rural population of Tarraconensis by *conventus* based on a projection of 1:3 with regards to urban

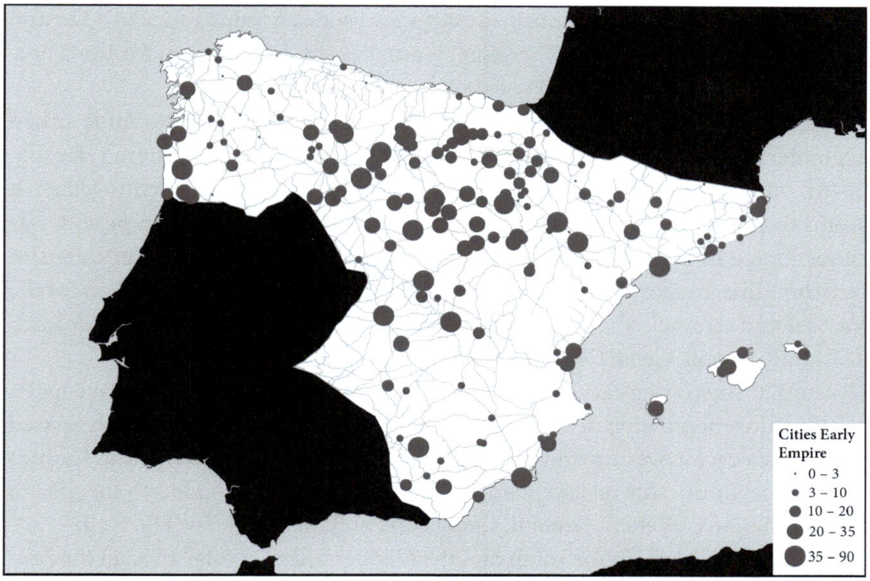


**Fig. 5.9** Distribution of the urban population of Hispania Tarraconensis (author: Pau De Soto)

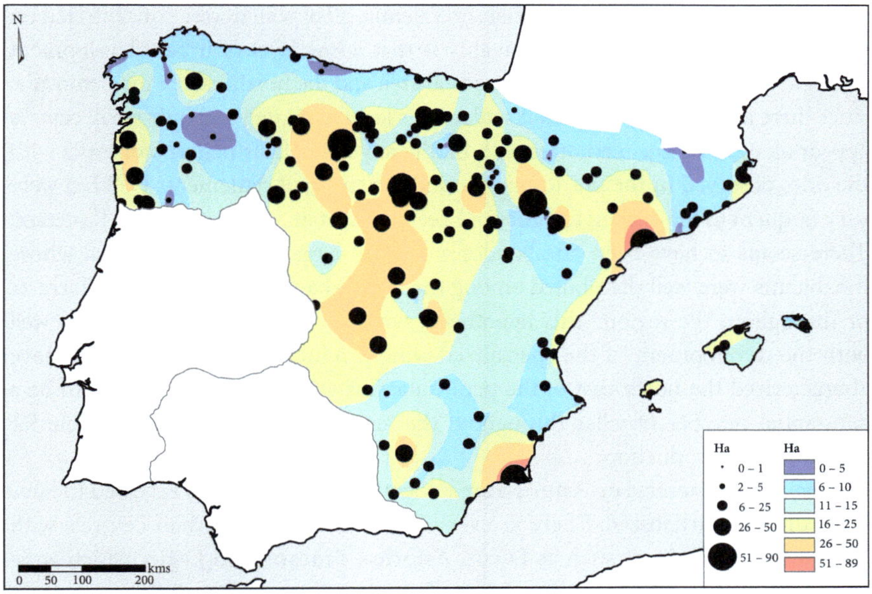


**Fig. 5.10** Heat map of the revised urban population of Hispania Tarraconensis (author: Pau De Soto)

dwellers except in the three north-western *conventus*, a value of 2,018,437 rural inhabitants can be obtained. Therefore, a possible total population for the whole province was around 2,598,240 people.

With the exception of Caesaraugusta and Clunia, there are no large urban agglomerations comparable to other provinces in the Western Empire (Hanson, 2016), but a substantial number of medium-sized cities are grouped together. It seems that the population, as was already the case in the pre-Roman period, was concentrated in large urban centres with the intention of exploiting an extensive territory. This territory included the upper Ebro valley, the ancient territory of the Vaccaei and Arevaci. The main urban centres were former Iron Age *oppida* such as Clunia, Lancia, Gella, Confluentia, or Lacobriga.

Another interesting fact is that the two central plateaux appear to have had a relatively low population density, with only a small number of quite widely spaced settlements each covering under 10 ha, with Complutum and Contrebia Carbica as the exceptions. This relatively uninhabited region corresponded to the area of the Celtiberians, Edetani, Oretani, Contestani, and Bastetani (see Fig. 5.10).

On the other hand, in the south and the Mediterranean coastal area, an interesting phenomenon can be detected. Large cities are scarce, and only Tarraco and Carthago Nova stand out, while medium-sized cities are somewhat more frequent. Inside this area in the east of the peninsula, the urban phenomenon is rather limited with small cities and large territories without remarkable urban concentrations. Although this would seem to be a contradiction given the importance that cities such as Tarraco, Saguntum, Emporiae, or Valentia, all of which were concentrated on the coastline, must have had, the reality is that a low level of urban development seems to be recorded for the eastern coastal area and the north-east of the peninsula, since there are very few significant settlements located inland, and only small centres appear alongside large territories with hardly any cities. This pattern contrasts with the ones observed in the pre-Roman period, when small settlements (< 3 ha) were very frequent in the ancient territory of Laeetani, Edetani, Contestani, and Bastetani. There seems to have been an abandonment of a large number of *oppida*, whose inhabitants were well distributed among the new urban centres, especially Tarraco, or throughout the region. This hypothesis, which is impossible to prove, fits well with the development of the specialized wine production that is known to have characterized the north-east of the peninsula; this viticulture needed there to be a substantial number of villas throughout the territory, which were responsible for structuring its production.

Finally, the Cantabrian-Asturian area, together with Galicia, is revealed to have been the least urbanized. There are very few medium-sized urban centres, with the exception of places such as Lucus, Asturica, Bracara, and Legio, which were consolidated as the largest urban poles. The importance of its mining resources, especially gold (see Fig. 5.11), and the need for its exploitation and administration by the Roman State may help to explain the policy of urban foundations,

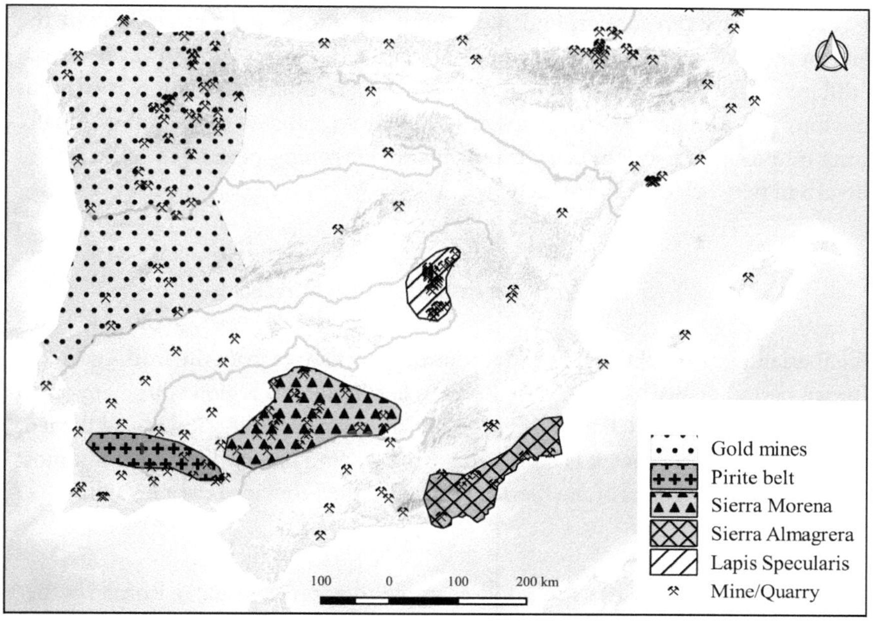


**Fig. 5.11** Location of the main mining districts in the Iberian peninsula

mostly *municipia*, in this part of the peninsula (Carreras, 2014: 63), which once again seems to reflect, in terms of both densities and location, the pattern established by the Iron Age peoples, who might have been structured by a system of heterarchical *castros* organized according to diverse groups, and thus without a clear urban centre, which were subsequently accepted as *civitates* (i.e. secondary agglomerations).

This urban fabric characteristic of the Early Empire that has just been described, including its population densities, can be explained from the structure of the road network in the Iberian peninsula, as well as that of the main navigable rivers, the Guadalquivir and the Ebro river valleys, and the Ruta de la Plata (the Silver Route) being the preferred axes, which were already exploited during the Iron Age. However, above all, this settlement pattern can be explained on the basis of the pre-existing urban framework that is known to have already been in place in the third century BCE (see Chapter 4). The comparison between the two periods not only demonstrates the considerable level of urban development existing in the Iberian peninsula before the arrival of Rome, but also the existence of solid foundations on which the province under study was built, both in terms of demography and settlement patterns during the Early Empire.

In fact, as we will show in the case studies discussed below, urbanism in Tarraconensis is an example of diversity and reflects the combination and negotiation between foreign and indigenous traditions and populations in the development of some of its most important cities. In other cases, however, we see a different process where foundations *ex novo* were established in areas without previous pre-Roman settlement to settle Italian veterans or cities that originally came into existence as legionary camps before becoming permanent elements of the urban network of the province.

## 5.1.1 Mediterranean Coastal Area

The Iberian Levant is the region with the strongest changes from the Iron Age to the Roman period. As we have seen, the Romans encountered a region with many small urban settlements (see Chapter 4, Fig. 4.28). In comparison the Roman settlement pattern has changed now; it is at this coast that we find one of the largest and most monumentalized centres of the Iberian peninsula: the provincial capital Tarraco.

### Tarraco (Tarragona)

The capital of the province is a good example to appreciate Early Roman settlement in Iberian territory during the Second Punic War. In 218 BCE, the Roman armies of the Scipio brothers landed and created their military base in allied territories, such as those of the Greek colony of Emporion, or at conquered *oppida* like Kese—a former Punic ally that became part of war booty (Liv., XXI, 60) (Mar and Ruiz de Arbulo, 2011: 210). The indigenous *oppidum* remained unaltered, but the Roman consuls built their *praesidium* and military camp on the nearby hill (see Fig. 5.12).

The first signs of urban planning in the lower town can be dated to the late second century BCE thanks to the *forma urbis Tarraco* documented by Macias et al. (2007). Combining the information of more than 30 excavations in the area of the lower city, a series of regular patterns were recorded. The evidence suggests a layout of *insulae* measuring 35 × 70 m (1 × 2 *actus*) together with streets 5.9 m wide (see Fig. 5.10) (Mar and Ruiz de Arbulo, 2011: 263–4).

The layout registered at least five *cardines* (N–S) and six *decumani* (E–W) adapted to the specific topography of the lower part of Tarraco. The perimeter wall seems to define an area of approximately 50 ha, in which the Roman military camp continued to exist in the upper part. If a constant of 250 inhabitants per hectare is applied, republican Tarraco accommodated 12,500 inhabitants. It is difficult to calculate the number of urbanized *insulae*; taking into account the number of *cardines* and *decumani*, there were a minimum of 42 *insulae* of 2,450 m$^2$ (35 × 70 m–1 *actus* × 2 *actus*). If we consider that at least 20 m$^2$ per person should be assigned as a minimum living space (see Chapter 3), it produces a total civilian population of 5,145, to which should be added the military personnel in the *praetorium*—perhaps another 5,000.

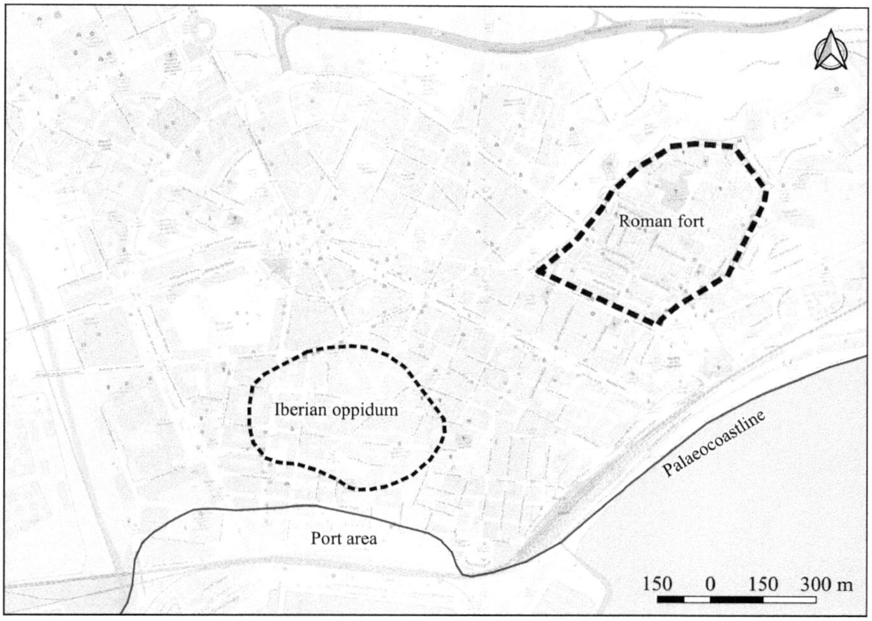


**Fig. 5.12** Location of the Iberian *oppidum* and the Roman military *praetorium* at Tarraco (Tarragona) during the Second Punic War (after Mar et al., 2012: 220)

Another important development was the port, which was initially a simple bay without protection and not very deep, similar to any other (*sálos*) or point of anchorage (*ankipobólion*). Since the Romans were aware of this problem, they decided to build a large wharf in the harbour and warehouses (Mar et al., 2012: 268). It constituted a new quarter of the city with industrial areas, baths, and also residences.

This early capital of the province had a mixed composition of indigenous Cossetani inhabitants (ancient Kese), the military garrison, and all the administrative staff attached to the provincial *praetor* (see Fig. 5.13). Besides, as time pregressed, the city became an attractive economic destination for Italians and traders from other lands as well as individuals from the Hispanic provinces, as the epigraphy reveals (Alföldy, 1975, see Chapter 7).

The city became a Roman colony between 44 and 36 BCE, which also supposed a land division (*centuriation*) and distribution of plots to the legionary veterans (*assignatio*), probably from the Civil Wars. There is a patron dedication from the new colony to Domitius Calvinus, who was provincial governor from 39–36 BCE. It seems that the late republican and early imperial city had two sectors, the upper military garrison and the lower urbanized town, with an empty space between. The two sectors were connected in the Flavian period with the construction of the central circus.

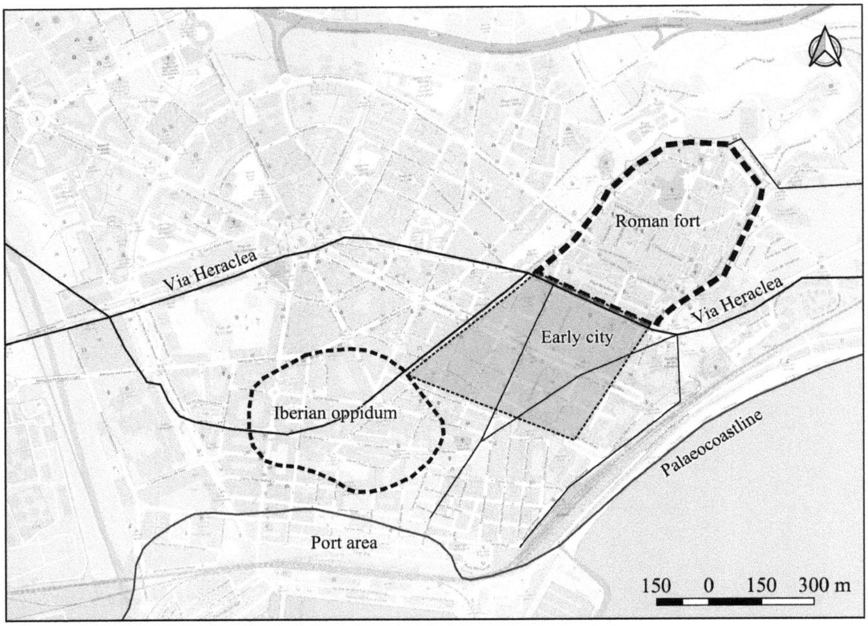


**Fig. 5.13** Location of the Iberian *oppidum* and the Roman town of Tarraco (Tarragona) (after Mar et al., 2012: 263)

According to the archaeological data, the Principate witnessed a growth of the city with even extramural *regiones* or *suburbia*. Macias (2013: 127) calculated an area of 90 ha for the Augustan period with 30–40 ha of peri-urban *regiones*, which expanded on the extramural side to the west.

Following the same method of calculation per hectare, the city housed approximately 22,500 inhabitants. During Augustus' reign, Tarraco became a *colonia* and later, in the Vespasianic period (*c.* 73 CE), Q. Vibius Crispius as *legatus augustus pro praetore in censibus accipiendis* with the help of Sextus Attius Suburanus as *adiutor* undertook a provincial census (Alföldy, 1969: 18–19). Those are probably the censuses consulted by C. Plinius Secundus, who was *procurator metallorum* at Asturica Augusta at that time.

## Carthago Nova (Cartagena)

Qart-Hadašt (New city) was the main Punic urban foundation in the Iberian peninsula. It was founded by Hasdrubal in 229–8 BCE on a peninsula with five hills and the port (see Fig. 5.14). The early city was surrounded by a circuit of walls 3 km in length, enclosing an area of approximately 43 ha. The *Arx Hasdrubalis* hill seems to have concentrated the palaces of the Punic elite. The rest of the town was occupied by a mixed indigenous and Punic population, who were basically involved in agricultural, mining, and commercial activities.

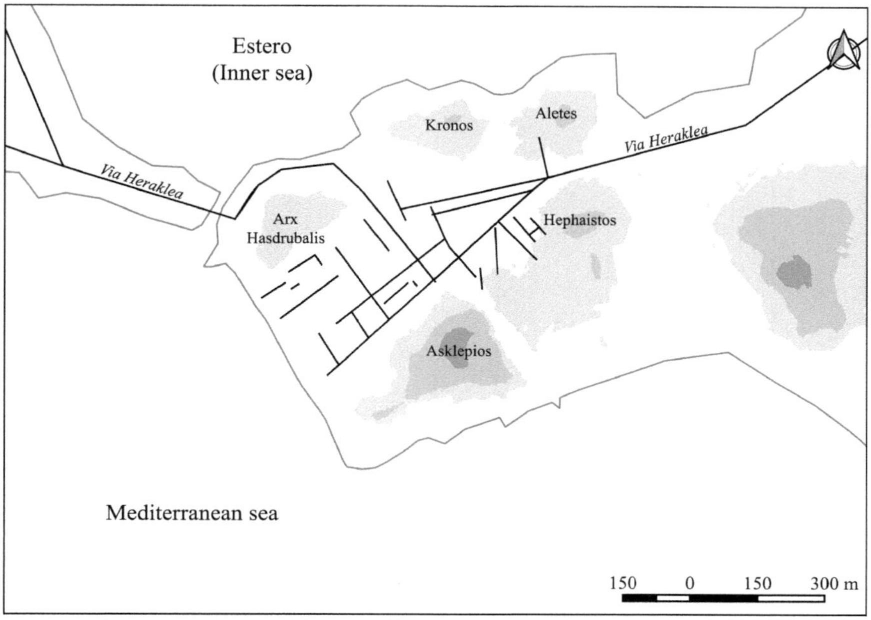


**Fig. 5.14** Map of early Qart-Hadašt (Cartagena)

After the Roman conquest during the Second Punic War, the city expanded and replaced part of the population with Italian immigrants. In fact, Carthago Nova—the city's new name—became one of the most successful ports in Hispania Citerior, as well as a place where traders from all around the Mediterranean settled (see Chapter 7). Strabo (III.2.10) explains that the silver mines of Carthago Nova were large and only 20 *stadia* away from the town. The whole mining district covered an area whose circular perimeter measured 400 *stadia* and occupied a stable working population of 40,000 people—probably slaves.

The influence of the port is also stated by Strabo (III.4.6):

> New Carthage is a rather important emporium, not only of imports from the sea for the inhabitants in the interior, but also of the exports from the interior for all the outside world.

For instance, the road to Segobriga enabled the *lapis specularis* extracted in this region, which was used all around the Mediterranean, to be exported. Therefore, it is not surprising that, after becoming the *Colonia Vrbs Ivlia Nova Carthago* (CVINC) in 44 BCE, it increased in size, reaching almost 80 ha in the first and early second centuries CE, and attaining a population around 20,000 inhabitants if we use a density of 250 inhabitants per hectare. The topography of the town consists of five hills located around a large southern bay with a small marsh on the northern side (see Fig. 5.15) (Ramallo and Martínez Andreu, 2010).

**Fig. 5.15** Plan of early imperial Carthago Nova (Cartagena)

The most well-known public buildings are the theatre, located in the south part of the town close to the port (Ramallo and Moneo, 2009), and the forum, distributed over three terraces. So far, the forum has provided significant buildings such as a curia of the local magistrates, a basilica, and also a *collegium* of the imperial cult. The city adopted an inicipient version of a grid plan to the space between the five hills, and also included an amphitheatre to the south.

Carthago Nova reached its peak in the first century CE, but in the second half of the second century CE, the urban area was reduced in size within what is considered a general economic and social crisis (Quevedo, 2012: 65) (see Chapter 6).

## Valentia (Valencia)

The city of Valentia (Valencia) was founded by the Romans in 138 BCE (Ribera and Jiménez, 2012), probably on an island surrounded by the marshland and the

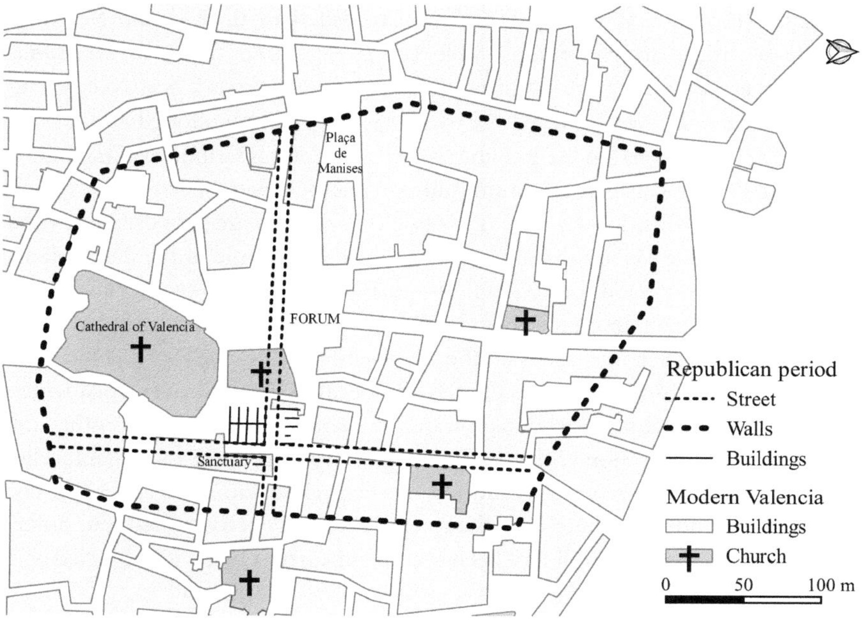


**Fig. 5.16** Early Republican Valentia (138–75 BCE) (Valencia)

waters of the Albufera lagoon (*amoenum stagnum*). Although Avienius (*Ora Marit.* 147) spoke about a former indigenous settlement, to date there are no signs of an Iberian site except for the presence of some Iberian pottery. Therefore, our present archaeological knowledge confirms an Italic foundation *ex novo* probably for the Italian veterans of the Lusitanian Wars during Decimus Iunius' praetorship (139–8 BCE ) (see Fig. 5.16).

The early town covered an area of 10 ha, and some poor houses and an early forum and bath complex, as well as foundational pits, have been identified (Ribera and Jiménez, 2012). The population of this first foundation was basically Italian, as appears to be demonstrated by the material culture as well as the Latin graffiti recorded (see Chapter 7). It is a good example of an Italic military foundation of the republican period. The sources do not provide the number of settlers that initially were settled in Valentia, but it seems feasible to suggest numbers between 2,500 and 3,000 individuals (estimates from 250 and 300 inhabitants per hectare, see Table 5.5 for Italic foundations).

However, the city did not succeed since it was completely destroyed as a result of the Sertorian War in 75 BCE. Valentia was abandoned for almost 100 years, with the exception of some specific areas, such as the sanctuary of Aesculapius. In the early first century CE there are the first signs of the city's recovery, but this was modest and without public epigraphy, until the first inscriptions appeared in the Flavian period (Ribera and Jiménez, 2012: 91).

Finally, the city was re-founded or re-established in the Claudio-Neronian period, according to Pomponius Mela (II, 6, 92), who refers to *notissimas Valentiam et Saguntum*. Other testimonies design Valentia as a new colony, and there may have been a new *deductio*, which also appears mentioned as a 'colony located 3000 steps from the sea' in Pliny (*NH* III.20). Later inscriptions (*CIL* II 3737; II 3739; II 3741) recorded two communities, namely *Valentiani veterani et veteres* or *uterque ordo Valentinorum* (*CIL* II 3745). The *Veterani* are supposed to be the new *coloni* and the *Veteres* the old inhabitants, perhaps some of the descendants of the republican-period foundation. The early imperial city covered an area of 20 ha, therefore doubling its size and probably population, and included some public buildings, such as a circus on the south-eastern side (see Fig. 5.17).

At the end of the first century CE, the city began to build a river port, which underwent extensive modifications towards the north in the second century CE, improving the connection with the sea. In the second century CE, Valentia displayed an orthogonal layout with a forum in a central position (see Fig. 5.17). The city was surrounded by water after the river waters had been diverted into different channels and a large wall had been erected in carrer Quart, which acted as a dam to avoid overflowing from the River Turia.

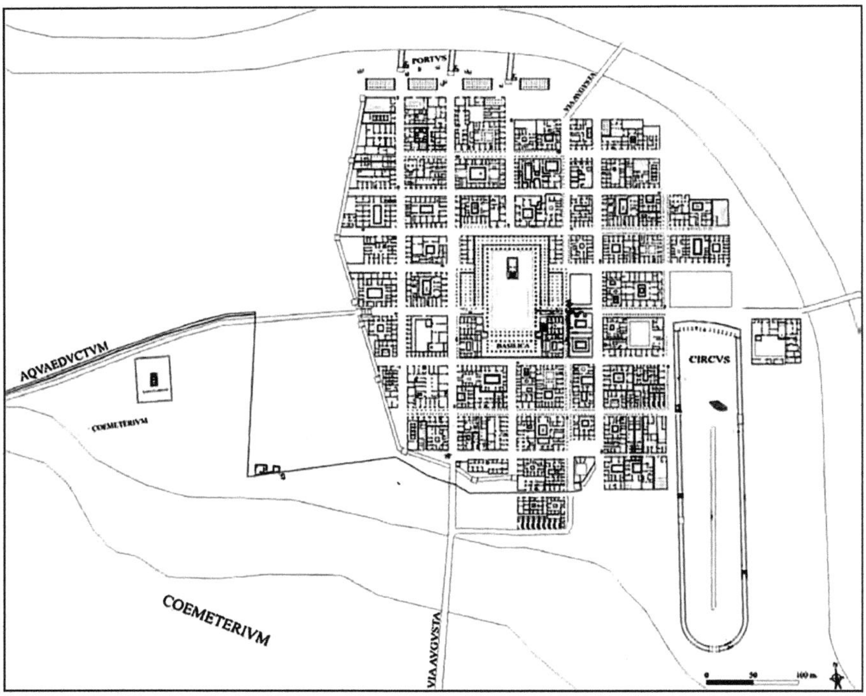


**Fig. 5.17** Early imperial Valentia (Valencia)

As we will see in Chapter 6, the city experienced far-reaching transformations from the third century onwards, with a series of destructions and fires that left sections of the town uninhabited. Although its extent did not change, not all the space inside the urban area was occupied (Ribera and Jiménez, 2012). For instance, in the northern part of the town numerous dumping areas and industrial workshops have been traced rather than residences.

## Demographic Analysis and Urbanization Rates

As the analysis above has made clear, there were quite some interventions in the urban settlement system from the conquest onward. Certainly this region where we find the Iberian groups has changed due to the imposition of some *coloniae*. Despite the large size of some of these new foundations, in general the cities remain small as Mela reminds us referring to the *parva oppida* of the coast (II, 80), in other words, there are signs of demographic continuity. As the area of the Mediterranean coast is roughly the same as the area of the Iberian group in Chapter 4 we can compare the RSA (Fig. 5.18).

In comparison to the Iberian pattern (Figs. 4.9 and 4.10) we observe that the system has become hierarchical, the *q*-value changing from 0.57 for the Iron Age to 0.834 for the imperial period. The more hierarchical system is due to the presence of the two large *coloniae* of Tarraco and Carthago Nova, both being capitals

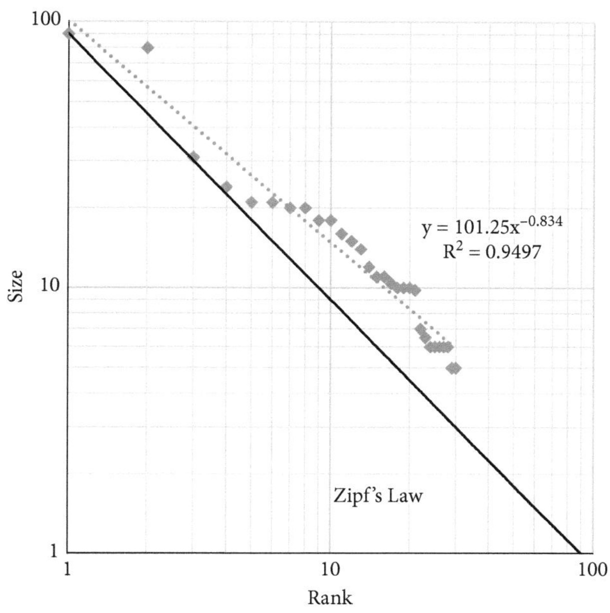


**Fig. 5.18** RSA of the imperial settlements of the Mediterranean coastal area over 5 ha (n = 30)

**Table 5.8** Estimates of urbanization rates for the Levant

| | 'Urban' | 30% | 25% | 20% |
|---|---|---|---|---|
| Low count | 105,000 | 350,000 | 420,000 | 525,000 |
| High count | 131,250 | 437,500 | 525,000 | 656,250 |

in different periods. However, even when we exclude the sizes of these two main centres we see that in general urban settlements have become larger. This raises the question whether we should consider this a concentration of the population or a demographic growth. On the one hand, we cannot conclude whether there is a concentration in the urban centres based on our density figures for imperial (200 to 250 inhab./ha) and Iron Age settlements (250–400 inhab./ha) (see Chapter 4), even though these are larger. In order to see whether we find a concentration we need to calculate the 'urban' population as we did in Chapter 4. The total urban surface, considering together all the sites larger than 5 ha, was 525 ha (Table 5.8).

Using the same urbanization rates as in Tables 4.5 and 4.6 for the Iberian groups we note that the urban population is quite similar. Hence we must conclude that the growth of the main urban centres allowed some of the rural dwellers to concentrate in larger cities where they lived in lower densities. On the other hand, we observe a continuity of the dense rural population (see section 5.4) in the region, which shows that the urban concentration phenomena did not take place everywhere and probably concentrated around Tarraco and Carthago Nova. As a result we find that in the Mediterranean coastal region the area may have seen some demographic growth between the Late Iron Age and the Roman period, but is likely to have been a small one and on the rural sector, something that has already been suggested for the territory of the Laeetani and the Indiketes in the north-east of the province (Sinner and Carreras, 2019). As we will see in Chapter 7, the stronger connections to the wider Mediterranean region from the Roman conquest onward led to a heightened commercial and economic growth, in this area related with a specialized economy based on wine production and the so-called villa system that may explain the population increase of the countryside.

### 5.1.2 Central Inland Area

Contrary to the changes of the urban centres of the Mediterranean coastal area, we see a stark continuation in the central territories of the province. Many Iron Age settlements continue well into the imperial period—in several cases even on the same site as the old city, thereby complicating the research into the size of the settlement over time. In order to establish the size for different periods we need geophysical and excavation data to allow the precise dating of the traces. Nonetheless, there are good examples of well-studied urban developments of Iron

Age *oppida* into Roman cities, such as Complutum shifting from a hill top location into the plain of the Henares river.

### Complutum (Alcalá de Henares)

Located on the central Meseta in the region of Carpetania, Complutum is a good example of how an Iron Age *oppidum* was transformed into a Roman city. The original settlement was located on the hilltop known as Cerro de San Juan de Viso, a Carpetanian site that covered a hill spur of 6–7 ha, which was later occupied by a military camp of 1.5 ha (Azcárraga and Ruiz, 2019). Most of the information comes from aerial photography, survey, and some test-pits, so it is still under discussion. Nevertheless, there was an Early Roman town covering an area of almost 35 ha confirmed by recent excavations that have provided evidence for a settlement lasting from 40 BCE to 40 CE. The *insula* module seems to be a square with 30 m sides, which together with the streets made a unit of 1 square *actus* (see Fig. 5.19).

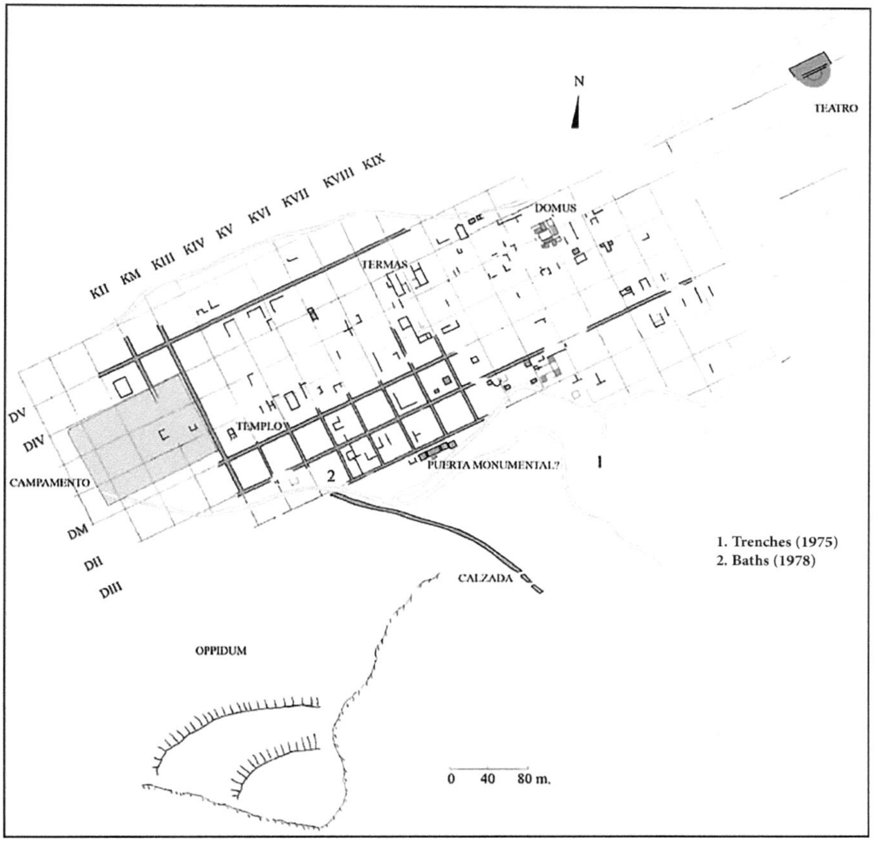


**Fig. 5.19** Proposed city plan of Cerro del Viso—Late Republican Complutum (Alcalá de Henares)

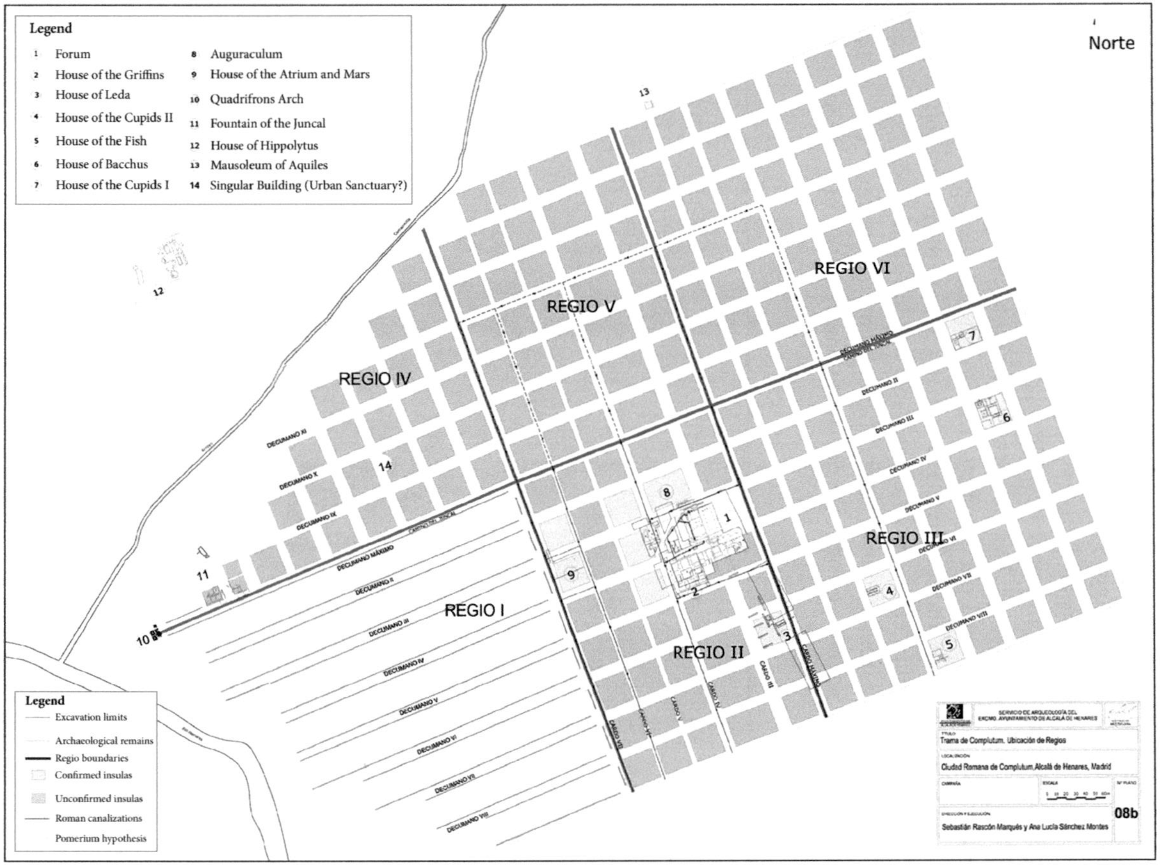


Fig. 5.20 Proposed urban plan of imperial Complutum (Alcalá de Henares)

However, the fertile Henares valley was a better location for an urban settlement, so Augustus designed a new town in the valley instead of on the hilltop. Although the initial occupation in the *regio* I are datable to the Augustan period, it seems that the construction of the city took more than 40 years.

The new settlement of Complutum was developed in the Claudian period, when the population of Cerro de San Juan de Viso probably moved to the new city, forming a town covering 50 ha divided into 5 *regios* (Carreras et al., 2017). The 50 ha size also covered the north-western and south-western suburbs, which included some religious buildings, *domus*, and a *fullonica*. Complutum became a *municipium* in 73–4 CE with the Flavian grant of *ius Latii*.

Initially, the city was believed to have had two different *insula* modules, one found in *regiones* II, III, V, and VI and another for the two western *regiones* I and IV. However, a recent geophysical survey in *regio* IV has confirmed the same module as in the eastern part. Therefore, it seems that the whole city was organized according to a regular grid plan with square *insulae* of 36 m including the porticoes, in other words a module of one *actus*.

In terms of urbanism, apart from *insulae* of 30 × 30 metres, there were two types of streets. The main streets, which included *decumani* III, IV, and V, were 12 metres in width, in which 3 metres on both sides were taken up by porticoes, leaving a 6-metre-wide central roadway. In contrast, the secondary streets also measured 6 metres in width, but without any signs of porticoes. The forum lay at the crossroads between the *cardo maximus* and *decumanus* III and contained monumental buildings such as a basilica, the northern baths and later curia, a cryptoporticus, the southern baths, a *macellum*, and a temple (see Fig. 5.20). The forum underwent a profound transformation in the third century CE (see Chapter 6).

The eastern part of the town was dominated by a residential area with large *domus* (e.g. those known as the houses of Bacchus, Leda, Cupids, and the Fish), which also continued in the eastern suburban area outside the walls. Besides, another suburban district, which includes luxurious residences such as the Hippolytus villa and a *fullonica* at La Camarilla, has been recorded to the north-west.

### Caesaraugusta (Zaragoza)

The foundation of Caesaraugusta in the middle Ebro valley was similar to other Roman foundations in Hispania Tarraconensis reflecting the importance of the Iron Age settlement. It was established by Augustus in 15–14 BCE on a small Iberian site known as Salduie. The newly founded city was laid out on a series of terraces shaped by the Rivers Ebro, Huerva, and Gallego and their possible flood plains (Longares et al., 2018).

The city was located in an area where the three cultural areas in the north-east—those of the Iberians, the Celtiberians, and the Vascones—represented by earlier *oppida* such as Salduie, Contrebia Belaisca, and Alaua (Alagón) met

(Beltrán Lloris, 2016: 303). It was another colonial *deductio* for the veteran legionaries of the IIII Macedonia, VI Victrix, and X Gemina legions, as is recorded on local coins and demonstrated by the legionary stamps recovered from the city. However, the local epigraphy also suggests a sizeable indigenous component in the colony's foundation, which reached an extent of 56 ha and 14,000 inhabitants (250 inhab/ha) at its peak under the Principate.

This mixture of populations was described by Strabo (III.2.15) with the term *sunkismenai*, which seems to refer not only to the presence of Italian veterans, but also to a combination of different indigenous cultures (Beltrán Lloris, 2016: 311). The early Augustan foundation only covered a limited area similar to that defined by the Late Roman walls, but in the Julio-Claudian period the city expanded towards the east and south, creating respectively what are known as the *barrio oriental* and *barrio meridional* (see Fig. 5.21). Besides, the western *suburbia*—present barrio del Gancho—included a necropolis and also an industrial area with pottery workshops.

The city reached its height in the second century CE with a large forum adjoining its northern limit, a riverside port, a theatre to the south, public baths, gardens, and long colonnaded avenues. The limits of the town at this period are clearly defined by the necropolis, landfill areas, as well as the sewerage systems (Escudero Escudero and Galve Izquierdo, 2013).

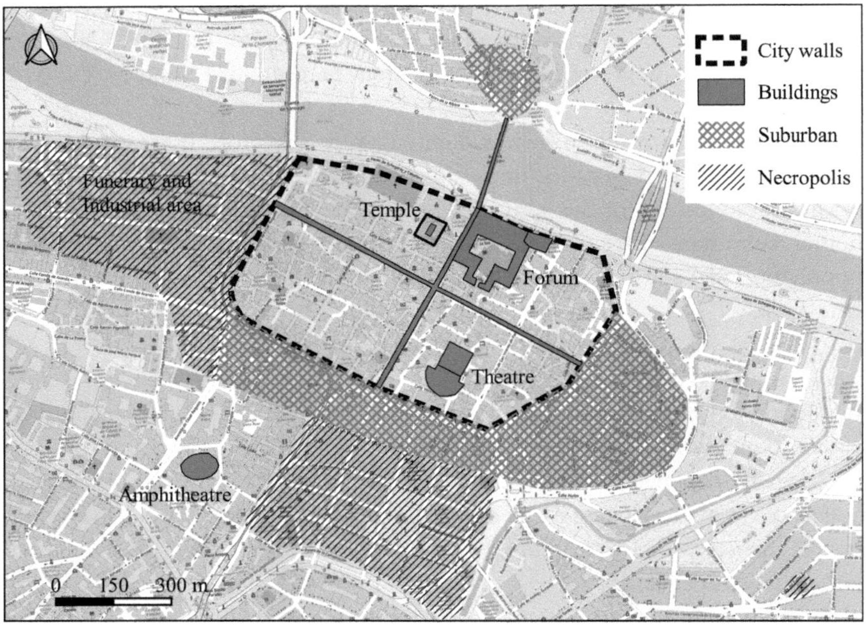


**Fig. 5.21** Proposed city plan of Caesaraugusta (Zaragoza)

## Demographic Analysis and Urbanization Rates in the Centre of Tarraconensis

As we have seen in Chapter 4, several of the groups in the inland had relatively high urbanization rates, that is to say their population tended to be centred on the large *oppida* within the territory. When turning to the Roman period we see a clear continuation of the centres in the settlement system, although in some cases the population had shifted the centre. The case of Complutum shows how the urban centre moved from the hill top to the plain. Whereas others were fully new foundations on the same site (Caesaraugusta) or near the old site (Clunia).

Calculating the population based on the total of 1,875 ha for the urban sizes with the urbanization rates is difficult. As we have seen, the Iron Age groups had different settlement systems and continue to do so in the Roman period. While we see a strong continuation in the Celtiberian and Carpetanian area, the Vacceans and Vettones seem more prone to shift towards urban centres abandoning the *oppida*. However, in the greater picture we see a slight rise in the urban area of the region as a whole (Fig. 5.22). As we have seen in Chapter 4, the groups must be considered rather urbanized taking into account the high urbanization rates that we obtained. As already stated for the central groups, their high urbanization rate in the Iron Age period may partially respond to the inclusion of rural sites due to the 3 ha cut-off point, which is rather low for the *oppidum* system characterized by large hillforts. For the Roman period we need to turn to lower urbanization rates, as the period sees a process of rural occupation through the

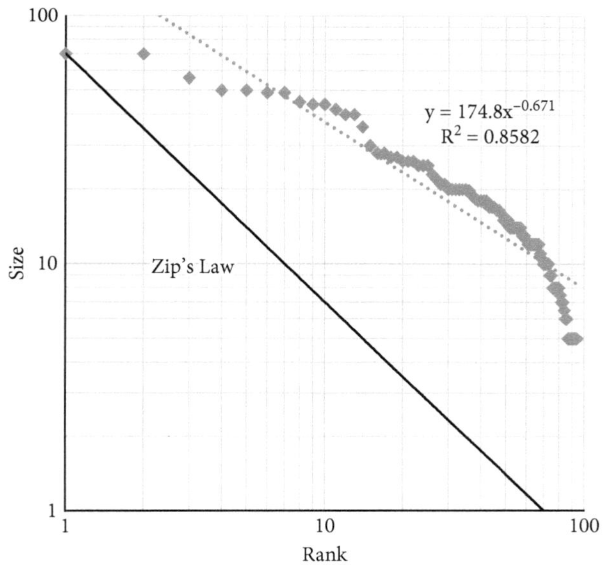


**Fig. 5.22** RSA of the imperial settlements in the centre of Tarraconensis over 5 ha

**Table 5.9** Estimates of urbanization rates for the centre of Tarraconensis

| | 'Urban' | 50% | 40% | 30% |
|---|---|---|---|---|
| Low count | 375,000 | 750,000 | 937,500 | 1,250,000 |
| High count | 468,750 | 937,500 | 1,171,875 | 1,562,500 |

foundation of *villae* and the organization of the urban territories (Table 5.9) (Burillo Mozota, 2008: 256; Noguera Celdrán, 2010: 17; see also below section 5.4).

An urbanization rate of 50% would be considered 'very high' (Bowman and Wilson, 2011: 12); a more realistic figure would be around 30% fitting the findings of Morley for Italy in the same period (1996: 182).

### 5.1.3 North-Western Coastal Area

As already stated in Chapter 4, we find the settlement system of the Castro Culture in the north-western region. These castros, or hillforts, tend to be rather small measuring only a few hectares, with the largest outliers reaching to 20 ha. In the north-western region almost all valleys are controlled by a castro, located within viewing distance of each other. This settlement system posed a challenge for the Roman conquest. Rather than conquering large sites and their large associated territories, the Romans needed to conquer each castro as the system was less hierarchical (Pereira Menaut, 1982: 255). Even though the Edict of Bierzo (*Hep* 7, 1997, 378) seems to indicate a hierarchical system, the *civitates* of the Susarri and Gigurri hold *castellae* as subordinate settlements. However the *castellum Paemeiobriga* belonging to the Susarri is granted *immunitas* as it sided with Rome. As the grant is not given to the *civitas* of the Susarri as a whole, it must be the case that the Paemeiobrigensis acted alone. This heterarchical system probably did not function well within the more centralized Roman state; as a result three new cities were founded functioning as *conventus* capitals: Bracara Augusta, Asturica Augusta, and Lucus Augusti.

#### Bracara Augusta (Braga)

The foundation process of the main capitals of the *conventus iuridici* in the north-west of Hispania Tarraconensis followed the same pattern. Bracara Augusta was an Augustan foundation dating to post 16 BCE in a region inhabited by the Bracari (Martins et al., 2012). The early town has produced evidence for a substantial indigenous presence in its epigraphy and material culture, although the city's layout is basically Roman (Fig. 5.23). The city was located alongside the course of the River Cávado on a 199- metre hilltop and exhibited a square grid plan.

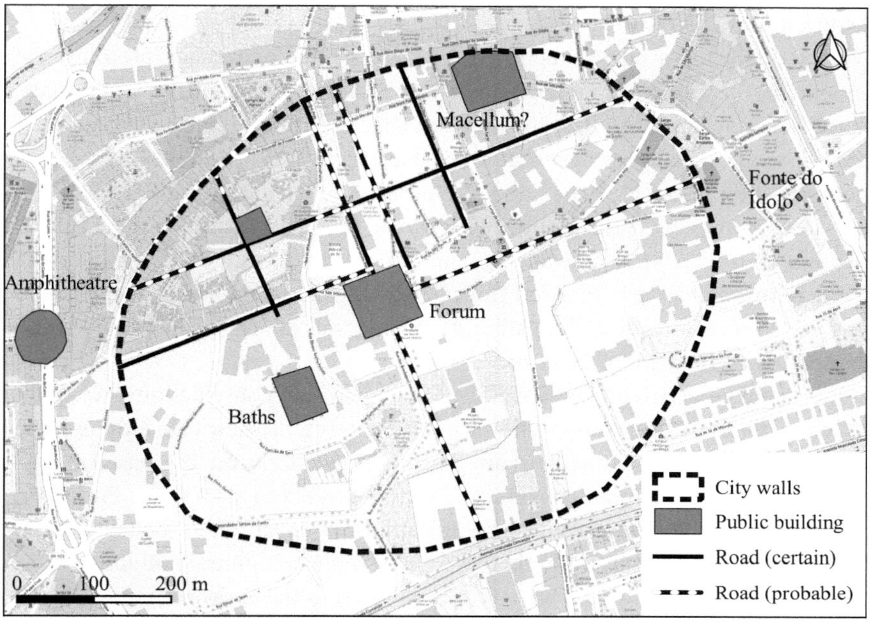


**Fig. 5.23** Proposed early imperial city plan of Bracara Augusta (Braga)

Although it was initially believed that there was an Iron Age *oppidum* in Bracara, more than 50 years of urban excavations have not provided any evidence for one. The earliest materials and built structures on the hill known as Colina do Alto da Cividade, where the forum is considered to have been located, can be dated to the Augustan period (Martins, 2004: 153). One of the earliest buildings on the hilltop is a bath-house.

However, earlier imperial remains are so few that it is difficult to recognize the urban plan of this time. The evidence increases in the Flavian period when the city's layout can be identified on the basis of some streets and sewers (see Fig. 5.23). Actually, the network of sewers seems to be datable to the first two decades of the first century CE. As far as it is known, there is a single urban layout for the city, so the Flavian plan must have been the same as the one in use in the initial period.

With regard to public buildings, a bath complex was found at the Alto da Cividade close to the city forum, which included a large *palaestra* with sides measuring 50 metres. In addition, there is a large building near the Cathedral (Sé Catedral) that was interpreted as a *macellum* due to the large amount of macrofauna remains, such as animal bones and oyster shells (Martins, 2004: 157–60).

Close to the bath complex at Alto da Cividade, a semi-circular structure with strong, solid foundations that seem to be identifiable as a theatre was discovered in 1998. In contrast, the amphitheatre seems to have disappeared, though seventeenth- and eighteenth-century antiquarian records indicate its existence.

### Asturica Augusta (Astorga)

Located on the top of an 869-metre hill without any sign of previous protohistoric settlement, the city of Asturica Augusta was born from a legionary camp established between the Rivers Tuerto and Jerga after the end of the Cantabrian Wars (29–19 BCE). Urban rescue excavations have detected a double ditch (*fossa fastigata*—first phase U-shaped and second phase V-shaped) of this early camp and some stones with the symbol LX, which probably identifies the Legio X Gemina (Burón, 2006). Nowadays, it is difficult to recognize the size of the original military camp (Vidal and González, 2018: 275–7). However, it appears to have covered an area of 26 ha with a perimeter wall of 2.1 km in length, being abandoned in the reign of Tiberius.

Afterwards, the two ditches were filled in and civilian constructions were built on top of them. A new stone wall was built enclosing the new city, although the site's topography constrained urban growth, particularly on the eastern spur where there is a steep gradient on its eastern and western slopes (see Fig. 5.24). Early imperial Asturica occupied an intramural area of 27 ha housing 6,750 inhabitants (250 inhab/ha), and there were also some extramural buildings.

A 5-metre-wide Early Roman wall was detected in the excavations in calle del Padre Blanco, which can be dated to the Claudian period. It seems that this early *emplecton* wall was complemented with circular towers 5 metres in diameter. The construction failed to last very long since by the end of the first century CE, it had been demolished partly to construct a private house (known as the *Domus de los Denarios*) (Vidal and González, 2018: 279–81).

The city's layout was adapted to the plateau with a completely rectangular area (430 × 380 metres) displaying orthogonal planning, and a triangular southern area, which included the forum and an irregular array of streets (see Fig. 5.24). The *insulae* in the orthogonal part are of different dimensions, ranging from a square block covering 3,700 $m^2$ to a rectangular one covering almost 1 ha (known as the House of the Great Peristyle) (Vidal and González, 2018: 281).

There was a main avenue (*cardo maximus*) that connected the rectangular and triangular regions and included some outstanding buildings such as the Greater Baths and the eastern side of the forum. This main thoroughfare was 10 metres wide and paved by large, flat, quartzite stones. The remaining streets were only between 4 and 7 metres wide and had porticoes along one of the sides. The central point of the city coincided with the Greater Baths at the junction between the north-west–south-east and north-east–south-west axes, which was also important underground as this was a point where the main sewers met (Vidal and González, 2018: 282). There were also Lesser Baths near the western wall, which may have belonged to a *collegium*.

The forum was located in the southern triangular region of the city, in which a three-sided colonnaded building, covering an area of 3 ha, appears to have been the most significant construction. On its western side, there is a small room

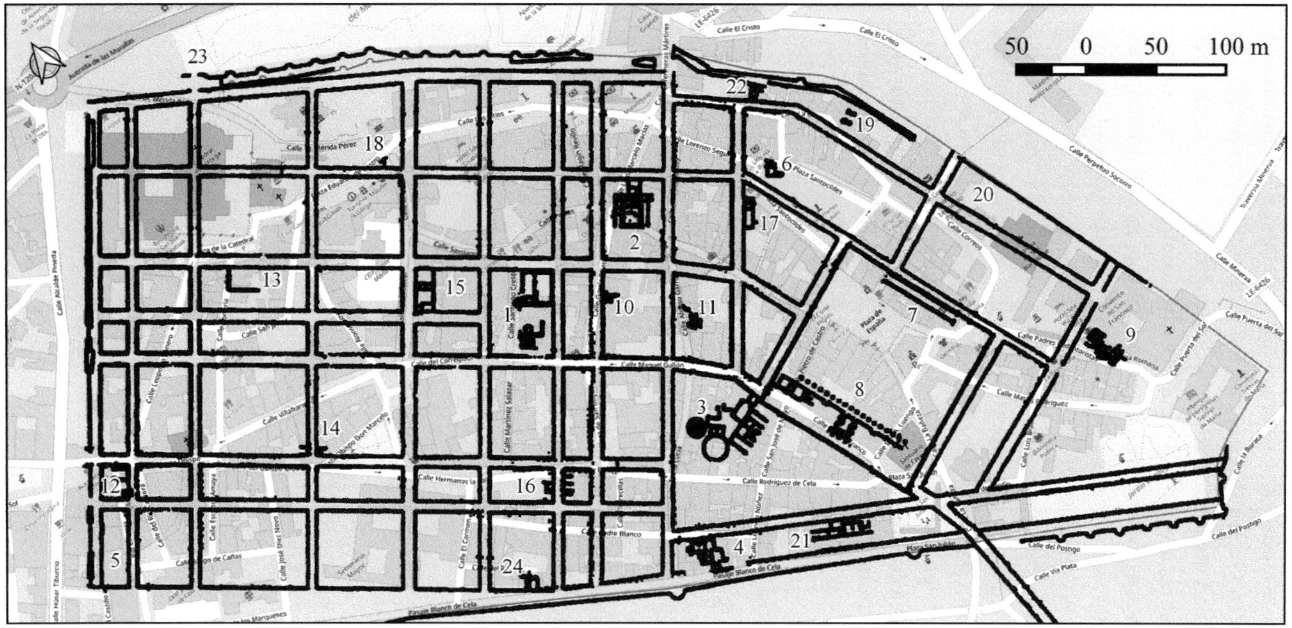


1 Large baths
2 House of the large peristyle
3 House of the opus signinum pavement
4 Small baths
5 House of the painted columns
6 House of the Pompeian paintings
7 Ergastual
8 Basilica
9 House of the mosaic with the bear and birds
10–11 Domus
12–18 possible workshops
19–20 other constructions
21 Domus
22 House at the wall
23 Roman gate
24 Moat of the encampment and later domus

**Fig. 5.24** Proposed city plan of imperial Asturica Augusta (redrawn after Vidal and González, 2018)

decorated with an *opus sectile* floor that was interpreted as an *aedes Augusti* or the curia. On the eastern side of the forum, rescue excavations detected a large, monumental exedra with a radius of 7 metres and walls of 1.5–1.7 metres in thickness under the modern Gullón theatre. The building continues towards the south with a rectangular plan measuring 90 metres in length and ends in another semi-circular exedra, creating a three-nave plan (with a central nave 13 metres wide and side ones 7 metres wide). Although excavation is still incomplete, archaeologists believe that it was a large basilica that imitated the shape of Trajan's Basilica in Rome (Vidal and González, 2018: 286–7).

As far as residential areas are concerned, numerous luxurious *domus* around the forum, which are named after the decoration of their mosaics and paintings (e.g. Domus of the Pompeian paintings, Domus of the Bear and the Bird mosaic), and the Major Baths have been traced in Asturica. According to local archaeologists, early imperial Asturica covered a similar area to the military camp, but with some extramural constructions (Vidal and González, 2018). Thus, it maintained the same area of 27 ha.

## Demographic Analysis and Urbanization Rates in the North-West of Tarraconensis

As was the case with the Mediterranean coast, the north-western area equates well with the Iron Age region, allowing a RSA comparison between both areas (Fig. 5.25). Unfortunately most research into the castros has one major issue, which is that most are identified and measured using remote sensing and lack ground trothing. As a result the data, such as the relation between built-up and

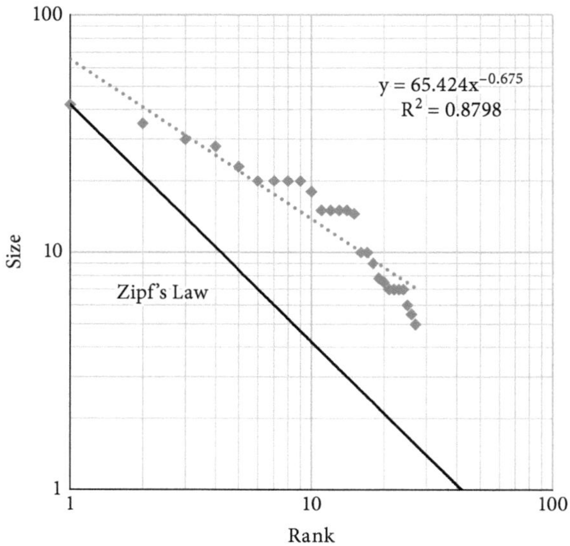


**Fig. 5.25** RSA of the imperial settlements of the north-western area over 5 ha (n = 27)

**Table 5.10** Estimates of urbanization rates for the north-western territories of Tarraconensis

| | 'Urban' | 20% | 15% | 10% |
|---|---|---|---|---|
| Low count | 84,000 | 420,000 | 560,000 | 840,000 |
| High count | 105,000 | 525,000 | 700,000 | 1,050,000 |

walled area, as well as dating, are uncertain and need to be improved in the future. Nonetheless, with the available data we can open the debate on suggesting a possible change in the settlement systems. Once again, the most notable difference is the overall larger size of cities in the imperial period. In the case of the north-west this increase also seems to be accompanied with a significant demographic growth, as the comparisons between Tables 4.16 and 5.10 show. In Chapter 4 we already discussed the exemplary situation of Citânia de Briteiros, where we observe the multiple extensions of the ramparts enclosing more space. Moreover, castros in the vicinity are abandoned, seemingly as the population moved to Citânia (Fonte et al., 2011: 362). The foundation of the *conventus* capitals in the region had a similar pull effect on *castros* in the wider region (see Chapter 7 on the case of Asturica Augusta). Despite the creation of the *conventus* capitals as new centres we see that the system with a $q$-value of 0.675 is not hierarchical. Admittedly, we are missing Tarraco as the capital of the province.

The Plinian account mentions that in this region we expect to find most of the dispersed *civitates* that are not centred on a city, but have one or more non-urban centres (Houten, 2021: 94). As a result of this non-urban organization of the region we expect a continuation of the low urbanization rate. Although Pliny mentions a total of 62 *civitates* for this region (Asturum (22), Lucensis (16), and Bracarum (24)), many of these might have been non-urban, partially explaining the low number of cities for the region. The total extension of the area can be estimated in 420 ha. Taking this as the ballpark figure for the urban extent of the region, we can calculate roughly the urbanization rates as shown in Table 5.10.

As we have already seen, Pliny provides census figures for a part of the region: 240,000 for Asturum, 166,000 for Lucensis, and 285,000 for Bracarum. This would give us a total population just shy of 700,000 people. Therefore, an urbanization rate between 12 and 15% depending on the low- or high-count estimations can be suggested.

## 5.2 Public Buildings and Infrastructure in Hispania Tarraconensis

As discussed in Chapter 3, among the more complicated and problematic proxies to estimate population numbers are urban features such as public buildings and infrastructure. As has been stated, by reading Vitruvius it might prove possible to relate fora and population size (Vitr. 5.1.2). In order to make this relationship feasible, Vitruvius must have been speaking about the size of the plaza as this is where the population would have gathered. As such it could provide us with a proxy for population numbers. Plotting the size in hectares against the size of the plaza we can begin to examine the relationship between these two proxies for population size (see Fig. 5.26). The provincial forum of Tarraco has been omitted from this estimate since its 11 ha would dwarf the other fora and make the graph unreadable. Unfortunately, the size of the so-called colonial forum of Tarraco is unknown. So far only the basilica has been excavated. If an attempt is made to reconstruct the size of the plaza based on comparable *basilicae*, the colonial forum would have been similar to that of Clunia. However, if we try to reconstruct the forum based on the assumption that the width of the basilica is the width of one of the sides of a square forum, we end up with a forum the size of that of Emporiae (Mar and Ruiz de Arbulo, 1987). Despite these uncertainties, the colonial forum of Tarraco most probably shared certain functions with the provincial forum in the upper city.

The graph shows that the trend is indeed that smaller cities would have had smaller fora, which is logical as there was less space for a large forum in a small place. Despite this logical trend, the spread is quite erratic, and it must be concluded that there is no direct relationship between forum size and city size. The largest fora belong to the *conventus* capitals. A few of these capitals are missing: the plaza size of Bracara Augusta is unknown; however, based on the six *insulae* of the city plan that seem to have contained the forum, we could infer a size of

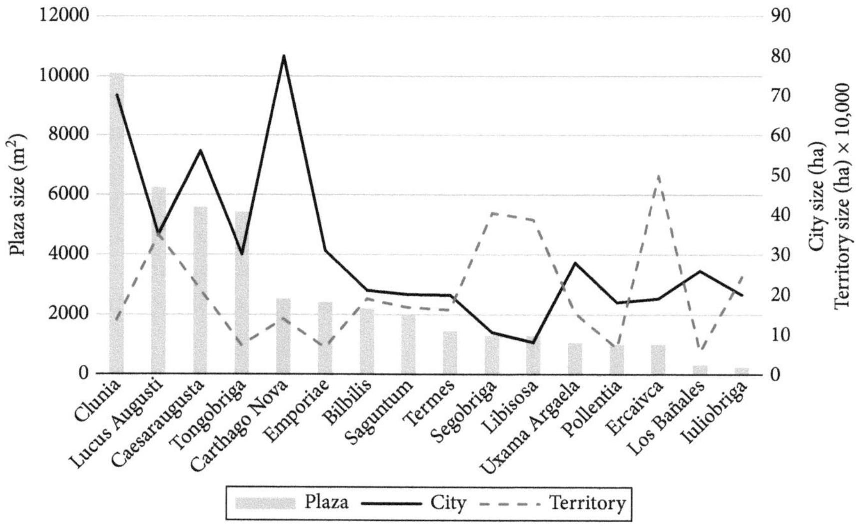


**Fig. 5.26** Forum plaza size compared with city and territory size

approximately 7,500 $m^2$ for the whole forum. This would include a rather large plaza. Similarly, we do not know the exact layout of the constituent parts of the forum of Asturica Augusta; however, the complete complex covered an area of approximately 31,000 $m^2$. The only *conventus* capital with a smaller forum is Carthago Nova; however, this is likely to have been the consequence of geographical constraints.

The forum of Tongobriga stands out. Even though the city itself is quite large, which has been estimated to have covered some 30 ha, its forum seems befitting for a *conventus* capital. As this is a city in a region with a low level of urbanization, it may have functioned, for example, as a marketplace for a wider region than its own *civitas* territory.

In the scholarly literature, monumental buildings are often related to the size of cities and their hinterland, based on the presumption that the whole, or at least the free population of the entire community should have been able to attend the spectacles organized (see Chapter 3). Unfortunately, the territories of the *civitates* are not known complicating our understanding of this issue. Nonetheless, through the use of Thiessen polygons calculated using least-cost paths, we can reconstruct territories including geographical limitations. Clearly these reconstructed territories are still very problematic, as the real territories were also created by the specific histories and evolution of each community. In those cases where scholars have reconstructed the most likely territory, this has been used. In other cases, we have used the Thiessen-polygon territory calculated; this would at least contrast less densely and more highly urbanized areas.

Turning to the relationship between forum and territory size, it can be observed that the line is very irregular. If we were to look for a trend, it would indicate a rise in territory parallel with declining forum size.

Another monument related to town-planning is the theatre. Although the theatre is one of the earliest Graeco-Roman monumental buildings, most of the theatres in Hispania were constructed in the Caesarean or Augustan period (Ramallo and Santiuste de Pablos, 1993; Ramallo, 2002; Sear, 2006; Noguera Giménez et al., 2011–12). As in the case of forum plaza size, this is one of the monuments most closely related to demographic estimates—the idea being that at least a part of the population would visit the theatre. For the theatres we can consider the *cavea* size, since this is where the attendants would sit, as the size of the whole theatre should not be related to the population. For the province under study there are only nine theatres for which the size of the *cavea* is known (see Fig. 5.27).

When considering theatres and their relationship to the size of a city or territory, it can be concluded that there is no relationship at all. The most striking case is that of Segisamo, a city of only 3.5 ha, which has a theatre with a *cavea* diameter of a massive 101 metres (Abásolo Álvarez, 1975; 1998; Olmo Martín, 2006). Since the theatre has not been excavated, and the measurement of the diameter of the

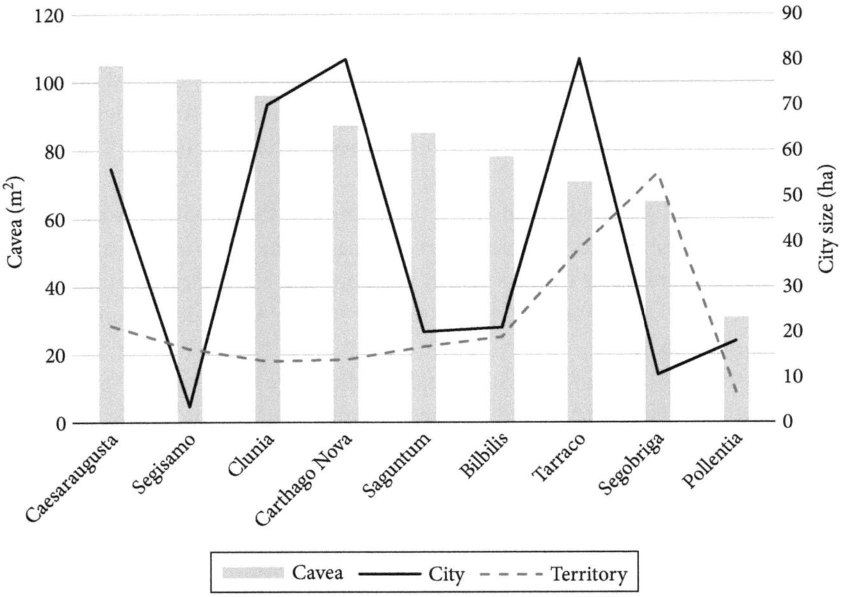


**Fig. 5.27** Theatre *cavea* size compared with city and territory size

*cavea* was made on the surface, it is quite likely to have been smaller. If the theatre was as large as proposed, the explanation may lie in the origin of the settlement as a military encampment (Flor. *Epit.* II 33.48; Oros. *Hist.* VI 21.3; Abásolo Álvarez, 1975; García Sánchez, 2016). Another possibility is that Segisamo was much larger than is generally thought. The estimated size of 3.5 ha is based on a suggestion put forward by Abásolo Álvarez in 1975. García Sánchez points out that the early city may have been larger than the modern town of Sasamón, as a few *insulae* can be observed continuing into the fields adjacent to the city (García Sánchez, 2016: 35).

Unfortunately, only a few amphitheatres are known in Hispania Tarraconensis. Among many probable amphitheatres, if we consider all the epigraphic documents mentioning gladiatorial games or even only expected due to the status of a settlement, there are seven certain examples. Our sample becomes scarcer when considering that there are only data referring to the size and capacity of four of these amphitheatres (Ceballos Hornero and Ceballos Hornero, 2003: 59). Even though a very small data set is under consideration, there appears to be no correlation between these parameters (Fig. 5.28). Although the large size of the amphitheatre of Segobriga might be explained by its extremely large territory.

The last spectacle building that allowed the masses to watch spectacles in a Roman town is the circus. Once again, the data set available is quite limited in size. In Hispania Tarraconensis there are 11 circuses recorded in the literature. From these, only six are documented archaeologically, and five have known sizes

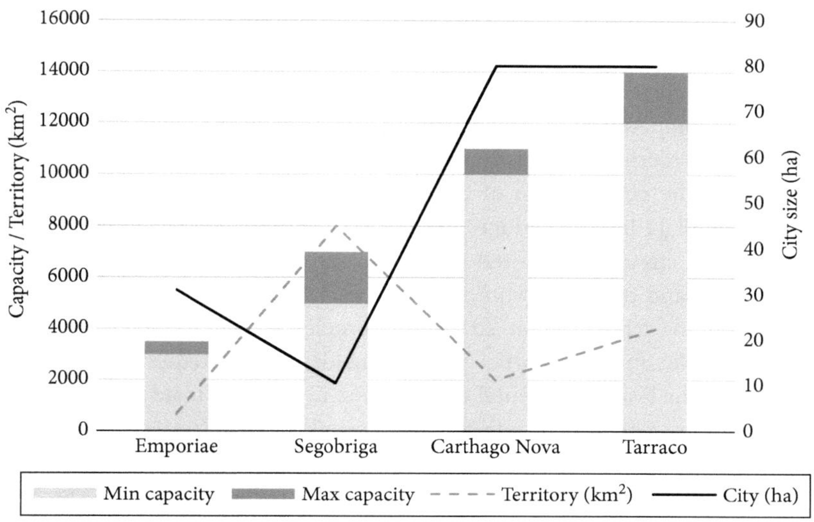


**Fig. 5.28** Amphitheatre arena size compared with city and territory size

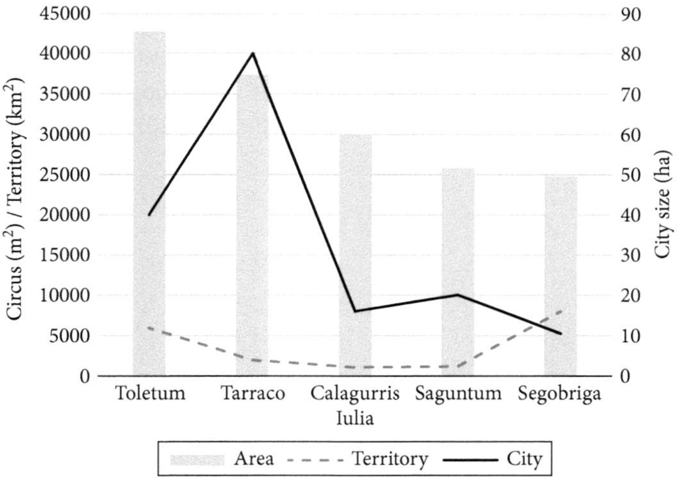


**Fig. 5.29** Circus size compared with city and territory size

(Fig. 5.29). There are two explanations for the small number of circuses: first, chariot and horse races could be held in any open field; second, and related to the first, circuses tended to be constructed at a later date than theatres and amphitheatres.

Sánchez-Palencia and Sáinz Pascual (2001) suggested that the Toletum circus may have been inspired by the construction of the one in Augusta Emerita. Since

Emerita has the largest circus found in the peninsula, this could explain the rather large circus of Toletum.

Conversely, Tarraco, one of the largest cities in the province, has a relatively small circus compared to the size of the city. The size of the circus is even more surprising considering the fact that it was part of the major renovations undertaken during the construction of the provincial forum by the Flavians, which covers a total of 11 ha. It could have been precisely this relationship between the forum and the circus that limited the size of the latter, as it had to fit between the *pomerium* and the new forum. Dupré (1997) postulated that the location of the circus may have been chosen so that the complex would resemble the complex of the Circus Maximus, the Portico of the Danaids, and the Temple of Apollo.

Turning to the last monumental construction used to calculate population, the aqueduct, it must be accepted yet again that we only have sufficient data in a small number of cases. The feature used to compare the different aqueducts is the size of the *specus* in square centimetres (after Martínez Jiménez, 2014) (see Fig. 5.30). Obviously a larger *specus* does not relate directly to a larger amount of water flow, as this depends on the source for the aqueduct as well as the capacity of the *castellum aquae*. For places with multiple aqueducts, we have totalled the area of the different *specus*, as these were most likely in operation at the same time. Moreover, as in the case of the circus, it is hard to draw conclusions from the low number of places with enough information. Nonetheless, it is apparent that there is no clear relationship between aqueduct capacity and city size. As has been stated by Martínez Jiménez, aqueducts were not key for the water supply required, but part of the monumentalization of the city (Martínez Jiménez, 2019).

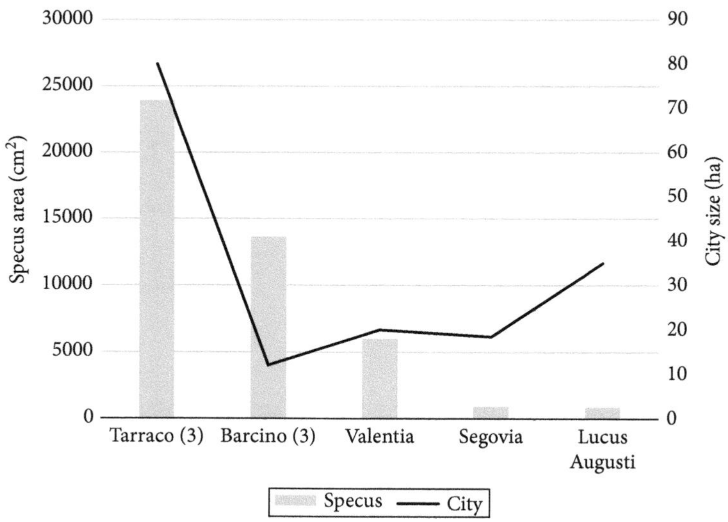


**Fig. 5.30** *Specus* area compared with city size

As has become clear, using the monumental constructions of different cities to calculate population is very problematic in general and certainly does not work for the case of Hispania Tarraconensis. First and foremost because the data needed are often lacking. The observant reader will have noticed that several cities constantly reappear in the different graphs. This is a consequence of research bias. Monumental cities such as Barcino, Tarraco, and Segobriga tend to draw the attention of researchers and funding; as a result, they are well studied. In order to draw conclusions, more research into the less well-known cities should be carried out. Moreover, and more importantly, from the small data sets it seems that there is no relationship between monuments and population. Even if the possible territory of a community is taken into account, this lack of connection appears to be true. Admittedly, this may be the result of the small size of the data set; however, there are other elements to bear in mind when turning to monumental buildings as a proxy for demography. As stated, the size of the monuments can be restricted by the geography of the city. Moreover, the size of a monument can be the result of the financial capacity of a community and/or its elites (Martínez Jiménez, 2019); we should understand the possibly never-used circus of Segobriga in this light. Peeking over the frontier of Tarraconensis, we can observe the largest amphitheatre in the West (excluding the Italian peninsula) in Italica. This monument was not the result of a large population but rather related to the city having been the birthplace of both Trajan and Hadrian. Italica became an imperial showcase to display the power and wealth of the emperor.

## 5.3 Secondary Agglomerations

The category of secondary agglomerations has led to extensive debates often defined by modern boundaries; in this category, we find the small towns of the English-speaking world and the 'agglomérations secondaires' of the Francophone debate (Houten, 2021: 130–74; 2022). In the Iberian peninsula there has been no overall discussion on this subject of significant urban and demographic importance. There are some publications dealing with 'aglomeraciones secundarias', but these are often regional studies without an overall understanding of the phenomenon. This section will only deal with four case studies in order to understand the role these settlements played and define the effect they had on the demography of the province.

To the south we find the port settlement of Portus Ilicitanus, which outgrew its primary centre. Thereafter, we turn to the inland region and consider the case of Segobriga to understand the relationship between a self-governing community and its mining settlements. Both these regions are relatively urbanized (see Figs. 5.9 and 5.10) and will give us insights into the urban–rural population ratio.

The third case study will turn to the north-west, where we examine Aquae Querquernae, a community with different centres each fulfilling its own function (bathing, *mansio*, military camp, and civic community). Lastly, we turn to the well-investigated settlement of Iturissa.

### 5.3.1 Portus Ilicitanus

The port settlement of Portus Ilicitanus (Santa Pola) worked in tandem with the *colonia inmunis Ilici*, which was located inland. The relationship between these two settlements pre-dates the Roman period and can be traced back as early as the fifth century BCE, when a fortified settlement was located on the shore of the *sinus* Ilicitanus (Márquez Villora, 1999; Molina Vidal, 2005). The port settlement at Santa Pola appeared in a period of enhanced trade with the Phoenicians, the port being located on the coastal route to Ebusus (Ibiza) and the Balearic Islands (Molina Vidal, 2004; 2005). In this period, the Iberian settlement of Ilici, possibly to be identified with Helike (Abad, 1984), must have been of great importance as can be observed from the impressive Iberian art found here, including the *Dama de Elche*. The connection between Ilici and the Mediterranean is evident from the artwork (Ramos Fernández and Ramos Molina, 2004) and the *Bronce de Alcudia*, Alcudia being the modern name for the site of the *colonia*; this land deed shows that the *coloni* were coming from different parts of the western Mediterranean: Icosium (3), Praeneste, Vibo Valentia, Ulia Fidentia, Malaca, Corduba, Aurelia Carissa, and the Balearic Islands (Díaz Ariño, 2008: 88).

The area of Santa Pola seems to have been abandoned, or at least activity there seems to have declined in the fourth century BCE, only to be reoccupied in the Roman period (Molina Vidal, 2005: 100). The natural harbour and the River Vinalopó created a favourable location for a port settlement. Molina Vidal suggests that the advantages prompted the Romans to reuse this place to construct a port settlement for the new *colonia* of Ilici (Molina Vidal, 2005: 87 and 100; Fumanal and Ferrer, 2007).

The *Bronce de Alcudia* gives 43 BCE as the foundation date (Chao Fernández et al., 1999). This early date of foundation is supported by coins from the city dating to the Second Triumvirate (Llorens, 1994: 170; Díaz Ariño, 2008: 88). However, an inscription referring to the *patronus* T. Statilius Taurus (*CIL* II 3556) points to a foundation date of around 27 BCE. The possibility of a double *deductio* would explain this inscription. It is possible that Ilici was founded during the Second Triumvirate and that veterans from the Cantabrian Wars were sent to Ilici in 27 BCE (Márquez Villora, 1999: 188). Nevertheless, it is generally accepted that Ilici was a self-governing community from at least 43 BCE onwards. Unfortunately, the archaeological record of both Ilici and Portus Ilicitanus is rather limited due to modern occupation of the region (Tendero Porros, 2004). Still, the connection between the two settlements can be asserted. The new *colonia* needed a connection to the Mediterranean, and the port settlement only 12 km from the *colonia* was the most logical site. Archaeologically, the reoccupation of the site at Santa Pola can be linked with the foundation of the *colonia* (Márquez Villora, 1999: 187; Molina Vidal, 2005: 100). Finally, there are indications in the epigraphic record that these two settlements were connected (Abascal, 1989: 14). That Ilici was an important Roman colony is certain. The evidence can be found in its coins with the legend C(olonia) I(ulia) I(ilici) A(ugusta), in its special status as a *colonia immunis* (Plin. *NH* III.19), in the large centuriated territory covering 11,340 ha (Chao Fernández et al., 1999: 423; Márquez Villora, 1999: 189), and in the monumentalization of the city.

An interesting feature of the settlement of Portus Ilicitanus is that it outgrew the city on which it depended. Carreras indicates 24 ha as the size of Portus whereas Ilici (Elche) only measured 9.8 ha. Admittedly, the port and the warehouses of the port settlement took up some considerable space. Nonetheless, we can be certain that the Santa Pola settlement was much larger than the area used by the port. Clearly, the port settlement became a centre for economic and demographic growth (see Fig. 5.31).

Situated near the boundary between Tarraconensis and Baetica, Portus Ilicitanus was a well-positioned stopping point for ships travelling from Spain to the Balearic Islands or North Africa (Fig. 5.31). Molina Vidal points to the predominance of non-locally produced Hispanic amphorae, which account for about 94% of the amphorae studied in Portus Ilicitanus and in the city itself (Molina Vidal, 2004: 193). During the Early Empire, imports from Baetica and the Atlantic coast make up 50–70% of the total imports recorded in Portus Ilicitanus (Márquez Villora, 1999: 206; Molina Vidal, 2005: 194). The large number of these products shows that the port of Ilici was a trans-shipment harbour for produce leaving the Iberian peninsula (Márquez Villora, 1999: 215; Molina Vidal, 2004: 195). In the first and second centuries, imports from outside the Iberian peninsula mainly came from the Italian peninsula. Products from North Africa started to arrive in the first century and took over the position of Hispanic products in the late third century, reaching 44.64% of the containers (Márquez Villora, 1999: 261). Products from the eastern Mediterranean do not seem to have arrived before the late third century; most probably these products were carried by ships sailing via Sicily, Sardinia, and the Balearic Islands (Márquez Villora, 1999: 289).

In the second half of the fourth century, Portus Ilicitanus also became a production settlement for *garum* and salted products. The port settlement declined in the late fifth or early sixth century (Molina Vidal, 2004: 195; 2005: 110). During

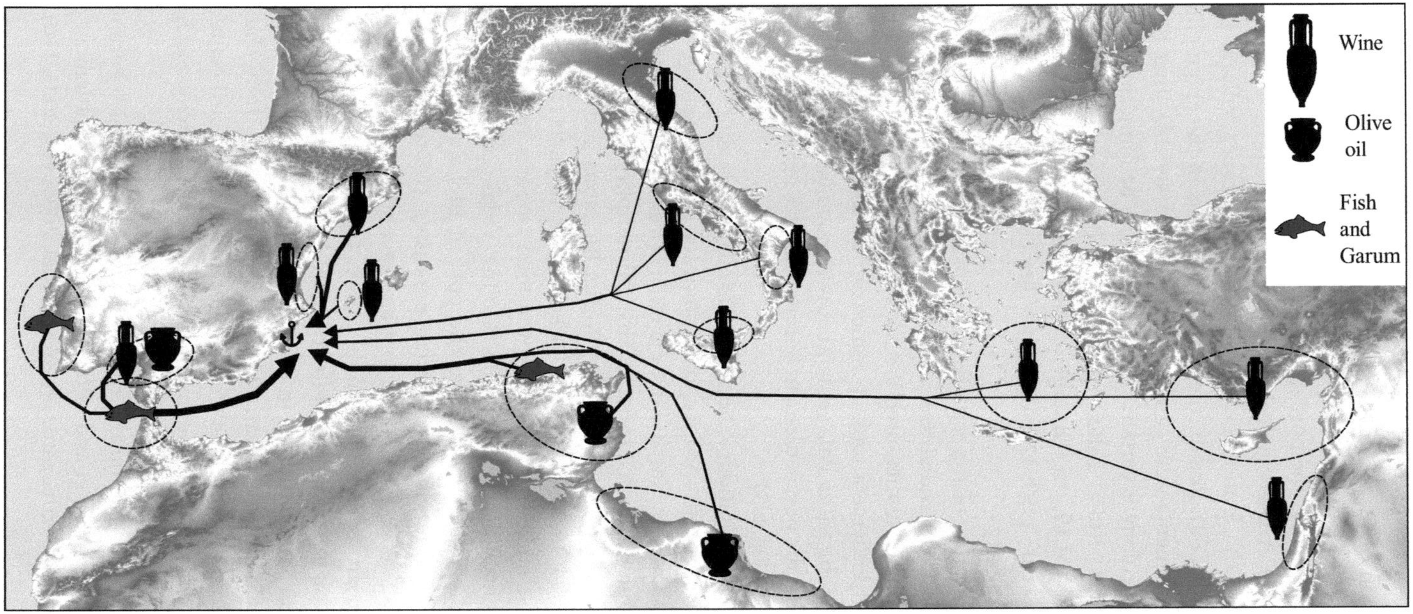


**Fig. 5.31** Portus Ilicitanus and its commercial connections in the first to fourth centuries (after Márquez Villora, 1999: 531)

this period, Ilici continued to develop and in the seventh century even became an episcopal seat (Gutiérrez Lloret, 2004).

### 5.3.2 Segobriga

The mining centre of Segobriga is one of the most studied and elusive settlements in the Iberian peninsula. The main city draws most of the attention of research due to its remarkable monumental nature; the 10.5-ha city boasted all three buildings for spectacles in addition to two bath complexes and a richly decorated forum (Almagro-Gorbea and Abascal Palazón, 1999). The city is rather small for such an array of monuments, and although only 20% has been excavated so far, it is expected that some other monuments, such as the main temple complex, still have to be uncovered. The question of where the population of this *civitas* lived must be raised. In order to understand the demography of this *civitas*, we have to turn to the ager Segobrigensis.

According to Pliny the Elder, *lapis specularis* mines could be found in a wide area around Segobriga (*NH* XXXVI.160). The comment by Pliny raises the question of whether he was referring to the territory of Segobriga or to the city as the

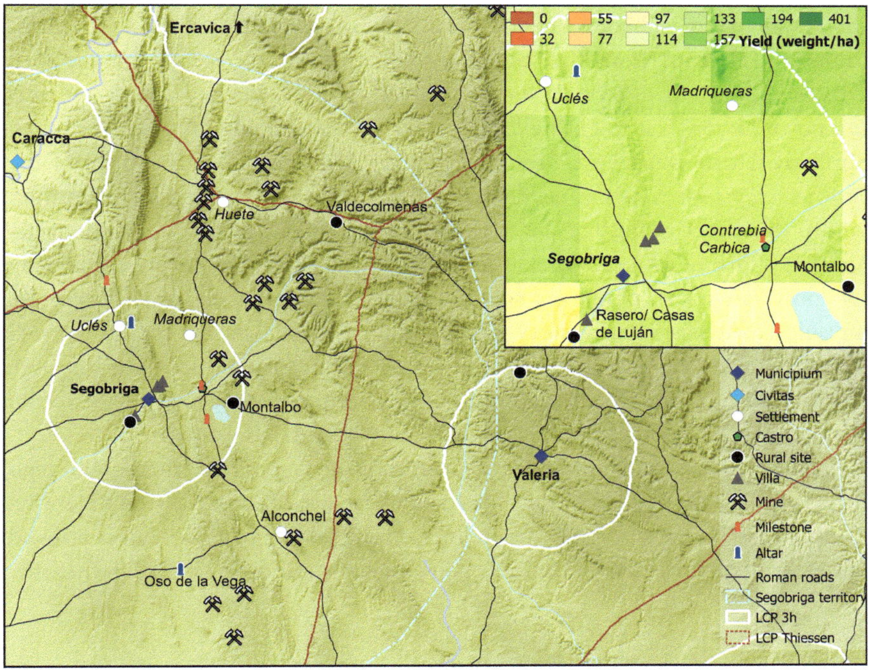


**Fig. 5.32** Territory controlled by Segobriga including the *lapis specularis* mines

focal point for the mines. By mapping the territory presented by Pliny together with the neighbouring *municipia*, it can be observed that most of the towns lie outside this large area, supporting the idea that Segobriga controlled the vast area containing the *lapis specularis* mines (see Figs. 5.32 and 5.11). Interestingly the settlements close to the major mining areas all fall within the weighted Thiessen polygons based on walking distances from the primary settlements (LCP Thiessen), strengthening the claim that Segobriga controlled the *lapis specularis* mines in the large area that Pliny discusses.

The secondary agglomerations in the Iberian peninsula need more attention and work. For the ager Segobrigensis we have a small well-studied section due to the efforts of the Audema group for the *Obras de Abastecimiento de Agua Potable desde el Acueducto Tajo-Segura a la Llanura Manchega* project (Morín de Pablos, 2014). This research has located and studied the different villas and some of the rural settlements in the vicinity of Segobriga. One of the important finds was the settlement of Madriqueras II, a Roman settlement measuring just under 10 ha (measured after Urbina Martínez et al., 2014a). The site had sewers, at least two of which have been identified, and a large building identified as a *horreum*. This site is a clearly a secondary agglomeration to Segobriga.[2]

Two other secondary agglomerations are Uclés (Oculis) and Opta (Huete). The site of Uclés has yielded a multitude of inscriptions. However, it should be borne in mind that the concentration of inscriptions at this site is a result of the *spolia* found embedded in the monastery of Uclés. Nonetheless, the most important element from this site is the altar to Aironis set up by the *gens* Ocules(is) (*CIL* II 5888). Unfortunately, the size of the settlement remains unknown although it might be expected to have occupied only a few hectares. Similarly, Huete must have been a secondary agglomeration in control of the northern *lapis specularis* mines (Macias, 2008). This is supported by its location within the direct vicinity of the important mines of Carrascosilla, La Mudarra, and Las Vidriosas. Moreover, it is located along an important route connecting two pre-Roman sites of marked significance: Ercavica and Contrebia Carbica. As a result, Huete has a long history starting in the Bronze Age and continuing well into the Roman period. The site of Contrebia Carbica is an important Iron Age *oppidum* in control of the larger area, but it went into decline after the Sertorian War and was replaced by Segobriga as the main centre in the region.

To the south we find another concentration of *lapis specularis* mines, although not as dense as the northern ones. The focus of this area must have been Alconchel (Macias, 2008). The site started as an important Iron Age *oppidum* but continued as a secondary agglomeration in the Roman period. It is likely that the

[2] The term *vicus* is often used in the research to indicate its secondary nature to the *civitas* capital. Even though the sites of Huete, Uclés, and Madriqueras are most likely *vici* in the official sense, there is no evidence for this juridical status and therefore the term will not be used.

concentration of three altars at Osa de la Vega indicates either a second focus for the southern mines or a sanctuary.

In addition to the secondary agglomerations, we find several sites with a clear Roman occupation layer, but not clearly identifiable as sites of major importance for the organization of the territory: Valdecolmenas, Montalbo, and the two sites at Rasero/Casas de Luján. To the south of Segobriga, 3.5 km down the River Cigüela, lie Rasero de Luján and Casas de Luján, both of which are clearly ceramic production sites facilitated by their location on the banks of the Cigüela. The main site here is the possible villa (or might it have been a secondary agglomeration?) of Casas de Luján, where a pottery kiln was found as well as a *balneum* (Urbina Martínez et al., 2014b). Lastly, there are some villas located in the ager Segobrigensis. However, a complete survey does not exist for the area and, therefore, we cannot be sure how many sites we would expect to find. Nonetheless, it shows the complexity of an urban territory. These villas were the closest agricultural production sites to Segobriga, with wine production being recorded at La Peña II and Llanos de Pinilla.

Macias divides the territories of the three *civitates* (Segobriga, Ercavica, and Valeria) into clear production regions. Obviously, this would not have been as strict as presented; nonetheless, it is interesting to reflect on different productive functions for the less understood sites. Montalbo, in tandem with the secondary agglomerations Uclés and Madriqueras, could well have been central to agricultural production for the territory. Turning to the agricultural production, an attempt can be made to understand the 500 km$^2$ of land under the plough today within a three-hour walking radius from Segobriga and to try to calculate the maximum population that could have been supported by this area in ancient times. The location of the three settlements at roughly two hours from each other and Segobriga gives the idea of an almost symmetrically divided territory. Moreover, the sites are in the higher yield area in the direct vicinity of Segobriga. Similarly, we find Valdecomas and Alconchel in higher yield areas within their territory.

Turning to the yield of cereals per hectare (Global Agro-Ecological Zones (GAEZ) web database http://gaez.fao.org/), the existing data make it feasible to estimate the land production capacity with different techniques based on a 30-year average (1961–90). The data set allows recalculations for arable cultivation without chemical fertilizers and modern irrigation. Note that the map indicates the output per hectare in cases where all the land was under cultivation. Hence the calculations present an overestimate of the population. Engels (1990) calculated the number based on the yield of barley: area of arable land * hectolitre yield per km$^2$ * fallowing of land = total hectolitre yield per year. The total yield then has to be converted into kilocalories and divided by the calorific intake per person per year. As we have the kg dry weight (DW) per hectare from the GAEZ data set we can simply calculate the calorific yield and divide this to get the population.

The total yield of the upper half of the territory within a three-hour walking distance from Segobriga, controlled by the secondary agglomerations, is 5,935,167 kg DW. This would support approximately 13,500 inhabitants. Note that this is a high-count number as it is based on all land under cultivation in the past 50 years. Segobriga with its 10 ha (excluding the spectacle buildings) would have had a maximum population of around 3,000 inhabitants. Estimating the three secondary agglomerations to have been no more than 10 ha, based on the size of Madriqueras, we would have a high estimate of 10,000 inhabitants in the direct vicinity of Segobriga, which would fit the maximum output of the land around the city. Taking Segobriga as the urban centre of the territory, we would have an urbanization rate of 30%.

### 5.3.3 Aquae Querquernae (Galicia)

The *populus* of Aquae Querquernae appears in Pliny, in Ptolemy, in the itineraries, and more importantly on the Padrão dos Povos, as a *civitas* (Plin. *NH* III.28: *Querquerni*; Ptol. II 6, 46: *Ὕδατα Κουακερνῶν*; Itin. Ant. 428.2: *Aquis Querquennis*; Ravenn. 320.3: *Aquis Cercenis*, *CIL* II 2477). The settlement system of Aquae Querquernae is rather interesting. The administrative centre seems to be Castro de Rubiás, a castro that continued to be occupied well into the Roman period (Rodríguez Colmenero et al., 1998: 905). Honorific inscriptions have been found in this castro, indicating its significance (AFFE nos. 591 and 608). Rodríguez Colmenero argues that this castro was the so-called '*civitas* capital'. Since the military camp was located along the main route, Ptolemy and the itineraries referred to Aquae Querquernae as the *polis* of the Querquernae without mentioning the castro (Rodríguez Colmenero et al., 1998: 908).

The fact that the area contains an auxiliary camp along the so-called *Via Nova* from Bracara Augusta to Asturica Augusta complicates the analysis (Rodríguez Colmenero, 2002; Vega Avelaira et al., 2009). The encampment probably belonged to the cohort III of the Legio VII Gemina. The camp follows the standard regular layout and was clearly created *ex novo*. Several buildings have been excavated or identified (Rodriguez Colmenero et al., 1998; Rodríguez Colmenero, 2002; Vega Avelaira et al., 2009). Measuring 2.31 ha, the camp is rather large for an auxiliary camp and seems more suitable for a cohort (Rodríguez Colmenero et al., 1998; Vega Avelaira et al., 2009).

In addition to the military camp and Castro de Rubiás, we find several secondary settlements; unfortunately, most are now (partially) submerged because of the construction of a hydroelectric dam. The largest secondary settlement is that of Baños de Bande (4.4 ha) (Rodríguez Colmenero, 1991; Rodríguez Colmenero et al., 1998: 905). This settlement is considered to be the military *vicus* and often used as the modern reference for Aquae Querquernae. Admittedly, the importance of this settlement cannot be ignored, as this was the site of the *mansio* that is mentioned in the Ravenna and Antonine Itinerary (Itin. Ant. 428.2; Ravenn. 320.3). Moreover, it was the location of the thermal springs and had a bathing complex, from which Aquae Querquernae took its name.

The military camp seems to have had settlements related to it. To the south-east we find the closest settlement, often considered to be the *canabae*, referred to as A Cidade (0.5 ha) (Palao Vicente, 2009). Again, not much is known about this settlement. On the other side of the River Limia, we find another settlement, Buraca da Moura, which was clearly related to the fort located to the north (Soares Fortes, 2008; Palao Vicente, 2009: 528). This has been interpreted as a gold-mining settlement.

Turning again to the population that this *civitas* could have supported, we find that the yield within the three-hour walking distance is far lower, with approximately 1,552,300 kg DW per year. Using the calculations proposed by Engels, a maximum population of 3,530 persons is obtained. Looking at the different settlements, an attempt can be made to calculate the total population. First, the auxiliary camp is considered to be a *cohorte quinquenaria*, which provides a total of 500 men (Pérez Losada, 2002: 187). The 0.5 ha *canabae* related to the camp would have housed about another 150 people. The civil settlement (4.4 ha) at the hot-water springs would have been composed of a maximum of 1,320 people (300 inhab/ha, 1100 using 250 inhab/ha). Adding the castros occupied in the Roman period would go beyond the three-hour walking area: Castro de Rubiás would have housed a maximum of 3,000 inhabitants. However, if we include the possible yield of the whole area, the maximum population that could have been supported would have been 7,500 inhabitants.

### 5.3.4 Iturissa

Another *mansio* of interest is Iturissa, which was situated about 30 km from Pompaelo along the route connecting Asturica Augusta with Burdigala (Itin. Ant. 455.6; Ravenn. 311.14). The name of the settlement is mentioned not only in the itineraries, but also in Ptolemy, indicating that we may be dealing with a settlement of some importance (Ptol. II 6.66). The settlement was partially surveyed and excavated in the late twentieth century (Pérex Agorreta and Unzu Urmeneta, 1990).

In recent years, various areas have been surveyed using a magnetometer (Garcia-Garcia et al., 2016: 243). In between the villages of Aurizberri/Espinal and Auritz/Burguete a densely inhabited area of at least 4.5 ha has been found. This settlement might have continued to the east filling the area up to the river and thus covering roughly 6 ha. The settlement is clearly a roadside settlement, as buildings are located along one main street, with some small perpendicular alley

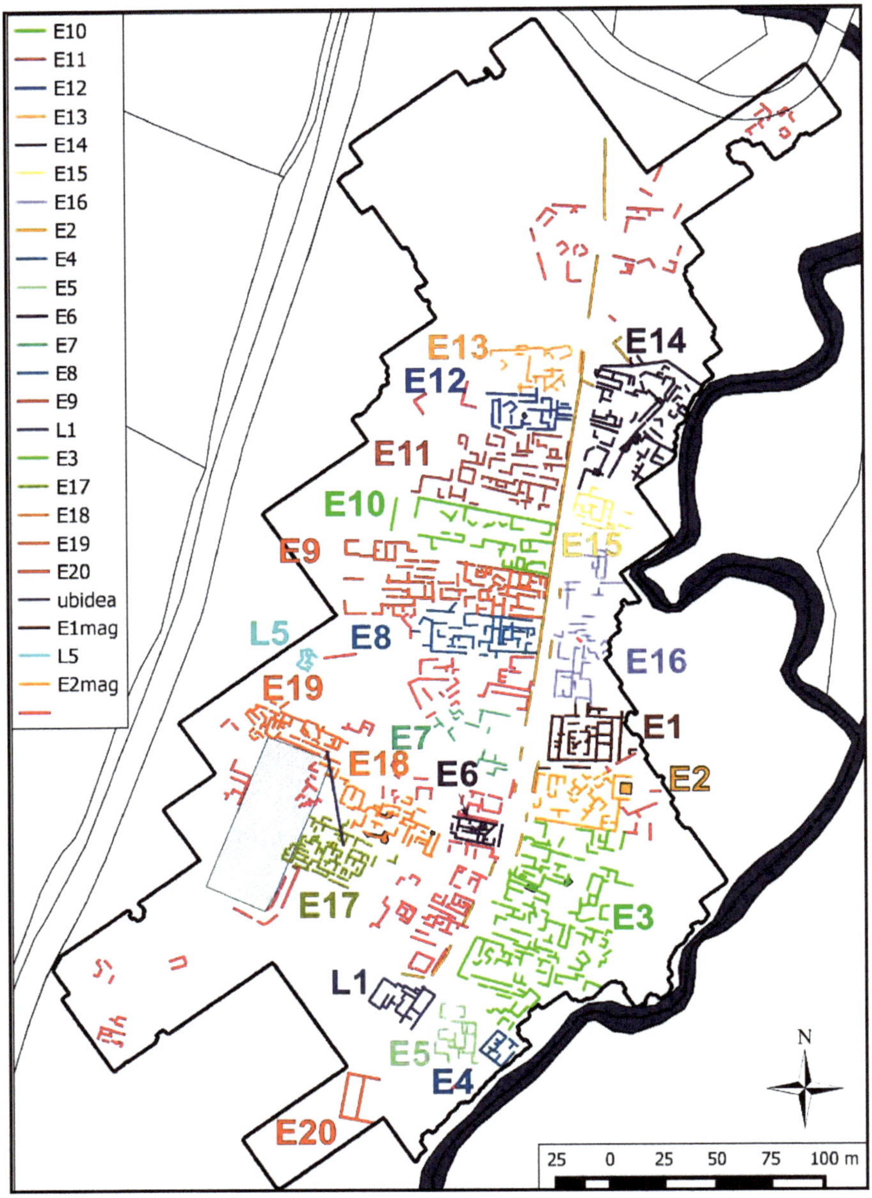


**Fig. 5.33** Results from the geophysical survey of Iturissa (Garcia-Garcia, 2017: fig. 4.3)

ways (Burnham and Wacher, 1990; Bénard et al., 1994: 46; Garcia-Garcia et al., 2016: 247). Garcia-Garcia (2017: 98) has identified several units within the small settlement based on their orientation (Fig. 5.33). Within the settlement a few buildings can be tentatively identified as houses. However, the variation in size makes it hard to give good estimations of population per unit. In addition, E4 and E15 could have been *domus* type houses. Whereas the row of structures in the west (E8 to E13) might be strip houses. Moreover, Garcia-Garcia and colleagues point out that these buildings do not cling closely to the main road. They argue that the houses were not built directly bordering the street but had porticoes. Porticoed streets are common for terraced houses in roadside settlements (Pérez Losada, 2002: 49; Garcia-Garcia et al., 2016: 247). The area to the south-east can be interpreted as industrial (Fig. 5.33: E3). To the south-west, we find a zone with limited magnetic activity that is delimited by linear structures (grey area between E17, 18, and 19), and to the east there is a rather large building complex (Garcia-Garcia et al., 2016: 250). This part of the site has been interpreted as a possible public area.

Population estimations for this small settlement are hard due to the irregular nature of its organization and the mixed purpose buildings. Despite these problems we see a rather dense pattern allowing us to use the estimations for the urban settlements (200 to 250 habitants per hectare). As such the settlement would have held between 1,200 and 1,800 inhabitants.

## 5.4 Rural Populations

As can be inferred from the previous pages, some secondary agglomerations acted as administrative centres in the countryside. They were more common in agricultural regions, mining districts, or territories where animal husbandry became one of the main economic sources. However, identifying distribution patterns of these rural populations over time is a rather complex task. In recent years, archaeological field surveys have provided alternative data that have shed some light on the rural demographic patterns (Hin, 2013). There has been a long tradition of field surveys by either foreign teams or local archaeologists in Mediterranean countries such as Italy or Greece, where there is a considerable volume of high-quality field survey data.

In contrast, the Iberian peninsula does not enjoy such a long tradition of field surveys, which have only been concentrated in particular regions and carried out by certain research teams (Knodell et al., 2023). Therefore, the currently available data are heterogeneous and provide a blurred image that may not be completely accurate. Normally, a number of sites of a certain period for a prospected region have been recorded, so a density of sites can be established, regardless of their dimensions. In spite of these difficulties, it has been possible to generate a map of rural distribution of the population in Roman times (from Augustus to the third century CE) from 72 surveys (Carreras, 2014: 69), with densities ranging from 0.02 to 1.75 archaeological sites per km$^2$. As the dimensions of each of them are unknown, a minimum low value of five people per site has been assigned to all sites (see Fig. 5.34) (Carreras, 2014: 69).

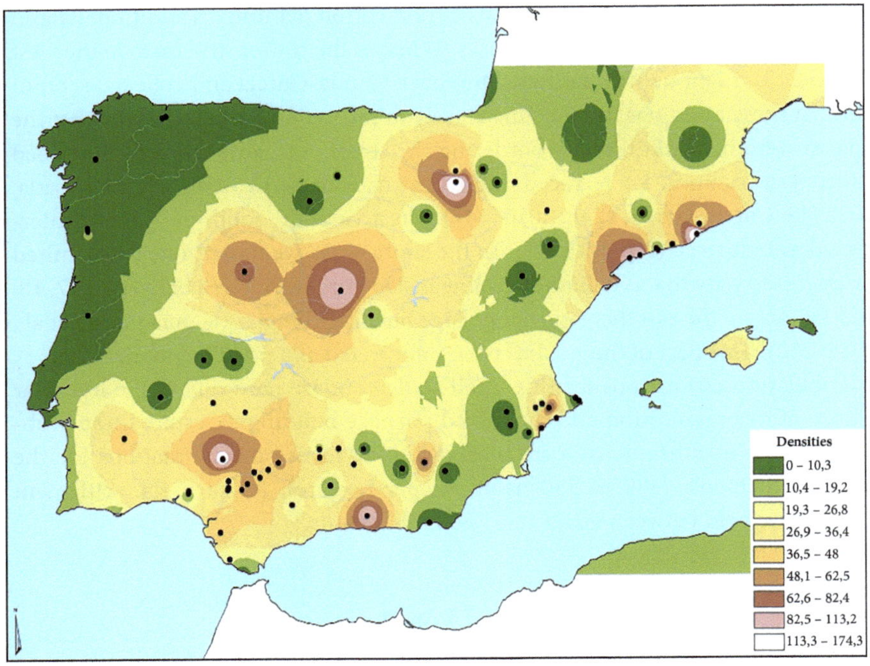


**Fig. 5.34** Distribution of rural populations according to field survey densities (Carreras, 2014: 69)

The number of field surveys has increased in recent years and, for instance, the list of prospections in Hispania Tarraconensis has reached a total of 55 instead of the 36 recorded in 2014 (Carreras, 2014) (see Appendix III). Despite the increase in surveys, the data are still poorly balanced, since there is a clear concentration of field surveys in the Mediterranean coastal strip, whereas the central plateau and the Atlantic north-west are still hardly surveyed at all so far (see Fig. 5.35).

Although the data are heterogeneous, a general trend can be inferred. For instance, very high densities of rural sites are recorded in the Catalan coastal strip from Tarraco to Iluro, which is consistent in all the surveys so far. A similar trend can be inferred from surveys in the Contestani region (Alicante–Elche), where the city of Ilici and its secondary agglomeration Portus Ilicitanus are located (see discussion above). There is also a medium density in the hinterland of Carthago Nova (as shown by the Tallante survey). Finally, the high density registered in the Huescar survey (Albacete) represents a strange case that requires further explanation.

Other high densities appear in the upper Ebro valley, which was a region of high urban concentration as well (see Figs. 5.9 and 5.10). In contrast, the low

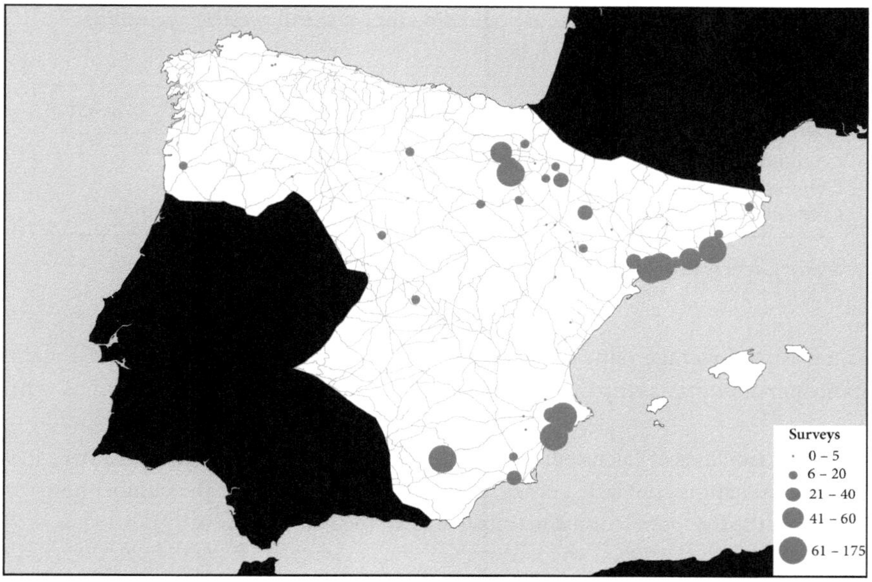


**Fig. 5.35** Location of 55 surveys recorded in the present study (density per km$^2$ of Roman sites)

densities of the central plateau and the north-west of the Iberian peninsula may be biased by the lack of surveys. Since most surveys do not provide information about the spread of archaeological material distribution, it is impossible to assign a site size and associated number of inhabitants (see Chapter 3). As an alternative a minimum number of five inhabitants per single site has been provided. Therefore, each set of survey data can be expressed not only as a density of sites per km$^2$, but also a conversion of density of inhabitants per km$^2$.

First, an attempt was made to connect field survey data with an ancient text by Pliny the Elder (*NH* III.4.28) that referred to the total population of the three north-western *conventus*. Houten (2021) has discussed Pliny the Elder's reliability on these specific data, since there appears to be a close relationship between the *conventus* population and the number of *populi*. Pliny (*NH* III.4.28) recorded that the *conventus* Asturum consisted of 22 *populi*, providing an average of 10,909 inhabitants per *populus*:

> Next upon these touch the twenty-two nations of the Astures, who are divided into the Augustani and the Transmontani, with the magnificent city of Asturica. Among these we have the Cigurri, the Pæsici, the Lancienses, and the Zoëlæ. The total number of the free population amounts to 240,000 persons.

**Table 5.11** Calculation of rural population for the north-western *conventus* from Pliny the Elder (*NH* III.4.28)

| | Total population | Countryside | Density inhab./km$^2$ |
|---|---|---|---|
| *Conventus* Asturum | 240,000 | 201,395 | 5.1 |
| *Conventus* Lucensis | 166,000 | 141,690 | 6.3 |
| *Conventus* Bracarum | 285,000 | 244,922 | 12.2 |

*Source*: Carreras (2014: table III).

Likewise, the average value obtained for the *conventus* Lucensis was 10,100 inhabitants per *populus*, taking into account a total number of 16 *populi*.

> The jurisdiction of Lucus embraces, besides the Celtici and the Lebuni, sixteen different nations, but little known and with barbarous names. The number however of the free population amounts to nearly 166,000. Pliny *NH* III.4.28

However, this argument does not work with the evidence from the *conventus* Bracarum, where 24 *populi* were listed by Pliny, which suggests an average of 7,291 inhabitants per *populus*.

> In a similar manner the twenty-four states of the jurisdiction of the Bracari contain a population of 175,000, among whom, besides the Bracari themselves, we may mention, without wearying the reader, the Bibali, the Cœlerni, the Gallæci, the Hequæsi, the Limici, and the Querquerni. Pliny *NH* III.4.28

Be that as it may, from the total populations of each particular *conventus*, one can subtract the urban population to reach a total rural population, which can later be divided into the area of each *conventus* (see Table 5.11) (Carreras, 1996; 2014: 64, table III).

These operations generate densities of rural inhabitants per km$^2$ in each *conventus*, which can be compared with the data obtained from field surveys in those regions and an average of 7.4 inhabitants per km$^2$. Unfortunately, only the Val do Cavado field and the Ave valley surveys near Braga are recorded in the area of the *conventus* Bracarum (Millett et al., 2000). The number of sites per km$^2$ was very low, an average of 0.06 sites per km$^2$. If a number of five people is considered for each site, the final result is 0.3 inhabitants per km$^2$, far from the 12.2 obtained from Pliny's data for this *conventus* or the 7.4 inhabitants per km$^2$ as the average value for the three *conventus*. Therefore, the rate of site recovery from archaeological field surveys makes it difficult to compare them to the historical data.

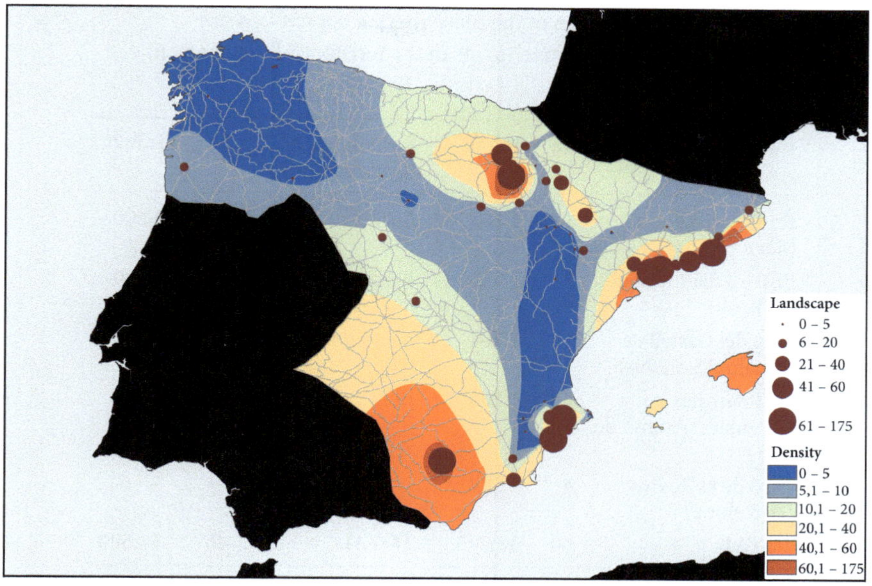


**Fig. 5.36** Heat map of the rural population based on 55 surveys recorded in the present study (density per km$^2$ of Roman sites) (author: Pau De Soto)

Other general densities for the Iberian peninsula in Roman times are supplied by Aüsbuttel (1998) and Corvisier and Suder (2000), who coincided in proposing an average of 10.1 inhab./km$^2$. Other nearby provinces to Hispania Tarraconensis, such as Gallia (7.7 inhab./km$^2$), Greece (7.5 inhab./km$^2$), or Africa (7.5 inhab./km$^2$), record lower densities that are similar to the average value (7.4 inhab./km$^2$) of our three *conventus* (Aüsbuttel, 1998). Despite the difficulties involved in relating field survey results to historical density data, field surveys still generate useful relative data to visualize the province of Hispania Tarraconensis as a whole. Fig. 5.36 illustrates a heat map with data from 55 surveys (Appendix III) and reinforces the idea of an irregular distribution of population.

One outstanding concentration of rural population appears on the north-east and central Mediterranean coast with high densities in the coastal strip from Tarraco to Iluro and around Ilici. This high density of rural occupation (Tarraco and Baetulo surveys, see Appendix III) contrasts with a low density of urban population (see Figs. 5.9 and 5.10) with the only exception of the city of Tarraco. If the population in the Iberian *oppida* is compared with the Roman towns in the Laeetani region (Sinner and Carreras, 2019: 318–19), there is hardly any difference (see Table 5.12).

Therefore, with the exception of Tarraco, the Roman conquest in the north-eastern coastal area of the province did not suppose a change in the urban

**Table 5.12** Comparison of the main Iberian *oppida* (> 4 ha) populations and the Roman towns in the territory of the Laeetani (NE Spain)

| **Iberian *oppida*** | **ha** | **Inhab.** | **Roman town (Carreras, 2014)** | **ha** | **Inhab.** |
|---|---|---|---|---|---|
| Burriac (Cabrera de Mar) | 10 | 4,260 | *Baetulo* | 14 | 3,500 |
| El Turó del Montgrós (El Brull) | 9 | 3,843 | *Barcino* | 12 | 3,000 |
| Puig del Castell de Samalús (Samalús) | 4 | 1,704 | *Blendium* | 10 | 2,500 |
| La Torre dels Encantats (Arenys de Mar) | 4 | 1,704 | *Iluro* | 10 | 2,500 |
| Turó de la Rovira (Barcelona) | 4 | 1,704 | — | — | — |
| TOTAL | **40** | 13,215 | TOTAL | **46** | 11,500 |

*Source*: Sinner and Carreras (2019: table 9).

populations as first thought, but probably a new pattern of distribution in the countryside. There are few Iberian farms in the Late Iron Age, which contrasts with the large number of farms, villas, and other rural sites in the republican and early imperial periods (see section 5.4.1 below). Most rural sites were close to the main urban centres such as Tarraco (effectively in the *suburbia*) and well-communicated with roads, rivers, and ports. A part of the agricultural production of those farms and villas was probably not only supplied to the nearby large urban centres, but also to distant markets (e.g. Tarraconensis wine) (Martín et al., 2020). The success of such long-distance trade may explain the new pattern of distribution of rural sites in the Laeetani countryside (see Chapter 7).

Likewise, the high rural densities around Ilici and Carthago Nova may have a similar explanation, although agricultural produce was chiefly destined for local or regional markets rather than more distant ones.

The other high density of rural population was recorded in the upper Ebro and Douro valleys (the territory of the Berones, Pelendones, Arevaci, and Turmogidi), where high urban densities were also recorded. Again, the Roman imperial peace facilitated the colonization of the territories of the nearby *oppida* (i.e. their *suburbia*) with different types of rural settlements, including villas focusing on intensive wine and olive oil production in regions such as Navarre. Apart from local consumption, some agricultural produce may have travelled via the main transport infrastructures (that is from rivers to roads) to medium-range markets. One of these potential medium-distance markets may have been the Roman army based in the north-west of the peninsular around the legionary fortress of *Legio* (León) (Carreras, 1997).

With regard to the regions with lower densities of rural population, such as the central plateau and the north-western district, the lack of surveys may have biased those values. Nevertheless, those regions also record low densities of urban population, so the results from the field surveys look relatively consistent. These regions offered poor conditions for agricultural produce with altitudes above 1,200 m (the Picos de Europa and Sistema Ibérico) and agricultural yields below 30% (the north-west of the Iberian peninsula) and precipitation below 400 ml/year (central plateau) (Houten, 2021). Therefore, the low densities of urban and rural population appear consistent with difficult conditions for agricultural production and a lack of transport infrastructure (see Chapter 7).

Historical comparisons may help to appreciate the diversity of population densities in the Iberian peninsula and compare them to the average density calculated for Hispania Tarraconensis (rural: 7.4 inhab./km$^2$ and total, including urban: 9.2 inhab./km$^2$). In the fourteenth century, the Christian kingdoms that occupied the former territory of Hispania Tarraconensis recorded slightly higher densities: Navarre (10.9 inhab./km$^2$), Aragon (7.72 inhab./km$^2$), and Castile (11.83 inhab./km$^2$) (Pérez, 2010). Before the arrival of the Black Death (1348), the different territories of the kingdom of Aragon also revealed some variations,

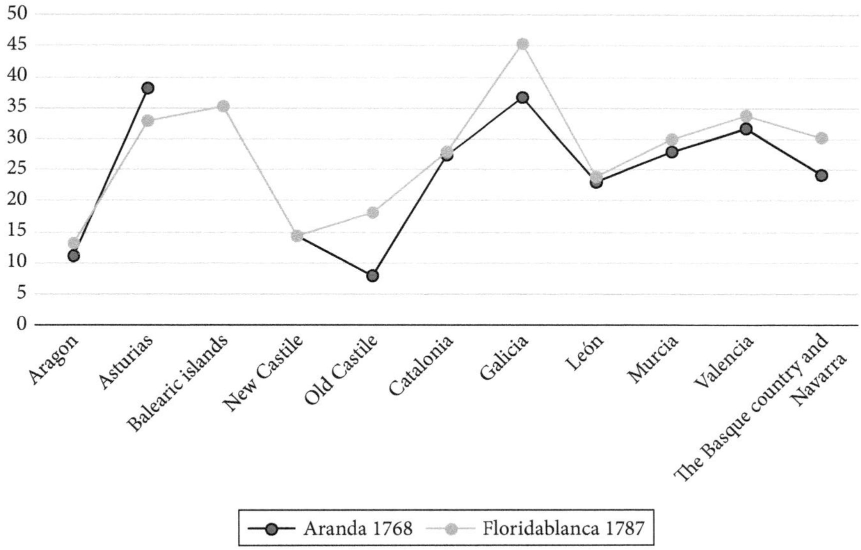


**Fig. 5.37** Population densities (km$^2$) in the north of Spain according to the official censuses by Aranda (1768) and Floridablanca (1787)

such as the principality of Catalonia (15.6 inhab./km$^2$), Aragon (5.23 inhab./km$^2$), Valencia (10.7 inhab./km$^2$), and the Balearic Islands (12 inhab./km$^2$).

Two centuries later, in 1553, the average density for the whole of the Iberian peninsula was around 9–10 inhabitants per km$^2$ (Iglesias, 1979). The major change in the demography of the peninsula was recorded in the eighteenth century with the first official censuses (1768: Aranda; 1787: Floridablanca) (see Fig. 5.37). Some peripheral regions, such as Galicia, the Basque Country, or the Balearic Islands reached as many as 25 to 35 inhab./km$^2$, whereas inland regions such as Aragon and the two Castiles attained between 8 and18 inhab./km$^2$. At that time, the distribution of population in the Iberian peninsula had changed completely since Roman times.

## 5.4.1 Ager Tarraconensis Surveys

There are only a few systematic surveys employing standard methodologies in Hispania Tarraconensis that provide good dating of the sites identified as well as details of their size and materials. This information allows us to infer the number of potential inhabitants and the evolution of the countryside. One of the areas that have enjoyed two systematic surveys with high-standard methods is the Ager Tarraconensis (Carreté et al., 1995; Prevosti and Guitart, 2011), in other words the *suburbia* that surrounded Tarraco, the ancient capital of the province.

The city of Tarraco, which reached a peak size of 90 ha including the extramural sites (see section 5.1.1), also recorded a very high density of population in its *ager* (106 sites per km$^2$ according to Carreté et al., 1995; or 93 sites per km$^2$ according to Prevosti and Guitart, 2011; cf. Schneider, 2017). Both field surveys have covered an area of 15 ha around the city and show similar densities and also evolution over time. They register a substantial increase in rural sites from the Iberian period towards the Republic and later into the Early Empire (see Table 5.13). This evolution of the Ager Tarraconensis does not differ much from that recorded by Launaro (2011) in different regions of Italy with an increase in farms (34%) and villas (68%) from the republican to the early imperial period. However, Hin (2013: 341) suggests that the increase in number of Italian rural sites is associated with a reduction in their size. The data from the Ager Tarraconensis survey (Prevosti and Guitart, 2011), which includes site dating and size, may be a good case study to evaluate this point. The survey includes detailed information from 23 rural sites dated between the Iberian era (fourth–third centuries BCE) and the Late Empire (third–fifth centuries CE), whose extent (see Table 5.13) enables us to point to a potential number of inhabitants for each period.

As pointed out in Chapter 3, the extent of material scatters from each individual site can generate a potential number of inhabitants on the basis of a site typology (see Table 5.14).

**Table 5.13** Extent of the 23 sites surveyed in hectares

| Site | Iberian | Republican | Early Empire | Late Empire |
|---|---|---|---|---|
| 1.1 | | 0.31 | | |
| 1.2 | | 5.48 | 0.94 | |
| 1.3 | | 0.26 | 0.26 | |
| 1.4 | 1.73 | 1.73 | 1.52 | |
| 1.5 | | 0.33 | | |
| 1.6 | 2.29 | 5.61 | 6.52 | 1.85 |
| 1.7 | | | 3.1 | 2.05 |
| 1.8 | | 2.69 | 2.75 | |
| 2.1 | | | 1.28 | 1.28 |
| 3.1 | | | | |
| 3.2 | | | 0.8 | 0.56 |
| 3.3 | | | | |
| 3.4 | | | | |
| 3.5 | | | 1.25 | 1.25 |
| 3.6 | | | | |
| MV | | | | |
| MP | | | 0.91 | |
| VS | | | | |
| MN | | | | |
| MM | | | 0.41 | |
| LB | | | 4.15 | 0.43 |
| EP | | | 2.45 | 0.29 |
| CC | | | 11.78 | 0.45 |

*Source*: Prevosti and Guitart (2011).

**Table 5.14** Conversion table of site categories from scatter extensions to inhabitants

| Typologies | Size ($m^2$) | Inhabitants |
|---|---|---|
| Large *vicus* | 800 | 80 |
| Large *villa* | 500 | 50 |
| Small *vicus* | 400 | 40 |
| Small *villa* | 300 | 30 |
| Large farm | 100 | 10 |
| Small farm | 60 | 5 |

The application of these conversion values generates a number of dwellers for each site over time, as well as total rural population for each period. Table 5.15 shows the number of inhabitants in this territory over time from the extent of the materials by fields and the calculation of inhabitants.

**Table 5.15** Number of inhabitants based on the site dimensions recorded by the Ager Tarraconensis survey

| Site | Iberian | Republican | Early Empire | Late Empire |
|---|---|---|---|---|
| 1.1 | | 62 | | |
| 1.2 | | 1,096 | 188 | |
| 1.3 | | 52 | 52 | |
| 1.4 | 346 | 346 | 304 | |
| 1.5 | | 66 | | |
| 1.6 | 458 | 1,122 | 1,304 | 370 |
| 1.7 | | | 620 | 410 |
| 1.8 | | 538 | 550 | |
| 2.1 | | | 256 | 256 |
| 3.1 | | | | |
| 3.2 | | | 160 | 112 |
| 3.3 | | | | |
| 3.4 | | | | |
| 3.5 | | | 250 | 250 |
| 3.6 | | | | |
| MV | | | | |
| MP | | | 182 | |
| VS | | | | |
| MN | | | | |
| MM | | | 82 | |
| LB | | | 830 | 86 |
| EP | | | 490 | 58 |
| CC | | | 2356 | 90 |
| TOTAL | 804 | 3,282 | 7,624 | 1,632 |

*Source*: Prevosti and Guitart (2011).

The overview of the population by periods makes the increase in the number of sites from the Iberian to the republican period from two to seven sites clear, with a fourfold increase in rural dwellers. From the republican to the early imperial period, the number of sites and population doubled. Contrary to Hin's (2013: 341) statement on villa size reduction from the time of the Republic to the Early Empire, the size of only 1 out of 14 declined, whereas most of them remained approximately the same size or were new foundations. The Ager Tarraconensis survey clearly demonstrates the potential of standardized surveys to shed some light on the evolution of rural populations.

## 5.5 Final Remarks

In the past century several estimations have been made for the population numbers of the Iberian peninsula in Roman times. These started out with high numbers from 6 up to 9 million by Beloch and have become more conservative as methodologies and research progressed; currently the estimations are around 5 million for the whole peninsula. As we have shown, the population numbers remain estimations based on the available, but incomplete, data. One of our main questions and challenges is to find the proxy that we can use to establish a population number. The most logical seems to be the size of a settlement, multiplied by a density per inhabitants number. However, as we have shown with the case studies, even when taking comparable cities from the Iberian peninsula, we end up with very different forms of urbanism and urban densities. The example of the 11-ha provincial forum of Tarraco shows that we need to be careful with proxies such as size. Similarly we have to consider differences between the walled area of a city and the actual built-up area. The case of Clunia shows that the walled area can easily include empty spaces whereas Tarraco has peri-urban areas.

As a method to circumvent these problems people have turned to other proxies such as forum size, seating areas in spectacle buildings, or water supply of aqueducts. However, we have shown that these proxies are similarly problematic. The first issue we have to deal with is the likelihood that the monuments of cities were not only for the urban population, but were meant for the whole community, including those living in the territory. Moreover, some of these buildings would have been created solely for intercity competition, leading to an oversized monument, giving space for more people than needed. In very specific cases we might see that the monuments had a supra-regional function. The fora of the *conventus* capitals tend to be larger as these cities were central not only to their own territory but to the whole *conventus iuridicus*.

Therefore we propose to continue to use the size of a settlement multiplied by a density number. Through our case studies we have established the density between 150/200 and 250/300 inhabitants per hectare for the early imperial period, based on a combination of archaeological evidence, census data from different periods, and the scarce information provided by the ancient sources. The size of the urban settlements have been based on the available data. When possible, we have used the established built-up area; in the cases where this is not specified we have to use the estimation available. As research into the settlements is a continuous process the size estimations are soon to be outdated. However, the general patterns will not change much with more fine-grained data due to the effect of diminishing returns.

In addition to the urban settlements, we have turned to the settlements in the territory. Unfortunately, the research into these settlement categories needs more work. In order to study the rural settlement systems we need extensive rural surveys. This type of research has only recently started to gain momentum on the Iberian peninsula. One of the early examples of such a study is the study of the territory of Tarraco, the Ager Tarraconensis. Similarly, we find that the intermediate settlements, the secondary agglomerations, between the rural and the urban are understudied on the Iberian peninsula. The few cases where we have been able to look at the secondary agglomerations show that they have an important demographic impact, making up a significant part of the non-urban population. Due to the amount of data that still need to be collected, we believe that future studies devoted to these settlements will aid in improving our demographic estimates.

The period of the Early Empire saw demographic growth in comparison to the low-count number of the Iron Age. This growth is expected when we accept the 0.15% growth per annum. Our estimations lead to an urban population of roughly 580,000 urban inhabitants and a total population of 2,600,000 people for the province of Hispania Tarraconensis. This leads to an urbanization rate of 22%, which in some regions would have been higher, reaching up to 30%. It is interesting to point out that the urbanization rate has lowered in comparison to the Iron Age and the demographic growth seems to take place in the countryside, something that is also confirmed by the existing surveys. We only see a significant urban demographic change in the north-west of the province. This difference, however, is likely to find its origins due to the clearer urban organization in the Roman period. With the given juridical status of communities, we can draw a line between what to consider urban and what not. It is quite likely that an important number of the 'urban' settlements of the Iron Age (see Appendix I and Chapter 4), are considered secondary agglomerations in the Roman period. Besides this shift due to definition, we see a clear change in the concentration of urban centres in some areas of Tarraconensis from the Iron Age into the Roman period. Although the large inland cities in the centre of the province continue, the Mediterranean coastal area sees a clear concentration of population in new and larger urban centres. The general pattern shows a relatively discrete trend of rising population from the Iron Age to the Early Empire. However, as we will see in the next chapter, this pattern of growth is halted in late antiquity.

*The Human Factor: The Demography of the Roman Province of Hispania Citerior/Tarraconensis.* Alejandro G. Sinner, Cèsar Carreras, and Pieter Houten, Oxford University Press. 
DOI: 10.1093/9780191943881.003.0005

# 6

# Population and Urbanization in the Late Roman Period

In the late second century or early third century CE, the province of Hispania Tarraconensis (see Fig. 1.1), divided after Diocletian reforms into Tarraconensis, Gallaecia, and Carthaginensis, experienced major economic changes that are evident from the reduction in size and even abandonment of some of its cities (Brassous and Quevedo, 2015; Andreu, 2017; Andreu and Blanco Pérez, 2019). Despite the fact that academic tradition dates the crisis of the cities of Hispania to the late third century CE, some archaeological evidence suggests an earlier urban crisis that affected each region in a different way. The traditional model of the late third-century crisis relied on limited literary evidence, such as that for the invasion of the *Mauri* in the reign of Marcus Aurelius and the Frankish raid (*c.* 260 CE) (Kulikowski, 2010: 86).

The third century also witnessed a substantial downturn in mining activity, although current research reveals that most mines continued to be exploited afterwards, but it was less intensive than in previous periods (Edmondson, 1989). The great extraction works (*metalla*) with hydraulic infrastructure probably declined (that is what are generally known as *ruina montium*), and mining administration also moved from public to private hands (Montero and Orejas, 2018). In this new context, the mining districts were no longer a pole of attraction for regional migration as discussed in Chapter 7.

Recent research on palaeoclimates has identified a major climate change in the late second century CE in the Western Roman Empire, when the Roman Climatic Optimum (RCO) (200 BCE–150 CE),[1] characterized by warmer temperatures, shifted to a cooler period with intervals of cold temperatures of 5° below zero and dry seasons alongside volcanic eruptions (*c.* 235–285 CE) (McCormick et al., 2012). It is still difficult to know how this change affected the province under study, but it may explain the depopulation of some cities and the renewed occupation of the countryside in the fourth century CE. Harper (2019) argues that this climate change triggered famines and the spread of pandemics (the Antonine plague) (see Chapter 8 for its impact on Hispania), which produced urban depopulation and a widespread demographic crisis in some Roman provinces.

[1] The chronology is based on Greenland ice cores, dendrodata of summer temperatures in the Austrian Alps, and evidence from Britain (Erdkamp, 2021).

Signs of urban abandonment are evident in Hispania Tarraconensis in fora modified or dismantled in the third century CE (e.g. Los Bañales, Segobriga, Llívia) as well as waste-dumping areas and burials inside the walls (e.g. Tarraco). This raises the question of whether this is proof of the city being abandoned or indicative that people were still using the urban site, albeit in a different way than expected for the imperial period. At the very least, it does indicate abandonment or reuse of certain sectors of the city. Besides, many cities refurbished their defences during the third century CE, perhaps as a response to the Frankish invasion (*c.* 260 CE), or possibly simply as a way of guaranteeing security. The perimeters of those cities walled in both the Principate and the Late Roman period, were reduced, except for the possible case of Bracara Augusta (Carreras, 2014; De Soto and Carreras, 2022). According to Ausonius in his letters to Paulinus (*Ep.* 29.50–1), some of the small towns in the Ebro valley exhibited signs of decadence. He described Ilerda as arid and in ruins, Bilbilis as inhospitable, and Calagurris as being in the same situation.

## 6.1 The Cities and Population in Hispania Tarraconensis in the Late Roman Period

Contrary to the opinion of Kulikowski (2010: 85), who argued that the largest cities in Roman Spain grew substantially in the Late Roman period, the archaeological data from Hispania Tarraconensis show a much more diverse reality. A clear reduction in size, at least in the Mediterranean region can be documented. The extent of the capital, Tarraco, was reduced by almost 66%, Carthago Nova by 50%, and Caesaraugusta by 20%. However, the *conventus* capitals in the north-west remained unaltered, and Bracara Augusta slightly increased in size. We should see this growth in the light of the creation of the new province of Gallaecia, with Bracara as its capital and its continuation as capital in the Suebic kingdom.

The urban system of late antiquity saw mayor changes. One of the most important ones in the period is the loss of significance of the Roman juridical status, even though it is unclear at what time the relevance of the status of *colonia* or *municipium* is lost. In late antiquity the importance of places was based on the presence of episcopal and metropolitan sees. Interestingly, these sees do not follow the old urban system; places like Urgellum, Brittonia, and Dumio are new centres that rose as they became episcopal sees (see Fig. 6.1). Similarly, we find Toletum, a rather standard *municipium* in the Early Empire, as the capital of the Visigothic kingdom. Despite these new towns, the limited number of cities that seem to continue could not have provided the same coverage as the administrative system of the Early Empire. This raises the, so far unanswered question, how to identify the cities or central places of late antique Hispania and how the vast peninsula was spatially organized (Houten and Panzram, forthcoming).

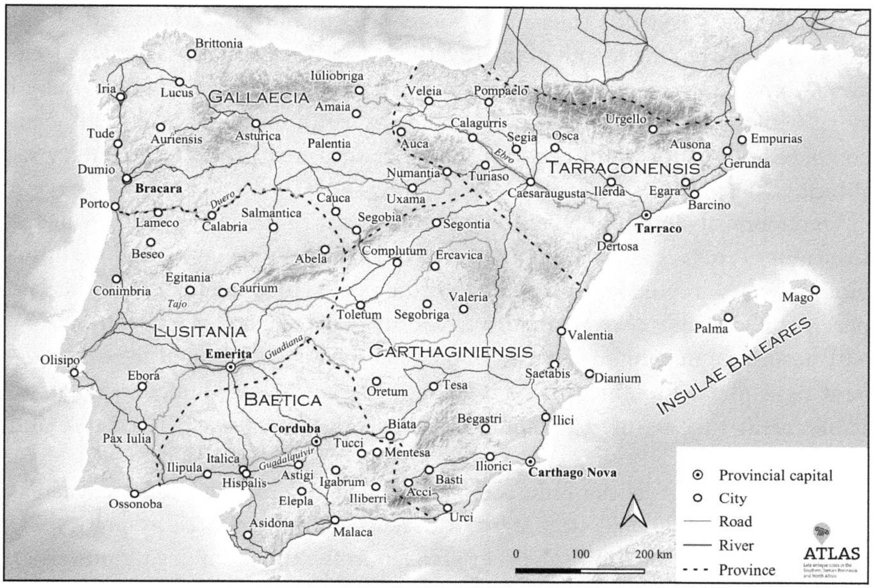


**Fig. 6.1** Map showing the cities of Hispania in the fourth century CE (after Panzram, 2019)

Without the administrative or juridical characterization of the Early Empire a definition of the late antique city needs to be made. However, creating such a definition goes beyond the scope of this book. Most likely this definition needs to be based on archaeological evidence as the civic epigraphy ends in the late fourth to early fifth century CE. As to be expected, the archaeological data for this period are hard to interpret. On the one hand, this is due to the historical interest in the imperial period in earlier excavations, ignoring and destroying late antique layers. On the other hand, as already stated, it is hard to define the boundaries or size of cities with partial abandonment or reuse of inner-city sectors and newly created *suburbia*. Nonetheless, a short survey of the seven early imperial cities described in Chapter 5 reveals that different urban realities and evolutions took place in Hispania Tarraconensis during this period, and in many cases clear signs of abandonment and size reduction were experienced during late antiquity.

### 6.1.1 Mediterranean Coastal Area

#### Tarraco (Tarragona)

The extent of the city seems to have contracted in the mid-second century CE to 50–60 ha. The whole urban change process ended in the late fourth century CE when Tarraco became a double city: an official, administrative centre in the upper part under the governor's rule, and a poorer settlement in the coastal strip from the ancient port to the mouth of the River Francolí. The coastal quarter was 1 km away from the upper urban core and consisted of humble houses made of reused stone without tiles and mortar, with the only exception of an extramural bath complex built in the third century CE and refurnished in the fifth century CE (Macias, 2000: 262).

Developments in the fifth century CE in the dual-centre city resulted with the Concilium Provinciae in the upper part of the urban area being reused for humble residences and the lower district near the port being maintained. In this late period, the city only covered an area of approximately 30 ha (Macias, 2013: 134), which means a maximum population of 7,500 inhabitants. One of the most evident signs of abandonment is the presence of large rubbish dumps in the main public areas such as the Concilium Provinciae in the upper part (Dupré and Remolà, 2002).

The upper city was the only completely inhabited part of the site, whereas the lower town exhibited clear signs of decadence (see Fig. 6.2). Actually, there were levels of destruction in the port area (from the third century CE onwards), and the forum of the colony was abandoned along with the lower urban area (Macias, 2000: 261), which is evident from the disuse of the sewer system. Besides,

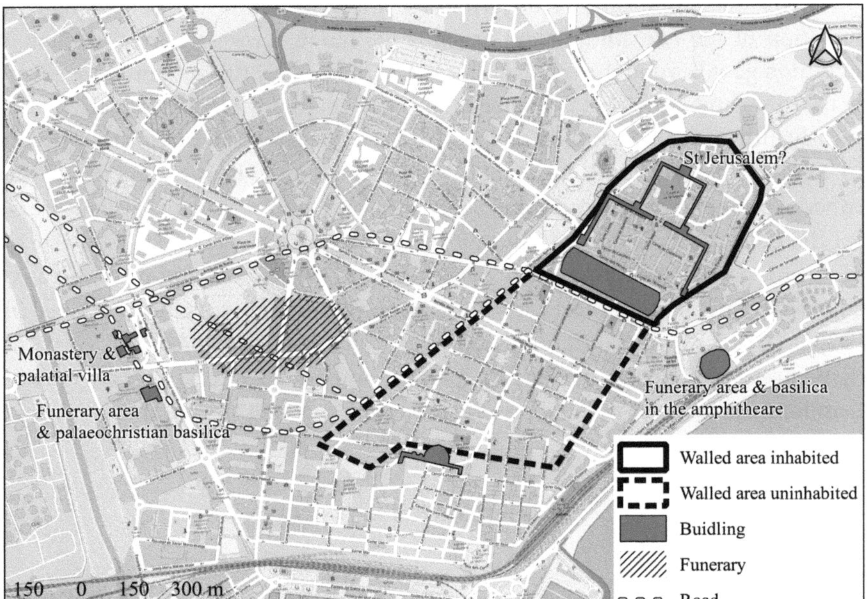


**Fig. 6.2** Map of Tarraco in late antiquity (after Macias, 2000: 259)

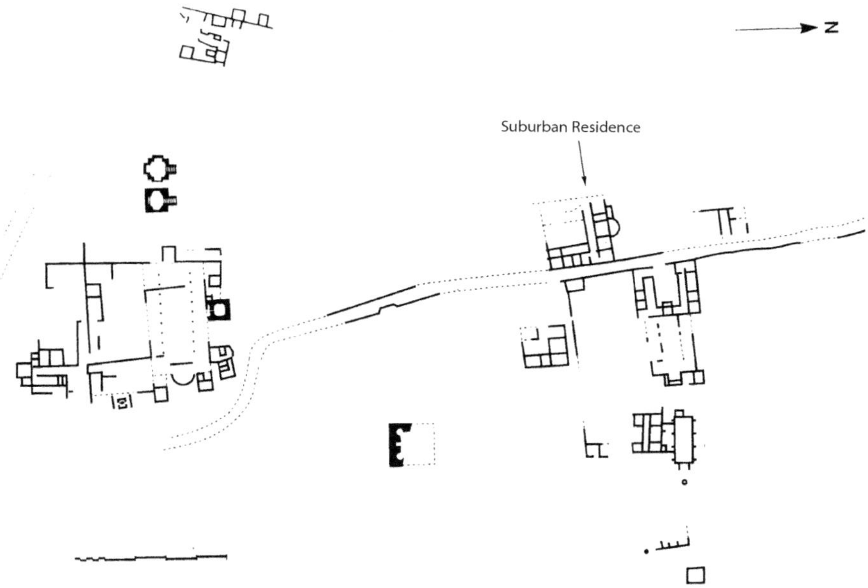


**Fig. 6.3** Plan of Tarraco's suburban Christian complex and *domus* (after de Palol and Pladevall, 1999)

the extramural suburban areas disappeared and were replaced by a late necropolis and early Christian buildings.

Apart from a reduction in size and the consequent decrease in population, Late Roman Tarraco displays distinctive features, with a series of Christian constructions in suburbs, such as a number of basilicas, a possible monastery, and cemeteries with ample evidence for the commemoration of the deceased (i.e. *laudatio*) (Fig. 6.3).

## Carthago Nova (Cartagena)

As happens in other Roman cities in the Iberian peninsula, by the end of the second century CE, the population of the city had decreased, probably due to a decline in the local mining industry. In late antiquity, the city contracted to half its former size, being reduced to some 40 ha, covering only an area known as Carthago Spartaria between the two hills of *Arx Hasdrubalis* and *Mons Asclepius* (see Fig. 6.4) (Quevedo, 2012). As happened at Tarraco, a series of landfills inside the city are recorded, which are indicative of the state of abandonment of these parts of the urban area (Vizcaino, 1999).

In 533/534 CE, the city was conquered by Byzantine troops after they defeated the Vandals in Africa and seized control over the Balearic Islands and Septem (Ceuta) (Ramallo, 2000: 581). The ancient sources reveal that Belisarius reinforced the walls

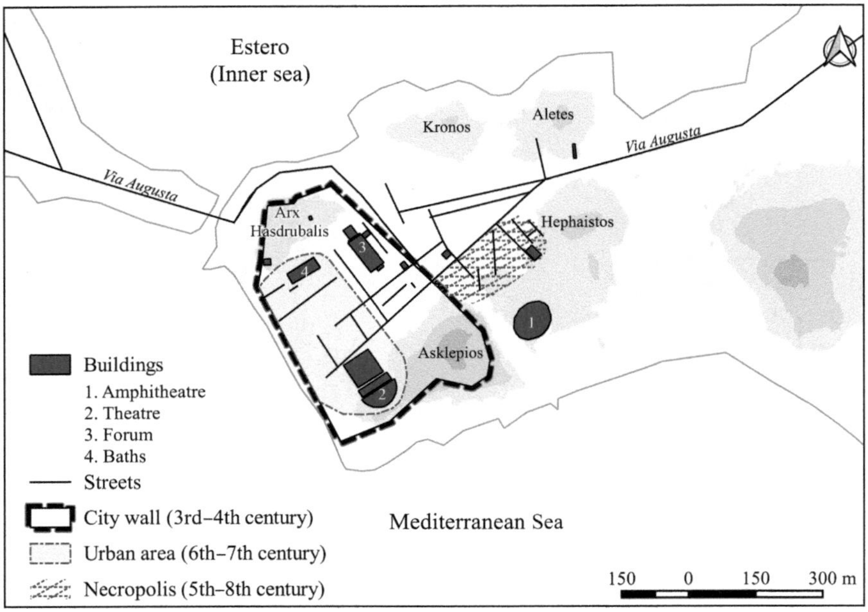


**Fig. 6.4** Map of Carthago Spartaria in late antiquity (Cartagena)

of Carthago Spartaria (Procop. *Bell. Vand.*, I, 23, 19–21; *Bell. Goth.* I, 14, 15), although archaeological remains of those reforms have only been identified at Cerro de San José. In a slightly later inscription, dated to 589–90, the general Comentiolus praises the walls and gates of the city (*CIL* II 3420). The Byzantine conquest did not represent a new influx of people since the soldiers that remained in the city were few in number, and probably insufficient to occupy the extensive perimeter of the existing city walls.

Between the second half of the fifth and the seventh century CE, some small *vici* and *pagi* around the city were reoccupied. This phenomenon probably suggests a partial abandonment on the part of the urban population. In other words, a trend towards de-urbanization (Ramallo, 2000: 604), or perhaps a rise in the rural population of the region (Murcia Muñoz, 2021: 564).

## Valentia (Valencia)

The city of Valentia underwent far-reaching transformations from the third century onwards, with a series of destructions and fires that led to the abandonment of whole sections of the urban area. Although its extent did not change, based on the defensive wall, not all the space inside the city was occupied (Ribera and Jiménez, 2012). For instance, in the northern part of the urban area, numerous landfill areas and industrial workshops rather than residences have been documented. It could be calculated that the residential space in the city was reduced by at least 10%. Valentia in late antiquity covered approximately 18 ha.

Some of the remains of the fourth-century CE reconstruction were related to the martyrdom of Saint Vincent, which was extremely important for the city in the Late Roman period as revealed by the excavations at the Pia Almoina (Ribera, 2016). It should be borne in mind that Valentia became the only bishopric see between Dertosa and Saetabi on the Levant (eastern coast). However, the city suffered a second destruction during the first half of the fifth century CE; afterwards, the urban impact of Christianity completely modified the intramural area (e.g. around the Pia Almoina), as well as some extramural parts such as La Roqueta (Ribera et al., 2020: 65).

In the early sixth century CE, there is evidence for a thriving period of construction in the episcopal centre under the leadership of the bishop, Justinian, combined with the urbanization of the circus area, which became a new urban quarter (70 × 250 metres). But the constructive dynamism of this century was cut short when the Justinianic plague reached the city in 542 CE (Procop. 2.22). A mass grave of 15 individuals (Tomb 41) in the episcopal cemetery is indicative of the impact of the epidemic in the city (Calvo, 2000; Ribera et al., 2020: 68).

At the end of the sixth century CE, a new fortified town was built only 16 km from Valentia, which probably became a new centre of power for a short period until the late seventh century or early eighth century CE (Ribera et al., 2020: 76–82). One of its most outstanding features is a defensive wall 2 metres in thickness, enclosing a perimeter of 1,000 metres, which had a series of 3 × 3 metre towers (Fig. 6.5). The site is currently under excavation by a team from the Institute of

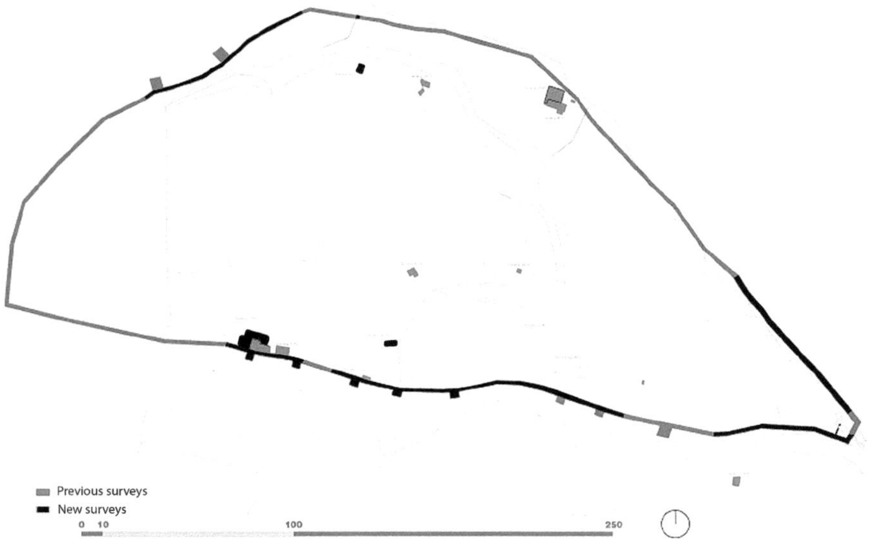


**Fig. 6.5** Map of the new foundation of Valencia la Vella (Ribera et al., 2020: fig. 7, 76)

Classical Archaeology of Catalonia (ICAC), and georadar survey has identified an urban settlement with a large building (25 × 7 metres) in the lower part adjoining the entrance as well as an important building at the top of the hill. The site was abandoned by the end of the seventh or early eighth century.

## 6.1.2 Central Inland Area

### Complutum (Alcalá de Henares)

Paulinus of Nola (*Epist. Ausonius* XXXI) described Complutum as a wealthy city of Hispania in 391–2 CE in the same way as Barcino, Tarraco, and Caesaraugusta. Archaeologically, in the Late Empire the city showed signs of dynamism with the reoccupation and rehabilitation of residences and public spaces such as the basilica (Rascón, 1999). The city, however, probably lost inhabitants and contracted to an area of 45 ha (see Fig. 6.6).

As any other city in Tarraconensis, Complutum underwent noteworthy topographical changes from the third century onwards, but it maintained a lively urban life as Paulinus of Nola documents in the late fourth century CE (Rascón and Sánchez, 2006: 267). Apart from Paulinus, other Christian sources (*Passio Iusti et Pastoris*, 7) refer to the martyrdom of the two brothers, Justus

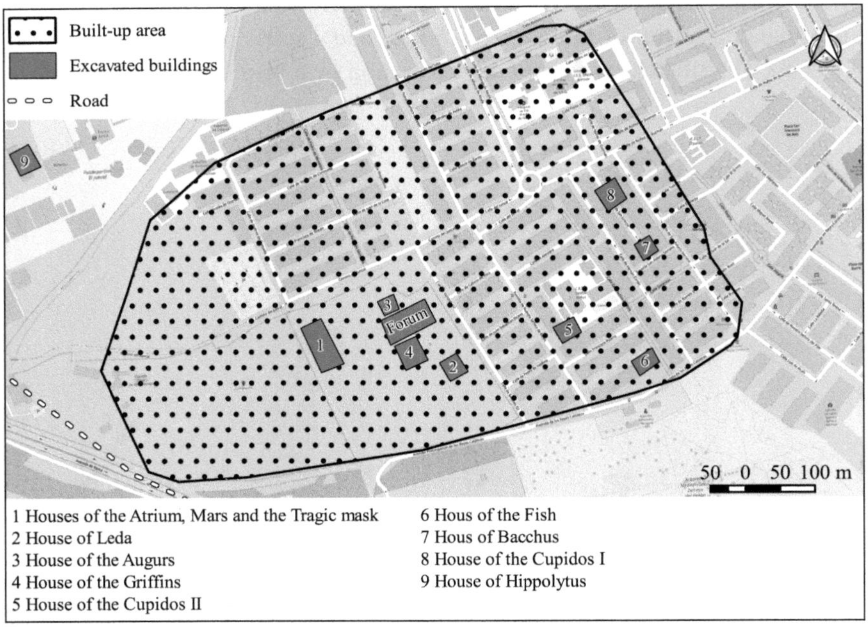


**Fig. 6.6** Plan of Complutum in late antiquity (Rascón and Sánchez, 2006: 270)

and Pastor, and the later construction of a martyrium. Near this cult building, Paulinus built his son's tomb, and there were also other religious spaces (Rascón and Sánchez, 2006: 268–9).

Furthermore, some of the architectural changes in Complutum in late antiquity affected public buildings. For instance, the forum was modified in the third century CE when the old basilica was transformed into a curia, cryptoporticus, and a possible *tabularium*, together with a refurbished basilica. The building included a monumental marble façade that suggests a thriving local economic urban life.

With regard to private architecture, some of the most luxurious domus such as the houses of Bacchus, Cupid, and Leda were built in the third and fourth centuries CE. This phenomenon is unusual in the Iberian peninsula in the Late Roman period, with the only exception of private residences at Emerita Augusta (Rascón and Sánchez, 2006: 271).

Other opulent residences can be detected in some suburban domus such as the house of Hippolytus and the villa of El Val. The house of Hippolytus was initially built in the first century CE but was completely transformed in phase III in the third century CE with modifications to rooms and mosaics, possibly becoming a *collegium*. Based on the mosaics researchers have suggested that the building was expanded during the third and early fourth centuries CE. In the Late Roman period it may have reached a total surface area of 5,800 $m^2$ (Arce et al., 2007: 320) (Fig. 6.7). The villa of El Val also underwent substantial reforms with the construction of a cross-shaped mausoleum in the third century CE and a major necropolis with more than a hundred burials (Rascón and Sánchez, 2006: 286).

### Caesaraugusta (Zaragoza)

During the Late Roman period, the total area covered by the city was reduced considerably from 56 ha to 44 ha. There is also evidence that the thickness of the early concrete (*opus caementicium*) wall of 2.85 m in width was increased by the addition of a third-century CE masonry wall externally, reaching a total thickness of 4.25 m (Escudero Escudero, 2014: 281). However, some scholars consider that this later circuit of walls should be dated to the Caliphal period (Paz, 2015).

Nevertheless, a thorough study of the archaeological evidence from the eastern external quarter reveals that it formed part of the walled city during the Early Empire before being totally abandoned in the third century CE with the construction of the new Late Roman wall (Galve, 2018–19: 59–61) (see Fig. 6.8).

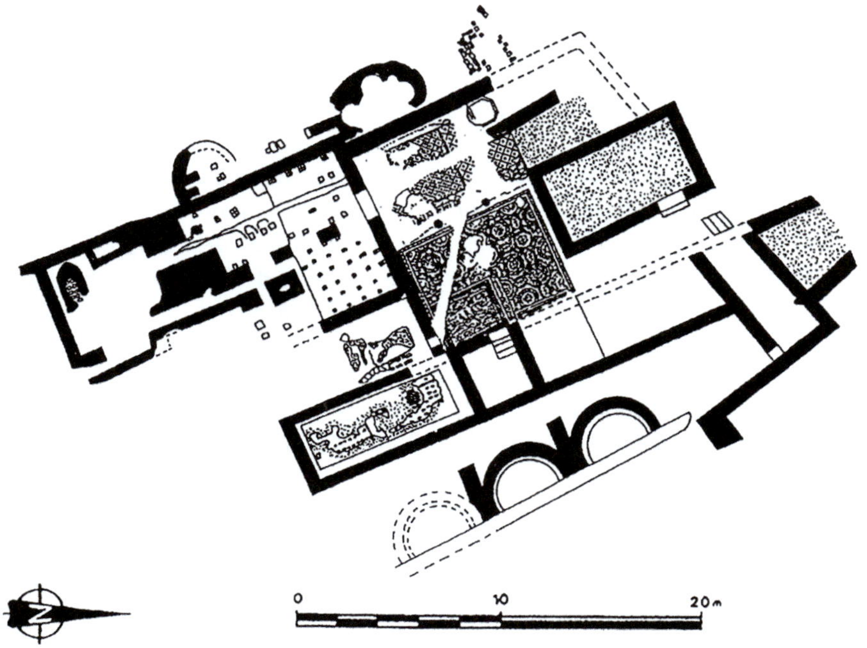


**Fig. 6.7** Complutum, plan of the bath complex in the House of Hyppolitus (Rascón Marqués, 2007)

**Fig. 6.8** Plan of Caesaraugusta in late antiquity (Escudero Escudero and Galve Izquierdo, 2013: fig. 370, 311)

This quarter was located in a low-lying area at the confluence of the Rivers Huerva and Ebro with the presence of amphora drains to avoid flooding. The area shows signs of occupation until the third century CE with modest domestic structures, sewers, and some artisan workshops.

The whole sewer system of this quarter went out of use in the late third century CE, and the area was occupied by mainly fourth-century CE burials (excavation at calle Barrioverde 12–16) including children buried in an amphora and a mausoleum (Galve, 2018–19: 69). Besides, some construction materials from this quarter were looted for reuse until the fifth century CE. Finally, a series of landfills are recorded across the whole area in the fourth and fifth centuries CE.

### 6.1.3 North-Western Coastal Area

Bracara Augusta (Braga)

The administrative reform introduced by Diocletian changed the role of Bracara, which became the capital of the new province of Gallaecia (Díaz, 2000: 403). Therefore, the city reached its peak from the third century CE onwards as Ausonius described (*Ordo nob. urb.* 11–14). In archaeological terms, the late third and early fourth century CE represented a period of dynamic urban development in the city with the refurbishment of public and private buildings (Martins et al., 2012: 156).

As far as is known, the city remained unaltered in the Late Empire and the walls of the Late Roman city enclosed an area of 48 ha, thus somewhat more than its extent in the early imperial period, including some nearby suburban neighbourhoods (*suburbia*). The Late Roman walls, built in the late third and early fourth centuries CE, changed the rigid grid layout of the city during the Early Empire. Some of early streets lost their initial function, and areas such as Carvalheiras or Frigideiras do Cantinho were included inside the walls (Fig. 6.9).

From 411 CE onwards, under the kingdom of the Suebi, Bracara became the capital, with a short interlude during the reign of Rechila (r. 438–48) when Emerita was the capital. The presence of the court of the Suebi in Bracara might help to explain the growth of the city in the late antique period. At a later date, the centre of the city shifted to the north and was fossilized in the medieval period by a wall, traces of which are still visible today. The medieval fortified city is estimated to be about half the size of the late antique one.

With regard to the public buildings, the baths of Alto do Cividade recorded a series of modifications in the mid-fourth century CE in the *frigidarium* area and the abandonment of the palaestra. Near the cathedral, the possible *macellum* was covered by an extensive pavement of *opus signinum* datable to the late third and fourth centuries CE (Martins, 2012: 158–60). As in the case of other cities, public buildings, such as the amphitheatre and theatre at Cividade de Cima,

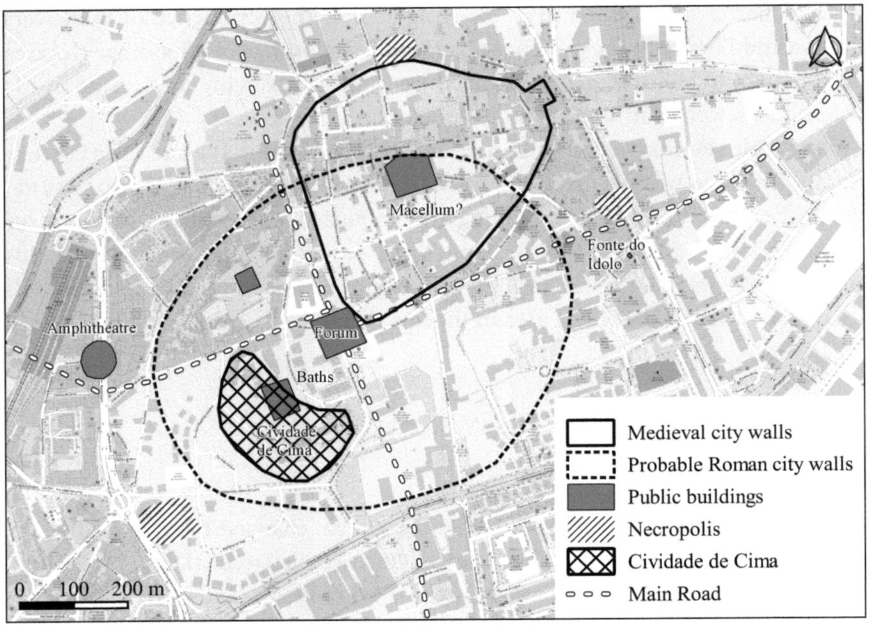


**Fig. 6.9** Proposed city plan of late antique Bracara Augusta

were abandoned in the early fourth century CE, probably because comedies and *munera* were no longer the most popular spectacles in the late antique city. Private architecture also reveals signs of continuity in the late period, although there are indications of abandonment in some parts of the classical city.

In 459 CE, the Visigoths routed the Suebi and ransacked the city as Hydatius (*Chron.* 177) explains. He described Suebian Bracara as a Christian Roman city destroyed by a barbarian horde of Visigoths. Nevertheless, the city showed signs of vitality in the sixth century CE when the monk Martin arrived to Bracara (*c.* 550 CE) to convert the Suebi to Catholicism. At this time, religious buildings such as the monastery of Dumium appeared in places on the periphery of the city, similar to what we see in other cities in the Iberian peninsula (Díaz, 2000: 414).

## Asturica Augusta (Astorga)

According to the archaeological evidence, Late Roman Asturica had a similar extent to its forerunner, but without extramural constructions (Vidal and González, 2018). Thus, it retained the same intramural area of 27 ha although some public spaces and buildings were now occupied by private constructions. Excavations in Astorga reveal that the street level was raised by several metres, especially in the area closest to the third- and fourth-century CE city wall (Fernández Ochoa and Morillo, 2005: 321).

The most outstanding public construction were the city walls with a solid base of *opus incertum* that lifted the street level almost 1 metre in comparison with earlier periods (García Marcos and Vidal, 1998; Gutiérrez González and Arias Páramo, 2009: 759). The wall seems to have reached a height of 15 metres, and it was intensively transformed between the fifth and seventh centuries CE (Fig. 6.10).

As far as public buildings are concerned, the main baths had late phases and were abandoned in the fifth century CE, whereas the lesser baths were already deserted as from the third century CE onwards (Vidal and González, 2018: 283). The luxurious domus in the town still appear to be occupied in later periods, and the date of abandonment remains unknown.

The phenomenon of city wall construction seems to cover not only the late third century, but also the fourth century in Hispania Tarraconensis (Fernández Ochoa and Morillo, 2005: 299). In terms of wall-circuits, many late fortifications were built following the alignment of the previous ones. If we look at their size and extent, some were reduced, but others, such as Bracara Augusta, even increased their area. Besides, the phenomenon seems to have been restricted to the provinces of Hispania Tarraconensis and Gallaecia, since it has hardly been documented in the other provinces of the Iberian peninsula, with a few exceptions such as Emerita or Italica. Late Roman walls were the most significant public work in any of the cities in the province, which demonstrates the economic potential that some of these urban centres still had.

Besides public works, the economic potential of a city, or at least its inhabitants, can be seen from private constructions. Whereas we might notice the abandonment of public buildings in the late third and fourth century, we should also call attention to the transformation of these buildings into housing (Arce et al., 2007: 306). In addition to the conversion of public buildings we observe a continuation and construction of several domus type houses.

### 6.1.4 General Overview

As mentioned above, ancient sources such as Paulinus of Nola provide a vivid image of the urban decay in Hispania Tarraconensis in the late fourth century CE, citing the decadent minor cities of Ilerda, Bilbilis, and Calagurris (Letter to *Ausonius* XXXI). However, in the same letter he praised the situation of other cities such as Barcino, Tarraco, Caesaraugusta, and Complutum, despite their reduction in size. Paulinus can be considered a reliable source since for a short time he lived in Complutum, where he is likely to have buried his son Celsus, and in Barcino, where he became a presbyter in 394 CE.

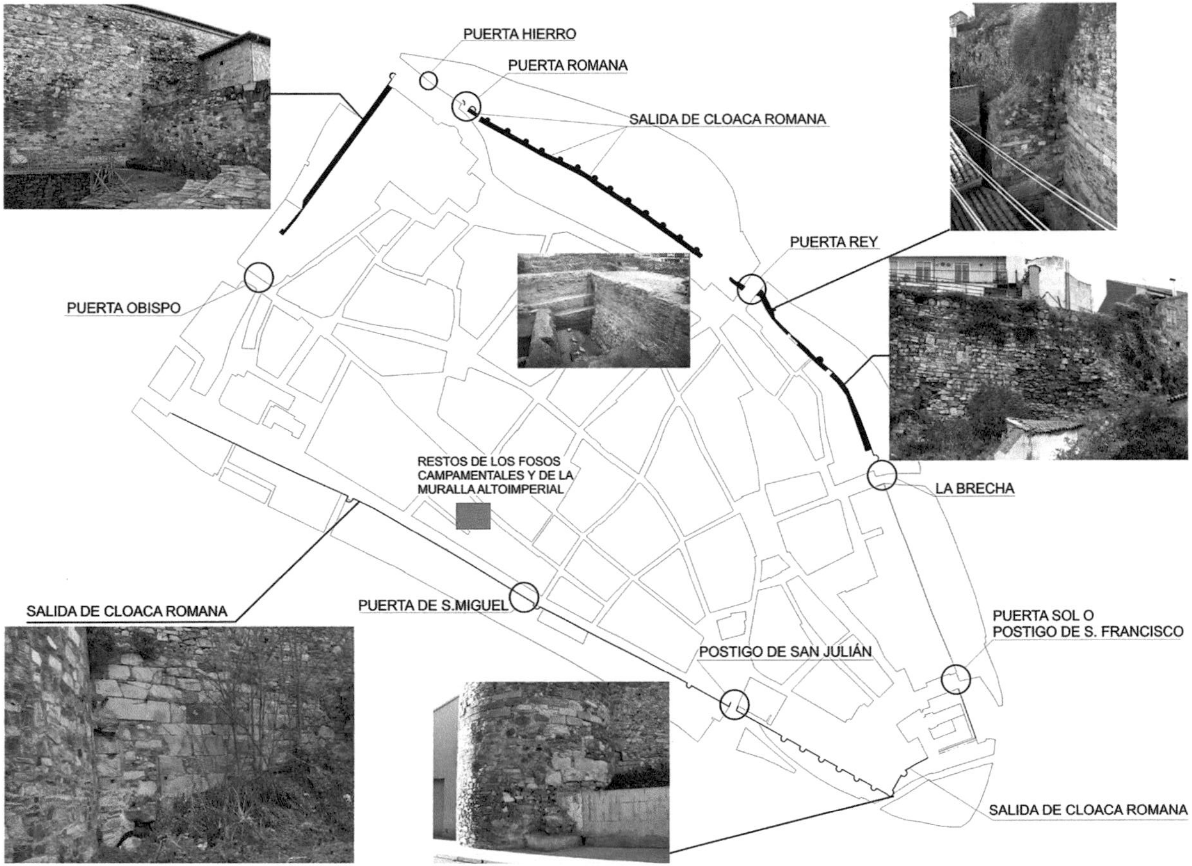


**Fig. 6.10** City plan of late antique Asturica Augusta (Gutiérrez González and Arias Páramo, 2009: 758, fig. 1)

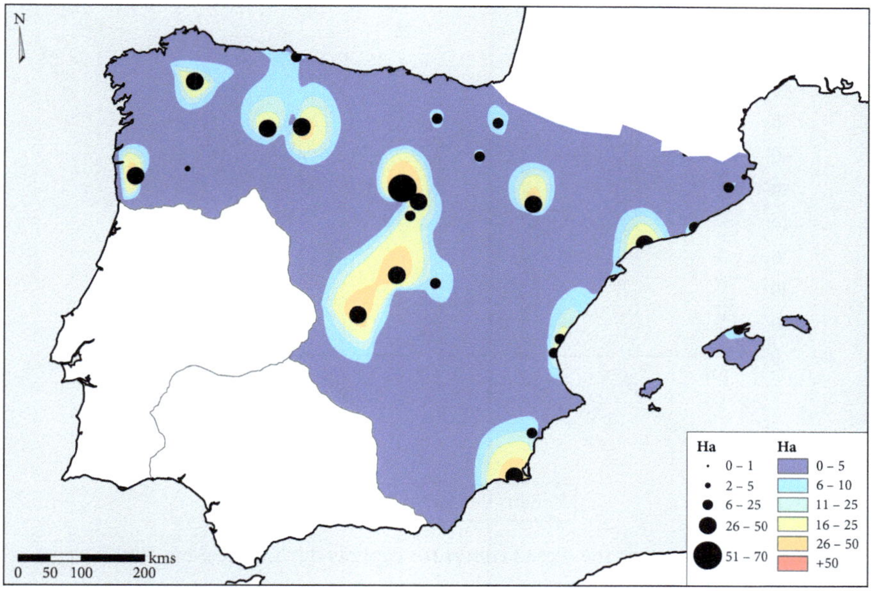


**Fig. 6.11** Urban population density (after De Soto and Carreras, 2022: fig. 2)

Unfortunately, research on the dimensions of late antique cities in Hispania Tarraconensis is very limited (Diarte Blasco, 2011). Nowadays only 25 late urban centres have well-documented perimeters. This is an extremely small number when compared to the 181 towns for which the extent is known in the Early Empire. Therefore, the distribution of the late urban population presented in Fig. 6.11 is only a projection of these 25 cities rather than a solid one from a statistically representative sample. Similarly, we cannot turn to a RSA or calculations of the urban population as we have done in Chapters 4 and 5, due to the limited number of urban areas for this Late Roman period. With all these limitations in mind, the density projection reveals some interesting patterns, such as a significant reduction of most coastal towns that largely depended on Mediterranean trade.

If the dimensions of cities are compared between the Early Empire and late antiquity, the overall picture becomes clearer. Fig. 6.12 shows the extent of the seven *conventus* capitals in Hispania Tarraconensis in hectares. There is a clear pattern of decrease in size for the Mediterranean capitals such as Tarraco and Carthago Spartaria, perhaps due to a fall in commercial opportunities. Caesaraugusta, which was 300 km away from the Mediterranean coast, underwent only a small adjustment in size, whereas the *conventus* capitals of the central plateau and north-west remained unaltered. The only possible increase in size is documented at Bracara Augusta as a result of the impact of becoming the Late Roman provincial capital of Gallaecia and the capital of the kingdom of the Suebi (see above).

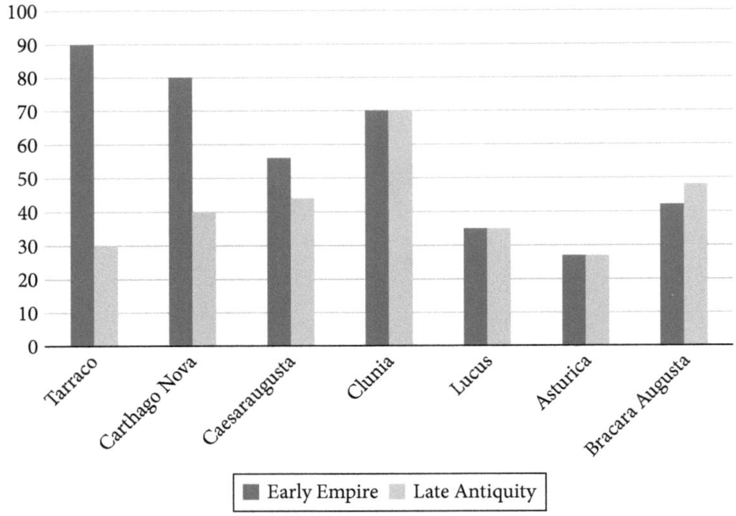


**Fig. 6.12** Comparison of the size of *conventus* capitals during the Early Empire and late antiquity

It is clear that the cities in the centre of the province, such as Clunia and Complutum, were able to maintain their size. It is also likely that they enjoyed a period of economic growth. For instance, Complutum was not an administrative capital, but local authorities were fostering public initiatives as the inscriptions from the basilica of the city record (Bowes, 2013: 214). The forum of the city also underwent a process of refurbishment in the third century CE (Rascón, 1999), while a bishop is also recorded in Complutum from the fifth century CE onwards, which reveals its increasing importance as an urban centre.

When we compare the sizes of cities that were not *conventus* capitals, the image of a stable urban population in inland regions is confirmed (see Fig. 6.13). In addition, a less pronounced drop in size in some Mediterranean coastal towns can be observed. Two large cities, to be more precise Complutum and Toletum, retained almost all their population, whereas Mediterranean coastal towns such as Valentia and Pollentia witnessed a small reduction in size. A special case is Ercavica, an inland Celtiberian *municipium* linked to the exploitation of the *lapis specularis* mines (see Chapter 5). With the decrease in maritime trade this commodity, which found its way to Cartagena, was affected as well. Perhaps the demographic decrease in this inland centre is related to the decrease in mining exploitation. In the late sixth century we might expect a second demographic decrease for cities in this specific area due to the foundation of Reccopolis (Olmo

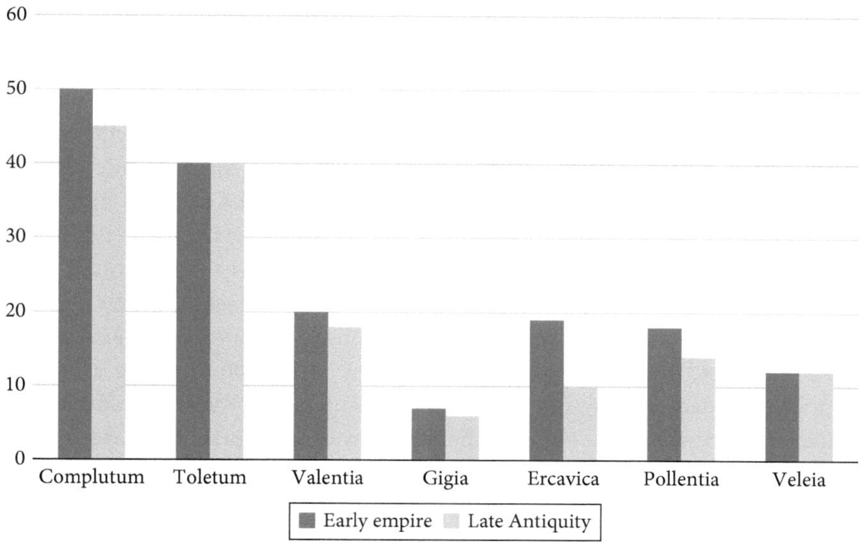


**Fig. 6.13** Comparison of the size of secondary centres during the Early Empire and late antiquity

Enciso et al., 2019: 108). The creation of such an urban centre must have had a pull effect on the neighbouring ones.

Two small northern towns, specifically Gigia and Veleia, saw only limited shrinking in population. Likewise, most north-western cities retained their importance and developed their commercial and trade contacts with other provinces from the fourth century CE onwards (e.g. *Vicus Spacorum*) (Fernández, 2014). What seems obvious from this urban picture is that the province evolved towards a regionalization of its economy. The gold mining continued, but the scale of extraction was limited, and it is quite likely that the Roman State did not participate directly. These small-scale exploitations may have been run by small communities living in *castra* or at other rural sites. The most likely explanation for the continuity of the north-western region is found in its peripheral position during the Early Empire. As the region was never fully integrated into the wider economic network, apart from the state extraction of gold, the economy had been regional from the start.

However, the general trend saw a shift in the urban layout away from orthogonal planning, with a narrowing of streets, the disuse of sewers and drains, and the abandonment and/or reuse of public buildings (Gurt, 2000–1; Diarte Blasco, 2015). There was also a change in the streets in later periods when they were covered by clay or rubble instead of the earlier stone paving. Furthermore, public structures were converted into modest domestic spaces, reflecting a general trend towards an increase in private space at the expense of public areas (Bravo, 2016: 149). The most outstanding examples are those buildings devoted to leisure such as baths, theatres, amphitheatres, and circuses. Pagan temples were converted or completely abandoned. Some of those abandoned public buildings and urban quarters became landfill areas or open spaces where neighbours burned their organic refuse. Furthermore, the late antique period witnessed a substantial decrease in monumental construction by private individuals and acts of euergetism, a trend that is well documented in the late second century CE or the early third century, and which became the norm in most of the main towns (Kulikowski, 2010: 94).

Until new data and more detailed information on the inhabited parts of the Late Roman settlements are provided it will not be feasible to obtain a clearer image of their demography, population numbers included. With the information available at present, it is obvious that there was an overall decrease in the urban population in the province of Hispania Tarraconensis, especially in the Mediterranean region, whereas the capital of Lusitania and the cities in the Guadalquivir valley maintained their status for a time. Despite this decrease in size, the city remained a focus of administrative, political, and religious power, and some of the elites continued to dwell in those late urban centres and helped to finance and reconstruct and build fortifications (Kulikowski, 2010; Martínez Jiménez et al., 2018: 69).

In the fifth century, the Christian religion generated a different pattern of urbanism in towns with religious buildings (e.g. basilicas) and episcopal palaces normally located in the city centres. This new Christian topography included intramural cemeteries as well as an increase in the urban development in the suburban areas, which sometimes included places of worship (Bravo, 2016: 153–7).

## 6.2 Outstanding Changes in the Countryside: From the Large Villas to Small Towns

In contrast to the signs of abandonment in the urban centres of Tarraconensis, in the countryside there is a concentration of monumental luxurious villas that continued to be occupied during the fourth and fifth centuries CE. This phenomenon is especially noticeable in the Ebro and Duero valleys (Chavarría, 2005: 519). The wealth of those rural residences has been interpreted as a result or consequence of an alleged ruralization of the province (Chavarría, 2005: 521). However, it should be emphasized than the concentration of wealthy rural villas (see Fig. 6.14) coincided with the most populated *conventus* (see Fig. 6.15). Therefore, it does not seem to be a change between urban and rural populations, but a decline of the coastal urban centres and nearby territories in favour of an economic expansion of other territories such as the Duero and Ebro valleys, as well as the region of

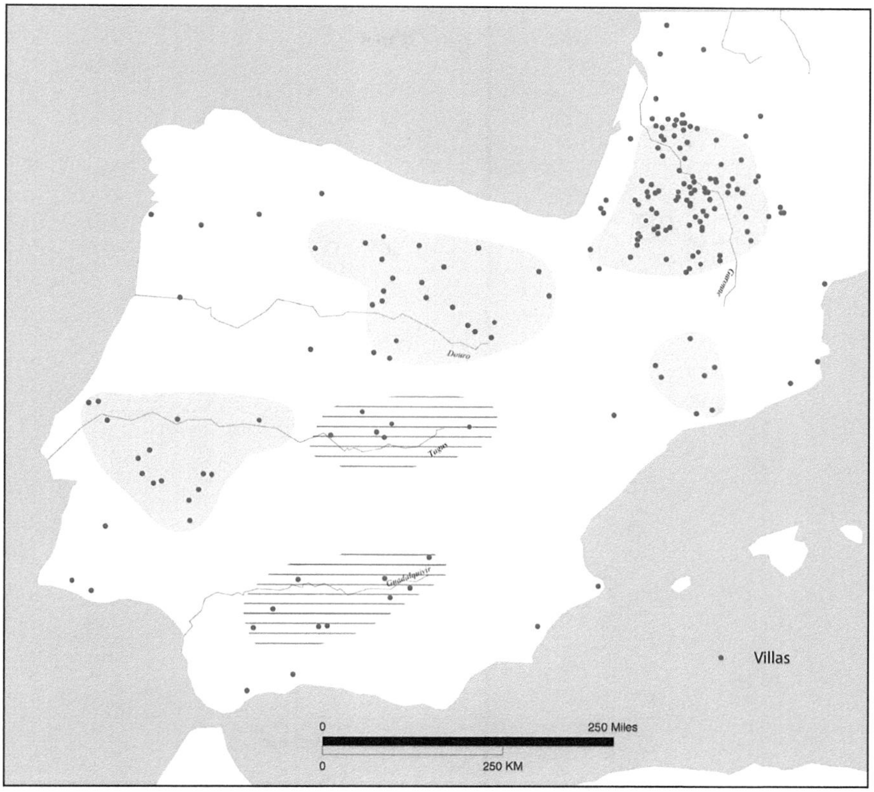


**Fig. 6.14** Distribution of monumental fourth-century Roman villas (after Chavarría, 2005)

Carpetania. Although those villas normally existed in the Early Empire, they were enlarged in the fourth century CE, becoming monumental residential complexes with large reception rooms and rich decorative programmes (e.g. mosaics, paintings, architectural decorations) (Ripoll, 2018). However, these sumptuous spaces are found alongside extensive areas devoted to production, including wine presses and warehouses (i.e. dolia and possible cereal *horrea*). Near those production quarters some dwelling structures are recorded, as in the case of the villas of El Ramalete, Los Quintanares, and La Olmeda. These may have been the homes of the dependent population (variously known as *tuguriae*, *casae*, *pagi*, or *vici*) (Chavarría, 2005: 526).

As Bowes (2013: 194) pointed out, these late villas cannot be understood as autarchic economic and administrative elements in the central and western parts of the peninsula, but as the result of social competition among the elites. This increased bureaucratic presence in particular regions responded to the

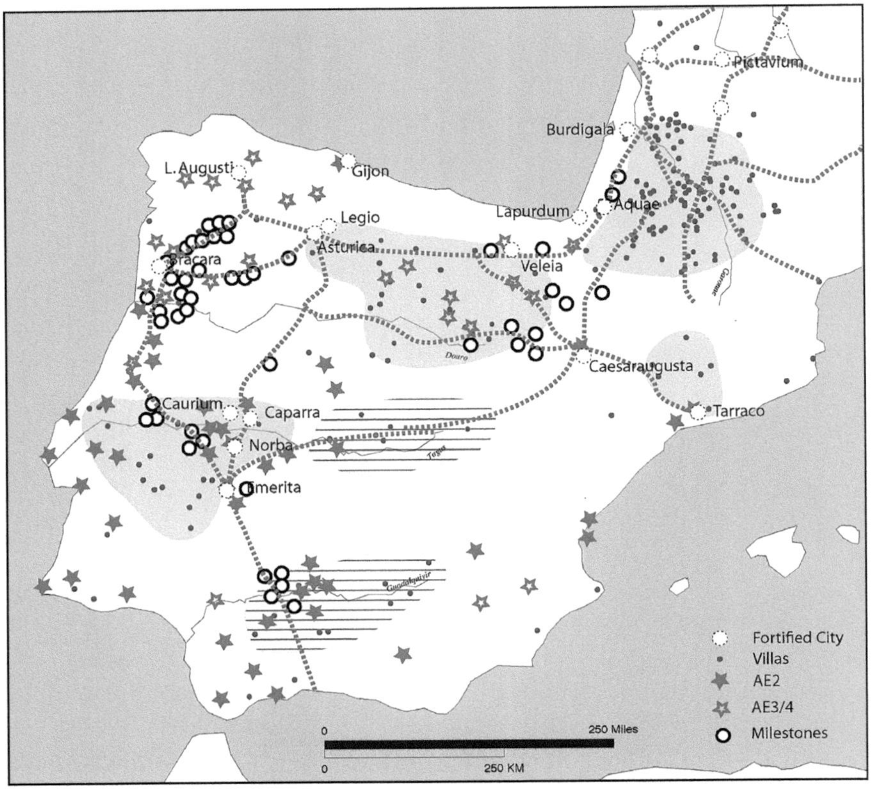


**Fig. 6.15** Concentration of villas related to coinage (AE2, AE3/4), fortified cities, and reconstruction of Roman roads (Bowes, 2013: fig. 5)

demands of taxation within an imperial framework that needed resources for their armies (i.e. the *annona militaris*).

Moreover, the owners of these monumental villas may not have been the same urban elites as in the coastal cities, but their wealth need not to have been only the result of agricultural surpluses. One possible explanation is that those wealthy landlords also acted as tax collectors in the countryside, in the same way as urban *duumviri* had done in previous periods. The development of the *iugum* as a unit of tax, and the notion of *origo* to attach tax responsibility to specific pieces of land, placed rural land at the centre of political-economic theory, while the development of agents like the *praepositus pagi*, as yet unattested in Spain but present in other western provinces, may have been those theories made flesh, in the form of a rurally-based officials charged with verifying the fairness of the tax levy (Bowes, 2013: 215). Therefore, the location of these luxurious villas should be connected with a new economic model for the province of Tarraconensis in late antiquity. The same regions also have the highest concentrations of Constantinian coinage (AE2, AE3, and AE4),[2] Roman road rebuilding, and some of the late urban defensive circuits (see Fig. 6.15). In other words, the new pattern of rural distribution was partially the result of a distinctive economic model, one in which direct agricultural production (e.g. cereals) was an important asset.

The owners of these magnificent rural villas are mostly unknown, but epigraphic evidence suggests that in some cases local and provincial administrators (local bureaucracy) were the proprietors of these villas. Some of them may have belonged to the imperial circle such as the Carranque *uilla* attributed to Maternus, lieutenant of Theodosius (Rodríguez Gutiérrez, 2011: 95); one cannot forget that Theodosius' family was originally from Cauca (Chavarría, 2005: 541).

There is significant variation in rural constructions in Late Roman Tarraconensis depending on the environmental conditions, traditions, and functionality (Chavarría, 2005: 522). However, most of the villas display similar layouts and decorative programmes, such as hunting scenes in their mosaics, many of which reproduced the owners' way of life. The most representative elements were the mosaics that combined geometric motifs with figurative scenes. Apart from the hunting scenes that identified the owners' lifestyle (e.g. Carranque, La Olmeda), mythological themes such as Dionysus (Baños de Valdearados) and Achilles (Carranque, La Olmeda), or circus races (Bell·lloc, Aguilafuente, Torre de Palma, and El Val) were also recurrent iconographic motifs (Chavarría, 2005: 539).

One of the most interesting economic features of Late Roman pottery production and distribution in the Diocesis Tarraconensis, as Bowes (2013: 216) indicates, is the coincidence with the Roman villas. In other words, the villas became economic poles of the province at the time, creating small-scale commercial circuits (micro-regional markets and networks) different from those on the coast, where foreign imports of pottery and amphorae were more common. Actually, the owners of those luxurious *villae* showed the same status as urban elites of the province cities during the Early Empire (Rodríguez Gutiérrez, 2011: 94).

The layout of the Olmeda villa (see Fig. 6.16) reveals the luxurious structure of such residential complexes, with a central courtyard surrounded by numerous rooms lavishly decorated with figurative mosaics and a private bath complex on the north side. Most luxurious decorations appeared in the reception rooms located on the central axis of the northern peristyle, opposite the main entrance (as at Cuevas de Soria or Aguilafuente), which displayed the social level of the owners (Chavarría, 2005: 535).

In the case of the villa of La Olmeda, apart from the owner's residence, there are other rural settlements nearby, inhabited by families of probable agricultural

[2] AE coin types are a series of bronze coins minted between CE 364 and 450 during the reigns of Valentinian I to III.

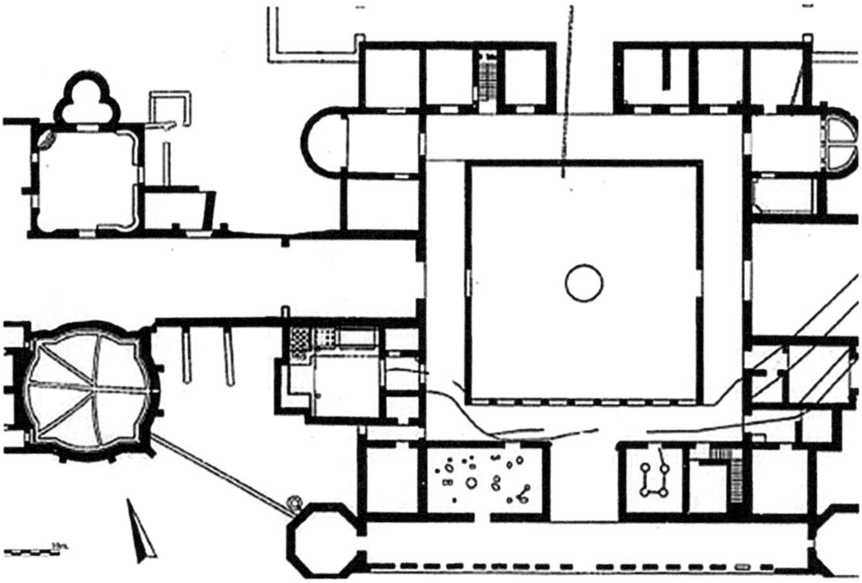

**Fig. 6.16** Plan of the villa of La Olmeda (Pedrosa de la Vega) (Chavarría, 2007: fig. 69)

workers. The villa's necropolis with a substantial number of burials demonstrates that villas tended to be population centres similar to *pagi*, *fora*, or *vici*.

A few recorded villas datable to the late fourth century CE and early fifth century CE in the Ebro valley were fortified, thus reflecting the insecurity in the countryside due to bands of *bagaudae* and the first waves of the so-called 'barbarian' invasions (Suebi, Alans, and Vandals). Examples of these fortified villas can be found at Granja d'Escarp (Lleida), Salillas de Buradón (Alava), Ortilla (Huesca), and Suellacabras (Soria) (Gómez, 2006: 174).

The term *bagaudae* appears to mean 'fighters' in Gaulish, derived from *baga-* related to war and *-auda* related to fighter (Sanz and Lázaro, 1995: 753). The *bagaudae* are identified as bands of free landless peasants that lived in Gaul and the Ebro valley, who attacked wealthy villas and church estates from the late third century CE onwards. Scholars do not agree on their origin; it has been proposed that the *bagaudae* were urban lower classes expelled from the cities, whereas others identified them as simple, landless peasants (cf. Arce, 2013: 160–6). In the Ebro valley, where they are also attached to the suburban areas of small towns, they are documented in the early fifth century CE (Sanz and Lázaro, 1995). Their most active period in Hispania Tarraconensis was between 441 and 454 CE when the emperor sent Flavius Asturius to quell them (Hydatius, *Chron.* 125). The revolt reached its peak when in 449 CE Basilius led a group of *bagaudae*, in the first instance against Turiaso, where the local bishop, Leon, was killed (Hydatius,

*Chron.* 141–2). The ecclesiastical authorities led the urban resistance in the Ebro valley against the *bagaudae*, and normally took refuge in the churches that were ultimately not respected. After the Turiaso episode, Basilius joined the king of the Suebi, Requiarius, to devastate the region of Caesaraugusta, sacking the city of Ilerda. Finally, the general Frederic, brother of Theodoric II, king of the Visigoths, was sent as a *foederatus* of Rome to fight against the *bagaudae* and Suebi. He subjected the last groups of *bagaudae* in 454 CE, although they reappeared in Gallaecia, where *bagaudae* also took part in the sacking of Bracara in 456 CE.

Scholars still debate whether the *bagaudae* should be seen as a new social group or class (Thompson, 1979; Sanz and Lázaro, 1995). According to Sánchez León (1996), the *bagaudae* consisted of groups of:

1. Free, freedmen, and slaves in terms of legal status;
2. *Vascones*, Celts, and Romans in terms of origin;
3. Small, ruined peasants, temporary agricultural labourers, army deserters, brigands, *coloni*, slaves, and marginalized urban residents (even former aristocrats).

The unstable situation of the countryside affected the luxurious villa model in place during the fourth century CE in the mid-Ebro valley (see Fig. 6.14). As a result, the villa-system adapted to the arrival of newcomers such as the Suebi or Visigoths, as well as overcoming the issues created by the peasant revolts of the *bagaudae*. Notwithstanding this, some of those large villas remained occupied in the fifth century, although they did not display the architectural luxury of previous periods (Diarte et al., 2020: 271). The main source of archaeological information on the countryside comes from field surveys normally carried out in the territories surrounding the towns and cities, but they are lacking in non-urban areas in which large villas or small towns were the principal settlements.

The recent survey of the territories of two north-western cities, namely Asturica and Albocela (Diarte et al., 2020), provides relevant information on the rural settlement transition in the province during late antiquity. For instance, both territories saw the reoccupation of Iron Age hillforts (the castro Iglesia Caída, Castro de Viso, Castro de Pedrero, and Teso de la Mora), probably due to the existence of a frontier between the Suebic and Visigothic kingdoms. The occupation of *castella*—'castros'—in the north-west was also documented in the written sources by Hydatius (*Chron.* 41), who acknowledged the presence of new settlement types (*castella, turris, palatia, ecclesiae*...) in zones controlled by the old *possessores*, the new Germanic populations, and autonomous agricultural communities (Díaz and Menéndez, 2016: 176). Although field surveys record less activity in the villas in the north-west (Diarte et al., 2020: 293), the power of those Roman proprietors cannot be disregarded.

Apart from the above mentioned typologies of rural properties of different sizes owned by traditional Roman landlords or newcomers, Guzman (2016: 23) reports a series of properties exploited by local peasants that did not belong to the previous groups. In archaeological terms, these properties can be identified by the presence of small communities (e.g. *pagi*, *vicus*) gathered together, which shared modest assemblages of material culture. In fact, Vigil-Escalera (2007) has also noted such micro-communities on the central plateau (Meseta) in the fifth century CE with new social relations that cannot be compared to the ones from earlier centuries:

> The consolidation of a dense network of stable peasant settlements that in many cases were located close to the old Late Roman estates as an economic strategy that enabled them to make savings in the supply of constructional material and to take advantage of the remains of agricultural infrastructure, which may not have been completely abandoned by previous generations. The possible colonization of virgin agricultural spaces, conversion of previous plots of land to new uses, and introduction of land management systems related to very strong bottom-up social systems, and an excellent practical knowledge of the environment, implied a substantial change in the rural landscape of large areas only comparable in scale to what had been initiated by the Roman conquest.
>
> Vigil-Escalera, 2007: 250–1

In late antiquity, most small towns continued as settlements in the countryside, acting as markets, as well as census and tax collection centres. They were the minimal administrative structure of the Roman province as Festus (502 and 508 L) and Isidore (*Etym.* 2.11–12) explained. Agricultural settlements, such as farms, could be dispersed, but they were part of those small towns, so *vici* and *pagi* only had those special administrative functions (Curchin, 1985: 328–38). Due to their nature as roadside settlements, the word *vicus* stems from *viae* because most of these villages grew along roads or at crossroads (Varro, *LL* V.159); the *vici* had a good communication infrastructure, which was required to establish the administrative units. However, some unfortified *vici* were abandoned in the fifth century CE due to violent conditions, looking for a safer settlement; but the fortified ones continued as fortified villas (Curchin, 1985: 338).

In the case of *pagi*, Isidore (*Etym.* 2.11–12) and Festus (502 and 508 L) indicated that they were popular associations in rural environments. Their rural nature is also confirmed by Varro (*LL* VI.26), who refers to agricultural festivals involving the whole *pagus*, called *Paganicae* (Curchin, 1985: 338). Some *pagi* in the Diocesis Tarraconensis include the epithet *Augusti*, so they were created by public initiative. Since *pagi* were in association with farms or disseminated dwellings, most of their legal problems were related to property rights, such as the conflict before the governor of Tarraconensis (193 CE) in which a *pagus* (*rivi Larensis*)[3] claimed a property or part of Valeria Faventina's plot:

> *Imp(eratore) Caes(are) P(ublio) Helvio / Pertinace princip(e) / senatus patre patriae / Q(uinto) Sosio Falcone C(aio) Iulio Eruci/o Claro co(n)s(ulibus) III Idus Febr(uarias) / sententiam quam tulit / L(ucius) Novius Rufus / leg(atus) Aug(usti) pr(o) / pr(aetore) v(ir) c(larissimus) inter* ***compaganos ri/vi Larensis*** *et Val(eriam) Faventinam / descriptam et propositam pr(idie) Non(as) / Novembr(es) in v(erba) i(nfra) s(cripta) Rufus leg(atus) c(um) c(onsilio) c(ollocutus) / decretum ex tilia recitavit / congruens est intentio mea qua / [- - -]tus proximae argumentis / [- - -] parte prolatis rei / [- - -] aput me actu[m] est d/[- - - i]nspectio itaq[ue / - - - q]ui in priva[- - - / - - -]a mox [- - - / - - - - - ?]* (*CIL* II 4125)

In addition, *pagi*, together with the *civitates*, were places from which taxes were collected, so any estate had to be declared as belonging to either a *civitas* or *pagus* (*Dig*. 50.15.1.4). As far as known, the *pagi* were concentrated in the form of agricultural lands in areas such as the Ebro valley, and in the central plateau, and the uplands of Cantabria. Scholars have argued that *pagi* were normally located in Romanized areas, whereas *vici* represented a continuity of Iron Age settlements, mainly in the north-west. One of the most well-known *vici* was *Vicus Spacorum*, modern-day Vigo (Fig. 6.17), whose economy was based on sea resources and salt from the first century CE until its abandonment in the Visigothic period.

During the Early Empire, the north-west, the later province of Gallaecia, had a rather low level of urbanization, the only large urban centres being the *conventus iuridicus* capitals. Therefore, the settlement system was organized differently, based more on rural populations and small agglomerations such as *vici* that also continued to exist in the Late Roman period (Bravo, 2016: 158). Besides, the ancient sources refer to other agglomerations such as *mansiones* and *stationes* along the old main Roman routes, and even simple houses such as *casae* and *tuguria*.

The Ager Tarraconensis survey (see Chapter 5) shows a projection of inhabitants in different types of settlement. The rural sites in late antiquity were fewer in number than in the Early Empire and smaller when compared with Republican sites (see Table 5.15). Therefore, the number of potential dwellers went down during the Late Roman period in accordance with the reduction in the size of Tarraco. Besides, Tarraco's territory included some luxurious villas such as Centcelles, in the modern-day municipality of Constantí or Els Munts (Altafulla). Also, the Ager Tarraconensis survey (Carreté et al., 1995) documented large archaeological scatters with late material that may identify other lavish rural residences.

[3] The *pagus rivi Larensis* has been identified as Lauro between Valentia and Saguntum (Alföldy, 1975: no. 143).

**Fig. 6.17** Salt museum in *Vicus Spacorum* (present Vigo)

Again, more surveys and research are required to complete the present image of the countryside during the Late Roman period. According to the available data, there is no direct transferral between urban populations and the countryside. The reduction of urban population also affected their own territories—as seen in the case of Tarraco—but it is unknown whether there was a general downturn of population or the occupation of new, completely rural regions.

## 6.3 Suebi, Alans, and Vandals: Migration or Invasion?

One of the obvious demographic changes in Late Roman Hispania Tarraconensis is the arrival of different groups from Central Europe. It is still under discussion whether these were military invasions or just migratory movements, but scholars agree that they created a disruption in the life of the province. The initial influx of Suebi, Alans, and Vandals took place in 409 CE, leading to the destruction of cities and villas during the first half of the fifth century CE (Chavarría, 2005: 554).

According to Hydatius (*Chron.* 41), the Alans settled in Lusitania and Carthaginensis and established their capital at Emerita from 412 to 418 CE, whereas the Siling Vandals settled in Baetica until 429 CE, when both tribes crossed the Mediterranean together to gain access to the north of Africa. The movement of those tribes in the peninsula has left little archaeological trace except for the above mentioned destruction levels in some towns and villas that seems to be chronologically connected with their arrival. This is the case of abandonment levels at the villas of El Romeral and El Val (Chavarría, 2005: 544–5).

The Suebi, on the other hand, settled in the province of Gallaecia and chose Bracara as their capital at a later date. Our main source for this period is Hydatius, bishop of Aquae Flavia, who referred to the Suebic conquest of Gallaecia. Hydatius (*Chron.* 41) comments that in 411 the surviving Hispani in Gallaecia agreed to live under the yoke of the Suebi, but some strongholds, including cities (e.g. Lucus Augusti) and *castella tutiora* (*castros* and *castella*) resisted the newcomers (Díaz and Menéndez, 2016: 177). There was at least one movement of local people that fled to those well-defended upland sites (Hydatius, *Chron.* 81), which were probably under the protection of large landowners (Valer. *Bergid. Ordo* 7, pp. 169, 5).

With diminishing imperial control over the provinces of Tarraconensis and Gallaecia, some of the Iron Age peoples such as Vascones, Cantabri, and Varduli reappeared in the classical sources (Hydatius, *Chron.* 164), as they attempted to create their own political institutions (Díaz and Menéndez, 2016: 181). Actually, the province of Tarraconensis continued to be ruled by imperial delegates, but the newcomers had full control of the situation. Orosius states that the Hispani in 417 CE lived better under barbarian authority than strangled by Roman fiscal greed:

> Nevertheless, soon afterwards, the barbarians came to detest their swords, betook themselves to the plough, and are affectionately treating the rest of the Romans as comrades and friends, so that now among them there may be found some Romans who, living with the barbarians, prefer freedom with poverty to tribute-paying with anxiety among their own people. Orosius VII.4.17

In 452 and 454 CE the Roman imperial embassies attempted to negotiate with the Suebi about returning the territory of Gallaecia to the Roman Empire (Hydatius, *Chron.* 155, 161). It was not until the direct intervention of the Visigoths in 456 CE under the leadership of Theodoric II that the situation in Tarraconensis changed (Guzman, 2016: 29). The Visigoths, whose capital at that time was Toulouse (Languedoc) in southern Gaul, first put down the Bagaudic rebellion in the Ebro valley and later fought against the Suebi (Hydatius, *Chron.* 161). Hence, the mid-fifth century CE in Hispania Tarraconensis and Gallaecia witnessed a period of serial pillaging and instability in the main urban centres (449: Caesaraugusta; 460: Lucus Augusti; 468: Asturica Augusta) (Hydatius, *Chron.* 250, 199, and 186).

The Visigoths inherited the situation created by Suebi and Alans in the North, where the Vascones, Cantabri, and Astures maintained their self-government, and remained in their own territories. The image can be completed with a letter from Pope Hilarus (*Ep.* 16.1), dating from 465, referring to *honorati et possessores* in the Ebro valley, who had written in defence of Silvanus, bishop of Calagurris, accused by the bishops of Tarraconensis of making improper ordinations. Therefore, those *possessores* were still an important civilian power in the countryside. The quote is complemented by another mention from Isidore of Seville (*HG* 34), who referred to the resistance of Roman landlords to Visigothic control (Chavarría, 2005: 546). It is to be expected that with de-urbanization, the role of the rural villas became increasingly important. Power was not derived from the *cursus honorum* in the city but the land held by the elite in the rural hinterland (Chavarría, 2007: 50). Some of the late antique villas would have covered over 5 ha, and although not all this area was inhabited, they were clearly larger in size than several imperial cities.

In the mid sixth-century CE, when a Visigothic faction asked the Byzantine emperor Justinian I for help, the political map left after those migratory movements could have been approximately the situation illustrated in Fig. 6.18. The emperor sent his troops to control Carthago Spartaria (ancient Carthago Nova) and part of the former province of Baetica.

One of the questions that arises from the Germanic migrations is what the number of newcomers actually was and where they settled. Most scholars seem to agree that the migrations did not represent a large number in terms of

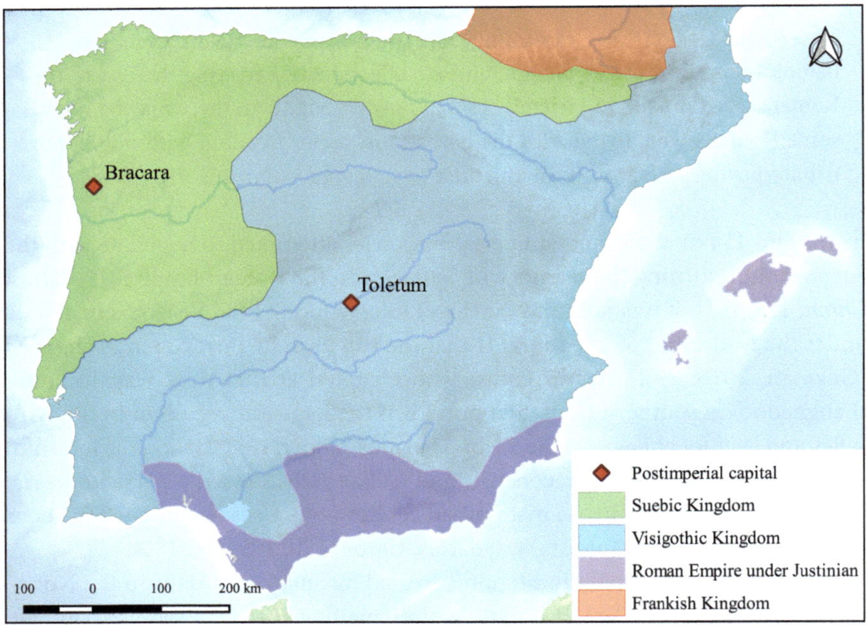


**Fig. 6.18** New political kingdoms in the mid-sixth century CE

population, since most of the groups consisted of small numbers of warriors with their families (López Quiroga, 2011: 44). Besides, some of their leaders were integrated within local Roman elites, following the example of Athaulf and the empress Galla Placidia (Sivan, 2011; Salisbury, 2015). Abadal (1959) put forward the hypothesis that the Visigothic aristocracy numbered around 1,500 families (*c.* 6,000–7,000 members), and their army was 10% of the total population. Reinhart (1945) established an approximate number of 80,000–100,000 Visigoths based on their settlements and cemeteries in the Iberian peninsula. If the total population of the Iberian peninsula remained similar to what it had been during the Early Empire, which was 4–4.5 million (Carreras, 2014), the percentage of Visigoths could have reached between 2 and 2.5% of the total population. Even if we accept a 20% contraction of the total population, the percentage that this group will have represented is still not very significant.

Likewise, Palol (1966) quantified the number of Visigoths according to the cemeteries known at that time, while Ripoll (1989: 392–5) updated this figure, reaching a total population of 80,000 people, taking into account that some Visigothic families remained in Aquitania and Narbonensis and never crossed into the Iberian peninsula.

In the case of Visigothic populations, excavated cemeteries enable us to discriminate them from local communities, since their religion and funerary practices differed from each other. It must be mentioned that some specialists no longer consider that this was necessarily the case. In other words, not everybody who wore 'Visigothic metalwork' was certainly a Visigoth, at least not after the mid-sixth century CE. Be that as it may, most of those necropolises are located on the northern Meseta in the same region with a concentration of urban centres and the luxurious fourth-century villas as Figs. 6.11 and 6.19 record. Apart from the excellent agricultural conditions of this area, it should be remembered that it also had the greatest density of population since the Iron Age (see Chapters 4 and 5).

The choice of an already densely-settled region as the area to establish themselves demonstrates the easy integration of the Visigoths among local Roman landlords. As a result of their small population numbers and quick integration, the Visigoths seem to have lost their language and left no signs in personal and place names (Ripoll, 1989: 399). The impact of the Visigoths in terms of Y-DNA has recently been studied, but it does not seem to be significant, probably because of admixture during their long stay in Eastern Europe (see Chapter 8). With regard to the Suebi, the other German tribe that remained in the Iberian peninsula, scholars calculated a total number of 20,000–25,000 people (Thompson, 1982: 158–9; Arce, 2013: 149), or perhaps 30,000–40,000 when they settled in Gallaecia (Orlandis, 1988). In terms of DNA, the Suebi brought a series of haplogroups, but only one of them, R1a, is found essentially in the western half of Iberia—especially in Portugal and Galicia—but also in northern Castile, Asturias, and Cantabria (see Chapter 8).

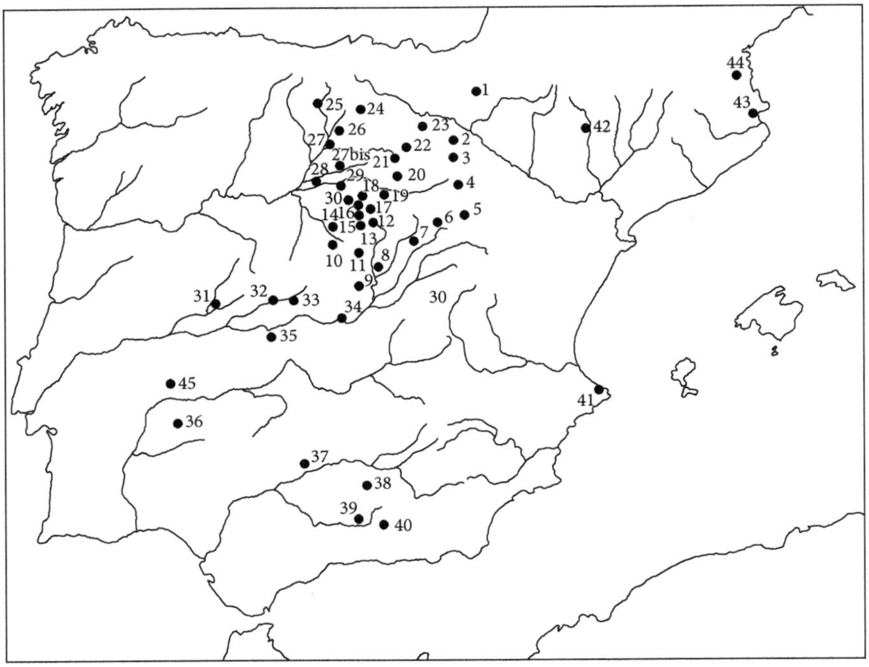


**Fig. 6.19** Location of the main Visigothic cemeteries according to Palol (1966)

As was mentioned above, Hydatius (*Chron.* 81) recorded that people fled to *castella* when the Suebi arrived, which in archaeological terms implied a reoccupation of the Iron Age castros. In recent years, archaeological excavations have registered around 114 hillforts in Gallaecia that were occupied from the fifth century CE onwards (Arias, 2018: table 1). Most late antique castros were located close to the main communication networks as Fig. 6.20 illustrates clearly, showing how important roads and rivers were in the formation of Late Roman settlement patterns.

## 6.4 Conclusions

The present chapter covers the changes in the urbanism and population in the Late Roman period in Hispania Tarraconensis, Carthaginensis, and Gallaecia. Those three provinces were the new provincial divisions of the previous Hispania Tarraconensis after Diocletian's reforms. As becomes obvious from the previous pages, the data of this period are still limited due to difficulties in defining the sizes of Late Roman cities. Urban archaeology has improved in recent years in Spain, and many new excavations often bring layers dated to late antiquity to light and provide some clues on the development of cities in this period. In general, there

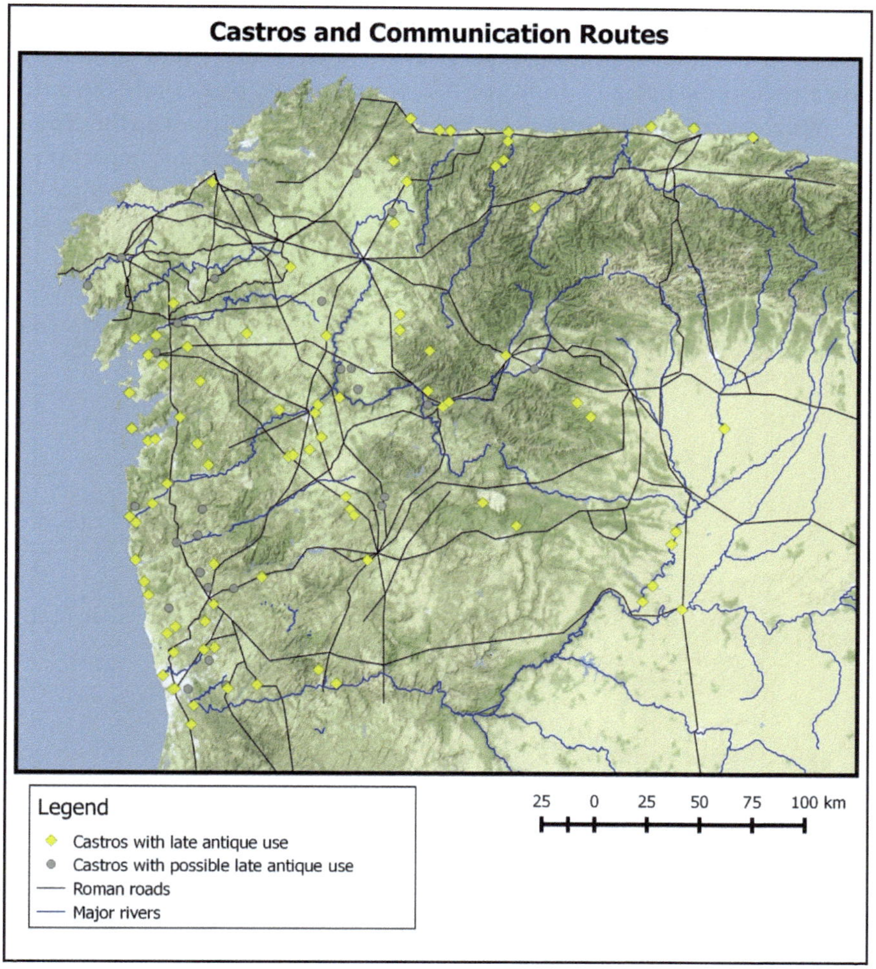


**Fig. 6.20** Map of castros with Late Roman occupation in north-western Gallaecia (Arias, 2018: fig. 2)

are signs of the abandonment of public spaces, burials, and the apparition of landfills inside towns together with evidence for de-urbanization. Although the downward trend appears to be general, there are some exceptions in particular cities such as Bracara Augusta, which became the new provincial capital and later capital of the Suebic kingdom.

The period also displays a phenomenon of luxurious residences in the countryside from the fourth century CE onwards. Such a pattern of rural settlement coincides with what is seen in the Gallic provinces and reveals a movement of the urban elites to the countryside. Unfortunately, field survey data are still too poor to recognize population movements from the city to the countryside.

The final feature of this period was the movement of peoples from Central Europe to the Iberian peninsula. Some of those Germanic tribes crossed the province before moving on to North Africa, and others, particularly the Suebi and Visigoths remained in Hispania, settling in the north-west and on the central plateau respectively. It is difficult to evaluate their real demographic impact since ancient sources tell us that they did not number more than 200,000 people. In terms of DNA, those migrations did not represent a noticeable genetic impact either (see Chapter 8).

*The Human Factor: The Demography of the Roman Province of Hispania Citerior/Tarraconensis*. Alejandro G. Sinner, Cèsar Carreras, and Pieter Houten, Oxford University Press. 
DOI: 10.1093/9780191943881.003.0006

# 7
# Connectivity, Migrations, Mobility, and Networks

During the last two decades, interest in theorizing, discussing, and tracing connectivity, mobility, migration, and, in general, movement in the Roman Mediterranean has expanded considerably among historians and archaeologists. The greater part of this scholarship has largely been oriented in two different but interconnected directions. First, the collection and analysis of archaeological data, focusing especially on studying the forms of production, distribution, and consumption that Roman economic networks triggered. Second, a substantial number of studies have converged in developing and integrating new theories and methods that can be applied to historical and archaeological research. As a result of these two profitable lines of research, a considerable number of contributions have been published recently (e.g. Pitts and Versluys, 2015; de Ligt and Tacoma, 2016a; Tacoma, 2016; Isayev, 2017; Lo Cascio and Tacoma, 2017). It is not without good reason that it has been suggested that the level of connectivity of a territory or region is the variable that makes it possible to estimate its social and economic features at a particular historical moment (Horden and Purcell, 2000).

Research on Roman roads, accessibility, and transportation costs in the Empire (Laurence, 1999; Kolb, 2019) and Hispania (Carreras and De Soto, 2010; 2013; De Soto, 2019) have witnessed major growth in recent years, especially since the use of GIS network applications was integrated into historical and archaeological research. A substantial number of publications on the Roman economy, commercial circuits, and trade networks have summarized large datasets of archaeological information providing new ways of visualizing and understanding connections across the ancient world. A well-known example is ORBIS, the Stanford Geospatial Network Model of the Roman World, which contains the basic routes of the Roman Empire. The project integrates data-based predictive geospatial modelling, providing tools that can help scholars to understand how travel and routes shifted, based on the type of transportation, medium used (i.e. road, river, or sea), season, or even month of the year. Concepts such as distance can be converted into variables (e.g. cost and time), and the subsequent creation of algorithms and models makes it feasible to analyse and interpret the rationale and functioning behind a transport network. Therefore, we are now in a position to be able to model—in economic and social terms—the potential of a specific transport infrastructure, thereby achieving an unprecedented capacity to understand how people moved, how long displacement took place, and at what cost. On the other hand, we should not forget that networks are means for the analysis of archaeological data but do not offer objective responses; they need to be interpreted and require accuracy when working at a provincial or regional level, a scale at which ORBIS is not accurate enough for the Hispaniae, since it only includes the main transportation routes, but misses many others, such as secondary roads, trackways, and river routes.[1]

Despite this increasing interest in migrations, mobility, and connectivity, and the huge technological, methodological, and theoretical advances that this field has accomplished, migrations have always been the least covered subject in demographic studies in antiquity, or as Voland (2000: 142) said a 'neglected step-child of research'. It is worth noting that this becomes a key element for the reproductive strategy in societies at critical times. Apart from the sustained growth of a population as a consequence of its fertility rate, its life expectancy, and its death rate (see Chapter 2), any population is affected by the sudden changes that migrations entail, both in individual movements and in the mobility of human groups (e.g. deportation, slavery, armies).

However, as Mary Beard has pointed out, mobility 'was not restricted to the axis between the metropolitan centre and the rest of the Roman world' (Beard, 2015: 508), and the fact that the majority of research involving mobility and connectivity still focuses on the flow of people, objects, and ideas in and out of Rome rather than other types of inter- and intra-provincial relations and connections is an issue that needs to be addressed. Similarly, the rural, productive, hilly, and other non-urban landscapes and their workers and inhabitants are commonly excluded from these type of studies—as happens in many cases in scholarship focusing on demography, creating an urbanocentric vision of migration and movement. Lastly, most of the literature concentrates on very specific and isolated case studies (local or regional) or exclusively on long-distance migrations (the shotgun picture), there being few studies that succeed in integrating diverse datasets diachronically and for a wide range of spatial scales, a weakness that frequently hints at how people experienced connectivity and mobility.

The Iberian peninsula in general and the province of Citerior/Tarraconensis in particular offer a perfect case study to illustrate many of the aforementioned problems. From the arrival of the Romans with the Scipio brothers in 218 BCE until late antiquity, the Iberian peninsula experienced a series of migratory processes that affected its territories in different ways and the province under study is

[1] The study of the transportation network of Hispania Mercator-e developed by P. de Soto is a much more accurate tool: https://www.arcgis.com/home/webmap/viewer.html?webmap=0178a2683de44c81b5839aac2b48411e&extent=-10.6672,36.3778,3.5162,43.5015.

not an exception. The origins, numbers, and social status of the protagonists in these movements changed over time as did their destination and the reasons behind their migratory processes, making the province of Citerior/Tarraconensis an excellent case study to see the overall picture. Moreover, several studies have been devoted to understanding such a phenomenon, providing us with a large body of data that has been constantly revised and updated (Brunt, 1971; Haley, 1991; Díaz Ariño, 2008; Stefanile, 2017; Ortiz Córdoba, 2019c). To do so, in this chapter we will discuss extra-provincial migrations from the late Republic down to the Late Roman period generically and the cases of migrations from Gallia, Africa, and Italy specifically.

Besides, Hispania Citerior also records at least one case of indigenous deportation when Pompey punished the communities that had supported Sertorius in 71 BCE (Plut. *Pomp.* 21, 1) (Pina Polo, 2009: 283). According to a late source (Hier. *adv. Vigil.*, 4 ed. Migne, *Patr. Lat.* 11, 389–90), the Pyrenean town of Lugdunum Convenarum was founded by transferring Vettones, Arevaci, and Celtiberians who had previously supported Sertorius, though archaeologically the new founded city does not show any sign of migration (Esmonde-Cleary, 2007). Other examples of the relocation of indigenous populations during the second-first centuries BCE transferred to newly founded cities by *imperatores* as a result of defeat and the following *deditio* are Gracchuris, Valeria, and perhpas Caepiana, Brutobriga and Pompaelo (Pina Polo, 2021).

Furthermore, in the Hispanic provinces, there was also a high degree of internal mobility, whether temporary or permanent, which can be very useful to grasp the detailed picture and its evolution over the course of time. To do so, we will analyse several case studies including those of Tarraco (in the north-east), Asturica Augusta (in the north-west), and Clunia and its territory (inland) in order to gain an appreciation of and visualize patterns and differences that may be representative of the diversity in existence in the province from an urban and rural perspective. Both the classical and the epigraphic sources provide extensive documentation on migrations that, in archaeological and especially genetic terms, are more complicated to assess (see Chapter 8). Once again, to conduct this 'small picture' analysis we have excellent tools (epigraphic corpora aside) such as the data from projects like MIGRA–UCAN and *Mapping Migration in Roman Iberia,* and monographic studies (Villalón, 2019).

Transport infrastructures in a huge province such as Hispania Citerior/Tarraconensis were the means by which people came to the province and moved around it. A thorough analysis of these infrastructures by GIS provides explanatory elements to understand accessibility between territories that were likely to receive or lose population. In the case of Hispania Citerior/Tarraconensis, there were two external interprovincial connections (namely, the Mediterranean and the Atlantic) that were linked by an extensive network of roads and rivers, though internal connectivity is the key element to understand the province's integration over the passage of time until modern periods (Ringrose, 1972).

Finally, the causes of this migration to and within the peninsula in Roman times were not so dissimilar to those of today, from access to new, previously underexploited territories (in other words ecological niches), employment opportunities (e.g. land shortages, urban centres, professions), political reasons (e.g. conflict, instability), or ethnic and religious ones (e.g. diasporas). As many have suggested, the term mobility is problematic since it encompasses a wide variety of social realities and other categories. Slaves, soldiers, merchants, workers, women, and others all moved, but they did so in heterogeneous ways, in response to diverse motivations and over different periods of time; some returned in days, others in months or even years, and many never saw their motherland again (Woolf, 2016: 193). Once again, by integrating case studies discussing mobility triggered by work—in many cases seasonal—opportunities (harvests and mining) to the long-distance migrations and the very localized or temporally specific datasets of specific case studies, we shall be able to explore how people experienced mobility and connectivity in the largest Hispanic province in quite a unique way.

## 7.1 Mediterranean Connectivity: Hispania Citerior—Italy

The premier source for interconnections with Italy during the late Republican period can be found in the arrival and distribution of Dressel 1 and Lamboglia 2 wine amphorae and Brindisi olive-oil amphorae and fine black-gloss tableware. During the second century BCE, Italic amphorae clearly outnumber the rest of imported amphorae (e.g. Punic, Greek). In the north-east of Citerior, in the second century BCE, these vessels represent close to 60% of the total sherds of imported amphorae in the selection of Iberian settlements studied by Asensio (2010: 31) (Fig. 7.1). Similar numbers of Italic amphorae are recorded in some of the case studies discussed in this text, for example in Ilduro, Italic amphorae account for approximately 69% of all the imported fragments.[2]

Molina Vidal's study (1997: 65) also highlights the predominance of Tyrrhenian amphorae in Citerior in the northern half of the coastal territories of the province. Of all amphorae imports from Italy, Dressel 1 containers (wine amphorae) represent 85–95% of the total. However, in the southern half of the province, these vessels only represent 45–50%, the Adriatic wines transported in Lamboglia 2 amphorae having been much more significant and especially high at Tossal de Manises (57%), La Alcudia (56%), or El Molinete (54%), revealing a different commercial dynamic from that found in the northern area (Molina Vidal, 1997:

[2] Numbers estimated from a sample of 5,538 fragments recovered from the Can Benet and Ca l'Arnau sectors (Stannard and Sinner, 2014: 174).

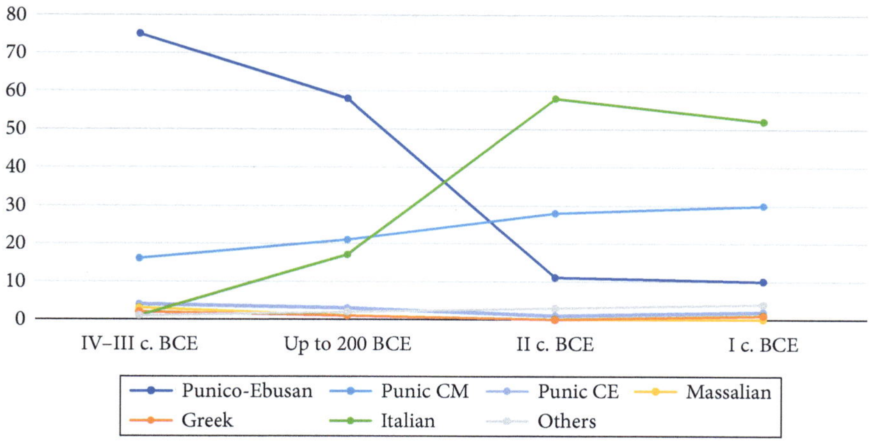


**Fig. 7.1** Percentage of fragments of Italic amphorae with respect to the fragments of amphorae from other provenances (note Punico-Ebusan amphorae) from a sample of five Iberian sites in the north-east of the Iberian Peninsula (fourth-third centuries BCE) (redrawn after Asensio, 2010)

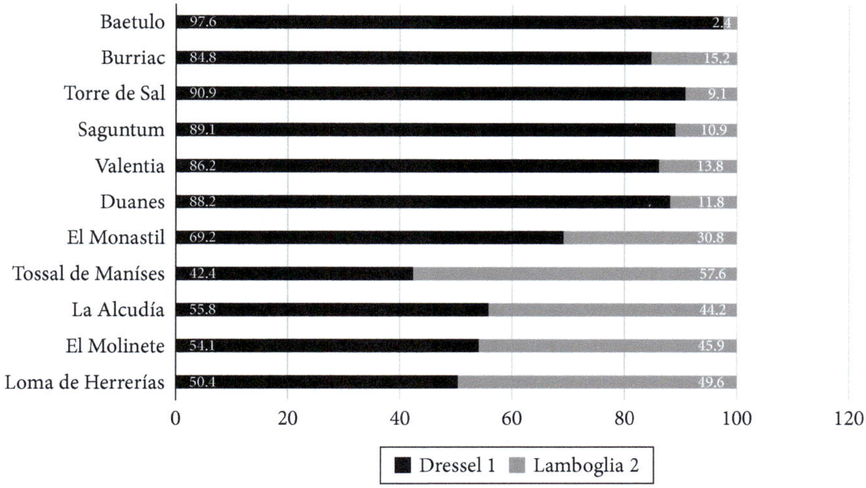


**Fig. 7.2** Regional distribution of Dressel 1 and Lamboglia 2 amphorae of Italic origin (redrawn after Molina Vidal, 1997: fig. 45)

65 and fig. 44) (Fig. 7.2) and highlighting the importance of understanding trade routes and connectivity at a regional and provincial level and beyond the division of the Mediterranean in the oriental and western markets (Tchernia, 1986: 68 and 74).

Further valuable archaeological evidence connecting Italy and north-eastern Spain is provided by shipwrecks (see Parker, 1992). From the mid-second century

BCE and down to the first half of the first century BCE, wrecks carrying containers of Italic origin are predominant in the western Mediterranean (Asensio, 2010: 31). These large volumes of imported Italic wines were in many cases accompanied by black-gloss wares as a secondary cargo, a commodity that was widely consumed and which is represented at almost every archaeological site on the Mediterranean shores of the province with archaeological levels datable to the second and early first centuries BCE.

Looking in the opposite direction, from Citerior to the Italian peninsula, the evidence of high connectivity between these two territories is well documented archaeologically and by the ancient sources, providing a good idea of the types of goods that were exported. The latter recurrently mention slaves and textiles among the cargoes that most probably filled the empty space left in the ships that transported the amphorae and fine tableware previously discussed to Hispania. Leaving aside the textiles from Lusitania (Plin. *NH* VIII.191) and Baetica, the wool from the latter province enjoyed fame during the reign of Augustus (Str. 3.2.6; Plin. *NH* VIII.191), the linen from Citerior, especially that of Saetabi (Catull. 12.14–15 and 25.6–7), Tarraco, and the variety made in Zoelae (Asturias) were widely exported and praised by ancient writers:

> But it is the province of Nearer Spain that produces a linen of the greatest lustre, an advantage which it owes to the waters of a stream which washes the city of Tarraco there. The fineness, too, of this linen is quite marvellous, and here it is that the first manufactories of cambric were established. From the same province, too, of Spain, the flax of Zoëla has of late years been introduced into Italy, and has been found extremely serviceable for the manufacture of hunting-nets. Zoëla is a city of Gallaecia, in the vicinity of the Ocean. Pliny *NH* XIX.2

Slaves were also commonly taken from Citerior to Italy, as the ancient sources give good account of this from the very first moment when Roman forces arrived in the province. As early as 218 BCE, after Cissa (Kese) was taken, a substantial contingent of captives was sold into slavery (Liv. 21.60.8). Without providing here an exhaustive list of each of these chapters, it is worth pointing out that the slave trade from the largest of Hispania's provinces towards Italy continued during most of the Republic. Livy (39.42.1) mentions how Terentius Varro sold the prisoners taken in the year 184 BCE after the capture of the Sussetani city of Corbion. Appian (*Iber.* 68) is even more specific and tells us that Q. Fabius Maximus Servilianus, proconsul in Spain in 141–140 BCE, sold 9,500 of the prisoners he took from various Iberian cities into slavery. As early as the beginning of the first century BCE, in the years 98–94, the consul Titus Didius after besieging and taking the city of Colenda, sold all the captives, including women and children (App. *Iber.* 99). Finally, the situation did not change during the Civil Wars or the Cantabrian Wars. In both conflicts, several chapters in which enemies were traded into slavery are narrated by the ancient sources. Perhaps two of the most iconic examples are the episode when Sertorius laid aside his former clemency and sold some of the sons of the Iberians who were being educated at Osca (Plut. *Sert.* 25.4.), or the chapter during the Cantabrian Wars when the Cantabri, seeing that they had no prospect of freedom, decided to end their lives:

> Nevertheless, he did not appear to them that sort of man when it came to action; for they were defeated and reduced to slavery by him, and the Astures likewise, since he also aided Carisius. Not many of the Cantabri were captured; for when they had no hope of freedom, they did not choose to live, either, but some set their forts on fire and cut their own throats, and others of their own choice remained with them and were consumed in the flames, while yet others took poison in the sight of all. Cassius Dio 65.5.2

In fact, it has been suggested, and is quite feasible, that a substantial number of the 40,000 men that worked in the Carthago Nova mines (Polyb. 34.9.9; Str. 3.2.10) in the middle of the first century BCE were the result of slaves being moved in the opposite direction and never leaving the province.

Archaeologically speaking, lead ingots are perhaps the best evidence for the maritime routes that connected the Iberian and Italic peninsulas as underwater finds seem to corroborate (Fig. 7.3). Ships loaded with lead ingots[3] frequently

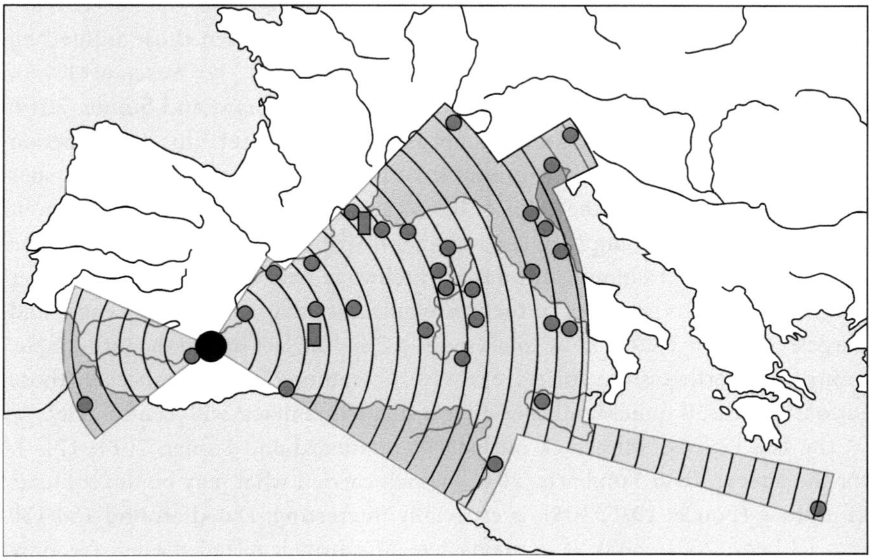

**Fig. 7.3** Lead ingots from Carthago Nova found in the Mediterranean (after Trincherini et al., 2009: 141, fig. 5)

[3] A complete corpus of lead ingots in Domergue and Rico (2023).

sailed between Carthago Nova towards Italy; the wrecks provide excellent proof of these commercial exchanges and trade routes (for a compilation of wrecks see Parker, 1992; provenance studies using lead isotope analysis Trincherini et al., 2001; 2009; Nesta et al., 2011; Domergue et al., 2012; 2016; Sinner, 2021). The suggestion that the lead business attracted Italians to Spain to exploit its economic potential in various forms is also well documented epigraphically. As we will discuss below, number of Italian *gentes* involved in this trade have been identified, particularly from Campania and Minturnae and its hinterland (Marín Díaz, 1986; Díaz Ariño, 2008; Orejas and Beltrán, 2010; Stefanile, 2014, 2017; Stannard et al., 2019).

Coinage can also provide interesting evidence of connectivity between Italy and Hispania Citerior. Stannard has been assembling a database of non-Roman coins that can be provenanced to the River Liri, at Minturnae, where the Via Appia crossed over a bridge connecting Latium to Campania.[4] The Liri database documents one of the largest known groups of foreign coins from any late Hellenistic site in Italy.

There is a substantial number of Spanish coins in the database. Mainland mints make up about 4.5% of the database (70 coins). In Citerior, the ports of Kese/Tarraco (18.6%) and Undikesken/Emporion (14.3%) are especially prominent while coins from Valentia (2.9%) and Carthago Nova (1.4%) have a smaller presence in the sample. If we look at the presence of Hispanic coins in the Liri database beyond the three main harbours of Citerior, coins of the Laeetani are relatively common (7.1%), and much more significant than those minted by the Iberian peoples located inland, such as the Sussetani (4.3%), Ausetani (1.4%), and the Lacetani and Ilergetes (2.9% combined) (Stannard and Sinner, 2014: fig. 9). Celtiberian issues are not even present in the Liri set. This phenomenon appears to be significant, because most of the Iberian and Celtiberian issues circulated locally, unlike the coins of Kese/Tarraco, which are found throughout Catalonia. A good example of the regional distribution of these issues can be seen in the coins circulating at Ilduro, which were overwhelming local (Sinner and Martí, 2012): the issues of the Cessetani, Ausetani, Laeetani, Lacetani, and Ilergetes make up 84.9% of the total (see Fig. 7.4). The fact that in the Liri sample, mints from north-eastern Spain are relatively common (Fig. 7.4), especially those in coastal areas, is quite significant since it suggests contacts with central Italy.

The Isla Pedrosa shipwreck off Estartit (Stannard and Sinner, 2014: 171–4; for the wreck: Vivar Lombarte, 2016), which carried what may be the contents of a purse (Ponce, 1975: 105), is especially interesting. Dated around 150/130 BCE (Ribera, 2001: 300), it contains five Minturnaean lead pieces, the only examples known from anywhere else, as well as Neapolitan coins. The purse

[4] Ruegg (1995); for the circumstances of these finds Stannard and Ranucci (2016: 158–61).

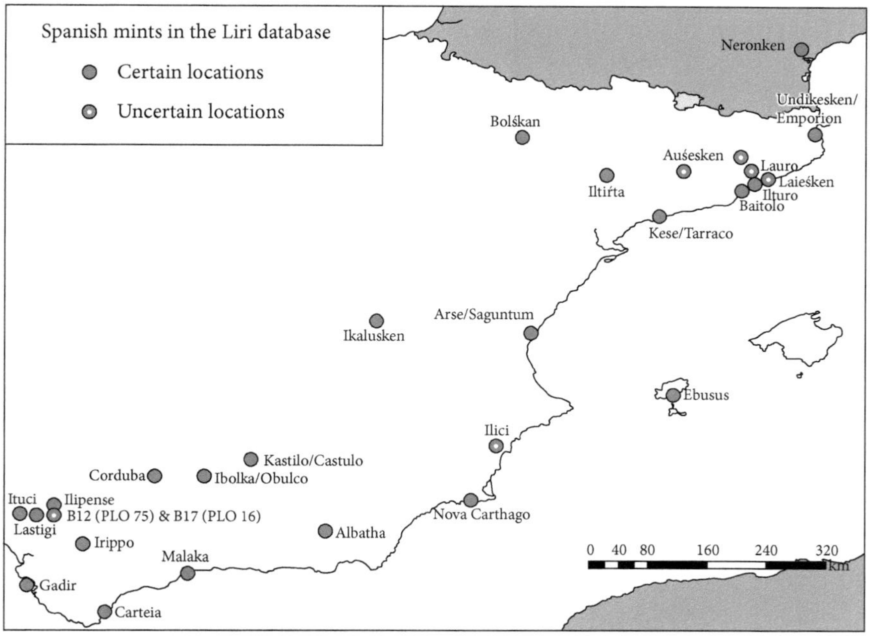


**Fig. 7.4** Hispanic mints recorded on the coins in the Liri database

probably belonged to a passenger from Minturnae who had boarded a south-bound cabotage vessel from the major entrepôt of Emporion, which was selling Campanian A black-gloss wares and local millstones down the Catalan coast (Arévalo and Delgado, 2016).

As can be seen, coinage, pottery assemblages (amphorae and black-gloss pottery), lead ingots, textiles, and the slave trade, all point towards the existence of a considerable degree of connectivity and intense commercial exchanges between Italy and Hispania Citerior during the last two centuries of the Republic. The ports of Minturnae and especially Puteoli, the latter a major harbour for the Roman world since the early second century BCE, were fundamental points on this connectivity network—as were those of Emporion, Tarraco, and Carthago Nova in Hispania and Massalia in southern Gaul—and help to explain the origin of the archaeological evidence described above and, as we will see later in this chapter (see section 7.4.3), the importance that Campanian and Minturnaean merchants gravitating around the Gulf of Naples and the River Liri had for the initial colonization of Citerior. The port of Puteoli, which experienced continuous commercial growth until the first century CE, was a place of contact between goods and merchants from very distant locations and a hub that connected Hispania Citerior with Campania (see Fig. 7.5).

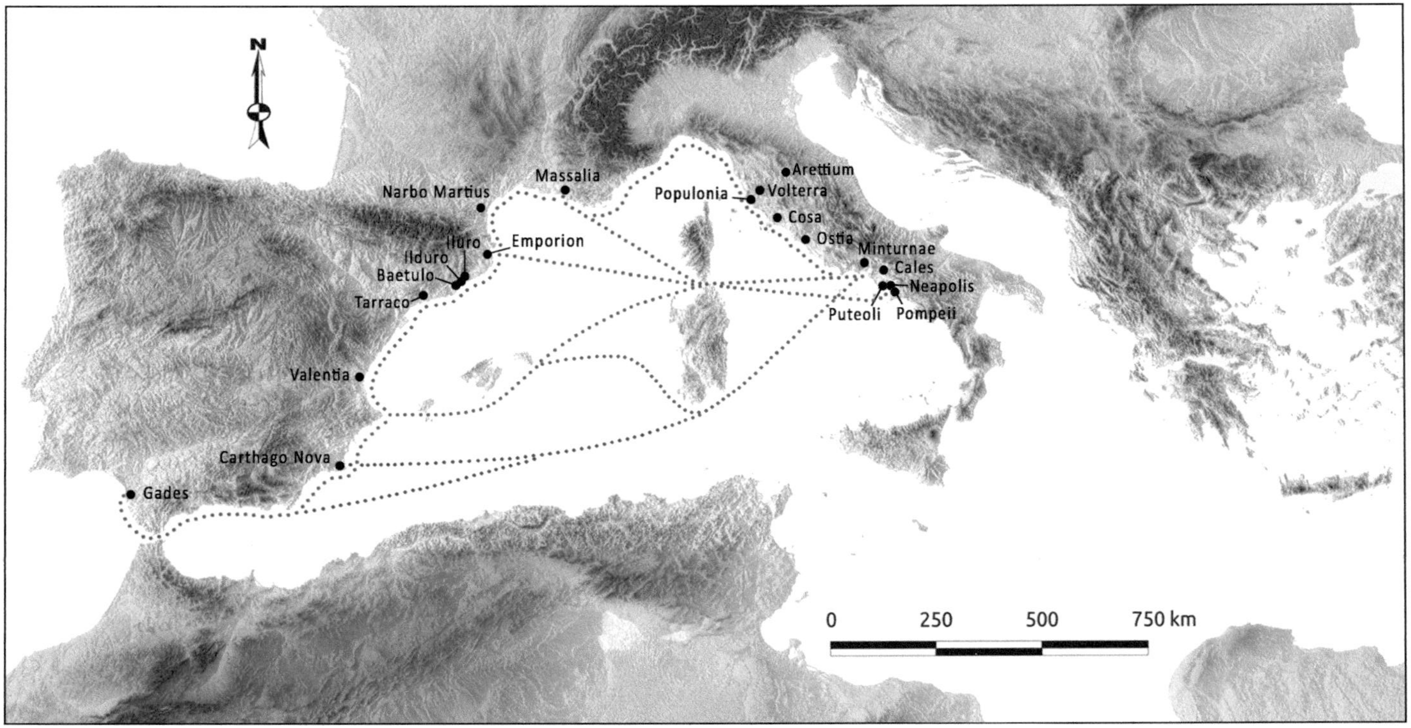


Fig. 7.5 Main overseas Mediterranean routes connecting Italy, Gaul, and Hispania Tarraconensis

## 7.2 The Atlantic: Connectivity between Citerior and the Outer Sea

Apart from the coastal Mediterranean access route, Hispania Citerior was conquered by the Romans from the Atlantic Ocean through a longer process. The first connection between the inner Mediterranean and the Atlantic was created by the Phoenicians of Tyre. At the end of the second millennium BCE, they founded the colony of Gadir, which became the colonial entrance to the Atlantic southern core, including present-day southern Portugal, western Andalusia, and north-western Morocco (Carreras and Morais, 2010; 2012). Gadir was a springboard for expeditionary missions to the west coast of Africa and the western seaboard of the Iberian peninsula (Fig. 7.6). It appears that these eastern colonizers were searching for tin along the Atlantic coasts, though the ancient sources are imprecise. Herodotus (*Hist.* 3.115) refers to his lack of knowledge: 'nor do I know of any islands called the Cassiterides whence the tin comes which we use'. These Cassiterides islands were supposed to be somewhere north-west of Iberia (Fonte et al., 2015); some authors even placed them in south-western Britain. New tin mines have been discovered in Portugal and Gallaecia (Meunier, 2019).

Another later ancient source is the *Ora maritima* of Avienius (fourth century CE), which encompasses earlier documents referring to the Oestrymnis, a place

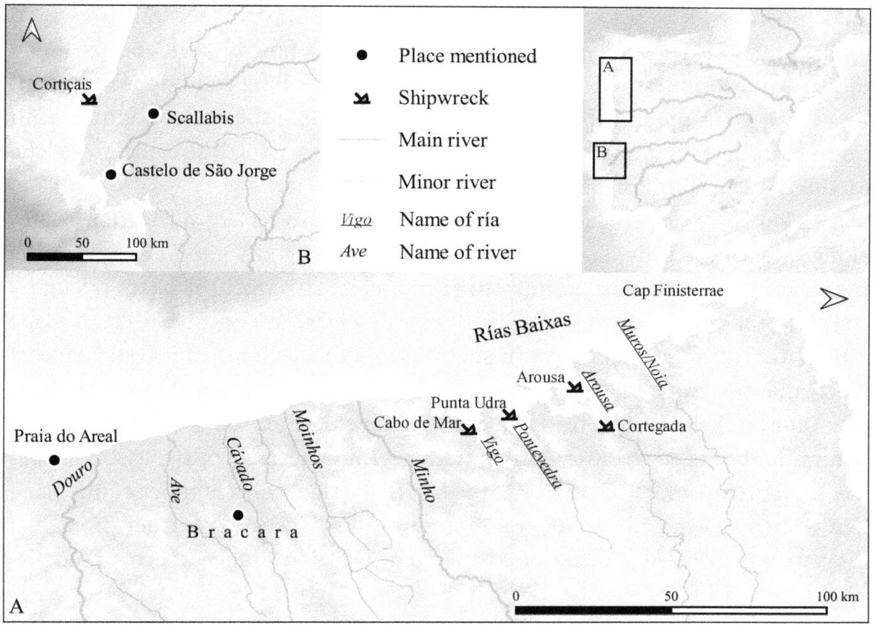


**Fig. 7.6** Map with the main sites, rivers and *rias* mentioned in the text

where people were wealthy in tin and lead and sailed in leather boats (*Ora maritima* 92–106). Nowadays, it is believed that Oestrymnis was located on the northern coast of Galicia where tin and lead mines are well documented (Fonte et al., 2015). The Phoenicians from Gadir controlled the tin trade of this western seaboard up to the Roman period, despite the fact that little Phoenician material (e.g. Phoenician amphorae) is recorded on the coasts of Portugal, Galicia, or the British Isles.

Therefore, the Atlantic became a unique exchange corridor where sailors could ship their merchandise from the southern to the northern end and the other way around. Nevertheless, a major change took place during the last two centuries BCE when the Romans began to make contact with populations living on the Atlantic coastline. According to Strabo (*Geog.* III.5.3), Gadir at that time was a place where: 'live the men, who are equipped with the most and largest merchant-vessels, from our sea (Mediterranean) and the outer sea (Atlantic)'. In addition to new political conditions and the Romans' quest for metals, the thriving trade on the western Atlantic seaboard was also the result of better weather conditions. Data obtained from an analysis of meteorological and oceanographic circumstances suggest that in Roman times different conditions existed, much more conducive to navigation than those of the present day.

There is evidence that climatic conditions, including prevailing winds on the western coast of Portugal before the Roman period, during the Roman era and even until 1000 CE, were quite different from today's strong north wind or 'nortada' (Soares, 1987). Since this publication, Soares' study was recently presented by the author as an academic thesis, and it indicates how the evidence of much milder wind conditions could help us to understand sailing conditions in ancient times, as well as the fact that the Atlantic Sea lanes had specific conditions, with tides bringing substantial changes to sea-levels and tidal streams from the Mediterranean (Blot, 2010: 83).

The Portuguese and Galician coastline offered a variety of navigation routes along estuaries, marine lagoons, and rivers (Figure 7.6). A good example is the Rías Baixas, as Fernández points out (Fernández, 2010: 229) it offers a lengthy coastline that begins at the estuary of the River Minho and goes up to Cape Finisterre with four major bays (namely, Vigo, Pontevedra, Arousa, and Muros/Noia) that penetrate inland. Thanks to this special coastal morphology, the castros (hillforts) situated in this area had the benefit of excellent conditions, with natural harbours suited to maritime trade (for an overview of the castros, location, and urbanism, see Chapter 4). The fact that a significant number of imported items, such as glass and coins, were found in these castros is further proof that they were privileged places, attracting trade goods produced throughout the Roman world.

However, one quickly realizes that the most abundant material excavated at them were amphorae of various types and fabrics, corresponding to the different periods when the territories were conquered. The study of the substantial number of amphorae discovered in this area, most probably unloaded on the well-known Areal beach, states first that the best represented period is that from the second century BCE to the first century CE (Fernández, 2010; Morais, 2010: 103–4) and then that the most common type is the Haltern 70 amphora, with about 1,000 individuals (Morais and Carreras, 2004: 93–112). The identification of a shipwreck in Ria de Arousa (Vilagarcía de Arousa, Pontevedra) reflects the importance of these places in Roman times.

According to Blot (2010: 85–6), the Romans chose places near river mouths and lagoons to establish their most important cities (see Chapter 5), which may explain the existence of an interconnection between their roads and the river and maritime routes. The Roman town of Bracara Augusta is one of the best examples of this interconnection of roads and waterways. The economic and commercial importance of this town has already been highlighted (Morais, 2010). It is unquestionable that Bracara Augusta was an important centre for the shipping and redistribution of food and manufactured commodities, which came from several large production centres—thus suggesting that this city was well integrated into the Empire, as can be seen from the quantity and types of amphorae found there (Morais, 2010: 216–18). Nevertheless, the city did not benefit directly from the ports-of-call along the Atlantic route, although it may have done through secondary ones involved in the traffic of both small and larger cabotage vessels that were situated at the mouths of the Rivers Ave and Cávado. The larger vessels, heading towards the main ports-of-call on the Rivers Douro and Minho, may well have unloaded part of their cargoes at the mouths of the Rivers Ave and Cávado.

Dependable evidence exists for shipwrecks along the Galician coast, even though no structural remains of Roman boats have actually been found there. Despite the problems of preservation—the dynamics of the seabed make locations difficult to trace—there are indications that suggest at least three shipwrecks (Naveiro, 1991: 63–7, fig. 14). The first may be situated in the Ria de Arousa, near the island of Cortegada (Vilagarcía de Arousa, Pontevedra), where at least 34 specimens of Haltern 70 amphorae were concentrated, 22 of which were unbroken or nearly unbroken: traces of resin inside (Morais and Carreras, 2004: 104) have been recovered (together with Southern Gaulish *terra sigillata* fragments). It is possible that the sandbar built up by the river may have been responsible for the shipwreck of this vessel. The second possible shipwreck may be located in Cabo de Mar, where a large number of Haltern 70 amphorae were found, four of which were unbroken. At this spot is a dangerous shoal that extends into the sea, and this might have been responsible for the sinking of the vessel. It is possible that these amphorae were intended for disembarkation at the nearby beach of Praia do Areal, as is suggested by the large number of amphora fragments collected in excavations there. The third place, situated at Punta Udra, may mark another shipwreck. Even though we are unaware of any cargo remains, three stumpy pieces of lead from a medium-sized vessel have been found in a relatively small area (about 12 $m^2$). There is further evidence of shipwrecks on the Portuguese coast. On the north coastline of Portugal, archaeological discoveries in the intertidal area of the mouth of the Peralto—the former estuary of the Rio de Moinhos (Esposende)—revealed several traces of Roman occupation.

Further to the south, at the underwater site of Cortiçais (Peniche), a shipwreck with Haltern 70 amphorae and thin-walled wares has been recorded, among which are more than two dozen Italian *sigillata* fragments from the time of Augustus. This shipwreck, situated off the southern coast near the city of Peniche, is situated at a shallow depth (between 4 and 6 m) and at a distance of 30 m from the coastline.

After the Lusitanian Wars (155–138 BCE), southern Lusitania, including part of the southern Atlantic core, came under Roman control. The movements of the Roman legions and the new urban settlements also brought new commercial trade in Mediterranean goods to the western Atlantic seafront. This first period of Roman commercial influence in the western Atlantic (155–50 BCE) was a collaboration with traders from Gadir, an allied city (*civitas foederata*), who had contacts with local communities and also had detailed knowledge of navigation in the Atlantic.

In terms of material culture, the evidence of such commercial dynamics is registered in the volume and distribution of the typical Roman wine amphorae of this period: Italic Dressel 1B, Adriatic Lamboglia 2, and North African Mañá C2c (T.7.4.3.3). The excavation of Castelo de São Jorge (Lisbon) provides a good example of this commercial trade during the Republican period, beginning with some Graeco-Italic amphorae, but with a significant presence of Dressel 1B, Mañá C2c (T.7.4.3.3), and Lamboglia 2 amphorae (Pimenta, 2005), together with other vessels from the Gulf of Cádiz (T.9.1.1.1). Graeco-Italic and Lamboglia 2 amphorae were not very popular and are present at only a few sites in southern Lusitania. The second most important vessel is the Phoenician Mañá C2c (T.7.4.3.3), spanning from the mid-second century BCE up to the Augustan period. It was initially produced in North African workshops and later imitated in the Baetican production centres. The Mañá C2c (T.7.4.3.3) amphorae are supposed to have contained fish-sauce products which were mainly consumed in southern Lusitania (Pimenta, 2005: 124) and in some northern castrejos (Fernández, 2010) close to the local sources of tin (*Oestrymnis*).

Perhaps the best-known indicator of these Republican trading networks are once again black-gloss wares and the Dressel 1 wine amphorae, with their three different variants (A, B, and C). Among these three variants, the Dressel 1B is the most widely distributed because of its long production date range from *c.* 100 BCE until the first decades CE. Probably most of them were traded during the first half of the first century BCE, at the time the Roman armies reached the north-west of the Iberian peninsula. Initially, Publius Crassus undertook a military expedition there in 96–94 BCE, while Julius Caesar as *praetor* reached the River Douro (Mt Herminius)—the limit of the province of Citerior—in his campaigns of 61–60 BCE. In these later campaigns, Julius Caesar received support from the people of Gadir, who provided a fleet of around 80 ships (Cass. Dio, 37, 52–3; *Zonaras* 10.6), and probably traded part of the spoils. As a result of this collaboration, Julius Caesar appointed L. Cornelius Balbus as *praefectus fabrum*, the chief engineer of his armies in Gaul: he became one of Caesar's closest advisers (Carreras, 2010: 249). Scallabis was the headquarters of Julius Caesar's armies at that time. It demonstrates a change in the sources of supply: apart from Italian amphorae and fine wares, there is now a wide variety of new forms of Baetican amphorae from the coast and the Guadalquivir valley (e.g. ovoids, Mañá C2c-T.7.4.3.3, Ovoide 1) (Almeida, 2008).

This trend increased during the principate of Augustus, when the emperor waged war against the Astures and Cantabri in the north-west of the Iberian peninsula (29–19 BCE) with five legions (I, II, IV, IX, and XX), and supplies had to be acquired from the Atlantic and Cantabrian ports. Most amphorae from this period came from Baetica, chiefly fish-sauce vessels (i.e. Dressel 7–11 and Dressel 12), or those for olive oil (i.e. Oberaden 83), and numerous contents in the case of Haltern 70 (i.e. wine, olives, *defrutum*, *muria*).

In conclusion, the large dimensions of Hispania Citerior and the fact that it was conquered in different phases from the Mediterranean and Atlantic coasts generated a heterogeneous development of its transport infrastructures that must be discussed to understand how, where, and why people moved. In fact there were two independent transport infrastructures that were connected by road in the territory of what became the future *conventus* Cluniensis.

## 7.3 A Province on the Move: Connectivity Inside Hispania Citerior/Tarraconensis

As mentioned earlier, research on Roman roads, accessibility, and transportation costs in Hispania has experienced considerable growth in recent years. Concepts such as distance can be converted into variables (e.g. cost and time), and the subsequent creation of algorithms and models makes it feasible to analyse and interpret the rationale and functioning behind a transport network (Carreras and De Soto, 2010; 2013; De Soto, 2019). These theoretical models are capable of displaying a picture of how accessible a city was or how connected a region could have been. An important aspect to do so is accuracy, since only a complete detailed network, including secondary roads and trackways as well as river waterways, can model connectivity in a complete province or region. Fortunately, thanks to the excellent research conducted in the last two decades (De Soto and Carreras, 2009;

Carreras and De Soto, 2010), we are now in a position to model the potential of the transport infrastructure of the province under study in economic and social terms (Brughmans, 2010; 2013).

When the Roman army first disembarked in Emporion in the late third century BCE, they probably followed the already existing Iron Age network of trackways and roads, whose layout is still not well known. In the last few years, some rescue excavations have managed to identify complex tracks below Roman roads, which are interpreted as Iberian trackways such as Font de la Figuera (Valencia) under the Via Augusta (Sánchez Priego, 2015). This Iberian track was a hollow trench 3–3.2 metres wide filled with gravels and sands, and it includes remains of wheel ruts. Besides, another Iberian track was identified at Faldetes (Moixent) close to the Via Augusta of a width that ranges from 4 to 9 metres (García Borja et al., 2012: 111). Finally, the last example of Iberian track comes from the mountainous region of Alt del Punxó (Alcoi), which registers a paved road of 5 metres wide and a slight gradient of 4% (Espi et al., 2009: 40–1). Although the Roman roads represented a planned infrastructure layout with high public investment, they took advantage of the Iberian tracks or pathways, which were already in place.[5]

In what is today modern Catalonia, at least from the third century BCE onwards, the orographic conditions had propitiated—and conditioned—the existence of a relatively dense communications network that included waterways such as the River Ebro as well as sections of the Rivers Besòs and the Llobregat. The land network ran in two directions: one set of tracks were parallel to the coastline, while a second group, perpendicular to the first one communicated inland areas with the coast. In the area of the Laeetani, the existence, since pre-Roman times, of different roads and paths following one of these two axes, which structured and communicated this territory, is well known: good examples of this are the Via Heraklea (Mayer and Rodà, 1986; Lostal Pros, 1992; Sillières, 1999), the Camí de la Carena, and the Camí dels Contrabandistes. By the mid-to-late second century BCE, this transportation system had been improved thanks to the creation of well-drained roads, the earliest example (120 BCE) being the road constructed by Manlius Sergius (Mayer and Rodà, 1986), which connected a small network of military posts, *vici* and *castella* (Padrós, 2010). Those early Republican roads soon became much more than mere corridors for military movements and army supply, acting as vectors that connected places, peoples, and things, true agents in the creation of material diasporas (Fig. 7.7).

After 218 BCE, the newcomers from Italy settled in coastal locations with good harbour facilities such as Emporion, Tarraco, or Carthago Nova. As discussed in section 7.1, these settlements combined good connections between Italy and their local populations with favourable infrastructures allowing easy and fast journeys

[5] A more complete study of Iron Age tracks and pathways in Hispania Citerior is required to assess the real contribution of the Romans to the development of transport infrastructures.

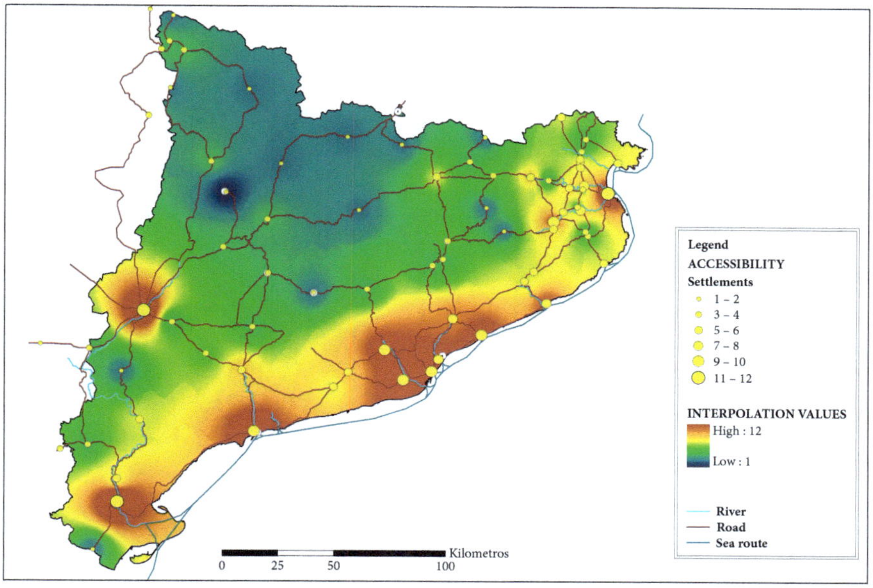


**Fig. 7.7** Accessibility map of north-eastern Hispania (author: Pau De Soto)

to Rome by sea. During the first decade of the conquest, only with some difficulty was Rome able to control a buffer zone along the Mediterranean coast, subjugating uprisings by the local Iberian groups (Cato's campaigns: Liv. 34.15.9; 39.42.7) and subduing their populations.

Despite the abundant literary sources mentioning Italian military sites in inland regions, only in the last few decades has archaeological research uncovered a series of such sites dated to the mid-second century BCE (Morillo, 2003; 2016; Pera et al., 2016). These Early Roman garrisons (*castella*, *praetoria*) were normally located in natural corridors (i.e. valleys) going from coastal towns to major inland Iberian *oppida* (see Fig. 7.8).

The Romans probably followed previous Iron Age tracks with a minimal infrastructure, but reinforcing those routes through the creation of well-drained roads defended by a protective network of *castella* (e.g. Puig Castellar de Biosca), some of which controlled the major rivers such as the Ebro and Guadalquivir. Those early Republican roads, datable only by their milestones and the assemblages at the forts along the roads, were secure corridors for military movements and army supply. In Hispania, the oldest dated milestones have been found in the north-eastern territories and have been dated between 120 and 110 BCE (Lostal Pros, 1992), a very short time after the Gracchi brothers, around 130–120 BCE, under whom milestones with the names of magistrates involved in the construction of roads in Italy were used for the first time in Roman history (Laurence, 1999). This initial road network connected the main coastal settlements with the first

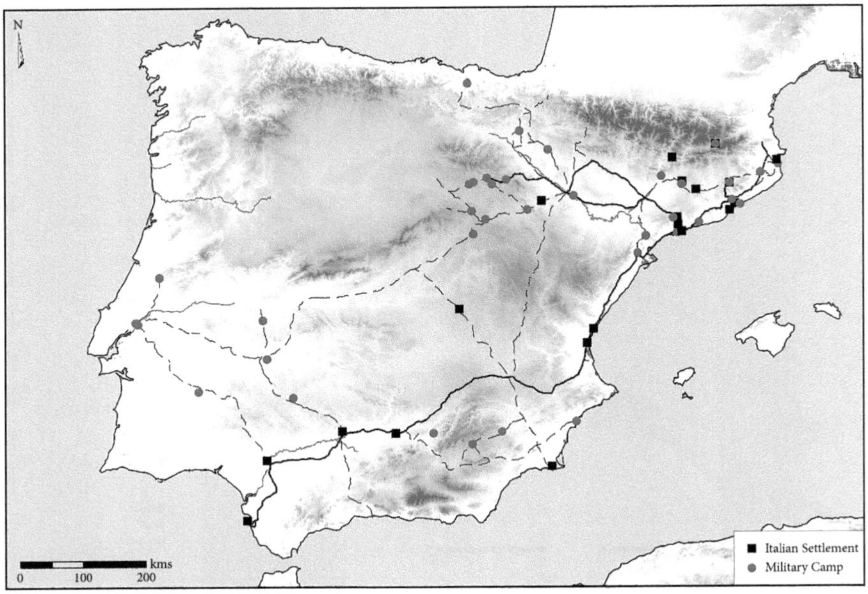


**Fig. 7.8** Roman military camps (dots), sites with italic architecture (squares) and probable main land routes in the Iberian peninsula in the mid-second century BCE (after De Soto and Carreras, 2022)

inland territories that were conquered, facilitating the creation of new military sites on the frontier, which in turn allowed the conquest of further territory, in a continuous process.

This kind of capillary advance explains the slowness in conquering the central areas of the Meseta (in the Celtiberian Wars) and Lusitania. The first road layout in the Iberian peninsula shows that its primary function was one of military connectivity, linking the Roman legions fighting in the Meseta and Lusitania with their coastal headquarters (*hiberna*). Similarly, Laurence explains how the Romans gained control of the Italian peninsula by creating a road network and a policy of founding colonies (312–44 BCE) (Laurence, 1999; see also Houten, 2021). Our research (see Chapters 4 and 5) allows for a more nuanced picture of this process, showing how the Iron Age settlement patterns and transportations networks laid the foundations of the Roman one. In this respect, the Iberian peninsula became an experimental territory to put into practice methods of military conquest and control in which the road system played a crucial role. A good example of this sensible strategy of appropriation, reuse, adaptation, and improvement of previous infrastructure can be seen when looking at the earliest urban centres founded by the Romans in the conquered areas: Tarraco (217 BCE) was built near the main hillfort of the Cessetani (Kese), Carthago Nova (209 BCE) was the capital of the Carthaginians in south-west Spain (Qart-Hadašt), and Italica

(206 BCE) was founded close to a native Turdetani town. These cities were always established near or over existing settlements that were well connected by sea or river routes, and also by some of the first known main roads in the Iberian peninsula, such as the coastal route known as the Via Heraklea, subsequently known as the Via Augusta (De Soto, 2010), and which also pre-dated the Roman arrival.

The ancient sources, basically Livy and Appian, provide accounts of troop numbers sent to Hispania Citerior during Republican times. They normally recorded the name of the governor when a change in troops and their composition took place (Solana, 1998). The histogram in Fig. 7.9 registers those numbers in addition to the projected number of troops from 197 to 73 BCE.

From 197 BCE to 153 BCE, the average number of troops deployed in Hispania Citerior was 15,000 soldiers, such as the one legion and around 2,150 infantrymen, 2,750 *socii* and auxiliaries during the praetorship of A. Terentius Varro (Liv. 39.38.3). Apart from the Roman origin of the legionaries, it is difficult to know where the other troops came from, since most of them were Italian *socii* and indigenous auxiliaries. During the Celtiberian Wars the number of troops increased to 40,000 soldiers (30,000 Roman or Italic in origin and 10,000 auxiliaries) (App. *Iber.* 84; 89; 95–7). After the Celtiberian Wars, the permanent troops in the province numbered 20,000, a figure that increased to 50,000 during the Sertorian Wars.

Numismatics offers the possibility of evaluating the areas where coinage was identified and used in detail, but also of how coins travelled. Coin distribution is an excellent marker to see how efficient the transport network in place was in northeastern Spain (roads and rivers) by the early first century BCE. The distribution of

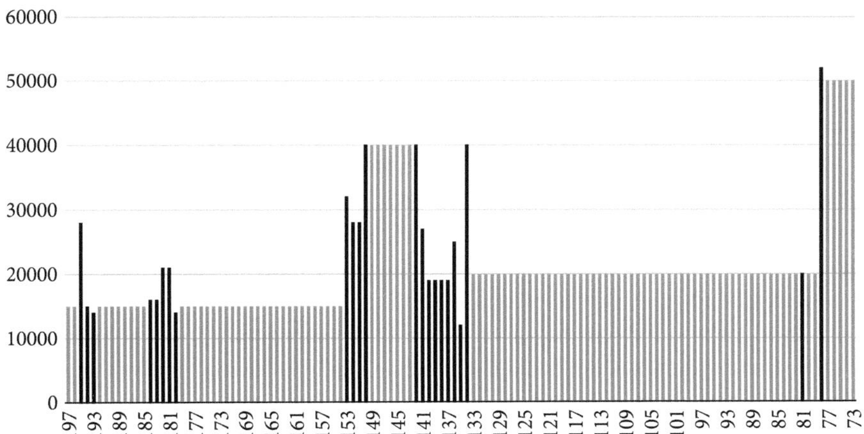


**Fig. 7.9** Roman military forces in Hispania Citerior in Republican times (197–73 BCE). In black, numbers extracted from the classical sources. In grey, projections based on those numbers

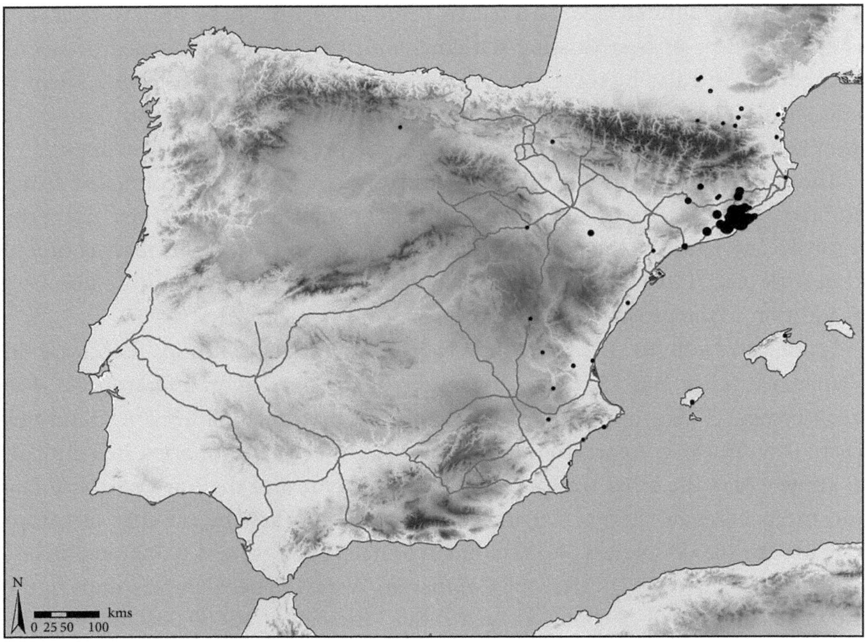


**Fig. 7.10** Layout of the Republican roads and the distribution of the Iberian coins of Ilduro

the Iberian coins of the Laeetani (Sinner, 2013), produced at four different coastal sites in the north-east of Citerior, namely Laieśken, Ilduro (Sinner, 2017), Lauro (Llorens and Ripollès, 1998), and Baitolo (Padrós, 2002; 2012), is a good case study. Even though the highest density of finds is located near these production centres, there was an active movement of coins following the main routes along the coast and the most important land routes that connected cities and towns (see Fig. 7.10 for Ilduro).

Other products that were also distributed following these same early transport networks include Apulian olive oil, transported in Brindisi amphorae, which were principally intended for Italian consumption (Carreras et al., 2016). Iberian tribes had already produced olive oil since the mid-fifth century BCE, but the production was small in scale, of limited quality, and not intended for export. As a result, these local olive oils were not used for military supply purposes at that time because the Italian army preferred the familiar Adriatic olive oil rather than local one. The distribution of Brindisi amphorae (see Fig. 7.11) therefore probably identifies, at least to a certain extent, the location of Roman military garrisons in the peninsula at the end of the second century BCE, given the close relationship between the distribution of Brindisi amphorae and the presence of Italics during the Republican period.

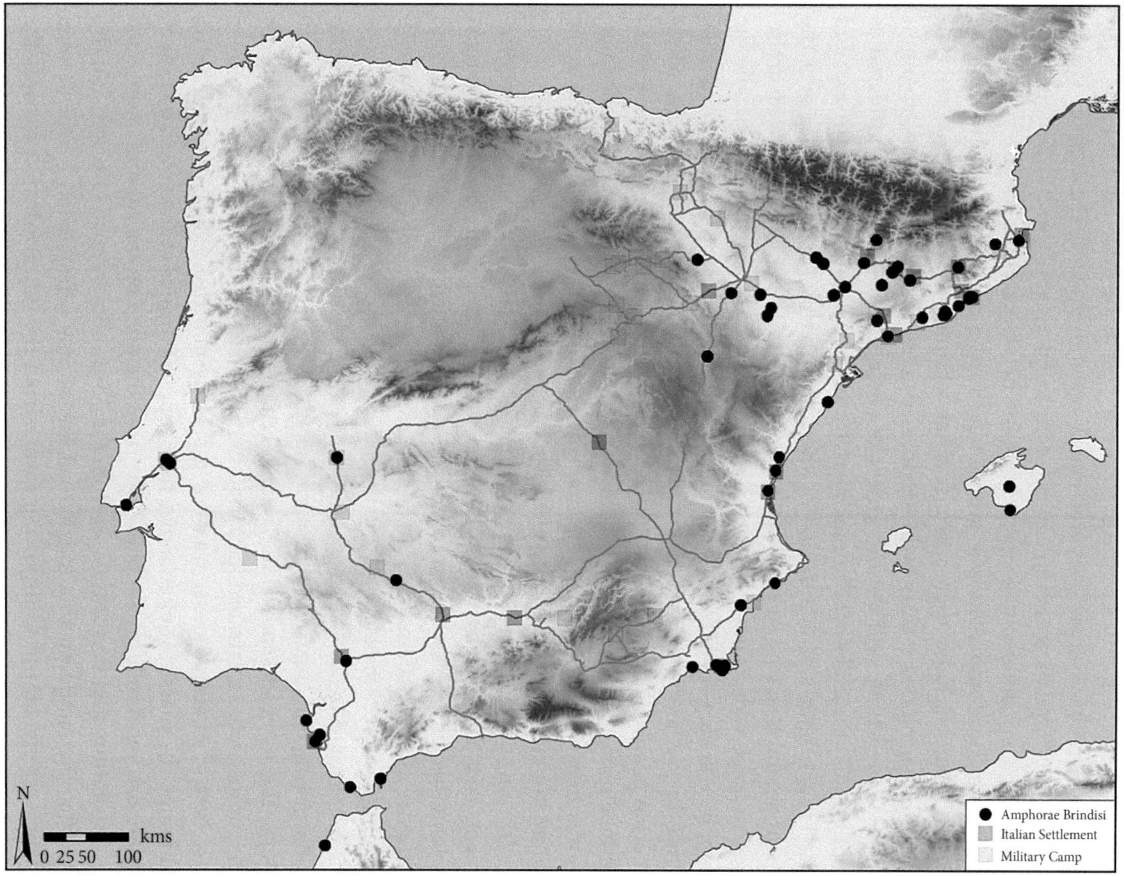


Fig. 7.11 Distribution of Brindisi amphorae in the Iberian peninsula (Carreras et al., 2016: 110, fig. 8)

For this early period when the road layout was still under construction, it is useless to generate connectivity maps, and transportation cost and time surfaces for the regions under the control of Celtiberian, Lusitanian, and Celtic groups, for two reasons. First, some parts of the Roman road system are still unknown. Second, the details of this Iron Age trackway system are undetermined, and what is known of this system does not match up entirely with the Roman layout. During the Republican period, there seem to have been two independent and technologically differently adapted transport networks in the Iberian peninsula, favouring social and economic accessibility to the different populations of the time. On the one hand, there was a local network inland created over several centuries and exploited mainly by indigenous societies that allowed local geographically limited trade and the movement of some foreign products considered as luxuries. On the other hand, an incipient transport network in the north-east and the Levant, built and maintained by the Roman army (in some cases over the main pre-existing Iron Age paths), was technologically adapted (e.g. paved, drainage systems, wide enough for carts to travel, etc.) to more efficiently handle the supply of Italic products to the military contingents deployed in the peninsula. Only in the late first century BCE and early first century CE, when the whole Iberian peninsula had been conquered and pacified, can we speak of a common unified transportation system that blended together the two aforementioned networks in existence, allowing the same efficiency in the supply of products to the entire population of the Iberian peninsula.

In sum, the early Republican transport network served the military requirements well, with safe harbours on the coast and secure road and river corridors inland that allowed the movement of legionaries and administrative personnel to support military operations. But it also supported the exploitation of the rich mining resources in places like Carthago Nova and the Sierra Morena.

With regard to the Atlantic coast, the process took place in a later period coinciding with the Augustan campaigns against the Cantabri and Astures (29–19 BCE). The armies assembled in the southern part of these regions since the Picos de Europa were an extraordinary mountain barrier and supply by tracks from the northern Cantabrian coast was not especially effective (Morillo et al., 2016), although the Classis Aquitania may have supplied armies in the years 26–25 BCE. Therefore, most military supplies came from the ports on the Atlantic coast, such as Brigantium and Portus Cale, or from the Ebro valley by road (De Soto, 2011b).

After the conquest, this initial road layout was consolidated by the Roman army with the aim of transporting metals from the mining district towards the main Atlantic and Mediterranean ports (see Fig. 7.12). Despite the existence of three ports on the Bay of Biscay, namely Oisasso, Gigia, and Portus Amanum (the later Flaviobriga), few products were channelled inland from those points.

Whereas the Mediterranean coast concentrated some of most essential urban centres, such as Emporion, Tarraco, Valentia, Saguntum, or Carthago Nova,

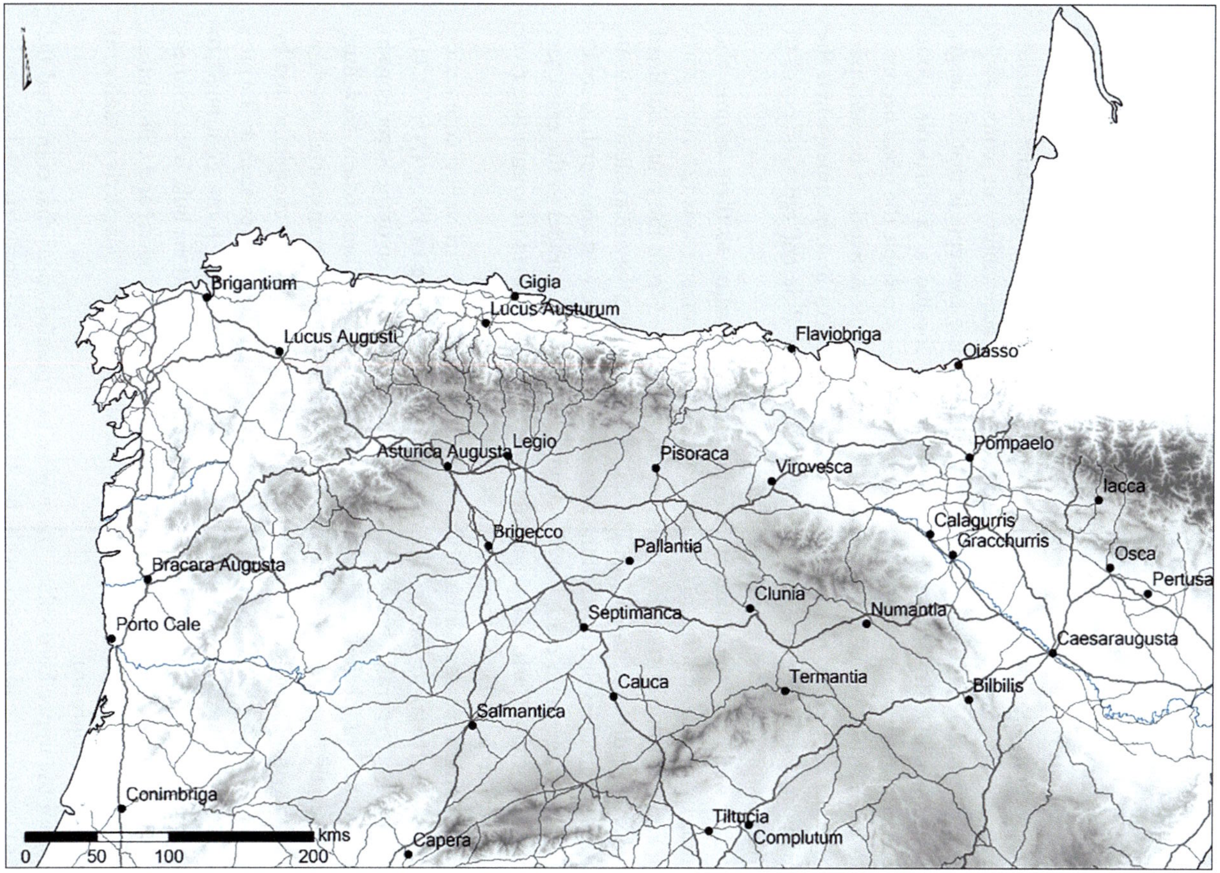


Fig. 7.12 The road layout in the north-west of Hispania Tarraconensis (De Soto, 2011b)

a completely different pattern was established on the Atlantic coastline, where inland centres became the most significant. The three capitals of the *conventus iuridici* (Bracara, Lucus, and Asturica Augusta) were inland towns far from the coast, so secondary centres such Portus Cale, Iria Flavia, Vicus Spartarius, or Brigantium were the main maritime redistribution centres facilitating the movement of merchandise and people. Therefore, the final road system of Hispania Citerior, renamed as Tarraconensis after 27 BCE, was the result of joining two independent land-transport infrastructures developed on the basis of the needs of each coast.

A second approach to the transportation network of Hispania Citerior/ Tarraconensis implies applying concepts such as accessibility or connectivity (Carreras and De Soto, 2010). The idea behind those concepts is that the larger the number of infrastructures that end or are located at a particular point (i.e. roads, maritime routes, or river ports), the more accessible the point becomes (De Soto, 2019). When any society builds its transport network, it benefits particular centres, ports, or roads. The same happened in Roman times when the legionaries built primary and secondary roads or different types of ports to enhance strategic urban centres and corridors.

After weighting the different infrastructures according to their volume and connectivity potential from secondary roads (1), primary roads (2), river ports (3), and maritime ports (4), a heat map can be created from the values obtained from each individual town (see Fig. 7.13). The connectivity map clearly reveals the main corridors that crossed the province from east to west and north to south. Apart from the main road, the Via Augusta, which ran parallel to the east coast from Iuncaria to Carthago Nova, there was a series of corridors combining river routes and roads that connected the coast to inland areas.

The earliest passage inland was the stretch of the Ebro valley connecting Dertosa (Tortosa) to Vareia (Logroño), which, according to Pliny (*NH* III.21), had vibrant river traffic between those two towns. Navigation of the River Ebro in later historical periods helps to identify critical locations when travelling upstream that may have required river boats to be towed or transported overland (Carreras and De Soto, 2010: 149–55). Besides, the route was complemented by roads that followed the Ebro valley after reaching it from cities such as Tarraco (Tarragona), Barcino (Barcelona), or Ilerda (Lleida). The route continued to Caesaraugusta (Zaragoza), which was a land communications hub, with connections towards the south to Saltigi (Chinchilla de Monte Aragón) and Complutum (Alcalá de Henares), and then followed the river as far as Calagurris (Calahorra) and Vareia (Logroño).

From the upper Ebro valley, there were two parallel roads that connected the Mediterranean road network with the Atlantic one. The northern road started at Calagurris-Vareia and followed a route towards the military district, crossing the lands of the Berones and Turmogi, linking the towns of Virovesca (Bribiesca), Pisoraca (Herrera de Pisuerga), Segisamo (Sasamón), Lancia (Villasabariego),

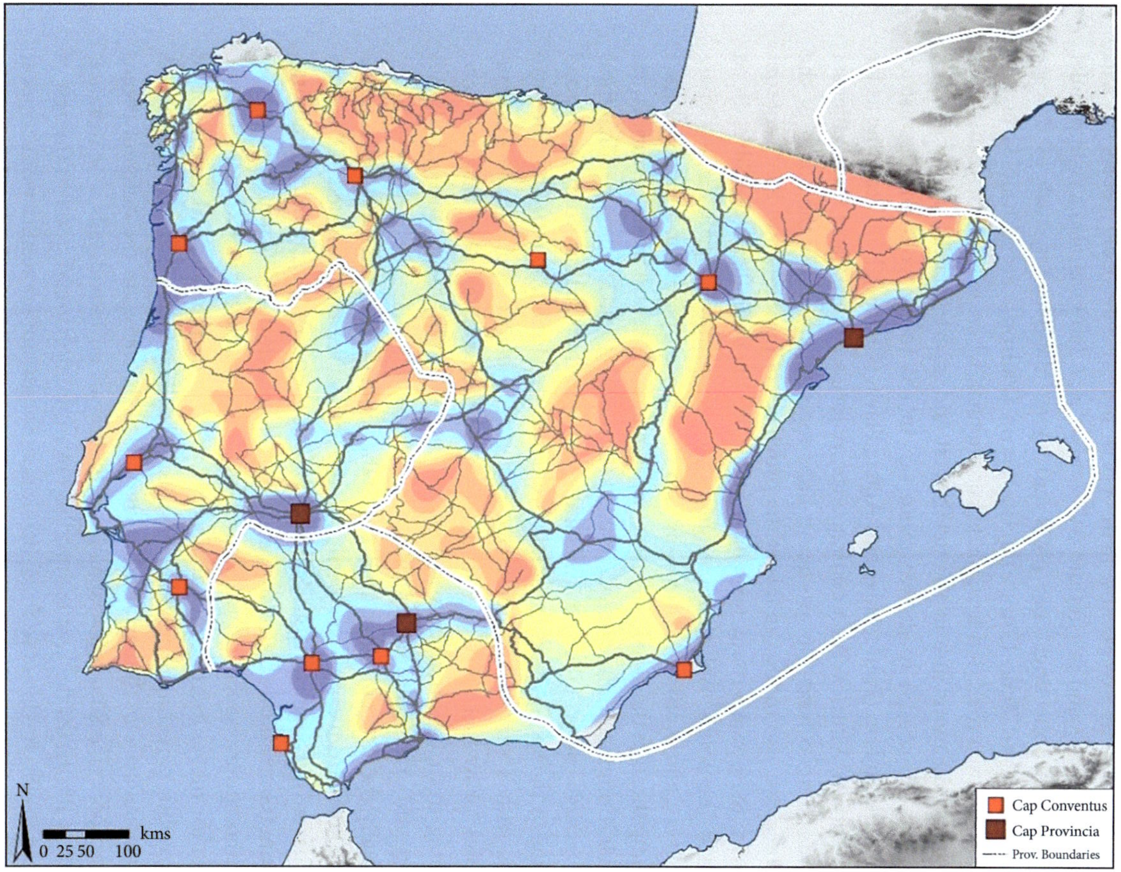


**Fig. 7.13** The transport connectivity map of the Iberian peninsula. In blue, corridors with the highest connectivity (De Soto and Carreras, 2022)

Legio (León), and Asturica Augusta (Astorga). The southern road crossed the uplands inhabited by the Arevaci and Vaccaei, passing through Turiaso (Tarazona), Augustobriga (Agreda), Numantia (Garray), Uxama Argaela (Osma), Clunia (Coruña del Conde), Brigaecium (Benavente), and Asturica Augusta (Astorga).

On the Atlantic coast, the main ports were Portus Cale (Porto), Vicus Spacorum (Vigo), and Brigantium (A Coruña), and there was also a road parallel to the coast connecting those ports and some inland towns, such as Bracara Augusta (Braga), Tude (Tui), and Iria Flavia (Padrón). From Iria Flavia and Brigantium, two roads led towards Lucus Augusti, whereas Bracara Augusta was the communications hub in the north-west and, apart from being the starting point for the coastal road, two more ran inland to the gold-mining district through Bergidum (Ponferrada) and Aquae Flavia (Chaves), both reaching as far as the city of Asturica. As a consequence, Asturica Augusta and Caesaraugusta became the two land transportation hubs for routes towards the south of the province and also to the capitals of the provinces of Lusitania and Baetica. From Asturica there was a route, nowadays called the Via de la Plata (the Silver Road towards the south to Emerita Augusta), via Salmantica (Salamanca), Capera (Caparra), and Norba. Asturica was also the starting point for a diagonal road running through the area known as Carpetania in the centre of the peninsula, via Segovia, Complutum, Toletum, Consabura (Consuegra), and Laminium (Alhambra) to Carthago Nova. Likewise, Caesaraugusta was the starting point for a road leading to the south towards Saltigi (Chinchilla de Monte Aragón) and Carthago Nova, with a variant that connected Saltigi to Saetabis (Xàtiva) and Dianium (Dènia), or to Ilici (Elx). It was also complemented by another diagonal road running from Caesaraugusta to Emerita Augusta and passing through Bilbilis (Calatayud), Complutum, and Toletum.

Finally, the last communication axis in the south of Hispania Tarraconensis was a road going from east to west similar to the Ebro valley axis. It started in Dianium and passed through Saetabis, Saltigi, Libisosa (Lezuza), Laminium (Alhambra), Oretum (Granátula de Calatrava), and Sisapo (Almodóvar del Campo).

Although transport infrastructures were developed by the Roman State to favour the movement of goods and people, the cost of transport and time involved in travelling constrained such movements. Modelling the cost of travelling in GIS network analysis in Roman times according to the values of the different means of transport (De Soto and Carreras, 2009) reveals curious details. For instance, Fig. 7.14 illustrates the cost of travelling from the north-east coast to the rest of the peninsula, in this case from Barcino although similar results would appear from Tarraco. It becomes clear that costs were relatively low when travelling by sea to any coast, even the Atlantic, but higher costs were generated when travelling inland except along the Ebro valley.

Therefore, the high costs of land transport (Carreras and De Soto, 2010: 81–91) were a serious impediment to inland communication. This was even more

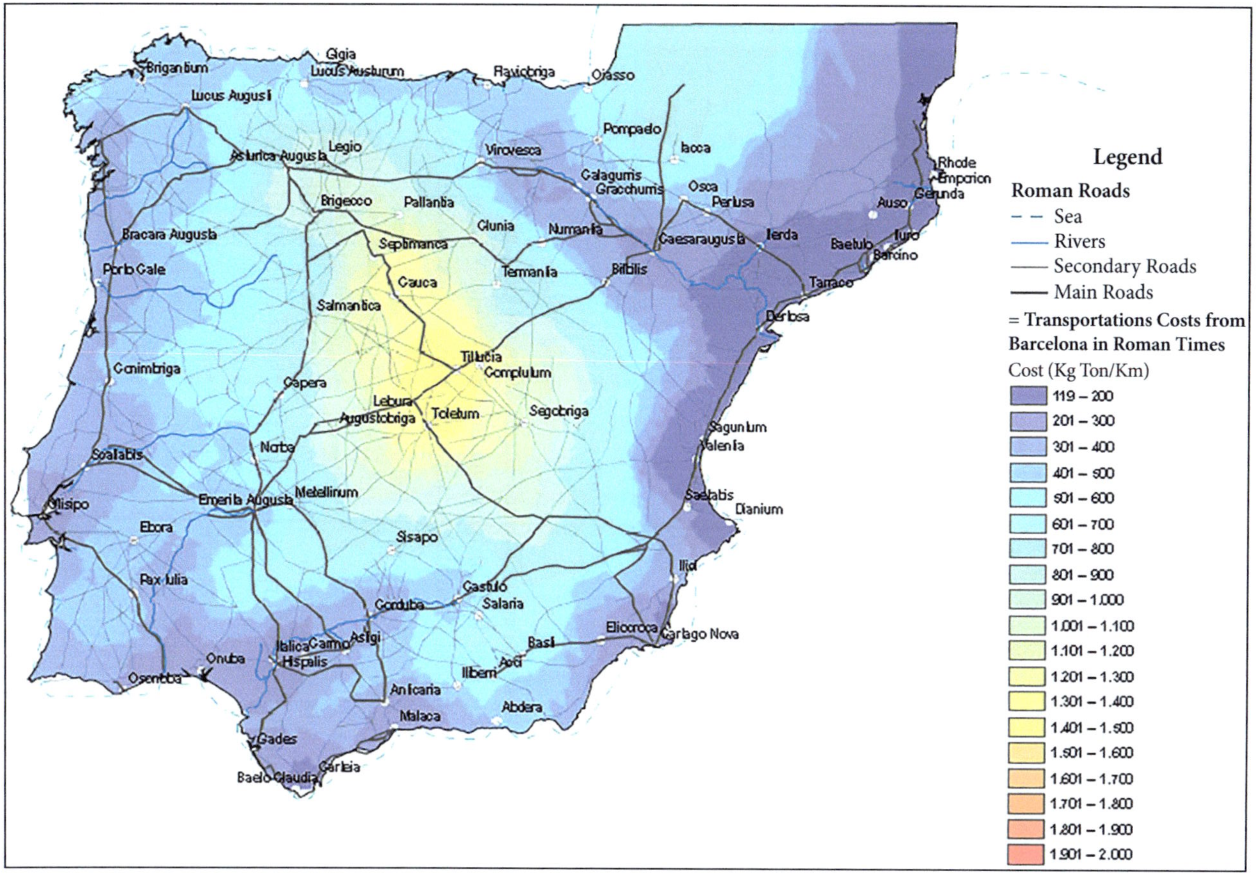


Fig. 7.14 Transport costs from Barcino (Carreras and De Soto, 2010: 206, fig. 70)

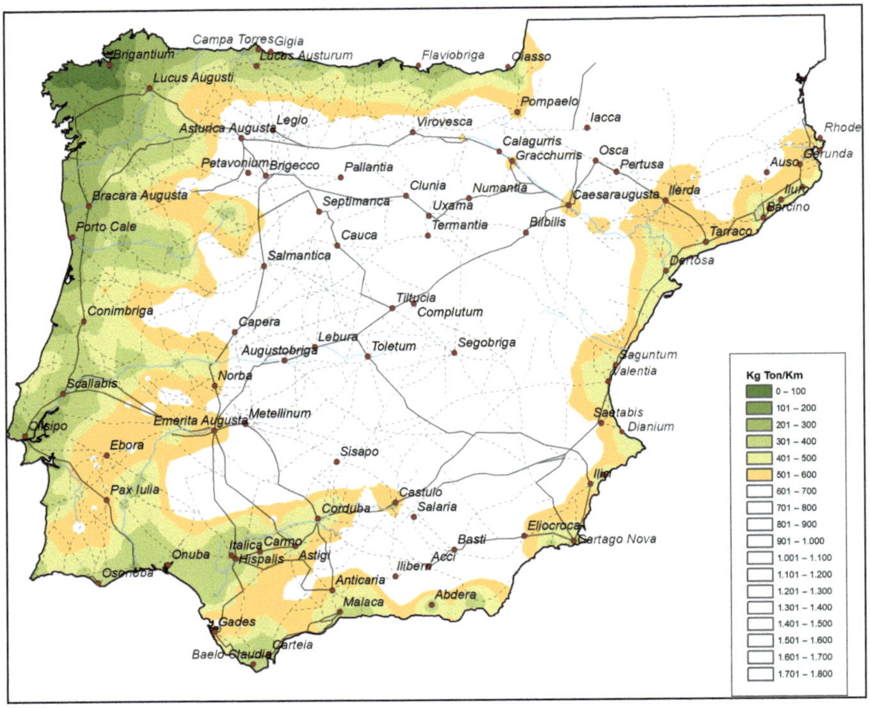


**Fig. 7.15** Transport costs from Brigantium (De Soto, 2011b)

evident in the Atlantic part of the province, where no large river could facilitate access inland. The cost from Brigantium appears in Fig. 7.15, which evidences difficulties in transport from the Atlantic ports to the gold-mining district and the Mediterranean coast.

The most isolated regions in terms of transport costs were the territories of the central Meseta (inhabited by the Arevaci, Vaccaei, Turmogi, Carpetani, Oretani, and Olcades), which could only sustain internal movement for both products and also their population, with restricted access to the coasts. Calculating transport costs from the city of Toletum produces a map that clearly defines the territory within which transport costs were very high limiting movement (above 25% of the final price of wheat; see Carreras and De Soto, 2010) (Fig. 7.16). Despite the fact that transport costs reduced the exchange of low-value products such as cereals, they only had a limited impact on high-value products such as metals, stones, or luxuries.

Perhaps the concept of cost may have been too abstract or at least perceived differently by Roman traders and travellers, but the time involved in covering such distances was more tangible. Applying GIS network analysis and taking into

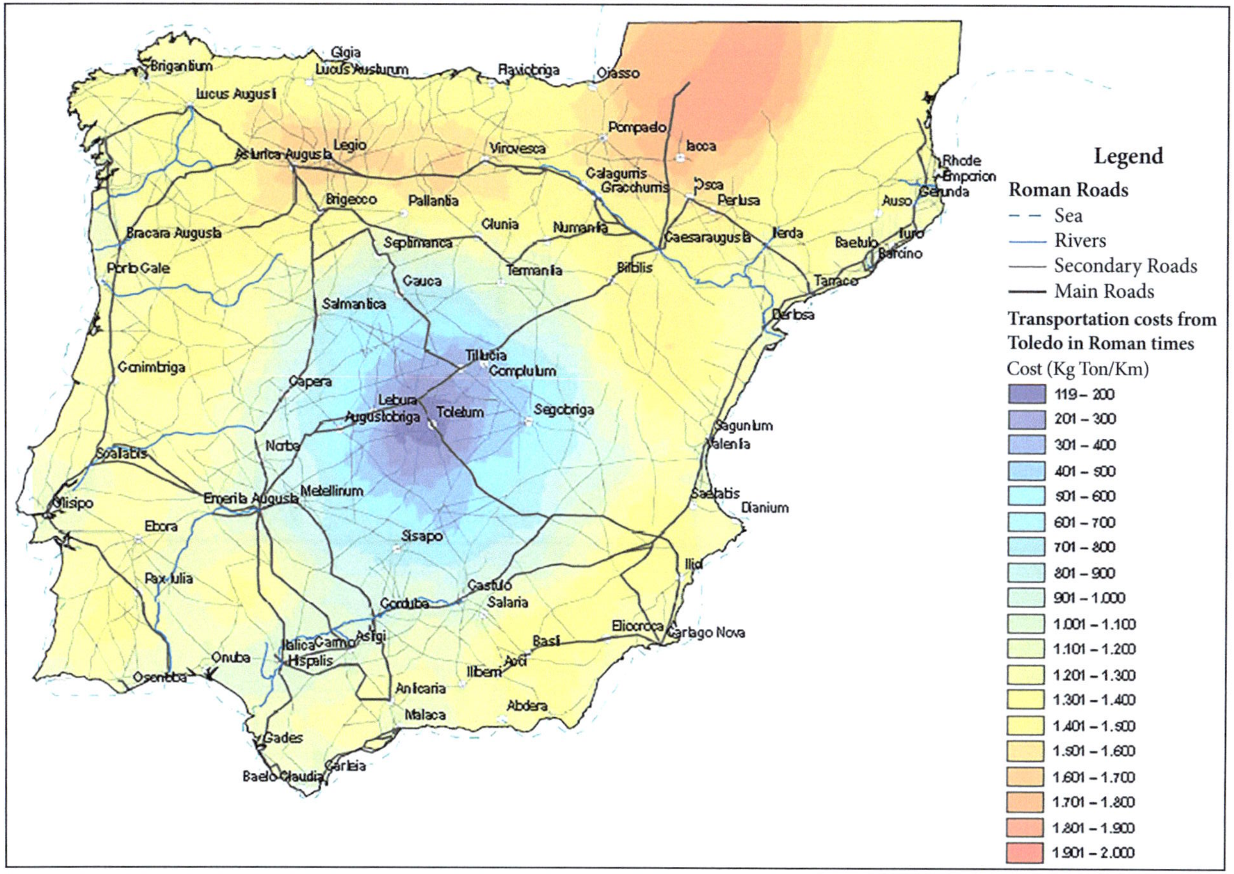

**Fig. 7.16** Transport costs from Toletum (Carreras and De Soto, 2010: 210, fig. 73)

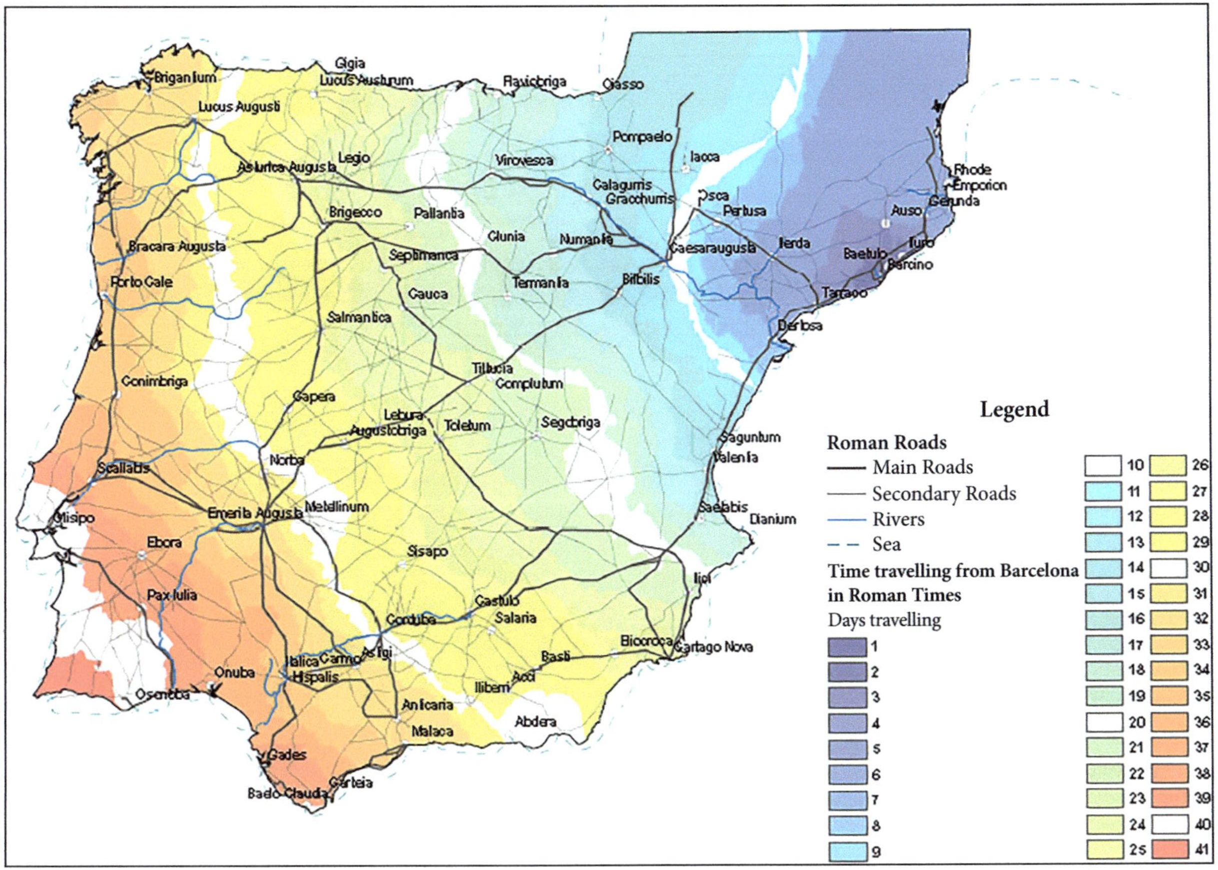


**Fig. 7.17** Transport time in days from Barcino (Carreras and De Soto, 2010: 181, fig. 52)

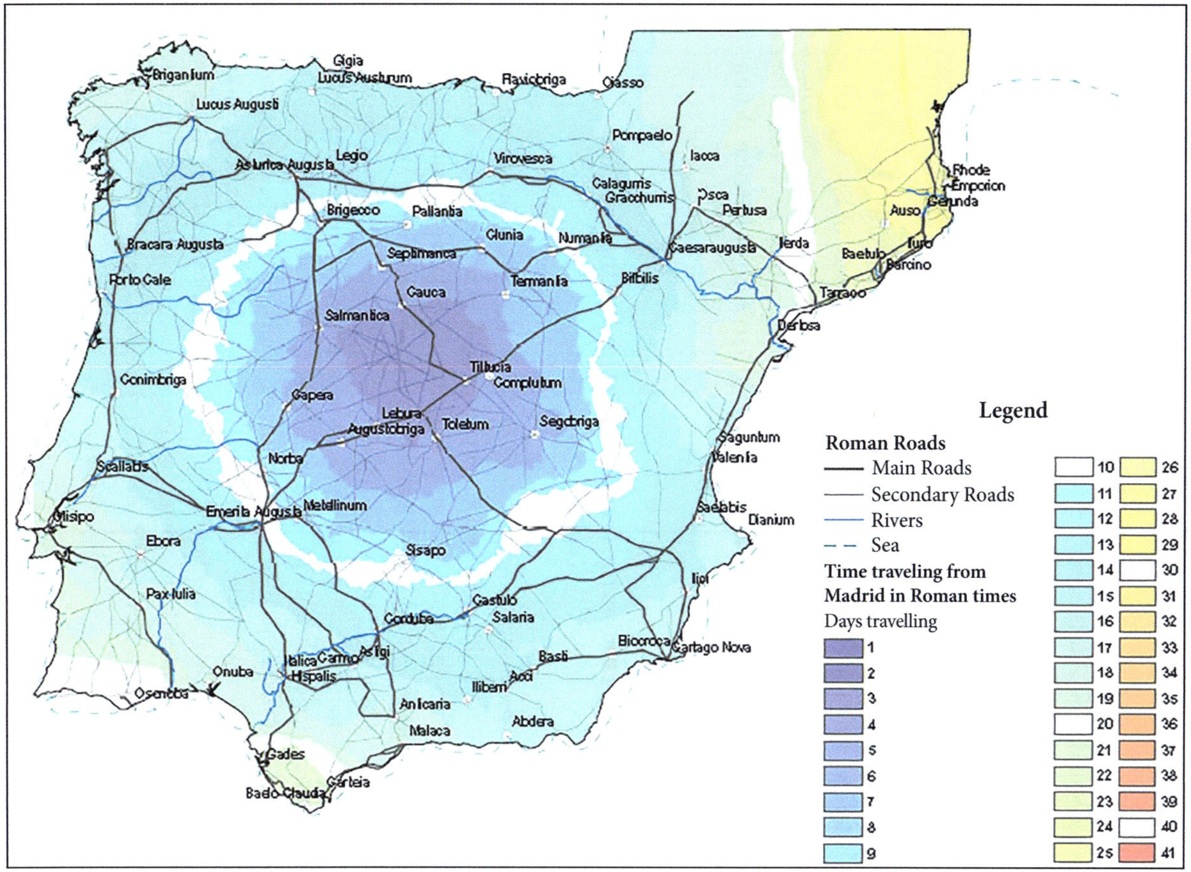


Fig. 7.18 Transport time in days from Complutum

account the speed of the diverse means of transport, an alternative image can be established (Carreras and De Soto, 2010: 180–4).

Fig. 7.17 depicts the time involved in travelling by wagon from Barcino to the rest of the Iberian peninsula, with the white strips indicating 10-day segments. For instance, the journey from Barcino to Asturica or Complutum took more than 20 days. Therefore, the most likely contact area was the territories within these 10-day boundaries. This is extremely meaningful and helps us to understand how inter- and intra-provincial relations, connections, mobility, and migrations took place (see below), especially if we bear in mind that travelling from Rome or almost anywhere else on the west coast of Italy to any point of Mediterranean side of the province (from Emporiae down to Carthago Nova) would not take more than 14 days.

Likewise, the 10-day boundary from the town of Complutum in the middle of the Meseta (see Fig. 7.18) defines the most likely exchanges of this central part only with other towns on the Meseta and the capital of the Lusitania (Emerita Augusta). The framework of transport infrastructures may have conditioned seasonal movements of traders and people (e.g. harvesting), but also definitive migrations within the province.

## 7.4 Migrations to Hispania Citerior during the Late Republican Period

In the Iberian peninsula, scholarly debates about the extent of the migration phenomenon during the late Republican period have been taking place for over half a century. Two opposed positions predominate. The first one contends that a major influx of Italics settled in Hispania after the Second Punic War (Wilson, 1966: 9–12; Marín Díaz, 1988: 47–109; González Román, 2010). Rome needed to maintain a permanent military presence,[6] and some believe that many soldiers settled after service (Brunt, 1971; Gabba, 1973).[7] García-Bellido (1966: 498) added that following and living off the troops, many peoples belonging to the lower strata of Roman society, such as merchants, fortune tellers, prostitutes, magicians, etc., as well as other kinds of intermediaries, such as agents and resellers, the latter mostly belonging to the equestrian order, also moved to Hispania. These people would frequently spread out through the rearguard in

[6] Among these troops, the percentage of Italic soldiers was always very high, to the point of reaching between 60 and 70% of the total; and, as is well known, the weight that the Sabelic-language communities of central and southern Italy had on the allies was considerable (Afzelius, 1944: 57–92; Brunt, 1971: 661–4; Cadiou, 2008: 85–171).

[7] The most obvious evidence of this Italian presence is from the onomastic and prosopographic analysis of some Hispanic epigraphic corpora (Díaz Ariño, 2008) and numismatic series, such as those of Valentia (Barreda Pascual, 1998: 352–75) and Saguntum (García-Bellido and Blázquez, 2001: 140–51).

search of and providing supplies and goods of all kinds (Liv. *Per.* 57; App. *Iber.* 85). Others have spoken of a 'migratory flow', which during the second century BCE was, in contrast to what happened in the first century BCE, of an eminently private nature, unrelated to any type of public organization (Marín Díaz, 1986: 53). Supporters of high levels of migrants argue that, as a result of economic migration, in addition to the military movement, people settled in the main urban centres on the eastern shores of the newly created province of Hispania Citerior and the nearby mining deposits (Marín Díaz, 1986: 63). Further studies have shown that a number of Italian *gentes*, many of them involved in the exploitation and commercialization of the lead and silver mines, have been identified in the south-east and the east of the peninsula, particularly from Campania and Minturnae and its hinterland (Díaz Ariño, 2008; Orejas and Beltrán, 2010; Stefanile, 2017; Stannard et al., 2019).

The second position is more circumspect, taking a critical view of the classical sources and tending to minimize the entity of migratory flows to the Iberian peninsula, or at least of those who permanently settled there (Le Roux, 1995; Cadiou, 2008: 627–61; Pina Polo, 2023). As will be seen below, however, while perhaps the second position reflects a closer picture of what migration from Italy (and elsewhere) represented numerically speaking for the province, it cannot be systematically extrapolated as the only existent reality. It is essential to highlight that differentiated regional situations existed not only in Hispania, but also inside Citerior during the second–first centuries BCE. They were the product of specific contact processes, resulting from the diverse combination of the original, unique situations. As we have highlighted in the previous section of this book (see Chapters 4–6), each territory in the province and its peoples and communities had its own social, cultural, and demographic particularities, in many cases with roots going back to the Iron Age period. Many factors including geographical location, topography, existing transportation network (see above), among others must be taken into account, and not only the purely military and economic ones—despite their importance—as well as the capacity for Roman action/strategies that existed at each specific moment. In this chapter, for the late Republican period we will focus on the cases of the north-east, the Levant (east), the Ebro valley, and the south-east (especially Carthago Nova) of Citerior, since it has been suggested that the limited immigration that did take place must have primarily focused on the major urban areas within the peaceful regions of the province, specifically along the Mediterranean coastline (Pina Polo, 2023: 86). Aditionally, the selected areas exemplify well how none of the two historically opposed positions towards migration from Italy discussed above were fully correct or completely wrong.[8] Instead, there is still much work to be done, and detailed local and regional analyses are

[8] It is important to remember that these areas are also the ones that concentrate the highest numbers of freedmen and slaves. See Chapter 2 in this volume.

necessary in order to understand the extent of migratory flows, and where and why they happened.

Migrant numbers and volumes aside, one aspect of this migratory process on which most scholars do seem to agree is the fact that the majority of this flow of peoples that arrived from Italy were not from Rome. In the words of Marín Díaz (1986: 63), there was a: 'dominancia de gentilicios itálicos en comparación con los romanos'[9] in the Latin onomastics documented in Hispania during the second century BCE. Marín Díaz explained this imbalance as the consequence of the presence of Italic contingents among the legionary troops (1986: 60). Among the *nomina* of freemen of Roman origin, Marín Díaz (1986: 58) also divided them into two groups: the ones belonging to the most noble Roman families (e.g. Lucretius in the case of Tarraco and Carthago Nova)—usually much more concentrated in the province of Ulterior—and those of plebeian origin (e.g. Munius and Numius in Valentia and Baebius in Carthago Nova).

While Marín Díaz was right and Italic names dominate the corpus, the label Italic is a heterogeneous one and, as Estarán (2019: 388) has appropriately pointed out, these migrants were mostly people that spoke Sabellic or Italic languages, which included the Umbrian, Oscan, and the so-called Sabellic dialects (Estarán, 2019: 388). As we have seen when discussing the connectivity between Italy and Hispania Citerior, and we will discuss in the following lines, most of these individuals were originally from two specific areas: the Bay of Naples via Puteoli and the Auruncan and Calenan region via the port of Minturnae on the River Liri (Stefanile, 2015: 171; 2017; Stannard et al., 2019).

This migration left its mark on place names and personal names as well as on the linguistic substrata of Hispania. From the point of view of place names, apart from the analogies proposed by Menéndez Pidal (1929), there is no doubt that certain city names (e.g. Italica) and personal names (e.g. Campanus: *CIL* II 750, 4974, 3860, 4199, 5774) constitute a clear indication of the possibly Italic origin of the first inhabitants of a series of urban settlements in Hispania (Marín Díaz, 1988: 54).

Finally, if one takes a look at the status of those who migrated and, bearing in mind the considerable limitations of the existing epigraphic corpus of inscriptions belonging to the Republican period (Alföldy, 1975: 1–11; Marín Díaz, 1986: 57; Díaz Ariño, 2008: 85–191), a great abundance of freedmen, apparently higher than in later periods (see section 7.5), can be detected. The cases of Tarraco and Carthago Nova are especially meaningful since we see freedmen associated with patrons who are members of professional *collegia* such as those in Capua and Minturnae. Nevertheless, in Marín Díaz's (1988) study discussing the provenance of 65 individuals who probably migrated to Hispania, the *ingenuii*, free individuals,

[9] 'there was a dominance of Italic onomastics in comparison with the Roman ones'.

were the largest group, numbering 45. It is important to bear in mind, however, that the magistrates recorded in coin legends were included in this group, notably skewing the data.

### 7.4.1 The North-East of Citerior

The north-eastern part of Citerior during the late Republic is a good case study.[10] It is the area where the Romans first disembarked in 218 BCE, and where they established two of their main military bases (Emporion and Tarraco). In addition, the ancient sources have left numerous accounts discussing the presence of *redemptores*, *mercatores*, and *mangones*. We see the activity of *redemptores* supplying the army from 195 BCE (Liv. 34. 9. 12), and the presence of *mercatores* is also well attested, purchasing the spoils of war as early as 200 BCE (Liv. 23. 22. 3).

Archaeologically speaking, in recent decades, research has uncovered a series of settlements of varied sizes and typologies, all of them dated around the mid-second century BCE, and which are characterized by the presence of public and private architecture in a marked Italic style (see Fig. 7.8). Substantial volumes of ceramics—especially black-gloss pottery and Dressel 1A and Brindisi amphorae—imported from Italy (Morillo, 2003; 2016; Sinner, 2015; Pera et al., 2016; Madrid and Sinner, 2021) are also a common denominator on these archaeological sites, indicating that the inhabitants of these settlements were strongly influenced by and in contact with a Romano-Italic culture. Some of these sites have been interpreted as Early Roman garrisons (*castella*, *praetoria*) and were usually located in strategic positions overlooking natural corridors (e.g. valleys, waterways) and connecting coastal towns to the major Iberian *oppida* located inland pointing to an east–west axis (Fig. 7.19). Following the general trends described above for the Mediterranean in general and Hispania in particular, scholars have tended to 'populate' these settlements with Italic peoples (*contra* Olesti, 2010; 2017; Sinner and Ferrer, 2016).

It has been argued that, in the north-east of the Iberian peninsula (modern-day Catalonia), during the second and up to the mid-first century BCE, a large degree of long-distance mobility is inferred when in reality what we see is a limited degree of mobility that sustained a high degree of connectivity between Italy and Spain (Sinner, 2024). Permanent mobility did exist, of course, and epigraphic and archaeological evidence supports it, but it was short-lived and minimal, took place mostly in the first century BCE, and was focused in Tarraco. The state of affairs in the rest of the region was different, being marked by the dynamism and capacity of adaptation, response, and renegotiation of the native peoples in

[10] This section draws heavily on the text in Sinner (2024).

relation to the new colonial culture to which they were now well connected. Overestimating the direct role played by Italic migrants in this process of economic, social, and cultural change, partially denies the capacity and agency that the indigenous peoples of Hispania Citerior had in building a provincial society.

### Kese/Tarraco

The capital of Citerior was the main stronghold of the Roman army during most of the Second Punic War and especially in the earlier stages of the conflict (Liv. 21.60–1; Plin. *NH* III.21).[11] It would be unsurprising that, during the second century BCE, the town experienced a substantial degree of long-distance mobility since it was the destination of soldiers as well as merchants and other suppliers of the army. In fact, one of the oldest Latin inscriptions engraved in the Iberian peninsula comes from its defensive town walls and reads M(anios) Vibio(s), honouring Minerva (*CIL* I$^2$ 3449; *CIL* II$^2$ 14 841; *AE* 1981, 573). This graffito points towards an example of migration related to the early moments of the Roman presence in Hispania. Moreover, the Latin epigraphy of Tarraco is nowadays one of the largest corpora of inscriptions in existence that we have for all Republican Hispania. Alföldy (1975: 1–11) catalogued 18 entries for this period while Díaz Ariño (2008: 146–63) compiled a total of 21 inscriptions, making it *a priori* an excellent case study to trace migrants. However, this is not the case. As Estarán (2019: 396–7) points out in her recent study, the Latin epigraphy of Tarraco is not significant—quantitatively speaking—until the first century BCE. The few inscriptions that can be ascribed to the second century BCE do not provide any evidence to identify *nomina* of Italic origin. On the other hand, the coinage issued by the mint of Kese, already active before 170 BCE (Villaronga, 2002: 38–9), and which continued until the early first century BCE, always used the Iberian script (Campo, 2002; *CNH* 158–71).

Republican-period cemeteries in Tarraco are almost unknown; however, funerary inscriptions reused in secondary contexts do provide some examples of migration as well as three cases of bilingual (Iberian-Latin) inscriptions (*ELRH* 65–6). In the early first century BCE, an inscription dedicated to Cn. Lucretius (*ELRH* C68) is of special interest. Made by his freedmen, it mentions the Scaptia tribe. Due to the rarity of this tribe in Hispania, together with the fact that one of the *coloni* in the Ilici bronze (C1) ascribed to the same tribe came from Praeneste, Díaz Ariño (2008: 155) has suggested an Italic origin for this individual. A similar situation occurs in the funerary inscription datable to the first half of the first century BCE of a freedman that was erected by his patron, Decimus Titurnius (*ELRH* C69). The presence of the *gentilicium* Titurnius, infrequent in the Hispanic corpus, could point towards an Italic origin for this family.

[11] For a diachronic evolution of the city and its population numbers, see Chapters 4, 5, and 6 in this volume.

Already in the second half of the first century BCE, a few more inscriptions enable us to trace the Italic origin of some individuals, the *nomina* A. Varaeus A. I. Philonicus and Varaeia A. I. Danais, freedmen from Tarraco (*ELRH* C70), being good examples. Two more freedmen from Tarraco belonging to the Nonia family could also reflect an Italic provenance, as Díaz Ariño has noted (*ELRH* C75). In fact, this family is present in the epigraphy of Samnium, Venetia, and especially Rome and Campania. Similarly, some of the individuals present in a collective funerary monument, perhaps belonging to a *collegium funeraticum* (Alföldy, 1981: 31–2; Beltrán Lloris, 2004: 166), could also have originated in Italy. This is the case of the *nomina* Veicius, unknown in Hispania but present in an inscription in Capua dated to 105 BCE (*CIL* I$^3$ 2947; Solin and Salomies, 1994: 200), and Annius, attested in an inscription in Aquileia and Delos (*CIL* I$^2$ 2648). Finally, the epitaph of a woman named Rubenia Sura—although its reconstruction is uncertain—could also have been of Italic origin. The name Rubenius is not recorded in Hispania and most likely to have originated in Etruria or Campania (Schulze, 1904: 220).

In sum, the evidence we have for mobility in Kese/Tarraco during the second century BCE is limited to the literary sources (Liv. *Per.* 21.61). This has led to the logical supposition that peoples coming from all over Italy might have gathered in this military outpost. However, the epigraphic record, so far very limited in size, suggests a scenario in which only a few of these individuals settled permanently in the city, so for the remaining cases it can be considered a temporary migration. A slightly different picture can be seen during the first century BCE, when the Latin epigraphic evidence increases significantly, allowing us to trace the Italic origin of some individuals, mostly freedmen and freedwomen. Whatever the case, during the last two centuries of the Republic, in one of the two most important cities in Hispania Citerior, less than a dozen cases of migrants from Italy can be traced.

### Emporion/Emporiae

After the foundation of the Neàpolis towards the end of the sixth or at the beginning of the fifth century BCE, Emporion soon became one of the main redistribution centres for the north-east of the Iberian peninsula. By the late third century BCE, the Greek city was the entrance point of the Roman army (Polyb. 3.76), housing first Scipio's troops (218–206 BCE) (Liv. 21.60.3-4; Polyb. 3.76.2.), and subsequently those of Cato (Liv. 34.11) (197–195 BCE). What appears to be a large military establishment dating to the central decades of the second century BCE has recently been identified. This site demonstrates the logistical and military importance that the city continued to have for the Roman administration in the middle of the century since it is believed that this settlement would have been used to levy native populations as auxiliary troops (Tremoleda et al., 2016). Therefore, if we look for case studies where migrants from Italy can be expected, Emporion is again an excellent candidate.

Epigraphically speaking, only one inscription has been recorded that can help us to testify the movements of Italic people into the city. The inscription, dating from around 250–225 BCE, pre-dates the arrival of the Roman army and reads *VR. CN. VESVIA*. This property mark can be read in two ways. The first one understands VR as the abbreviation of the word *urna*, referring to the vessel on which the inscription was engraved, and therefore providing the name Cn. Vesuia(ni) (cf. *ELRH* C88). The second, reads VR (—) as a *praenomen*, CN(AEI) as the gamonimic, and VESVIA as a *nomen*. In this reading, our individual would be an Italic woman.

Starting in the second century BCE (Campo, 2002: 80–1) and down to the early first century BCE, the city minted a significant number of bronze issues under the name of Undikesken/Emporiae, first using Iberian script (*CNH* 141–51) and later Latin (*CNH* 151–7). Some of the issues included the name of the magistrates and can offer information about the ethnic composition of the elites of the city, a social group in which Italic origins might be expected. Contrary to what we find in other cases such as Valentia (Pena, 1986; Ripollès, 1988: 17–21), where the magistrates recorded on the coins are mostly of Italic origin, magistrates on the coins of Undikesken are mostly, if not always, Iberian.

Graffiti in Emporion are perhaps the best documents we have to demonstrate the heterogeneity of the peoples who once inhabited this settlement. Greek inscriptions are concentrated between the sixth and the fourth centuries BCE. Graffiti written in Iberian (13) (*MLH* III C1.9–23) or Latin (7), on the other hand, are recorded between the third and the first centuries BCE. Those employing the Latin language cluster in the first century BCE but are of little help in determining whether their makers were of Italic origin.

In short, prior to the period of the Civil Wars, all the available evidence seems to point towards a Latinization of Greek and Iberian peoples, a process in which the establishment of the Roman city certainly had a key role, rather than a substantial migratory phenomenon.

### Ilduro/Iluro

The ancient settlement of Ilduro (later Iluro), located in the valley of the modern town of Cabrera de Mar (Barcelona), occupied a strategic position at a point on the coastline of north-eastern Citerior, equidistant from the main harbours as well as the *castra-hiberna* of Tarraco (to the south) and Emporion (to the north) (Fig. 7.19), both approximately 120 km away. The two largest settlements in the valley, the *oppidum* at Burriac (Zamora, 2006–7) and the late Republican settlement, both incorporated construction techniques, materials, and ceramics typical of the Italian peninsula, more specifically from Campania (Stannard and Sinner, 2014; Sinner, 2015: 8–20; Madrid and Sinner 2019). The late Republican settlement presents a range of building types that had a public or private function, and which appear to point towards building activities promoted by outsiders. Perhaps

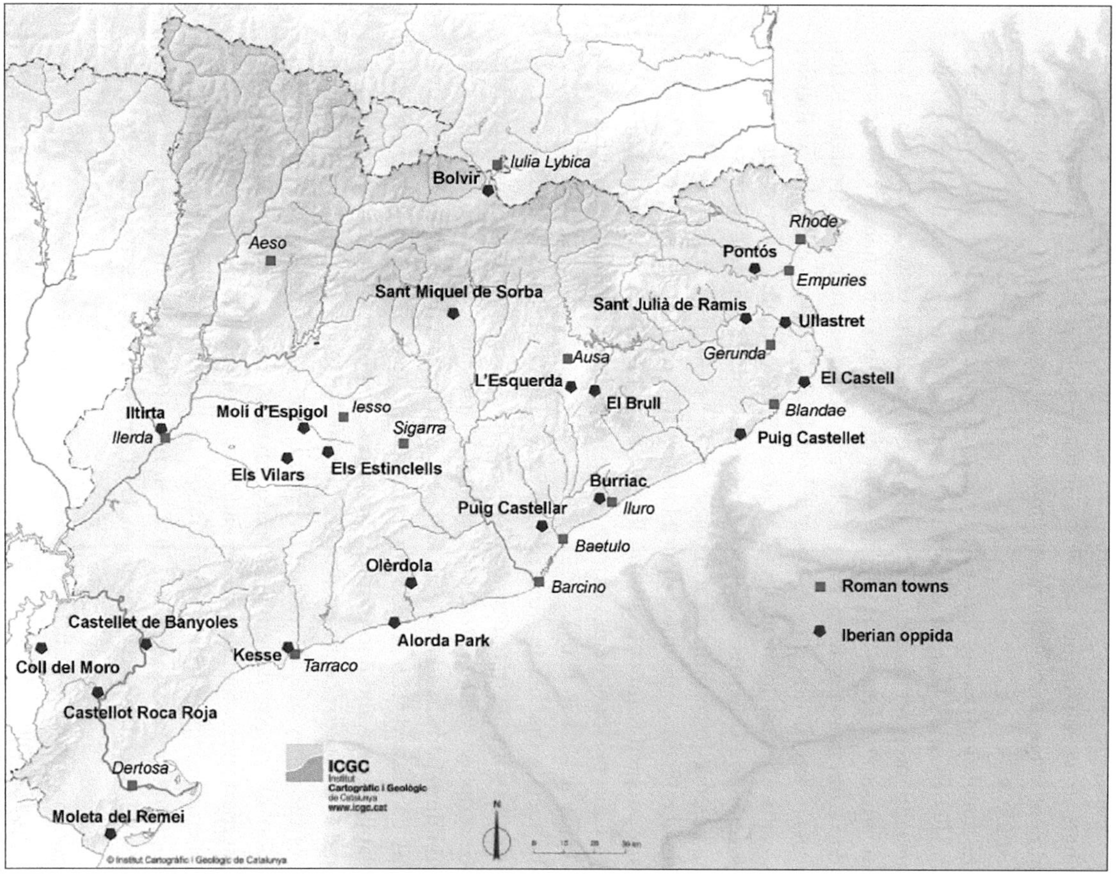


**Fig. 7.19** Map including some of the main Iberian *oppida* and the main Roman towns in north-eastern Hispania, including those mentioned in this text

the best examples are the public baths of Ca l'Arnau and what is known as the domus of Can Benet (García et al., 2000; Martín and García, 2002). The settlement seems to have been built *c.*150 BCE and was abandoned as an urban centre during the first quarter of the first century BCE.

Currently, the corpus of well-studied Iberian inscriptions from Cabrera de Mar numbers almost 80 (Sinner and Ferrer 2016; 2018). It is therefore one of the most prominent epigraphic assemblages among the Iberian corpus and a meaningful case study.

The majority of inscriptions with more than one sign are *post coctem* graffiti on ceramics—mostly black-gloss pottery—bearing isolated personal names. These are usually interpreted as the name of the owner of the vessel, e.g. sosian (a full list in Sinner and Ferrer, 2016: 215). A few of these personal names could correspond to Latin names written using the Iberian script, as is the case of bilake (Latin Flaccus) or kai (Latin Gaius). However, both bilake and kai could also be Iberian personal names, as Moncunill and Velaza (2011: footnote 7) have suggested for the former and Untermann (1990: no. 66) for the later (kaisur). In the event of it being possible to confirm a Latin origin for these two personal names (kai/Gaius and bilake/Flaccus), the most plausible scenario is that they were natives that had already adopted Latin onomastics. This would not be a strange practice, since the use of Latin personal names among the Iberians is well attested in the Bronze of Ascoli (89 BCE) (*CIL* I 709).[12]

The fact is that during the second and first centuries BCE only one Latin inscription with the *tria nomina* A.VAL.A[13] has been recorded in this settlement. This inscription can be dated to the second quarter of the first century BCE, a time when Ilduro had already been abandoned as an urban centre (Sinner et al., 2014). If this contrasted with the 63 inscriptions and over 20 personal names using Iberian language and onomastics from this site, it becomes clear that during the second and the first centuries BCE, the Iberian language was used by the inhabitants of the valley of Cabrera de Mar. This is also indicative that the ethnic composition of its population was predominantly indigenous. Even in its Latin counterpart, Iluro, founded around 80/70 BCE on the site of present-day Mataró, the Iberian script remains predominant in the foundational levels and Latin inscriptions are scarce (García, 2017; Sinner et al., 2021). In sum, the towns of Ilduro/Iluro received very few migrants (if any) from the Italian peninsula.

## Baitolo/Baetulo and Ieso/Iesso

The epigraphic and linguistic situation of Ilduro is similar to that of other important late Republican cities that were founded in north-eastern Spain during the first

[12] A recent study suggests the possibility that some members of the *Turma Salluitana* could have stayed in Italy, showing a case of permanent long-distance mobility in the other direction (Velaza, 2021).

[13] There is a second inscription bearing the same *tria nomina* that remains unpublished.

quarter of the first century BCE and which, as Ilduro did (Sinner, 2017), minted coinage using the Iberian script (Padrós, 2012). Baitolo/Baetulo (Torra, 2009) and Ieso/Iesso (Pera, 2005) are the best documented examples. In both cities, a clear predominance of the Iberian script over Latin is attested, making it quite feasible to suggest that the presence of Italic settlers was minimal during the last two centuries before the Common Era.

Baetulo, modern-day Badalona, the Latin adaptation of the Iberian Baitolo, is identified by the classical sources written in the first century BCE as the name of a city located between Barcino (Iberian Barkeno and modern Barcelona) and Iluro (Iberian Ilduro) (Plin. *NH* 3.22; Ptol. 2.16.18; Mela 2.90) (Fig. 7.19)—also as the name of a small nearby river, usually identified as the modern Besòs, which is probably the origin of the city's name Sinner and Ferrer, 2020: 367–8).

If we look into the ethnic composition of the inhabitants of Baitolo/Baetulo, it seems possible to suggest that most of them were natives. Of the epigraphic corpus recovered from the excavations in the city, all the inscriptions belonging to the foundational phases of the town and during most of the first century BCE use the Iberian script (Torra, 2009). Finally, references to the Latin name Baetulo, both from the ancient sources and from the oldest inscriptions, date from the late first century CE, as is the case of the Baetulonenses who are mentioned in an inscription of 98 CE (*IRC* I, 139) (Sinner and Ferrer, 2020: 371–2).

A similar situation can be documented in Iesso, an *ex novo* foundation (*c.* 120 BCE) (Guitart et al., 1998) of a marked strategic nature, designed to control the territory, as shown by its location with respect to other Republican urban centres such as Ilerda, Tarraco, Aeso, and Ausa, all of them at a distance of about 80 km (Fig. 7.19).

As with Ilduro/Iluro and Baitolo/Baetulo, Iberian epigraphy is the norm for inscriptions from the foundational levels of Iesso (late second and early first centuries BCE). So far, 38 Iberian inscriptions—in addition to coins issued by the city, which also used the Iberian script (Pera, 2001)—on different supports (mostly ceramics) have been published (Pera, 2003; 2005). In contrast, no Latin onomastics have been documented to date during the first century BCE. Even at a later time, of the four preserved Latin inscriptions that are legible, two of them (*IRC* II, 75 and 83) name individuals with *cognomina* of indigenous tradition (Kajanto, 1965). Therefore, the currently available data suggest that most of the early inhabitants of Iesso were natives as well.

Finally, it is also quite possible that even the elites and town magistrates in most (if not all) of the newly founded towns discussed here were natives. They were in charge of deciding the language and legends employed on their coins—almost always selecting the Iberian script (Sinner and Ferrer, 2016; Amela, 2018; Houten 2023)—and when magistrates appear on the coins, as in the case of Undikesken, their onomastics also point towards indigenous individuals. Additionally, the presence of native peoples (Ceretani) as part of municipal elites has recently been documented in Iulia Libica (Ferrer et al., 2018) (Fig. 7.19), another town founded *ex novo* during this dynamic period of transformations. In Iulia Libica, three magistrates (*quattorvirii*) were still using Iberian onomastics during the Augustan period, and a fourth, while having a Latin name, maintained an Iberian filiation (Ferrer i Jané et al. 2018).[14]

### 7.4.2 The Ebro Valley, the Levant, and South-Eastern Citerior

Other areas that historians have considered to have been strongholds of Italic presence in Hispania Citerior during the Republican period are the Ebro valley, the Levant (eastern Spain), and the south-east of the Iberian peninsula. The existence and repetition of place names that may indicate an Italic origin, such as Benavente (from Beneventum, attested 10 times), Abella (from Avella, 5 times), and Lavern(ia) (from Lavernium, 2 times) among many others (see Stefanile, 2017: 59–60), as well as place names derived from the root Osci (Huesca da Osca, Villanueva de Oscos, Santa Eufemia de Oscos, and Santa Eulalia de Oscos) have been interpreted, in the past, as evidence that demonstrates the impact of Italic emigration from Italy to the Hispanic province.

More precisely, the concentration of these place names in a limited area of the province of Citerior, along the natural east–west corridor that the Ebro valley provided and, specifically, in the area located near Osca (present-day Huesca, Aragon), led Menéndez Pidal (1969) to associate this fact with the presence of Oscan-speaking colonists. It is worth highlighting, however, that Adams (2007: 407) rejected this possibility by relating the root of the place name Osca to Bolskan, well known among the corpus of Iberian inscriptions thanks to its coin legends (Mon. 40). However, as Stefanile (2017: 60) has suggested, the possible relationship between the presence of peoples from Campania in the area and some of the other place names mentioned above cannot be totally discarded.

Be that as it may, it is the archaeological and especially the epigraphic evidence that can be useful to study and, to a certain extent, quantify the existence of Italic migrants in these territories towards the end of the Republic. While the number of Republican inscriptions—including graffiti—found in excavations in the main urban centres located in these three densely populated regions of Citerior (see Chapters 4–5) can be counted in their hundreds, most of them are written in Palaeohispanic scripts, and those using the Latin language are clustered in no more than five or six settlements. In this section, therefore, we will discuss only the three cities that have so far provided the largest number of Latin inscriptions, and which have also been the subject of detailed studies: Valentia (Levant, 34 inscr.),

[14] *Bella · Gaisco · f(ilius) / Bella · Bastobles · f(ilius) / Adinildir · Betepe[- · f(ilius)] / Corneli · Erdoild[ir · f(ilius)] / scriptum · est · IIII · viratum.*

La Cabañeta (*Castra Aelia*?, 53 inscr.), and Carthago Nova (40+ inscr.). These cities are also the ones where the presence of Italic migrants can be attested in the largest numbers in the province of Citerior during the Republican period.

Finally, as will be seen in some of the case studies discussed below, it is worth highlighting the fact that, as also happened later during the imperial period (see below), the distribution of the *gentes* who moved to Hispania Citerior reveals profound differences in the nature of the migratory flow towards the peninsula. In Carthago Nova, and to a lesser extent in the cities slightly further north, most individuals seem to have been of civil origin and can be linked with the exploitation of the mines and other commercial and agricultural activities. On the other hand, in cities like Valentia, the presence of individuals related with the military is marked, and the presence of businessmen is harder to attest (Stefanile, 2017: 65).

### Valentia

The truth is that very little is known about the first inhabitants of this Latin colony. However, the epigraphic (Arasa, 2012; de Hoz et al., 2013; Houten, 2023), numismatic (Pena, 1986; Ripollès, 1988), archaeological (Ribera, 2007), and architectural evidence (Marín and Ribera, 1999), apart from, of course, the status given to the city, all seem to suggest that most of its early inhabitants could trace their origins to the Italic peninsula, and that they are likely to have been Italian veterans of the Lusitanian Wars that took place during Decimus Iunius' praetorship (139–138 BCE):

> In Hispania, consul Iunius Brutus gave land and a town, called Valentia, to those who had fought under Viriathus. Livy, *Per.* 55.4

The sentence in the Periochae should therefore be interpreted as indicating that Brutus allocated land to soldiers who had fought for the Roman army against Viriathus, rather than to Lusitanians who had served under Viriathus' leadership (Pina Polo, 2004: 231). Especially relevant to support an Italic origin for these settlers is the fact that 34 graffiti inscribed on ceramics are known from the early city, and they are mostly written in Latin (Bonet and Mata, 1989: 142–5; de Hoz et al., 2013) (Table 7.1). The use of Latin in this chronological context is meaningful in itself since, during the second half of the second century BCE, most of the local groups were still using Palaeohispanic scrips, as we have seen in the north-east of Citerior (see above) and a substantial number of the inscriptions discussed here were recovered from two interrelated archaeological contexts belonging to the foundational levels of Valentia, datable to around 138 BCE (de Hoz et al., 2013: 409).

While most of the inscriptions are very brief and do not provide much information, some of them can help us to trace the ethnicity and geographical origins of some of the inhabitants of the early city.

**Table 7.1** Graffiti on ceramics documented in the Republican levels of Valentia

| Latin | Greek | Iberian | Marks/ uncertain | total | Ref. |
|---|---|---|---|---|---|
| 16 | 3 | 1 | 5 | 25 | De Hoz et al., 2013 |
| 3 | – | 6 | – | 9 | Bonet and Mata, 1989 |

*Source*: de Hoz et al. (2013).

Two of the graffiti (de Hoz et al., 2013: nos. 2 and 25) can be reconstructed as C(aius) · P(—) (75 BCE) and M(arci) · Ca(—) respectively, making it possible to detect the use of a shortened Roman onomastic formula consisting of a *praenomen* and *nomen* among the first inhabitants of Valentia. The latter inscription is of particular interest. Interpreted as a property mark, this graffito expresses a Roman name and was found in an archaeological context that can be dated close to the foundation of the city (de Hoz et al., 2013: 418).

A better picture of the provenance of some of the early inhabitants of Valentia can be seen thanks to the coin legends used by the mint of the city. The civic magistrates recorded in the issues of Valentia (C. LUCIEN., C. MUNI., T. AHI. T. F., L. TRINI. L. F., L. CORANI., and C. NUMI.) provide valuable onomastic information and have been the subject of several studies (Pena, 1986; Ripollès, 1988; Estarán, 2019, 398–9). While Munius, Nummius, and Trinius are difficult to ascribe to a specific geographical location inside the Italic peninsula, it does seem possible to suggest an origin in the interior of Campania and Samnium for Ahius, and a Campanian or Calenan origin for Coranius, based on the onomastic repertory of this *nomen* (Estarán, 2019: 398–9).[15]

## La Cabañeta (Castra Aelia?)

Located in the modern town of El Burgo de Ebro, in the middle reaches of the River Ebro and 17 km from the modern city of Zaragoza, was an urban settlement founded *ex novo* and covering an area of approximately 20 ha. The site shares a very similar chronology to that of the Republican city of Valentia. Founded in the second half of the second century BCE, probably after 133 BCE, it was destroyed and abandoned during the Sertorian Wars (Mínguez and Díaz Ariño, 2011: 51–4 with bibliography).

It has been suggested that La Cabañeta might have originally been a military camp, perhaps identifiable as the *oppidum* of Castra Aelia, later transformed into a civilian site (Mínguez and Díaz Ariño, 2011: 51):

[15] An Etruscan provenance for the *nomen* Coranius cannot be ruled out completely (Ripollès, 1988: 19; Estarán, 2019: 399).

> Contrebia was reduced after forty-four days with a large loss of soldiers. Sertorius left Lucius Insteius in the town with a strong garrison, and led his own force to the Ebro River. There he constructed winter quarters by the town called Camp Aelia, and remained there with his forces; by day he held a conference in the town of the cities allied with him. Livy 91.3

As in Valentia, the architectural characteristics of the excavated buildings (including a bath complex, a forum, and a large *horrea* complex), and the urban planning of the settlement, which follows a orthogonal layout, seem to conform to Italic models (Mínguez and Díaz Ariño, 2011: 52). It is also important to highlight that as opposed to what is found at most of the sites in the area during the second century BCE (e.g. Caminreal, Botorrita, Azaila, etc.), at La Cabañeta only 1.6% of the ceramics are local, whereas imports clearly predominate (Mínguez and Ferreruela Gonzalvo, 2012: 269–70).

Additionally, an important inscription, integrated within the *opus signinum* floor that paved a cultic space in the *horrea* of the settlement (*AE* 2001, 1237 = *ELRH* C105) (see Fig. 7.20), records the place as the headquarters of a *collegium* of merchants made up of Italic migrants (Ferreruela Gonzalvo and Mínguez, 2001). In addition to this important inscription, crucial for our purposes of identifying migrants, another 52 inscriptions have been recovered from La Cabañeta (50 graffiti, Mínguez and Díaz Ariño, 2011; and two inscriptions on stone, Mínguez and Díaz Ariño, 2019) (Table 7.2).

Both inscriptions on stone bear several texts and/or schematic images; however, only two texts, one from each inscription, are of interest to document migrants among the inhabitants of La Cabañeta. The first text reads L(ucius) · RVELI(us), Ruelius being a very rare *nomen* only recorded in one other inscription from Cisterna di Latina (Lazio)—now lost—that can be dated to the first century CE (*CIL* X 6494). The lack of filiation makes it impossible to say whether our individual, who has been interpreted as the stonecutter or the owner or supervisor of the workshop in which the stone block was cut, was a freeman or freedman (Mínguez and Díaz Ariño, 2019: 244). The second text (*vac.*)R(*vac.*) / [.?]BOSI++ is much more complex to interpret, and up to three possibilities of how to reconstruct this text have been suggested (see Mínguez and Díaz Ariño, 2019: 246). With all the caution that is required in this case, however, we agree with Mínguez and Díaz Ariño that the most plausible reconstruction of the text is [-] B'R'OSI(us) Ḷ(ucii) F(ịlius). If this reconstruction is correct and, as these scholars have well pointed out, Brosius/Prosius is an extremely rare *nomen*, only documented in Italy in the areas of Latium, Samnium, and Campania (*CIL* IX 2282; X 4306, 5513, and 6695; XIV 4242; AE 1931, 13; 1993, 559; 2005, 434; Stefanile, 2017: 297–8). Outside Italy, only one inscription from Germania (*AE* 1931, 13) is attested, while in Hispania, the *nomen* appears exclusively in two inscriptions from Carthago Nova, datable around

**Fig. 7.20** Forum and *horrea* at La Cabañeta (el Burgo del Ebro) (Photograph: J. M. Minguez)

**Table 7.2** Number of inscriptions divided by the language in which they were written

| Latin | Greek | Iberian | Marks/uncertain | Total | Ref. |
|---|---|---|---|---|---|
| 22 | 14 | 2 | 12 | 50 | 2011 |

*Source*: Mínguez and Díaz Ariño (2011).

the end of the Republic thanks to palaeographic study (*CIL* $I^2$ 2271; Mínguez and Díaz Ariño, 2019: 246).

If we accept the interpretation of Mínguez and Díaz Ariño (2019: 247) of these two texts as the names of artisans instead of quarry marks, it is plausible to consider that stone cutting workshops existed at La Cabañeta as early as the last third of the second century BCE and the beginning of the following century. The participation of immigrants from Italy in these workshops would be clearly attested by the two aforementioned inscriptions.

On the other hand, only a few of the 22 Latin graffiti on ceramics can inform us about the presence of migrants among the individuals that once marked these objects as their belongings. Number 18 could be interpreted as a Latin name, with the *praenomen* L(ucius) abbreviated and followed by the *nomen*, of which only the first letter was preserved (M [---] or V [---]) (Mínguez and Díaz Ariño, 2011: 52). Other examples of graffiti at La Cabañeta using the structure *praenomen* + *nomen* are known; however, the most interesting text and the only one that can really offer detailed information on the area in Italy that the migrant came from is graffiti number 24: C(aii) · PVMPV[nii?]. The text belongs to an archaeological level located in the *horrea*, which can be dated during the Sertorian Wars. The form Pumpu[---] should be read as an archaic or dialectal variant of the *nomen* Pomponius, and therefore related to the Oscan **pumpe* (five) (Vetter, 1953: 74; Untermann, 2000: 601–3). This is especially interesting because it mentions an individual with a probable origin in central Italy, matching the origin of the magistrates whose names were written on the *opus signinum* that once paved the floor of the cultic space located in the building of the association that they presided over (Mínguez and Díaz Ariño, 2011: 83).

In brief, based on the predominance of the Latin script among the inscriptions at La Cabañeta, as well as the fact that at least a number of its inhabitants were indeed migrants from central Italy, it seems feasible to suggest that the majority of its peoples were originally from the Italian peninsula and, therefore, had a different origin from those recorded in the contemporary epigraphic corpora in the area. This may have been because it was the first city founded by the veterans from the Numantine Wars. At Azaila (Cabezo de Alcalá, Teruel) (*MLH* III, E.1.1–453; Díaz Ariño and Mayayo, 2008), La Caridad (Caminreal, Teruel) (*MLH* IV K.5.1–10; Herce et al., 1993), Contrebia Belaisca (Botorrita, Zaragoza) (*MLH* IV K.1.4–23; Díaz and Jordán, 2001; Estarán et al., 2011), and Gracchuris (Velaza Frías 2009: 612–613; Martínez Torrecilla and Jordán Cólera, 2016) all of them important settlements located along the Ebro valley, the epigraphy mainly employs Palaeohispanic scripts (Iberian and Celtiberian), showing that the abundant use of Latin at La Cabañeta seems to be the exception rather than the rule. The best-case study to exemplify this reality is Azaila (Beltrán Fortes, 1995; 2013). There, more than 450 graffiti inscribed on different kinds of objects and vessels are known, but only seven can certainly be identified as Latin texts (*ELRH* C97–C104). This picture should not surprise us, since it is fairly similar to what we have seen for the north-east of the province, where Tarraco is the exception and concentrates most of the existing Latin inscriptions in the region. In contrast, in other cities such as Baitolo/Baetulo, Ilduro/Iluro, and Iesso/Ieso, the use of the Iberian language seems to have been the norm rather than the exception. It is worth to note, that in most ot the case studies dicussed above (e.g. Valentia, Azaila, La Cabañeta, Tarraco), despite of the script (Iberian, Latin, Greek) and ethnic substrata that predominates (italic or indigenous), we see diferent examples—not two are the same—of multilingual communities and ethnically mixed populations. These diversity is likely to represent—at least to some extent—the type of comunities that were formed in Hispania Citerior during the late republic, and poses interesting questions on how these groups were able (or unable) to integrate in cultural terms (Pina Polo, 2023).

### Carthago Nova

There is no doubt that due to its outstanding mining potential, natural resources, and strategic location—including one of the finest harbours in the western Mediterranean—if there is one place in Hispania Citerior where the arrival of Italic migrants was numerically larger than anywhere else in the province—or at least better attested—that is the city of Carthago Nova and its hinterland. The city was probably one of the first, if not the first, urban centre showing contacts with the Italian peninsula, even before the Second Punic War, as attested by the finds of ancient Greek amphorae (Márquez Villora and Molina Vidal, 2005; Stefanile, 2017).

Additionally, the probable establishment of Italic colonists in 209 BCE, after the city had been conquered by Scipio, could certainly have favoured the migratory process. Recently, it has also been suggested, based on a study of some of the city's coin issues, that many veterans settled in Carthago Nova after they served in the Misenum fleet, taking part in military campaigns between 31 BCE and 41 CE (López, 2012).

Finally, during the late Republican period, the mining concessions of silver-bearing galena exploitations were primarily rented out to societies, families, or individuals, who paid a percentage of their profits to the Roman state (Rico, 2010; Sanz, 2012). This arrangement of the mining exploitations certainly encouraged individuals to migrate towards mining districts:

> When the Romans took control of Iberia, a crowd of Italians filled the mines and bore off great wealth through their lust for profit. After purchasing a multitude of slaves, they turn them over to the overseers of the mine workings, and these, opening up shafts in many places and digging deep into the earth, search for the strata rich in silver and gold. Diod. Sic., *History* 5.36

Stefanile's analysis of the names stamped on lead ingots produced in the mining districts in the territory of Carthago Nova seems to fit well with Diodorus' account and further reinforces the presence of Italian immigrants in the city (Stefanile, 2013; 2015; 2017). His study suggests that families originating in northern Campania and the Gulf of Naples made up 63% of those marking ingots, while 18% came from other places in Italy (Stefanile, 2015: 176).

Furthermore, Carthago Nova has not only provided most of the Latin inscriptions in the Hispanic corpus for the second century BCE, but also many texts that can help us to detect better the arrival, settlement, and ways of association of these migrants coming from the Italic peninsula during the second and first centuries BCE (Abascal and Ramallo, 1997; *ELRH*, 99–130 among others).

Estarán's (2019: 414–15) data reflect the importance of the Italic presence in the city in comparison to the other cities of Citerior prior to the Civil Wars very well. Of the 48 individuals in her list, 22 bear a probable Italic *nomen*, but only two of those belong to the territories in north-eastern Citerior (one in Tarraco and one in Emporion), three are attested in Valentia, and the rest are all recorded in Carthago Nova (17).

As can be seen, there is a certain consensus among scholars, the ancient sources, and the archaeological and epigraphic record as regards the idea that Italic contingents migrated to the city during the late Republican period. Therefore, it does not seem necessary to review all the inscriptions and other evidence mentioned above in detail, especially because some of this material will be discussed in the next two sections devoted to showing how many of the migrants that moved to Hispania Citerior during the late Republic could trace their origins to central Italy. As we shall see below, the area of Campania—especially the Bay of Naples—via the harbour of Puteoli, and the Auruncan and Calenan territories, slightly further north, via the river port of Minturnae, were the regions where many of the immigrants arriving in Citerior had their origins.

### 7.4.3 Central Italic and Campanian Emigration to Hispania Citerior

The pattern of individuals migrating from Campania to Hispania can be traced in almost every case study discussed above. In the defensive walls of Tarraco, the inscription of Manio Vibio honouring Minerva stands out as one of the oldest in Hispania (*CIL* $I^2$ 3449; *CIL* $II^2$ 14 841; *AE* 1981, 573). If we examine where the Vibii are known in Italy, the towns of Capua, Abellinum, Cumae, and Herculaneum (Salomies, 2012: 179; Alföldy, 1981) appear at the top of the list. Based on the epigraphic evidence, it seems quite reasonable to suggest a Campanian origin for the author of the graffito in Tarraco (Estarán, 2019: 396).

In addition, in the capital of the province but already in the second half of the first century BCE, the freedmen from Tarraco (*ELRH* C70) A. Varaeus A. l. Philonicus and Varaeia A. l. Danais, may have been migrants from Campania, since the -aei-/-ae- shift noted in the case of the Caeicius from Cartago Nova (*ELRH* C50) can be detected (Estarán, 2019: 407). If, indeed, it is the Varius *nomen*, its Oscan equivalent is well documented in the Italic corpus (Salomies, 2012: 177).

Another example of a migrant of Campanian origin is Vr. Cn. Vesuia from Emporion. As Estarán (2019: 395) has recently suggested, the family name points towards a Sabellic origin, the name N. Vesui(us) being documented in Capua

(*CIL* I² 2949) and the forms Vesuius, Vesbius, and Vesuuius in Pompeii (*CIL* IV 19, 52, 71, 1495, 2512, 2889, 9824).

Moving south, in Valentia a possible origin in the interior of Campania and Samnium has been suggested for Ahius, while a Campanian or Calenan origin for Coranius is quite feasible following the onomastic repertory of this *nomen* (Estarán, 2019: 398–9).

Similarly, if the reconstruction of B'r'osi(us) Ḷ(ucii) f(ịlius) for one of the artisans from La Cabañeta is accepted and, considering the fact that Brosius/Prosius is an uncommon *nomen* only recorded in Italy in the areas of Latium, Samnium, and Campania, it seems acceptable to suggest a central Italic origin for this individual. Additionally, the members of the *collegium* established at La Cabañeta also seem to be migrants from these central Italic regions.

In Carthago Nova, this pattern is even more accentuated. Of the list of ten magistrates of a *collegium* who financed the construction of religious building (*ELRH* 10), a large majority had a central Italic origin. These individuals, who seem to be permanently based in the city due to their commercial and mining activities, can be divided equally between *ingenui* and freedmen. If we examine the names of the former slaves, Puupius, Luucius, Prosius, Titius, and Vereius are all well documented in Oscan epigraphy as well as in the Latin epigraphy of the regions where Oscan was spoken (Estarán, 2019: 401). Furthermore, the origin of the demonym Pupius is attested in the Latin epigraphy in Benevento, Telesia, Atela, Capua, and Pompeii, among others, while it is known that luvkiis is the Italic equivalent of the Latin Lucius in Oscan personal names. The demonym luvkiis/loucies, of central Italic origin, found throughout the Pelgina and Campanian regions in pre-Roman times, was later Latinized in the form Lucius or Lucceius (Salomies, 2012: 158; Nonnis, 2015: 269). Prosius is also well attested in the Latin epigraphy of Macchia d'Isernia and Isernia (*AE* 2005: 434; *AE* 1993: 559; Estarán, 2019: 403) in the heart of the Oscan-speaking territories. Similarly, while the *nomen* Titius is widely distributed in the Republican period in the areas of Etruria, Lazio, Campania, Samnium, and Apulia (Nonnis, 2015: 430), the demonym tittiis is very frequent in Oscan inscriptions and the *praenomen* *N(umerius)* has been suggested by Salomies (2012: 138–9) as an indicator of attachment to Oscan-speaking regions. As can be seen, a central Italic origin for most of these individuals can be suggested.

The study of the second inscription from a *collegium* (*ELRH* C50) in Carthago Nova, including the names of slaves, freedmen, and two *ingenui*, seems to point towards a more diverse origin—compared with the previous one—for the individuals listed (Estarán, 2019: 407–9). The names, M. Caeici N. C. l., L. Paqui X l. Silo, Q. Verati C. s., and Pil. Pontili M. C. s., are also likely to be migrants from Oscan-speaking territories (Estarán, 2019: 409).

The cases of the Appuleii from Carthago Nova, one who was the *IIvir quinquennalis* of 29/28 BCE (L. Appuleius Rufus) and the other the individual

(L. Appuleius L.l. P(h)ilo), who stamped the ingot recovered from the Mal di Ventre wreck, are also interesting. Both shared the *praenomen* Lucius, a significant clue that may lead us to relate them to the Gulf of Naples, thanks to the comparison with Herculaneum (Stefanile, 2017: 140–1).

If we now move on to the inscriptions on lead ingots, the presence of a large number of individuals from Italy and more specifically from Campania in the exploitation of the Iberian silver and lead mines was first mentioned by Domergue many years ago (1990). However, the arguments to support this hypothesis were sometimes limited (Stefanile, 2017: 60). Stefanile's recent analysis, however, has shown that a detailed study of the stamps on the lead ingots from Carthago Nova not only confirms Domergue's theory but raises the number of Campanian people among the Italic individuals recorded in the city considerably, reaching as many as 63% of the total (Stefanile, 2013; 2017) (Fig. 7.21). The picture that arises from the analysis of this epigraphic evidence is one of dozens of stories of men, of families, freedmen, slaves, who travelled and may have migrated from Campania to Hispania (Stefanile, 2017: 64).

A broader picture of the importance of Campanian migration to Citerior can be obtained by analysing all the epigraphic evidence from the cities discussed in Stefanile's study (2017). The percentage of the *gentes* with a strong probability of having an origin in the Campanian region is quite significant, reaching 21% of the total—although a part of his data refers to the Early Empire. Forty-five *gentes*, out of the 280 attested in the cities of Carthago Nova, Ilici, Lucentum, Dianium, Edeta, Saetabis, Valentia, and Saguntum have been traced, in the course of his research, to a Campanian origin; the number may have been even larger since Stefanile (2017: 64) did not include those widespread *gens*, for which it is complicated to trace a certain origin, in this list.

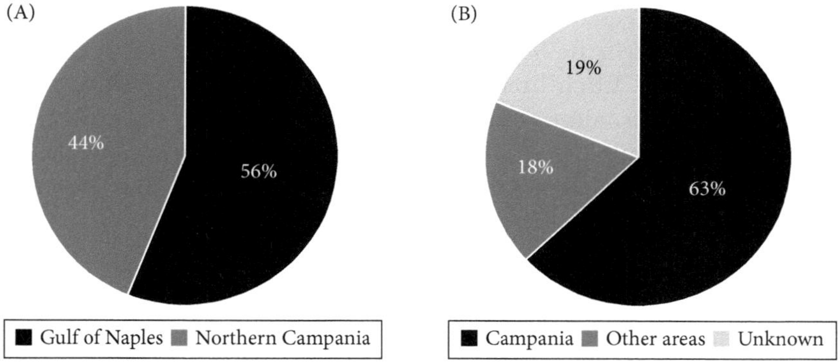


**Fig. 7.21** (A) Origin of the *gens* attested on the lead ingots from Carthago Nova. (B) origin of the Campanian families attested on the lead ingots from Carthago Nova (after Stefanile, 2015)

## Minturnae and the Auruncan-Calenan Migration towards Citerior

Thanks to several recent studies (Stefanile, 2017; Estarán, 2019; Stannard et al., 2019), we can now start to see how the Auruncan-Calenan territories, located in the northern part of Campania, also seem to have been the origin of many individuals that migrated towards Citerior, the cities of Minturnae, Cales, and Teanum Sidicinum being especially important in this migratory movement (Stefanile, 2017: 31).

Although the scale of this phenomenon is still smaller and less well documented than its counterpart in the Bay of Naples—and also less studied—Stefanile (2017: 175–7) suggests that northern Campanians, including those with the names Aurunculeii, Calvii, Carulii, Cornelii Polliones, Fiduii, Furii, Messi, Planii, Geminii, and Roscii departed from the port of Minturnae and that several families, such as the Saufeii from Praeneste, attested three times in Dianium and the area of Safor, were likely to have been based in Minturnae (Stefanile, 2017: 97). Some of them will be discussed briefly.

A connection between the Fannius from Carthago Nova (C. Fannius Latini f. Censorinus) and those Fannii established in Minturnae by the end of the second century BCE (Pesando and Guidobaldi, 1989: 71–2) has also been proposed (Stefanile, 2017: 196–7). Among the Fannii from Minturnae, it is worth mentioning the *eques* and *publicanus* Cn. Fannius (Verr. 1.128), who participated in a chapter of the life of Marius, when he was arrested at Minturnae in 88 BCE in the house of a woman named Fannia (Val. Max. 8.2.3; Plut. *Marius* 30). Finally, another member of the family, L. Fannius, was sent to Hispania in 85 BCE, in the company of L. Magius, to negotiate with Sertorius (Stefanile, 2017: 197).

A similar case can be made for the members of the *gens* Fufii recorded in Carthago Nova (Fufia; L. Fufius L. l. Varus), for which Stefanile (2017: 205–8) has put forward a very plausible origin in the Fufii Caleni, well attested in both the literary sources (Cic. *Phil.*, 8.13; *Phil.*, 2.41) and the epigraphic record of Cales and Capua (Barreda Pascual, 1998; Pena, 2009: 15).

Moreover, an origin in Minturnae has also been suggested as the most likely origin for the Titinii from Carthago Nova (Alexander, L. Titini servus; L. Titinius P.f.; Titinia mulieris l. Mart(h)a), attested in the city between the end of the second century BCE and the early first century BCE, as suggested by the epigraphic (Pesando and Guidobaldi, 1989) and literary evidence (Plut. *Mar.* 38.4; Val. Max. 8.2.3) of a similar date (Stefanile, 2017: 313–17).

Furthermore, an Auruncan origin seems to be the most probable option for the Lucilius documented in Saguntum (L. Lucilius L.f., a *duumvir* who participated in the reconstruction of the walls) and Saetabis (L. Lucilius). It is true that it is not possible to exclude an origin in other areas of Campania; however, the presence of servants of the family in the port of Minturnae in some of the most significant texts referring to the city, in which almost all the names are also present in Hispania, should be mentioned. These include the story of the poet Lucilius, who fought in Numantia alongside Scipio Aemilianus Africanus,[16] and this seems to serve the hypothesis of an origin among the Aurunci (Stefanile, 2017: 240).

In a recent study, Stannard et al. (2019: 150–7) have identified at least one probable *societas* trading with Carthago Nova from Minturnae, through the abbreviated *nomina* FVRI, C·BAIBI, L·NVM, C·NVM, and C·SAM/IR recorded on the small lead series from Minturnae. These lead pieces show that members of these *gentes* collaborated in Italy, and indeed were close enough to create a single die-linked lead issue associating their names. While the existence of a company from Minturnae trading with Carthago Nova does not directly prove a constant migratory flow from one place to the other, it adds to the above mentioned cases discussed. In addition, Orejas and Sánchez-Palencia (2002) list the Furii, the Baebii, and the Numisii among the 16 most important families of the city of Carthago Nova on the basis of inscriptions (Fig. 7.22).

Furthermore, members of these *gentes* are also well documented along the eastern coast of Citerior, as Stefanile's work has shown (Table 7.3). It is important to be aware that not all of them need to have been related to the Italic *gentes*, since individuals with the same *nomen* might, of course, belong to more than one family, as is the case of the Baebii, one of the most important families in Saguntum,

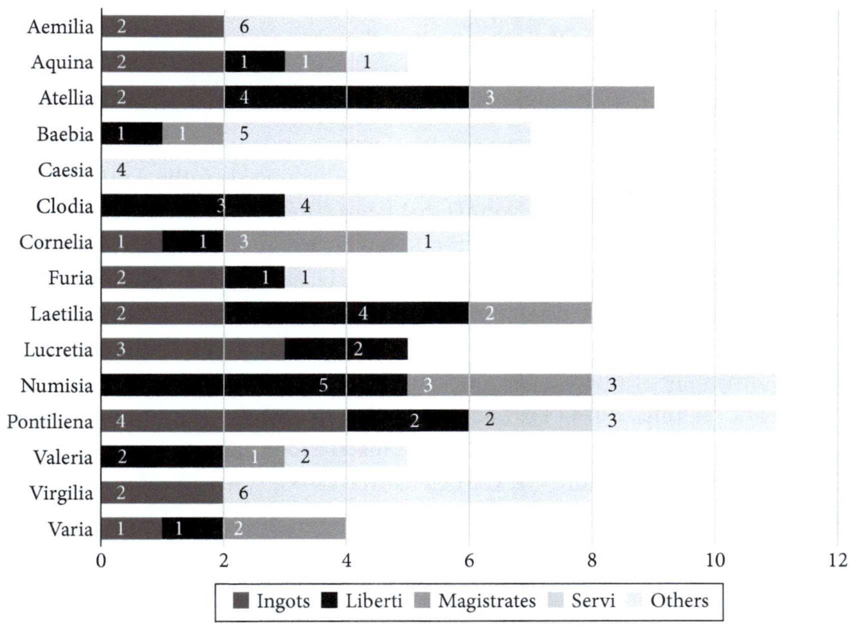


**Fig. 7.22** Epigraphic representation of the most important families of the city of Carthago Nova (redrawn after Orejas and Sánchez-Palencia, 2002: 548, fig. 543)

16 *Celebre et Lucilii nomen fuit, qui sub P. Africano Numantino bello eques militaverat* (Vell. 2.9.4).

**Table 7.3** FVRI, C·BAIBI, L·NVM, C·NVM and presence of these *gentes* in the towns considered by Stefanile (2017)

| Minturnae | Gentes | Place documented | Date | Stefanile |
|---|---|---|---|---|
| FVRI | Furii | Ilici | 1st c. BCE and 1st c. CE | Fig. 28 |
| | | Lucentum | 1st c. BCE and 1st c. CE | Fig. 33 |
| | | Saetabis | All dates | Fig. 44 |
| C·BAIBI | Baebii | Dianium, La Safor, Saetabis, | Until the mid-1st c. CE | Fig. 38 |
| | | Edeta | All dates | Fig. 49 |
| | | Valentia | 2nd c. BCE and 1st c. CE | Fig. 53 |
| L·NVM C·NVM | Numisii | Dianium, La Safor | Until the mid-1st c. CE | Fig. 38 |

who are unlikely to have been of Italic origin, but rather descendants of the local aristocracy that received citizenship in the second century BCE.

The 29 lists of magistrates of *collegia* honouring gods at Minturnae, however, are a valuable resource to document the *gentes* in this city between 90 and 50 BCE (Barreda Pascual, 1998: 103). Many of the magistrates were of servile condition, thus facilitating the names of their *domini* as well. It is important to note that servile magistrates are known only in Italy and Carthago Nova in Republican times.[17]

The Furii are attested six times as *domini* of magistrates at Minturnae (Gregori and Nonnis, 2014: 106). The praenomina (Gnaeus and Aulus) used by two of these *domini*, suggest that they are likely to have belonged to the Minturnaean branch of the *gens* (Gregori and Nonnis, 2014: 94). The Furii also exploited silver/lead mines at Carthago Nova during the Republic and produced ingots, such as the one signed by A· and P· Furii, freedmen of C·, L·, and P· Furii. These are some of the earliest ingots and could support the idea of the company having played an early role in the lead trade.

The Numisii are attested three times at Minturnae, as *domini* of magistrates (Gregori and Nonnis, 2014: 110) and were also one of the leading families of Carthago Nova over a long period of time, as inscriptions indicate well. They were also connected with the mines in Cartagena-Mazarron, since a Sextus Numisius appears as a donor of an altar to the Lares in an inscription found in the vicinity of the San Rámon mine in the Boltada ravine (Portmán). This is probably because companies specialized, some in mining and some in metalworking, the Numisii being among the latter (Díaz Ariño and Antolinos, 2013: 541–3).

[17] *'Per l'età repubblicana magistri di condizione servile (da soli o insieme a liberti) sono finora attestati in area laziale e campana, oltre che a Minturnae, solo a Praeneste, Cora e Pompei e, nelle province occidentali, a Carthago Nova'* (Gregori and Nonnis, 2014: 96).

The Baebii are attested at Minturnae by the *domina* of a magistrate. The Baebii are also documented in imperial times, as an important *gens* in the mining area of Turobriga and Arucci in the Sierra Morena (Orejas and Beltrán, 2010: 408–9). Members of the *gens* are attested as magistrates of the city during the first century (Orejas and Ramallo, 2004: 111, fig. 112).

Stefanile (2017: figs. 390, 49, 53, and 57) points to Cornelii from Dianium and Safor in the first centuries BCE and CE, and in Edeta in the first century BCE, in Valentia between the second century BCE and the first century CE, and Saguntum in the first centuries BCE and CE. Orejas and Sánchez-Palencia (2002: 548) list Cornelia as one of the 16 most attested *gentes* at Carthago Nova insofar as the inscriptions are concerned (Fig. 7.22), and more importantly, P. Cornelius Pollio, of the tribe of Aimilia, signed ingots as P·CORNEL L·F POLLION FORMIAN GAL, specifying his origin in the town of Formia, immediately to the north of Minturnae (Domergue, 1990: 254, table 4, no. 1013).

Finally, as Stefanile (2017: 64) has correctly pointed out, one must also bear in mind that the origin of a family does not necessarily coincide with the starting point of the migration towards Citerior. There are numerous cases of ancient families with roots in the Lazio region that, by the end of the Republic, had consolidated a branch in Minturnae. It is therefore from this city, and not from their motherland, that the members of the family sailed towards the recently conquered Hispanic territories.

As can be seen in this, by no means exhaustive, account, of the available data (see Stannard et al., 2019 and especially Stefanile, 2017 for a much more detailed picture), the evidence of migrants from the Auruncan-Calenan area and especially from Minturnae is of considerable importance and should be taken into account together with its Campanian counterpart. In short, there were two areas in central Italy that seem to have been fundamental in the migratory process of Italics towards Hispania Citerior during the late republican period: on the one hand, the Gulf of Naples, certainly gravitating around the port of Puteoli; on the other, the lands once inhabited by the Aurunci, in the northern part of the region, presumably gravitating towards the port and the city of Minturnae (Stefanile, 2017: 66).

## 7.4.4 Greek Migrants in Hispania Citerior

To date, an in-depth study of the Republican-period Greek inscriptions in Hispania Citerior is still lacking. However, a brief consideration of the state of knowledge which provided interesting results was undertaken by de Hoz et al. (2013). To the already mentioned Greek graffiti from Valentia and La Cabañeta, those recorded in Carthago Nova—whose interpretation should be taken with great caution (*HEp* 6, 657; Ramallo and Ruiz, 1994: 97–8)—and Emporion (de Hoz, 1997: 33–56) should be added. Additionally, two more graffiti have been recorded in the Iberian *oppidum* of Ca n'Oliver (Cerdanyola del Vallès, Barcelona) (Francès et al., 2008: 224–5), one from the modern town of Roses (Canòs 2002: no. 190), one at La Alcudia (a property mark, *HEp* 14, 12), and one from the archaeological site of Na Guardis in Majorca (de Hoz 1997: 88). Finally, if we follow Alföldy's proposal, a couple of tombstones from Tarraco should also be added to this list (Alföldy, 2011a: 90–2 and 98–9).

Despite the small sample, we agree with de Hoz et al. (2013: 420) when they suggest that the presence of Greek-speaking people in Republican Citerior would have been a fairly frequent situation, especially in coastal cities or towns and *oppida* with a marked mercantile profile, La Cabañeta being a good example of the former and Ca n'Oliver of the latter.

Two facts prevent us from interpreting the individuals behind these texts as freedmen or slaves of oriental provenance: in the first place, freedmen's inscriptions on stone seem to have systematically used the Latin language, regardless of what their mother tongue was (Beltrán Lloris, 2004). This phenomenon is also documented in the domestic sphere, where property marks on ceramics show that Greek *cognomina* are inscribed using the Latin alphabet (*ELRH* C94, C95; de Hoz et al., 2013: 421). Second, the few known public inscriptions erected by *peregrini* of Greek origin are always written in their vernacular language or are bilingual (de Hoz, 1997: 34–9; de Hoz et al., 2013: 421), suggesting that the authors of the aforementioned graffiti using the Greek language are likely to have been merchants or immigrants.

Of course, many would have belonged to the first category, but it seems reasonable to suggest that some were also migrants, especially considering the proximity of Emporion and Rhodes and the many contacts that existed with the peoples and the Greek colonies, especially Massalia, in the Gulf of Lion. The only Republican-period Greek tombstone from Emporion is dedicated to an individual from Massalia (de Hoz, 1997: 34–5), perhaps embodying the mobility in existence between these territories. A Campanian origin also seems quite feasible; we have seen the prominence that this region had in Italic migration towards Citerior, and the individual commemorated in one of the two Greek tombstones from Tarraco is also considered to have probably been a Neapolitan (*CIL* II$^2$ 14 G 3; de Hoz et al., 2013: 421). Finally, even though it is less likely, but not impossible, a more distant origin, in the central or even eastern Mediterranean might be considered for these migrants. As de Hoz et al. (2013: 421) have pointed out, the owner of the *ostrakon* with a mention of the Cabiros from la Albufereta, or some of the merchants who transported the Rhodian, Cnidian, and Chios amphorae that are not uncommon on the archaeological sites of coastal Citerior and even Ulterior (Molina Vidal, 1997; Mateo, 2016) must have come from such areas. Neither should we forget that Numas, the Greek who financed the construction of the sanctuary dedicated to Serapis in Emporion in the first century BCE was from Alexandria (*ELRH* C79; de Hoz, 1997: 36–7).

## 7.5 Migrations to Hispania Tarraconensis during the Empire

The consolidation and deeper integration of the provinces of Hispania favoured the development of mobility of different types during the Empire. The moment of greatest demographic impact was probably brought about by the Caesarian and Augustan colonization, whose quantitative importance was underlined by the classical sources. In this short chronological period, a wider phenomenon of organized migration based on the foundation of colonies seems to have taken place. Suetonius (*Caes.* XLII) indicated that 80,000 citizens were distributed in overseas colonies; that is, the new provinces of Achaia, Africa, Gaul, and the Hispaniae. In his *Res Gestae*, Augustus himself provided the figure of 300,000 veterans who were supposedly established during his reign in various colonies located throughout Italy and the provinces (RGDA, 3). The impact for the Hispaniae was clear; there were at least 22 colonies that helped to reinforce the administrative and economic structure of Hispania, and 10 of them are documented during this period in Citerior: Tarraco, Emporiae, Carthago Nova, Celsa, Acci, Barcino, Caesaraugusta, Ilici, Libisosa, and Tucci.

In fact, most of the Augustan colonies were to become the cities that housed the largest concentrations of population; they were located in the Guadalquivir valley, on the Mediterranean coast, in the Ebro valley—now pacified and under Roman control—which was where almost all the colonies in Citerior were founded, and on the River Tagus and the Guadiana (Fig. 7.23). Much of the central plateau, as well as the northern and north-western parts of the peninsula, did not witness any of these foundations. Perhaps that explains why the residence of the *legatus iuridici* is found in Calagurris even when he was likely to be active in the north-west, in regions that had a noticeable presence of military detachments. During Augustus' campaigns in the north-western territories of the province under study (29–19 BCE), more than 20,000 legionaries were permanently deployed in these areas. However, the real impact of this isolated phenomenon is unclear, since most of them never finally settled in the province and returned to their home towns.

The Early Empire also brought with it greater diversity as regards the origins of the migratory flows that arrived in the Iberian peninsula. On the other hand, only a few new colonies were founded after Augustus, the most important ones being Clunia, Flaviobriga, and Italica. The epigraphic record enables us to document the movement of Italics towards Hispania, but also the arrival of people of Gallic and African origin, the latter being quite numerous in the coastal cities

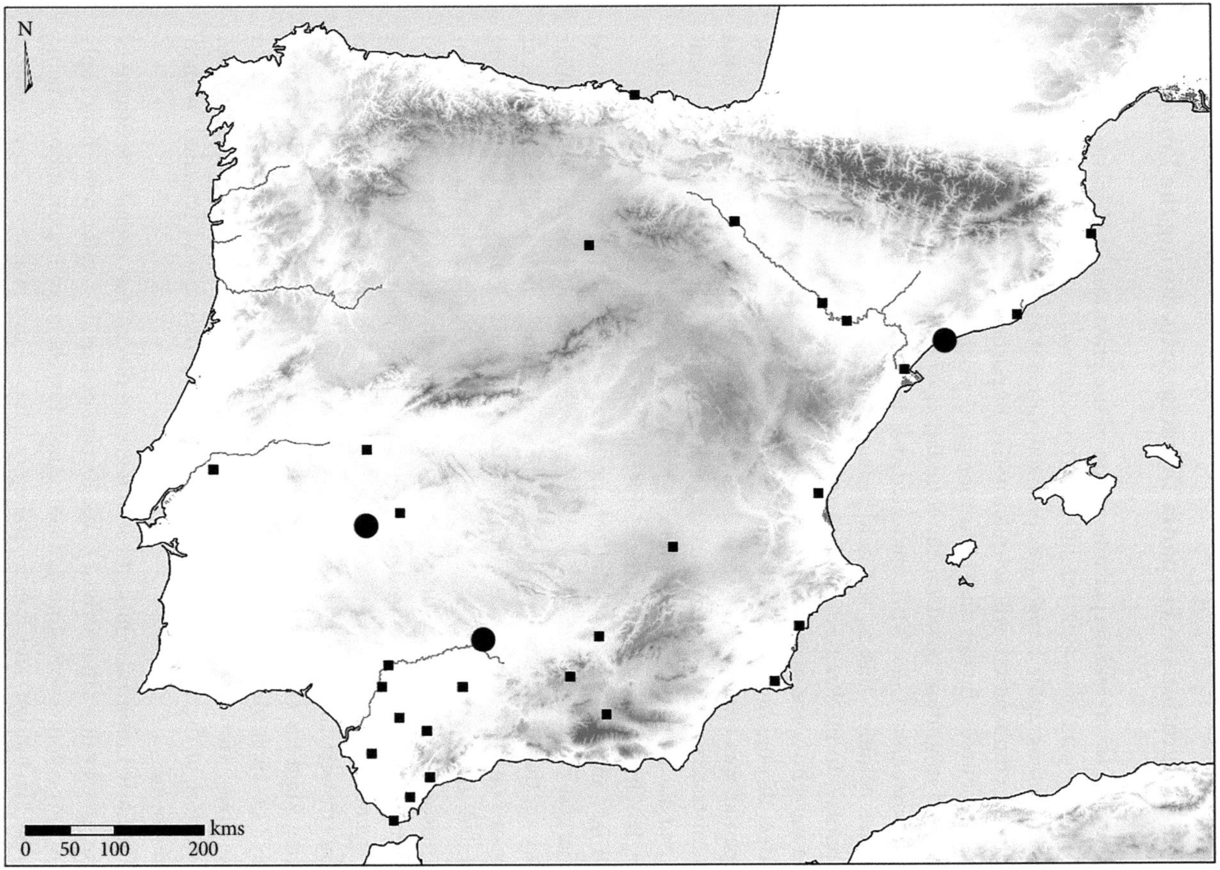


**Fig. 7.23** Distribution of the Roman colonies of Hispania. Larger circles indicate provincial capitals

(e.g. Barcino and Tarraco); it should be noted that the Iberian peninsula had close commercial contacts with these two regions in particular from the second century onwards. To a lesser extent, more distant immigrants from Greece and the eastern Mediterranean are also attested, together with a small contingent of migrants from the provinces along the Rhine and the Danube (Haley, 1991: 27–52; Ortiz Córdoba, 2019a: 156). Even considering all the above, it is important to highlight that Haley's study on immigration into the Hispanic provinces during the Empire revealed that migrants to the Iberian peninsula only represented fewer than 5% of the total population attested in the epigraphic record (Haley, 1991). Besides, he confirms that Tarraco concentrated most of the immigrants entering Hispania Tarraconensis (see Fig. 7.24).

In subsequent centuries, the sources record invasions by '*Mauri*' in Baetica in the time of Marcus Aurelius (Cass. Dio, 52.25.4–5; 53.15.3), some of whom finally settled in the peninsula. In the middle of the third century CE, the invasions of the Franks and other Germanic groups deeply affected the province (see Chapter 6), initiating a period of continuous population movements (Suevi, Alans, Vandals, Visigoths). Their numerical contribution was surely limited, but today it is difficult to determine. Epigraphically, the Late Roman period is characterized by a smaller number of inscriptions, but a great diversity of origins. In addition to the arrival of Italics, Africans, and people from the Danube provinces, immigrants from the eastern provinces are recorded for the first time (Fig. 7.25).

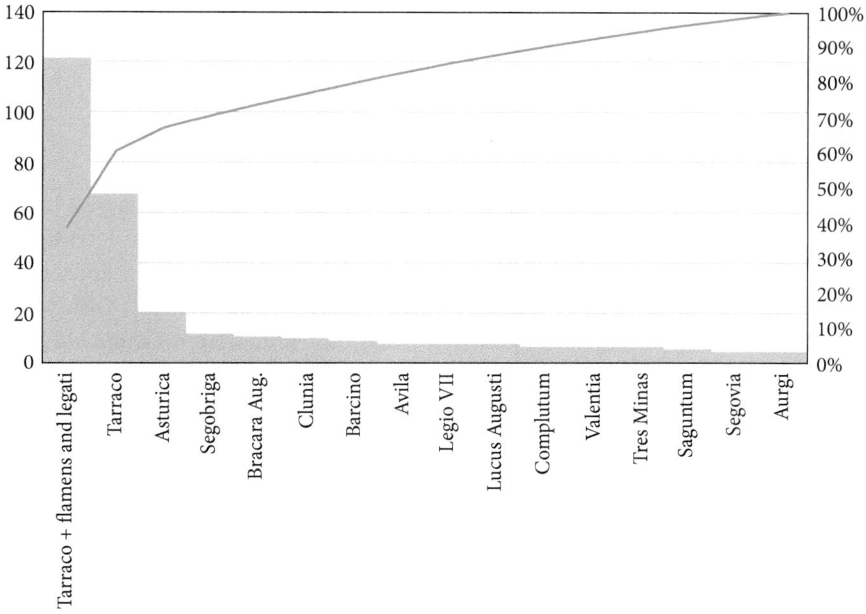


**Fig. 7.24** Number of *alieni* in the cities of Hispania Tarraconensis (after Haley, 1991)

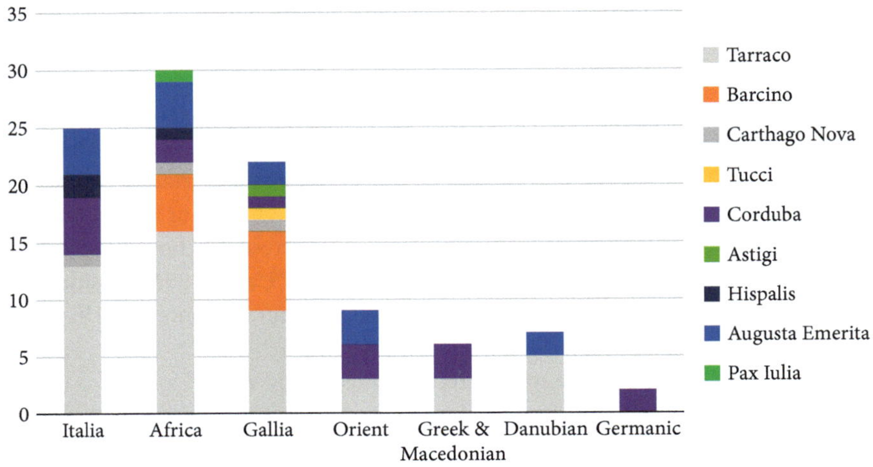


**Fig. 7.25** Distribution of the origin of extra-peninsular immigration (Ortíz Córdoba, 2019c: chart 15)

Finally, it is important to underline that in this section (7.5) a type of mobility that is characterized by being permanent in nature, in other words one that led to the migrants settling in their places of destination, will be discussed. This is important because it differentiates this type of movements from others that will be discussed later (7.6), which were temporary in nature since they involved the return of the new arrivals to their place of origin.

## 7.5.1 Italic Migrants

For the early imperial period, Hispania Tarraconensis produces the largest body of evidence for people from Italy migrating to the peninsula. When looking at the places of origin in Italy of these individuals, the great majority came from Rome and the north of the Italian peninsula, a picture that contrasts with what was recorded for the Republican period, when individuals from Campania and central Italy made up the majority of emigrants (Haley, 1991: 33). Moreover, those related with the movements of the army are the most frequently represented among the sample, reflecting both its military make-up and the importance of northern Italy as a source of legionary recruits during the first two centuries of the Empire.

One special case study is Herrera de Pisuerga (Pisoraca) in the north-west of the Iberian peninsula, which was supposed to be the headquarters of Legio IIII Macedonica (Pérez González, 1989; Pérez González and Illaguerri, 1992). The legion seems to have arrived in Herrera *c.* 20 BCE as part of the military contingent deployed in the Cantabrian Wars and departed for Mogontiacum around 39 CE. The legion took part in the Civil Wars—with great loses at the Battle of Phillippi in 42 BCE—and later fought on the side of Octavian against Lucius Antonius at the siege of Mutina. Some of its veterans were settled in northern Italian towns such as Firmo (ILS 2340-CVSI 72), Aeste, and Veneto (CVSI 22, 24, 25), where there were probably new recruits among local populations. In other words, most of the soldiers in Legio IIII were from the northern Adriatic regions (Picenum, Umbria, Aemilia, Venetia, and Histria).

The archaeological material of the early first century CE from Herrera is outstanding in terms of volume and variety, with a large quantity of Italian samian ware and especially vases by a potter probably from northern Italy named L. Terentius, who imitated Italian samian at Herrera (Pérez González, 1989). Besides, recent amphora studies confirm a particular assemblage with a substantial percentage of north Adriatic wine amphorae and stamps (Pérez González and Arribas, 2021) unparalleled in the rest of Citerior. It seems that soldiers from this particular region brought their consumption preferences with them, even though such goods may have been more expensive and difficult to obtain. This is not a unique case, since a similar example of an African military contingent at York in the Severan period was associated with African red-slip pottery, together with local imitations, imported amphorae, and also African skeletons.[18]

With regard to the epigraphic evidence in Tarraconensis, five of these inscriptions can be dated before the Flavian period, and the number rises to seven after 68 CE (Haley, 1991: 30–1). These data coincide with the presence of up to seven legions in Hispania between 30 BCE and 68 CE (Haley, 1991: 28). Among the civilian inscriptions, six come from the province under study and two of them are from the north-western territories, a freeborn from Caesaraugusta and a series of honorary inscriptions from Carthago Nova and Asso (Caravaca) highlight the presence of the *scrib(a) quaestorius et aedilicius L. Aemilius M.f. M.nep. Quir(ina) Rectus domo Roma*. This individual, in addition to possessing the citizenship of the Sicellitani, Assotani, and Bastetani in Tarraconensis and of Sparta and Argos, was an aedile in Carthago Nova, suggesting that he spent long periods of time in that city (Haley, 1991: 32).

To summarize, even if only those inscriptions that can most probably be related to an Italic origin and therefore associated with a process of migration into Hispania Tarraconensis are considered, the province records a total of 27 individuals. If we now examine the status of the migrants, *ingenui* (16) dominate over those of servile condition (2) and freedmen (5) (Fig. 7.26a). Four of our individuals are

[18] Swan (1992) was the first author that identified African red slip in good numbers as well as imitations at the Legio VI headquarters in York during the Severan campaigns in northern Britain. Such African presence was also confirmed with an unparalleled number of northern African amphorae by Williams and Carreras (1995). Recent isotope analysis of skeletons has confirmed the presence of African population at York and allows an update of this temporary movement of troops (Pitts, 2021).

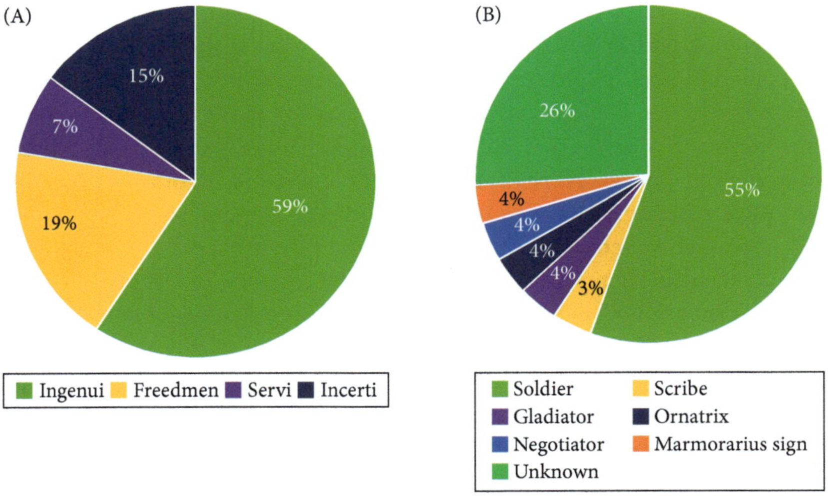


**Fig. 7.26** (A) Status and (B) professions of the Italian migrants (27 individuals)

*incerti*. If the sample is now divided by profession, soldiers (15), as stated above, clearly constitute a majority, and are the only category that allows a clear pattern of mobility towards the province to be pointed out. As for all the other professions (scribe, gladiator, negotiator, etc.), there is only one attested case of each, and therefore no conclusions can be drawn from the evidence (Fig. 7.26b).

### 7.5.2 Gallic Immigration into Tarraconensis

The immigration of individuals from the nearby territory of Gaul is quite remarkable under the Empire, the only period for which inscriptions are available, with a total of 29 inscriptions that mention 31 individuals (Haley, 1991: 36; Ortiz Córdoba, 2019a: 160). This is not surprising since, as has been seen above, both provinces are well connected by land and especially by the Mediterranean Sea and the Atlantic Ocean. At this point, it is worth mentioning that, when discussing the population of Gallic origin settled in Tarraconensis, all those individuals not only from the province of Narbonensis, but also from the other three Galliae, the vast territory that under Roman rule was organized into the provinces of Aquitainia, Lugdunensis, and Belgica, are included under the collective name of Gauls (Ortiz Córdoba, 2019a: 157).

Most of the immigration from the Galliae to Hispania was concentrated in the Tarraconensis province, particularly in its north-eastern parts (Fig. 7.27). A closer examination reveals a preference for the coastal cities, with Tarraco and Barcino standing out above all the others, combining a total of 16 inscriptions, which record 18 individuals. Tarraco seems to be the preferred destination since up to

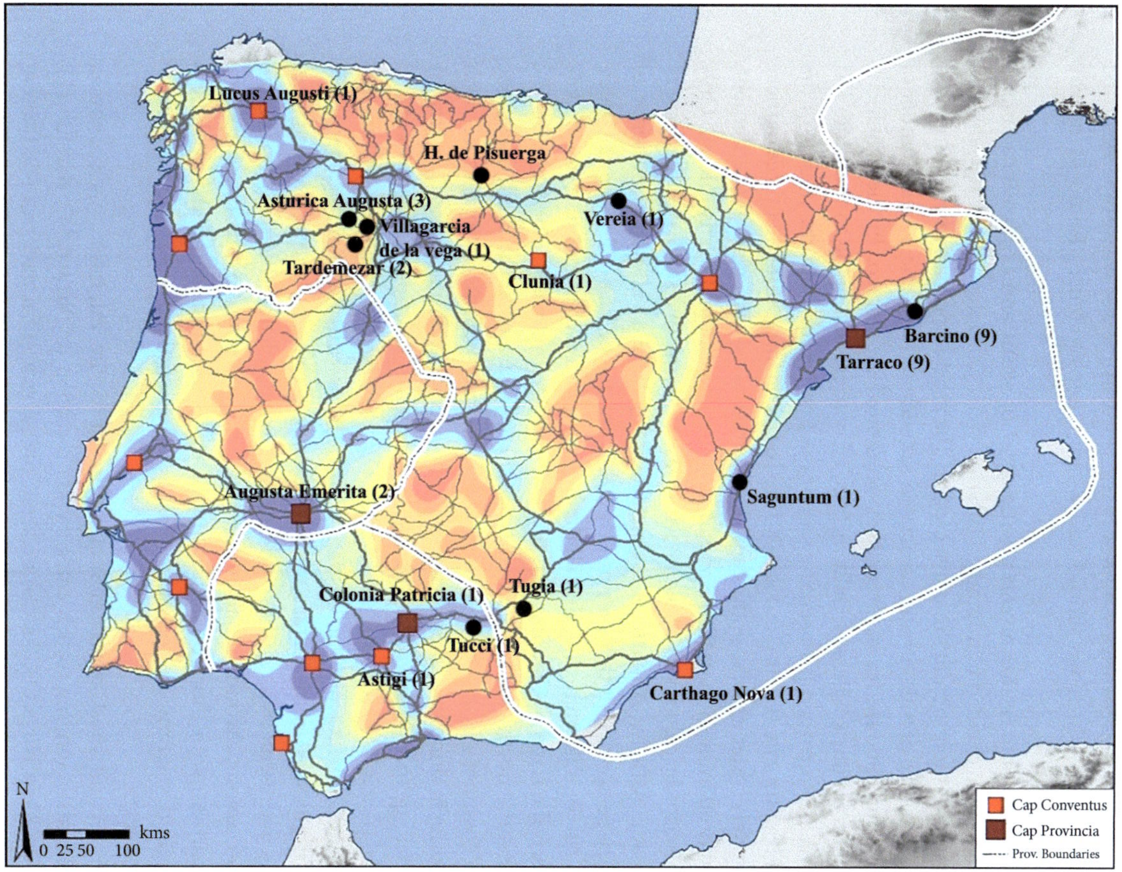


**Fig. 7.27** Geographical distribution of the recorded Gallic immigrants superimposed on the connectivity map of the Iberian peninsula. The number of individuals found in each city is indicated in brackets (after Ortíz Córdoba, 2019c: fig. 1)

nine possible migrants are recorded there (Haley, 1991: 34–5). Barcino (9) also seems to be a destination for those Gauls who migrated to Tarraconensis as suggested by two inscriptions that certainly indicate a Gallic origin and several others that are possible candidates on the basis of the evidence of their tribe (Haley, 1991: 36). Asturica Augusta is the third in the list with three recorded individuals, to which we should add a few other references found in nearby towns (Fig. 7.27).

The epigraphic record reveals a wide array of status and occupations among the Gauls who decided to migrate to Citerior. Ortiz Córdoba (2019a: 163) divided the causes of their mobility into five groups. The most important one is comprised by the presence of military and associated individuals (12). The largest number of inscriptions alluding to the army is concentrated in Tarraco. In the provincial capital up to four soldiers of Gallic origin, all of them belonging to the Legio VII Gemina, are recorded between the end of the first century and the middle of the second century CE (Ortiz Córdoba, 2019a: 164). It is interesting that three of these individuals (veterans) chose the capital of Tarraconensis as a place for retirement, probably an indication of the remarkable opportunities that the city offered. Only one inscription alludes to a soldier who was still on active service at the time of his death. Asturica Augusta is the next city (3), with a substantial presence of military personnel, in this case mostly belonging to the Legio X Gemina (Haley, 1991: 34–5); it is interesting that all the inscriptions are clustered in terms of date between the reign of Claudius and that of Nero (Ortiz Córdoba, 2019a: 166). The fact that the north-western *conventus* capital may have been the residence of one of the governor's *legati* also helps to explain this group of inscriptions, especially if it is borne in mind that the inscriptions from Herrera de Pisuerga and Tardemazar also belong to this category. The last two military inscriptions were found in Clunia (Peñalba de Castro) and Vareia (Varea) and can be dated to the first century CE (Ortiz Córdoba, 2019a: 169–71). It is worth highlighting that while the inscriptions from Tarraco mostly represent veterans, the remaining ones largely represent *milites*, thus indicating two completely different motives to migrate among the individuals in this category, which also explain their specific destinations, with those on active duty being recorded in inland areas, whereas the retired veterans are found in coastal regions (inland = service vs. coast = retirement).

The second most common motivation for Gallic migrants was economic. Individuals belonging to this category are recorded in Tarraco (4), Barcino (1), and Carthago Nova (1). As can be seen, the geographical pattern of settlement stands in complete contrast with the previous category, shifting from the Meseta and the interior of the north-western territories to the main cities on the Mediterranean coast of the province. This pattern of mobility makes sense since these individuals include a *negotiator*, one *mercator*, an *inaurator*, a *decurio larum*, and the patron of two corporations (Ortiz Córdoba, 2019a: 178);

they were therefore clearly looking for the opportunities and markets offered by the high degree of connectivity that these cities and their harbours presented (Fig. 7.28). This epigraphic evidence can be connected to the presence of Gaulish Samian ware, Gaulish amphorae and roof tiles, and even local workshops in the *conventus* Tarraconensis that may have belonged to Gaulish societies or individuals (Mayoral et al., forthcoming).

It is interesting to note that all the inscriptions in the province belonging to the group classified as colonists by Ortiz Córdoba can be traced to the same city, Barcino. The early date of the two known inscriptions (first half of the first century BCE) (*IRC* IV, 57; *CIL* II 4589) in which four individuals are mentioned (three of them from the same family), has been used to suggest the participation of Gallic individuals—from Arelate and Gallia Narbonensis—in the foundation of this colony (Haley, 1991: 36). Particularly significant is the case of Caius Coelius, who was *duumvir quinquennalis* in the Augustan period,[19] since he may well have been one of the earliest magistrates of the city (Curchin, 1990: 182, no. 420) and, consequently, part of the population contingent settled during the *deductio* of the colony (Ortiz Córdoba, 2019a: 180).

Lastly, it should be noted that there is a group of 10 inscriptions whose texts do not enable the causes that motivated the displacement of the people they record to be determined. Most of these come from the coastal cities of Barcino (4), Tarraco (1), and Saguntum (1) (Ortiz Córdoba, 2019a: 182).

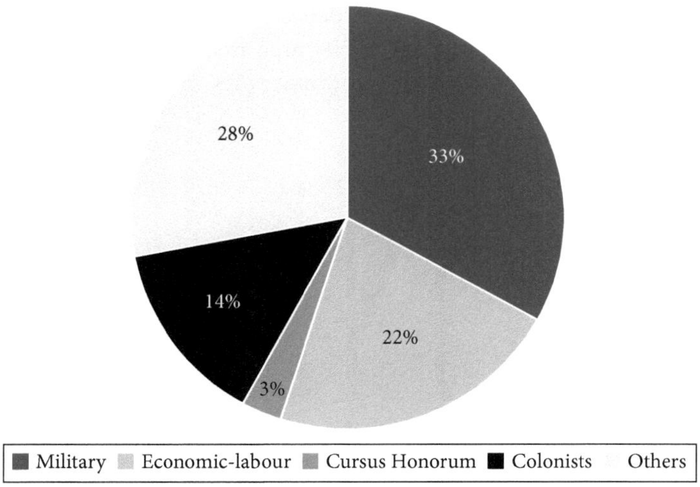


**Fig. 7.28** Distribution of the Gallic migrants in Hispania according to reasons for mobility (Ortíz Córdoba, 2019c: chart 3)

[19] *IRC* IV, 57: *C(aius) Coelius Atisi f(ilius) / IIvir quin(quennalis) mur(os) / turres portas / fac(iendas) coer(avit).*

If we now consider the status and demographics of this migration, two facts soon stand out: in the first place, there is a clear predominance of male migrants. Only two migrants are women: Usulenia Valentina, probably a native of Gallia Narbonensis, who died in Barcino, and Augustina, perhaps originally from Arelate, who lived in Tugia. As regards the social status of the immigrants, *ingenui* make up the majority (28), in comparison with those of servile condition (3) and freedmen (3) (Haley, 1991: 36; Ortiz Córdoba, 2019c: 192) (Fig. 7.29).

In short, several facts stand out when looking for patterns that can explain these movements: in the first place, Gallic military recruitment seems to be the main cause of migration to Tarraconensis, as it was for those migrants from Italy. This explains well the gender imbalance as well as the concentration in the capital and the north-west of the province, reflecting the presence of the Roman army in Hispania during the Early Empire. Second, a category of mobility related to economic activities and work opportunities can also be inferred to have been important. The participants in this movement settled in densely populated and well-connected coastal cities such as Tarraco, Barcino, and Carthago Nova.

Third, if one analyses the origin—when known—of these individuals, most of those reaching the north-east of the province came from areas and cities that were relatively close and, most importantly, well connected with their destinations. Twenty-nine of the 36 individuals studied by Ortiz Córdoba (2019a) came from Gallia Narbonensis, only three individuals from cities in Aquitaine, and one appears to have originated in Lugdunensis. The remaining three mention their Gallic origin in a generic way (Ortiz Córdoba, 2019a: 160). The most common cities of origin for those who migrated to Hispania are Arelate (7), Narbo Martius (3), and Vienna (4). The first two were important ports on the Gulf of Lion as well

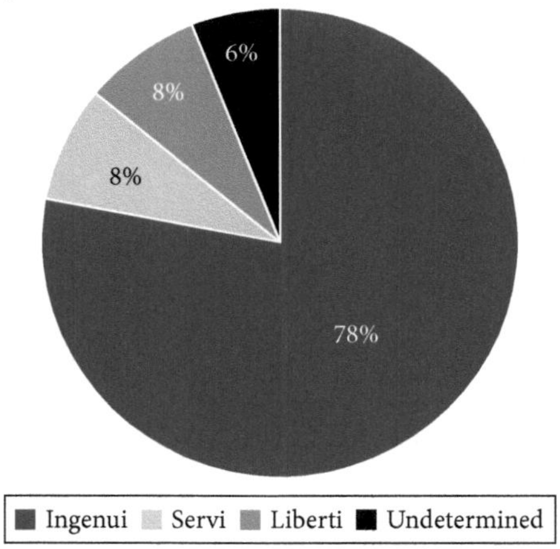


**Fig. 7.29** Distribution of the Gallic migrants based on their social status (Ortíz Córdoba, 2019c: chart 8)

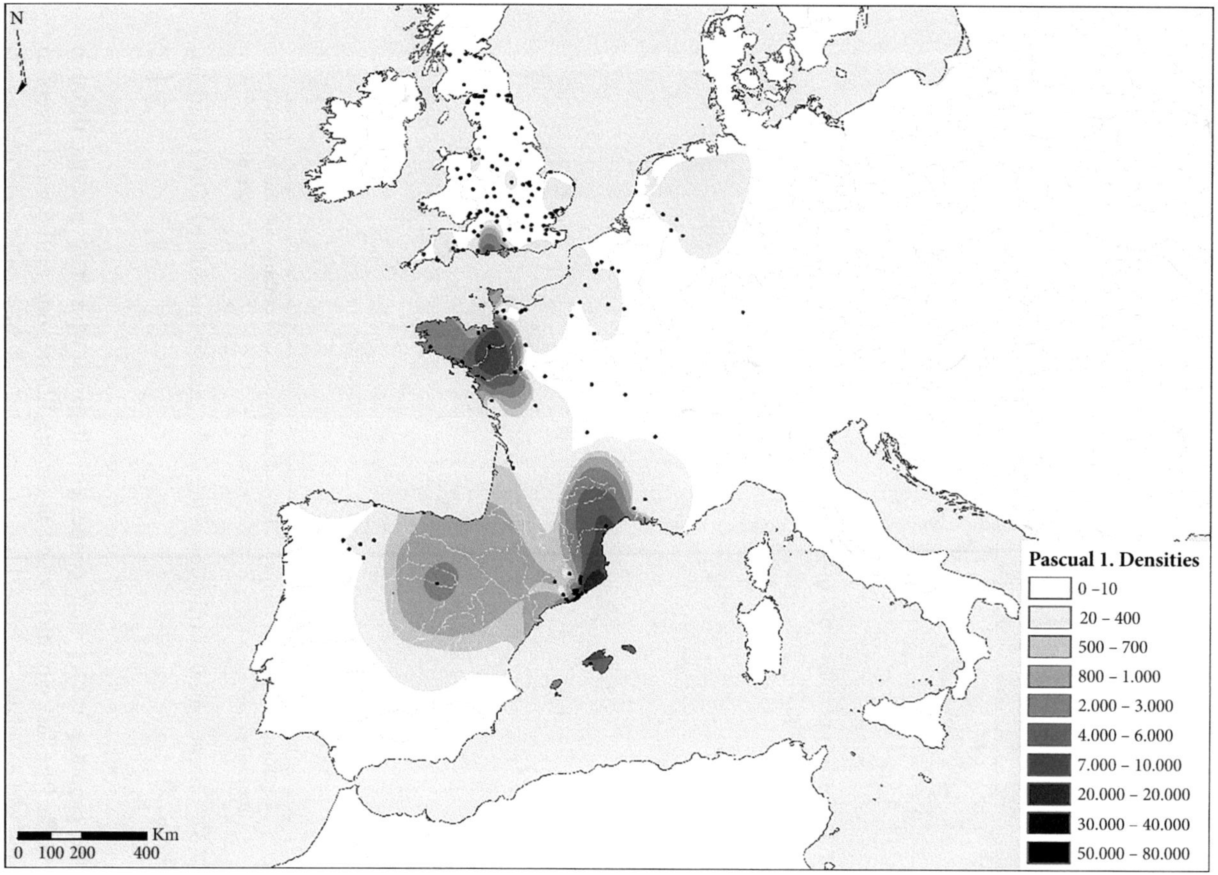


**Fig. 7.30** Distribution of Pascual 1 amphorae produced in Citerior (densities cg/m$^2$) (Carreras and van den Berg, 2017: 379, fig. 34)

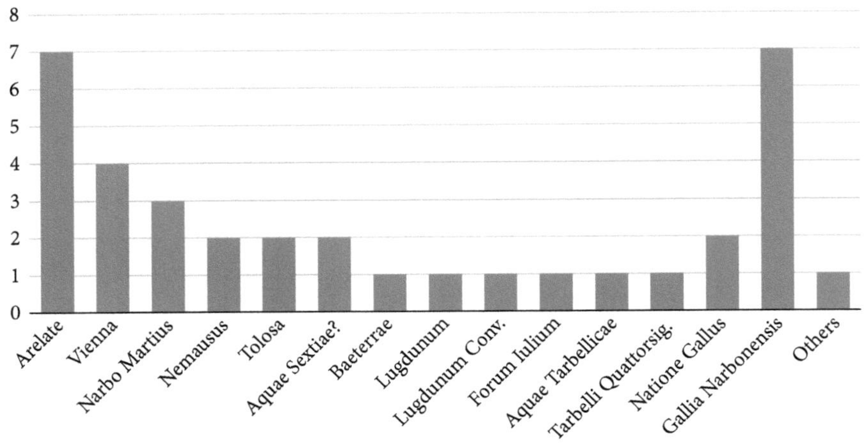


**Fig. 7.31** Distribution by cities of origin of the Gallic immigrants studied (Ortíz Córdoba, 2019c: fig. 2)

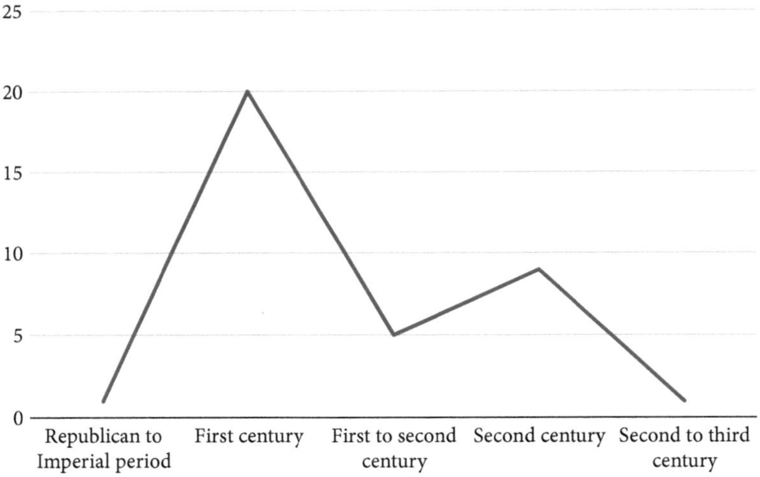


**Fig. 7.32** Chronological distribution of the Gallic immigrants studied (Ortíz Córdoba, 2019c: fig. 7)

as the cabotage routes that connected Hispania with Italy passing through Marseille. The last city mentioned is on the Rhône, one of the main rivers in Europe and navigable as far as Lyon in antiquity. All these cities were major consumption and redistribution centres for the products exported from Hispania in general and from Tarraconensis in particular, such as the Pascual 1 amphorae (Fig. 7.30). The overlapping in the distribution of the small bronzes of Massalia in the Gulf of Lion (especially in Narbo and Lattes) and the north-east of the peninsula (Emporion, Iluro, Baetulo, and Barcino) and the distribution of Tarraconense and Pascual 1 stamps (Sinner and Martí, 2022: 96–101 and fig. 7), are a great indicator that the origin of the migrants clearly illustrates the fundamental role played by connectivity and exchange in the movement of peoples and commodities (Fig. 7.31).

From a chronological point of view, it is possible to say that this immigration of Gallic origin into the province under study is concentrated within a very specific time span. Turning to the epigraphic record we can observe it occurred mainly in the first century CE. This migratory flow started to decrease in the second century CE, to the extent that it was almost negligible by the end of the century (Ortiz Córdoba, 2019c: 189) (Fig. 7.32). Clearly we have to take the epigraphic patterns into account: the sole reference to a Gallic migrant in the Republican period is partially due to the few inscription we have for this period (*c.* 150). However, the concentration in the first century CE cannot be a result of the epigraphic record; when we turn to all the dated inscriptions for the Iberian peninsula we observe that the first century has roughly 600 dated inscriptions, whereas the second century almost reaches 1,500 dated inscriptions, clearly highlighting the importance of Gallic migrants during this period.[20]

To conclude, Italic and Gallic migration into Tarraconensis seem to follow comparable patterns: they are similar numerically speaking (27 vs. 29), and both migratory processes reached their peak in the first century CE, and the majority of those taking part were freemen (16 vs. 28). In both cases, the main driving force seems to be military in nature (including the administration) (15 vs. 12) and, second, motivated by commercial and/or work-related circumstances (4 vs. 6).

### 7.5.3 From Africa to Hispania Tarraconensis

The third most important group of immigrants came from the African provinces, although only 17 explicitly indicate their African origin (Haley, 1991: 44). Despite the fact that some identifications are still under discussion because they are attributed on the basis of their family names, so far 48 Africani have been identified in the Iberian peninsula. The status of these African individuals was basically *ingenui* (22), freedmen (2), and *servi* (1), together with 23 of unknown status (Fig. 7.33). Most of their inscriptions are datable to the second or third centuries CE, when African products (e.g. amphorae, fine and coarse ware) were extremely common in the coastal strip of the province (Reynolds, 2010).

[20] These rough numbers have been obtained through the LatinNow webgis: gis.latinnow.eu (accessed 8 February 2023).

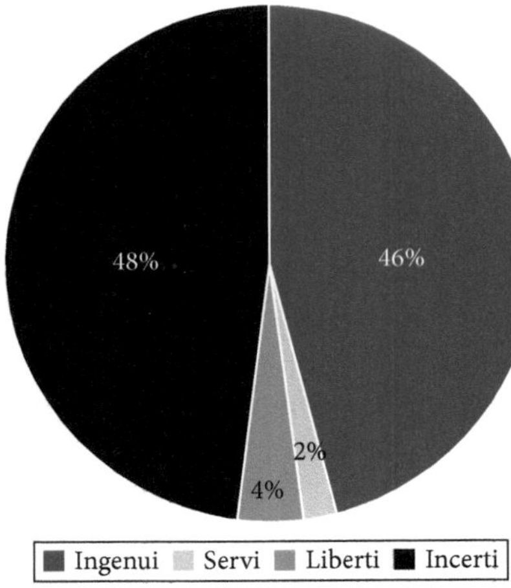


**Fig. 7.33** Status of the African immigrants

At least 22 of them lived in the major Mediterranean coastal towns such as Tarraco (16), Barcino (5), and Carthago Nova (1) (Ortiz Córdoba, 2019c: 832) as their funerary inscriptions demonstrate.[21] The extraordinary number of Africani at Tarraco reveals the importance of the governor's *officium* for attracting administrative and military staff as happens in the case of immigration from Gaul. With regard to their professions, only 25 inscriptions record their main occupations (see Fig. 7.34). More than 50% of them were military staff in the governor's *officium* at Tarraco with special tasks as *principales*. For instance, inscriptions from Tarraco record at least three *beneficiarii consularis* (Antonius Saturnius–*CIL* II$^2$ 14,1046; Lucius Anfidius Felix–*CIL* II$^2$ 14,1047; Lucius Valerius Barbarus–*CIL* II$^2$ 14,1058), which was a post responsible for military supply to the armies as well as the police (Carreras, 1997). Their inscriptions in Tarraconensis are recorded in the military district and the routes towards it, together with the examples from the governor's *officium*. For instance, the inscription of M. Sellius Honoratus from *Choba ex provincia Mauretania* (*AE* 1963, 13), who was *praefectum equitum* of the *II ala Flavia Hispanorum*, comes from Petavonium (Rosinos de Vidriales).

Other military positions recorded at Tarraco include a speculator (explorer) (Gargilius Rufus–*CIL* II$^2$ 14,1047) and a *praefectus I Cohors celtiberum* (Caius Iulius

[21] There is the special case of Ilici (Elx), where Pliny (*NH* III.4.19–20) states that the city had Icositani as contributors. Some scholars have identified the Icositani as the inhabitants of the African town of Icosium, although other authors such as Mayer and Olesti (2001) believe that they were neighbours of a town close to Ilici. However, it is likely that the city of Icosium in Africa was contributed to Ilici, as Zilil was part of Baetica (Plin. *NH* V.2). Houten argues that before the creation of the province of Mauretania Caesariensis these cities needed to be part of an existing provincial, thus Baetica and Tarraconensis were chosen as the provinces these places were part of (Houten, 2021: 138).

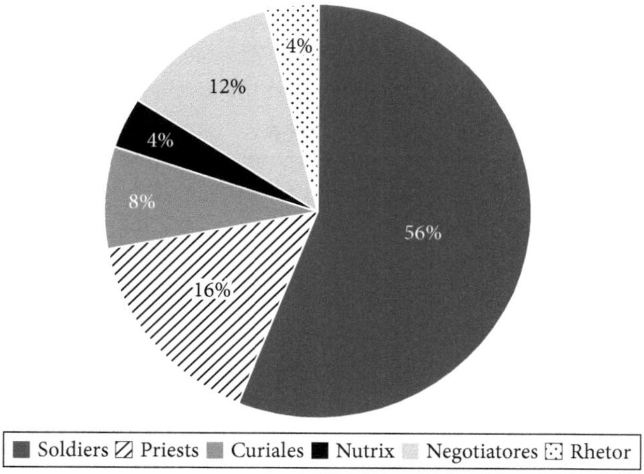


**Fig. 7.34** Professions of African immigrants

Speratianus-*CIL* II² 14,1018) while the remaining examples were legionaries of the Legio VII (Ortiz Córdoba, 2019c, 832–8).

As regards the chronology, as has been pointed out, most inscriptions are dated in the second and third centuries CE when Africans were promoted with the arrival of the Severan dynasty. Only the inscription of Caius Iulius Speratianus can be dated to the last quarter of the first century CE. Apart from Tarraco, another African called Publius Anfidius Exoratus (*IRC* IV.44) who was a *centurio* of the Legio III Augusta settled in the city of Barcino after finishing his service.

There was a lower proportion of Africani in the army than Italians or Gauls (29%). This is likely to have been a consequence of the relatively late recruitment of Africani into the Roman army when the number of troops in the province declined from the second century CE onwards (Haley, 1991: 49).

When the inscriptions refer to professions (see Fig. 7.34), they make it clear that Africani were involved in other activities than those connected with military matters. A substantial proportion were priests or *decurioni* in their local communities, but a large number were traders as indicated not only by the inscriptions, but also by the large number of African products (e.g. amphorae, cooking wares, etc.) found in the main coastal Mediterranean towns in Tarraconensis (Reynolds, 2010).

A *negotiator* called Quintus Ovilius Venustianus (*CIL* II² 14,1289), whose African *nomen* is also attested at Ostia and in North Africa, is recorded in the capital Tarraco. He may be an example of a commercial agent of an African company working in three Mediterranean ports, namely Carthage, Ostia, and Tarraco. Another possible trader was Lucius Caecilius Porcianus (late second–third century CE), described as coming *ex provincia Africa* (*CIL* II² 14,1204), who became *decurion adlectus* at Tarraco. Archaeologically, the importance of the African trade in the provincial capital is more than evident since most of the amphorae imported from the second century onwards are of North African origin (Remolà, 2000), containing olive oil, *garum*, and wine. Besides, a wide variety of products were imported alongside those transported in the amphorae, such as African red slip ware, cooking wares, or lamps.

Other noteworthy funerary inscriptions from Tarraco recorded a manumitted public slave named Publicius Ziogas from Leptis, who died at the age of 92 (*CIL* II 6116; third century CE), and a rhetor called P. Annius Florus, who ran a school in Tarraco during the reign of Domitian (Flor. *Verg.*) (Haley, 1991: 45).

Likewise, the city of Barcino received African traders who also developed thriving commercial contacts with the African coastal towns. The local epigraphy registers the name of Quintus Cornelius Secundus (*IRC* IV.59) from Carthago Magna, whose son Q. Cornelius Seranus even became a local aedile and *duumvir* in the colony of Barcino. In terms of archaeological evidence, the case of Barcino is similar to Tarraco with high levels of imports of African products from the second century onwards (Carreras and Berni, 2005).

Finally, the epigraphic evidence only records a few cases in which the deceased indicated his or her place of birth. The few examples from Citerior mention places of origin such as Cartago Magna, Lixus, Cirta, Sicca Veneria, or Leptis Magna. All were densely populated cities in Africa Proconsularis and Numidia, which may have been involved in business with the main ports of Tarraconensis such as Tarraco or Barcino (Haley, 1991: 50).

### 7.5.4 Military, Religious, and Administrative Migration

Nevertheless, most of the epigraphic evidence recorded in the province does not imply the existence of economic motives for migrating (Haley, 1991: 88). Instead, it reveals that the vast majority of inscriptions concerned soldiers, priests, civil servants, and slaves. For instance, Haley (1991: 83) registers at least 37 *alieni* soldiers and 76 priests, which was the most common occupation for immigrants. Of course, slaves underwent compulsory migration as a cheap source of labour for specialized occupations such as doctors or rhetors, but they were mainly engaged in unspecialized heavy manual work in the mining industry (Haley, 1991: 89–94).

During the Cantabrian and Asturian Wars (29–19 BCE), an unknown number of legions was deployed in the north-west of the province. When the conflict ended, three legions remained in the same region: the IIII Macedonia at Herrera de Pisuerga (Palencia)—already discussed—VI Victrix at León, and X Gemina at Rosinos de Vidriales (Zamora) (Morillo, 2005: 21). However, this situation did not last long since the Legio IIII Macedonia moved to Mogontiacum (Germania Superior) in 39 CE and the X Gemina to Carnutum (Pannonia) in 63 CE. In the Year of the Four Emperors (69 CE), the Legio VI Victrix proclaimed Galba emperor; he also created a new local legion called VII Galbiana to overthrow

Nero (Morillo, 2005: 22). The same year two legions returned to Hispania Tarraconensis (X Gemina and I Adiutrix), but all of them left the province in 69/70 CE to crush the Batavian rebellion led by Civilis. Finally, the Legio VII returned to the province and established its headquarters as the only *legio* in the whole Iberian peninsula at León (*Legio*) (García- Bellido, 1976).

At its peak, the number of soldiers in the province during the Early Empire was probably around 40,000, including legionaries and auxiliaries, but this figure was reduced to only 8,000 from the Flavian period onwards. If the total population in Tarraconensis was around 2.5 million inhabitants during the Early Empire (see section 5), less than 0.02% of the population before the Flavian period were related to the army, so the proportion of inscriptions overrepresents this social group. It must be borne in mind that Roman soldiers did not have any food or accommodation expenses since the army discounted them from payments to them (*stipendium–ad victum*). Therefore, they could save a great part of their salary and spend it on an appropriate grave and inscription. Moreover, the habit of erecting funerary epigraphy for soldiers seems to be related to those who died while serving in the army. Carroll points out that in the case of the Treveri, it seems that this custom was not taken home; the custom of commemoration might have remained strictly within the military sphere (Carroll, 2006: 65).

Most military inscriptions can be found in the north-western territories, where Roman troops were based at the main headquarters of Rosinos de Vidriales, Herrera de Pisuerga, and León as well as secondary military garrisons (e.g. Aqua Querquensis). These soldiers were largely of Italian (see section 7.5.1) and Gaulish origin (see section 7.5.2) in the first century CE, but from Hispania from the first century onwards (Ortiz Córdoba, 2019b). As for auxiliary troops, apart from local *cohortes* and *alae* (*Ala II Flavia Hispanorum*–Rosinos, *Cohors I Celtiberorum*–Sobrado dos Monxes, *Cohors III Lucensis*–Lugo), there were two Gallic cohorts, namely I *Gallica Equitata* at Herrera de Pisuerga and *II Gallica* whose camp is unknown, as well as the *ala Thracia* at Calagurris.

Other auxiliary troops levied in Hispania Tarraconensis were sent to other provinces in the Empire. Again, the north-western district was the most popular region for army conscription from the *civitates* of the Bracari, Lucenses, Astures, Cantabri, Vascones, or Arevaci (see Fig. 7.35) (García- Bellido, 1976).

Individual soldiers from Tarraconensis joined their detachments and ended up in different locations. Ortiz Córdoba (2019b) has recorded 25 inscriptions of soldiers levied from the main colonies in the province (5–20%) or abroad (20–80%), of which 11 refer to people from Clunia and nine from Caesaraugusta, compared to only one from Tarraco and one from Carthago Nova. Therefore, the soldiers joining the Roman armies were mainly from the central inland *conventus* in addition to the native troops from the north-western region of the peninsula.

When soldiers retired, it was difficult to settle in colonies after their foundation (*deductio*), as suggested by the case of four soldiers from Caesaraugusta (tribu

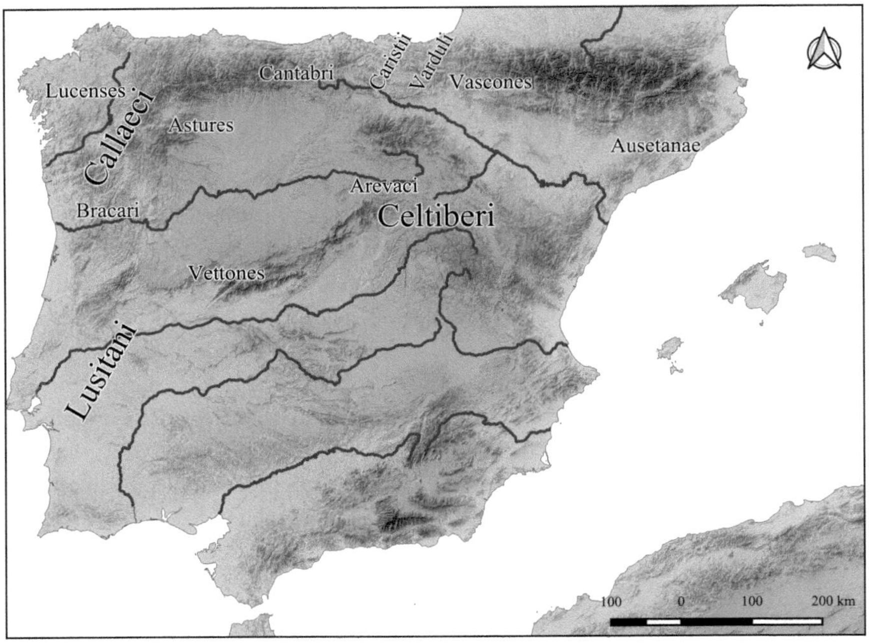


**Fig. 7.35** Local auxiliary troops levied in Hispania Tarraconensis (after García-Bellido, 1976)

Aniensis), who did not remain in the colony but died in places such as Vareia, Clunia, Petavorium, or Alburquerque (Ortiz Córdoba, 2019b: 77). Another special pattern is military migration to the capital, Tarraco, where the administration of the province (the governor's office, *procurator*) was concentrated. At least 17 inscriptions of *milites* with diverse origins are recorded, most of them from the north-west of the province (4 Bracarenses, 4 from the north-west, 1 Asturicense) (Ortiz Córdoba, 2019c: 677–8).

### Tarraco

The capital of the province obviously had all three migratory forms discussed in this section. As a *castra hiberna* and later *praesidium* in the early stages of the conquest, it was a military city from its onset and as such had a steady influx of troops. The earliest inscription from the city immediately confirms the presence of the military: M(anios) Vibio(s) Men(e)rua (*CIL* I$^3$ 34491). This inscription found on the so-called Torre de Minerva is part of the earliest sections of the walls of Tarraco, dated to the time of the Second Punic War (Díaz Ariño, 2008: 147; Panzram, 2002: 29). The name Manios Vibios is considered to be of Roman or Italic origin (see section 7.4.1). After the Second Punic War, the Roman presence continued on the site of Tarraco. The much later opistographic inscription confirms the military importance of the city, and the logically temporary, but also possibly permanent migration of soldiers to Tarraco. On the one side of the limestone plaque, there is an inscription commemorating Pompey (*CIL* I$^3$ 2964); the obvious dating for this honorific inscription would be 72–71 BCE at the time of Pompey's victory over Sertorius. Interestingly, the inscription was later used to commemorate a Publius Mucius Scaevola. Despite the uncertainties around the identification of this member of the Scaevola family, it is accepted that he must have been a legate for Caesar around 49 BCE (Panzram, 2002: 30).

When turning to the migrants in Tarraco with some reference to their place of origin, it can be seen that, out of the 79 recorded migrants with an origin, 21 also record their military role.[22] The majority of these listed Legio VII Gemina as at least one of the legions they served in during their career. This is hardly surprising as the legion was stationed within the province at modern-day León. As the soldiers used to continue the custom of mentioning their service, we should also include funerary inscriptions referring to the Legio VII Gemina as migrants into Tarraco. This gives us a total of 46 military migrants, encompassing funerary epigraphy, altars set up by soldiers, and the two honorific inscriptions to the provincial legate Hedius L. f. Rufus Lollianus Gentianus, who started his military career as a *tribunus militum* in the Legio VII Gemina (*CIL* II 4121/4122 = RIT 139–40, Mennen, 2011: 106).

One of the interesting migrants is M. Aurelius Lucilius from Poetovium, modern-day Ptuj in Slovenia (*CIL* II 4147; RIT 178). He is among the few that came from the eastern half of the Empire, his 40-year-long career had clearly taken him far and wide. He had served as an *eques singularis* and afterwards as a centurion in the following legions: I Adiutrix (Pannonia Superior), II Traiana (unknown), VIII Augusta (*Germania*), XIII Gemina (Pannonia), VII Claudia (*Moesia*?), and his last post with VII Gemina (Hispania Citerior), for which it is specified he was *hastatus prior*. The list of legions indicates that he must have served under or after the reign of Trajan, the inscription being dated to the late second or early third century CE. The presence of such an experienced veteran begs the question of why he moved to Tarraco. Ruiz de Arbulo (2011–12: 557) argued for a *campus* at Tarraco where recruits were trained by experienced veterans and proposed that M. Aurelius Lucilius should be included among the veteran instructors. The presence of such a training camp would indeed support the residence of experienced veterans there and also draw in even more prospective military migrants (Fig. 7.36).

Six of the migrants mentioning their military career migrated to Tarraco and took up the position of provincial *flamen* (*CIL* II 4203; 4205; 4213; 4240; 4245; 4251).

[22] We owe thanks to Claire Holleran who was so kind as to provide us with the data on migration in the *conventus* Lucensis, Cluniensis, and Tarraco for analysis (part of the project Mapping Migration in Roman Iberia).

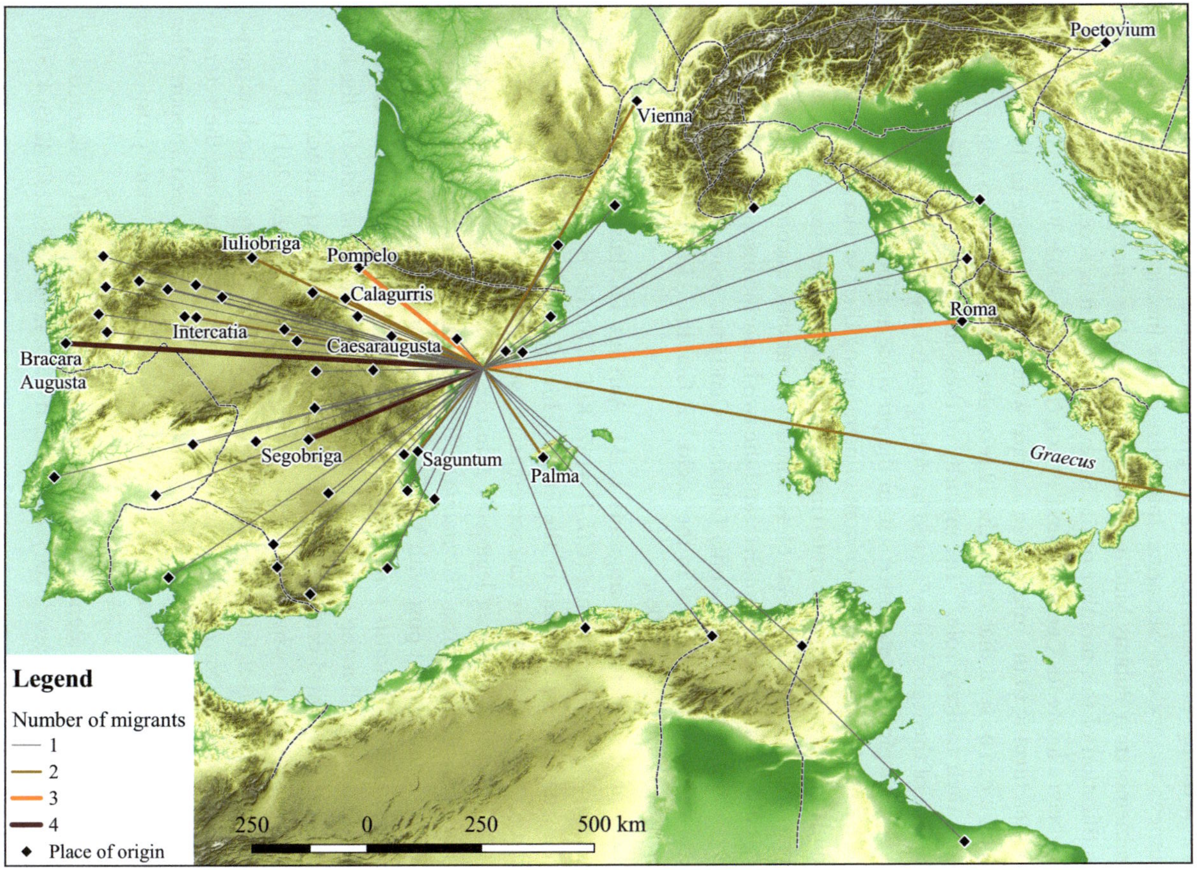


**Fig. 7.36** Migration towards Tarraco

The *flamen provinciae Hispaniae citerioris* was the highest priestly office in the province and taken up by the elite for a year. The *flamines* were honoured with inscriptions, which are an important source to study the careers and migration of the provincial elite (Alföldy, 2011b: 202). With the 75 *flamines* recorded by Alföldy (1973), we can analyse the details of migration towards Tarraco for this office. It is of interest that the majority of them are from regions relatively close to the city. The *conventus* of Tarraconensis provides 20 *flamines*, the adjoining *conventus* of Carthaginiensis and Caesaraugustanus supplied 21 and 12 respectively.

Turning to the specific places from which this migration occurred, unsurprisingly, it can be observed that the capital itself provided the highest number; Alföldy counted 13 from Tarraco, of which seven are uncertain. This is closely followed by Caesaraugustanus with possibly eight *flamines*. However, six are uncertain as these are only attributable to Caesaraugustanus on the grounds of their tribal affiliation to the Aniensis tribe. Interestingly, the two that did move from their position in Caesaraugustanus to Tarraco were both *adlecti* (Curchin, 1990: 26), who came from Grallia and Damania. This clearly indicates that magistrates could move up from their 'small town' through the *conventus* capital to a position at the provincial capital. Interestingly, the *conventus* capital Carthago Nova with its two *flamines* is outnumbered by Segobriga, which could boast four *flamines* that recorded the city as their home.

In addition to the *flamines*, we also find 12 *flameninicae provinciae Hispaniae citerioris* (Alföldy, 1973), which offers us an opportunity to consider the migration of elite women. At Tarraco 12 have been recorded, two of whom were from the city itself. The other 10 were from different corners of the province. Similar to those of the men, the inscriptions are mostly honorific, put up to commemorate the *flaminicae*. Outside Tarraco we find two inscriptions indicating that these migrations could have been temporary and related to the position. In Bracara Augusta there is a funerary inscription to Nigrina, who died at the age of 50 and held the position of *flaminica* (*CIL* II 2427). In Peal de Becerro, ancient Tugia, we find the inscription to L. Postumius Q. f. Serg. Fabullus and Manlia L. f. Silana, who were married, and both held the provincial position (*CIL* II 3329). Interestingly, the *colonia* Salaria is mentioned as the place where Fabullus held the position of *duumvir*. The fact that this honorific inscription was erected in Tugia indicates the high mobility of the elite. They were in Salaria for the duumvirate of Fabullus, then in Tarraco for some time, where they both took up the provincial priestship. The inscription in Tugia raises the question of why it was erected there. Were they, or one of them, originally from this city or did they only spend a while there before moving on to the next position?

In sum, the city of Tarraco was also a religious capital; as we have seen at least 55 inscriptions of *flamines* and *flaminicae* from different parts of the province, from Bracara to Libisosa, totalling more than 38 different places, have been identified. The most common places of origin for these priests were Caesaraugusta

(5), Palma (4), Segobriga, Lucus, Avobriga, and Dianium (2 flamines) (Haley, 1991: 77–82). Such a wide range of origins for priests connected with the provincial capital may suggest a temporary presence in the capital with more permanent activity taking place in the local communities.

Unsurprisingly, the epigraphy of the migrants mostly mentions people from the upper classes. The overrepresentation of the higher classes is, on the one hand, the result of the active participation of these elite groups in the epigraphic culture. Setting up an inscription was costly and not economically accessible for all classes in Roman society. Moreover, as considered above, the higher classes held positions that were commemorated and required movement (e.g. provincial *flamines*). Among the 'commoners' we could count the eight *milites* without higher offices. Examples include men from different parts of the Empire. However, all of them served in the Legio VII Gemina Felix. The legionary fort was located at modern-day León. That said, finding *milites* as migrants is hardly surprising, since their profession is necessarily one that involves mobility.

Keeping our attention on the inscriptions recording the *origo*, some *liberti* are also recorded. These show that both social and geographical mobility were possible. L. Aemilius Hippolytus was commemorated by his *collibertus* L. Aemilius Euhodus. The only record of an enslaved person is the funerary inscription for the 19-year-old Agathocules, a gilder (*inaurator*) from Vienne in Narbonensis (*CIL* II 6107). The inscription was set up by his *domina*, Cornelia Cruseidis, indicating that he is most likely to have travelled with her to Tarraco.

Based on the *tribus* we can identify some more possible migrants. The citizens of privileged communities were enlisted in one of the 35 *tribus* (Haley, 1991: 15; Houten, 2021: 79). The citizens of Tarraco were enlisted in the *tribus* Galeria, and so records of other *tribus* in the city indicate migrants or descendants of migrants (Haley, 1991: 26). In Tarraco, 31 people mention a different tribal affiliation from Galeria. Of these, only eight did not mention their *origo*. Seemingly most migrants with citizenship mention their place of origin when mentioning their tribal affiliation. Moreover, most of these men held high offices as, for instance *flamines* or administrative positions. Two were military men, of whom one also became *decurionus adlectus* of Tarraco (RIT 172). Nevertheless, the scope for using the *tribus* as a means to study migrants is very limited. We must also take into account the possibility of migrants from elsewhere with the *Galeria tribus*, such as those from other communities awarded privileges under Augustus (e.g. Edeta, Calagurris, Castulo). Those from Galeria that do not mention their *origo*, cannot be recognized. More importantly, as the *tribus* is the result of citizenship, we are unable to progress beyond this elite. This contrast between elite and non-elite is even starker in the Iberian peninsula, where most communities held the *ius Latii*, meaning that citizenship was obtained after holding a magistracy in the *municipium*.

### Asturica Augusta

One of the three *conventus* capitals in the north-west of the province was Asturica Augusta, where the military camp of the Legio X Gemina was initially established during Augustus' campaigns against the Astures and Cantabri. The camp was dismantled in the Tiberian period, when the surrounding trench was filled in, and subsequently a civilian settlement was created. No signs of an early pre-Roman settlement have been discovered, so it would seem that the Roman military camp and the later town were founded *ex novo*. Therefore, most of the initial settlers came from elsewhere; in fact, Haley (1991: 71–2) notes 21 inscriptions of *alieni* (foreigners), almost 12% of the population at an epigraphic level (Table 7.4).

Asturica Augusta is the city in Hispania Tarraconensis with the second highest proportion of military staff (9 inscriptions out of 33), in this case some of them belonging to the Legio X Gemina (Haley, 1991: 34–5). It is of interest that all the inscriptions are clustered in terms of chronology between the reign of Claudius and that of Nero (Ortiz Córdoba, 2019a: 166). The origin of two legionaries from the Legio X Gemina is recorded in the inscription (L. Octavius Magius–Baeterensis: *AE* 1928, 163 and Persius–*Hasta*: *AE* 1904, 160. *CIL* II 5076. *CIL* II 5662). There were also *milites* from other legions, for example the Legio IIII Macedonica (L. Terentius: *AE* 1994, 961), Legio VII Gemina (Granio Forti: *AE* 1928, 166), and a *vexillatio* of the same legion at the nearby site of Luyego (*AE* 1967, 229).

**Table 7.4** Inscriptions of *alieni* at Asturica Augusta

| Epigraphy | Origin | No. |
|---|---|---|
| *CIL* II 2904 = 5657 | *Celtica Supertamarica* (castello) *Elaniobrensi* | 1 |
| *CIL* II 2902 = 5081 | *Celtica Supertamarica* | 1 |
| CM León 22 | *Supertamaricus* | 1 |
| *CIL* II 2633 | *Zoelae* | 2 |
| *CIL* II 2651 | *Zoela* | 1 |
| *AE* 1982, 575 | *Lemavi* (castello) *Eritaeco* | 2 |
| ENAR 31 | *Domo Tabalaca* | 2 |
| *CIL* II 2639 (p. 707) | *(domo) Bracara* | 1 |
| CM León 21, no. 15 | *(domo) Bracara* | 1 |
| HAE 2183 | *Brigiaecina* | 1 |
| *CIL* II 5077 | *Uxsamensis* | 1 |
| EE IX 292e | *Uxama Ibarcensis* | 1 |
| *CIL* II 2649 | *Cilena* | 1 |
| *CIL* II 2641 | *ex municipia Castulonensi* | 1 |
| *CIL* II 2633 | *ex gentes Avolgigorum... Omiacus* | 1 |
| *CIL* II 2638 | *Caesaraugustanus* | 1 |
| EE IX 292f | *Seurrus Transminiensis* | 1 |

*Source*: Haley (1991: 71–2).

In addition, some inscriptions refer to soldiers from auxiliary units levied in their own *civitates*, such as Fuscus Dorilsis from Serdus (*cohors Thracum*: *AE* 1928, 165), Domitio from Tabalaca (*alae II Flavia Hispanorum*: *AE* 1961, 338), and Iunius Capitonius at Luyego (*cohors I Gallicae*). Finally, Pompeius Faventinus was an official, a *tribunus militum*, of the Legio VI Victrix and later *praefectus cohors VI Asturum* (*AE* 1966, 187; *CIL* II 2637). This is an excellent sample of the social composition of a military and administrative city in the middle of a region with a low level of adoption of Roman material culture and architecture such as Asturias. In the north-west, Hirt observed an abandonment of castros in the first century; however, in the vicinity of the mines, and processing sites, there is a reoccupation and even a denser pattern of castros (Hirt, 2010: 230). It is clear from the reorganization of the castro settlement structure and focus around productive sites that the local population were the labour force employed in the exploitation of the mines. However, as Florus (2.33.59–60; 2.33.52) and Cassius Dio (54.11.5) mentioned, some of them were moved to the new city of Asturica.

As Santos Yanguas (2017) pointed out, the north-western *conventus* capitals developed at a later date, so some of their functions and the associated administrative personnel probably appeared in the mid-first century CE, coinciding with the water engineering exploitation of the gold in the mining districts (e.g. Las Médulas). The most important administrative position in Asturica was of the *legatus iudicus*, an itinerant legal assistant to the governor (see section 7.7), which on occasions delivered justice in the *conventus* capital, as the inscription of *Flaminius Priscus* (*AE* 1823, 102) demonstrates.

The second most important civil servant in Asturica was the *procurator metallorum*, who was the person responsible for the accounting of public mining production in the region of the River Órbigo. Modern estimates suggest that between 4,000 and 6,000 workers were employed at the gold mines at Valduerna and 10,000 to 15,000 at Las Médulas (Holleran, 2016: 101). The importance of the post may have resulted in the majority of the *procuratores* known at Asturica having been of Italian origin, C. Plinius Secundus (*c*. 73 CE) being the first recorded. The other inscriptions that mention *procuratores* are L. Arruntius Maximus (*CIL* II 2477) (*c*.79 CE), Q. Petronius Modestus from Tergeste (Trieste) (*CIL* V 534 and 535) (*c*. 96–102 CE), Sextus Truttedius Clemens (*CIL* II 2643) (*c*. 106–38 CE), Caius Iunius Flavianus, probably from Rome (*CIL* VI 1620; XIII 1812) (*c*. 138–61 CE), and Gaius Otacilius Saturninus (*BRAH* 163, 1968, 191–209, no. 8) (*c*. 193–211 CE).

Migration from other *conventus* capitals was limited but reveals the special relationships between those centres. Asturica records two migrants from Bracara Augusta (*CIL* II 2639; CM León 21, no. 15) and one from Caesaraugusta (*CIL* II 2638). As was explained in section 7.3, Bracara and Caesaraugusta were two of the *conventus* capitals with the best connectivity with Asturica

Augusta by overland transport. In the opposite direction, two Asturicense were recorded in the epigraphy of Lucus Augusti (EE VIII 330) and Aurium (Orense) (HAE 2720), which are the two closest western urban centres towards the Atlantic coast.

As the urban centre of the gold mining district in the north-west of the province, Asturica attracted people from other *civitates* in the province, for instance *Celtici Supertamarci/Supertamarici*, *ERPLeón*, nos. 140, 170, and 248; Cluniensis, *ERPLeón*, nos. 247 and 282; Lemavi, *ERPLeón*, no. 155; Vxsamensis, *ERPLeón*, no. 224; Vxamibarcensis, *ERPLeón*, no. 130; and Zoela, *ERPLeón*, no. 316 (Rabanal and García Marínez, 2001). Therefore, as the main urban centre the *conventus* capital had a special power of attraction for the rural population in its administrative district. It is difficult to know whether it was planned as a temporary migration or definitive one. It must be borne in mind that most groups referred to in the local epigraphy were populations living close to the gold mines on the River Turienzo (e.g. the Supertamarici and Cileni), so they were probably involved in the mining industry (Holleran, 2016: 116).

## 7.6 Mobility and Work

Migration is commonly differentiated as seasonal, temporary, or permanent. The latter is what has been discussed so far because permanent migration leaves more archaeological traces, such as epigraphy. However, temporary migration implies a type of mobility that only occupies a certain period in one's life, sometimes being only a short seasonal or an annual movement, taking advantage of transport infrastructure. Both types of migration were also important in antiquity.

The principle behind seasonal mobility is that in certain seasons people can earn a higher income elsewhere than by staying within their own household (Erdkamp, 2008: 417). There were different Latin terms that described seasonal mobility, such as *incola*, *absens*, *hospes*, *inquilinus*, *fugitivus*, *peregrinus*, or *mutatio soli* (a lasting move) (Moatti, 2017: 224). Some agricultural and maritime activities involved a strict calendar that covered only the warm months from April to October, so the rest of the year people could earn an extra income by taking on secondary activities, which implied moving from the local household (*peregrinus*) to a working destination that ought not to be too far from home.

Similarly, the agricultural calendar created peaks in labour demand, when grain, olives, or grapes were harvested (Erdkamp, 2008). In the case of Hispania Citerior/Tarraconensis, most intensive production crops, such as grapes or olives, were concentrated in the coastal strip that could obtain seasonal workers from the nearby towns (e.g. Iluro, Barcino, Baetulo, Tarraco, Valentia, Denia, Ilici,

Carthago Nova) (Martín et al., 2020). The practice is well known from the so-called agro-towns in Roman Italy from Cato (*De Agr.* 136 and 144) or Suetonius (*Vesp.* 1.4) when he said that the emperor's grandfather was: 'a contractor for the day-labourers who come regularly every year from Umbria to the Sabine district, to till the fields'.

Although the evidence of such seasonal agricultural work is scarce, there is a famous second-century inscription from Mactar (Tunisia), in which a local farmer stated that he travelled to Cirta (Numidia) at harvest-time to later become head of the harvesters (Krenkel, 1965). The image is not dissimilar from the situation that arose in Spain in the eighteenth and nineteenth centuries when harvesters from Galicia and Asturias moved to the south of the Iberian peninsula and moved back northwards to their homes while working for payment (i.e. *jornaleros*) (Sarausa, 2006: 421). In modern times, seasonal harvesters only migrated to cereal regions (e.g. Castilla La Mancha, Extremadura, Andalusia) because these areas had large estates, whereas intensive crops such as vines and olive trees were harvested by populations living nearby (Sarausa, 2006). Hispania Tarraconensis is believed to have made use of a similar pattern of seasonal agricultural work with movements of rural populations from high-density territories towards places with large estates. Among other reasons, this seasonal activity may explain the final migration of people from *conventus* Cluniensis (Villalón, 2019).

Coastal towns were also familiar with temporary migration since shipping activities came to an end during the *maris clausum* from November to March, so sailors had to remain in port: needless to say, other related activities such as loading and unloading cargoes also stopped for five months. Besides, building activities were limited to the months of April to November with good weather (Frontin. *De Aquis*. 123); therefore, workers involved in building activities also had to stop work in winter. Some of them returned to the countryside whereas others survived the whole winter in town. It seems clear that the economy of cities was subject to annual cycles of expansion in warmer months (e.g. construction and shipping) and contraction in winter (Erdkamp, 2016: 34).

Transportation by pack animals was an alternative occupation in winter periods when farmers had fewer agricultural activities, so they could employ their donkeys and mules for short-distance transportation. This practice was recorded in central Spain in the eighteenth century by Ringrose (1972), so one can imagine similar practices in earlier historical periods. The conditions of overland roads probably made transport by wagons impossible in winter, so the peasants' pack animals were an excellent temporary alternative. This seasonal migration has left no evidence in the archaeological record, and hardly any literary references, but it seems more than feasible.

### 7.6.1 Transhumance

Perhaps the most obvious seasonal migration is long-distance transhumance, which was a long-standing tradition in the province under study. Flocks of sheep normally spent summers in the uplands with good pastures and returned to the plains in winter, following the same pattern as the Italian Apennines. Varro (2.1.16) describes how flocks of sheep were driven to the Apennines in the Samnium region in summer, whereas they were transferred to the Apulian plains in winter.

In the case of Hispania Citerior/Tarraconensis, flocks were sent to the mountain regions of the Pyrenees in summer (Colominas et al., 2019) while they were brought back to the coastal plains in winter. Likewise, shepherds from the mountain ranges of the Picos de Europa and the Iberian System behaved in a similar way taking their herds to the uplands in summer whereas they drove them back to the prairies in winter. However, the Meseta (central plateau) of the Iberian peninsula had a longer circuit with a pattern of transhumance from the northern Meseta in summer to the grasslands of Lusitania, Baetica, and the lands of the Carpetani and Olcades in winter (Sánchez Moreno, 1998: 54).

According to Livy (21.43.8–9), the Celtiberians were a pastoralist society that lived on the Meseta, so they followed those north–south transhumance routes along the main gorges. In medieval times, there was a transhumance institution called La Mesta that moved flocks of sheep from north to south, probably following similar routes or *cañadas* (Sánchez Moreno, 1998: 69). The medieval routes were the Silver or Vizana gorge, the western Leonesa route (from Asturica to Emerita), the eastern Leonesa route, and the western Soriana route.

Some scholars, such as Gómez Pantoja (1995: 497; 2001), are of the opinion that migration from the cities of Uxama Argaela and Clunia was related to this transhumance route, which leads from the *conventus* Cluniensis to Lusitania or Baetica. As mentioned above, the *conventus* Cluniensis had a high density of population from pre-Roman to early imperial times, so migration was a way to relieve demographic pressure. Epigraphy reveals that natives from Uxama and Clunia moved to towns further west in the north-western mining district and southern Lusitania (see Fig. 7.37). Transhumance as well as good road connections may have been a reason for such a distribution of inscriptions (see section 7.3), but there were probably other economic attractions offered by the final destinations.

What is apparent is that the number of emigrants from the *conventus* Cluniensis was not paralleled in other *conventus* in the province of Tarraconensis. They represent almost 12.5% of the total *alieni* recorded in the Iberian peninsula (Haley, 1991: 87–8). Their exodus took place inside the province, so it seems likely that it was due to temporary or seasonal migration.

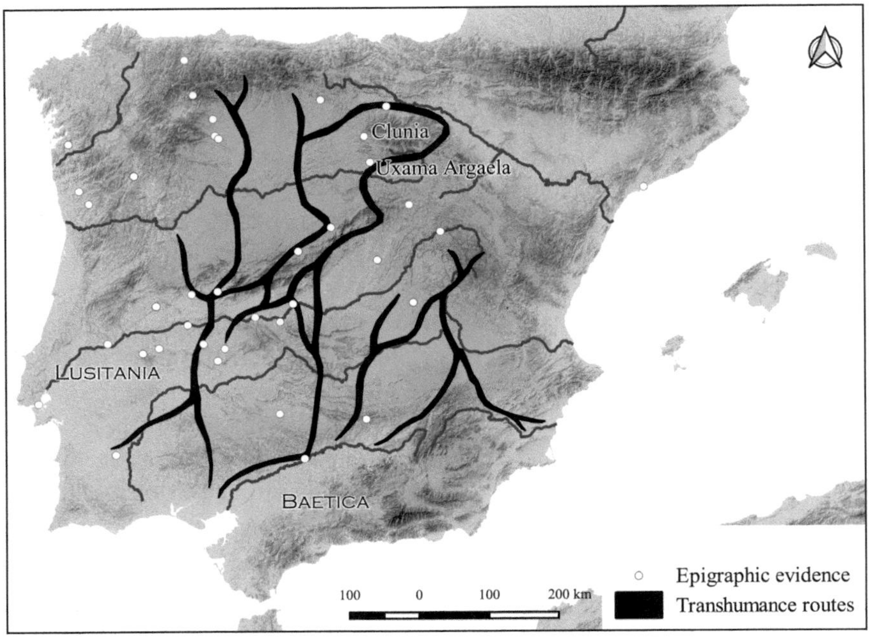


**Fig. 7.37** Main medieval transhumance routes of La Mesta and distribution of inscriptions of natives from Uxama and Clunia (after Gómez Pantoja, 1995: 499)

## 7.6.2 Temporary Migrants: Army, Mines, and Domestic Service

It is not unusual for individuals to migrate temporarily to another town or region at some stage in their life. Most temporary migrants return to their original home when they have completed their temporary professional activity. One of the most popular temporary migratory activities for adult males was the army, where young men could find a livelihood in a dangerous profession, but one that could provide them with employment for 25 years of their lives, which enabled them to be discharged in their 40s. Due to the risk of the military profession, most of them never managed to retire from the army, so their military inscriptions reveal the distribution of such temporary migrants.

Another activity that required an enormous workforce was mining. From Republican times onwards, numerous Italians (Diod. Sic. 5.36.3.4) arrived in Iberia—mainly at the mines of Carthago Nova—as mine exploiters or overseers (Holleran, 2016: 111) using slaves as the basic workforce (Diod. Sic. 5.38). Strabo (III 2.10) quoting Polybius indicated that the mines of Carthago Nova employed almost 40,000 people. However, the situation in the early imperial period changed, and the labour force was mixed, combining slaves, criminals (Ulpian, *Dig*. 48.19.8.4), and free labour.

A large number of inscriptions recording migrants from other parts of Hispania Tarraconensis that also had local mines have been found in the mining districts of the north-west. These long-distance movements far from their original homes might be explained by the possibility of specialized work or better incomes (e.g. in gold mines). There are clusters of migrants from the province to the north-western and Lusitanian mines from places such as Clunia, Nova Augusta, Uxama Argaela, Uxama Barca, Libia, and Victoriacum (Holleran, 2016: 115) (Fig. 7.38). Perhaps the most fascinating case is offered by the people from Clunia that are recorded in the mines of Tres Minas and Monfortinho. The six examples of Clunienses recorded at Tres Minas were males, who died between the ages of 20 and 40, perhaps temporary migrants who never returned to their place of origin (Holleran, 2016: 115). A final good example is an association of Bracari (*sodalicium Bracarorum*) (*HE* 23699) discovered from an inscription found at Pax Iulia near the Vipasca mines.

Most seasonal and temporary migration involved males, with the exception of domestic service, which was especially suitable for young teenagers, who entered wealthy households normally of town-dwelling relatives. When they reached marriageable age, these young women returned to create their own household. As concerns the distances involved, domestic service migration normally took place within the same *conventus*.

A closer look at the epigraphy of the *conventus* Caesaraugustanus shows that more than 19% of the inscriptions commemorate people that were not born in this *conventus* (Magallón and Navarro, 1992). Most of them are military personnel concentrated along the northern route between the Ebro valley and the north-west military district with four individuals at Calagurris (three *equites* of the *ala Taurorum* from Bessus: *CIL* II 2984 and a legionary from Legio VI from *Bononia*), five legionaries and their relatives at Tritium Magallum (*CIL* II 2887, 2088, 2089, 2090, 2091—one is from Lancia and another from Toletum) (Navarro, 1989–90), one legionary at Vareia from Narbo (IRR no. 20), and another legionary at San Millán (*CIL* II 2901).

Most conventual magistrates were probably *alieni* as their post in the *conventus* was a step in their *cursus honorum*. The epigraphy records six inscriptions with conventual posts (e.g. *proconsul ext. imperatoris*, *iuridicus*, *censitor*), and only three of them for whom a birthplace is recorded were of foreign origin (*Iuirici*: Puteoli-*CIL* II 2888; Augusta Taurica-*CIL* V 6987; Nemausus-*CIL* XII 3167) (Magallón and Navarro, 1992).

Another example of temporary migration is evident in a dedication erected by a couple from Clunia, who set up an inscription to Hercules at Complutum (*CIL* II 5855), a nearby town located on the main overland corridors. Another Cluniensis was the *grammaticus* L. Memmius Probus (*CIL* II 2892), who created an academy at Tritium Magallum, also a well-connected, nearby city. As the epigraphy reveals,

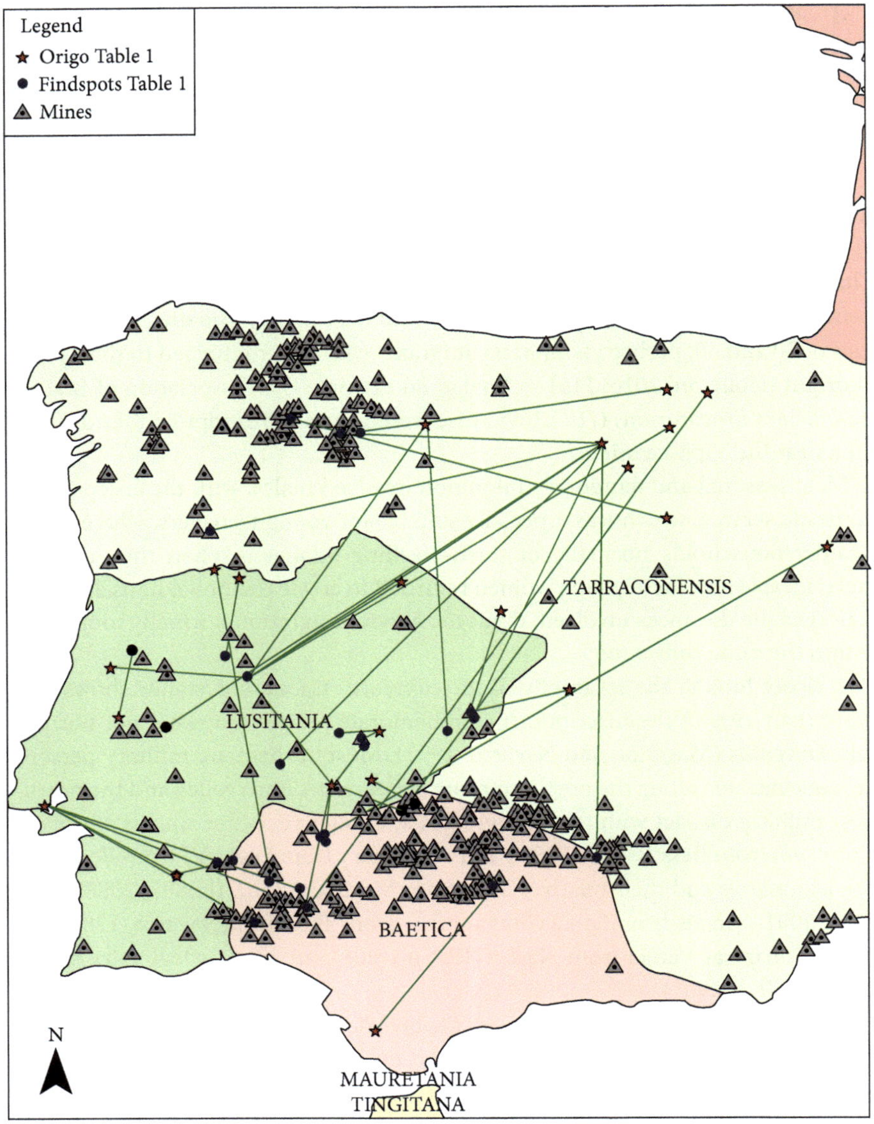


**Fig. 7.38** Map with mines (triangles), the *origo* (stars), and locations of burial (circles) of individuals that migrated to mining districts (Holleran, 2016: fig. 6.1)

most seasonal and temporary migration was local and involved very short distances, such as the cases of a Carensis (a Basque *civitas*) who died in the nearby town of Carcastillo (*CIL* II 2962) and an Andelonensis buried at Cara (*CIL* II 2963), together with an Eturissensis in Campo Real (Sos) (Magallón and Navarro, 1992). In all those cases, there are secondary roads connecting their place of origin with their final residence.

### 7.6.3 Mobility and Administration: The Conventus Iuridici

The *conventus iuridici* were administrative divisions within the Tarraconensis province with the initial function of providing justice to the provincials (Albertini, 1923). With the help of a *legatus iuridicus*, the governor used to tour all the *conventus* capitals to provide justice to their *civitates* (tribes) during a three-day *concilium* (meeting). The *conventus* capitals did not only offer courts of justice, but were also religious centres, where the imperial family was worshipped, as well as being seats of fiscal and census administration seats (Ozcáriz, 2013).

In relation to migration, the *conventus* capitals were probably the closest urban centre for temporary or seasonal migrations. They were the largest cities in the immediate region that could offer a variety of positions in the service sector that would attract young people (temporary jobs) as well as seasonal work in some periods of the year (e.g. in transportation or construction). As considered above, some of the higher magistrates from 'small towns' were able to move to the *conventus* capital as *adlecti*. In a large province such as Hispania Tarraconensis, the provincial capital was far away from most of its citizens, particularly in the north-western district and the central Meseta. The *conventus* capitals provided a centre within a closer range, normally being located at a distance of 50 hours (five days) from any region of its territory (see Fig. 7.39) (Carreras and De Soto, 2022). There was only one large region in the central Meseta (Carpetania, Olcades) and another in the Levant (Edetania) probably with a lower density of population that were at a distance of more than 50 hours' travelling time from their capitals. Actually, the size of the *conventus* Caesaraugustanus and Carthaginensis was unnaturally large since they included those central regions of Carpetania and the Olcades, which may have deserved to be part of another new *conventus*.

#### Clunia

The *conventus* Cluniensis, had its centre in the *colonia* Clunia Sulpicia, and covered the upper Duero valley and the Cantabrian coastal area. According to Pliny (*NH* III.26) the *conventus* included several peoples: Varduli, Turmogidi, Carietes and Vennenses, Vaccaei, Cantabri, Autrigones, and several of the Celtiberian tribes. It is noteworthy that the *conventus* division did not follow tribal organizations. The Celtiberian tribes, for example, were divided between Cluniensis, Caesaraugustanus, and Carthaginensis. The *conventus* provides an interesting case study, as it is understood to have been a centre of dispersion rather than one of attraction (Haley, 1991: 87–8; Curchin, 2011: 124). We shall start by looking at the migrants moving into Cluniensis (Fig. 7.40) and then turn to the emigrants.

Within the *conventus* we find at least 34 migrants referring to their migratory status (Table 7.5).

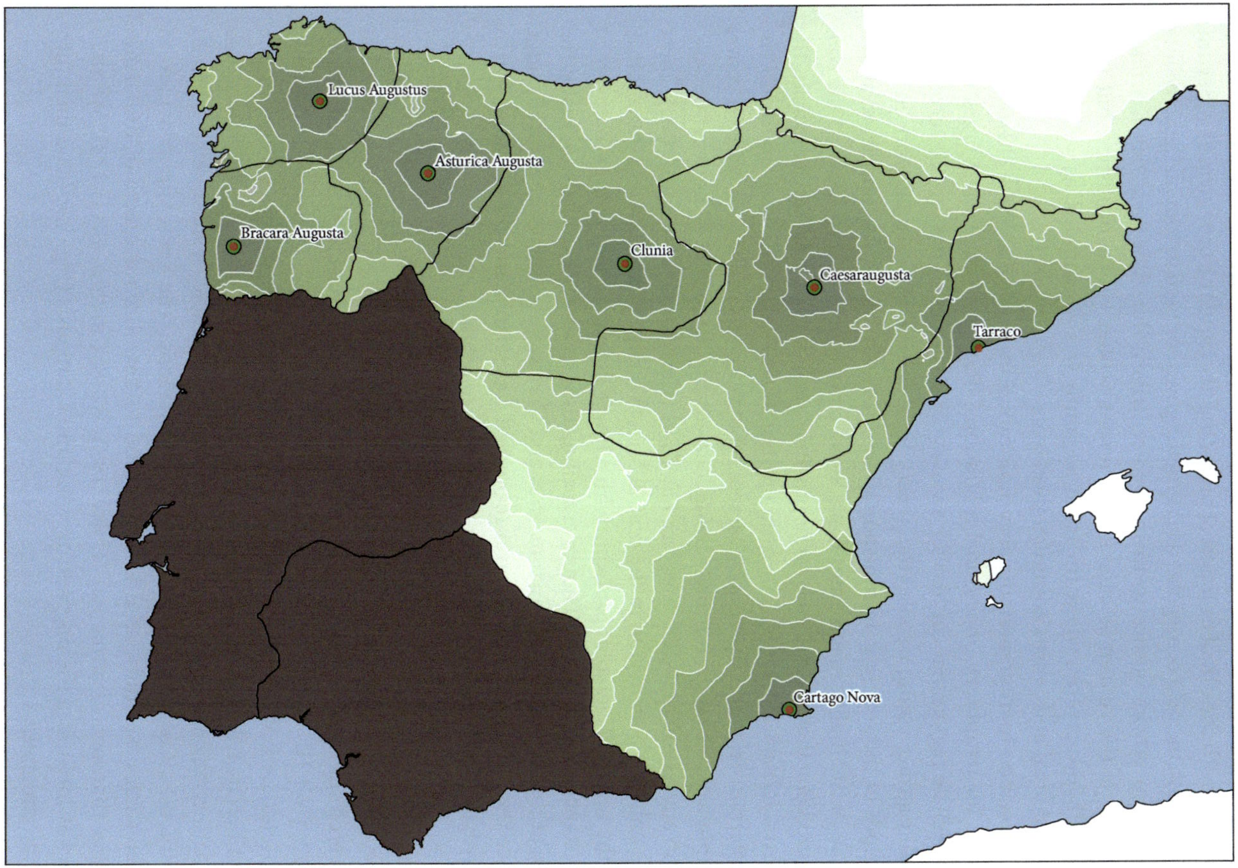


**Fig. 7.39** Distance in hours (10h buffer) from the *conventus* capitals (Carreras and De Soto, 2022)

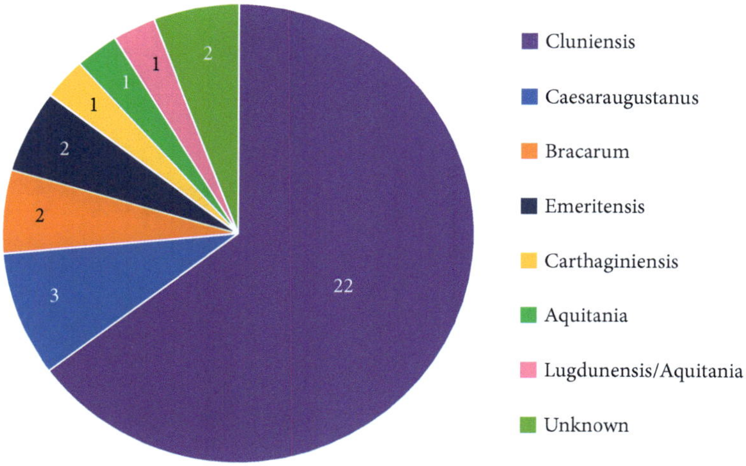


**Fig. 7.40** Migrants to Clunia according to *conventus* or province

The majority of the movements took place within the *conventus*. This low migration from beyond the *conventus* might support the idea that the economic possibilities were limited. From the *conventus* capital of Caesaraugusta, there are three recorded migrants towards Cluniensis. A veteran and an (unrelated) freedwoman are recorded in Clunia, while in Pallantia we find a man of uncertain standing, who has the *tria nomina*. From the *conventus* Bracarum we can observe that the two migrants both originate from the Interamici. The Interamici was one of the ten *civitates* involved in the construction of the bridge crossing over the River Tamega at Chaves (*CIL* II 2477). The location of the Interamici is uncertain; however, Castro da Cibdá de Arméa seems a likely candidate (Houten, 2021: 88). Despite the relatively high numbers from Interamicia and Caesaraugusta, these remain stray finds. The 12 migrants from outside the *conventus* can be broken down as follows: *ingenui* (7); *Liberti* (1); *Servi* (0); *Incerti* (4).

It is noteworthy that two *servi*, 18-year-old Secundius and 5-year-old Celadus, were buried with the sole *liberta* Iulleia Araucia; they could possibly be added to the migrants, although this remains uncertain. Military migrants make up a large part of this small selection. The *ingenui* include four soldiers, among whom one mentions the Legio VII Gemina. The veteran from Lugdunum, although it remains uncertain whether this was Lugdunum Convenarum or the capital of Gallia, was a *duplicarius*. The migration recorded towards the *conventus* Cluniensis is very limited and provides no clearly distinguishable groups.

Turning to the emigrants we see an interesting pattern; unlike the other *conventus* capitals, Clunia seems to have a high outward movement. Forty-eight inscriptions recorded Clunia as their origin. It has been suggested by several

**Table 7.5** Epigraphic evidence for migrants to Clunia

| Findspot | Findspot(modern) | Origin | Region | Epigraphic ref | Haley (1990) | # |
|---|---|---|---|---|---|---|
| | Trévago, Soria | Augustobriga | Eme | *AE* 2002, 794 | 485 | 1 |
| Clunia | Peñalba de Castro, Burgos | Brigiaecum | Clu | *CIL* II 6338 | 479 | 1 |
| Clunia | Peñalba de Castro, Burgos | Caesaraugusta | Cae | *AE* 1976, 357; EC 102 | 474; 475 | 2 |
| Pallantia | Palencia | Caesaraugusta | Cae | *CIL* II 5764 | 463 | 1 |
| Amallobriga | Montalegre | Cauca | Clu | *AE* 1985, 581 | 465 | 1 |
| Segovia | Segovia | Cauca | Clu | *CIL* II 2729 | 469 | 1 |
| | Duratón | Cauca | Clu | AHH IV 1948, 79 | 471 | 1 |
| Nova Augusta | Lara de los Infantes, Burgos | Clunia | Clu | *AE* 1956, 25 | 487 | 1 |
| Pisoraca | Herrera de Pisuerga, Palencia | Consabura | Car | *AE* 1967, 239 | 460 | 1 |
| Termes | Tiermes | Dercinoassedenses vicani Cluniensium | Clu | *AE* 1953, 267 | 483 | 1 |
| Clunia | Peñalba de Castro, Burgos | Emerita Augusta | Eme | | 480 | 1 |
| Pallantia | Palencia | Interamici | Bra | *CIL* II 5765; AFFE I 310 | 464 | 1 |
| Segovia | Segovia | Interamici | Bra | *CIL* II 2730 | 470 | 1 |
| | Coruña del Conde, Burgos | Intercatia | Clu | *CIL* II 2786 = AE 1956, 27 | 477 | 1 |
| Palantia | Palencia | Intercatia | Clu | *CIL* II 5763 | 462 | 1 |
| Pisoraca | Herrera de Pisuerga, Palencia | Lugdunum? | Gal? Aqu? | *CIL* II 2912 | | 1 |
| Vellica | Monte Cildá | Orgenomescum | Clu | *CIL* II 6301 | 492 | 1 |
| Nova Augusta | Lara de los Infantes, Burgos | Pomptina tribus | ? | *CIL* II 2852 | 488 | 1 |
| Clunia | Peñalba de Castro, Burgos | Quirina tribus | ? | *CIL* II 2798 | 481 | 1 |
| Segisamo | Sasamón, Burgos | Suessatium (Suestatio) | Clu | *AE* 1911, 130; *AE* 1920, 80 | 490; 491 | 2 |
| Uxama | Osma | Termes | Clu | *AE* 1980, 588 | 482 | 1 |
| Clunia | Peñalba de Castro, Burgos | Tolosa | Aqu | *AE* 1988, 787 | | 1 |
| Clunia | Peñalba de Castro, Burgos | Uxama (Argaela) | Clu | *CIL* II 2787 | 478 | 1 |

| | | | | | | |
|---|---|---|---|---|---|---|
| Segovia | Segovia | Uxama (Argaela) | Clu | *CIL* II 2733; *CIL* II 2732; *CIL* II 2731 | 466; 467; 468 | 3 |
| Palantia | Palencia | Uxama (Argaela) | Clu | *CIL* II 5762 | 461 | 1 |
| Amaia | Amaya, Burgos | Uxama (Argaela) | Clu | ERPSoria 168 | 489 | 1 |
| | Peña del Castillo (Buenafuente de Sisal) | Uxama Argaela | Clu | EE VII 140b | 473 | 1 |
| | Quintanilla de las Viñas, Burgos | Uxama Barca | Clu | *CIL* II 2854 | 486 | 1 |
| | Duratón | Vadinia | Clu | AHH IV 1948, 22 | 472 | 1 |
| Clunia | Peñalba de Castro, Burgos | Vindeleia | Clu | *AE* 1920, 80 | 476 | 1 |

authors that this could easily be the result of including those that recorded the *conventus* of the same name (Curchin, 2011: 124; Villalón, 2019: 277). However, in the immediate vicinity there is Uxama Argaela with another large number of emigrants: no fewer than 20 people. This seems to support the idea of high levels of emigration from the upper Duero basin. However, it should be borne in mind that the higher occurrence might be the result of a local custom to record the *origo*, rather than this being a valid reflection of higher outward migration. Even considering the possibility that we need to allow for a possible overrepresentation, migration patterns from the *conventus* towards the south and the west can be observed (Fig. 7.41).

Grouping the use of the term Clunienses together as a possible reference to the city of Clunia, we can start to look at this group and observe some patterns. The first striking observation is the shift to the west. The sole eastern occurrence of a Cluniensis is the honorific inscription in Tarraco to the *flaminica* Aurelia Marcellina reading EX CLUNIENS(I) (*CIL* II 4198; Alföldy, 1973: 94). Only one reference to the *origo* Cluniensis is found in Baetica, where Titus Pompeius Fraternus died at the age of 15 and was commemorated by his father (*AE* 1922, 8). This inscription was found close to the mines at El Centenillo. This observation leads us to other concentrations of emigrants.

When the mining areas and concentrations of mines are examined, a correlation can be observed (Fig. 7.42). The idea of Clunienses moving to mining regions is supported by the higher concentrations in the Tresminas region and the city of Igaeditania, both important gold-mining areas. Domergue (1990: 345) pointed out that there was a high demand for manual labour at the mines. At the western end of the Sierra de Gredos, around the ancient city of Capera, eight natives with the *origo* Clunienses are recorded, all of them in the vicinity, but not in the city itself. Of interest is the inscription put up by a vicinia Cluniensum (*CIL* II 821). Vicinia has been read as the name of a *serva*, where Cluniensium would indicate this was a public slave of the city of Clunia (Haley, 1991: 19). A second possible interpretation proposes that it should be read as a reference to a neighbourhood association of Clunienses that put up the epitaph. If it is a neighbourhood association, then we have evidence for a wider organized community of Clunienses. Nonetheless, the high number of Clunienses in this region raises the question of why they moved there. Río-Miranda (2011: 68) argues that the people could have been drawn in as manual labour for the mines of Capera. The occurrence of specific groups of people at specific mines could be explained by the effect of communication between the migrants and the home region. Successful compatriots would share their experience and attract more people from their place of origin.

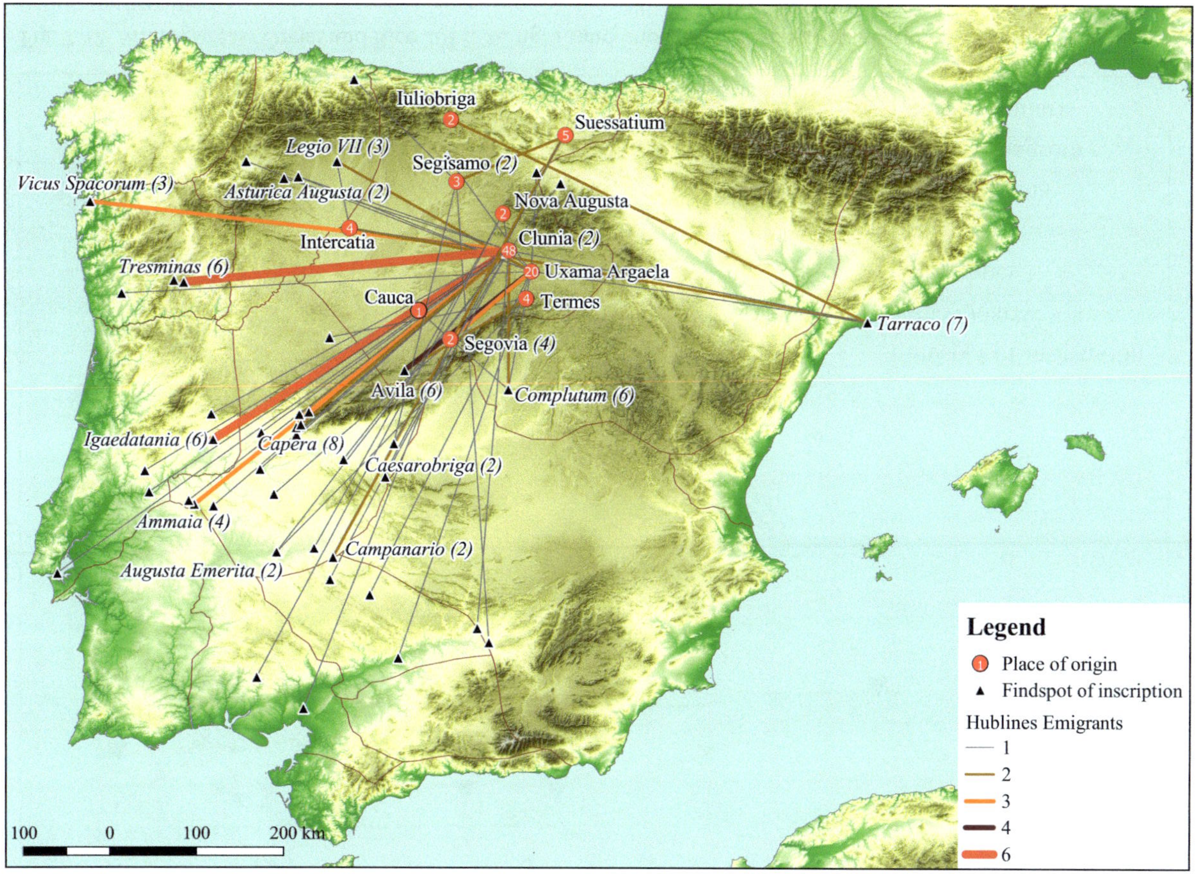


**Fig. 7.41** Emigrants from Cluniensis. Names and numbers in italics give the findspot of the inscriptions

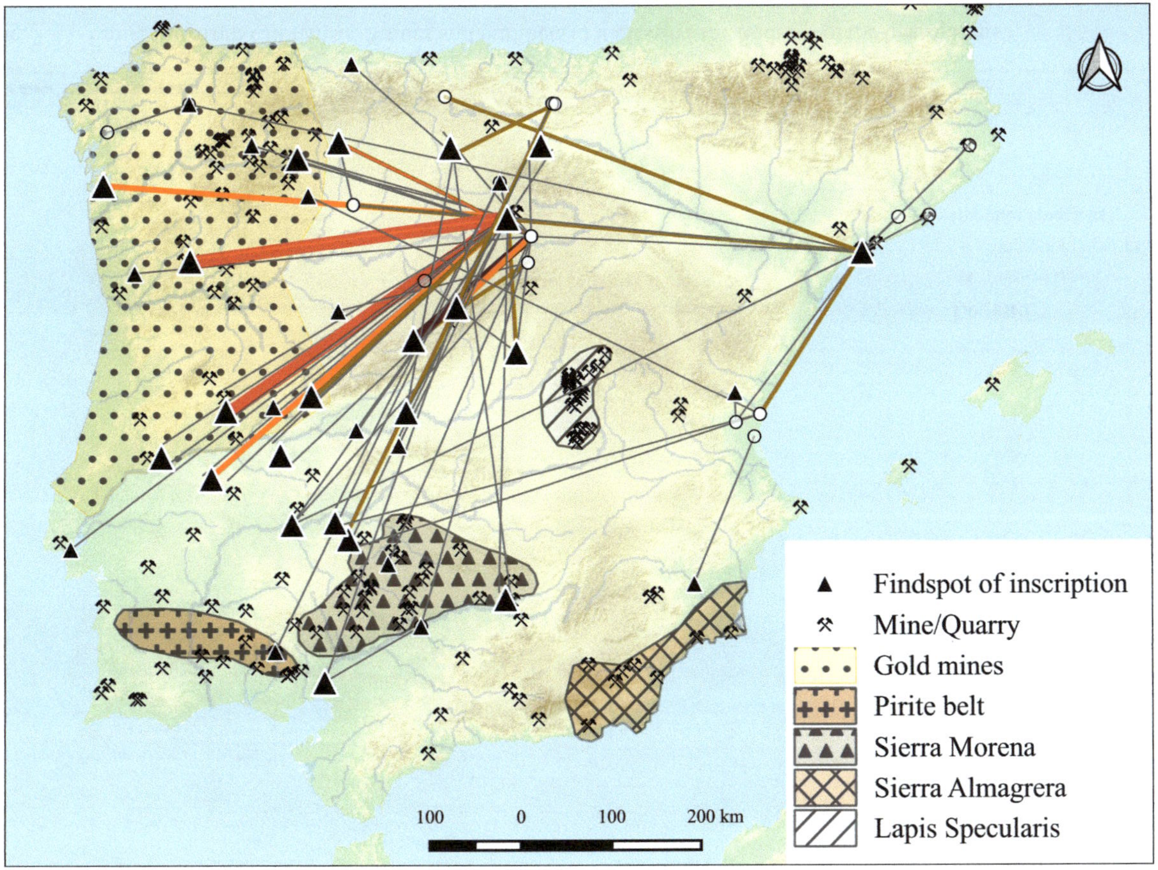


**Fig. 7.42** Mining areas (Orejas and Rico 2012: 32. fig. 1) and findspots of inscription mentioning an *origo* from places within the province

### 7.6.4 The Case of Carthago Nova

The city of Carthago Nova (Cartagena) is of interest as an important trading centre for the southern part of Hispania Citerior/Tarraconensis. Due to its strategic position on a small peninsula (40 ha) that protected the entrance to a well-sheltered bay, the settlement became the site of the Barcid economic and military capital Qart-Hadašt in 228 BCE (Diod. Sic. 25.12; Polyb. II 13.1; Noguera Celdrán, 2012: 124). After the Roman conquest in 209 BCE, the city was renamed Carthago Nova and remained a key centre in the Iberian peninsula due to its strategic position. The port city enabled access to the North African coast and a fast connection with the Italic peninsula via the Balearic Islands. In addition, the territory of Carthago Nova contained silver and lead mines. These were of such great importance that the first migrants from the Italian peninsula to Carthago Nova were families forming a mining elite (Stefanile, 2017: 48) (see section 7.4.3). In the Republican period, these Italic families held important positions such as the magistracies.

With the arrival of the imperial period, these families from the Italian peninsula continued to be of importance; a famous example of a member of this elite originally from Rome is L. Aemilius Rectus, who invested in Carthago Nova and became an *adlectus* to the *ordo* (*CIL* II 3423; II 3424; II 5941; Haley, 1991: 32). Surprisingly, very few people with a clear *origo* outside Carthago Nova are found in the epigraphic record. This might have been a consequence of there being a difference in epigraphic customs regarding the addition of the *origo* in Carthago Nova. It should be taken into account that the culture of the Punic community in the Iberian peninsula did not include extensive use of inscriptions (Zamora López, 2005: 164). However, we must account for another factor: forced labour. In addition to the elite moving in, a large workforce was needed for the mines; as a result, the city became a significant port of call for many migrants and enslaved people.

As a mining centre, Carthago Nova absorbed many slaves; this form of forced mobility leaves few traces and is hard to appreciate. There is some evidence for this group in the Republican period in Carthago Nova (De la Escosura Balbás, 2021: 37).

Fig. 7.43 shows the people attested in the Republican period by their juridical status according to De la Escosura Balbás. The total number of people recognized by De la Escosura Balbás for Carthago Nova in the Republican period is 122, of whom 11 were women. Of these people 10 men held Roman citizenship (ROM), of whom 8 were directly related to mining as they can be recognized through the stamps on lead ingots. The Roman citizens in this period all originated from the Italian peninsula (De la Escosura Balbás, 2021: 40). The two BOH categories are those where the juridical status remained unidentified, with BOH.FIL as the category where a filiation is mentioned. Of special interest regarding the use of forced labour are the LIB, 28 *liberti*, and SER, the 11 enslaved people. De la

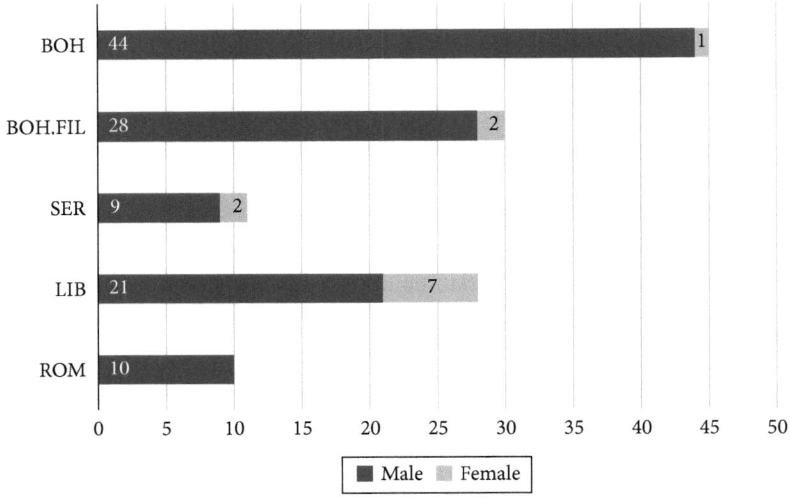


**Fig. 7.43** Attested Republican population categorized by status (De la Escosura Balbás, 2021: 33, fig. 2.2)

Escosura Balbás states that the status of Carthago Nova as a 'Ciudad de libertos' (city of freedmen/women) is false when the total number of *liberti* in relation to freeborn individuals is reconsidered (102/110). However, the enslaved and freed individuals are normally underrepresented and the relatively high number, in comparison with the Roman citizens, seems to indicate we might be dealing with a rather large number of enslaved and freed people in the Republican city of Carthago Nova. However, we must account for the fact that we have a Republican inscription recording five *servi* and five *liberti* as the magistrates of a *collegium* (*ELRH* C10; *CIL* I 1477). The former slaves are a more visible group, although their origin often remains hidden. Nonetheless, two *liberti*, L. Auius Antipho and A. Auius Eclectus, dedicated an altar to the Gaditanian Hercules (*CIL* II 3409). It has been hypothesized that this singular offering to the Gaditanian Hercules indicates that these *liberti* originally came from Gades (De la Escosura Balbás, 2021: 49).

## 7.7 Conclusions

The present chapter illustrates the significance of transport networks in the movements of people, whether for the purpose of conquest, trade, or any kind of migration. However, the development of those infrastructures in Hispania Citerior/Tarraconensis was not linear, but instead involved a continuous construction of ports and roads on the basis of previous native trackways and settlement patterns. The Roman military disembarkment in the late third century BCE forced them to create the first harbour infrastructures in the Mediterranean ports of Emporion, Tarraco, and Carthago Nova, which went on to witness a lively movement of amphorae, black-gloss pottery, and coins from the Italian peninsula. Moving inland from these Mediterranean ports, which acted as springboards, legionaries and traders followed the newly built roads that ran parallel to the River Ebro. In this initial stage, military priorities determined the movement of people in the new province.

We must stress the fact that inscriptions—our best and most employed tool of analysis in the chapter to trace mobility—while providing some key information, represent a skewed sample of the total population. Therefore, many of the conclusions in this chapter need to be read in the context of the silence of large segments of the population who did not erect inscriptions and are therefore invisible to us.

It is difficult to evaluate the significance of early Republican migrations, but it seems to have been minimal, since most legionaries returned to Italy whereas the inscriptions do not reveal any major contingent of Italian origin in the province. The *nomina* suggest that most Italian immigrants came from the Tyrrhenian coast, from the Gulf of Naples to the region of Minturnae. Such a preferential relationship between the coast of Hispania Citerior and these southern Italian regions is also indicated by pottery assemblages and coin circulation. The city of Carthago Nova and its nearby mines may have received the majority of newcomers whether to work in the mines (e.g. as slaves or traders) or to participate in the commercial networks with the Italian homeland. With regard to the new urban foundations, graffiti and epigraphy suggest that most inhabitants were of local origin (e.g. Iberian graffiti in places such as Iesso or Ilduro), although with some exceptions with a strong Italic component (e.g. La Cabañeta). In accordance with our present state of knowledge, it does not seem likely that the Italian migration towards Citerior in the Republican period was substantial in volume, except in some cities in particular coastal regions. A further movement of people that it is difficult to document was of slaves that were sent from Citerior to Italy in Republican times, but also the prisoners taken by the Roman army and employed in the mines of Citerior (e.g. Carthago Nova).

The Atlantic side of the province was basically conquered in the first century BCE and exhibited a similar process with the creation of port infrastructures in some river estuaries, which became the starting point for a road network that probably followed preceding indigenous trackways. The process increased in pace during the Cantabrian Wars (29–19 BCE) since it involved the settlement of four legions and auxiliary troops as well as the creation of reliable supply routes in the north-west of the province. The presence of the Roman army in the north-west favoured migration to this region, at least during the first century CE, and this appears to be evident in *conventus* capitals such as Asturica Augusta. Roman legionaries were temporary migrants that moved to new provincial destinations as soon as the region was pacified. Only a few of them remained in the province either in the legionary settlement or the main coastal towns.

In the Early Empire, a different background among foreign migrants can be seen in Tarraconensis, with a wider range of origins according to the epigraphic evidence (Haley, 1991). Most permanent migrants came from Italy, but not only from the the Campania and the Auruncan-Calenan territories but also from northern Italy, in some cases due to legionary levies in these regions. The second most important regions of origin were the Gaulish provinces and North Africa; these migrants shared a similar profile, with some coming for administrative reasons linked to their *cursus honorum*, while others had purely economic motives due to the proximity of those territories.

Apart from permanent migration, the development of the transport network favoured temporary and seasonal movements within the province. Some agricultural, trading, construction, and harbour tasks were limited to the spring and summer seasons, so populations could move to another town in the winter and autumn. Other professional occupations, such as military ones and domestic service, involved young age groups who moved to urban or military sites for a limited period and then returned home in adulthood. The epigraphic record of Hispania Tarraconensis provides some unique case studies of this seasonal and temporary migration, for instance the movement in the *conventus* Cluniensis along the traditional transhumance routes and migration to areas close to mining districts, especially the case of Carthago Nova with the presence of Italian family traders and slaves in its mining complexes.

*The Human Factor: The Demography of the Roman Province of Hispania Citerior/Tarraconensis.* Alejandro G. Sinner, Cèsar Carreras, and Pieter Houten, Oxford University Press. 
DOI: 10.1093/9780191943881.003.0007

# 8

# Future Directions and New Approaches to Study Ancient Populations

Research on palaeopathology or aDNA in Physical Anthropology is still quite a young field in Portugal and Spain. There are only few studies of Roman archaeology from the province of Hispania Citerior/Tarraconensis covering those topics. Of course, there are excellent case studies from very particular excavations, but so far, the territory lacks an overall view of the province as a whole. Initially, the idea was to include in this book particular chapters covering those topics; however, the quantity and quality of their data could not match the level of detail or analysis employed in other chapters in this volume.

Studies in other Roman provinces such as Britain or Italy have shown the great potential of these approaches to observe ancient populations from different perspectives overcoming some traditional visions and prejudices. Understanding causes of ancient death, either natural or provoked, may help us understand changes in population and patterns of disease. Besides, there is a recent interest in modelling ancient epidemics and comparing their death toll with that caused by present diseases (Newfield et al., 2022).

A large percentage of the evidence presented in Chapter 2, comes from the epigraphic record; which, as we have discussed in this volume, presents some bias (see Chapters 2 and 3). Comparing such data with physical anthropology obtained from well-studied Roman necropoleis in the province could be an excellent alternative. Moreover, relating disease outbreaks with particular mass graves may shed some light on how new diseases and epidemics affected a provincial society.

On the other hand, aDNA studies can offer new insights about migrations (see Chapter 7) and the genetic composition of the populations of Hispania from the Iron Age down to the Late Roman period, providing an alternative way to quantify the importance of the Italic colonization in Republican times. Furthermore, research on aDNA may help us to analyse local communities and familial relationships in relatively reduced territories, especially from a matrilineal perspective.

Although such studies are still in an initial stage, this chapter attempts to illustrate their potential in future research based on specific case studies from the province that have been documented and studied in detail providing accurate and valuable data. It is expected that future breakthroughs in those fields will change our views of the population in the province. As will be seen later, palaeogenomics studies are just beginning. Interest in this type of analysis is increasing day after day, seeing its potential, constant improvements in its methodology, and the number and quality of the datasets. Now only a small window has opened, but when enough data are available, we will be able to get a reasonably accurate picture of how the peoples of the Iberian peninsula were characterized genetically.

## 8.1 Thinking of Past Health and Disease

The study of pathologies based on skeletal remains is still a young field in the territory of Hispania Citerior/Tarraconensis, despite the fact of excellent singular research conducted in particular rescue archaeological excavations. Of course, it is a relevant subject, which was also underlined by the classical authors such as Herophilus of Cos (382–322 BCE):

> When health is absent, wisdom cannot reveal itself, strength cannot fight, intelligence cannot be applied, art cannot become manifest, wealth becomes useless.

Discussing health and illness through the analysis of archaeological human remains invites one to reflect on the concepts that concern them over the course of time. Every society lives and feels health and sickness in a different way, since they are not immutable realities. On the contrary, they are concepts constructed in a variable way according to space and time (Vergara, 2007). These two are social rather than strictly biological concepts because they permanently need to be balanced with the economic, political, cultural, and social reality of each period. In other words, they are arbitrary and changeable throughout the history of humankind (Molina Vidal, 1997).

Assuming the present definition of 'health' in the Western world as a 'complete state of physical, psychic and social welfare' (OMS, 1948), it probably had little to do with what ancient people understood by health. This chapter attempts to offer an approach to the contributions that biological anthropology or osteoarchaeology can make to the knowledge of health among the communities of the territory under study.

The human bones recovered in an archaeological context can provide a large amount of data on the health of people from the past. The anthropological study of bones allows analyses of pathological conditions and injuries produced by certain diseases as well as of past ways of life. Besides, bone modifications of non-pathological origin can be related to everyday activities or cultural aspects. Furthermore, skeletal remains can provide a biological profile, not only of an individual, but also of the whole population, which enables us to focus on aspects from palaeogeography to population history (Ledermann, 1969; Masset, 1986;

Sellier, 1995). The combination of all this information, together with basic field data on burial type and the individual's deposition, can shed light on particular aspects of health and disease, including hygiene, medicine, physiological stress, violence, physical activities, teeth use, diet, and the demographic history of archaeological populations (Larsen, 2002; 2015; Isidro and Malgosa, 2003).

But discussing health and disease through skeletal remains is a challenge not only due to the difficulty of integrating concepts accurately, but also because only a small percentage of known diseases leave traces on bones (Ortner, 2011), and absence of skeletal alterations does not necessarily imply good health. Furthermore, different diseases may generate similar bone injuries, or a particular disease may produce different kinds of bone injuries. Notwithstanding its limits, bone is a tissue sensitive to stress and is susceptible to environmental and/or nutritional changes. Therefore, our lives and way of living may have repercussions on our bones.

Palaeopathology, palaeostomatology, and palaeodentistry cover the study of pathological episodes that may leave traces in our skeleton, helping us to explore health conditions. Palaeopathology can be defined as 'the science that studies variants, anomalies, lesions and diseases from the past, from all the traces and pieces of evidence left' (Villalaín Blanco, 2007: 45). Palaeopathological studies allow us to interpret traces that remain in bones and link them with different disorders and organism alterations, including palaeostomatology analyses and the origin of alterations in teeth which may be pathological or non-pathological but related to food consumption. This area can be defined as the 'branch of odontostomatology that covers the study of structures, functions and diseases of the mastication apparatus from the human and animal remains from the ancient times' (Chimenos et al., 1992). Thus, it is possible to improve our knowledge of health in antiquity if archaeological information and field anthropology are integrated with direct information about bones.

## 8.2 Palaeopathology

Not all human diseases leave traces on bones. Normally, if a disease becomes fatal quickly, this will not be registered on the skeleton as even the fastest of bone reactions—periosteal new bone formation—can take a few days to develop. If the disease was slow-progressing or chronic, it is then more likely to have left skeletal lesions.

The most common palaeopathological lesion observed in human skeletal remains from Hispania Citerior/Tarraconensis is related to a group of alterations produced by porous phenomena such as cribra orbitalia and femoralis (Polo-Cerdá and Villalaín Blanco, 2001; Subirà et al., 2002), parietal thinning, cranial vault porosity with or without bone thickening, as well as periosteal reactions on the diaphysis or metaphysis of long bones. Sometimes, porous phenomena come together with slight bone deformations. Despite these being unspecific alterations, they are normally related to metabolic deficiencies or infectious processes and are thus related to individual health and nutrition (Herrerín et al., 2011). Anaemia has been considered a possible aetiology for these lesions (Guerrero and Ribas, 1997; Subirà et al., 2002); however, these could also be associated with vitamin deficiencies or with a reduction in the individual's immune capacity (Polo-Cerdá and Villalaín Blanco, 2001).

Before starting on the case studies illustrating the importance and amount of information that can be obtained from skeletal remains, it is important to consider that the analysis of archaeological human remains is not only crucial to understand aspects of the health, diet, and illness from ancient populations, but also to investigate palaeodemography (Masset, 1990; Konigsberg and Frankenberg, 1992). From the osteoarchaeological perspective, palaeodemography is approached by assessing sex and age estimating the remains of the adult and non-adult individuals recovered (Wiedemann, 1989; see Chapter 2).

The methods available to accurately estimate the age and sex vary depending on the stage of skeletal development, so the first step is to differentiate between adult and juvenile individuals, and this is established by analysing epiphyseal fusion. That is to say that if the long bone epiphyses are not fused, the individual is classified as juvenile and, if they are, the individual is classified as adult. The sternal epiphysis of the clavicle, the iliac crest, the annular rings of the vertebral bodies, and the fusion between the first and second sacral vertebrae, which are late fusion epiphyses, are not considered for this classification.

In this discussion, we will not attempt to provide an exhaustive account of the methods used for sex assessment, age estimation, and metric and non-metric analysis of human remains, as there are several resources that cover these topics and their associated challenges and caveats at length (see for example Ferembach et al., 1980; Walker et al., 1988; Cox and Mays, 2000; Buckberry, 2018). However, it is important to consider the demographic profile of the population of Hispania Citerior/Tarraconensis.

At a demographic level, this population presents an age structure similar to those of modern developing countries (Parkin, 1992; Corvisier and Bellancourt-Valdher, 1999). These pyramids are characterized by a wide base—the infancy and childhood cohort is the largest—and a large percentage of women at a reproductive age. These populations, as discussed in Chapter 2, are also characterized by high numbers of infant mortality; half of the individuals born die before reaching the age of 25 (Ledermann, 1969; Masset, 1986; Sellier, 1995). Nowadays, some common causes of death in children below five years of age are pneumonia, diarrhoea, and birth complications, although infectious diseases are the most frequent of all (Black et al., 2010; Liu et al., 2015). Malnourishment is the cause of death of 54% of the infants dying between the ages of one and four; however, the synergy between malnourishment and infection cannot be disregarded (Pelletier et al., 1995).

In the adult segment of the archaeological population, other signs that can usually be observed are degenerative changes (Campillo, 1993; Baxarias, 2002). In the past, they were normally linked to old age or physical activity. Lesions of traumatic and microtraumatic origin, which can be linked to generalized or occasional violence as well as to accidents, are common; underlying pathologies can be interesting from the point of view of care and medical practices since if these are not suitably treated, they can result in bone deformation or shortening (Guerra, 1982; Aufderheide and Rodríguez-Martin, 1998).

Enthesopathies, bone adaptations, and non-pathological alterations are also common findings in skeletal remains in the province. Enthesopathies have been studied as occupational stress markers when aiming to analyse ways of life and activity patterns. However, the development of enthesopathies is not only related to a way of life, but also to the individual's age, so interpretation of those markers is not always simple and straightforward (Cunha and Umbelino, 1995; Robb, 1998; Villotte et al., 2010). Likewise, non-pathological alterations to bone shape are studied to infer physical activities and weight-bearing patterns. However, it should be considered that bone shape is affected by genetics and individual age, and bone tissue seems to be more susceptible to changes in charge patterns during its development (Ruff et al., 2006; Shaw and Stock, 2009).

In Roman society, there was one form of medicine reserved for the wealthy population, and another for the lower strata of society, and this difference is nowhere more obvious than when assessing healed trauma (Díaz González, 1950; Schulten, 1952). The pathological data from Hispania Tarraconensis suggest that traumatic lesion can be found in 18% of the Roman urban population with a clear predominance in the trunk (47%)—especially the parts that correspond to the ribs and clavicles. In general, there are very few cases of polytrauma; individuals displaying more than one fracture with signs of survival do not represent more than 1–2% of the population. With regard to non-deadly complications, non-united healed fractures (or pseudoarthrosis) and secondary infections (post-traumatic osteomyelitis) are the most frequent findings and yet are still rare. Forty per cent of the fractures in long bones either show no sign of reduction or have healed but show displacements, angulations, lateral deviations, rotations, and even overlapping. Pseudoarthrosis, or failure in the final consolidation of broken limbs, is as high as 5% if limb long bones are considered. These data contrast with the detailed therapeutic descriptions obtained from classical sources about reductions of fractures and dislocations (Apollonius of Citium, first century BCE; Baxarias, 2002), as well as temporary immobilizations depending on the type and seriousness of the fracture. It seems feasible that this contrast reflects social and economic differentiation, or even individual factors related to the choice of a more empirical or magical or religious form of medicine (Baxarias, 2002).

Neoplasms and developmental or congenital anomalies are less frequent. Most neoplastic lesions detected on bone remains are benign (Armentano et al., 2012), mainly button osteomas on the cranial vault. The prevalence of malignant tumours is quite low (around 0.4%), although many tumours do not leave any trace in bone tissue. A reduced life expectancy in the Roman population and a smaller number of environmental factors conducive to cancer could also explain this low prevalence. With regard to congenital pathologies or non-metrical anatomical variants, lumbosacral transition is present in approximately 3% of individuals, affecting men and women at the same rate. Sternal variants and spina bifida occulta exhibit prevalence rates below 5% (Baxarias, 2007).

It is worth reminding that the absence of evidence of pathology is not evidence of health, and that the high mortality associated with malnourishment and infections may have left no or non-specific bone lesions.

## 8.3 Evidence of Palaeopathologies in Context: Some Case Studies

The development of osteoarchaeology in the northern Iberian peninsula is relatively recent, so there are isolated case studies, but not yet enough material to put together an overall study on the province. There are insufficient quantitative data to provide a general overview of pathologies in Hispania Citerior/Tarraconensis. Although there have been attempts to extend the evidence of a single case study, a cemetery at Tarraco (Baxarias, 2002), to the health situation of the whole territory, in fact there were only few examples of each type. Other scholars, such as Menéndez Bueyes (2013; 2016), have covered specific periods, such as late antiquity, similarly also drawing on a small number of case studies.

It is clear that there are excellent studies of particular necropoleis, such as the one analysing the episcopal cemetery at Valencia (Calvo, 2000) or Vila de Madrid (Barcelona; Jordana and Malgosa, 2007); however, these are all treated in isolation. Therefore, this section attempts to illustrate the potential of those case studies to create a general view of palaeopathologies in Hispania Citerior/Tarraconensis in the future. To do so, a series of well-researched examples are put forward here to show the potential of osteoarchaeology to understand health and disease from burial practices in the province.

### 8.3.1 The Case of Can Mitjans

#### Field Anthropology

Early in 2017 in the Vallès Occidental, a pit one metre in diameter and one and a half metres deep was identified; it contained human skeletal remains and pottery of the early imperial period (first–second centuries CE), a period in which inhumation was the most common burial practice. The pit was located at La Carena de Can

Mitjans (Viladecavalls), a few kilometres from the city of Terrassa (ancient Egara). Egara became a Roman *municipium* in the Flavian period after Vespasian's Latin rights (*ius latii*) reforms affected the towns of Hispania. In the same region as Can Mitjans, there was also the Roman villa of Camp d'en Ventura (Santa Perpètua de Mogoda), the important villa of la Salut (Sabadell) (Casas i Genover et al., 1995), as well as the rural sites of Can Cabassa (Sant Cugat del Vallès) and Can Ubach (Sant Cugat del Vallès), among others (AAVV, 2007).

An anthropological field study allowed the recognition of human skeletal remains belonging to two well-articulated individuals squeezed inside the feature in a forced position (Brothwell, 1987).

Individual 1 was found in supine position lateralized to the left as the body occupied the western half of the pit. Its skull was found close to the southern side of the feature, and forced to the right side, in contact with the right shoulder. The left arm was extended against the south-western side, whereas the right one was bent with the hand resting at the abdominal level. The lower part of the body presented a right rotation to the torso and the lower limbs were almost in supine position, with the right leg semi-flexed to the left. The left knee was in contact with the western side of the pit. Its tibiae, fibulae, and other foot bone elements were below the remains of individual 2. Most of the skeletal elements, except for the right hand and foot, were in complete articulation.

The second body was found lying in a forced position. The individual lay on its left side with the anterior aspect of the body following the northern wall of the pit, over the legs and feet of individual 1. The remains followed the pit wall, from the skull to the femora, the feet in the centre of the feature and the right foot over the right elbow of individual 1. The right arm was semi-flexed, and the left one hyperflexed, with the hand by the neck. The temporomandibular joint remained articulated with the mouth half-open. The lower limbs display hip extension and bent knees. All the skeletal elements were in complete articulation.

The strict maintenance of the articulation on the labile joints suggests that the pit was soon filled in once the two individuals had been deposited (Brothwell, 1987; Duday, 2009), and the partial overlapping of individual 2 over individual 1 suggests simultaneous inhumation with individual 1 being laid in the pit before individual 2.

## Osteological Analysis and Laboratory Anthropology

The study of the remains in the laboratory confirms that there were two inhumations, a male and a female (Fig. 8.1). The remains of individual 1, which were in a perfect state of preservation (Walker et al., 1988), belong to a male individual aged 11 years old (11±2 years old) at the time of death considering the state of epiphyseal fusion and tooth development (Crétot, 1978; Ferembach et al., 1980; Krogman and Iscan, 1986; Brothwell, 1987; Alduc-LeBagousse, 1988; Schutkowski, 1993; Buikstra and Ubelaker, 1994; Scheuer and Black, 2000) and an estimated stature

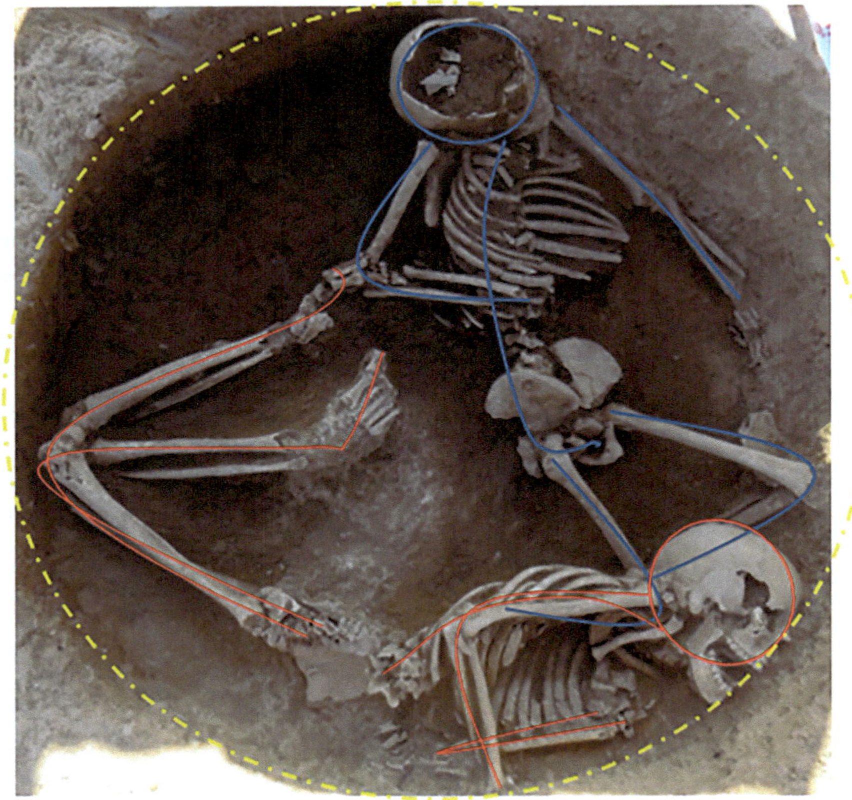

**Fig. 8.1** *In situ* position of the two individuals found in the pit at Can Mitjans (Catalonia). This was an undisturbed simultaneous primary burial where the individuals had been laid out in a forced position

of between 138.5 and 141 cm (Martin and Saller, 1957; Olivier, 1960; Krogman and Iscan, 1986).

The remains of individual 2, in an excellent (95%) degree of preservation (Walker et al., 1988), belong to a female between 21 and 24 years old at the time of death considering the late fusion epiphyses and the eruption and development of the third molar (Crétot, 1978; Ferembach et al., 1980; Krogman and Iscan, 1986; Brothwell, 1987; Buikstra and Ubelaker, 1994). This individual's stature was approximately 144.99 cm as measured from the upper right long bones. The upper and lower dentition were recovered in full and exhibit no pathology, but there was distal rotation of the left maxillary canine (23), non-generalized periodontal disease, and seemingly advanced wear on the first molars and incisors considering the estimated age at death. On the right medial femoral condyle there is a round lesion with well-defined margins measuring 16.5 × 12.3 mm compatible with an osteochondritis dissecans of microtraumatic ethology.

Even though individual 2 is older than individual 1, the skull of the juvenile individual was larger and more robust than that of the adult individual. On the posterior aspect of the skull, individual 1 presents an inca bone as well as wormian bones at the lambdoidal suture, epigenetic characteristics not observed on the skull of individual 2 (adult). However, the second individual presents visible obelic or parietal holes (Hauser and DeStefano, 1989). Post-cranially, individual 2 shows bilateral medio-lateral bending of both femora and ossification of the ligamentum flava on two lower dorsal vertebrae.

Individual 1 presented an abnormal bone thickening for the upper extremities (humeri, ulnae, and radii) as well as at the tibiae. Femora and fibulae present an abnormal mediolateral bending. Individual 2 exhibits bone alterations to the lower limbs which are similar to those observed in individual 1. These skeletal deformities are compatible with residual vitamin D deficiency or rickets (Isidro and Malgosa, 2003; Brickley et al., 2020). Additionally, this individual also has dental calculus and excessive wear of the deciduous teeth (Chimenos et al., 1999).

Rickets is a metabolic disease associated with a lack of vitamin D during human development. Nowadays, the disease has its highest incidence in infants aged between 3 and 18 months (Brickley and Ives, 2008: 91). This hormone is produced in deep layers of the skin when sunlight interacts with the vitamin provider (Lewis, 2007: 119) and its deficiency may be due to a lack of sunlight, lack of food containing this vitamin (e.g. milk and eggs), or genetic factors (Brickley and Ives, 2008: 83). Since this vitamin acts at the intestinal level, facilitating the absorption and homeostatic control of calcium and phosphorus, as well as calcium deposition on the osteoid matrix (Ortner, 2011: 393; Brickley and Ives, 2008: 90), its deficiency affects bone maturation and mineralization, resulting in characteristic bone deformations (Brickley and Ives, 2008). At the clinical level, individuals with rickets also display nervous symptoms and other manifestations such as immunodeficiency and skin lesions (Isidro and Malgosa, 2003). Young individuals that manage to overcome rickets can, in adulthood, exhibit sequels of the disease. Residual rickets can be characterized by exaggerated curvature of bones in the limbs, although normal bone remodelling may produce less obvious deformation (Brickley and Ives, 2008: 91, 112). Other cases of active and residual rickets have been diagnosed in other contemporary sites of Hispania Tarraconensis such as in Barcino (Mays et al., 2018).

## Data Integration and Interpretation

The skeletal remains from the pit at Carena de Can Mitjans correspond to two young individuals, a female between 21 and 24 years old, and a male between 10 and 12 years old. Palaeopathological analysis of the skeletal remains revealed observable bone deformations compatible with rickets (Fig. 8.2). Therefore,

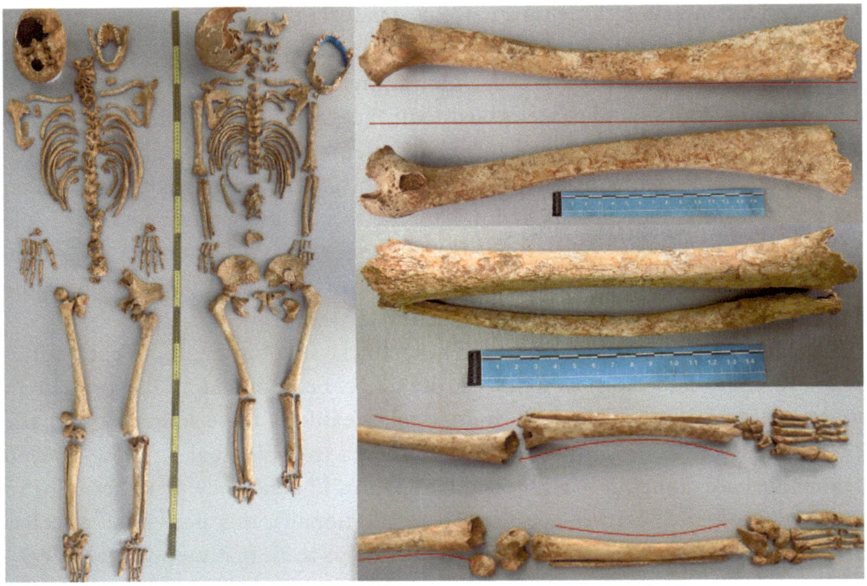

**Fig. 8.2** Left: Layout of the skeletal remains from the two individuals from Can Mitjans in the anthropological laboratory. Right: Notice the diaphyseal torsion and thickening of the long bones of the legs (Photograph: N. Armentano)

they show restricted living conditions and shortcomings. These two individuals died at an early age and may have had a poor or unvaried diet, which consisted of food groups deficient in vitamin D and possibly other vitamins and vital elements necessary for the body to develop and grow successfully. The microtraumatic injury to the medial femoral condyle of individual 2 could suggest repetitive physical activities and imply strong muscular development.

Both individuals were buried in a reused storage structure, and the retention of articulated small joints suggests that it was a primary double burial carried out without care as the position of the skeletal remains suggests the individuals were dumped in the pit. The right to burial was sacred in Roman society, for whom anything deemed 'sacra' meant that it was inviolable and forever (Remesal Rodríguez, 2002). However, given that the normal burial rite at this moment in time was single inhumation in a grave, the Can Mitjans double pit burial was non-normative (González Villaescusa, 2001; Sevilla, 2014).

The combination of osteological analysis with the associated pathology and funerary context suggests that these individuals may have belonged to the lowest and most humble levels of Roman society; although they were buried, they neither enjoyed a proper funerary ritual and nor did this follow the normative procedures or take place in the appropriate spaces for Roman society (Polo-Cerdá and García-Prósper, 2001; 2002).

It is not strange to find burials in pits, wells, or spaces that were not truly funerary in nature in antiquity (García-Prósper, 2001; Vaquerizo, 2014), and it should be borne in mind that these individuals may have been on the fringes of society but were still important and fundamental to it. These are the live stories that may be invisible in the Latin epigraphic records discussed in this book (especially Chapters 2 and 7), but where anthropology can help by providing information about their life, health, and death.

In the Iberian peninsula, more extensive studies are required to contrast and complement knowledge acquired from historical sources (Desiderio, 2007). Currently, palaeopathological studies are scarce in the Iberian peninsula and are based on limited series of data, as well as case studies of specific pathologies (Campillo and Tarrats, 1991; Benet et al., 1992; Vilaseca and Foguet, 1995; García-Prósper et al., 2007; Jordana and Malgosa, 2007; Gómez-González et al., 2011; Menchón, 2012; Puerta López and Garcia Rosselló, 2012; Escala et al., 2013; Armentano and Nociarová, 2015). Despite this situation, analyses of human remains and their funerary contexts suggest that there were differences in certain areas of the Roman Empire as well as at the provincial level in terms of health or disease as well as regarding treatment after death.

### 8.3.2 Two Cases of Traumatism at Can Colomer

Trauma is an acute physical injury or wound affecting the tissues of the body (Roberts and Manchester, 1995). In life, these could include superficial scratches, cuts, and bruises, but these are mostly invisible in skeletal remains. As such, the types of trauma observable in human remains are fractures (including trepanation, amputation, and gunshot wounds), dislocations, and secondary complications of severe soft tissue trauma. Fractures can be classified according to their aetiology, so depending on whether they have been caused by a sudden injury (such as a fall or as a consequence of interpersonal violence), as a result of fatigue or repeated stresses, or are secondary to pathologies that weaken the bone structure (such as osteoporosis or osteomalacia). But they can also be classified according to their patterns of fracture (e.g. transverse, oblique, spiral, comminute, compression, and greenstick fractures).

In osteoarchaeology, one of the most important aspects to consider when analysing trauma is when it happened: did it happen well before death and therefore healed, or does it show signs of healing, or did it happen around the time of death? The process of healing is generally well understood, and some aspects of it are visible in dry bone. Initially, a blood clot forms around the fracture site; this is followed by the laying out of an intercellular substance that becomes calcified and forms a structure of woven bone also known as callus. The repair process then continues, and the woven bone is remodelled to lamellar bone and finally to normal bone.

It is not uncommon to see healed fractures in archaeological human remains; however, on many occasions, they are not well-aligned and often show signs of infection. In the past, unless there had been a reduction and immobilization of the fracture, many fractures healed misaligned, meaning that the bone no longer retains its normal shape. It is this malalignment, along with the buttressing associated with the callus, that usually gives away a healed fracture. Finally, wound infection was (and still is) one of the most dangerous complications of fractures, mainly of those where the skin may have been torn, and the wound is then infected by micro-organisms from outside the body.

Here two cases of trauma at Can Colomer will be discussed, and by looking closely at the lesion, we will endeavour to understand how these injuries happened and how they may have impacted the individual's life.

## Field Anthropology

In 2008, an excavation was undertaken at a Late Roman cemetery (second–eighth century CE) in the Vallès Occidental region, close to the modern city of Terrassa (ancient Egara), known as the Camps de Can Colomer necropolis. The archaeological fieldwork consisted of the excavation and recording of 39 funerary units. The burials mainly consist of tombs covered by two sets of flat roofing tiles (*tegulae*) placed in a pitched arrangement and simple graves. There were also four cases of inhumations in pits, two cases of stone tombs with lime mortar, and an inhumation inside a reused amphora.

The skeletal remains studied belonged to a minimum number of 50 individuals since, although most of the funerary structures contained skeletal remains of only one individual, there were at least 10 funerary units that contained remains of more than one (Fig. 8.3). Those multiple burials could represent reused tombs, or double or triple burials. Interestingly, all these multiple burials were located close to each other in the south-eastern sector, and they were tombs with two rows of *tegulae* propped up against each other. As all the individuals in the multiple simultaneous burials were juvenile or young adult individuals, it seems that age may have been a factor in this burial rite.

## Osteological Analysis and Data Integration

The palaeopathological study of this group records cases of degenerative pathologies (24%), mainly affecting their vertebrae. This was consistent with the findings from the skeletal remains from Tarraco, where the most common location of degenerative changes, for both sexes, was in the lumbar spine, with 20% of individuals to some degree affected, followed by the dorsal and cervical vertebrae. The second joint most affected among the Tarraco skeletons was the knee, affecting 10% of individuals. Similar data come from the necropolis of Eucaliptal (Huelva), with a predominance of spine discarthrosis, and hip and knee osteoarthritis (Baxarias, 2007). If the data are classified according to sex, female Roman

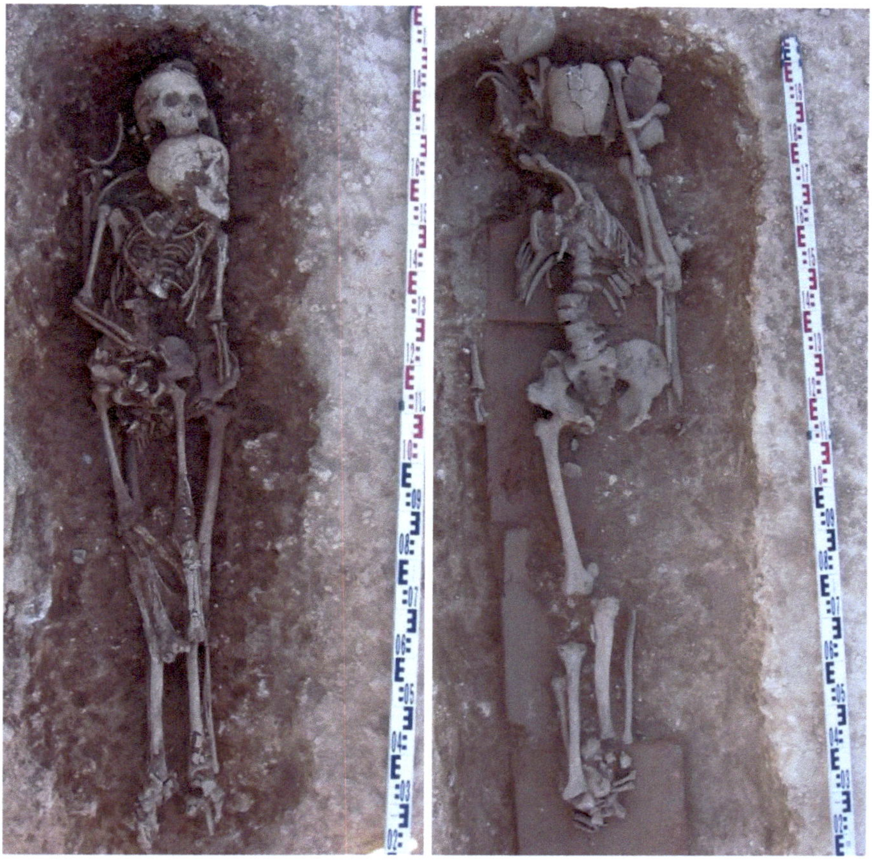

**Fig. 8.3** Examples of burial types in the Camps de Can Colomer necropolis: undisturbed simultaneous double burial in a simple grave (left), and partially disturbed single burial in a grave with two rows of tiles (Photograph: N. Armentano)

individuals in Hispania Tarraconensis had a higher prevalence of gonarthrosis (knee arthrosis) and temporomandibular osteoarthritis. In contrast, male individuals had higher prevalence rates of elbow or wrist osteoarthritis, which could be related to intensive manual effort; the right arm was more affected than the left. Data on the high frequency of talar and ankle osteoarthritis present among 8% of the total population in the Tarraco necropolis can be explained by different factors, such as type of shoes worn, the custom of walking long distances on foot, or the lack of correction for common foot deformations (varus foot, flatfoot, cavus foot etc.). Written sources reveal that the most common foot malformations were known in the Roman world, and they were treated with chalk and special lead boots (Baxarias, 2002).

There are also cases of traumatic lesions (8%) and some cases of infectious diseases. Less frequent are microtraumatic injuries, such as osteochondritis dissecans, periostosis, or enthesopaties. At a dental level, cases of oral pathologies are common in the form of serious periodontal disease. Physiological stress markers, such as linear enamel hypoplasia, are also commonly found.

Funerary unit 25 consisted of a tomb covered by inclined *tegulae* with the remains of an adult individual in supine position, with the arms half-flexed and the hands on the abdomen (Fig. 8.4). The individual was oriented north–south with the head towards the north facing east. The long extremity bones presented a lateral rotation, the right radius was displaced, the hand bones were disarticulated, and the pelvic waist was opened, which suggests that this individual decomposed in a tomb with empty space, without sediments. Apart from the bones of this articulated skeleton, the coccyx and a femur from another individual were identified in the laboratory, which is evidence of the tomb's reuse.

The main burial was of a female individual aged between 35 and 45 years old at the time of death and a stature of 152.8 cm. The long bones show limited

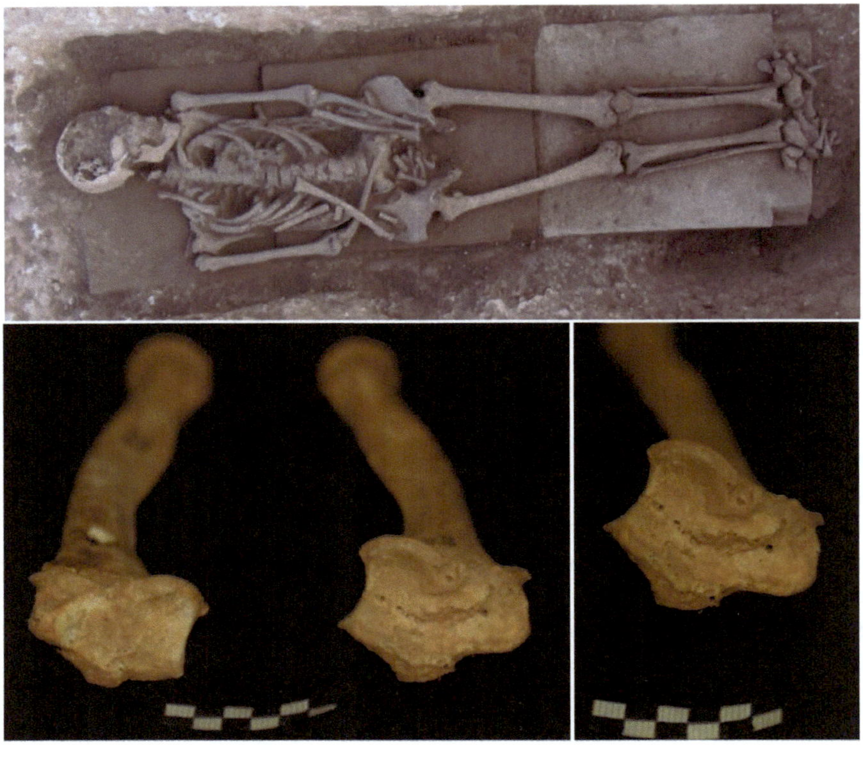

**Fig. 8.4** Funerary unit 25 from Camps de Can Colomer: skeletal remains of a female individual with a well-healed fracture at the distal epiphysis of the radius

bone muscular remodelling. In terms of pathology, the individual exhibits signs of degeneration compatible with degenerative changes affecting the spine, also known as discarthrosis of the dorsal vertebrae, as well as osteoarthritis at the shoulder, hip, and knee joints showing osteophytic changes and eburnation to the articular surfaces. At a dental level, the individual displays significant destruction in the lower part of the right maxilla due to a fistula process. The dental wear was very advanced, and in some cases only the root remained of the tooth as well as generalized alveolar resorption measuring more than 3 mm.

There were also major alterations to the bones of the left hand, with eburnation of the trapezius and scaphoid, and to the right one, with bone exostosis in the first metacarpal and the first proximal and distal phalanges. The distal epiphysis of the left radius presents an alteration compatible with a consolidated fracture, and the osteoarthritis observed in the left hand could be secondary to this injury. This is because this distal articular facet was uneven and would have resulted in an abnormal contact between this and the lunate and scaphoid bones.

These fractures of the distal epiphysis of the radius or Colles fractures are frequent in human archaeological remains and are associated with a fall with outstretched arms that are likely to have been rotated sidewards. Therefore, it would lead to a rear displacement of the radius. In the modern world, there is a predominance of Colles fractures in post-menopausal women, between the ages of 50 and 60, associated with bone loss. However, these kinds of fractures can occur to any individual as a result of an accident (Brickley and Ives, 2008: 161–2).

The second case that will be discussed is that of the individuals from funerary unit 26, which comprised a tomb covered by two rows of inclined *tegulae* with remains of a young adult male individual in supine position, with semi-flexed arms and hands on the abdomen (Fig. 8.5). The individual was oriented north–south, with the head towards the north and facing westwards. An external rotation of femora and tibiae was recorded, as well as the disarticulation of some skeletal elements, suggesting this individual also decomposed in an empty tomb.

The skeletal remains studied belong to an individual of 18–20 years old at the time of death. There are no signs of epiphyseal fusion; however, the epiphyseal line is clearly visible on the humeral and femoral heads, femoral condyles, tibial plateau, and ischial tuberosity. Despite not having fully finished growing, this individual had an estimated stature of 156.3 cm as calculated from the radius. The skull fragments preserved appear to belong to a gracile skull with small mastoid processes. The preserved molars show advanced dental wear considering the individual's young age. With regards to the individual's health, there is bilateral cribra femoralis, and the right third metatarsal shows thickening compatible with a consolidated fracture. In this case, there is a correct reduction of the fracture and lack of inflammatory signs or related infectious processes. This type of traumatic injury affecting the foot bones may be related to walking on irregular or difficult surfaces, or even not using suitable shoes.

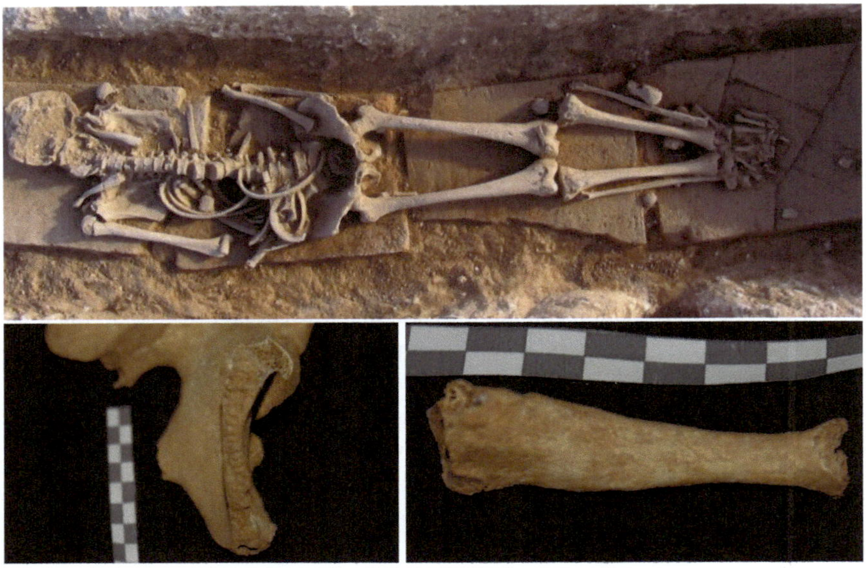

**Fig. 8.5** Funerary unit 26 from Camps de Can Colomer: skeletal remains of a young adult male individual with a well-healed fracture in the right third metatarsal

## 8.4 Diseases and Pandemics

Causes of death in antiquity were diverse and are sometimes difficult to establish on the basis of taphonomic remains present in the necropoleis. Apart from violent deaths, with evidence of irreversible fractures, most of the deceased do not provide details on the cause of death. There is general agreement that most deaths were produced by stomach and intestinal problems because most deaths were recorded in late August and early September. Early Christian data from Alexandria and Rome (period 250–550 CE) reveal deaths at the end of summer and in early autumn, coinciding with the first torrential rains (Harper, 2019: 108). These data coincide with a predominance of seasonal diseases produced by food poisoning and water contamination (acute diarrhoea—*shigellosis*, which includes cholera—and typhus—*salmonelosis*).

Epidemics were not unknown in the ancient world, and they were probably responsible, at least in part, for the high mortality among past populations (Fig. 8.6). Infections are related to environmental conditions and create havoc when there is a confluence of diverse circumstances, such as population movements, poverty, wars, famines, etc., since they contribute decisively to their evolution. At a skeletal level, these infectious diseases can hardly be detected since they are usually resolved quickly, whether the individual recovers or not, and thus do not leave any trace in bone tissue (Polo-Cerdá and García-Prósper, 2011; Nociarová and Armentano, 2013). It is in these cases where molecular analysis may help to correctly detect the pathogen causing the disease. The population of Hispania Citerior/Tarraconensis, without antibiotics, was probably exposed to the thousands of millions of microscopic bacteria that normally live on the skin, in the digestive system, mouth, and throat that may have caused a higher mortality among the most vulnerable sections of the population. The most frequent infections detected in Roman human remains are dental. Approximately 10% of the population endured or had suffered an infectious process associated with carious lesions and periodontitis, with numerous abscesses being recorded (Baxarias, 2002).

The dissemination of many of those diseases was favoured by malnutrition in certain regions and particular social groups. Most ancient populations concatenated infectious diseases due to the lack of food and malnutrition, which was sometimes combined with bad hygienic conditions, mainly in urban centres (e.g. cholera) (Menéndez Bueyes, 2013: 137).

One of the diseases that spread from the fifth century BCE around the Mediterranean was malaria (*falciparum malaria*—whose name comes from 'bad air') and which spreads from mosquitoes present in marshes (Sallares, 2002; Sallares et al., 2004). It was documented in central and southern Italy in Roman times (texts by Celsus, *De Re Medica* 8.3.3) in wetlands, but it may also have been common in cities in Hispania Tarraconensis close to marshes or rivers such as Barcino, Caesaraugusta, or Valentia. The only alternative to avoid spreading malaria was draining wetlands or selecting higher zones with good winds as residences (as Liv. 5.54.4 suggests). Malaria generates genetic mutations (CD39) in populations that suffered it; therefore, it can be detected from DNA analysis of the bones. It seems that the Roman expansion led to a spread of malaria to northern Africa and Hispania (Sallares, 2002). However, neither the ancient sources nor DNA analyses are enough to provide the real extent and its distribution in the province under study.

Other diseases present among the populations of the peninsula included tuberculosis and leprosy, as well as venereal diseases. Regarding tuberculosis, at least five cases are documented in Roman Spain (Menéndez Bueyes, 2016: 230). The *M.Bovis* variant seems to have spread through milk consumption or milking, affecting those regions of the province where stock-breeding was most frequent, such as the north-west and the Pyrenees in particular. Leprosy—the Hansen bacillus—was another contagious disease that appears at early age and in adolescence because of problems of hygiene. In Hispania Tarraconensis, there is evidence for leprosy at Pamplona, Gomacín, and Valencia. The disease has been recorded in Europe since 250–200 BCE and can be identified at the level of bones by the traces that it leaves on faces. Finally, another common disease, in this case of venereal transmission, was syphilis, which arrived from Africa and reached Southern Europe in the third millennium BCE, which also leaves traces in bones. The origin of some of those diseases lay in the combination of the population's unequal access to health resources and poor conditions of hygiene, which favoured the spread of contagious pathologies (Menéndez Bueyes, 2016).

Archaeologically, dental health provides us with data about social differences regarding health. Most of our information about diseases in antiquity comes from the medical literature documented in the middle of the second century CE from the works of doctors such as Galenus, who described the health situation in the central and eastern Mediterranean in detail. In the Iberian peninsula, only 26 doctors are recorded from the first-century CE epigraphy. Most of them seem to have been freedmen or slaves with Greek names. Incidentally, among the most prestigious doctors in Hispania was a Greek physician called Antonius Musa, who was responsible for the health of Augustus while he was in Tarraco in the year 23 BCE, and Tiberius Claudius Apolicenius, a freedman who also practised in Tarraco.

Apart from common diseases, the classical sources mention a series of pandemics that struck the Roman Empire as a whole in particular periods of its history (Figure 8.6). In recent years, those historical references from ancient sources have been placed alongside the archaeological data (Harper, 2019). The first great

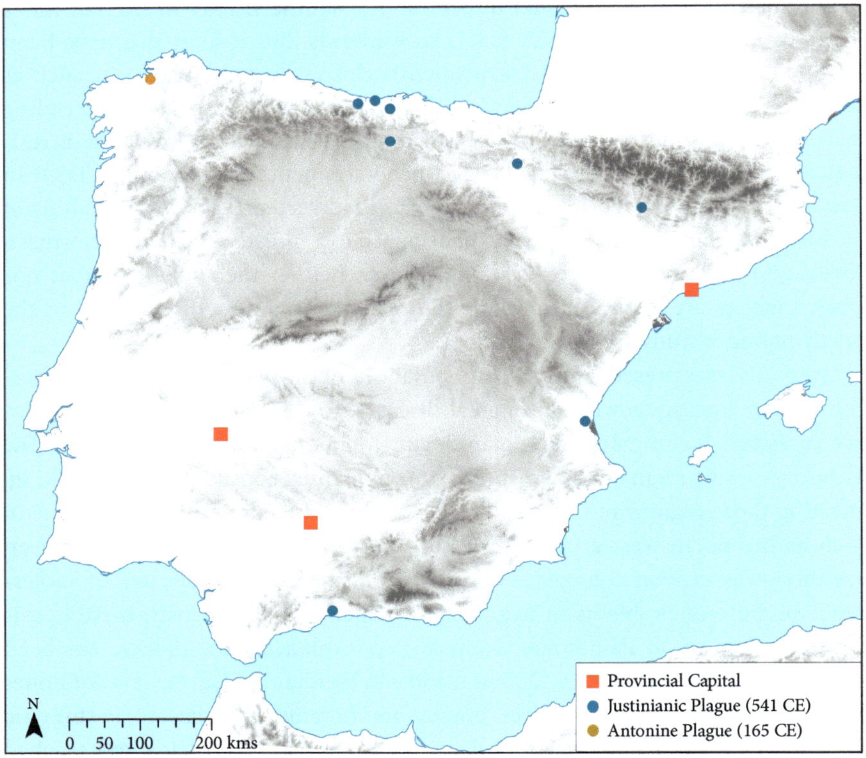


**Fig. 8.6** Map with evidence for epidemics in the Iberian peninsula (after McCormick, 2015: fig. 1; Harper, 2019: fig. 10)

epidemic occurred in the Antonine period during Lucius Verus' campaign in Seleucia against Parthia, which, as Ammianus Marcellinus (*Res Gest.* 23.6.24) said 'polluted everything with contagion and death, from the frontiers of Persia all the way to the Rhine and to Gaul'. This pandemic described by Galenus himself, meant the death of 2% of the Roman population in the Empire as a whole, and in some places such as Aquileia it decimated 15–20% of the army stationed there. From the description of its features, the disease seems to have been *Variola major* (smallpox), of which there were different waves in Egypt (178–9 CE), Noricum (181–3 CE), and Rome itself (191 CE) (Harper, 2019: 130–50). Despite the fact that the pandemic may have affected Hispania Tarraconensis, there is no direct evidence, except an inscription from Brigantium (La Coruña), which has been tentatively associated with it (Harper, 2019: map 10).

The next great pandemic appeared in the time of Cyprian, when he was bishop of Carthage (*c.* 249 CE). It was a plague that lasted 20 years, until 270 CE, and as Orosius (*Hist. Adv. Pag.* 7.21.5–6) said it affected most large cities in the Empire: 'Hardly a Roman province, city, or house escaped being smitten and desolated by that widespread pestilence'. For some authors, the disease can be identified as cholera or typhus (Fuentes, 1992) or even smallpox, but descriptions were contradictory. Another alternative was influenza, since it was a winter disease, which brought about the death of half the population. In the fifth century CE, in the year 410 CE, Hydatius, bishop of Aquae Flaviae (Chaves) (*Chron.* 17.48) talked about a plague in his diocese in Hispania Tarraconensis (Fuentes, 1992), which coincided with a climate of conflict and the invasion of the Suevi and Alans (see Chapter 6).

The only well-recorded great pandemic is the first bubonic plague, when rats spread it in Justinian's reign in 579 CE (Kulikowski, 2006). Victor of Tunnuna (*Chronicon* 44) explains that the bubonic plague affected the whole of Hispania, and he himself also died because of it. Archaeologically, a series of collective tombs datable to this period have been identified and seem to reflect deaths caused by the pest. For instance, in Tarraconensis, there are 21 mid-sixth-century tombs in the city of Valentia or the San Antón necropolis at Cartagena, and perhaps, the contemporary tombs of Contrebia Leukade (McCormick, 2015; 2016). The plague spread from Hispania reaching other provinces such as Gaul, as Gregory of Tours (*Hist. Franc.* 9.22) explains, where in 584 CE traders from Hispania brought the plague to the city of Marseille.

Outbreaks of bubonic plague continued during the period of the Visigoth kingdom, and the Mozarabic chronicle points out that they affected Egica's reign (687–702 CE). An Arab source (*Akhbar Majmu'a*) reveals that the plague reduced the population of Hispania by half between 707 and 709 CE. In this period collective burials can be dated, for instance, the ones in Cantabrian caves, such as Las Penas, Riocueva or La Garma; la Cueva Foradada (Huesca) or Cueva Larga (Palencia).

## 8.5 DNA and Genetic Studies

The Iberian peninsula, between Europe and Africa, has always been a place of contact between people and cultures. As regards ancient times, who took part in these contacts and how and to what extent they participated in them is a difficult question to clarify. Although different categories of evidence provide information, this is frequently inconclusive. Also, it is often complicated to separate the biological and cultural influences, but genetic studies of ancient material can shed some light on this still poorly known field. The increase in the amount of ancient DNA (aDNA) that can be recovered from remains and the improvements in its quality have led to enormous advances in aDNA methodologies and studies over the last 10 years. These improvements allow us to begin to appreciate migratory processes in the past from a new perspective. The possibility of obtaining thousands of informative DNA positions and even complete genomes provides population data, family relationships, or information about individuals (phenotype, ancestry, pathology), in order to understand the past and its people.

In general, the main palaeogenetic studies have focused on very ancient times, substantial population movements, broad sweeps of history, and large tracts of land. However, the Iberian peninsula, despite being an important crucible of cultures, was little studied until recently. Like other Mediterranean regions, the history of the Iberian peninsula was strongly marked by the Romans and their influence can be seen elsewhere: language, architecture, law, etc. But, what about the people themselves?

The second half of the chapter aims to compile the few genetic evidences available so far that can contribute to answer the question of whether culture or genetics was the key to the transformations that we see in Hispania from the Iron Age down to the Late Roman period, whether admixture or replacement occurred, and if that is the case, where it took place. The answer can be sought in the knowledge that we have derived from the few individual and population genetic studies carried out to date. We will also point out the main milestones that we need to surpass in order to acquire a general picture of Hispania.

### 8.5.1 Palaeogenetics and Palaeogenomics

Knowledge of the human past can be obtained from many different sources and different fields of research. Science is constantly advancing, and all disciplines, including archaeology and anthropology, are adapting to the new methodologies that science continues to offer. One of the best tools to interpret ancient populations is palaeogenetics, because it is independent from the observer and offers objective information. In recent years, we have witnessed an enormous development of genetic studies carried out on the basis of ancient human remains although mainly focusing on the early stages of European and American history (e.g. Fu et al., 2016; Moreno-Mayar et al., 2018).

The term 'palaeogenetics' was introduced in 1963 (Pauling and Zuckerkand, 1963), but the application of the knowledge arising from this field to human remains began in 1985 when Svante Pääbo published the retrieval of DNA from an ancient Egyptian mummy (Pääbo, 1985). This was the first step that the scientific community needed to initiate an enormous effort to fill a new field: palaeogenetics and specifically human palaeogenetics. During those first years, some researchers were able to obtain DNA from mummies, although they were unable to do more than merely retrieve it. No information about the individuals analysed was established in this period.

The second milestone was the revolution triggered by Polymerase Chain Reaction (PCR) (Mullis et al., 1986). This method was essential to analyse the scarce and fragmented DNA obtained from organic material (Pääbo and Wilson, 1988; Pääbo et al., 1988), bones, and teeth (Hagelberg et al., 1989; Horai et al., 1989). PCR is a quick and easy way to create an unlimited number of copies of DNA from a single or few original templates. However, not only that; PCR enables millions of copies to be created in just a few hours. This amount of DNA can be reliably used in a variety of tests to detect the presence of a specific variant of a gene, or it can be compared among individuals, for example, to detect differences so as to identify them, or to identify the presence of other organisms. The introduction of PCR inaugurated a period of several years in which the DNA obtained started to provide information about the people from whom it was obtained and, therefore, we were able to begin to appreciate an individual's genetic data and to improve our understanding of past populations and their structure.

In those initial years, when the methodologies for retrieving and amplifying DNA from ancient remains were not sufficiently specific for critical samples, analysis of mitochondrial DNA (mtDNA) was an excellent option. MtDNA is found in every cell of our body outside the nucleus, in the organelles called mitochondria, which are the main source of chemical energy for cells. For the study of ancient remains, this type of DNA has the advantage that in each cell there are hundreds of mitochondria, each one with a significant number of mitochondrial DNA molecules, all of them equal. Therefore, in a single cell there are thousands of copies of mtDNA, between 1,000 and 10,000 copies depending on the cell type (Bodenhagen and Clayton, 1974). Moreover, despite its relatively small size (16,569 base pairs (bp) in humans), this genome accumulated a great amount of variation during human evolution and dispersion. In contrast, nuclear DNA (nDNA) is much larger and is organized into different chromosomes, namely 23 pairs. In each cell, there are only two copies of nuclear genetic information, one from the father and the other from the mother. The high number of copies of mtDNA is the main feature that makes it easier to retrieve, analyse, and compare than nDNA. Other characteristics such as maternal inheritance, the absence of recombination, and the high mutation rate (Ramakrishnan and Hadly, 2009) also make mtDNA particularly amenable to ancient genetic analysis. For these reasons, the genetic information available from ancient skeletal remains analysed in that period came mainly from mtDNA (e.g. Gill et al., 1994; Montiel et al., 2001; Lalueza-Fox et al., 2005; Nesheva, 2014), and specifically from its non-coding region, which contains high variability zones. Moreover, some fragments of specific nuclear genes or repetitive regions were also studied. Among them, Y-chromosome markers were the focus of interest as regards the sex diagnosis of remains (e.g. Caramelli et al., 2007), and to follow male lineages (Kivisild, 2017). In addition, fragments of genes related to morphological characteristics, human pathologies, or pathogens (e.g. Montiel et al., 2001; Malgosa et al., 2005; Anastasiou and Mitchell, 2013) were tested.

The third milestone was the birth of palaeogenomics (Slatkin and Racimo, 2016). Previously, palaeogenetics using PCR-based approaches could only study relatively short, isolated DNA fragments from a limited number of genes and samples that were not excessively old, at the most 100,000 years old (Orlando et al., 2006). However, the improvement of new amplification methodologies, sequencing, and the application of bioinformatics enabled new information to be produced from more and smaller DNA fragments, making it possible to analyse more genes and more ancient remains. Thus, palaeogenomics, in contrast with palaeogenetics, studies all the genes and fragments of DNA that can be recovered from an organism. Human palaeogenomics emerged from studies on Neanderthals (Green et al., 2006; Noonan et al., 2006), but it is now applied to all periods of our history, and to all kinds of organisms (Serrano et al., 2021). It is currently driving molecular studies on ancient remains. It has been transformed from achieving the partial genome of one individual to obtaining hundreds or thousands of genomes from ancient humans (e.g. Skoglund and Mathieson, 2018; Brunson and Reich, 2019). The development of palaeogenomics has been characterized by the improvement of DNA extraction from ancient samples and from sediments, but its flowering benefits from the advances in Next Generation Sequencing (NGS) in particular. Currently, NGS of double strand and single strand DNA libraries are used as the basis of palaeogenomic studies; however, in many cases, whole genome enrichment is performed before sequencing.

Nevertheless, as can be seen, palaeogenetics and palaeogenomics are together a field of knowledge that has only developed very recently (Montiel et al., 2007; Hagelberg et al., 2015; Simón and Malgosa, 2016). In its short life, this new discipline has displayed all the stages of scientific growth: the beginning of a new technology that triggers a disproportionate euphoria that led to amazing, but false results; followed by a stage of demotivation and disillusionment because of the problems and the reality check; and finally, the current stage of maturity and stability in this scientific area (Chrzanová Pečnerová, 2017). Now it is a flourishing science that surprises us every day with new data.

### 8.5.2 Genetic Data from the Iberian Peninsula

In the first 20 years of Spanish palaeogenetics, few Iberian individuals and populations have been studied. Certainly, DNA studies are time consuming and very demanding, because of the high cost of human and financial resources (Shapiro and Hofreiter, 2014). This is due both to the characteristics of the samples (damage and scarcity of endogenous DNA, and the high probability of contamination with recent DNA) and to the processes and laboratory requirements associated with authentication (high sterility, replication, bioinformatics requirements, etc.). Conversely, they have not been a priority in the allocation of funds for Spanish palaeogenetic research in recent years, and this has been a major challenge in order to achieve a corpus of data on ancient human populations. Despite this, knowledge of the past is important for the future in many ways (e.g. Zeberg and Pääbo, 2021) and aDNA in Spain has generated new important data.

Nonetheless, the Iberian peninsula is present in the most important palaeogenomic works about European and Eurasian prehistory (e.g. Olalde et al., 2018; 2019; Kocher et al., 2021). Geographical location and climate are fundamental factors that enabled ancient populations to develop and flourish in accordance with the natural resources available during cooler times, or as a bridge between continents and societies. That is the reason why the Iberian peninsula has produced the most ancient genetically characterized hominin remains, those from Atapuerca (Meyer et al., 2014).

At present, the spectrum of DNA studies of prehistoric hominins in the Iberian peninsula ranges from the Palaeolithic (e.g. Hervella et al., 2012; Olalde et al., 2014), via the Neolithic from Barcelona (e.g. Olalde et al., 2015) to Lugo (e.g. González-Fortes et al., 2019), from the north (e.g. Hervella et al., 2012; Haak et al., 2015) to the south (e.g. Fregel et al., 2018), to the present. However, samples are too few to reflect the variability of populations and periods. To date, the widest study of ancient Iberian peninsula populations is that of Olalde et al. (2019), which analyses the genetic evolution of the Iberian peninsula from Palaeolithic times onwards including interesting data for the study of our province. More recently, 140 new genomes (18 with low SNP coverage that limit population analysis) were reported focused mainly in Bronze Age Argar society from the south-east of the Iberian peninsula (Villalba-Mouco et al., 2021; 2022).

## 8.6 The Challenges of aDNA

The mains challenges of aDNA studies come from the preservation of the DNA molecule, which is directly linked to skeletal tissue preservation. All organic material begins to decay at the very moment of death. When hypoxia is established in the body, autolysis begins. Subsequently, the decomposition caused by other organisms, mainly endogenous, as well as exogenous bacteria and insects, progresses. When it comes to skeletonization, decomposition is further aggravated by the environmental conditions of burial, temperature, pH, and the chemical composition of the soil (Gill-King, 1996; Janaway et al., 2009).

Time plays against DNA preservation. The older the remains are, the easier it will be for them to be in poor condition, and the harder it will be to extract DNA from them. But such difficulties are not only caused by the passage of time, but also by the place where the remains lie. Burials often took place in places near water, in damp caves, in warm places, in clandestine mass graves, or were undertaken without care, or the remains were even abandoned on the surface. All these situations allow the intervention of different organisms (scavengers, plants, insects, and bacteria), alongside physical and chemical activity, leading to poor conservation of the remains themselves. Exposure to these issues causes increased hydrolytic attacks, endogenous endonuclease activity, and oxidative activity via free radicals, which are directly responsible for DNA breakdown. Fragmentation and damage are the result. Consequently, cold, dry, and abiotic environments constitute the best ecosystems for DNA preservation.

Linked to the poor conservation of skeletal remains is the high possibility of contamination with current DNA. Traces of DNA from our hair, epithelial cells, sweat, and aerosol drops from nasal, bronchial, or saliva secretion have greater possibilities of being amplified and analysed than the DNA recovered from the skeletal remains—what palaeogeneticists call endogenous DNA. So, in inadequate conditions of analysis, modern DNA is much more likely to be amplified than ancient DNA, and therefore to give us erroneous data.

Therefore, the main characteristics of DNA from ancient contexts are fragmentation, damage, and contamination. Together, these factors prevent the accurate extraction and analysis of ancient DNA.

Regarding the provenance of the source of DNA, different types of tissues have been used to obtain DNA, both organic and inorganic. Today it is possible to obtain DNA from almost every material and site: bone, teeth, keratinous tissues such as hair and nails (Gilbert et al., 2004; 2008), even from soils (Slon et al., 2017; Zhang et al., 2020). The question is: how well preserved is this DNA? Traditionally, teeth have been ranked first among the tissues used as a source of DNA in palaeogenetic studies. However, the petrous part of the temporal bone has become very prominent recently, as it contains one of the areas with the hardest and densest bone tissue in the human skeleton (Pinhasi et al., 2015). For this reason, the petrous bone retains more and better quality DNA. In both the petrous bone and the teeth, this hardness and resistance defend them from most environmental effects such as desiccation and decomposition (Patidar et al., 2010) and therefore largely protect them from environmental and physical conditions that accelerate DNA decomposition (Alvarez García et al., 1996).

The main problem is being able to achieve enough samples derived from archaeological sites of interest (well dated, archaeologically or historically well documented, and/or representative of the population or geographical space), and which are sufficiently well preserved to provide DNA of quality. Palaeogenetics and palaeogenomics have a lot of work ahead.

## 8.7 Roman Genetic Studies in Spain

There are very few genetically studied individuals in Hispania (Fig. 8.7), and they come from a broader study that includes individuals from other periods (Palomo-Díez et al., 2019). To be more precise, seven Roman individuals from the site of Segobriga (Cuenca, central-eastern Spain) dating from the Late Roman period (fifth century CE) were analysed; however, this study also included individuals until the end of the Muslim period. Genetic characterization was based on the analysis of mtDNA hypervariable regions I and II by amplifying overlapping fragments. Only samples from two individuals were well amplified, and both correspond to mtDNA haplogroup H, (amplification length: 16105–16399); for the other five individuals, shorter fragments were recovered, and the haplogroup cannot be reliably assigned. Thus, so far, DNA analysis based on PCR methods

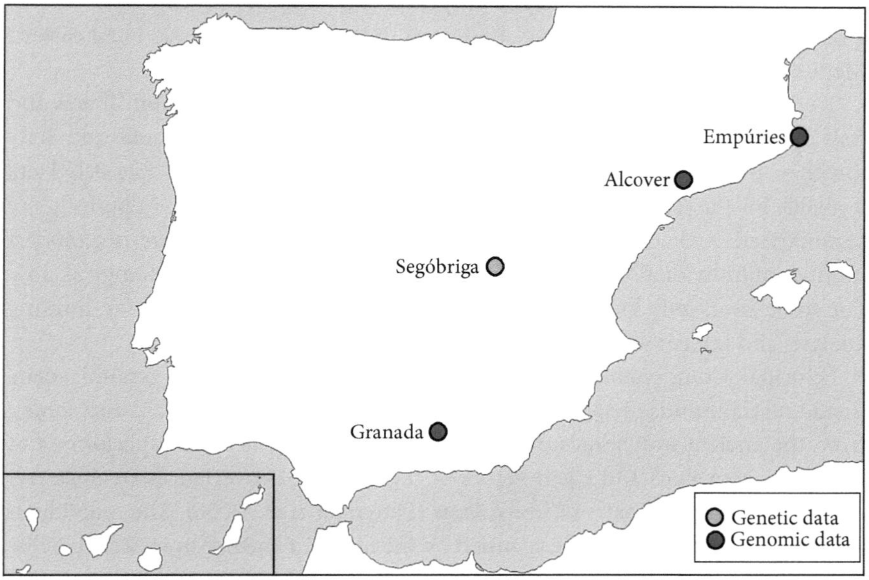


**Fig. 8.7** Spanish locations of archaeological sites with Roman genetic and genomic data

has, in general, been of lower quality and has not enabled an accurate genetic profile of Roman individuals from the Iberian peninsula to be obtained.

Some further information has recently been obtained from genomic studies (Olalde et al., 2019). However, to date, characterization of Roman individuals from the Iberian peninsula at the genomic level is also very scarce, including only 13 individuals from the north-east of the peninsula and four from the south-east. Specifically, these 17 Roman individuals come from three archaeological sites: Empúries (L'Escala, Girona; 43–500 CE), Mas Gassol (Alcover, Tarragona; 200–500 CE), and Plaza Einstein (Granada; 200–400 CE) in the east and south of the Iberian peninsula. These individuals were characterized by thousands of SNPs of the entire genome.

Olalde et al. (2019) analysed the ancient genomic variation of Iberians from the Mesolithic until historical times, revealing that the Roman presence in the peninsula had a substantial genetic impact. Although some Roman individuals cluster with Iron Age individuals from the Iberian peninsula, others fall outside this group and lie closer to eastern Mediterranean populations (see principal component analysis in Olalde et al., 2019).

As far as other European regions are concerned, a detailed study using genomes from people buried since the Mesolithic until the medieval period at 29 archaeological sites in and around the city of Rome (Italy) was recently published (Antonio et al., 2019). The people of ancient Rome from the city's earliest stages and from after the decline of the Western Empire in the fourth century CE genetically resembled other Western Europeans. But during the imperial period, greater diversity can be observed, and most of the residents sampled had eastern Mediterranean or Middle Eastern ancestry.

To date, there are no analyses combining Roman individuals from Iberia and Italy. In this context, we analyse data from the Iberian peninsula and Italy together, including ancient samples and markers displayed in Table 8.1. Data available for the Roman period, but also for previous and subsequent periods, are summarized. As can be observed (Table 8.1), for each period there is a modest number of individuals analysed, and they come from several archaeological sites. For some sites, only low resolution mtDNA results are available so far, limiting analysis and interpretations.

Principal Component Analysis (PCA) was performed using genomic data, including thousands of SNPs from nuclear genomes, specifically from autosomes, from the ancient individuals detailed in Table 8.1. PCA is usually performed to find the eigenvalues and eigenvectors of the matrix of covariances of allele frequencies between all pairs of individuals (Patterson et al., 2006). The individuals are often plotted on the plane spanned by the first two eigenvectors. Relative distances in this space indicate their overall similarity. PCA is convenient, because it is both easy to use and provides a very visual result (Slatkin, 2016). Ancient individuals were projected onto the components computed on present-day Eurasian

**Table 8.1** Populations and individuals included in Principal Component Analysis based on genomic data and in correspondence analysis of mtDNA and Y-Chr haplogroups

| Pop. | Pop. code | No. indiv. Gen. Data | No. indiv. mtDNA | No. indiv. Y-Chr | Sites | Reference |
|---|---|---|---|---|---|---|
| Iberian peninsula Bronze Age | IP_BronzeA | 1 | 1 | 0 | El Portalon Cave, Sierra de Atapuerca | Günther et al., 2015 |
| | | 4 | 4 | 3 | Monte do Gato de Cima 3, Brinches, Beja Monte do Vale do Ouro 2, Ferreira do. Alentejo, Beja Torre Velha 3, Serpa, Beja | Martiniano et al., 2017 |
| | | 53 | 53 | 30 | Bray Cave, Gibraltar Cabezo Redondo, Villena, Alacant/Alicante, Valencian Community Can Roqueta II, Sabadell, Barcelona, Catalonia Casas Velhas, Melides, Setúbal Castillejo del Bonete, Terrinches, Ciudad Real, Castilla-La Mancha Cerro de la Virgen, Orce, Granada, Andalusia Cova del Gegant, Sitges, Barcelona, Catalonia Coveta del Frare, La Font de la Figuera, València/Valencia, Valencian Community El Cerro, La Horra, Burgos, Castilla y León El Sotillo, Laguardia, Araba/Álava, Basque Country Fuente la Mora, Valladolid, Castilla y León Galls Carboners, Mont-ral, Tarragona, Catalonia Gruta do Medronhal, Arrifana, Coimbra Humanejos, Parla, Community of Madrid La Requejada, San Román de Hornija, Valladolid, Castilla y León Lloma de Betxí, Paterna, València/Valencia, Valencian Community Loma del Puerco, Chiclana de la Frontera, Cádiz, Andalusia Monte da Cabida 3, São Manços, Évora Ondarre, Aralar, Gipuzkoa, Basque Country Tordillos, Aldeaseca de la Frontera, Salamanca, Castilla y León Túmulo Mortorum, Cabanes, Castelló/Castellón, Valencian Community Valdescusa, Hervías, La Rioja Virgazal, Tablada de Rudrón, Burgos, Castilla y León | Olalde et al., 2019 |
| | | 2 | 2 | 2 | Cueva de los Lagos, Aguilar de Alhama, La Rioja Pirulejo, Priego de Córdoba, Córdoba, Andalusia | Valdiosera et al., 2018 |
| | | 0 | 8* | 0 | Montanisell Cave | Simón et al., 2011 |
| | | 0 | 1* | 0 | Maçanet cave, Castellón, Valencian Community | Gamba et al., 2008 |

*Continued*

Table 8.1 *Continued*

| Pop. | Pop. code | No. indiv. Gen. Data | No. indiv. mtDNA | No. indiv. Y-Chr | Sites | Reference |
|---|---|---|---|---|---|---|
| Iberian peninsula Iron Age | IP_IronA | 17 | 17 | 11 | Can Roqueta II, Sabadell, Barcelona, Catalonia Can Roqueta-Can Revella, Sabadell, Barcelona, Catalonia Els Estrets de la Rata, Vilafamés, Castelló/Castellón, Valencian Community Font de la Canya, Avinyonet del Penedés, Barcelona, Catalonia Hort d'en Grimau, Castellví de la Marca, Barcelona, Catalonia Mas d'en Boixos-1, Pacs del Penedès, Barcelona, Catalonia Puig de la Misericordia, Vinaròs, Castelló/Castellón, Valencian Community Puig de Sant Andreu, Ullastret, Girona, Catalonia Turó de Ca n'Oliver, Cerdanyola, Barcelona, Catalonia | Olalde et al., 2019 |
| | | 0 | 10* | 0 | Castellet de Bernabé, Líria, Valencian Community Los Villares, Castellón, Valencian Community Puig de la Nau, Castellón, Valencian Community Torreló Bonerot, Castellón, Valencian Community Tossal de Sant Miquel, Líria, Valencian Community | Gamba et al., 2008 |
| | | 0 | 2* | 0 | Besora, Sta. Maria de Besora, Catalonia | Unpublished data from A. Malgosa and C. Santos Group |
| | | 0 | 11* | 0 | Camp de les Lloses, Tona, Catalonia | Unpublished data from A. Malgosa and C. Santos Group |
| | | 0 | 17* | 0 | Puig de Sant Andreu, Ullastret, Catalonia Illa d'en Reixac, Ullastret, Catalonia Mas Castellar, Pontós, Catalonia | Sampietro et al., 2005 |
| South-west Iberia Tartessian | IP_IronA_Tartessian_SW | 4 | 4 | 1 | La Angorrilla, Alcalá del Río, Sevilla, Andalusia | Olalde et al., 2019 |
| North-east Iberian peninsula Greeks | IPNE_Greek_ClasA | 10 | 10 | 6 | Empúries, Girona, Catalonia | Olalde et al., 2019 |

| | | | | | | |
|---|---|---|---|---|---|---|
| North-east Iberian peninsula Hellenistic | IPNE_Hellen_ClasA | 5 | 5 | 3 | Empúries, Girona, Catalonia | Olalde et al., 2019 |
| North-east Iberian peninsula | IPNE_Roman_ClasA | 13 | 13 | 6 | Empúries, Girona, Catalonia Mas Gassol, Alcover, Tarragona, Catalonia | Olalde et al., 2019 |
| Romans | | 0 | 1* | 0 | Mas d'Arago, Castellón, Valencian Community | |
| South-east Iberian peninsula Romans | IPSE_Roman_ClasA | 4 | 4 | 3 | Plaza Einstein, Granada, Andalusia | Olalde et al., 2019 |
| | | 1 | 1 | 0 | Segobriga, Saelices, Castilla-La Mancha | Palomo-Díez et al., 2019* |
| Iberian peninsula Visigoth and Carolingian | IP_Visi_Car | 19 | 19 | 10 | Pla de l'Horta, Sarrià de Ter, Girona, Catalonia L'Esquerda, Roda de Ter, Barcelona, Catalonia | Olalde et al., 2019 |
| | | 0 | 63* | 0 | Aldaieta (Basque country) | Alzualde et al., 2006 |
| Italy Copper and Bronze age | It_Copper_BronzeA | - | 8 | 3 | Martinsicuro Su Crocefissu | Antonio et al., 2019 |
| Italy Imperial period | It_Imperial | 10 | 10 | 8 | Civitanova Marche Mazzano Romano Monterotondo | Antonio et al., 2019 |
| Italy Imperial Rome | It_ImpRome | 37 | 37 | 15 | ANAS (Azienda Nazionale Autonoma delle Strada), Centocelle Isola Sacra Palestrina, Antina Via Paisiello (Necropoli Salaria), Viale Rossini (Necropoli Salaria) | Antonio et al., 2019 |
| Italy Iron Age | It_IronA | 10 | 10 | 7 | Ardea Boville Ernica Castel di Decima Veio Grotta Gramiccia Civitavecchia Palestrina Colombella Palestrina Selciata | Antonio et al., 2019 |
| Italy late antiquity | It_LateAnt | 20 | 20 | 12 | Celio Crypta Balbi Marcellino & Pietro San Ercolano | Antonio et al., 2019 |
| Italy late antiquity and early medieval | It_LateAnt_Emediev | 5 | 5 | 5 | Mausoleo di Augusto | Antonio et al., 2019 |
| Greece Bronze Age | Gre_BronzeA | 15 | 15 | 4 | Agia Kyriaki. Salamis Armenoi. Crete Crete. Lassithi Lassithi. Crete Peloponnese. Galatas Apatheia Phaestos. South-western Crete Pylos Tryfilia. Peloponnese | Lazaridis et al., 2017 |

* Low resolution data based only on HVRI and HVRII of mtDNA.

and North African individuals. Present-day individual data compiled from published papers were downloaded from David Reich's laboratory repository (reich.hms.harvard.edu). PCA (Fig. 8.8) shows that only a few Roman individuals from Iberia cluster with Roman individuals from Italy. Several individuals cluster with Iron Age individuals from Iberia and Italy. The remaining Iberian Roman individuals were set apart from Roman individuals from Italy, Iberian individuals of different dates, and Iron Age Italians.

Focusing on monoparental markers, mitochondrial DNA (mtDNA) (Table 8.2), and Y-chromosomes (Y-Chr) (Table 8.3), high-resolution haplogroup frequencies were established for each period and region. For mtDNA, although there are some data at low resolution (Table 8.1), only high-resolution analyses were considered since considerable diversity is lost if low resolution grouping is considered, particularly for haplogroups H and U.

To relate the distribution of haplogroups in different populations from different periods, a correspondence analysis was performed for mtDNA and Y-Chr haplogroups, and the results are shown in Figs. 8.9 and 8.10 respectively.

If the mtDNA haplogroup distribution is considered (Fig. 8.9a), with the exception of the Bronze Age, a clear separation between the Iberian and Italian populations of all the periods can be observed. Considering the Roman period, samples from north-eastern Iberia, mainly from the site of Empúries, cluster with those of Bronze Age date from Iberia and Italy and are close to Iron Age Iberians, denoting a certain mtDNA continuity from the Iron Age to the Roman period. By contrast, samples from the Roman period from south-eastern Iberia form a set apart and are close to Visigoths and Carolingians in the Iberian peninsula. This grouping is mainly determined by the presence of the H4 mtDNA haplogroup in both groups (Fig. 8.9b), which is also present in the Tartessian culture of south-western Iberia. Globally, with the mtDNA data available so far for Hispania, it appears that maternal lineages largely demonstrate continuity from the Bronze and Iron Age populations that occupied the Iberian peninsula, reinforcing some of the conclusions obtained in Chapter 7.

Concerning Y-Chromosome haplogroup distribution (Fig. 8.10), as for mtDNA, a differentiation between the Iberian and Italian populations can be observed. The Roman-period samples from the north-east of the Iberian peninsula cluster with other Iberians from the classical age, denoting continuity since the Bronze–Iron Age (Sinner 2024), with the dominance of Y-Chr haplogroup R1b1a1 (Fig. 8.10b). However, they form a set in the negative quadrant for dimension 2 together with the Roman population from Italy and also that from the south-eastern Iberia cluster with a predominance of the J Y-Chr haplogroup (Fig. 8.10b). To a great extent, with the Y-Chr data available so far for Romans in the Iberian peninsula, it appears that during Roman occupation some male influence was established in Iberian territory.

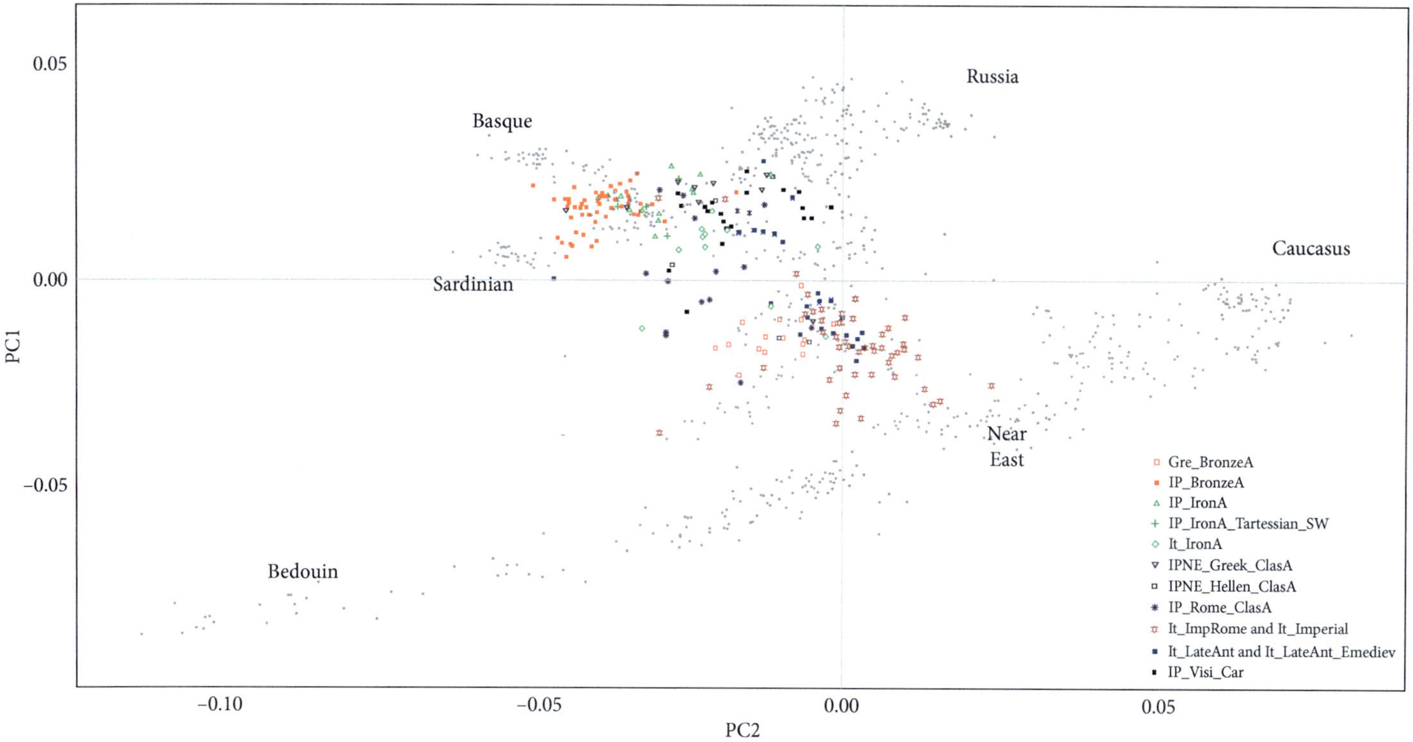


**Fig. 8.8** PCA of present-day Eurasian individuals (grey dots), with ancient individuals from Iberia and Italy (different colours and marks according to population and chronology)

**Table 8.2** Frequency of mtDNA haplogroups, based on high resolution data, for ancient Iberian and Italian populations

| mtDNA haplogroup | | Gre_ BronzeA | IP_ BronzeA | IP_ IronA | IP_IronA_ Tartessian_SW | IP_Visi_ Car | IPNE_ Greek_ ClasA | IPNE_ Hellen_ ClasA | IPNE_ Roman_ ClasA | IPSE_ Roman_ ClasA | It_Copper_ BronzeA | It_ Imperial | It_ ImpRome | It_ IronA | It_ LateAnt | It_ LateAnt_ Emediev |
|---|---|---|---|---|---|---|---|---|---|---|---|---|---|---|---|---|
| C4a1a | N | 0 | 0 | 0 | 0 | 2 | 0 | 0 | 0 | 0 | 0 | 0 | 0 | 0 | 0 | 0 |
| | % | 0.0% | 0.0% | 0.0% | 0.0% | 10.0% | 0.0% | 0.0% | 0.0% | 0.0% | 0.0% | 0.0% | 0.0% | 0.0% | 0.0% | 0.0% |
| D4j11 | N | 0 | 0 | 0 | 0 | 0 | 0 | 0 | 0 | 0 | 0 | 0 | 1 | 0 | 0 | 0 |
| | % | 0.0% | 0.0% | 0.0% | 0.0% | 0.0% | 0.0% | 0.0% | 0.0% | 0.0% | 0.0% | 0.0% | 2.7% | 0.0% | 0.0% | 0.0% |
| H | N | 4 | 0 | 2 | 0 | 0 | 1 | 3 | 0 | 0 | 0 | 2 | 3 | 3 | 3 | 1 |
| | % | 26.7% | 0.0% | 11.8% | 0.0% | 0.0% | 10.0% | 60.0% | 0.0% | 0.0% | 0.0% | 20.0% | 8.1% | 30.0% | 15.0% | 20.0% |
| H1 | N | 1 | 12 | 4 | 1 | 1 | 1 | 1 | 1 | 0 | 2 | 1 | 1 | 1 | 3 | 0 |
| | % | 6.7% | 20.0% | 23.5% | 25.0% | 5.0% | 10.0% | 20.0% | 7.7% | 0.0% | 25.0% | 10.0% | 2.7% | 10.0% | 15.0% | 0.0% |
| H2 | N | 0 | 0 | 0 | 0 | 0 | 0 | 0 | 0 | 0 | 0 | 2 | 0 | 1 | 0 | 1 |
| | % | 0.0% | 0.0% | 0.0% | 0.0% | 0.0% | 0.0% | 0.0% | 0.0% | 0.0% | 0.0% | 20.0% | 0.0% | 10.0% | 0.0% | 20.0% |
| H3 | N | 0 | 3 | 1 | 0 | 1 | 2 | 0 | 0 | 0 | 0 | 0 | 0 | 0 | 0 | 0 |
| | % | 0.0% | 5.0% | 5.9% | 0.0% | 5.0% | 20.0% | 0.0% | 0.0% | 0.0% | 0.0% | 0.0% | 0.0% | 0.0% | 0.0% | 0.0% |
| H4 | N | 0 | 0 | 0 | 1 | 2 | 0 | 0 | 1 | 2 | 0 | 0 | 0 | 0 | 0 | 0 |
| | % | 0.0% | 0.0% | 0.0% | 25.0% | 10.0% | 0.0% | 0.0% | 7.7% | 50.0% | 0.0% | 0.0% | 0.0% | 0.0% | 0.0% | 0.0% |
| H5 | N | 1 | 0 | 0 | 0 | 0 | 0 | 0 | 0 | 0 | 0 | 1 | 3 | 0 | 0 | 0 |
| | % | 6.7% | 0.0% | 0.0% | 0.0% | 0.0% | 0.0% | 0.0% | 0.0% | 0.0% | 0.0% | 10.0% | 8.1% | 0.0% | 0.0% | 0.0% |
| H7 | N | 0 | 0 | 0 | 0 | 0 | 0 | 1 | 0 | 0 | 0 | 0 | 1 | 0 | 0 | 0 |
| | % | 0.0% | 0.0% | 0.0% | 0.0% | 0.0% | 0.0% | 20.0% | 0.0% | 0.0% | 0.0% | 0.0% | 2.7% | 0.0% | 0.0% | 0.0% |
| HV | N | 0 | 0 | 0 | 0 | 0 | 1 | 0 | 0 | 0 | 0 | 0 | 1 | 0 | 1 | 0 |
| | % | 0.0% | 0.0% | 0.0% | 0.0% | 0.0% | 10.0% | 0.0% | 0.0% | 0.0% | 0.0% | 0.0% | 2.7% | 0.0% | 5.0% | 0.0% |
| HV0 | N | 0 | 4 | 2 | 0 | 0 | 1 | 0 | 1 | 1 | 1 | 0 | 0 | 0 | 0 | 0 |
| | % | 0.0% | 6.7% | 11.8% | 0.0% | 0.0% | 10.0% | 0.0% | 7.7% | 25.0% | 12.5% | 0.0% | 0.0% | 0.0% | 0.0% | 0.0% |

| | | | | | | | | | | | | | | | | |
|---|---|---|---|---|---|---|---|---|---|---|---|---|---|---|---|---|
| I | N | 1 | 0 | 1 | 0 | 0 | 0 | 0 | 0 | 0 | 0 | 0 | 0 | 0 | 1 | 0 |
| | % | 6.7% | 0.0% | 5.9% | 0.0% | 0.0% | 0.0% | 0.0% | 0.0% | 0.0% | 0.0% | 0.0% | 0.0% | 0.0% | 5.0% | 0.0% |
| J1c | N | 0 | 6 | 2 | 1 | 1 | 0 | 0 | 1 | 0 | 1 | 1 | 1 | 0 | 1 | 0 |
| | % | 0.0% | 10.0% | 11.8% | 25.0% | 5.0% | 0.0% | 0.0% | 7.7% | 0.0% | 12.5% | 10.0% | 2.7% | 0.0% | 5.0% | 0.0% |
| J2a | N | 0 | 1 | 1 | 0 | 0 | 0 | 0 | 0 | 0 | 0 | 0 | 1 | 0 | 1 | 0 |
| | % | 0.0% | 1.7% | 5.9% | 0.0% | 0.0% | 0.0% | 0.0% | 0.0% | 0.0% | 0.0% | 0.0% | 2.7% | 0.0% | 5.0% | 0.0% |
| J2b | N | 1 | 3 | 1 | 0 | 1 | 0 | 0 | 0 | 0 | 1 | 0 | 1 | 0 | 0 | 0 |
| | % | 6.7% | 5.0% | 5.9% | 0.0% | 5.0% | 0.0% | 0.0% | 0.0% | 0.0% | 12.5% | 0.0% | 2.7% | 0.0% | 0.0% | 0.0% |
| K1a | N | 1 | 10 | 1 | 0 | 0 | 1 | 0 | 1 | 0 | 1 | 1 | 1 | 1 | 1 | 1 |
| | % | 6.7% | 16.7% | 5.9% | 0.0% | 0.0% | 10.0% | 0.0% | 7.7% | 0.0% | 12.5% | 10.0% | 2.7% | 10.0% | 5.0% | 20.0% |
| K1b | N | 0 | 2 | 0 | 0 | 0 | 0 | 0 | 1 | 0 | 0 | 0 | 1 | 0 | 0 | 0 |
| | % | 0.0% | 3.3% | 0.0% | 0.0% | 0.0% | 0.0% | 0.0% | 7.7% | 0.0% | 0.0% | 0.0% | 2.7% | 0.0% | 0.0% | 0.0% |
| K1c | N | 0 | 0 | 0 | 0 | 0 | 0 | 0 | 1 | 0 | 0 | 0 | 0 | 0 | 0 | 1 |
| | % | 0.0% | 0.0% | 0.0% | 0.0% | 0.0% | 0.0% | 0.0% | 7.7% | 0.0% | 0.0% | 0.0% | 0.0% | 0.0% | 0.0% | 20.0% |
| K2a | N | 0 | 0 | 0 | 0 | 0 | 1 | 0 | 0 | 0 | 0 | 0 | 0 | 0 | 0 | 0 |
| | % | 0.0% | 0.0% | 0.0% | 0.0% | 0.0% | 10.0% | 0.0% | 0.0% | 0.0% | 0.0% | 0.0% | 0.0% | 0.0% | 0.0% | 0.0% |
| K2b | N | 0 | 0 | 0 | 0 | 0 | 0 | 0 | 1 | 0 | 0 | 0 | 0 | 0 | 0 | 0 |
| | % | 0.0% | 0.0% | 0.0% | 0.0% | 0.0% | 0.0% | 0.0% | 7.7% | 0.0% | 0.0% | 0.0% | 0.0% | 0.0% | 0.0% | 0.0% |
| L4a2 | N | 0 | 0 | 0 | 0 | 0 | 0 | 0 | 0 | 0 | 0 | 0 | 0 | 0 | 0 | 1 |
| | % | 0.0% | 0.0% | 0.0% | 0.0% | 0.0% | 0.0% | 0.0% | 0.0% | 0.0% | 0.0% | 0.0% | 0.0% | 0.0% | 0.0% | 20.0% |
| R0 | N | 0 | 0 | 0 | 0 | 0 | 0 | 0 | 0 | 0 | 0 | 0 | 0 | 0 | 1 | 0 |
| | % | 0.0% | 0.0% | 0.0% | 0.0% | 0.0% | 0.0% | 0.0% | 0.0% | 0.0% | 0.0% | 0.0% | 0.0% | 0.0% | 5.0% | 0.0% |
| T1a | N | 0 | 0 | 0 | 0 | 0 | 0 | 0 | 0 | 0 | 0 | 0 | 2 | 0 | 2 | 0 |
| | % | 0.0% | 0.0% | 0.0% | 0.0% | 0.0% | 0.0% | 0.0% | 0.0% | 0.0% | 0.0% | 0.0% | 5.4% | 0.0% | 10.0% | 0.0% |

*Continued*

**Table 8.2** *Continued*

| mtDNA haplogroup | | Gre_ BronzeA | IP_ BronzeA | IP_ IronA | IP_IronA_ Tartessian_SW | IP_Visi_ Car | IPNE_ Greek_ ClasA | IPNE_ Hellen_ ClasA | IPNE_ Roman_ ClasA | IPSE_ Roman_ ClasA | It_Copper_ BronzeA | It_ Imperial | It_ ImpRome | It_ IronA | It_ LateAnt | It_ LateAnt_ Emediev |
|---|---|---|---|---|---|---|---|---|---|---|---|---|---|---|---|---|
| T2 | N | 0 | 0 | 0 | 0 | 1 | 0 | 0 | 0 | 0 | 0 | 0 | 4 | 0 | 1 | 0 |
| | % | 0.0% | 0.0% | 0.0% | 0.0% | 5.0% | 0.0% | 0.0% | 0.0% | 0.0% | 0.0% | 0.0% | 10.8% | 0.0% | 5.0% | 0.0% |
| T2a | N | 0 | 0 | 0 | 0 | 0 | 0 | 0 | 0 | 0 | 0 | 0 | 1 | 0 | 0 | 0 |
| | % | 0.0% | 0.0% | 0.0% | 0.0% | 0.0% | 0.0% | 0.0% | 0.0% | 0.0% | 0.0% | 0.0% | 2.7% | 0.0% | 0.0% | 0.0% |
| T2b | N | 0 | 1 | 0 | 1 | 0 | 0 | 0 | 3 | 0 | 0 | 0 | 0 | 1 | 2 | 0 |
| | % | 0.0% | 1.7% | 0.0% | 25.0% | 0.0% | 0.0% | 0.0% | 23.1% | 0.0% | 0.0% | 0.0% | 0.0% | 10.0% | 10.0% | 0.0% |
| T2c | N | 0 | 0 | 0 | 0 | 0 | 0 | 0 | 0 | 0 | 0 | 1 | 2 | 1 | 0 | 0 |
| | % | 0.0% | 0.0% | 0.0% | 0.0% | 0.0% | 0.0% | 0.0% | 0.0% | 0.0% | 0.0% | 10.0% | 5.4% | 10.0% | 0.0% | 0.0% |
| T2d | N | 0 | 0 | 0 | 0 | 0 | 0 | 0 | 0 | 0 | 0 | 0 | 1 | 0 | 1 | 0 |
| | % | 0.0% | 0.0% | 0.0% | 0.0% | 0.0% | 0.0% | 0.0% | 0.0% | 0.0% | 0.0% | 0.0% | 2.7% | 0.0% | 5.0% | 0.0% |
| T2e | N | 0 | 2 | 0 | 0 | 0 | 0 | 0 | 0 | 0 | 0 | 0 | 0 | 0 | 0 | 0 |
| | % | 0.0% | 3.3% | 0.0% | 0.0% | 0.0% | 0.0% | 0.0% | 0.0% | 0.0% | 0.0% | 0.0% | 0.0% | 0.0% | 0.0% | 0.0% |
| U1 | N | 0 | 0 | 0 | 0 | 0 | 1 | 0 | 0 | 0 | 0 | 0 | 2 | 0 | 0 | 0 |
| | % | 0.0% | 0.0% | 0.0% | 0.0% | 0.0% | 10.0% | 0.0% | 0.0% | 0.0% | 0.0% | 0.0% | 5.4% | 0.0% | 0.0% | 0.0% |
| U3a | N | 0 | 0 | 1 | 0 | 1 | 0 | 0 | 0 | 1 | 0 | 0 | 1 | 0 | 0 | 0 |
| | % | 0.0% | 0.0% | 5.9% | 0.0% | 5.0% | 0.0% | 0.0% | 0.0% | 25.0% | 0.0% | 0.0% | 2.7% | 0.0% | 0.0% | 0.0% |
| U3b | N | 1 | 0 | 0 | 0 | 0 | 0 | 0 | 0 | 0 | 0 | 0 | 2 | 0 | 0 | 0 |
| | % | 6.7% | 0.0% | 0.0% | 0.0% | 0.0% | 0.0% | 0.0% | 0.0% | 0.0% | 0.0% | 0.0% | 5.4% | 0.0% | 0.0% | 0.0% |
| U4 | N | 0 | 0 | 0 | 0 | 0 | 0 | 0 | 0 | 0 | 0 | 0 | 1 | 1 | 0 | 0 |
| | % | 0.0% | 0.0% | 0.0% | 0.0% | 0.0% | 0.0% | 0.0% | 0.0% | 0.0% | 0.0% | 0.0% | 2.7% | 10.0% | 0.0% | 0.0% |
| U5a | N | 2 | 1 | 0 | 0 | 5 | 0 | 0 | 2 | 0 | 1 | 0 | 0 | 1 | 0 | 0 |
| | % | 13.3% | 1.7% | 0.0% | 0.0% | 25.0% | 0.0% | 0.0% | 15.4% | 0.0% | 12.5% | 0.0% | 0.0% | 10.0% | 0.0% | 0.0% |

| | | | | | | | | | | | | | | | | |
|---|---|---|---|---|---|---|---|---|---|---|---|---|---|---|---|---|
| U5b | N | 0 | 1 | 0 | 0 | 0 | 0 | 0 | 0 | 0 | 0 | 0 | 0 | 0 | 0 | 0 |
| | % | 0.0% | 1.7% | 0.0% | 0.0% | 0.0% | 0.0% | 0.0% | 0.0% | 0.0% | 0.0% | 0.0% | 0.0% | 0.0% | 0.0% | 0.0% |
| U5b1 | N | 0 | 7 | 0 | 0 | 1 | 0 | 0 | 0 | 0 | 0 | 0 | 0 | 0 | 0 | 0 |
| | % | 0.0% | 11.7% | 0.0% | 0.0% | 5.0% | 0.0% | 0.0% | 0.0% | 0.0% | 0.0% | 0.0% | 0.0% | 0.0% | 0.0% | 0.0% |
| U5b2 | N | 0 | 0 | 0 | 0 | 0 | 0 | 0 | 0 | 0 | 0 | 1 | 0 | 0 | 1 | 0 |
| | % | 0.0% | 0.0% | 0.0% | 0.0% | 0.0% | 0.0% | 0.0% | 0.0% | 0.0% | 0.0% | 10.0% | 0.0% | 0.0% | 5.0% | 0.0% |
| U5b3 | N | 0 | 3 | 0 | 0 | 0 | 1 | 0 | 0 | 0 | 0 | 0 | 1 | 0 | 1 | 0 |
| | % | 0.0% | 5.0% | 0.0% | 0.0% | 0.0% | 10.0% | 0.0% | 0.0% | 0.0% | 0.0% | 0.0% | 2.7% | 0.0% | 5.0% | 0.0% |
| U6a | N | 0 | 0 | 0 | 0 | 0 | 0 | 0 | 0 | 0 | 0 | 0 | 3 | 0 | 0 | 0 |
| | % | 0.0% | 0.0% | 0.0% | 0.0% | 0.0% | 0.0% | 0.0% | 0.0% | 0.0% | 0.0% | 0.0% | 8.1% | 0.0% | 0.0% | 0.0% |
| U7a | N | 0 | 0 | 0 | 0 | 0 | 0 | 0 | 0 | 0 | 0 | 0 | 1 | 0 | 0 | 0 |
| | % | 0.0% | 0.0% | 0.0% | 0.0% | 0.0% | 0.0% | 0.0% | 0.0% | 0.0% | 0.0% | 0.0% | 2.7% | 0.0% | 0.0% | 0.0% |
| U8b | N | 0 | 0 | 0 | 0 | 0 | 0 | 0 | 0 | 0 | 1 | 0 | 0 | 0 | 0 | 0 |
| | % | 0.0% | 0.0% | 0.0% | 0.0% | 0.0% | 0.0% | 0.0% | 0.0% | 0.0% | 12.5% | 0.0% | 0.0% | 0.0% | 0.0% | 0.0% |
| V | N | 0 | 2 | 0 | 0 | 2 | 0 | 0 | 0 | 0 | 0 | 0 | 0 | 0 | 0 | 0 |
| | % | 0.0% | 3.3% | 0.0% | 0.0% | 10.0% | 0.0% | 0.0% | 0.0% | 0.0% | 0.0% | 0.0% | 0.0% | 0.0% | 0.0% | 0.0% |
| W | N | 0 | 0 | 0 | 0 | 2 | 0 | 0 | 0 | 0 | 0 | 0 | 0 | 0 | 0 | 0 |
| | % | 0.0% | 0.0% | 0.0% | 0.0% | 10.0% | 0.0% | 0.0% | 0.0% | 0.0% | 0.0% | 0.0% | 0.0% | 0.0% | 0.0% | 0.0% |
| X2 | N | 2 | 0 | 0 | 0 | 0 | 0 | 0 | 0 | 0 | 0 | 0 | 1 | 0 | 0 | 0 |
| | % | 13.3% | 0.0% | 0.0% | 0.0% | 0.0% | 0.0% | 0.0% | 0.0% | 0.0% | 0.0% | 0.0% | 2.7% | 0.0% | 0.0% | 0.0% |
| X2b | N | 0 | 2 | 1 | 0 | 0 | 0 | 0 | 0 | 0 | 0 | 0 | 0 | 0 | 0 | 0 |
| | % | 0.0% | 3.3% | 5.9% | 0.0% | 0.0% | 0.0% | 0.0% | 0.0% | 0.0% | 0.0% | 0.0% | 0.0% | 0.0% | 0.0% | 0.0% |
| X2d | N | 1 | 0 | 0 | 0 | 0 | 0 | 0 | 0 | 0 | 0 | 0 | 0 | 0 | 0 | 0 |
| | % | 6.7% | 0.0% | 0.0% | 0.0% | 0.0% | 0.0% | 0.0% | 0.0% | 0.0% | 0.0% | 0.0% | 0.0% | 0.0% | 0.0% | 0.0% |

**Table 8.3** Frequency of Y-chromosome haplogroups, based on high resolution data, for ancient Iberian and Italian populations

| Y-Chr Haplogroup | | Gre_ Bronze age | IP_ Bronze Age | IP_ ClaAge_ Greek | IP_ClaAge_ Hellenistic | IP_Iron Age | IP_Visi_ Car | IPNE_ ClaAge_ Roman | IPSE_ ClaAge_ Roman | IP_IronA_ Tartessian_ SW | It_Copper_ Bronze Age | It_ Imperial | It_ Imperial Rome | It_Iron Age | It_Late Antiquity | Late Antiquity/ Early Medie |
|---|---|---|---|---|---|---|---|---|---|---|---|---|---|---|---|---|
| BT | N | 0 | 1 | 0 | 0 | 0 | 1 | 0 | 0 | 0 | 0 | 0 | 0 | 0 | 0 | 0 |
| | % | 0.0% | 2.9% | 0.0% | 0.0% | 0.0% | 10.0% | 0.0% | 0.0% | 0.0% | 0.0% | 0.0% | 0.0% | 0.0% | 0.0% | 0.0% |
| E1b | N | 0 | 0 | 0 | 0 | 0 | 1 | 0 | 0 | 0 | 0 | 0 | 1 | 0 | 1 | 0 |
| | % | 0.0% | 0.0% | 0.0% | 0.0% | 0.0% | 10.0% | 0.0% | 0.0% | 0.0% | 0.0% | 0.0% | 6.7% | 0.0% | 8.3% | 0.0% |
| G2a2b1 | N | 0 | 0 | 0 | 0 | 0 | 0 | 0 | 0 | 0 | 0 | 0 | 2 | 0 | 0 | 0 |
| | % | 0.0% | 0.0% | 0.0% | 0.0% | 0.0% | 0.0% | 0.0% | 0.0% | 0.0% | 0.0% | 0.0% | 13.3% | 0.0% | 0.0% | 0.0% |
| G2a2b2 | N | 1 | 0 | 0 | 0 | 0 | 0 | 0 | 0 | 0 | 1 | 1 | 1 | 0 | 2 | 1 |
| | % | 25.0% | 0.0% | 0.0% | 0.0% | 0.0% | 0.0% | 0.0% | 0.0% | 0.0% | 33.3% | 12.5% | 6.7% | 0.0% | 16.7% | 20.0% |
| H2 | N | 0 | 0 | 0 | 0 | 0 | 0 | 0 | 0 | 0 | 0 | 0 | 0 | 0 | 1 | 0 |
| | % | 0.0% | 0.0% | 0.0% | 0.0% | 0.0% | 0.0% | 0.0% | 0.0% | 0.0% | 0.0% | 0.0% | 0.0% | 0.0% | 8.3% | 0.0% |
| HIJK | N | 0 | 0 | 0 | 0 | 0 | 0 | 1 | 1 | 0 | 0 | 0 | 0 | 0 | 0 | 0 |
| | % | 0.0% | 0.0% | 0.0% | 0.0% | 0.0% | 0.0% | 16.7% | 33.3% | 0.0% | 0.0% | 0.0% | 0.0% | 0.0% | 0.0% | 0.0% |
| I | N | 0 | 0 | 0 | 0 | 0 | 1 | 0 | 0 | 0 | 0 | 0 | 0 | 0 | 0 | 0 |
| | % | 0.0% | 0.0% | 0.0% | 0.0% | 0.0% | 10.0% | 0.0% | 0.0% | 0.0% | 0.0% | 0.0% | 0.0% | 0.0% | 0.0% | 0.0% |
| I1 | N | 0 | 0 | 0 | 0 | 0 | 0 | 0 | 0 | 0 | 0 | 0 | 0 | 0 | 1 | 0 |
| | % | 0.0% | 0.0% | 0.0% | 0.0% | 0.0% | 0.0% | 0.0% | 0.0% | 0.0% | 0.0% | 0.0% | 0.0% | 0.0% | 8.3% | 0.0% |
| I2a1 | N | 0 | 0 | 0 | 0 | 0 | 0 | 0 | 0 | 0 | 2 | 0 | 0 | 0 | 1 | 1 |
| | % | 0.0% | 0.0% | 0.0% | 0.0% | 0.0% | 0.0% | 0.0% | 0.0% | 0.0% | 66.7% | 0.0% | 0.0% | 0.0% | 8.3% | 20.0% |

| | | | | | | | | | | | | | | | | |
|---|---|---|---|---|---|---|---|---|---|---|---|---|---|---|---|---|
| J | N | 0 | 0 | 0 | 2 | 0 | 0 | 1 | 1 | 0 | 0 | 0 | 2 | 0 | 0 | 0 |
| | % | 0.0% | 0.0% | 0.0% | 66.7% | 0.0% | 0.0% | 16.7% | 33.3% | 0.0% | 0.0% | 0.0% | 13.3% | 0.0% | 0.0% | 0.0% |
| J1 | N | 0 | 0 | 0 | 0 | 0 | 0 | 0 | 0 | 0 | 0 | 3 | 1 | 0 | 2 | 0 |
| | % | 0.0% | 0.0% | 0.0% | 0.0% | 0.0% | 0.0% | 0.0% | 0.0% | 0.0% | 0.0% | 37.5% | 6.7% | 0.0% | 16.7% | 0.0% |
| J2 | N | 3 | 0 | 0 | 0 | 0 | 1 | 0 | 1 | 0 | 0 | 2 | 5 | 1 | 2 | 1 |
| | % | 75.0% | 0.0% | 0.0% | 0.0% | 0.0% | 10.0% | 0.0% | 33.3% | 0.0% | 0.0% | 25.0% | 33.3% | 14.3% | 16.7% | 20.0% |
| P | N | 0 | 0 | 0 | 0 | 0 | 1 | 0 | 0 | 0 | 0 | 0 | 0 | 0 | 0 | 0 |
| | % | 0.0% | 0.0% | 0.0% | 0.0% | 0.0% | 10.0% | 0.0% | 0.0% | 0.0% | 0.0% | 0.0% | 0.0% | 0.0% | 0.0% | 0.0% |
| R | N | 0 | 0 | 2 | 0 | 0 | 0 | 1 | 0 | 0 | 0 | 0 | 1 | 0 | 0 | 0 |
| | % | 0.0% | 0.0% | 33.3% | 0.0% | 0.0% | 0.0% | 16.7% | 0.0% | 0.0% | 0.0% | 0.0% | 6.7% | 0.0% | 0.0% | 0.0% |
| R1a1 | N | 0 | 0 | 0 | 0 | 0 | 0 | 0 | 0 | 0 | 0 | 1 | 0 | 0 | 0 | 0 |
| | % | 0.0% | 0.0% | 0.0% | 0.0% | 0.0% | 0.0% | 0.0% | 0.0% | 0.0% | 0.0% | 12.5% | 0.0% | 0.0% | 0.0% | 0.0% |
| R1b1 | N | 0 | 0 | 0 | 0 | 0 | 1 | 0 | 0 | 0 | 0 | 0 | 0 | 0 | 0 | 0 |
| | % | 0.0% | 0.0% | 0.0% | 0.0% | 0.0% | 10.0% | 0.0% | 0.0% | 0.0% | 0.0% | 0.0% | 0.0% | 0.0% | 0.0% | 0.0% |
| R1b1a1 | N | 0 | 34 | 4 | 1 | 11 | 4 | 3 | 0 | 1 | 0 | 0 | 1 | 3 | 1 | 2 |
| | % | 0.0% | 97.1% | 66.7% | 33.3% | 100.0% | 40.0% | 50.0% | 0.0% | 100.0% | 0.0% | 0.0% | 6.7% | 42.9% | 8.3% | 40.0% |
| R1b1a2 | N | 0 | 0 | 0 | 0 | 0 | 0 | 0 | 0 | 0 | 0 | 0 | 1 | 2 | 0 | 0 |
| | % | 0.0% | 0.0% | 0.0% | 0.0% | 0.0% | 0.0% | 0.0% | 0.0% | 0.0% | 0.0% | 0.0% | 6.7% | 28.6% | 0.0% | 0.0% |
| T1a1a | N | 0 | 0 | 0 | 0 | 0 | 0 | 0 | 0 | 0 | 0 | 1 | 0 | 1 | 0 | 0 |
| | % | 0.0% | 0.0% | 0.0% | 0.0% | 0.0% | 0.0% | 0.0% | 0.0% | 0.0% | 0.0% | 12.5% | 0.0% | 14.3% | 0.0% | 0.0% |
| T1a2b | N | 0 | 0 | 0 | 0 | 0 | 0 | 0 | 0 | 0 | 0 | 0 | 0 | 0 | 1 | 0 |
| | % | 0.0% | 0.0% | 0.0% | 0.0% | 0.0% | 0.0% | 0.0% | 0.0% | 0.0% | 0.0% | 0.0% | 0.0% | 0.0% | 8.3% | 0.0% |

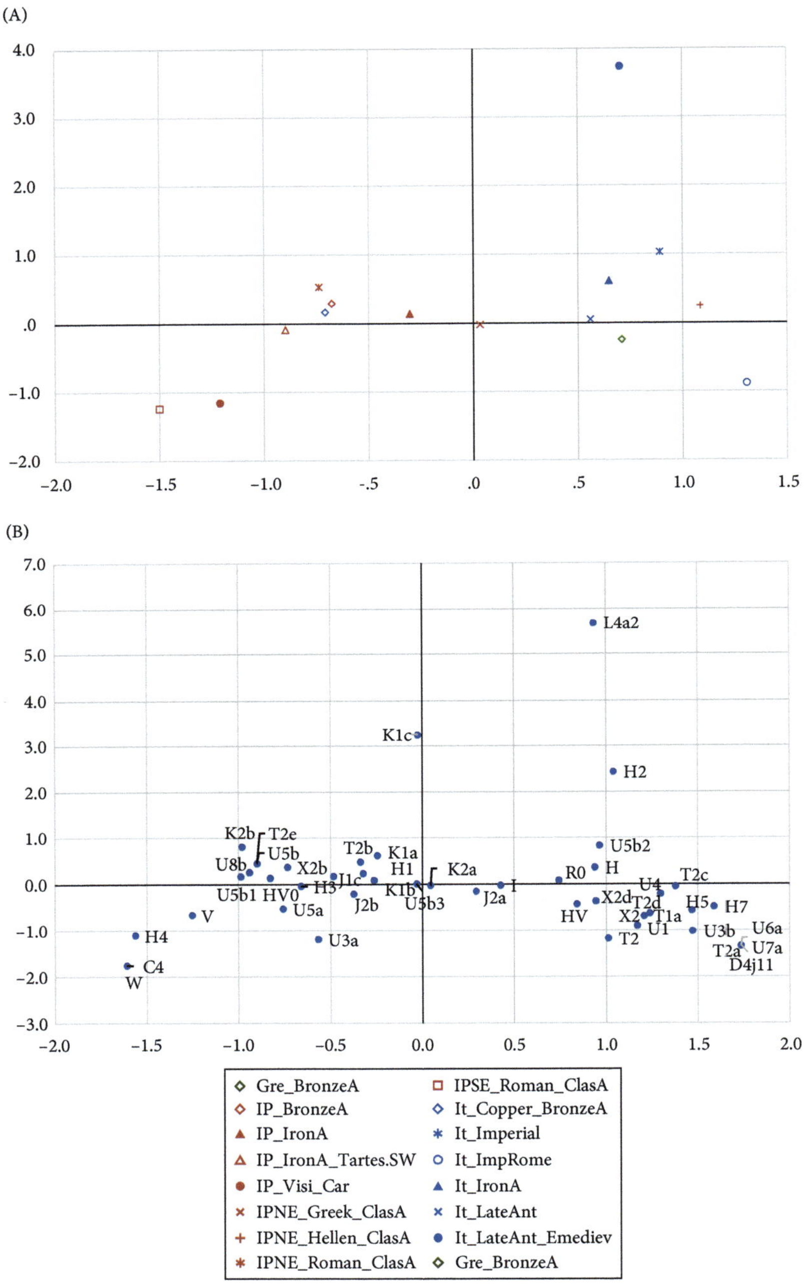


**Fig. 8.9** Correspondence analysis of mtDNA. (A) Population representation. (B) mtDNA haplogroup representation

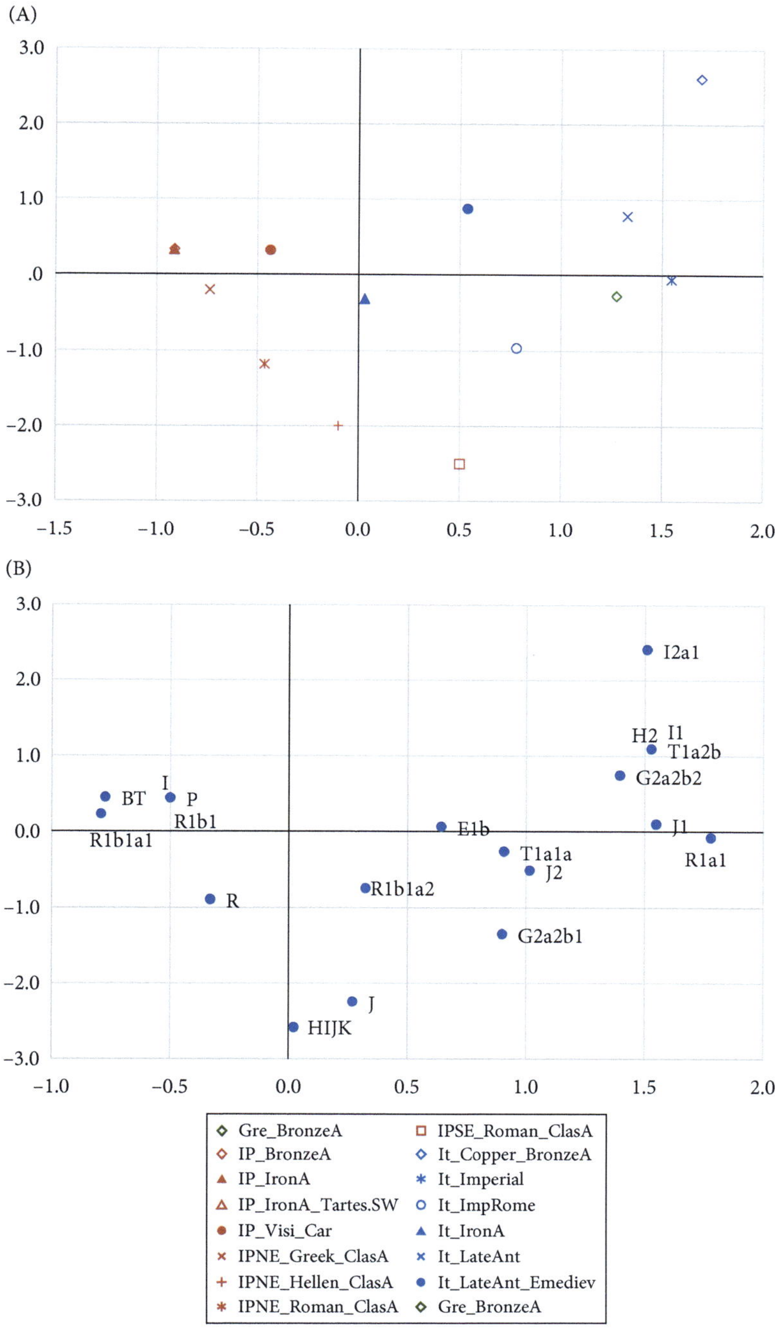


**Fig. 8.10** Correspondence analysis of Y-chromosome. (A) Population representation. (B) Y-chromosome haplogroup representation

Considering our analysis and those of Olalde et al. (2019) from previous cultural periods, genetic flows into Iberia were recorded in the Late Bronze Age or Early Iron Age; in contrast, in the Roman period, southern Iberia bears witness to a major impact of North African ancestry according to Olalde et al. (2019). They associated this relationship to the high levels of mobility during the Roman Empire or to the earlier Phoenician-Punic presence. The authors also state that the Roman presence in the peninsula had a notable cultural impact and a substantial genetic impact as well, but a lower long-term demographic impact. From our analysis, this relationship is linked to a male movement according to the Y-chromosome data. In addition, the relationship of Roman Iberian series with later Visigothic and Carolingian mtDNA suggests a continuity of female lineages.

## 8.8 Conclusions and Future Directions

Archaeological human remains are an incomparable source of data which, combined with information obtained from other sources, especially epigraphic evidence and demographic data, can help create richer images of how people lived and died in Roman Hispania Citerior/Tarraconensis. It is for this reason that it is so important to combine data obtained from different sources and disciplines. For example, in the study of health and disease, it is also essential to consider research on tools and instruments related to medical practice in the province (Floriano, 1941; Borobia Melendo, 1992). Tweezers, spatulas, medicine boxes, scalpels, scissors, probes, tongs, razors, ointments, needles, among others, are surgical, medical, and pharmaceutical instruments—as well as cosmetic ones—which have been found in archaeological and funerary contexts, and which contribute to our knowledge of the art of healing in antiquity (Jackson, 1993; Baker, 2013). This archaeological evidence demonstrates that, while the art of healing was often closer to the Roman gods than to empirical science (González Zymla, 2007; King and Dasen, 2008; Da sen, 2011), there were certainly people with the ability, skills, and talent necessary to undertake surgical interventions such as cataract removal (Bailly, 1994), limb amputations (Casas i Genover, 1993), trepanations, c-sections (Bliquez, 2010), or to treat dental ailments successfully (Borobia Melendo and Parra, 1992). Moreover, there was extensive knowledge and understanding of the properties of many plants that were used to make different remedies and medicines with a variety of effects (anaesthetics, sleep-inducing, anti-inflammatory, aphrodisiac, euthanasic, etc.) (Abreu, 2011). Thus, while the majority of the medical practices and knowledge that existed in the past would not have left any traces on the skeletal remains that we study, the presence of these tools and instruments confirms the existence of some pathologies—and their attempts to cure them—that are currently invisible in human remains.

The pathologies observed in the province are the same as those observed in other periods or locations; however, the two case studies show how lifestyle and social status, ways of life, diet, and access to foodstuffs can influence an individual's health and disease status. In particular, the first case also demonstrates the need to consider the funerary context to understand past societies. It is vital to emphasize, however, that extensive and interdisciplinary research is needed to improve our knowledge of these populations and have an overall understanding of the province population as a whole.

Besides, the outbreaks of pandemics that reached the Roman Empire from the mid-second century CE to late antiquity may have affected the province of Tarraconensis, although the direct evidence is not so clear. The high mortality of those outbreaks may well have influenced the living conditions of contemporary populations noticeably.

On the other hand, as noted in Chapter 7, from the period when the Romans arrived until late antiquity, the Iberian peninsula was involved in continuous processes of migration of different origins, numbers, and objectives, leading to the formation of a diverse provincial society. A large amount of indirect information allows us to obtain a good picture of some periods. This is the case of the Roman advance in Iberia. The impact of Rome can be seen in the archaeological remains (amphorae and other types of pottery), the evidence of its roads and trade, its constructions, its written texts, place names, funerary stelae, and, of course, in the language.

At the genetic level, however, the question is difficult to understand with the data currently available. Palaeogenetic analyses related to the population of Hispania are very scarce and often unspecific. Palaeogenomics is a newly-born academic field. Genomic data are more abundant, but still insufficient and often intricate. The same is true for populations from previous and later times, the Bronze and Iron Ages, and late antiquity. But the main problem we face in order to measure the impact of Rome in the Iberian peninsula in genetic terms is the scant knowledge we have about who the Romans that came to Iberia were, what their population structure was, and how to define them genetically. Certainly, as mentioned above, there are Roman texts and inscriptions that refer to legionaries and auxiliaries, but where did they come from and who accompanied them (see Chapter 7)?

Palaeogenetics and palaeogenomics base their deductions on statistical analysis. Numbers are necessary and precise; therefore, the more data available, the more accurate they are. Concerning materials of the peninsula, we have very few data from the first genetic studies using mtDNA. Only the incomplete sequences of seven individuals from Segobriga (Late Roman Empire) are available for Roman times. From earlier periods, the Bronze and Iron Ages, we have somewhat more data, but it is far from abundant: sequences of nine Bronze Age individuals from two archaeological sites and 40 from four Iron Age sites (Table 8.1). All these sequences of the non-coding region of mtDNA based on PCR analysis are incomplete and unevenly long. Consequently, the analysis cannot make use of all the fragments produced and some potential information is lost. For this reason, it was decided to collect all these data as a reference for a possible individual inference, but not to focus our interpretation on them.

The available palaeogenomics data, although there is a modest number of samples, offer more information and are more accurate. Seventeen Roman individuals are available, mainly from the site of Empúries in the north-east, and another in the south. While the data have limitations, there is a substantial set of data from the Bronze and Iron Ages and Iberian times, and, most important, there are genomic data for Etruscans (Posth et al., 2021) and Roman-period inhabitants of the area near Rome itself (Antonio et al., 2019). If the identity of the individuals who arrived as a consequence of the Roman conquest remains unknown—at least in part, see Chapter 7—at minimum there is a point of reference provided as regards the people who lived near the city of Rome itself.

Bearing in mind the limitations of the number of individuals, some extrapolations can be made. First, the projection/superimposition of the ancient individuals over the distribution of present-day European and North African populations (Fig. 8.8) reveals two clusters. One includes populations in the Iberian peninsula (Bronze and Iron Age, plus Classical Greek and Hellenistic populations, and the Visigothic and Carolingian series) and Iron Age Italian populations. The other one clusters Roman-period individuals in Italy. While individuals in Italy in late antiquity are distributed in both groups, Roman individuals in the Iberian peninsula lie between the two groups.

Second, this means that there are not many differences between the ancient populations. Thus, the mixed positions of individuals show that the migrations defining Eurasian populations reached as far as the south; furthermore, there was also a certain continuity between all of these pre-Roman populations. It can be assumed that the ancient population of the Iberian peninsula is blurred among other European populations, at least those of the south.

However, Roman civilization introduced elements of contrast. These new features arrived not from the north but from North Africa and the Mediterranean in general. New genomes were introduced through the expansive nature of Roman colonialism, and they arrived in the peninsula where they mixed with the previous genetic pool.

It is also interesting to have the view of genetic relationships among populations based on monoparental genetic markers. The continuity of female and male lineages seems to offer different histories for the population as a whole. The distribution of mtDNA shows that individuals of the Iberian and Italian Bronze Age were mapped together. Conversely, as regards the Iron Age, segregation between the Iberian and the Italian peninsula can be observed. However, there is a continuity of female lineages until the Iron Age. In the Roman period, a bias between the two Iberian groups can be observed: the north-eastern mitochondrial genomes are closer to those of the Bronze and Iron Ages; for this reason, one can argue for a degree of continuity (Sinner, 2024). Meanwhile, southern Iberian Roman genomes, as identified in the Late Roman necropolis of Granada (Navas et al., 2009), were mapped with later Iberian populations—late antiquity and the Carolingian series which includes North African and Near Eastern mtDNA haplotypes; this shows the always close relationship with Africa, which was strengthened in the Roman period. In fact, people from the African provinces are the third most important group of immigrants that came to Tarraconensis after Italic and Gallic migrants as discussed in Chapter 7.

The Y-chromosome markers (Fig. 8.10) show a dissociation between the Iberian and Italian male lineages. The former show the presence of R1b, a typically Western Europe Y-haplogroup, while the latter reveal haplogroups I1, I2a1, and R1a of Eastern Europe and the Germanic tribes (I1), J1, a dominant Arabic haplogroup, or J2, a west Asian and Graeco-Roman paternal lineage (Eupedia.com, Manco et al., 2018; Sahakyan et al., 2021).

It seems that maternal lineages (mtDNA) were maintained in the Iberian peninsula at least from the Bronze Age onwards, and they do not differ very much from the Italian ones. However, a difference began to appear from the south with the introduction of new foreign haplogroups, mainly from North Africa and the Near East in the Late Roman period. Meanwhile, male lineages (Y-chromosome) reveal greater differences. From the Bronze Age to the Visigothic and Carolingian periods, the map of Y-haplogroups differs between the two peninsulas, reflecting a different history. On the basis of these data, it can be suggested that the main migrators were men who contributed to generating more diversity in the Iberian peninsula. The male lineages that arrived to the province under study are likely to have been from Italy, North Africa, and the Near East, mainly Carthaginians and Phoenicians in the south, matching the data obtained from the evidence for trade, military activity, and slavery (see Chapter 7).

These hypotheses come from palaeogenomic data from studies conducted in the Iberian peninsula and Rome. However, as has already been emphasized, they are statistical inferences contrasted with historical and archaeological studies. If the latter are based on larger datasets, the genetic data we can provide is important but still scarce. Therefore, we need to increase the number of samples to obtain a clear panorama of Hispania in Roman period.

Some goals need to be achieved. Above, reference was made to the challenges presented by the number of samples, their documentation and representativeness, and the work ahead for the genetic study of antiquity. Therefore, the first objective is obtaining meaningful, valid, and sufficient samples. This would enable us to acquire an overview of the pre-Roman genetic situation in the Iberian peninsula. At present, the around 200 genomes available (with a very heterogeneous distribution) from the Bronze Age to the Iron Age must cover a period of 2,000 years and 596,740 $km^2$ (INE, 2018). Compiling more genomes is a priority. The same aims can be established for the Roman period. More genomes are needed, but here the distribution of power could be of interest. Therefore, data must be obtained from the main cities of Hispania, to gain an understanding of the different influences created as a result of the main activities carried out in them. At present, the data mainly come from a single city, Emporion/Emporiae; a few data come from two villas, one in Granada near the city of Iliberri-Florentia, and the other in Alcover (Tarragona). It is no less important to have a picture of what is happening in the rest of the Mediterranean, but especially in Rome, since it was the metropolis that pulled the strings in this period. For this reason, increasing the number of genomes is the main step to create a genetic map of antiquity.

The second milestone is related to methodological improvements: DNA extraction and amplification and bioinformatics, all this in connection with open-access information.

Finally, yet importantly, joint work and collaborative efforts are needed to be able to link the genetic data with the entire range of documentary, archaeological, historiographical, and anthropological information; a truly interdisciplinary task such as the one started in this volume is indispensable and must be a priority of future studies.

*The Human Factor: The Demography of the Roman Province of Hispania Citerior/Tarraconensis.* Alejandro G. Sinner, Cèsar Carreras, and Pieter Houten, Oxford University Press. 
DOI: 10.1093/9780191943881.003.0008

# 9
# Conclusions

Providing new insights into the demography of Hispania Citerior/Tarraconensis by employing an integrating and interdisciplinary approach has been the main objective of this volume. In the previous eight chapters we have combined archaeological, anthropological, historical, genetic, and epigraphic evidence, to portray a picture that allows for a more comprehensive understanding of the population characteristics, numbers, movements, and settlement patterns of this Roman province diachronically, from the Late Iron Age (third–fourth centuries BCE) down to the Late Roman period.

When looking at the characteristics of the inhabitants of Citerior/Tarraconensis (Chapter 2), it is important to acknowledge the challenges that come with studying life expectancy, mortality, fertility, pathologies, and diseases. The available sources, including epigraphic data, censuses, ancient sources, life tables, and osteological analysis of human remains, all present limitations and must be approached with caution, combined and never in isolation. Epigraphic records, for example, lack information on newborn and infant deaths and often round off ages at death, making demographic estimates not representative of the population of the province. Literary sources have similar limitations, often focusing on the upper classes in Rome from a male and urban perspective. Whereas censuses and life tables are more realistic in their data, they are geographically restricted and not directly applicable to the province under study. Necropoleis are a valuable source of information, but also have limitations. Infant deaths are often underrepresented, and it is difficult to know what percentage of the original burial area has survived. Moreover, cemeteries were often in use for long periods of time, covering several centuries with varying living standards. It is also challenging to determine the social and juridical status of those buried in them. In order to gain a clearer understanding of the demographic characteristics of an ancient population, it is important to combine and compare all the above sources and datasets, using their strengths to balance their respective limitations. When considering life expectancy and mortality in Hispania Citerior/Tarraconensis through integration of all these sources, a life expectancy at birth of around 25 years can be suggested, with a marked difference in the peak period of fertility between males and females. A Total Fertility Rate between four and six children seems plausible based on the available evidence. Due to the high perinatal mortality, the ratio

Gross Reproduction Rate between mothers and daughters must have reached 2.8, making it possible to keep the population numbers of this provincial society stable generation after generation.

In chapter 8, when looking at pathologies and the skeletal remains of individuals from the studied region—although the sample is still small—common palaeopathological lesions related to porous phenomena, including cribra orbitalia and femoralis, parietal thinning, cranial vault porosity with or without bone thickening, as well as periosteal reactions on the long bone diaphysis or metaphysis, can be detected. These alterations are often linked to metabolic deficiencies or infectious processes, indicating a correlation with individual health and nutrition. Anaemia has been proposed as a possible cause of these lesions, but they could also be associated with vitamin deficiencies or reduced immune function of the individual. Skeletal remains in the province also commonly exhibit enthesopathies, bone adaptations, and non-pathological alterations. Enthesopathies have been examined as markers of occupational stress in order to understand activity patterns and ways of life. However, the development of enthesopathies is not solely dependent on occupation, but also influenced by age, making interpretation of these markers complex. Benign neoplastic lesions, such as button osteomas on the cranial vault, are the most observed tumours. Malignant tumours are rare and may not leave any trace in bone tissue. The lower prevalence of cancer may be due to reduced life expectancy in the Roman population as well as to fewer environmental factors conducive to cancer. The prevalence of congenital pathologies or non-metrical anatomical variants is generally low. Degenerative pathologies are recorded in the necropoleis near ancient Egara and Tarraco. In the former, they affected the vertebrae of one of every four individuals. In the latter, the lumbar spine was the most common location for degenerative changes in both sexes, and the knee was the second most affected joint. When the data are revised by sex, female individuals had a higher prevalence of knee and temporomandibular osteoarthritis, while males had higher prevalence rates of elbow or wrist osteoarthritis. Traumatic lesions and infectious diseases are less frequent, while cases of oral pathologies, such as serious periodontal disease, and physiological stress markers, such as linear enamel hypoplasia, are common.

Epidemics and infectious diseases were common in the ancient world, and the population of Hispania Tarraconensis was likely exposed to various diseases due to environmental and social conditions. Malnutrition and poor hygiene, especially in urban centres, contributed to the spread of infectious diseases such as cholera. Malaria, spread by mosquitoes present in marshes, was documented in central and southern Italy in Roman times, and may have been common in the cities in Hispania Tarraconensis near marshes or rivers. Tuberculosis, leprosy, and venereal diseases such as syphilis were also present among the population. The first great epidemic that affected Roman populations took place in the Antonine period seems to have been Variola major (smallpox), and it caused the death of 2% of the inhabitants of the Empire as a whole. The next great pandemic, during the time of Cyprian, lasted for 20 years and affected most large cities in the Empire—most likely, also in the large cities of Hispania Tarraconensis, such as Tarraco and Carthago Nova. Some authors identify it as cholera or typhus, or even smallpox or influenza. In the fifth century CE, there was a plague in Hispania Tarraconensis, but the only well-recorded great pandemic is the first bubonic plague, which affected the whole of the Iberian peninsula in Justinian's reign (579 CE). The bubonic plague reappeared one more time in the Iberian peninsula during the Visigothic period during Egica's reign (687–702 CE). Between 707 and 709, another plague outbreak reduced the population of Hispania by half. The province continued to have periodic outbreaks throughout the Middle Ages and beyond.

Moving from the population characteristics into the population numbers, quantifying the inhabitants of a territory from archaeological, anthropological, and historical evidence is also a challenging task. Despite various methods being employed, none of them can be used alone to accurately calculate demographic figures due to the fragmentary and subjective nature of the data, resulting in large margins of error. For example, data from cemeteries are difficult to quantify as the universe of the population is unknown, and the survival of remains can be influenced by factors such as the funerary and burial rite used. Similarly, epigraphic evidence can provide valuable demographic numbers in rare and specific cases, but interpretation issues can arise due to the fragmentary and decontextualized nature of the texts. Public buildings, urban infrastructures, and water supply also fail in providing reliable estimates for Hispania Tarraconensis. While estimating the capacities of public buildings can provide valuable information, they tend to surpass the total population of a city as they were meant to accommodate the inhabitants of rural areas and nearby cities. Water supply can also be misleading, as water in ancient towns may have been used for purposes other than drinking, and therefore may not correlate with population numbers.

'Density by area' or 'people per area' is a popular method used to estimate population numbers, but it also has significant limitations. It fails to consider the possibility of vertical constructions, and there is no standard density value for Roman cities that can simply be applied to all case studies. Moreover, estimating the size of a city is often difficult. The used walled area can only be seen as a very rough estimation, as cities could outgrow their walls, or pastures and other uninhabited areas might have been included in the walled perimeter. On the other hand, the housing unit method, while considered to be the 'less inaccurate' method of all the methods discussed in Chapter 3, is also problematic and suffers from several methodological issues. It can be difficult to define what a 'household' is, and the area, layout, and plan, and number of inhabitants of a household can vary significantly based on the type of family structure. Additionally, it is impossible to estimate the total number of inhabitants if we do not know how many people were living in each domestic unit, so an average value is needed, which is archaeologically invisible and cannot be calculated from the archaeological record. In sum, while various methods can be employed to estimate population numbers, they all have limitations and require careful consideration, contextualization, and customization.

With all the above in mind and with the aim of reaching an estimate for the population numbers of the territory under study during the Late Iron Age, and to lay down the basis of the later diachronic comparison, in Chapter 4 we have improved the existing methodological apparatus for conducting demographic calculations, urbanization rates, and interpreting and comparing different urban systems in the Iberian peninsula during the fourth and third centuries BCE. When studying *oppida*, it is important to consider the unique characteristics of each site, such as its size, intramural built up density, urban configuration, and way of life. Extrapolating a specific density/hectare number to all *oppida* or using the same density/hectare to all *oppida* belonging to a specific group can be misleading and result in inaccurate conclusions. With that in mind, it is also true that our work shows how some of the variables needed for reliable demographic estimates are relatively homogeneous among some—but never all—of the studied Iron Age groups. For example, household average sizes between 70 and 100 square metres were the norm in most of the large Iron Age *oppida*, and ratios of 30–40% of communal/public space vs. 60–70% of household space seem to exist in most of the analysed Iberian, Celtiberian, Carpetani, and Vaccean settlements. However, our research also shows that customized calculations are always necessary because even within the same Iron Age group, settlement systems and household sizes can sometimes vary greatly.

As a direct consequence of improving the methodological apparatus, our results provide new insights on how the settlement patterns of the Iron Age groups that populated Iberia were diverse and varied, depending on factors such as geography, size of settlements, and social and urban organization. Coastal areas tended to have a high number of smaller settlements, leading to a mix of hierarchical and heterarchical settlement systems with low urbanization rates, as is the case of the Iberians and the groups in the north-western territories. With that in mind, few differences in the average size, distribution, and hierarchies between the northern and southern Iberian *oppida* exist. While the northern Iberians had a settlement pattern characterized by relatively small but numerous *oppida*, the Oretani in the south had larger *oppida* organized in a hierarchical system. The more heterarchical system observed among the northern Iberians might be due to the existence of a multitude of independent groups in the region, as mentioned in classical sources, and may show that, under the term Iberian, we tend to group together diverse realities. Similarly, while the north-west is generally characterized by relatively small castros, the Cantabrians and Asturians had some larger primary centres, which may have been the result of Roman policies and a later conquest. Inland groups such as the Celtiberians, Carpetani, and Vaccaei had larger settlements and a hierarchical organization. The urbanization rates of these groups were relatively high, and they were likely organized following a city-state model. The Vettones require further research due to their small sample size in our dataset (see Appendix I), but show a very specific type of settlement that has no parallel among any other of the studied groups, including large settlements and very low population densities. Turning back into population numbers, our estimates have suggested a total population between 2,000,000 (low count) and 2,500,000 (high count) inhabitants for the lands that later will become the province of Hispania Citerior/Tarraconensis.

Estimating the population of the Tarraconensis province in the Early Empire is no less of a challenging task. With all, based on the available evidence discussed in Chapter 5, which includes literary sources, archaeological estimates, and census data from different periods, we decided to use a population density range for Hispania Tarraconensis between 150/200 and 250/300 inhabitants per hectare in the estimates we conducted by using the density by area method. However, it is important to keep in mind that there was likely a substantial variation in population density within the region. Similarly, there is still much work to be done in studying the rural and intermediate settlements' 'secondary agglomerations' of Hispania Tarraconensis. The lack of data and research into these settlement categories is hindering our ability to make accurate demographic estimates for the countryside and the region. However, recent studies into the territory of Tarraco and other areas show that there is potential for growth in this field of research. By conducting extensive rural surveys with accurate and standardized methodologies and studying the secondary agglomerations, we can gain a better understanding of the population patterns and demographic changes in the province.

Our calculations have estimated an urban population of 580,000 and a total population of 2,600,000 for the province of Hispania Tarraconensis during the Early Empire, with an urbanization rate of 22% that could have reached 30% in the more densely urbanized territories of the province. While a shy population growth that took place in the territory rather than in urban centres can be suggested from the Iron Age to the Early Empire, the urbanization rate decreased during the Roman period in comparison to the Iron Age. There was also a significant urban demographic change in the north-west of the province, likely due to clearer urban organization in the Roman period. The juridical status of communities allowed for a clearer distinction between urban and non-urban settlements, which may have resulted in some settlements classified as secondary agglomerations in the Roman period instead of urban. The cut-off point of what *oppida* should be considered urban or rural is unclear for the Iron Age, and may have varied between different groups, hindering our capacity, at least to some extent, to accurately estimate urbanization rates during this period. What does seem clear is that there was a shift in the concentration towards few large urban centres in Tarraconensis during the Roman period, with new and larger cities emerging in the Mediterranean coastal area and that acted as attraction poles for the population.

Despite all the efforts made in Chapter 6, the evolution of the Late Roman city in the Iberian peninsula is perhaps the hardest to evaluate from a population perspective. Whether there was an overall decline or a shift towards rural areas is hard to say. Quantifying urban decline is not feasible, as there are only a few Late Roman cities whose perimeter walls or urban occupation have been calculated so far, making impossible the task of estimating and comparing population numbers as we have done for the Iron Age and the Early Empire. Similarly, due to the scarcity of the existent datasets, we have been unable to estimate urbanization rates or to create an RSA model for the urban system of the period in the province, a task that is left for future studies. On the other hand, thanks to a series of well-studied case studies, we have been able to document the development of luxurious *villae* in the countryside, revealing a dynamic territory in constant evolution rather than one in decline or crisis, one in which some of the urban elites are moving and investing into rural areas. From an urban perspective, the Late Roman period in Hispania Tarraconensis, Carthaginensis, and Gallaecia seems to be characterized by a general trend of de-urbanization, with signs of abandonment of public spaces, and the appearance of burials and landfills inside towns. We do observe an urban shift towards the interior as large cities such as Tarraco and Carthago Nova seem to shrink whereas the capitals of the new kingdoms, such as Bracara for the Suebi, have a pull effect on the population. Finally, there were movements of Germanic tribes from Central Europe to the Iberian peninsula, but their demographic impact is difficult to evaluate due to limited ancient sources and lack of genetic impact.

If we move now into the third pillar of any demographic study, mobility and connectivity, the development of transport networks played a significant role in the movement of the peoples in Hispania Citerior/Tarraconensis. The construction of ports and roads was not linear, but instead partially built upon previous native trackways and settlement patterns. The Roman military disembarkment in the late third century BCE forced the creation of the first harbour infrastructures in the Mediterranean ports of Emporion, Tarraco, and Carthago Nova, which saw the movement of amphorae, black-gloss pottery, and coins from the Italian peninsula and that serve as good indicators of how frequently contacts between Hispania and Italy took place.

Based on the available evidence discussed in Chapter 7, it appears that early Republican migrations to Hispania Citerior were not significant in terms of population size. Most legionaries returned to Italy, and there are no major inscriptions suggesting a large Italian presence in the province. However, there is some indication that immigrants from southern Italian regions, particularly the Tyrrhenian coast from the Gulf of Naples to the region of Minturnae, had a preferential relationship with the coast of Hispania Citerior. The city of Carthago Nova and its nearby mines may have received most newcomers, whether as slaves, traders, or participants in commercial networks with Italy. The new urban foundations also appear to have been largely composed of local inhabitants, as the epigraphic evidence from the Ebro valley, the north-east, and the Levant of the province seem to suggest. That said, some exceptions did exist, and settlements like Valentia or La Cabañeta did have a strong Italic component, showing once again no grand narrative works for every city in the province. Many urban realities existed in Hispania Citerior in terms of language, culture, and ethnicity. Overall, while there were some migrations to specific cities and coastal regions, it does not seem likely that the Italic migrations towards the province in the Republican period were substantial in volume.

The Atlantic side of the province was conquered in the first century BCE, and port infrastructures were created in some river estuaries. The process increased during the Cantabrian Wars (29–19 BCE), which involved the settlement of four legions and auxiliary troops, as well as the creation of reliable supply routes in the north-west of the province. The presence of the Roman army in the north-west favoured migration to this region, at least during the first century CE. In the Early Empire, a wider range of foreign migrants can be detected in Hispania Tarraconensis, although they still represent a small percentage of the total population. A significant number were coming from northern Italy due to legionary levies in these regions, showing an interesting change in the origin of the Italic migrants between the Late Republic and the Early Empire. The Gaulish provinces and North Africa were the second and third most important regions of origin respectively. Some of these migrants moved due to military and administrative reasons, while others came for economic ones, such as trade or investment opportunities that were available due to the province's proximity to their home regions and the existence of well-established trade routes.

It is important to note that temporary and seasonal movements were common in the province of Hispania Tarraconensis and over time may have mobilized an important number of individuals. Due to the development of the transport network in the Republican and imperial period, people were able to move more freely and easily within the province. Many duties, such as agricultural work, trading, construction, and harbour tasks, were limited to certain seasons, so populations would often move to another town during the off-season. In addition to this, certain professional occupations, such as military service and domestic work, involved young people who would move to urban or military sites for a limited period. The epigraphic record of Hispania Tarraconensis provides some unique case studies of this seasonal and temporary migration, such as the movement along traditional transhumance routes in the *conventus* Cluniensis and the migration to areas close to mining districts. One particularly interesting case is that of Carthago Nova, which had a significant presence of Italic traders and slaves in its mining complexes. These migrants likely came to the area for economic reasons and would have worked in the mines for a limited period before returning to their homes. Overall, the development of the transport network and the availability of seasonal work opportunities made temporary and seasonal migration a common practice in Hispania Tarraconensis and may have impacted the demography and population numbers of certain regions, either in a positive or negative way, cyclically.

In recent years, the discipline of bioarchaeology is taking a biocultural approach. This new bioarchaeological model integrates biology, archaeology, and social theory to provide all the necessary contextual information. Looking into groups of people who share the same lifestyle, physiological stress, mechanical stress, diet, diseases, grave goods, type of burial, forms of commemoration, etc., is now as important as looking into kinship relations and genetic data. Additionally, other factors such economy, environment, identity, and power are also considered. This integrated approach is necessary and will be key in the future to any ancient demography studies, but is especially relevant for the Roman period, where thanks to the epigraphic material and the ancient sources, we know well that kinship could also include social bonds unrelated to genetic kin or biological relatedness.

With the above in mind, the available data for palaeogenetics and palaeogenomics—although they are limited—for Hispania is discussed in Chapter 8. When integrated with the other historic, epigraphic, and archaeological datasets explored in this book, can offer alternative and very revealing information that helps to interpret and better understand the migratory movements and pathologies of its populations. The studies conducted up to date in Hispania reveal that new genetic elements are introduced during the Roman period, as a result of the expansive nature of Roman colonialism mixing with the previous genetic pool. The genetic relationships among populations based on monoparental genetic markers reveal different histories for the inhabitants of the territory under study. The continuity of female lineages until the Iron Age is observed, but in the Roman period, a difference between the two Iberian groups is seen. The north-eastern mitochondrial genomes are closer to those of the Bronze and Iron Ages, while southern genomes are grouped with later Iberian populations and North African and Near Eastern mtDNA haplotypes.

The Y-chromosome markers, on the other hand, show a dissociation between the Iberian and Italic male lineages, with the former showing the presence of R1b, a typically Western Europe Y-haplogroup, and the latter revealing haplogroups I1, I2a1, and R1a of Eastern Europe and the Germanic tribes (I1), J1, a dominant Arabic haplogroup, or J2, a West Asian and Graeco-Roman haplogroup. It is interesting to note that the differences in the Y-chromosome map suggest that the migratory patterns and genetic contribution of males differed from those of females. This could be attributed to factors such as intermarriage between local women and foreign men, a common practice in colonial processes. The presence of male lineages from Italy, North Africa, and the Near East, as suggested by the Y-chromosome map, is consistent with historical and archaeological evidence of trade, military activity, and slavery in the region. The Carthaginians and Phoenicians, who were known to have a strong presence in the southern part of the Iberian peninsula, are likely to have contributed to this genetic diversity. These findings provide insight into the complex history of migration and settlement in the Iberian peninsula, and highlight the importance of considering both maternal and paternal lineages when studying population genetics.

To conclude, the collaborative efforts of geneticists, archaeologists, historians, anthropologists, and other experts can play a crucial role in the study of ancient demography. Each field brings a unique perspective and set of tools to the table, and by integrating them and engaging in constructive dialogues we can develop a more comprehensive understanding of ancient populations and how they changed and evolved over time. Our interdisciplinary study of the demography of Hispania Citerior/Tarraconensis has allowed us to reconstruct important aspects of its population characteristics, numbers, movements, settlement patterns, and urbanization rates over time. By critically revising previous estimates of population numbers and providing new ones backed up by robust analysis of the available data, we offer a novel picture and a deeper understanding of how the human factor, in its purer demographic expression, is core to the processes of cultural, economic, and social change that occurred during the conquest and subsequent colonial process down to the fall of the Western Roman Empire in Hispania Citerior/Tarraconensis. We cannot forget that population size, its distribution, and movements are important indicators of economic growth, and can shed light on the development of collective identities and cultural exchange. We cannot close these final remarks without saying that this book aims to start the demographic debate for Hispania Citerior/Tarraconensis in particular and for the Iberian peninsula more generally. There is still much work to be done, our datasets and sources must be expanded, methodologies improved, theories and interpretations nuanced and revisited. With further research and future studies, this field will achieve a comprehensive understanding of the complex demographic dynamics that characterized the Iberian peninsula over time.

*The Human Factor: The Demography of the Roman Province of Hispania Citerior/Tarraconensis.* Alejandro G. Sinner, Cèsar Carreras, and Pieter Houten, Oxford University Press. 
DOI: 10.1093/9780191943881.003.0009

# Appendices

## APPENDIX I

## Iron Age sizes

| Settlement | COOR_X | COOR_Y | Ha | Group | Bibliography |
|---|---|---|---|---|---|
| Boya | 41.9228433 | −6.3565555 | 6 | Asturians | Almagro (1995) |
| Campa Torres | 43.5696334 | −5.7093608 | 10.27 | Asturians | Maya (1998); Maya & Cuesta (2001) |
| Capara | 42.5760108 | −5.4806066 | 15 | Asturians | Almagro (1995) |
| Castro de La Campa Torres | 43.56941 | −5.70279 | 8.6 | Asturians | Torres Martínez (2011) 268 |
| Fresno de Carballeda | 41.9995626 | −6.3477284 | 3.5 | Asturians | Almagro (1995) |
| La Almena | 42.1244561 | −6.1635419 | 3 | Asturians | Almagro (1995) |
| Labradas | 43.0295159 | −8.8554278 | 23 | Asturians | Almagro (1995) |
| Lancia | 42.532073 | −5.4128322 | 40 | Asturians | Almagro (1995) |
| Manganeses de la Polvorosa (Zamora) | 42.03624 | −5.746381 | 11 | Asturians | Delibes & Romero (2011) |
| Noega | 43.5140354 | −5.6867486 | 12 | Asturians | Almagro (1995) |
| Peña Piñera | 42.73488 | −6.68033 | 13 | Asturians | Celis & Muños (2015) |
| Bagunte | 41.3713325 | −8.6602145 | 15 | Callaeci | Almagro (1995) |
| Briteiros | 41.522528 | −8.304305 | 20.5 | Callaeci | Almagro (1995); Torres Martínez (2011) |
| Castro da Graña | 42.971966 | −7.972827 | 10 | Callaeci | |
| Castro da Subidá | 42.3825139 | −8.70915556 | 3 | Callaeci | PXOM (2012) |
| Castro das Travesas | 43.1654306 | −8.35855556 | 12 | Callaeci | PXOM |
| Castro de Cambre | 43.2919935 | −8.3482183 | 3 | Callaeci | |

*Continued*

| Settlement | COOR_X | COOR_Y | Ha | Group | Bibliography |
|---|---|---|---|---|---|
| Castro de Castromaior | 42.833211 | −7.719879 | 4.3 | Callaeci | PXOM |
| Castro de Elviña | 43.3296667 | −8.41533333 | 4 | Callaeci | PXOM |
| Castro de Fazouro | 43.6035 | −7.2985 | 6 | Callaeci | PXOM (2012) |
| Castro de Formigueiros | 42.705719 | −7.353395 | 5 | Callaeci | PXOM |
| Castro de Meangos | 43.2280521 | −8.2583444 | 3.17 | Callaeci | PXOM (2012) |
| Castro de Rañobre | 43.3377778 | −8.48861111 | 4 | Callaeci | PXOM (1996) |
| Castro de San Cibrán de Lás | 42.361 | −8.03 | 9.5 | Callaeci | Carballo Arceo (1996); Torres Martínez (2011) |
| Castro de Santa Trega | 41.89276 | −8.869351 | 20 | Callaeci | Carballo Arceo (1996) |
| Castro de Santaia | 43.1154583 | −8.041875 | 4 | Callaeci | PXOM |
| Castro de Santo Tomás | 43.59203 | −8.18717 | 3.2 | Callaeci | PXOM |
| Castro de Vigo | 42.2230802 | −8.73127831 | 17 | Callaeci | Hidalgo Cuñarro & Viñas Cué (1998) |
| Castro de Viladonga | 43.1611667 | −7.38866667 | 4 | Callaeci | PXOM (2012) |
| Castro de Vilar | 43.256111 | −8.273283 | 5.14 | Callaeci | PXOM (2012) |
| Castro do Foro | 43.5841643 | −8.1331655 | 4 | Callaeci | PXOM |
| Castro do Monte da Guía (Teis) | 42.2574975 | −8.70030164 | 6.43 | Callaeci | Hidalgo Cuñarro & Viñas Cué (1998) |
| Castro do Sino (Teis) | 42.2588035 | −8.68356439 | 3.58 | Callaeci | Hidalgo Cuñarro & Viñas Cué (1998) |
| El Castro (Os Mazos) | 43.43289 | −6.79253 | 3 | Callaeci | |
| Lansbrica | 42.3734131 | −8.0720856 | 8.8 | Callaeci | Almagro (1995) |
| Monte Mozinho | 41.1483682 | −8.3174734 | 20 | Callaeci | Almagro (1995); Torres Martínez (2011) |
| Samoedo | 43.33107 | −8.27348 | 6 | Callaeci | Almagro (1995) |
| Sanfins | 41.5803917 | −8.7786806 | 15.4 | Callaeci | Almagro (1995); Torres Martínez (2011) |
| Santa Tecla | 42.3886108 | −7.4531977 | 21 | Callaeci | Almagro (1995) |
| Souteliño | 42.0539195 | −7.4737491 | 4 | Callaeci | Almagro (1995) |
| Tontobriga | 40.6182559 | −7.0077208 | 32.6 | Callaeci | Almagro (1995) |
| Viladonga | 43.0648669 | −7.6497661 | 4.4 | Callaeci | Almagro (1995) |
| Castilnegro | 43.37225 | −3.80287 | 5.5 | Cantabrians | Fernández Acebo et al. (2010a) 475 |
| Ceja de las Lombas | 43.20647 | −4.09066 | 5.4 | Cantabrians | Fernández Acebo et al. (2010a) 247 |
| Cueto de Mogro | 43.42232 | −3.97342 | 5.5 | Cantabrians | Fernández Acebo et al. (2010a) 219 |
| Cueto de Moroso | 43.22693 | −4.05332 | 5 | Cantabrians | Fernández Acebo et al. (2010a) 257 |
| El Castillo de Prellezo | 43.39371 | −4.45213 | 3 | Cantabrians | Fernández Acebo et al. (2010a) 175; Torres Martínez (2011) 268 |

| | | | | | |
|---|---|---|---|---|---|
| El Castrejón | 43.02218 | −4.2465 | 4.2 | Cantabrians | Fernández Acebo et al. (2010a) 345 |
| El Castro (Campoo-Los Valles) | 42.93148 | −3.85624 | 9 | Cantabrians | Fernández Acebo et al. (2010a) 451 |
| Iuliobriga | 42.98511 | −4.11392 | 7.5 | Cantabrians | Almagro (1995) |
| La Campana | 43.02781 | −4.19839 | 3.2 | Cantabrians | Fernández Acebo et al. (2010a) 365 |
| La Guariza | 43.00998 | −4.18248 | 4 | Cantabrians | Fernández Acebo et al. (2010a) 371 |
| La Lomba | 43.02965 | −4.09455 | 5 | Cantabrians | Fernández Acebo et al. (2010a) 435 |
| La Masera | 43.40223 | −4.04064 | 5.35 | Cantabrians | Fernández Acebo et al. (2010a) 183 |
| La Peñuco | 43.20152 | −4.62806 | 3.3 | Cantabrians | Fernández Acebo et al. (2010a) 151 |
| Las Rabas | 42.95572 | −4.12682 | 10 | Cantabrians | Fernández Acebo et al. (2010a) 405 |
| Lerones | 43.09981 | −4.5479 | 3.2 | Cantabrians | Fernández Acebo et al. (2010a) 157 |
| Llan de La Peña | 43.10494 | −4.69105 | 4.6 | Cantabrians | Fernández Acebo et al. (2010a) 137 |
| Los Cantones | 43.15806 | −4.54472 | 9 | Cantabrians | Fernández Acebo et al. (2010a) 161 |
| Mizmaya | 43.38141 | −3.69783 | 3.5 | Cantabrians | Fernández Acebo et al. (2010a) 497 |
| Monte Bernorio | 42.7944422 | −4.1938071 | 28 | Cantabrians | Torres Martinez (2011) 269 |
| Peña de Sámano | 43.34366 | −3.23324 | 10 | Cantabrians | Fernández Acebo et al. (2010a) 571 |
| Sebrango | 43.1468 | −4.72141 | 3 | Cantabrians | Fernández Acebo et al. (2010a) 145 |
| Vellica | 42.7492463 | −4.2753585 | 10 | Cantabrians | Almagro (1995) |
| Alharilla | 40.118056 | −3.160278 | 6 | Carpetani | Urbina (2007) |
| Arroyo de los Castrejones | 40.109167 | −3.386944 | 3.5 | Carpetani | Urbina Martínez (2000) |
| Atalaya | 39.836921 | −3.571782 | 14 | Carpetani | Urbina Martínez (2000) |
| C Yepes | 39.9 | −3.628889 | 15 | Carpetani | Urbina Martínez (2000) |
| Castejón | 40.5310008 | −3.0315552 | 3.5 | Carpetani | Almagro (1995) |
| Castellar | 39.983333 | −3.366667 | 6.9 | Carpetani | Urbina Martínez (2000) |
| Cerro de La Gavia | 40.383333 | −3.616667 | 4 | Carpetani | |
| Cerro del Gollino | 39.759444 | −3.165 | 18 | Carpetani | Almagro (1995); Torres Rodríguez (2012) |
| Cerro del Gollino | 39.72286 | −3.3054972 | 15 | Carpetani | Almagro (1995) |
| Cerro de Manroyo | | | 6 | Carpetani | Urbina (2007) |
| Ciruelos | 39.933333 | −3.6 | 20 | Carpetani | Urbina Martínez (2000) |
| Complutum | 40.4818396 | −3.3644973 | 68 | Carpetani | Almagro (1995) |

*Continued*

| Settlement | COOR_X | COOR_Y | Ha | Group | Bibliography |
|---|---|---|---|---|---|
| Consabura | 39.460918 | −3.6070786 | 30 | Carpetani | Almagro (1995) |
| Contrebia Carbica | 40.143961 | −2.6912644 | 45 | Carpetani | Almagro (1995); Lorrio (1997) |
| Dehesa de Oliva | 40.8831251 | −3.4815582 | 26.5 | Carpetani | Almagro (1995) |
| Ecce Homo | 40.4833679 | −3.3233621 | 6 | Carpetani | Almagro (1995); Lorrio (1997) |
| El Albornoz | 40.466667 | −3.366667 | 4 | Carpetani | Azcárraga (2014) |
| El Cerro de las Fuentes | 40.6553548 | −3.05560147 | 4 | Carpetani | Azcárraga (2014) |
| El Cervero I | 39.639148 | −3.081738 | 10 | Carpetani | Domingo et al. (2007) |
| El Llano de la Horca | 40.478013 | −3.233821 | 10 | Carpetani | Baquedano Pérez et al. (2007) 380 |
| Esperillas | 39.976667 | −3.190833 | 12 | Carpetani | Urbina Martínez (2000) |
| Fuente Berrato | 40.03675 | −3.45956 | 12.5 | Carpetani | Urbina Martínez (2000) |
| Fuente Calzada | 39.976667 | −3.190833 | 11.7 | Carpetani | Urbina Martínez (2000) |
| Fuente de la Mora | 40.354207 | −3.756708 | 8 | Carpetani | |
| Fuente Pozuelo | 40.560833 | −4.016944 | 3.8 | Carpetani | Urbina Martínez (2000) |
| Hoyo Serna | 39.983333 | −3.366667 | 12.2 | Carpetani | Urbina Martínez (2000) |
| La Piojosa (Villalbilla) | 40.433889 | −3.298889 | 3 | Carpetani | Azcárraga (2014) |
| La Plata | 39.81448 | −3.490423 | 11 | Carpetani | Urbina Martínez (2000) |
| Las Minas | 40.0699 | −3.358 | 3.7 | Carpetani | Urbina Martínez (2000) |
| Melgar | 39.838734 | −3.65701 | 10.2 | Carpetani | Urbina Martínez (2000) |
| Montealegre | 39.835679 | −3.290283 | 13 | Carpetani | Urbina Martínez (2000) |
| Muela de Taracena | 40.6536654 | −3.1264137 | 5 | Carpetani | Almagro (1995) |
| Oreja | 40.109167 | −3.386944 | 8.6 | Carpetani | Urbina Martínez (2000) |
| Peña de la Muela | 40.033333 | −3.133333 | 7.4 | Carpetani | Urbina Martínez (2000) |
| San Cristobal (Yepes) | 39.902778 | −3.623611 | 3.8 | Carpetani | Urbina Martínez (2000) |
| San Ildefonso | 39.8 | −3.416667 | 16 | Carpetani | Urbina Martínez (2000); in other texts Urbina says 10 ha |
| San Juan del Viso | 40.15 | −3.916667 | 6 | Carpetani | Azcárraga (2017) |
| Santorcaz | 40.4715789 | −3.2335594 | 14 | Carpetani | Almagro (1995) |
| Sotomayor | 40.039483 | −3.528212 | 7.5 | Carpetani | Urbina Martínez (2000) |
| Titulcia | 40.1379148 | −3.5709978 | 12 | Carpetani | Almagro (1995); Polo López and Valenciano Prieto (2013) |
| Toletum | 39.8560679 | −4.0239568 | 40 | Carpetani | Almagro (1995); Lorrio (1997) |
| Valdajos | 39.983333 | −3.366667 | 7.9 | Carpetani | Urbina Martínez (2000) |
| Valdeibáñez | 40.474722 | −3.23 | 3 | Carpetani | Azcárraga (2014) |

| | | | | | |
|---|---|---|---|---|---|
| Valdelacierva | 39.983333 | −3.433333 | 13 | Carpetani | Urbina Martínez (2000) |
| Valdelascasas | 40.0295556 | −3.5769412 | 7.8 | Carpetani | Urbina Martínez (2000) |
| Venta de Juan Cano | 39.855452 | −3.213098 | 13.2 | Carpetani | Urbina Martínez (2000) |
| Ventorra de Rufino (Villalbilla) | 40.4338 | −3.298 | 3 | Carpetani | Azcárraga (2014) |
| Villamejor | 40.033333 | −3.602778 | 17 | Carpetani | Urbina Martínez (2000) |
| Villares | 39.956944 | −3.496667 | 22.5 | Carpetani | Urbina Martínez (2000); Salvador Conejo (2016) 174 gives 30 ha |
| Villasequilla | 39.883333 | −3.716667 | 11.5 | Carpetani | Urbina Martínez (2000) |
| Villatobas | 39.9 | −3.333333 | 12 | Carpetani | Urbina Martínez (2000) |
| Viloria | 39.987018 | −3.264759 | 36.3 | Carpetani | Urbina Martínez (2000); Urbina Martínez (2014a) gives 36.3 |
| Yeles | 40.1197677 | −3.8042363 | 3.5 | Carpetani | Almagro (1995) |
| Alto de la Solana de Sagides | 41.1483328 | −2.29721546 | 3 | Celtiberians | Lorrio (1997) |
| Arcóbriga | 41.2958857 | −2.1380916 | 7.75 | Celtiberians | Almagro (1995); Lorrio (1997) |
| Augustobriga – Arekorata | 41.8314 | −1.9848 | 49 | Celtiberians | Jimeno Martínez (2011) |
| Bilbilis | 41.3527628 | −1.6422977 | 21 | Celtiberians | Almagro (1995); Lorrio (1997) |
| Cabezo del Cuervo – Alcañiz | 41.050254 | −0.1329565 | 18 | Celtiberians | Almagro (1995) |
| Canales de la Sierra | 42.141111 | −3.024167 | 11 | Celtiberians | Lorrio (1997) |
| Castellar de Frías | 42.76225 | −3.29394 | 7.4 | Celtiberians | Almagro (1995) |
| Cerrillo Carraconchel | 41.1759043 | −2.0165062 | 10 | Celtiberians | Lorrio (1997) |
| Clunia – Alto del Cuerno | 41.7741442 | −3.35846901 | 18 | Celtiberians | Lorrio (1997) |
| Contrebia Belaisca | 41.5067282 | −1.0301073 | 12 | Celtiberians | Almagro (1995); Lorrio (1997) |
| Contrebia Leukade | 42.3495152 | −3.9160008 | 13.5 | Celtiberians | Almagro (1995); Lorrio (1997); Torres Martínez (2011) 268 |
| El Castejón (Luzaga) | 40.9766682 | −2.4456489 | 5.5 | Celtiberians | Lorrio (1997) |
| El Castellar (Frías de Albarracín) | 40.3377207 | −1.61599875 | 7.4 | Celtiberians | Lorrio (1997) |
| El Castillejo de La Laguna | 42.056115 | −2.419842 | 4 | Celtiberians | Jimeno Martínez (2011) |
| El Piquete de la Atalaya | 41.252813 | −0.868697 | 12 | Celtiberians | Lorrio (1997) |
| Ercavica | 40.4302018 | −2.6699792 | 7 | Celtiberians | Almagro (1995) |
| Kelin | 39.558333 | −1.278611 | 10 | Celtiberians | Moreno Martín & Valor Abad (2010) 251–3; Almagro (1995); Lorrio (1997) gives 6 ha for Los Villares de Ventosa |

*Continued*

| Settlement | COOR_X | COOR_Y | Ha | Group | Bibliography |
|---|---|---|---|---|---|
| La Caridad de Caminreal | 40.8388234 | −1.3209427 | 12.5 | Celtiberians | Almagro (1995); Lorrio (1997) |
| La Corona (Almazán) | 41.478566 | −2.54332 | 5.5 | Celtiberians | Lorrio (1997); Romero & Lorrio (2011) |
| La Coronilla de Velilla de Medinaceli | 41.1782 | −2.34056 | 6 | Celtiberians | Lorrio (1997) |
| La Custodia (Viana, Navarra) | 42.504492 | −2.390282 | 12.5 | Celtiberians | Torres Martínez (2011) 268 |
| Los Rodiles | 40.89722 | −1.782222 | 5 | Celtiberians | Diario Official Castilla-La Mancha 18-09-2012; Arenas Esteban (2011) |
| Luzón | 41.0266841 | −2.2766738 | 5 | Celtiberians | Almagro (1995) |
| Numantia | 41.8150617 | −2.4460875 | 7.6 | Celtiberians | Almagro (1995) |
| Ocenilla | 41.7927724 | −2.621681 | 7 | Celtiberians | Lorrio (1997) |
| Ocilis | 41.1723392 | −2.4353741 | 20 | Celtiberians | Almagro (1995) |
| Pinilla Trasmonte | 41.86709 | −3.58951 | 18 | Celtiberians | Lorrio (1997); Jimeno Martínez (2011) |
| Poyo del Cid | 40.8828637 | −1.333201 | 10 | Celtiberians | Almagro (1995); Lorrio (1997) |
| Secaisa | 41.2990588 | −1.5165816 | 15 | Celtiberians | Almagro (1995) |
| Segeda | 41.28913 | −1.51768 | 17 | Celtiberians | Lorrio (1997); Burillo Mozota (2011) |
| Segobriga | 39.9207771 | −2.8045626 | 10.5 | Celtiberians | Almagro (1995); Lorrio (1997) |
| Segontia | 41.0680324 | −2.6405659 | 20 | Celtiberians | Almagro (1995) |
| Segontia Lanca | 41.60985 | −3.40061 | 60 | Celtiberians | Almagro (1995); Lorrio (1997) |
| Solarana | 41.97 | −3.66 | 21 | Celtiberians | Lorrio (1997); Jimeno Martínez (2011) |
| Termes | 41.3687938 | −3.1993534 | 21 | Celtiberians | Almagro (1995) |
| Uxama Argaela | 42.8946583 | −3.0442915 | 30 | Celtiberians | Almagro (1995) |
| Valeria | 39.8125272 | −2.1470902 | 8 | Celtiberians | Almagro (1995); Lorrio (1997) |
| Villar del Río | 42.075381 | −2.351508 | 10 | Celtiberians | Lorrio (1997) |
| Villavieja de Muño | 42.2596641 | −3.8929133 | 12 | Celtiberians | Almagro (1995) |
| Alarcos | 38.9357165 | −3.9838385 | 12 | Iberians | Huerta y Morales (2011); Soria & Mata (2015) |
| Alarcos (Ciudad Real) | 38.9571 | −4.01017 | 18 | Iberians | Manzaneda Martín (2017) |
| Almedina | 38.6240327 | −2.954419 | 15 | Iberians | Almagro (1995) |
| Arse -Sagunt | 39.6791712 | −0.2774146 | 11.5 | Iberians | Pers. Comm. I. Grau |
| Burriac (Cabrera de Mar, Barcelona) | 41.5375667 | 2.3872475 | 10 | Iberians | Moret (1996); Zamora (2006–2007) |
| Cabeza de Buey | 38.626888 | −3.2030952 | 6 | Iberians | Almagro (1995) |

| | | | | | |
|---|---|---|---|---|---|
| Cabeza de Buey (Torre de Juan Abad) | 38.629336 | −3.203266 | 8 | Iberians | Manzaneda Martín (2017) |
| Calatrava la Vieja (Carrión de Calatrava) | 39.073824 | −3.835168 | 6 | Iberians | Manzaneda Martín (2017) |
| Castellar de la Meca | 38.959999 | −1.1550662 | 15 | Iberians | Pers. Comm. I. Grau; Lorrio Alvarado and Simón García (2016) |
| Castellet de Banyoles | 41.061389 | 0.668056 | 4.4 | Iberians | Asensio et al. (2012); Moret (1996) |
| Cástulo | 38.034757 | −3.6229968 | 44 | Iberians | Manzaneda Martín (2017) |
| Cerro de la Virgen (Membrilla) | 38.972435 | −3.354343 | 5 | Iberians | Manzaneda Martín (2017) |
| Cerro de las Cabezas (Valdepeñas) | 38.7594573 | −3.3847392 | 14 | Iberians | Almagro (1995); Manzaneda Martín (2017) |
| Cerro de las Monas (Chillón) | 38.72551 | −4.846443 | 4 | Iberians | Manzaneda Martín (2017) |
| Cerro de las Nieves – Calatrava la Vieja | 37.7767062 | −4.1636799 | 5 | Iberians | Huerta y Morales (2011) |
| Collado de los Jardines (Santa Elena) | 38.391223 | −3.498317 | 4 | Iberians | Manzaneda Martín (2017) |
| Collado del Herrerillo (Almuradiel) | 38.512293 | −3.494763 | 5 | Iberians | Manzaneda Martín (2017) |
| Darró | 41.2241992 | 1.7256327 | 4 | Iberians | Mullor & Fierro (1988); |
| El Castellón (Castellar de Santiago) | 38.56118 | −3.302812 | 4 | Iberians | Manzaneda Martín (2017) |
| El Castillo (Alcubillas) | 38.74972 | −3.117135 | 6 | Iberians | Manzaneda Martín (2017) |
| El Monastil | 38.4939926 | −0.7962546 | 3.5 | Iberians | Pers. Comm. I. Grau |
| El Turo del Montgros (El Brull, Barcelona) | 41.81657 | 2.30531 | 9 | Iberians | Moret (1996) |
| El Vilar (Valls) | 41.28728 | 1.25891 | 6 | Iberians | Soria & Mata (2015) |
| Giribaile (Vilches) | 38.121416 | −3.484662 | 14.56 | Iberians | Manzaneda Martín (2017) |
| Ilici | 39.1947105 | −0.5042406 | 10 | Iberians | Pers. Comm. I. Grau |
| Kese | 41.1172364 | 1.2546057 | 10 | Iberians | Otiña Hermoso & Ruiz de Arbulo (2000) |
| La Bastida de Alcusses | 38.8155018 | −0.8054577 | 6.9 | Iberians | Soria & Mata (2015) |
| La Bienvenida | 38.6461088 | −4.5175612 | 10 | Iberians | Almagro (1995) |
| La Carència | 39.3889439 | −0.7174489 | 7.4 | Iberians | Pers. Comm. I. Grau |
| La Piedra de Peñarrubia | 38.43099 | −2.168453 | 6 | Iberians | Soria & Mata (2015) |
| La Serreta (Alcoi) | 38.69189 | −0.446706 | 5.5 | Iberians | Soria & Mata (2015) |
| La Solivella -Alcalá de Chivert | 40.3041662 | 0.2252763 | 5 | Iberians | |
| La Torre dels Encantats | 41.5797031 | 2.5491562 | 4 | Iberians | Moret (1996); Garcès et al. (2013) 13 |

*Continued*

| Settlement | COOR_X | COOR_Y | Ha | Group | Bibliography |
|---|---|---|---|---|---|
| Laminium | 38.8995809 | −3.0528676 | 8 | Iberians | Manzaneda Martín (2017) |
| Les Masies de Sant Miquel | 41.2778415 | 1.4905591 | 4 | Iberians | Guitart et al. (2011); Noguera et al., (2020) provide 3.5 ha |
| Lezuza | 38.9491417 | −2.3539771 | 8 | Iberians | |
| Libisosa | 38.94158 | −2.3545 | 7.5 | Iberians | Manzaneda Martín (2017) |
| Los Miradores (Caracuel de Calatrava) | 38.846466 | −4.056011 | 5 | Iberians | Manzaneda Martín (2017) |
| Los Terreros (Torrebaja) | 40.113593 | −1.244609 | 4 | Iberians | Soria & Mata (2015) |
| Los Villares | 38.9644548 | −2.8844161 | 10 | Iberians | Almagro (1995) |
| Los Villares de Caudete | 38.7185793 | −0.9534242 | 10 | Iberians | Pers. Comm. I. Grau |
| Los Villaricos | 38.0418669 | −1.4906872 | 7 | Iberians | |
| Mairena (Puebla del Principe) | 38.547138 | −2.92755 | 3 | Iberians | Manzaneda Martín (2017) |
| Meca | 38.9589152 | −1.2311299 | 15 | Iberians | Almagro (1995) |
| Mentesa Oretana (Villanueva de la Fuente) | 38.69219 | −2.69485 | 10 | Iberians | Manzaneda Martín (2017) |
| Noria de Juan Muñoz (Viso del Marqués) | 38.609111 | −3.606704 | 4 | Iberians | Manzaneda Martín (2017) |
| Olerdola (Barcelona) | 41.3214216 | 1.7234463 | 3.5 | Iberians | Moret (1996); Soria & Mata (2015) |
| Oretum | 38.7601631 | −3.7180125 | 16.5 | Iberians | Almagro (1995); Manzaneda Martín (2017) gives 8 |
| Peñas de San Pedro | 38.729188 | −2.000971 | 4.5 | Iberians | Manzaneda Martín (2017) |
| Plaza de Moros (Malagón) | 39.852049 | −3.324757 | 4 | Iberians | Manzaneda Martín (2017) |
| Puente del Obispo (Baeza) | 37.954235 | −3.539518 | 3 | Iberians | Manzaneda Martín (2017) |
| Puig de la Nao (Benicarló) | 40.4180244 | 0.4229813 | 5 | Iberians | |
| Puig del Castell de Samalús | 41.7072824 | 2.3382536 | 4 | Iberians | Guàrdia (2015) |
| Saitabi | 38.9887291 | −0.5191539 | 10 | Iberians | Pers. Comm. I. Grau |
| Sant Miquel de Lliria | 39.63333 | −0.6 | 10 | Iberians | Pers. Comm. I. Grau |

| | | | | | |
|---|---|---|---|---|---|
| Santuario de la Virgen de Criptaza (Campo de Criptana) | 39.406302 | −3.091471 | 6 | Iberians | Manzaneda Martín (2017) |
| Serreta de Alcoi | 38.6850443 | −0.4282519 | 5 | Iberians | Pers. Comm. I. Grau |
| Sisapo | 38.64644 | −4.5183 | 10 | Iberians | Manzaneda Martín (2017) |
| Son Catlar | 39.9543406 | 3.8736999 | 3.75 | Iberians | Soria & Mata (2015) |
| Sucro | 39.1512424 | −0.4346133 | 12.5 | Iberians | Pers. Comm. I. Grau |
| Toriles o Casas Altas (Villarubia de los Ojos) | 39.133636 | −3.523268 | 12 | Iberians | Manzaneda Martín (2017) |
| Torre la Sal | 40.1562497 | 0.0438339 | 10 | Iberians | |
| Tossal de Morquí | 38.9020344 | −0.3092391 | 5 | Iberians | Pers. Comm. I. Grau |
| Tossal de Sant Miquel | 39.620798 | −0.597836 | 15 | Iberians | Soria & Mata (1997) |
| Ullastret | 42.0008975 | 3.0689759 | 5.2 | Iberians | Moret (1996) |
| Valdarachas (Ciudad Real) | 38.89936 | −3.975886 | 3 | Iberians | Manzaneda Martín (2017) |
| Villarejo de San Antón (La Solana) | 38.954443 | −3.266935 | 3 | Iberians | Manzaneda Martín (2017) |
| Xàtiva | 38.990278 | −0.521111 | 8 | Iberians | Soria & Mata (2015) |
| Bagunte | 41.3713325 | −8.6602145 | 15 | North-west | Almagro (1995) |
| Boya | 41.9228433 | −6.3565555 | 6 | North-west | Almagro (1995) |
| Briteiros | 41.522528 | −8.304305 | 20.5 | North-west | Almagro (1995); Torres Martínez (2011) |
| Campa Torres | 43.5696334 | −5.7093608 | 10.27 | North-west | Maya (1998); Maya & Cuesta (2001) |
| Capara | 42.5760108 | −5.4806066 | 15 | North-west | Almagro (1995) |
| Castilnegro | 43.37225 | −3.80287 | 5.5 | North-west | Fernández Acebo et al. (2010a) 475 |
| Castro da Graña | 42.971966 | −7.972827 | 10 | North-west | |
| Castro da Subidá | 42.3825139 | −8.7091556 | 3 | North-west | PXOM (2012) |
| Castro das Travesas | 43.1654306 | −8.3585556 | 12 | North-west | PXOM |
| Castro de Cambre | 43.2919935 | −8.3482183 | 3 | North-west | |
| Castro de Castromaior | 42.833211 | −7.719879 | 4.3 | North-west | PXOM |
| Castro de Elviña | 43.3296667 | −8.4153333 | 4 | North-west | PXOM |
| Castro de Fazouro | 43.6035 | −7.2985 | 6 | North-west | PXOM (2012) |
| Castro de Formigueiros | 42.705719 | −7.353395 | 5 | North-west | PXOM |
| Castro de La Campa Torres | 43.56941 | −5.70279 | 8.6 | North-west | Torres Martínez (2011) 268 |
| Castro de Meangos | 43.2280521 | −8.2583444 | 3.17 | North-west | PXOM (2012) |

*Continued*

| Settlement | COOR_X | COOR_Y | Ha | Group | Bibliography |
|---|---|---|---|---|---|
| Castro de Rañobre | 43.3377778 | −8.4886111 | 4 | North-west | PXOM (1996) |
| Castro de San Cibrán de Lás | 42.361 | −8.03 | 9.5 | North-west | Carballo Arceo (1996); Torres Martínez (2011) |
| Castro de Santa Trega | 41.89276 | −8.869351 | 20 | North-west | Carballo Arceo (1996) |
| Castro de Santaia | 43.1154583 | −8.041875 | 4 | North-west | PXOM |
| Castro de Santo Tomás | 43.59203 | −8.18717 | 3.2 | North-west | PXOM |
| Castro de Vigo | 42.2230802 | −8.7312783 | 17 | North-west | Largest extent in 1st century CE |
| Castro de Viladonga | 43.1611667 | −7.3886667 | 4 | North-west | PXOM (2012) |
| Castro de Vilar | 43.256111 | −8.273283 | 5.14 | North-west | PXOM (2012) |
| Castro do Foro | 43.5841643 | −8.1331655 | 4 | North-west | PXOM |
| Ceja de las Lombas | 43.20647 | −4.09066 | 5.4 | North-west | Fernández Acebo et al. (2010a) 247 |
| Cueto de Mogro | 43.42232 | −3.97342 | 5.5 | North-west | Fernández Acebo et al. (2010a) 219 |
| Cueto de Moroso | 43.22693 | −4.05332 | 5 | North-west | Fernández Acebo et al. (2010a) 257 |
| El Castillo de Prellezo | 43.39371 | −4.45213 | 3 | North-west | Fernández Acebo et al. (2010a) 175; Torres Martínez (2011) 268 |
| El Castrejón | 43.02218 | −4.2465 | 4.2 | North-west | Fernández Acebo et al. (2010a) 345 |
| El Castro (Campoo-Los Valles) | 42.93148 | −3.85624 | 9 | North-west | Fernández Acebo et al. (2010a) 451 |
| El Castro (Os Mazos) | 43.43289 | −6.79253 | 3 | North-west | |
| Fresno de Carballeda | 41.9995626 | −6.3477284 | 3.5 | North-west | Almagro (1995) |
| Iuliobriga | 42.98511 | −4.11392 | 7.5 | North-west | Almagro (1995) |
| La Almena | 42.1244561 | −6.1635419 | 3 | North-west | Almagro (1995) |
| La Campana | 43.02781 | −4.19839 | 3.2 | North-west | Fernández Acebo et al. (2010a) 365 |
| La Guariza | 43.00998 | −4.18248 | 4 | North-west | Fernández Acebo et al. (2010a) 371 |
| La Lomba | 43.02965 | −4.09455 | 5 | North-west | Fernández Acebo et al. (2010a) 435 |
| La Masera | 43.40223 | −4.04064 | 5.35 | North-west | Fernández Acebo et al. (2010a) 183 |
| La Peñuco | 43.20152 | −4.62806 | 3.3 | North-west | Fernández Acebo et al. (2010a) 151 |
| Labradas | 42.100418 | −5.909733 | 23 | North-west | Almagro (1995) |
| Lancia | 42.532073 | −5.4128322 | 40 | North-west | Almagro (1995) |
| Lansbrica | 42.3734131 | −8.0720856 | 8.8 | North-west | Almagro (1995) |
| Las Rabas | 42.95572 | −4.12682 | 10 | North-west | Fernández Acebo et al. (2010a) 405 |

| | | | | | |
|---|---|---|---|---|---|
| Lerones | 43.09981 | −4.5479 | 3.2 | North-west | Fernández Acebo et al. (2010a) 157 |
| Llan de La Peña | 43.10494 | −4.69105 | 4.6 | North-west | Fernández Acebo et al. (2010a) 137 |
| Los Cantones | 43.15806 | −4.54472 | 9 | North-west | Fernández Acebo et al. (2010a) 161 |
| Manganeses de la Polvorosa (Zamora) | 42.03624 | −5.746381 | 11 | North-west | Delibes & Romero (2011) |
| Mizmaya | 43.38141 | −3.69783 | 3.5 | North-west | Fernández Acebo et al. (2010a) 497 |
| Monte Bernorio | 42.7944422 | −4.1938071 | 28 | North-west | Torres Martinez (2011) 269 |
| Monte Mozinho | 41.1483682 | −8.3174734 | 20 | North-west | Almagro (1995); Torres Martínez (2011) |
| Noega | 43.5140354 | −5.6867486 | 12 | North-west | Almagro (1995) |
| Peña Piñera | 42.73488 | −6.68033 | 13 | North-west | Celis & Muños (2015) |
| Samoedo | 43.33107 | −8.27348 | 6 | North-west | Almagro (1995) |
| Sanfins | 41.5803917 | −8.7786806 | 15.4 | North-west | Almagro (1995); Torres Martínez (2011) |
| Santa Tecla | 42.3886108 | −7.4531977 | 21 | North-west | Almagro (1995) |
| Sebrango | 43.1468 | −4.72141 | 3 | North-west | Fernández Acebo et al. (2010a) 145 |
| Souteliño | 42.0539195 | −7.4737491 | 4 | North-west | Almagro (1995) |
| Tongobriga | 41.16202 | −8.1468 | 32.6 | North-west | Almagro (1995) |
| Tontobriga | 40.6182559 | −7.0077208 | 32.6 | North-west | Almagro (1995) |
| Vellica | 42.7492463 | −4.2753585 | 10 | North-west | Almagro (1995) |
| Viladonga | 43.0648669 | −7.6497661 | 4.4 | North-west | Almagro (1995) |
| Aguilar de Campos | 41.9840369 | −5.1807319 | 4 | Vacceans | Almagro (1995) |
| Amallobriga | 41.71829 | −4.1103 | 14 | Vacceans | Almagro (1995) |
| Cauca | 41.2176667 | −4.5228361 | 15 | Vacceans | Almagro (1995) |
| Cerro de San Andrés | 41.918372 | −5.069169 | 3.6 | Vacceans | Almagro (1995) |
| Cuéllar | 41.3997643 | −4.3150702 | 7 | Vacceans | Almagro (1995) |
| Cuenca de Campos | 42.0585105 | −5.0547427 | 10 | Vacceans | Almagro (1995) |
| Cuestacastro | 41.6337 | −5.17712 | 4.3 | Vacceans | Almagro (1995) |
| Intercatia | 42.1528695 | −4.6922384 | 49 | Vacceans | Almagro (1995) |
| La Peña | 42.0613419 | −2.3861318 | 55 | Vacceans | Almagro (1995); Lorrio (1997) |
| Las Quintanas | 41.6127047 | −4.1631678 | 26.3 | Vacceans | Almagro (1995) |
| Medina de Rioseco | 41.8836792 | −5.0433596 | 7.5 | Vacceans | Almagro (1995) |
| Melgar de Abajo | 42.2432398 | −5.1421583 | 34 | Vacceans | Almagro (1995) |
| Oceloduri | 41.5056574 | −5.7448039 | 25.5 | Vacceans | Almagro (1995) |
| Olmillos de Sasamón | 42.390004 | −4.0528 | 26 | Vacceans | Sancristán de Lama (2011) |

*Continued*

| Settlement | COOR_X | COOR_Y | Ha | Group | Bibliography |
|---|---|---|---|---|---|
| Pago de Gorita | 41.679448 | −4.671052 | 6 | Vacceans | Almagro (1995) |
| Pago de Grimata | 41.6492976 | −5.0241153 | 5.2 | Vacceans | Almagro (1995) |
| Pallantia | 42.2149995 | −4.3431765 | 110 | Vacceans | Almagro (1995) |
| Peña Amaya | 42.655556 | −4.15417 | 42 | Vacceans | Cisneros et al. (2005) |
| Peña Ulaña | 42.64917 | −4.05611 | 285 | Vacceans | Torres Martinez (2011) 269 |
| Pintia | 41.77754 | −4.4997 | 25 | Vacceans | Sancristán de Lama (2011) 7,000 inhabitants based on 280 inhab./ha |
| Rauda | 41.6966212 | −3.9284274 | 13.5 | Vacceans | Almagro (1995) |
| Septimanca | 41.5904328 | −4.8268456 | 7.1 | Vacceans | Almagro (1995) |
| Soto de Medinilla | 41.6856612 | −4.7155626 | 11.7 | Vacceans | Almagro (1995); Delibes & Romero (2011) |
| Teso del Cementerio | 42.031753 | −5.081657 | 5.7 | Vacceans | Almagro (1995) |
| Teso Mimbre | 41.7813337 | −5.1930752 | 3.6 | Vacceans | Almagro (1995) |
| Viminatium | 42.3288907 | −4.8039484 | 15 | Vacceans | Almagro (1995) |
| Zorita | 39.2841602 | −5.6989098 | 3.2 | Vacceans | Almagro (1995) |
| Calagurris | 42.3035212 | −1.9648758 | 10 | Vascones | Almagro (1995) |
| Carasta (Caicedo Sopeña, Álava) | 42.7783 | −2.9224 | 27 | Vascones | Torres Martínez (2011) 268; Almagro (1995) gives 17 ha |
| Castro de Intxur (Tolosa-Albistur, Guipúzcoa) | 43.115152 | −2.146265 | 17 | Vascones | Torres Martínez (2011) 268 |
| Castros de Lastra (Caranca, Álava) | 42.862483 | −3.061752 | 15.6 | Vascones | Torres Martínez (2011) 268 |
| Kosmoaga | 43.3215488 | −2.5844368 | 3.5 | Vascones | Almagro (1995) |
| La Hoya | 42.5535011 | −2.5850848 | 4 | Vascones | Almagro (1995) |
| Marazuela | 40.9798126 | −4.3655121 | 8 | Vascones | Almagro (1995) |
| Osca | 42.1360614 | −0.0298027 | 15 | Vascones | Almagro (1995) |
| Pompaelo | 42.8184538 | −1.6442556 | 3.2 | Vascones | Almagro (1995) |
| San Formerio | 42.7388693 | −2.8277064 | 4.4 | Vascones | Almagro (1995) |
| Santa Colomba | 42.767396 | −2.67754 | 14.5 | Vascones | Almagro (1995) |
| Santuste | 42.7607768 | −2.7758725 | 18.5 | Vascones | Almagro (1995) |
| Veleia | 42.842117 | −2.78728 | 11 | Vascones | Almagro (1995) |
| Albocela | 41.4941665 | −5.5892394 | 20 | Vettones | Almagro (1995) |

| | | | | | |
|---|---|---|---|---|---|
| Arroyo Manzanas | 39.9010452 | −4.8705161 | 20 | Vettones | Almagro (1995) |
| El Raso | 40.1557248 | −5.2409617 | 20 | Vettones | Almagro (1995); Álvarez Sanchís (2011) |
| Irueña | 40.443611 | −6.581667 | 9 | Vettones | Álvarez Sanchís (2011) |
| Las Cogotas | 40.7440033 | −4.7449591 | 14.5 | Vettones | Almagro (1995); Álvarez Sanchís (2011) |
| Las Merchanas | 40.9725654 | −6.6559365 | 5.2 | Vettones | Almagro (1995) |
| Ledesma | 41.09144 | −5.99906 | 11 | Vettones | Álvarez Sanchís (2011) |
| Ledesma (Bletisama) | 41.09144 | −5.99906 | 11 | Vettones | Álvarez Sanchís (2011); Almagro (1995) |
| Mesas de Miranda | 41.8571703 | −2.5112844 | 37.5 | Vettones | Almagro (1995); Álvarez Sanchís (2011) |
| Salmantica | 40.9651572 | −5.6640182 | 20 | Vettones | Almagro (1995); Álvarez Sanchís (2011) |
| Sanchorreja | 40.6646581 | −4.9146123 | 27.5 | Vettones | Almagro (1995) |
| Segovia | 40.94919 | −4.11934 | 20 | Vettones | Lorrio (1997) |
| Ulaca | 40.6475461 | −4.8120387 | 60 | Vettones | Almagro (1995); Lorrio (1997); Álvarez Sanchís (2011) |
| Yecla de Yeltes | 40.9595529 | −6.488173 | 4.3 | Vettones | Almagro (1995) |

APPENDIX II

# Imperial and Late Antique sizes

Sizes obtained from Carreras (1996), Carreras (2014), and Houten (2021).

| Ancient name | Modern name | COOR_X | COOR_Y | Imperial | Late Antique |
|---|---|---|---|---|---|
| Acci | Guadix | 37.3011351 | −3.1403255 | 15 | |
| Aeminium | Coimbra | 40.2033145 | −8.4102573 | 9 | |
| Aeso | Isona | 42.1185205 | 1.04653359 | 18 | |
| Alba Varduli | San Román de San Millán | 42.8653508 | −2.31285739 | 10 | |
| Albocela | Toro | 41.5274417 | −5.39133749 | 20 | |
| Alonis | La Vilajoyosa | 39.4839053 | −0.5293554 | 6 | |
| Amaia | Amaya | 42.6422226 | −4.1638541 | 42 | |
| Amallobriga | Tiedra (VA) | 41.6540243 | −5.2645258 | 14 | |
| Andelos | Muruzabal de Andión (Mendigorria) | 42.6281524 | −1.8354908 | 18 | |
| Aquae Calidae | Caldes de Montbui | 41.6512425 | 2.13520389 | 6 | |
| Aquae Celenae | Caldas do Reis | 42.6353087 | −8.6380598 | 6 | |
| Aquae Flavia | Chaves | 41.741781 | −7.4731647 | 14.5 | 5 |
| Aquae Querquernae | Baños de Bande, Porto Quintela | 41.9716507 | −7.9850020 | 7.8 | |
| Araceli | Araciel | 42.0666452 | −1.6180616 | 5 | |
| Arcobriga | Cerro Vilar (Monreal de Ariza) | 41.290499 | −2.1069816 | 14 | |
| Asso | Caravaca | 38.1041892 | −1.8609152 | 7 | |
| Asturica Augusta | Astorga | 42.4549303 | −6.0532511 | 27 | 27 |
| Augustobriga Pelendones | Muro de Agreda | 41.8336855 | −1.9886880 | 49 | |

| | | | | | |
|---|---|---|---|---|---|
| Aurienses | Orense | 42.3357893 | −7.8638809 | 7 | |
| Avilam | Avila | 40.656685 | −4.6812085 | 9 | |
| Baedunia | San Martin de Torres | 42.2702475 | −5.8514308 | 10 | |
| Baetulo | Badalona | 41.4469883 | 2.24503249 | 11 | |
| Barbotum | Torre Cillas | 42.0360435 | 0.12844040 | 8 | |
| Barcino | Barcelona | 41.3850639 | 2.17340349 | 10.4 | 10.4 |
| Baria | Villaricos | 37.2510185 | −1.7695909 | 11 | |
| Basti | Cerro Cepero | 37.4862228 | −2.7769903 | 6 | |
| Begastri | Cehegin | 38.0931302 | −1.7940581 | 5 | |
| Beligiom | Azaila | 41.2904702 | −0.4933037 | 7 | |
| Bergidum Flavium | Cacabelos | 42.598666 | −6.7259138 | 5.5 | |
| Bilbilis | Calatayud | 41.3531678 | −1.6468455 | 21 | |
| Blandae | Blanes | 41.6759954 | 2.79022889 | 10 | |
| Boletum | Barbastro | 42.035291 | 0.1273884 | 8 | |
| Bracara Augusta | Braga | 41.5454486 | −8.4265070 | 42 | 48 |
| Brigaecium | Fuentes de Ropel | 42.0043798 | −5.5466347 | 22 | |
| Bursao | Borja | 41.8337231 | −1.5341785 | 9 | |
| Caesaraugusta | Zaragoza | 41.6488226 | −0.8890853 | 56 | 44 |
| Caesarobriga | Talavera de la Reina | 39.962884 | −4.8304536 | 24 | |
| Calagurris Iulia | Calahorra | 42.3073551 | −1.9673133 | 16 | 8 |
| Cale | Gaia | 41.1238759 | −8.6117851 | 15 | |
| Cara | Santacara | 42.3753822 | −1.5517379 | 17 | |
| Caracca | Diebres | 40.2454017 | −3.0419719 | 8 | |
| Carissa | Bornos | 36.8159238 | −5.7433561 | 10 | |
| Carthago Nova | Cartagena | 37.6256827 | −0.9965839 | 80 | 40 |
| Castellum Tyde | Tüy | 42.049155 | −8.6466098 | 28 | |
| Castra Aelia | La Cabañeta | 39.6428055 | 2.75418009 | 21 | |
| Castulo | Cazorla | 37.9124527 | −3.0038121 | 40 | |
| Cauca | Coca | 41.2157967 | −4.5220553 | 26 | |

*Continued*

| Ancient name | Modern name | COOR_X | COOR_Y | Imperial | Late Antique |
|---|---|---|---|---|---|
| Celsa | Velilla del Ebro | 41.3743809 | −0.4369722 | 44 | |
| Civitas Maggaviensium | Olleros de Pisuerga | 42.7438526 | −4.2868697 | 13 | |
| Clunia | Coruña del Conde | 41.7660841 | −3.3911802 | 70 | 70 |
| Complutum | Alcalá de Henares | 40.4819791 | −3.3635421 | 50 | 45 |
| Confluentia | Paredes de los Mercados | 41.2324226 | −3.7158233 | 50 | |
| Consabura | Consuegra | 39.4642436 | −3.6091169 | 30 | |
| Contrebia Belaskia | Botorrita | 41.5054446 | −1.0286955 | 5 | |
| Contrebia Carbica | Villas Viejas (CU) | 39.904133 | −2.7190774 | 45 | |
| Contrebia Leukade | Aguilar-Inestrillas | 41.97 | −1.9852779 | 17 | |
| Deóbriga | Puentelarrá | 42.749717 | −3.0464330 | 26 | |
| Dertosa | Tortosa | 40.8125777 | 0.52144230 | 15 | |
| Dianium | Dènia | 38.8387992 | 0.10505570 | 6.5 | |
| Ebussus | Eivissa | 38.9067339 | 1.4205983 | 21 | |
| Edeta | Lliria | 39.6274082 | −0.5968562 | 10 | |
| Egara | Terrassa | 41.563211 | 2.00887470 | 6 | |
| Emporiae | Empúries | 42.1340179 | 3.11242800 | 31 | 5 |
| Ercavica | Cañaveruelas | 40.400659 | −2.6369180 | 19 | 10 |
| Flaviobriga | Castro Urdiales | 43.3688221 | −3.2156354 | 10 | |
| Flavium Brigantium | La Coruña | 43.3623436 | −8.4115401 | 7 | |
| Forum Gigurrorum | A Proba | 42.9641691 | −7.0063228 | 7.5 | |
| Forum Limicorum | Monte do Viso (Xinzo di Limia) | 42.0631102 | −7.7259471 | 5 | |
| Gella | Montealegre de Campos | 41.9015654 | −4.8981036 | 49 | |
| Gerunda | Girona | 41.9794005 | 2.82142640 | 6 | 6 |
| Gigia | Gijón | 43.5322015 | −5.6611195 | 7 | 6 |
| Graccuris | Alfaro | 42.1772977 | −1.7502311 | 17 | |
| Iacca | Jaca | 42.5717166 | −0.5470554 | 7.5 | |
| Iammon | Mahón | 39.8873296 | 4.25961950 | 5 | |
| Iesso | Guissona | 41.784519 | 1.2903074 | 18 | |
| Ilerda | Lérida | 41.6175899 | 0.6200146 | 23 | |
| Ilici | Elche | 38.2699329 | −0.7125608 | 9.8 | 9.8 |
| Ilinum | Hellín | 38.5068902 | −1.6979398 | 10 | |

| | | | | | |
|---|---|---|---|---|---|
| Iluro | Mataró | 41.5381124 | 2.4447406 | 7 | |
| Intercatia Vaccea | Paredes de Nava | 42.151599 | −4.692841 | 25 | |
| Iria Flavia | Padrón | 42.7381033 | −8.6607662 | 23 | |
| Iuliobriga | Retortillo | 40.8016566 | −6.3595042 | 20 | |
| Labitolosa | Puebla de Castro (Huesca) | 42.1439442 | 0.2872454 | 12 | |
| Lacóbriga | Carrión de los Condes | 42.3373375 | −4.6024326 | 70 | |
| Lancia | Villasabariego (León) | 42.5317351 | −5.4129363 | 44 | 40 |
| Lansbrica | San Cibrán de Lás | 42.3732068 | −8.0722034 | 9 | |
| Lassira | Moleta dels Frares (El Forcall) | 40.645299 | −0.20043740 | 8 | |
| Legio | León | 42.5987263 | −5.56709590 | 20 | |
| Leonica | Poyo del Cid (Teruel) | 40.9173028 | −1.2999390 | 10 | |
| Libisosa | Lezuza | 38.9496492 | −2.3554527 | 8 | |
| Lucentum | Tossal de Manisses | 38.3459963 | −0.4906855 | 5 | |
| Lucus Augustus | Lugo | 43.0097384 | −7.5567582 | 35 | 35 |
| Mago | Mahón | 39.9148178 | 4.2230836 | 16 | |
| Mundobriga | Munébrega (Zaragoza) | 41.2513238 | −1.7058403 | 20 | |
| Numantia | Garray | 41.8173792 | −2.4449638 | 11 | |
| Ocelum Duri | Zamora | 41.5034712 | −5.7467879 | 25.5 | |
| Ocilis | Medinaceli | 41.1717207 | −2.4338427 | 20 | |
| Oiasso | Oyarzun | 43.298838 | −1.8624156 | 15 | |
| Oretum | Granatula de Calatrava | 38.7987129 | −3.7422395 | 16.5 | |
| Osca | Huesca | 42.131845 | −0.40780580 | 16.5 | |
| Osicerda | El Palao (Alcañiz) | 41.0247826 | −0.1841673 | 5 | |
| Pallantia Vaccea | Palencia | 42.0096857 | −4.5288016 | 15 | |
| Palma | Mallorca | 39.5696005 | 2.65016030 | 14 | |
| Pentavonium | Rosinos de Vidriales | 42.089989 | −5.9833890 | 5 | |
| Pintia | Padilla de Duero | 41.6126361 | −4.1635342 | 25 | |
| Pisoraca | Herrera de Pisuerga | 42.5953655 | −4.3321114 | 6 | |
| Pollentia | Pollensa | 39.8771939 | 3.01620260 | 18 | 14 |
| Pompaelo | Pamplona | 42.812526 | −1.6457745 | 12 | |

*Continued*

| Ancient name | Modern name | COOR_X | COOR_Y | Imperial | Late Antique |
|---|---|---|---|---|---|
| Portus Illicitanus | Santa Pola | 38.1965614 | −0.5612438 | 24 | |
| Rauda | Roa de Duero | 41.7040526 | −3.9164585 | 14 | |
| Rhode | Rosas | 42.2632018 | 3.1755328 | 12 | |
| Saetabis | Xàtiva | 38.9899566 | −0.5235474 | 10 | |
| Saguntum | Sagunto | 39.6798633 | −0.27843845 | 20 | 20 |
| Salaria | Úbeda la Vieja | 38.0115293 | −3.37215630 | 10 | |
| Salmantica | Salamanca | 40.9701039 | −5.6635397 | 18 | |
| Sanisera | Sa Nitja | 40.071276 | 4.089033 | 6 | |
| Santa Criz | Santa Criz de Eslava | 42.5453584 | −1.450943 | 13 | |
| Segeda | Villalba del Perejil | 41.3275363 | −1.5493155 | 15 | |
| Segisama Iulia | Villadiego? | 42.5147918 | −4.0107323 | 12 | |
| Segobriga | Cabezo del Griego | 39.9204907 | −2.8041276 | 10.5 | |
| Segontia | Sigüenza | 41.067066 | −2.6462262 | 21 | |
| Segontia Lanka | Cuesta del Moro (Langa) | 41.6096487 | −3.4006360 | 35.7 | |
| Segovia Carpetania | Segovia | 40.9429032 | −4.1088090 | 18.4 | |
| Sisapo | Almaden de la Plata | 37.8730224 | −6.0815246 | 12 | |
| Suestatium | Arcaya | 42.8418263 | −2.6343862 | 18 | |
| Tagili | Armuna de Almanzora, Tijola | 37.34606 | −2.43326 | 25 | |
| Tamagani | Verín | 41.9402591 | −7.4349526 | 7 | |
| Tarraco | Tarragona | 41.1188827 | 1.2444909 | 90 | 30 |
| Tarraga | Los Bañales – Uncastillo | 42.3599895 | −1.131704 | 26 | |
| Termantia | Tiermes | 41.3685994 | −3.1994652 | 19.8 | 19.8 |
| Titulcia | Bayona de Tajuña | 40.2313 | −3.35021 | 12 | |
| Toletum | Toledo | 39.8628316 | −4.027323 | 40 | 40 |
| Tongobriga | Freixo | 41.1620191 | −8.146018 | 30 | |
| Trifinium | Villahizán de Treviño (Burgos) | 42.4782257 | −4.1059699 | 5 | |
| Tritium Autrigonum | Monasterio de Rodilla (Burgos) | 42.4575341 | −3.4694014 | 14 | |
| Tritium Magallum | Tricio | 42.4022984 | −2.7170297 | 5 | |
| Tritium Tuboricum | Astigarribiz, Mendaco, Motrico | 43.30643 | −2.38517 | 15 | |
| Turóbriga | Aroche | 37.9436991 | −6.9544649 | 6 | 6 |

| | | | | | |
|---|---|---|---|---|---|
| Tutugi | Galera | 37.7420931 | −2.5513692 | 6.5 | |
| Uxama Argaela | Osma | 41.587565 | −3.0668549 | 28 | 28 |
| Uxama Barca | Osma de Valdegobia | 42.8420421 | −3.0776568 | 28 | |
| Uxamilla | Belorado | 42.4195677 | −3.1917747 | 14 | |
| Valentia | Valencia | 39.4699075 | −0.37628810 | 20 | 18 |
| Valeria | Las Valeras | 39.7865213 | −2.1548473 | 14 | |
| Vareia | Varea | 42.463611 | −2.407222 | 27 | |
| Veleia | Iruña de Oca | 42.8192346 | −2.8277963 | 12 | |
| Vindelecia | Cubo de Bureba | 42.6402706 | −3.2062153 | 12 | |
| Visontium | Vinuesa | 41.9101058 | −2.7618028 | 20 | |
| | Cerro de las Cabezas – Valdepeñas | 38.760524 | −3.3876074 | 5 | |
| | La Caridad (Caminreal, TE) | 40.8393218 | −1.3230581 | 12.5 | |
| | Monte Mozinho | 41.2052808 | −8.2891305 | 20 | |
| | Sanfins | 40.9305632 | −8.5226706 | 15 | |
| | Santa Tegra | 41.8924795 | −8.8697056 | 20 | |
| | Villalba (SO) | 41.461667 | −2.482778 | 20 | |
| | Villavieja de Muño (BU) | 42.2593648 | −3.8932162 | 12 | |

APPENDIX III

# Rural prospection data

| Prospection | Area | Sites | Density (site/Km$^2$)×100 |
|---|---|---|---|
| Baetulo | 210 | 41 | 162 |
| Tarraco – Keay | 15 | 16 | 106 |
| Tarraco – Guitart-Prevosti | 15 | 14 | 93 |
| Cuenca de Nava (Palencia) | 875 | 50 | 5 |
| Val do Cavado (Braga) | 418 | 26 | 6 |
| Pinoso (Murcia) | 126 | 4 | 3 |
| Lerín (Navarra) | 100 | 20 | 20 |
| Altiplanicie soriana | 750 | 26 | 6 |
| Penedès | 450 | 29 | 6 |
| Monegros | 60 | 20 | 33 |
| Escatrón | 144 | 9 | 6 |
| Cuencas mineras turolesas | 21 | 1 | 4 |
| Arba de Biel | 72 | 19 | 26 |
| Taramundi | 81 | 3 | 3 |
| Oscos | 343 | 15 | 4 |
| Yecla | 660 | 9 | 1 |
| Huescar | 45 | 38 | 68 |
| Trasdeza | 170 | 8 | 4 |
| Tajuña | 216 | 29 | 13 |
| Sierra de Ujué | 120 | 6 | 5 |
| Javea | 266 | 10 | 3 |
| Segisamo | 10 | 1 | 10 |
| Penaguila (Alcoy) | 0.1 | 1 | 100 |
| Los Bañales (Uncastillo) | 144 | 9 | 6 |
| Polop Alt | 0.3 | 1 | 33 |
| Miranda de Azan (Salamanca) | 15 | 10 | 66 |
| Vallès Oriental | 500 | 54 | 18 |
| Guissona | 1225 | 73 | 5 |
| Cossetània – Baix Penedès | 300 | 37 | 12 |
| Garraf | 75 | 32 | 42 |
| Calagurris | 4 | 7 | 175 |
| Vall d'Alcoi | 576 | 40 | 6 |
| Dianium | 2400 | 139 | 5 |
| Vila Joiosa | 250 | 42 | 16 |
| Lucentum | 60 | 37 | 61 |
| Ilici | 3200 | 79 | 2 |
| Ribera de Duero | 231 | 10 | 4 |
| Río Arga (Navarra) | 120 | 10 | 8 |
| Cuarte de Huerva | 890 | 14 | 1 |
| Tarazona | 80 | 8 | 10 |
| Font Molar | 4 | 1 | 25 |
| Lauro | 66.7 | 5 | 7 |
| Campo Cartagena – Tallante | 20 | 5 | 25 |

| | | | |
|---|---|---|---|
| Rabanales | 89 | 4 | 4 |
| La Armuña (Salamanca) | 25 | 3 | 12 |
| Sorlada (Navarra) | 15 | 9 | 60 |
| Vall d'Onsella (Navarra) | 350 | 64 | 18 |
| Alcantarilla (Murcia) | 250 | 16 | 6 |
| Báscara (Alt Empordà) | 75 | 7 | 9 |
| Azaila (Teruel) | 200 | 7 | 3 |
| Ballobar (Huesca) | 150 | 6 | 4 |
| Costera (València) | 1500 | 55 | 3 |
| Fuentes de Ebro (Zaragoza) | 4000 | 10 | 1 |
| Hoya de Zucaina (Castellón) | 132 | 0 | 0 |
| La Muela (Zaragoza) | 7500 | 9 | 1 |

# Bibliography


AAVV. 2007. *Revisió del Pla Especial de Protecció del Patrimoni Arquitectònic*. Catàleg de Sant Cugat del Vallès. Ajuntament de Sant Cugat del Vallès.

Abad Casal, L. 1984. *Los orígenes de la ciudad de Alicante*. Alicante: Instituto Juan Gil Albert.

Abadal, R. 1959. 'A propos du legs visigothique en Espagne'. In *Caralteri del secólo Vil in Occidente*, pp. 541–85. Spoleto: Centri italiano di studi sull'alto Medioevo.

Abascal, J. M. 1989. *La circulación monetaria del Portus Ilicitanus*. Valencia: Conselleria de Cultura, Educació i Ciència.

Abascal, J. M. and S. F. Ramallo. 1997. *La ciudad de Carthago Nova: La documentación epigráfica*. Murcia: Universidad de Murcia.

Abásolo Álvarez, J. A. 1975. 'Notas sobre el campamento romano de Sasamón (Burgos)'. *Pyrenae* 11: pp. 127–32 and I–IV.

Abásolo Álvarez, J. A. 1998. 'La ciudad de Segisamo'. In *Los Orígenes de la ciudad en el Noroeste Hispánico*, edited by A. Rodríguez Colmenero, pp. 585–98. Lugo: Diputación Provincial de Lugo.

Abreu, A. M. 2011. *Compositiones Medicamentorum de Escribónio Largo. Substâncias vegetais com valor medicinal*. Lisboa: Universidade de Lisboa.

Adams, J. N. 2007. *The regional diversification of Latin*. Cambridge: Cambridge University Press.

Afzelius, A. 1944. *Die römische Kriegsmacht während der Auseinandersetzung mit den hellenistischen Grossmächten*. Aarhus: Universitetsforlaget.

Akrigg, B. 2019. *Population and economy in Classical Athens*. Cambridge: Cambridge University Press.

Aktüre, Z. 2007. 'Geographic distribution and architectural characteristics of the ancient theatres in modern Spain: A structuralist interpretation'. In *TRAC 2006: Proceedings of the sixteenth Annual Theoretical Roman Archaeology Conference*, edited by B. Croxford et al., pp. 17–33. Oxford: Oxbow.

Alarcão, J. de. 1988. *Roman Portugal*. Warminster: Aris & Philips.

Alberch, R. and N. Castells. 1985. *La població de Girona (segles XIV–XX)*. Girona: Institut d'Estudis Gironins.

Albertini, E. 1923. *Les divisions administratives de l'Espagne romaine*. Paris: Éditions de Boccard.

Alcock, S. and J. Cherry. 2004. *Side-by-side survey: Comparative regional studies in the Mediterranean world*. Oxford: Oxbow.

Alduc-Le Bagousse, A. 1988. 'Estimation de l'âge des non-adultes: Maduration dentaire et croissance osseuse. Données comparatives pour deux nécropoles médiévales bas-normandes'. In *Actes des 3èmes Journées Anthropologiques. Notes et Monographies Techniques, no. 24*, pp. 81–103. Paris: CNRS.

Alfaro, C. 2001. 'Vías pecuarias y romanización en la Península Ibérica'. In *Los rebaños de Gerión. Pastores y transhumancia en Iberia antigua y medieval*, edited by J. Gómez-Pantoja, pp. 215–32. Madrid: Casa de Velázquez.

Alfaro, C. 2010. 'La mujer y el trabajo en la Hispania prerromana y romana: Actividades domésticas y profesionales'. In *El trabajo de las mujeres en España. Desde la antigüedad hasta el siglo XX*, edited by Mª I. Del Val Valdivieso, pp. 15–38. Madrid: Casa de Velázquez.

Alföldy, G. 1969. *Fasti Hispanienses. Senatorische Reichsbeamte und Offiziere in den spanischen Provinzen des römischen Reiches von Augustus bis Diokletian.* Wiesbaden: Frank Steiner Verlag.

Alföldy, G. 1973. *Flamines provinciae Hispaniae Citerioris.* Madrid: CSIC.

Alföldy, G. 1975. *Die Römischen Inschriften von Tarraco.* Berlin: de Gruyter.

Alföldy, G. 1981. 'Die älteste römische Inschrift der Iberischen Halbinsel'. *Zeitschrift für Papyrologie und Epigraphik* 43: pp. 1–12.

Alföldy, G. 2011a. 'Griechische Inschriften und griechische Kultur in Tarraco'. *Zeitschrift für Papyrologie und Epigraphik* 178: pp. 87–125.

Alföldy, G. 2011b. 'Tausend Jahre epigraphische Kultur im römischen Hispanien: Inschriften, Selbstdarstellung und Sozialordnung'. *Lucentum* XXX: pp. 187–220.

Allison, P. M. 2006. 'Mapping for gender: Interpreting artefact distribution in Roman military forts in Germany'. *Archaeological Dialogues* 13(1): pp. 1–48.

Allison, P. M. 2013a. *People and spaces in Roman military bases.* Cambridge: Cambridge University Press.

Allison, P. M. 2013b. 'Female networks in the military communities of the Roman West: A view from the Vindolanda tablets'. In *Women and the Roman city in the Latin West: Mnemosyne Journal Supplement*, edited by E. Hemelrijk and G. Woolf, pp. 369–90. Leiden: Brill.

Allison, P. M. 2015. 'Characterising Roman artefacts for investigating gendered practices in contexts without sexed bodies'. *American Journal of Archaeology* 119(1): pp. 103–23. https://doi.org/10.3764/aja.119.1.0103.

Almagro-Gorbea, M. 1988. 'El área superficial de las poblaciones ibéricas'. In *Los asentamientos ibéricos ante la romanización*, pp. 21–34. Madrid: Casa de Velázquez.

Almagro-Gorbea, M. 1994. 'El urbanismo en la Hispania Céltica: Castros y oppida'. *Complutum* 4: pp. 13–76.

Almagro-Gorbea, M. 2001. 'Aproximaciones a la demografía de la Celtiberia'. In *Entre Celtas e Iberos: Las poblaciones protohistóricas de las Galias e Hispanias*, edited by L. Berrocal Rangel and P. Gardes, pp. 45–60. Madrid: Real Academia de la Historia.

Almagro-Gorbea, M. and A. F. Dávila. 1995. 'El Área Superficial de Los Oppida En La Hispania Céltica'. *Complutum* 4: pp. 209–34.

Almagro-Gorbea, M. and J. M. Abascal Palazón. 1999. *Segobriga y su conjunto arqueológico.* Madrid: Real Academia de la Historia.

Almeida, A. M. A. 2011. *Compositiones Medicamentorum de Escribónio Largo. Substâncias vegetais com valor medicinal.* PhD thesis. Lisboa.

Almeida, R. 2008. *Las Ánforas del Guadalquivir en 'Scallabis' (Santarém, Portugal). Una aportación al conocimiento de los tipos minoritarios.* Barcelona: Universidad de Barcelona.

Alonso, J. 2018. 'Demografía romana en Hispania a través de la epigrafía funeraria'. *Revista de Demografía Histórica* XXXVI(II): pp. 15–53.

Alonso, M. A. A. 2011. 'Los medici en la epigrafía de la Hispania romana'. *Veleia* 28: pp. 83–107.

AlQahtani, S. J., M. P. Hector, and H. M. Liversidge. 2010. 'Brief communication: The London Atlas of Human Tooth Development and Eruption'. *American Journal of Physical Anthropology* 142: pp. 481–90. https://doi.org/10.1002/ajpa.21258.

AlQahtani, S. J., Hector, M. P., and H. M. Liversidge. 2014. 'Accuracy of dental age estimation charts: Schour and Massler, Ubelaker and the London Atlas'. *American Journal of Physical Anthropology* 154(1): pp. 70–8. https://doi.org/10.1002/ajpa.22473.

Alston, R. 2002. *The city in Roman and Byzantine Egypt*. London: Routledge.
Alvarez García, A., I. Muñoz, C. Pestoni, M. V. Lareu, M. S. Rodríguez-Calvo, and A. Carracedo. 1996. 'Effect of environmental factors on PCR-DNA analysis from dental pulp'. *International Journal of Legal Medicine* 109(3): pp. 125–9. http://dx.doi.org/10.1007/BF01369671.
Álvarez Sanchís, J. R. 1999. *Los Vettones Biblioteca Archaeologica Hispana*. Madrid: Real Academia de la Historia.
Álvarez Sanchís, J. 2011. 'Ciudades vettonas'. *Complutum*, 22(2): pp. 147–84.
Álvarez Sanchís, J., C. Marín Suárez, Á. Falquina Aparicio, and G. Ruiz Zapatero. 2008. 'El "oppidum" vettón de Ulaca (Solosancho, Avila) y su necrópolis'. *Zona arqueológica* 12: pp. 338–63.
Álvarez Sanchís, J. and G. Ruiz Zapatero. 2001. 'Cementerios y asentamientos: Bases para una demografía arqueológica de la Meseta en la Edad del Hierro'. In *Entre Celtas e Iberos: Las poblaciones protohistóricas de las Galias e Hispanias*, edited by L. Berrocal Rangel and P. Gardes, pp. 61–76. Madrid: Real Academia de la Historia.
Alzualde, A., N. Izagirre, S. Alonso, A. Alonso, C. Albarrán, A. Azkarate, and C. de la Rúa. 2006. 'Insights into the "isolation" of the Basques: mtDNA lineages from the historical site of Aldaieta (6th–7th centuries AD)'. *American Journal of Physical Anthropology* 130(3): pp. 394–404.
Amela, L. 2018. 'Baitolo'. *Varia Nummorum* VIII: pp. 85–97.
Anastasiou, E. and P. D. Mitchell. 2013. 'Palaeopathology and genes: Investigating the genetics of infectious diseases in excavated human skeletal remains and mummies from past populations'. *Gene* 528(1): pp. 33–40. doi:10.1016/j.gene.2013.06.017.
Andreu, J. (ed.) 2009. *Fundamentos de Epigrafía latina*. Pamplona: Liceus.
Andreu, J. 2013. 'Movilidad de personas y relaciones entre ciudades en época romana en el conventus de Caesar Augusta: Aspectos epigráficos y prosopográficos'. *Veleia* 30: pp. 75–93.
Andreu, J. 2017. *Oppida labentia. Transformaciones, cambios y alteración en las ciudades hispanas entre el siglo II y la tardoantigüedad*. Tudela: Fundación Uncastillo.
Andreu, J. and A. Blanco Pérez (eds.) 2019. *Signs of weakness and crisis in the Western cities of the Roman Empire (c. II–III AD)*. Stuttgart: Franz Steiner Verlag.
Andreu, J., J. Cabrero, and I. Rodà. 2009. *Hispaniae. Las provincias hispanas en el mundo romano*. Tarragona: Documenta.
Antonio, M. L., Z. Gao, H. M. Moots, et al. 2019. 'Ancient Rome: A genetic crossroads of Europe and the Mediterranean'. *Science* 366(6466): pp. 708–14. doi:10.1126/science.aay6826.
Aranda. 1768. *Censo de Aranda*. Madrid.
Arasa, F. 2012. 'Apuntes sobre la epigrafía romana de Valentia'. *Espacio, Tiempo y Forma, s. II. Historia Antigua* 25: pp. 281–304.
Arce, J. 1997. *El último siglo de la España romana (284–409)*. Madrid: Alianza.
Arce, J. 2013. *Bárbaros y romanos en Hispania (400–507 A.D.)*. Madrid: Marcial Pons Historia.
Arce, J., A. Chavarría, and G. Ripoll. 2007. 'The urban domus in late antique Hispania: Examples from Emerita, Barcino and Complutum'. In *Housing in late antiquity: From palaces to shops*, edited by L. Lavan, L. Özgenel, and A. Sarantis, pp. 305–36. Leiden: Brill.
Arenas Esteban. 2011. 'El poblamiento prerromano en el área Alto Tajo-Alto Jalón'. In: *El origen del urbanismo en la Meseta Norte. Aldeas y ciudades en el I milenio a.C*, edited by G. Ruiz, A. Jimeno, and J. Álvarez. Complutum Extra 22/2. Madrid.
Arévalo, A. and F. Delgado. 2016. 'Las monedas y su propietario: Dinero de bolsillo en una pequeña embarcación'. In *Illa Pedrosa. Comerç marítim i xarxes de redistribuciò en època*

*tardorepublicana al mediterrani centreoccidental*, edited by G. Vivar Lombarte, pp. 118–32. Girona: Museu d'Arqueologia de Catalunya.

Arias, J. 2018. 'Late antique castros and their spatial milieu in Northwestern Iberia'. *Visigothic Symposium* 2: pp. 1–20.

Armentano, N. and A. Malgosa. 2002. 'Enterramientos primarios *versus* enterramientos secundarios'. In *Antropología y biodiversidad Vol. 1*, edited by A. Malgosa, R. Nogés, and M. P. Aluja, pp. 38–49. Barcelona: Edicions Bellaterra.

Armentano, N. and D. Nociarová. 2015. *Anàlisi antropològica de les restes esquelètiques recuperades durant la segona fase d'excavació a la necròpolis d'Empúries*. Barcelona: Servei d'Arqueologia de Catalunya, unpublished archaeological report.

Armentano, N., M. Subirana, A. Isidro, O. Escala, and A. Malgosa. 2012. 'An ovarian teratoma of late Roman age'. *International Journal of Paleopathology* 2(4): pp. 236–9.

Arroyo-Pardo, E., M. A. Ocana, J. J. Arroyo, et al. 2002. 'HPLC and UV-spectrophotometry examination of ancient DNA and PCR inhibitors in old human remains'. *Ancient Biomolecules* 4(1): pp. 33–41. doi:10.1080/13586120290018518.

Asensio, D. 2010. 'El comercio de ánforas itálicas en la Península Ibérica entre los siglos IV y I a.C. y la problemática en torno a las modalidades de producción y distribución'. *Bollettino di Archeologia online I 2010/Volume speciale* B/B8/3: pp. 23–41.

Asensio, D., J. Morer, J. Pou, J. Sanmarti, and J. Santacana. 2005. 'Evidències arqueològiques del procés d'emergència "d'élites" aristocràtiques a la ciutadella ibèricad d'Alorda Park (Calafell, Baix Penedès)'. In *Món Ibèric als Països Catalans, XIII Colloqui Internacional d'Arqueologia de Puigcerdà*, vol. 1, pp. 597–613. Puigcerdà.

Asensio, D., J.Sanmartí, R. Jornet, and M. T. Miró. 2012. 'L'urbanisme i l'arquitectura domèstica de la ciutat ibèrica del Castellet de Banyoles (Tivissa, Ribera d'Ebre)'. In *Íberos del Ebro. Actas del II Congreso Internacional (Barcelona)*, edited by M. C. Belarte, J. A. Benavente, L. Fatás, J. Diloli, P. Moret, and J. Noguera, pp. 173–93. Tarragona: ICAC.

Attema, P. and T. de Haas. 2011. 'Rural settlement and population extrapolation: A case study from the ager of Antium, central Italy (350 BC–AD 400)'. In *Settlement, urbanization, and population*, edited by A. Bowman and A. Wilson, pp. 97–140. Oxford: Oxford University Press.

Aufderheide, A. and C. Rodríguez-Martin. 1998. *The Cambridge encyclopedia of human paleopathology*. Cambridge: Cambridge University Press.

Aüsbuttel, F. M. 1998. *Die Verwaltung des Römischen Kaiserreiches. Von der Herrschaft des Augustus bis zum Niedergang des Weströmischen Reiches*. Darmstadt: Wissenschaftliche Buchgesellschaft.

Azcárraga. 2014. '"Nuevos datos sobre la romanización de la Car-petania centro-septentrional", I Simposio sobre los Car-petanos: Arqueología e Historia de un pueblo de la Edad del Hierro (12–14 marzo 2013, Museo ArqueológicoRegional de la Comunidad de Madrid)', *Zona Arqueológi-ca* 17: pp. 435–45.

Azcárraga, S. and A. Ruiz. 2019. 'El Proyecto Primitiva Complutum: Breve avance de las campañas de excavación de 2017 y 2018 en el Cerro de San Juan del Viso (Villalbilla, Madrid)'. *Actas RAM*: pp. 91–9.

Bagnall, R. S. and B. W. Frier. 1994. *The demography of Roman Egypt*. Cambridge: Cambridge University Press.

Bailón, M. 2012. 'El papel social y religioso de la mujer romana: Fortuna Muliebris como forma de integración en los cultos oficiales'. *Habis* 43: pp. 101–18.

Bailly, L. 1994. 'Les instruments liés aux soins de l'oeil: Une approche de la chirurgie oculaire romaine'. In *L'oeil dans l'antiquité romaine*, edited by M.-J. Roulière-Lambert, pp. 39–49. Lons-le-Saunier: Centre Jurassien du Patrimoine.

Baker, 2013. *The archaeology of medicine in the Greco-Roman world*. Cambridge: Cambridge University Press.

Balil, A. 1955. 'La duración media de la vida en la Carpetania romana'. *RABM* 61: pp. 287–92.

Balsera, V., P. Díaz-del-Río, A. Gilman, et al. 2015. 'Approaching the demography of late prehistoric Iberia through summed calibrated date probability distributions (7000–2000 cal BC)'. *Quaternary International* 386: pp. 208–11.

Banks, J. 1981. *The topography of the city of Barcelona and its urban context in Eastern Catalonia: From the third to the twelfth centuries*. PhD thesis, University of Nottingham.

Banks, P. 2005. 'El creixement físic de Barcelona, segles X–XIII'. *Quaderns d'Història* 8: pp. 11–33.

Banning, E. B. 2002. *Archaeological survey*. New York: Kluwer Academic/Plenum Publishers.

Baquedano Pérez, E., M. Contreras Martínez, G. Märtens Alfaro, and G. Ruiz Zapatero. 2007. 'El oppidum carpetano de "El Llano de la Horca" (Santorcaz, Madrid)'. *Zona Arqueológica* 10(2): pp. 374–94.

Barker, G. and D. J. Mattingly. 1999–2000. *The archaeology of Mediterranean landscapes*. Volumes 1–5. Oxford: Oxbow Books.

Barrat, A., M. Barthélémy, R. Pastor-Satorras, and A. Vespignani. 2004. 'The architecture of complex weighted networks'. *Proceedings of the National Academy of Sciences* 101(11): pp. 3747–52.

Barreda Pascual, A. 1998. *Gentes itálicas en Hispania Citerior (218–14 d. C.). Los casos de Tarraco, Carthago Noua y Valentia*. PhD thesis, Universidad Autónoma de Barcelona.

Barthélemy, M. 2011. 'Spatial networks'. *Physics Reports* 499(1–3): pp. 1–101.

Bass, W. M. 1995. *Human osteology: A laboratory and field manual*. Columbia: Missouri Archaeological Society.

Baxarias, J. 1997. 'Estudio paleopatológico de un caso de osteomelitis cervicodorsal de la necrópolis tardorromana de Prat de la Riba (Tarragona)'. In *La enfermedad en los restos humanos arqueológicos. Actualización conceptual y metodológica*, pp. 399–406. Cádiz: Universidad de Cádiz.

Baxarias, J. 2002. *La enfermedad en la Hispania romana. Estudio de una necrópolis tarraconense*. Zaragoza: Libros Pórtico.

Baxarias, J. 2007. 'Estado de la cuestión de los estudios paleoptaológicos realizados en las poblaciones romanas y tardoantiguas'. In *Enfermedad, muerte y cultura en las sociedades del pasado*, Vol. I., edited by J. Barca and J. Jiménez, pp. 123–33. Cáceres: Fundación Academia Europea e Iberoamericana de Yuste.

Baxarias, J., D. Campillo, M. E. Subirà, J. A. Ginestà, and M. J. Martínez. 2003. 'Complicaciones en el tratamiento de las fracturas en época tardorromana'. In *¿Dónde estampos? Pasado, presente y future de la paleopatología*, pp. 180–5. Madrid: Universidad Autónoma de Madrid.

Baxarias, J., L. Devant, M. E. Subirà, et al. 2005. 'Concentraciones de plomo en la población romana hispana: ¿Era el saturnismo una enfermedad prevalente en la tarrago imperial?' In *Nuevas perspectivas del diagnóstico diferencial en Paleopatología*, pp. 291–6. Mahón (Menorca): A. Cañellas.

Beard, M. 2015. *SPQR: A history of ancient Rome*. London: Profile Books.

Belarte, C. 2010. 'Los individuos en el espacio doméstico en la protohistoria de Cataluña'. *Arqueología Espacial* 28: pp. 109–34.

Belcastro, M. G., E. Rastelli, and V. Mariotti. 2008. 'Variation of the degree of sacral vertebral body fusion in adulthood in two European modern skeletal collections'. *American Journal of Physical Anthropology* 135(2): pp. 149–60. https://doi.org/10.1002/ajpa.20716.

Beloch, K. J. 1909. *La popolazione del mondo greco-romano*. Milan: V. Pareto.

Beltrán, M. A. 1987. 'Los asentamientos ibéricos ante la romanización en el Valle del Ebro: los casos de Celsa, Azaila y Botorrita'. In: *Los asentamientos ibéricos ante la romanización*, pp. 101–10. Madrid: Ministerio de Cultura, Departamento de Arqueología.

Beltrán Fortes, M. 1995. *Azaila. Nuevas aportaciones deducidas de la documentación inédita de Juan Cabré Aguiló*. Zaragoza: Institución Fernando el Católico.

Beltrán Fortes, M. 2013. *Azaila. Estado de la cuestión en el año 2013 (contiene documentación inédita de Juan Cabré)*. Zaragoza: Institución Fernando el Católico.

Beltrán Lloris, F. 2004. 'Libertos y cultura epigráfica en la Hispania republicana'. In *Vivir en tierra extraña emigración e integración cultural en el mundo antiguo: actas de la reunión realizada en Zaragoza los días 2 y 3 de junio de 2003*, edited by F. M. Simón, F. P. Polo, and J. Remesal Rodríguez, pp. 151–75. Barcelona: Publicacions i Edicions Universitat de Barcelona-IFC.

Beltrán Lloris, F. 2011. '¿Firmas de artesano o sedes de asociaciones comerciales? A propósito de los epígrafes musivos de Caminreal (E.7.1), Andelo (K.28.1) y El Burgo de Ebro (HEp 11, 2001, 621 = AE 2001, 1237)'. In *A Greek man in the Iberian street: Papers in linguistics and epigraphy in honour of Javier de Hoz*, edited by E. Luján and J. M. García Alonso, pp. 139–47. Innsbruck: Institut für Sprachen und Literaturen der Universität Innsbruck.

Beltrán Lloris, F. 2016. 'Colonia Caesar Augusta: El impacto sobre el territorio y las comunidades indígenas'. *Revista de historiografía* 25: pp. 301–5.

Beltrán Lloris, F. 2023. 'Latinization, Citizenship and the Epigraphic Habit'. In: *Social Factors in the Latinization of the Roman West*, edited by A. Mullen, pp. 24–50. Oxford: Oxford University Press.

Benet, C., X. Fábrega, J. M. Macías, and J. A. Remolà. 1992. 'L'àrea d'enterraments baix imperial de Mas Rimbau/Mas Mallol, Tarragona'. *Acta Arqueològica* V (1991–2): pp. 72–85.

Bénard, J., M. Mangin, R. Goguey, and L. Roussel. 1994. *Les agglomérations antiques de Côte d'Or*. Paris: Les Belles Lettres.

Bermejo, J. 2014. *Arqueología biopolítica: La sintaxis espacial de la arquitectura doméstica romana en la meseta oriental*. Madrid: La Ergástula.

Birch-Chapman, S., E. Jenkins, F. Coward, et al. 2017. 'Estimating population size, density and dynamics of Pre-Pottery Neolithic villages in the central and southern Levant: An analysis of Beidha, southern Jordan'. *Levant* 49(1): pp. 1–23.

Black III, T. K. 1978. 'Sexual dimorphism in the tooth-crown diameters of the deciduous teeth'. *American Journal of Physical Anthropology* 48(1): pp. 77–82. https://doi.org/10.1002/ajpa.1330480111.

Black, R. E., S. Cousens, H. L. Johnson, et al. 2010. 'Global, regional, and national causes of child mortality in 2008: A systematic analysis. Child Health Epidemiology Reference Group of WHO and UNICEF'. *Lancet* 375(9730): pp. 1969–87.

Blanco, J. F. 2018. 'La ciudad vaccea de Cauca'. In *Novedades arqueológicas en cuatro ciudades vacceas. Dessobriga, Intercatia, Pintia y Cauca*, edited by C. Sanz and J. F. Blanco, pp. 155–78. Valladolid: Universidad de Valladolid.

Bliquez, L. J. 2010. 'Gynecological surgery from the Hippocratics to the fall of the Roman Empire, Medicina nei secoli'. *Arte e Scienza* 22(2/3): pp. 25–64.

Blot, M. L. 2010. 'Seaports and fluvial harbours in Portuguese territory: The options for ancient harbour activities within a changing nautical landscape'. In *The Western Roman Atlantic façade: A study of the economy and trade in the Mar Exterior from the Republic to the Principate*, edited by C. Carreras and R. Morais, pp. 81–90. Oxford: Archaeopress.

Bodel, J., A. Bendlin, S. Bernard, et al. 2019. 'Notes on the elogium of a benefactor at Pompeii'. *Journal of Roman Archaeology* 32: pp. 148–82.

Bogenhagen, D. and D. A. Clayton. 'The number of mitochondrial deoxyribonucleic acid genomes in mouse L and human HeLa cells. Quantitative isolation of mitochondrial deoxyribonucleic acid'. *Journal of Biological Chemistry* 249(24):7991–5.

Bonet, H. and C. Mata. 1989. 'Nuevos grafitos e inscripciones ibéricos valencianos'. *Archivo de Prehistoria Levantina* 19: pp. 131–48.

Bonet, H., C. Mata, and A. Moreno Martín. 2008. 'Iron Age landscape and rural habitat in the Edetan Territory, Iberia (4th–3rd centuries BC)'. *Journal of Mediterranean Archaeology* 21: 165–89.

Borobia Melendo, E. L. 1992. *Instrumental médico quirúrgico en la Hispania Romana*. Sautuola: Revista del Instituto de Prehistoria y Arqueología Sautuola.

Borobia Melendo, E. L. and M. L. Parra. 1992. 'Instrumentos quirúrgicos en odontología de época clásica. Influencias en el diagnóstico paleopatológico'. *Munibe Suplemento* 8: pp. 227–30.

Bowes, K. 2010. *Houses and society in the Later Roman Empire*. London: Bristol Classical Press.

Bowes, K. 2013. 'Villas, taxes and trade in the fourth century Hispania'. In *Local economies? Production and exchange of inland regions in Late Antiquity*, edited by L. Lavan, pp. 191–226. Leiden: Brill.

Bowman, A. and A. Wilson. 2011. 'Introduction'. In *Settlement, urbanization, and population*, edited by A. Bowman and A. Wilson, pp. 1–14. Oxford: Oxford University Press.

Bradley, K. R. 1985. 'Child labour in the Roman world'. *Historical Reflections* 12(2): pp. 311–30.

Bradley, K. R. 1986. 'Wet-nursing at Rome: A study in social relations'. In *The family in ancient Rome: New perspectives*, edited by B. Rawson, pp. 201–29. London: Croom Helm.

Bradley, K. R. 1991. *Discovering the Roman family: Studies in Roman social history*. New York: Oxford University Press.

Brassous, L. and A. Quevedo. 2015. *Urbanisme civique en temps de crise. Les espaces publiques d'Hispanie et de l'Occident romain entre le IIe et le IVe siècle*. Madrid: Casa de Velázquez.

Bravo, M. J. 2016. 'Urban planning and territory in Hispania in Late Antiquity'. *Revista Digital de Derecho Administrativo* 16: pp. 145–91.

Brickley, M. and R. Ives. 2008. *The bioarchaeology of metabolic bone disease*. Amsterdam: Elsevier/Academic Press.

Brickley, M., R. Ives, and S. Mays. 2020. *The bioarchaeology of metabolic bone disease*, 2nd edition. Amsterdam: Elsevier/Academic Press.

Brooks, S. and J. Suchey. 1990. 'Skeletal age determination based on the os pubis: A comparison of the Acsádi-Nemeskéri and Suchey-Brooks methods'. *Human Evolution* 5(3): pp. 227–38. https://doi.org/10.1007/BF02437238.

Brothwell, D. R. 1987. *Desenterrando huesos: La excavación, tratamiento y estudio de restos del esqueleto humano*. México: Fondo de cultura económica.

Brughmans, T. 2010. 'Connecting the dots: Towards archaeological network analysis'. *Oxford Journal of Archaeology* 29(3): pp. 277–303.

Brughmans, T. 2013. 'Thinking through networks: A review of formal network methods in archaeology'. *Journal of Archaeological Method and Theory* 20: pp. 623–62.

Brunson, K. and D. Reich. 2019. 'The promise of paleogenomics beyond our own species'. *Trends in Genetics* 35(5): pp. 319–29. doi:10.1016/j.tig.2019.02.006.

Brunt, P. A. 1971. *Italian manpower 225 B.C.–A.D. 14*. Oxford: Oxford University Press.

Buckberry, J. 2018. 'Techniques for identifying the age and sex of children at death'. In *The Oxford handbook of the archaeology of childhood*, edited by S. Crawford, D. M. Hadley, and G. Shepherd, pp. 55–70. Oxford: Oxford University Press.

Buckberry, J. L. and A. T. Chamberlain. 2002. 'Age estimation from the auricular surface of the ilium: A revised method'. *American Journal of Physical Anthropology* 11 (3): pp. 231–9. https://doi.org/10.1002/ajpa.10130.

Buikstra, J. E. 1976. *Hopewell in the Lower Illinois Valley: A regional approach to the study of biological variability and mortuary activity*. Evanston: Northwestern University Archeological Program, Scientific Papers, No. 2.

Buikstra, J. E. and D. H. Ubelaker. 1994. *Standards for data collection from human skeletal remains*. Fayetteville: Arkansas Archaeological Survey.

Burillo Mozota, F. 2008. *Los Celtíberos. Etnias y estados*. Barcelona: Crítica.

Burillo Mozota, F. 2011. 'Oppida y "ciudades estado" celtibéricos'. *Complutum* 22(2): pp. 277–95.

Burnham, B. C. and J. S. Wacher. 1990. *The 'small towns' of Roman Britain*. London: Batsford.

Burón, M. 2006. 'El trazado urbano de Asturica Augusta: Genesis y evolución. Nuevos elementos de ingeniería romana'. In *III Congreso de Obras Públicas romanas*, pp. 289–312. Astorga: Junta de Castilla y León, Consejería de Cultura y Turismo.

Byrd, B. F. 2005. *Early village life at Beidha, Jordan: Neolithic spatial organization and vernacular architecture—the excavations of Mrs Diana Kirkbride-Helbæk*. Oxford: Oxford University Press.

Cadiou, F. 2008. *Hibera in terra miles. Les armées romaines et la conquête de l'Hispanie sous la République (218–45 av. J.-C.)*. Madrid: Casa de Velázquez.

Caldwell, J. C. 1982. *Theory of fertility decline*. London: Academic Press.

Caldwell, J. C. 2006. *Demographic transition theory*. Dordrecht: Springer.

Calvo, M. 2000. 'El cementerio del área episcopal de Valencia en la época visigoda'. In *Los orígenes del Cristianismo en Valencia y su entorno*, edited by A. Ribera, pp. 193–206. Valencia: Ajuntament de València.

Cambi, F. 1999. 'Demography and Romanization in central Italy'. In *Reconstructing past population trends in Mediterranean Europe (3000 BC–AD 1800)*, edited by J. Bintliff and K. Sbonias, pp. 115–27. Oxford: Oxbow Books.

Camino Mayor, J. 1995. *Los castros marítimos en Asturias*. Oviedo: Real Instituto de Estudios Asturianos.

Campillo, D. 1993. *Els primers vestigis de la malaltia*. Barcelona: Fundació Uriach.

Campillo, D. 2001. *Introducción a la paleopatología*. Barcelona: Bellaterra.

Campillo, D. and F. Tarrats. 1991. 'Anthropological identification and paleopathological study of a skeleton, probably pertaining to the Roman doctor from the II–I centuries BC, Tiberius Claudius Apollinarius (Tarragona, Spain)'. *Dynamis* II: pp. 387–414.

Campo, M. 2002. 'La producció d'Untikesken i Kese: Funció i circulació a la ciutat i el territori'. In *Funció i producció de les seques indígenes, VI Curs d'Història monetària d'Hispània*, edited by Curs d'Història monetària d'Hispània, pp. 77–104. Barcelona: Museu Nacional d'Art de Catalunya.

Canòs, I. 2002. *L'epigrafia grega a Catalunya*. Debrecen: Dept. of Ancient History, University of Debrecen.

Caramelli, D., C. Lalueza-Fox, C. Capelli, et al. 2007. 'Genetic analysis of the skeletal remains attributed to Francesco Petrarca'. *Forensic Science International* 173(1): pp. 36–40. doi:10.1016/j.forsciint.2007.01.020.

Carballo Arceo, L. X. 1996. 'Os castros galegos espacio e arquitectura'. *Gallaecia: revista de arqueoloxía e antigüidade* 14–15: pp. 309–57.

Cardona, F. 2009. 'Resultados del estudio antropológico de la necrópolis del foro de Pollentia (Alcudia, Mallorca): Campañas 2004–2008'. *CPAG* 19: pp. 429–47.

Cardoso, H. F. and S. R. Saunders. 2008. 'Two arch criteria of the ilium for sex determination of immature skeletal remains: A test of their accuracy and an assessment of intra- and inter-observer error'. *Forensic Science International* 178(1): pp. 24–9. https://doi.org/10.1016/j.forsciint.2008.01.012.

Carnicero, S. 2017. 'Estudio antropológico de los restos humanos hallados en la necrópolis de Iuliobriga (Retortillo, Cantabria)'. *Sautuola* XXII: pp. 275–87.

Caro Baroja, J. 1976. *Los pueblos de España*. Madrid: Istmo.

Carreras, C. 1996. 'Una nueva perspectiva para el estudio demográfico de la Hispania romana'. *BSAAV* 62: pp. 95–122.

Carreras, C. 1997. 'Los beneficiarii y la red de aprovisionamiento militar de Britannia e Hispania'. *Gerión* 15: pp. 151–76.

Carreras, C. 2010. 'The Gaditan elites and the figure of L. Cornelius Balbus'. In *The Western Roman Atlantic façade: A study of the economy and trade in the Mar Exterior from the Republic to the Principate*, edited by C. Carreras and R. Morais, pp. 249–53. Oxford: Archaeopress.

Carreras, C. 2014. 'Nuevas tendencias y datos sobre la demografía romana en la Península Ibérica'. *BSSA* LXXX: pp. 53–82.

Carreras, C. and P. Berni. 2005. 'Late Roman amphorae in the City of Barcino (Barcelona)'. In *Late Roman coarse wares, cooking wares and amphorae in the Mediterranean: Archaeology and archaeometry* (= LRCW I), edited by J. M. Gurt., J. Buxeda, and M. A. Cau, pp. 165–78. Oxford: BAR.

Carreras, C. and P. De Soto. 2010. *Historia de la movilidad en la Península Ibérica. Redes de transporte en SIG*. Barcelona: Editorial OUC.

Carreras, C. and P. De Soto. 2013. 'The Roman transport network: A precedent for the integration of the European mobility'. *Historical Methods: A Journal of Quantitative and Interdisciplinary History* 46(3): pp. 117–33.

Carreras, C. and P. De Soto. 2022. 'Los conventus iuridici en Hispania Citerior: Una explicación demográfica y espacial'. *Pyrenae* 53(2): pp. 1–28.

Carreras, C., A. Martin, J. Pera, et al. 2016. 'Las ánforas de Brindisi en Hispania Citerior. Pautas de distribución y de consumo'. *Saguntum* 48: pp. 103–21.

Carreras, C. and R. Morais (eds.) 2010. *The Western Roman Atlantic façade: A study of the economy and trade in the Mar Exterior from the Republic to the Principate*. Oxford: Archaeopress.

Carreras, C. and R. Morais. 2012. 'The Atlantic Roman trade during the Principate: New evidence from the Western façade'. *Oxford Journal of Archaeology* 31(4): pp. 419–41.

Carreras, C., P. Olmos, S. Rascón Marqués, et al. 2017. 'El diseño urbano de la *Regio IV* de Complutum (Alcalá de Henares). Estudios a partir de la prospección geofísica'. *Lucentum* XXXVI: pp. 221–37.

Carreras, C. and J. van den Berg. 2017. 'Conclusions: Kops Plateau in context'. In *Amphorae from Kops Plateau: Trade and supply to the Lower-Rhineland from the Augustan period to AD 69/7*, edited by C. Carreras and J. van den Berg, pp. 355–80. Oxford: Archaeopress Publishing.

Carreté, J. M., S. J. Keay, and M. Millett. 1995. *A Roman provincial capital and its hinterland: The survey of the territory of Tarragona, Spain, 1985–1990*. Ann Arbor: Journal of Roman Archaeology.

Carroll, M. 2006. *Spirits of the dead: Roman funerary commemoration in Western Europe*. Oxford: Oxford University Press.

Carroll, M. 2011. 'Infant death and burial in Roman Italy'. *Journal of Roman Archaeology* 24: pp. 99–120.

Casas i Genover, J. 1993. 'Instruments de cirurgia en villes romanes de les comarques de Girona'. *Annals de l'Institut d'Estudis Gironins* 32: pp. 9–20.

Casas i Genover, J., P. Castanyer, J. M. Nolla, and J. Tremoleda. 1995. *El món rural d'època romana a Catalunya. L'exemple del nord-est, Girona*. Girona: Centre d'Investigacions Arqueològiques de Girona.

Catalano, P., G. Amicucci, V. Benassi, et al. 2006. 'Gli insiemi funerari d'epoca imperiale: l'indagine antropologica di campo'. In *Memorie dal sottosuolo. Ritrovamenti archeologici 1980–2006*, edited by A. Tomei, pp. 560–3. Rome: Electa.

Celis Sánchez, J., and F. Muñoz Villarejo. 2015. 'Veinte Años En La Investigación de La Edad Del Hierro En Las Tierras de León'. In *ArqueoLeón II: Historia de León a Través de La Arqueología (Noviembre 2013 / Marzo 2014)*, edited by L. A. Grau Lobo, pp. 43–64. León: Museo de León & Junta de Castillia y León.

Ceballos Hornero, A. and D. Ceballos Hornero. 2003. 'Los espectáculos del anfiteatro en Hispania'. *Iberia* 6: pp. 57–70.

Chamberlain, A. T. 2006. *Demography in archaeology*. Cambridge: Cambridge University Press.

Chao Fernández, J. J., J. F. Mesa-Sanz, and M. Serrano. 1999. 'Un nuevo bronce hallado en la Alcudia'. In *Ciudades privilegiadas en el Occidente Romano*, edited by J. González Fernández, pp. 417–24. Seville: Universidad de Sevilla and Diputación de Sevilla.

Chavarría, A. 2005. 'Villas in Hispania during the fourth and fifth centuries'. In *Hispania in late antiquity: Current perspectives*, edited by K. Bowes and M. Kulikowski, pp. 519–52. Leiden: Brill.

Chavarría, A. 2007. *El final de las villae en Hispania (siglos IV–VII D.C.)*. Seville: Universidad de Sevilla.

Chimenos, E., A. Malgosa, and M. Subirá. 1992. 'Paleopatología oral y analisis de elementos traza en el estudio de la dieta de la población epipaleolítica de "El Collado" (Oliva, Valencia)'. *Munibe. Antropologia-Arkeologia* 8: pp. 177–82.

Chimenos, E., S. Safont, A. Alesán, et al. 1999. 'Propuesta de protocolo de valoración de parámetros en Paleodontología'. *Gaceta dental* 102: pp. 44–52.

Chrzanová Pečnerová, P. 2017. 'The hype cycle of ancient DNA'. *The Molecular Ecologist*. https://www.molecularecologist.com/2017/04/20/the-hype-cycle-of-ancient-dna/.

Cisneros, M. 2004. 'El oppidum de La Ulaña en la frontera meridional de los cántabros'. *Palaeohispanica* 4: pp. 89–109.

Cisneros, M., J. Quintana, and J. L. Ramírez. 2005. 'Peña Amaya y Peña Ulaña: Toponimia y arqueología prerromanas'. *Palaeohispanica* 5: pp. 565–84.

Clarke, S. K. 1974. 'A method for the estimation of prehistoric pueblo population'. *Kiva* 39: pp. 283–7.

Claus, M., A. Kolb, and W. A. Slaby. 2008. *Epigraphik-Datenbank Clauss/Slaby*. http://www.manfredclauss.de/index.html.

Coale, A. J. and P. Demeny. 1983. *Regional model life tables and stable populations*. New York: Academic Press.

Coelho Ferreira da Silva, A. 1995a. 'A evolução do hábitat castrejo e o procesode proto-urbanização no noroeste de Portugal durante o I milénio a.C.: Revista da Facultade de Letras'. *Historia* 12(505–46): p. 517.

Coelho Ferreira da Silva, A. 1995b. 'Portuguese Castros: The evolution of the habitat and the proto-urbanization process'. In *Social complexity and the development of towns in Iberia: From the Copper Age to the second century AD*, edited by B. Cunliffe and S. Keay, pp. 263–89. Oxford: Oxford University Press.

Coelho Ferreira da Silva, A. 2007. 'A evolução do sistema defensivo castrejo no Noroeste Peninsular'. In *Paisajes fortificados de la Edad del Hierro*, edited by L. Berrocal-Rangel and P. Moret, pp. 99–111. Madrid: Casa de Velázquez.

Collard, M., K. Edinborough, S. Shennan, et al. 2010. 'Radiocarbon evidence indicates that migrants introduced farming to Britain'. *Journal of Archaeological Science* 37: pp. 866–70.

Colominas, L., A. Evin, J. Burch, et al. 2019. 'Behind the steps of ancient sheep mobility in Iberia: New insights from a geometric morphometric approach'. *Archaeological and Anthropological Sciences* 11(9): pp. 4971–82.

Contreras, D. A., G. Märtens Alfaro, G. Ruiz Zapatero, and E. Baquedano Pérez. 2014. 'Oppidum, urbanismo y organización de los espacios de hábitat en El Llano de la Horca (Santorcaz, Madrid)'. *Zona Arqueológica* 17: pp. 111–24.

Contreras, D. A. and J. Meadows. 2014. 'Summed radiocarbon calibrations as a population proxy: A critical evaluation using a realistic simulation approach'. *Journal of Archaeological Science* 52: pp. 591–608.

Cook, S. F. and R. F. Heizer. 1968. 'Relationships among houses, settlement areas, and population in aboriginal California'. In *Settlement archaeology*, edited by K. C. Chang, pp. 79–116. Palo Alto: National Press.

Cope, D. J. 2008. *Bent bones: The pathological assessment of two fetal skeletons from the Dakleh Oasis, Egypt*. Orlando: University of Central Florida.

Correira, P. M. M. 1997. 'Fire modification of bone: A review from the literature'. In *Forensic taphonomy: The postmortem fate of human remains*, edited by H. W. Haglund and M. H. Sorg, pp. 275–94. Boca Raton: CRC Press.

Cortés, A. 2014. *L'arquitectura domèstica d'època tardorepublicana i altimperial a les ciutats romanes de Catalunya*. Barcelona: Institut d'Estudis Catalans.

Cortijo, M. 1993. *La administración territorial de la Bética romana*. Córdoba: Caja Provincial de Ahorros de Córdoba.

Corvisier, J. N. and M. Bellancourt-Valdher. 1999. *La démographie historique antique*. Arras: Artois Presses Université.

Corvisier, J. N. and W. Suder. 2000. *La population de l'antiquité classique*. Paris: Presses Universitaires de France.

Cox, M. and S. Mays (eds.) 2000. *Human osteology in archaeology and forensic science*. Cambridge: Cambridge University Press.

Crétot, M. 1978. *L'arcade dentaire humaine (Morphologie)*. Paris: Editione Julien Prélat.

Cruz, G. 2015. 'O surgimento do espaço urbano no Noroeste da Ibéria. Uma reflexão sobre os oppida pré-romanos'. In *I Jornadas Internacionales sobre la Evolución de los espacios urbanos y sus territorios en el Noroeste de la Península Ibérica*, edited by R. Martínez-Peñín and G. Cavero-Domínguez, pp. 407–28. Léon/Minho: Universidad de Léon/ Universidade do Minho.

Cuhna, E. and C. Umbelino. 1995. 'What can bones tell about labour and occupation: The analysis of skeletal markers of occupational stress in the Identified Skeletal Collection of the Anthropological Museum of the University of Coimbra (preliminary results)'. *Anthropologia Portuguesa* 13: pp. 49–98.

Cunliffe, B. 1995. 'Diversity in the landscape: The geographical background to urbanism in Iberia'. In *Social complexity and the development of towns in Iberia: From the Copper Age to the second century AD*, edited by B. Cunliffe and S. Keay, pp. 5–28. Oxford: Oxford University Press.

Curchin, L. 1985. 'Vici and pagi in Roman Spain'. *Revue des Études Anciennes* 87(3–4): pp. 327–43.

Curchin, L. 1990. *The local magistrates of Spain*. Toronto: University of Toronto Press.

Curchin, L. 2000–1. 'The Roman family: Recent interpretations'. *Zephyrus* 53–4: pp. 535–50.
Curchin, L. 2011. *The Romanization of central Spain: Complexity, diversity and change in a provincial hinterland*. London: Routledge.
D'Arms, J. H. 2000. 'P. Lucilius Gamala's feasts for the Ostians and their Roman models'. *Journal of Roman Archaeology* 13: pp. 192–200.
Dasen, V. 2011. 'Médicin, religión et magie'. In *La medicina à l'époque romaine. Quoi de neuf, doctor?*, edited by M. Lioux and J. Santrot, pp. 39–41. Lyon: Département du Rhône.
Dasen, V. 2013. 'Becoming human: From the embryo to the newborn child'. In *The Oxford handbook of childhood and education in the classical world*, edited by E. Grubbs, T. Parkin, and R. Bell, pp. 17–39. Oxford: Oxford University Press.
Dávila, A. F. 2007. 'La Edad del Hierro en la Carpetania: Una historia a medio contar'. *Zona Arqueológica* 10(1): pp. 15–34.
De Almeida, R. 2008. *Las ánforas del Guadalquivir en Scallabis (Santarém, Portugal). Una aportación al conocimiento de los tipos minoritarios*. Barcelona: Universitat de Barcelona.
De Hoz, M. P. 1997. 'Epigrafía Griega en Hispania'. *Epigraphica* 59: pp. 29–94.
De Hoz, M. P., B. Díaz, and A. Ribera. 2013. 'Grafitos sobre cerámica procedentes de los niveles romanorrepublicanos de "Valentia" (Valencia, España)'. *Palaeohispánica* 13: pp. 407–29.
De la Escosura Balbás, M. C. 2021. *La población de Carthago Nova de la conquista al principado. Epigrafía y onomástica*. Barcelona: Publicacions de la Universitat de Barcelona.
De la Rúa, C., C. Castro, A. Alonso, et al. 1992. 'Extracción y caracterización del DNA procedente del hueso esponjoso reciente y de los siglos XVI y XVII'. *Munibe Suplemento* 8: pp. 209–12.
De Ligt, L. 2012. *Peasants, citizens and soldiers: Studies in the demographic history of Roman Italy, 225 BC—AD 100*. Cambridge and New York: Cambridge University Press.
De Ligt, L. 2016. 'Urban systems and the political and economic structures of early-imperial Italy'. *Rivista di storia economica* XXXII(1): pp. 17–76.
De Ligt, L. and S. Northwood. 2008. *People, land, and politics: Demographic developments and the transformation of Roman Italy, 300 BC–AD 14*. Leiden: Brill.
De Ligt, L. and L. E. Tacoma. 2016a. *Migration and mobility in the early Roman Empire*. Leiden: Brill.
De Ligt, L. and L. E. Tacoma. 2016b. 'Approaching migration in the Early Empire'. In *Migration and mobility in the early Roman Empire*, edited by L. de Ligt and L. E. Tacoma Leiden, pp. 1–22. Leiden: Brill.
De Miguel-Ibáñez, M. P., J. M. Ballesteros Herráiz, M. Unzu Urmeneta, et al. 2011. 'Tres posibles casos de lepra en la plaza del Castillo (Pamplona, Navarra)'. In *Paleopatología. Ciencia multidisciplinar. Actas del X Congreso de Paleopatologias*, edited by A. González Martín, O. Cambra Moo, J. Rascón Pérez, et al., pp. 355–65. Madrid: Sociedad Española de Paleopatología.
De Palol, P. 1966. 'Demografia y arqueología hispánicas. Siglos IV–VIII. Ensayo de cartografía'. *BSAA* 32, pp. 5–67.
de Palol, P. and A. Pladevall (eds.) 1999. *Del romà al romànic. Història, art i cultura de laTarraconense Mediterrània entre els segles IV i X*. Barcelona: Enciclopèdia Catalana.
De Paz Fernández, F. J., J. F. Pastor Vázquez, and M. Barbosa Cachorro. 2014. 'Estudio antropológico de las cremaciones de la necrópolis vacceo-romana de Pintia (Padilla de Duero, Valladolid)'. *Anales de la Real Academia de Medicina y Cirugía de Valladolid* 51: pp. 103–11.

De Simone, G. F. 2017. 'The agricultural economy of Pompeii: Surplus and dependence'. In *The economy of Pompeii*, edited by M. Flohr and A. Wilson, pp. 23–51. Oxford: Oxford University Press.

De Soto, P. 2010. *Anàlisi de la xarxa de comunicacions i de transport a la Catalunya romana. Estudis de distribució i mobilitat*. PhD thesis, Universidad de Barcelona.

De Soto, P. 2011a. 'SIG y Network Analysis en el estudio de las redes de comunicación de la Cataluña'. In *Tecnologías de información geográfica y análisis arqueológico del territorio. Actas del V Simposio Internacional de Arqueología de Mérida*, edited by C. Mayoral and S. Celestino, pp. 651–65. Madrid: Consejo Superior de Investigaciones Científicas.

De Soto, P. 2011b. 'La configuración territorial del NO. Análisis desde una perspectiva de la accesibilidad y los costes de transporte'. In *Las ánforas de Lugo*, edited by C. Carreras, R. Morais, and E. González, pp. 99–132. Lugo: Concello de Lugo.

De Soto, P. 2019. 'Network analysis to model and analyse Roman transport and mobility'. In *Finding the limits of the limes: Modelling demography, economy and transport on the edge of the Roman Empire*, edited by P. Verhagen, J. Joyce, and M. Groenhuijzen, pp. 271–89. Cham: Springer International Publishing.

De Soto, P. and C. Carreras. 2009. 'La movilidad en época romana en Hispania: Análisis de aplicaciones de redes (SIG) para el estudio diacrónico de las infraestructuras de transporte'. *Habis* 40: pp. 302–24.

De Soto, P. and C. Carreras. 2022 'The economic and social evolution of the Iberian Peninsula as revealed through analysis of the Roman transport infrastructure'. In *Simulating Roman economies: Theories, methods, and computational models*, edited by T. Brughmans and A. Wilson, pp. 226–53. Oxford: Oxford University Press.

Dedet, B. 1987. *Habitat et vie quotidienne Languedoc au milieu de l'âge du Fer: L'unité domestique n° 1 de Gailhan, Gard*. Paris: CNRS.

Dedet, B. 1999. 'La maison de l'oppidum languedocien durant la Protohistoire: Forme et utilisation de l'espace'. *Gallia* 56: pp. 313–55.

Delibes, G. and F. Romero. 2011. 'La plena colonización agraria delValle Medio del Duero'. *Complutum* 22 (2): pp. 49–94. http://dx.doi.org/10.5209/rev_CMPL.2011.v22.n2.37727.

Deman, A. 1987. 'Réflexions sur la navigation fluviale dans l'antiquité romaine'. In *Histoire economique de l'antiquité*, edited by T. Hackens and P. Marchetti, pp. 79–106. Louvain-la-Neuve: Séminaire de numismatique Marcel Hoc Collège Érasme.

Desiderio, G. 2007. 'La muerte en la Hispania Romana. Ideología y prácticas'. In *Enfermedad, muerte y cultura en las sociedades del pasado Vol. I.*, edited by J. Barca and J. Jiménez, pp. 135–58. Cáceres: Fundación Academia Europea e Iberoamericana de Yuste.

Devore, J. L. 2012. *Probability and statistics for engineering and the sciences*, 8th edition. Boston, MA: Brooks/Cole, Cengage Learning.

Dewar, R. E. (1991). 'Incorporating variation in occupation span into settlement-pattern analysis'. *American Antiquity* 56(4): pp. 604–20.

Diamond, J. 2006. *Effondrement: Comment les sociétés décident de leur disparition ou de leur survie*. Paris: INCA.

Diarte, P., E. Ariño, and M. Pérez-Polo. 2020. '*Asturica* (Astorga, León) y *Albocela* (Villalazán, Zamora) entre la Antigüedad y la Edad Media: Análisis comparativo de sus territorios'. *SPAL* 29(1): pp. 271–99.

Diarte Blasco, P. 2011. *Morfología del cambio urbano en Hispania: La adaptación de los espacios públicos romanos a la nueva realidad tardoantigua*. PhD thesis, Universidad de Zaragoza.

Diarte Blasco, P. 2015. 'La convivencia de lo público y lo privado: el establecimiento de unidades domésticas y artesanales en los espacios cívicos huspanos'. In *Urbanisme civique en temps de crise: Les espaces publics d'Hispanie et de l'occident romain entre le IIe et le IVe siècle*, edited by L. Brassous and A. Quevedo, pp. 289–307. Madrid: Casa de Velázquez.

Díaz, M. A. and C. Jordán. 2001. 'Grafitos procedentes de Contrebia Belaisca'. *Palaeohispanica* 1: pp. 301–33.

Díaz, P. 2000. 'El reino suevo de Hispania y su sede en Bracara'. *Memorias de la Real Academia de Buenas Letras de Barcelona* 25: pp. 403–23.

Díaz, P. and L. R. Menéndez. 2016. 'Romanos, visigodos e indigenas: Las comunidades del Norte de Hispania en los inicios de la Edad Media [cuarenta años después]'. *Anejos de Nailos* 3: pp. 161–89.

Díaz Ariño, B. 2008. *Epigrafía latina republicana de Hispania* (= *ELRH*). Barcelona: Ediciones de la Universitat de Barcelona.

Díaz Ariño, B. and J. Antolinos. 2013. 'The organisation of mining and metal production in Carthago Nova between the late Republic and early Empire'. *Athenaeum: Studi Periodici di Letteratura e Storia* 101(2): pp. 535–53.

Díaz Ariño, B. and A. Mayayo. 2008. 'Cuatro nuevos grafitos procedentes de Azaila'. *Palaeohispanica* 8: pp. 197–202.

Díaz González, J. 1950. *Historia de la medicina en la Antigüedad*. Barcelona: Universidad de los Andes.

Diéguez Ramírez, J. P., I. Alemán Aguilera, and G. Moreno-Rueda. 2010. 'Estudio antropológico del Sector C de la necrópolis tardoantigua del Cortijo Coracho (Lucena, Córdoba)'. In *Esperanza Gutiérrez Redomero*, edited by A. Sánchez Andrés and V. Galera Olmo, pp. 245–54. Madrid: Universidad de Alcalá.

Domergue, C. 1990. *Les mines de la Péninsule Ibérique dans l'Antiquité Romaine*. Rome: École Française de Rome.

Domergue, C. and C. Rico. 2023. *Lateres plumbei hispani. Production et commerce du plomb hispanique à l'époque romaine (II^e^ siècle av. J.-C – I^er^ siècle apr. J.-C.)*. Madrid: Collection de la Casa de Velázquez no 195.

Domergue, C., P. Quarati, and A. Nesta. 2012. 'Les isotopes du plomb et l'identification des lingots de plomb romains des mines de Sierra Moderna: Questions de méthode: l'example des lingosts de l'épave "Cabrera 4"'. *Pallas* 90: pp. 243–56.

Domergue, C., M. L. di Vacri, A. Fernández Izquierdo, et al. 2016. 'Les lingots de plomb hispano-romains de Q. Vireius'. *Quaderns de prehistòria i arqueologia de Castelló* 34: pp. 177–96.

Domingo, L. A., J. M. Magariños, and A. Aldecoa. 2007. 'Nuevos datos sobre el poblamiento en la Carpetania meridional: el valle medio del Cigüela. En: Estudios sobre la Edad del Hierro en la Carpetania'. *Zona Arqueológica* 10: 218–37.

Domínguez, O. A. 1963. *La sociedad española del siglo XVII*. Madrid: CSIC.

Dopico, M. D. and J. Santos Yanguas. 2016. 'La creación de la red de ciudades del poder en la Citerior'. *Revista de historiografia* 25: pp. 111–31.

Downey, S. S., E. Bocaege, T. Kerig, et al. 2014. 'The Neolithic demographic transition in Europe: Correlation with Juvenility Index supports interpretation of the summed calibrated radiocarbon date probability distribution (SCDPD) as a valid demographic proxy'. *PLOS One* 9(8): e105730.

DuBois, P. 2019. *Slavery: Antiquity and its legacy*. Oxford: Oxford University Press.

Duday, H. 2009. *The archaeology of the death: Lectures in archaeothanatology*. Oxford: Oxbow Books.

Duncan-Jones, R. P. 1974. *The economy of the Roman Empire: Quantitative studies*. Cambridge: Cambridge University Press.

Duncan-Jones, R. P. 1977. 'Age-rounding, illiteracy and social differentiation in the Roman world'. *Chiron* 7: pp. 333–53.

Duncan-Jones, R. P. 1977–8. 'Aqueduct capacity and city populations'. *Libyan Studies* 9: p. 51.

Duncan-Jones, R. P. 2010. *Structure and scale in the Roman economy*. Cambridge: Cambridge University Press.

Dupré, X. 1997. 'El foro en las Provincias Hispánicas'. In *Hispania Romana: Desde tierra de conquista a provincia del imperio*, edited by J. Arce, S. Ensoli, and E. La Rocca, pp. 156–60. Madrid: Electa.

Dupré, X. and J. A. Remolà. 2002. 'A propósito de la gestión de los residuos urbanos en Hispania'. *Romula* 1: pp. 52–3.

Eckardt, H. 2010. *Roman diasporas: Archaeological approaches to mobility and diversity in the Roman Empire*. Portsmouth: Journal of Roman Archaeology.

Edmondson, J. 1989. 'Mining in the later Roman empire and beyond: Continuity or disruption?' *Journal of Roman Studies* 79: pp. 84–102.

Edmondson, J., T. N. Basarrate, and W. Trillmich. 2001. *Imagen y memoria: Monumentos funerarios con retratos en la colonia Augusta Emerita*. Madrid: Museo Nacional de Arte Romano.

Engels, D. W. 1990. *Roman Corinth: An alternative model for the classical city*. Chicago: University of Chicago Press.

Erdkamp, P. 2008. 'Mobility and migration in Italy in the second century BC'. In *People, land, and politics: Demographic developments and the transformation of Roman Italy, 300 BC–AD 14*, edited by L. de Ligt and S. J. Northwood, pp. 417–49. Leiden: Brill.

Erdkamp, P. 2016. 'Seasonal labour and rural-urban migration in Roman Italy'. In *Migration and mobility in the early Roman Empire*, edited by L. de Ligt and L. E. Tacoma, pp. 33–49. Leiden: Brill.

Erdkamp, P. 2021. 'A historian's introduction to paleoclimatology'. In *Climate change and ancient societies in Europe and the Near East*, edited by P. Erdkamp, J. G. Manning, and K. Verboven, pp. 1–24. Cham: Palgrave Macmillan.

Escala, O., A. Moya, E. Tartera, et al. 2013. *La Fogonussa (Sant Martí de Riucorb). Ibers, romans i visigots a la comarca de l'Urgell*. Barcelona: Tribuna d'Arqueologia.

Escudero Escudero, F. 2014. 'Ensayo sobre la estructura de la muralla romana de Zaragoza y tramo de la calle de los Mártires'. In *Homenaje a Guillermo Fatás*, edited by G. Fatás Cabeza and A. Duplá Ansuátegui, pp. 279–91. Zaragoza: Zaragoza Institución Fernando el Católico.

Escudero Escudero, F. and M. P. Galve. 2013. *Las cloacas de Caesaraugusta y elementos de urbanismo y topografía de la ciudad Antigua*. Madrid: Institución Fernando el Cátolico.

Esmonde-Cleary, S. 2007. *Rome in the Pyrenees: Lugdunum and the convenae from the first century B.C. to the seventh century A.D.* London: Routledge.

Espí, I., I. Grau, E. López, et al. 2009. 'L'aldea ibérica de l'Alt del Punxó: Producción agricola y asentamiento campesino en el área central de la Contestania'. *Lucentum* XXVIII: pp. 23–50.

Estarán, M. J. 2019. '¿Hablantes de lenguas itálicas en Hispania? Un análisis onomástico y sociolingüístico de la epigrafía latina hispana del siglo II a.C'. *Athenaeum* 107(2): pp. 388–423.

Estarán, M. J., G. Sopeña, F. J. Gutiérrez, and J. A. Hernández. 2011. 'Nuevos esgrafiados procedentes de Contrebia Belaisca'. *Palaeohispanica* 11: pp. 249–63.

Etxeberria, F. 1994. 'Aspectos macroscópicos del hueso sometido al fuego. Revisión de las cremaciones descritas en el País Vasco desde la Arqueología'. *Munibe* 46: pp. 111–16.

Eupedia. Genetics. *Y-DNA haplogroups*. Eupedia.com/Genetics. Visited December 2021.

Ezquerra, B. 2005. 'La ciudad romana de La Caridad'. In *Celtíberos. Tras la estela de Numancia*, edited by A. Chaín and J. I. de la Torre, pp. 205–12. Soria: Diputación Provincial de Soria.

Fentress, E. 2009. 'Peopling the countryside: Roman demography in the Albegna Valley and Jerba'. In *Quantifying the Roman economy: Methods and problems*, edited by A. Bowman and A. Wilson, pp. 127–61. Oxford: Oxford University Press.

Ferembach, D., I. Schwidetzky, and M. Stloukal. 1980. 'Recommendations for age and sex diagnoses of skeletons'. *Journal of Human Evolution* 9: pp. 517–49.

Fernández, A. 2010. 'Rías Baixas and Bigo (Vicus Eleni)'. In *The Western Roman Atlantic façade: A study of the economy and trade in the Mar Exterior from the Republic to the Principate*, edited by C. Carreras and R. Morais, pp. 229–38. Oxford: Archaeopress.

Fernández, A. 2014. *El comercio tardoantigua (s.IV–VII dC) en el Noroeste peninsular a través del registro cerámico de Vigo*. Oxford: Archaeopress.

Fernández Acebo, V., A. Martínez Velasco, and M. L. Serna Gancedo (eds.) 2010a. *Castros y castra en Cantabria*. Madrid: Acanto.

Fernández Acebo, V., A. Martínez Velasco, and M. L. Serna Gancedo. 2010b. 'Los poblados fortificados de la Edad del Hierro y las estructuras campamentales romanas en Cantabria: Reflexiones sobre el poblamiento, el reparto geográfico y la configuración'. In *Castros y castra en Cantabria*, edited by M. L. Serna Gancedo, A. Martínez Velasco, and V. Fernández Acebo, pp. 588–641. Madrid: Acanto.

Fernández Gómez, F. 1986. *Excavaciones arqueológicas en El Raso de Candeleda*. Avila: Diputación Provincial, Institución 'Gran Duque de Alba'.

Fernández Gómez, F. 2011. *El poblado fortificado de "El Raso de Candeleda" (Ávila): el núcleo D. Un poblado de la III Edad del Hierro en la Meseta de Castilla*. Sevilla: Universidad de Sevilla-Institución Gran Duque de Alba-Real Academia de la Historia.

Fernández Ochoa, C. and A. Morillo. 2005. 'Walls in the urban landscape of Late Roman Spain: Defense an imperial strategy'. In *Hispania in late antiquity*, edited by K. Bowles and M. Kulikowski, pp. 299–321. Leiden: Brill.

Fernández Ochoa, C., P. Salido, and M. Zarzalejos. 2014. 'Las formas de ocupación rural en Hispania. Entre la terminología y la práxis arqueológica'. *CuPAUAM* 40: pp. 111–36.

Ferrer, J., O. Olesti, and J. Velaza. 2018. 'Nuevas inscripciones rupestres latinas de Oceja y los IIIIviri ibéricos de Iulia Lybica'. *Dialogues d'histoire ancienne* 44(1): pp. 169–220.

Ferrer Sierra, S., A. Rodríguez Colmenero, and F. Hervés Raigoso. 1998. 'El Complejo arqueológico romano de "Aquis Querquernnis" Porto Quintela (Ourense)'. In *Los Orígenes de la ciudad en el Noroeste Hispánico II*, edited by A. Rodríguez Colmenero, pp. 891–910. Lugo: Diputación Provincial de Lugo.

Ferreruela Gonzalvo, A. and J. A. Mínguez. 2001. 'Un nuevo descubrimiento epigráfico romanorrepublicano en el valle del Ebro'. In *Élites Hispaniques*, edited by M. Navarro and S. Demougin, pp. 241–9. Burdeos: Pessac Ausonius Édition.

Flohr, M. 2017. 'Quantifying Pompeii: Population, inequality, and the urban economy'. In *The economy of Pompeii*, edited by M. Flohr and A. I. Wilson, pp. 53–86. Oxford: Oxford University Press.

Flohr, M. and V. Hunink. 2019. 'Een gulle gever zonder naam. De nieuwe grafinscriptie uit Pompeii'. *Hermeneus* 91: pp. 26–32.

Floriano, A. 1941. 'Aportaciones arqueológicas a la medicina romana'. *Archivo Español de Arqueología* 44: pp. 415–33.

Floridablanca, J. 1787. *Censo español executado de Orden del Rey, comunicada por el Excelentísimo Señor Conde de Floridablanca, Primer Secretario de Estado y del Despacho, en el año de 1787*. Madrid: Imprenta Real.

Fonte, J., B. Comendador, B. Lackinger, et al. 2015. 'Estaño y paisajes del agua en el noroeste peninsular'. In *Paisajes culturales del agua*, edited by V. Méndez Hernán, pp. 57–70. Ourense: Universidad de Extremadura.

Fonte, J., J. Valdez, F. S. Lemos, et al. 2011. 'Citânia de Briteiros e médio vale do Ave (NW de Portugal): SIG e análise arqueológica do território'. In *Tecnologías de Información Geográfi ca y Análisis Arqueológico Bibliography 419 del Territorio. Actas del V Simposio Internacional de Arqueología de Mérida*, edited by V. Mayoral Herrera and S. Celestino Pérez, pp. 359–66. Mérida: IAM.

Francès, J., J. Velaza, and N. Moncunill. 2008. 'Los esgrafiados sobre cerámica de Ca n'Oliver (Cerdanyola del Vallès)'. *Palaeohispanica* 8: pp. 217–42.

Fregel, R., F. L. Méndez, Y. Bokbot, et al. 2018. 'Ancient genomes from North Africa evidence prehistoric migrations to the Maghreb from both the Levant and Europe'. *Proceedings of the National Academy of Sciences of the United States of America* 115(26): pp. 6774–9. doi:10.1073/pnas.1800851115. Erratum in: *PNAS* 115(30): E7231.

Frier, B. W. 1982. 'Roman life expectancy: Ulpian's evidence'. *Harvard Studies in Classical Philology* 86: pp. 213–51.

Frier, B. W. 2000. 'Demography'. In *The Cambridge ancient history vol. XI: The high Empire: AD 70–192*, edited by A. Bowman, P. Garnsey, and P. Rathbone, pp. 787–816. Cambridge: Cambridge University Press.

Fu, Q., C. Posth, M. Hajdinjak, et al. 2016. 'The genetic history of Ice Age Europe'. *Nature* 534(7606): pp. 200–5. doi:10.1038/nature17993.

Fuentes, P. 1992. 'Las grandes epidemias en la temprana Edad Media y su proyección sobre la Península Ibérica'. *España Medieval* 15: pp. 9–29.

Fumanal, M. P. and C. Ferrer. 2007. 'El yacimiento arqueológico de La Picola (litoral de Santa Pola, España): Estudio geomorfológico y sedimentológico'. *Cuaternario y Geomorfología* 12(1–2): pp. 77–93.

Gabba, E. 1973. *Esercito e società nella tarda repubblica romana*. Florence: La Nuova Italia.

Galve, M. P. 2018–19. 'De vicus a suburbium: El barrio oriental de Caesaraugusta'. *Salduie* 18–19: pp. 59–119.

Gamba, C., E. Fernández, A. Oliver, et al. 2008. 'Population genetics and DNA preservation in ancient human remains from Eastern Spain'. *Forensic Science International* Genetics Supplement Series 1(1), pp. 462–64.

Gamo, E. and J. Fernández Ortea. 2019. 'Las termas públicas de Caraca y su contexto urbano'. In *En ningún lugar . . . Caraca y la romanización de la Hispania interior*, edited by E. Gamos, J. Fernández Ortea, and D. Álvarez Jiménez, pp. 43–70. Guadalajara: Diputación Provincial de Guadalajara.

Garcés, I. 2013. *Catàleg dels materials arqueològics de la Torre dels Encantats*. Arenys de Mar: Col·lecció del Museu d'Arenys de Mar.

García, J. 2017. *Gènesi, fundació i període republicà de la ciutat romana d'Iluro (Hispania Citerior)*. Mataró: Ajuntament de Mataró.

García, J., A. Martín, and X. Cela. 2000. 'Nuevas aportaciones sobre la romanización en el territorio de *Iluro* (Hispania Tarraconensis)'. *Empúries* 52: pp. 29–54.

García-Bellido, A. 1942. 'El castro de Coaña (Asturias). Nuevas aportaciones'. *Archivo Español de Arqueología* XV(48): pp. 216–44.

García-Bellido, A. 1954. 'El promedio de vida en la España romana'. *Archivo Español de Arqueología* 27: pp. 254–8.

García-Bellido, A. 1966. 'Los "mercatores", "negotiatores" y "publicani" como vehiculos de romanización en la España romana preimperial'. *Hispania: Revista española de historia* 104: pp. 497–512.

García-Bellido, A. 1976. 'El ejército romano en Hispania'. *Archivo Español de Arqueología* 49: pp. 59–101.

García-Bellido, M. P. and C. Blázquez. 2001. *Diccionario de cecas y pueblos hispánicos: I*. Madrid: CSIC.

García Borja, P., D. López Serrano, and J. L. Jiménez. 2012. *Al pie de la via Augusta. El yacimiento romano de Faldetes (Moixent, Valencia)*. Alcoy: P. García.

Garcia-Garcia, E. 2017. *Geofisika tekniken karakterizazioa Euskal Herriko Antzinaroko aztarnategi arkeologikoetan*. Doctoral dissertation, Leioa: Euskal Herriko Unibersitatea—Universidad del País Vasco.

Garcia-Garcia, E., J. M. Mtz Txoperena, R. Sala, et al. 2016. 'Magnetometer survey at the newly discovered Roman city of Auritz/Burguete (Navarre): Results and preliminary archaeological interpretation'. *Archaeological Prospection* 23: pp. 243–56.

García Marcos, V. and J. Vidal. 1998. '*Asturica Augusta*: De asentamiento militar a *urbs magnifica*'. In *Congreso Internacional sobre los orígenes de la ciudad en el Noroeste hispánico*, edited by A. Rodríguez Colmenero, pp. 911–44. Lugo: Diputación Provincial de Lugo.

Garcia Martinez, S. M. 1997. 'El fenomeno de la esclavitud en el noroeste hispanorromano según la evidencia epigrafica'. *Memorias de Historia Antigua* 18: pp. 195–218.

García Merino, C. 1976. *Población y poblamiento en Hispania romana: el Conventus Cluniensis*. Valladolid: Universidad de Valladolid.

García Merino, C. 2007. 'Problemas y soluciones al abastecimiento de agua a Uxama Argaela'. In *El agua y las ciudades romanas*, edited by J. Mangas and S. Martínez, pp. 213–35. Madrid: Ediciones 2007.

García Merino, C. and M. Sánchez-Simón. 2020. 'Una necrópolis postimperial de la villa de Almenara de Adaja-Puras (Valladolid)'. *Zephyrus* LXXXV: pp. 185–206.

García-Prósper, E. 2001. 'Algunos apuntes sobre las prácticas funerarias de época romana en Valentia'. *Saguntum* 33: pp. 75–84.

García-Prósper, E., I. López, and M. Polo-Cerdá. 2009. 'Esclavitud, cautividad y muerte en Hispania: A propósito de los casos de Valentia, Ilipa y Gades'. In *Actas del IX Congreso Nacional de Paleopatología*, edited by M. Polo-Cerdá and E. García-Prósper, pp. 719–28. Valencia: Sociedad Española de Paleopatología y Grupo Paleolab.

García-Prósper, E., M. Polo-Cerdá, and N. P. Guérin. 2007. 'Aproximación a la arqueología funeraria romana de Valencia a través de la necrópolis de la calle Quart (ss. II aC–III dC): Estudio preliminar de los rituales funerarios, bioantropología y paleopatología'. In *Enfermedad, muerte y cultura en las sociedades del pasado Vol. I*, edited by J. Barca and J. Jiménez, pp. 159–87. Cáceres: Actas del VIII Congreso Nacional de Paleopatología.

García Sánchez, J. 2016. 'Aerial survey of the Ager Segisamonensis: A Roman landscape revisited (Sasamón, Spain)'. *AARGnews* 52: pp. 34–42.

Garn, S. M., A. B. Lewis, and R. S. Kerewsky. 1966. 'Sexual dimorphism in the buccolingual tooth diameter'. *Journal of Dental Research* 4(6): p. 1819.

Garn, S. M., R. H. Osborne, and K. D. McCabe. 1979. 'The effect of prenatal factors on crown dimensions'. *American Journal of Physical Anthropology* 51(4): pp. 665–78. https://doi.org/10.1002/ajpa.1330510416.

Garnsey, P. 1991. 'Child rearing in ancient Italy'. In *The family in Italy from antiquity to the present*, edited by D. Kertzer and R. Saller, pp. 48–65. New Haven: Yale University Press.

Germoni, P., S. Keay, M. Millett, and K. Strutt. 2019. 'Ostia beyond the Tiber: Recent archaeological discoveries in the Isola Sacra'. In *Ricerche su Ostia e it suo territorio: Atti del Terzo Seminario Ostiense (Roma, École française de Rome, 21–22 ottobre 2015)*, edited by M. Cébeillac-Gervasoni, N. Laubry, and F. Zevi, pp. 149–68. Rome: L'École française de Rome.

Gilbert, M. T., T. Kivisild, B. Grønnow, et al. 2008. 'Paleo-Eskimo mtDNA genome reveals matrilineal discontinuity in Greenland'. *Science* 320(5884): pp. 1787–9. doi:10.1126/science.1159750.

Gilbert, M. T., A. Wilson, M. Bunce, et al. 2004. 'Ancient mitochondrial DNA from hair'. *Current Biology* 14(12): pp. R463–4. doi:10.1016/j.cub.2004.06.008.

Gill, P., P. L. Ivanov, C. Kimpton, et al. 1994. 'Identification of the remains of the Romanov family by DNA analysis'. *Nature Genetics* 6(2): pp. 130–5.

Gill-King, H. 1996. 'Chemical and ultrastructural aspects of decomposition'. In *Forensic taphonomy: The postmortem fate of human remains*, edited by H. W. Haglund and M. H. Sorg, pp. 93–108. Boca Raton: CRC Press.

Golden, M. 1988. 'Did the ancients care when children died?' *Greece & Rome* 35(2): pp. 152–63.

Goldsmith, N. and B. Graziosi. 2018. *Tombs of ancient poets: Between literary reception and material culture*. Oxford: Oxford University Press.

Gómez, F. J. 2006. 'La decadencia urbana y bajoimperial en la Diocesis hispaniarum: La primacia del argumento del declive, sobre el de la metamorfosis ciudadana'. *Historia Antiqua* 30: pp. 167–208.

Gómez-Bellard, F. 1996. 'El anàlisis antropológico de las cremaciones'. *Contemplum Extra* 6: pp. 55–64.

Gómez-Gonález, S., C. Roca de Togores, A. Romero, et al. 2011. 'Espondilitis anquilopoyética en la necrópolis tardorromana de Polisisto (Concentaina, Alicante)'. In *Paleopatología: Ciencia multidisciplinar*, edited by A. González-Martin, O. Cambra-Moo, J. Rascón Pérez, et al., pp. 477–81. Madrid: Sociedad Española de Paleopatología.

Gómez Pantoja, J. 1995. 'Pastores y trashumantes de Hispania'. In *Poblamiento celtibérico*, edited by F. Burillo Mozota, pp. 495–505. Zaragoza: Institución Fernando el Católico.

Gómez Pantoja, J. 2001. 'Pastio agrestis'. In *Los rebaños de Gerión. Pastores y transhumancia en Iberia antigua y medieval*, edited by J. Gómez-Pantoja, pp. 177–214. Madrid: Casa de Velázquez.

González-Fortes, G., F. Tassi, E. Trucchi, et al. 2019. 'A western route of prehistoric human migration from Africa into the Iberian Peninsula'. *Proceedings of the Royal Society B: Biological Sciences* 286(1895): 20182288. doi:10.1098/rspb.2018.2288.

González Román, C. 2010. 'Romanos e itálicos en la Hispania republicana'. In *Hispania et Gallia: Dos provincias del Occidente romano*, edited by L. Pons, pp. 13–32. Barcelona: Universitat de Barcelona.

González Ruibal, A. 2006. *Galaicos: Poder y comunidad en el Noroeste de la Península Ibérica (1200 a.C.–50 d.C.)*. A Coruña: Museo Arqueolóxico e Histórico and Castelo de San Antón.

González Villaescusa, R. 2001. *El mundo funerario romano en el País Valenciano. Monumentos funerarios y sepulturas entre los siglos I a. de C.–VII d. de C. Madrid: Casa de Velázquez*. Alicante: Instituto Alicantino de Cultura 'Juan Gil-Albert'.

González Zymla, H. 2007. 'En torno a la iconografía de la serpiente de Asclepio: Símbolo sanador de cuerpos y almas'. *Akros* 6: pp. 55–72.

Gowland, R. L., A. Chamberlain, and R. C. Redfern. 2014. 'On the brink of being: Re-evaluating infanticide and infant burial in Roman Britain'. *Journal of Roman Archaeology Supplementary Series* 96: pp. 69–88.

Gowland, R. and R. Redfern. 2010. 'Childhood health in the Roman world: Perspectives from the centre and margin of the Empire'. *Childhood in the Past* 3(1): pp. 15–42.

Gozalbez, E. and I. García. 2010. 'En torno a la medicina romana'. *Hispania Antiqua* XXXIII–XXXIV: pp. 323–36.

Gozalbes Cravioto, E. 2001. 'La proporción de las mujeres en la epigrafía funeraria romana del interior de Hispania'. *Espacio, Tiempo y Forma. Serie II. Historia Antigua* 14: pp. 95–114.

Gozalbes Cravioto, E. 2003. 'Aspectos de la sociología funeraria en la Celtiberia meridional'. *Wad-al-Hayara. Revista de Estudios de Guadalajara* 30: pp. 19–42.

Gozalbes Cravioto, E. 2007. 'La demografía de la Hispania romana tres décadas después'. *Historia Antiqua* XXXI: pp. 181–208.

Gracia Alonso, F. 1998. 'Arquitectura y poder en las estructuras de poblamiento ibéricas. Esfuerzo de trabajo y corveas'. In *Los Iberos. Príncipes de Occidente*, edited by C. Aranegui Gascó, P. Rouillard, and J. P. Mohen, pp. 99–114. Barcelona: Fundación 'La Caixa'.

Gracia Alonso, F., G. Munilla, E. García, et al. 1996. 'Demografía y superficie de poblamiento en los asentamientos ibéricos del NE peninsular'. *Complutum Extra* 6(11): pp. 177–91.

Grau, I. 2014. 'The Iron Age landscape of Alcoi valley, eastern Iberia: Agricultural intensification and sociopolitical dynamics'. *Journal of Field Archaeology* 39(2): pp. 124–33.

Grau, I. 2015. 'Sintaxis espacial en el *oppidum* ibérico. Reflexiones sobre los modelos espaciales y sociales'. *Arqueología de la arquitectura* 12: pp. 1–15.

Grau, I. and J. Moratalla Jávega. 2004. 'El paisaje antiguo'. In *Iberia, Hispania, Spania: Una mirada desde Ilici*, edited by L. Abad Casal and M. S. Hernández Pérez, pp. 111–18. Alicante: Caja de Ahorros del Mediterráneo.

Green, E. 2015. 'Conubium cum uxoribus: Wives and children in the Roman military diplomas'. *Journal of Roman Archaeology* 28: pp. 125–59.

Green, R. E., J. Krause, S. P. Ptak, et al. 2006. 'Analysis of one million base pairs of Neanderthal DNA'. *Nature* 444(7117): pp. 330–6. doi:10.1038/nature05336.

Gregori, G. L. and D. Nonnis. 2014. 'Il porto di *Minturnae* in età repubblicana: Il contributo delle fonti epigraphiche (con un'Appendice onomastica)'. In *l'epigrafia dei porti. Atti della XVIIe Rencontre sur l'Épigraphie du Monde Roman: Aquileia, 14–16 ottobre 2010*, edited by C. Zaccaria, pp. 80–122. Trieste: Antichità Altoadriatiche.

Grubbs, J. E. 2013. 'Infant exposure and infanticide'. In *The Oxford handbook of childhood and education in the classical world*, edited by J. E. Grubbs and T. Parkin, pp. 83–107. New York: Oxford University Press.

Guàrdia, M. 2015. 'A les portes de Lauro: el poblat ibèric del Puig del Castell de Samalús (Cànoves i Samalús)', *Ponències* 19: 73–108.

Guerin, P. (ed.) 2003. *El Castellet de Bernabé y el horizonte ibérico pleno edetano*. Valencia: Servei d'Investigació Prehistòrica.

Guerra, F. 1982. *Historia de la medicina*. Madrid: Norma.

Guerrero, L. and D. Ribas. 1997. 'Caracterización paleopatológica de la población prehistórica de Can Bosc de Monistrol de Rajadell (Bages, Barcelona)'. In *Actas IV Congreso Nacional de Paleopatología*, pp. 325–34. San Fernando de Cádiz: Universidad de Cádiz.

Guitart, J., J. Pera, and C. Carreras. 1998. 'La presencia del vi itàlic a les fundacions urbanes del segle I aC a l'interior de Catalunya: L'exemple d'Iesso'. In *En El Vi a l'antiguitat. Economia, producció i comerç al Mediterrani occidental: II Colloqui Internacional d'Arqueologia Romana, actes (Barcelona 6–9 de maig de 1998)*, pp. 39–65. Badalona: Museu de Badalona.

Guitart, J., J. M. Palet, M. Prevosti, and C. Ruestes. 2011. 'Ocupación y estructuración de la Cossetania Oriental (Tarragona) de época ibérica al Bajo Imperio'. In *Tecnologías de información geográfica y análisis arqueológico del territorio: Actas del V Simposio Internacional de Arqueología de Mérida (Anejos de AespA LIX)*, edited by V. Mayoral

Herrera and S. Celestino Pérez, pp. 221–32. https://www.academia.edu/30164188/Ocupaci%C3%B3n_y_estructuraci%C3%B3n_de_la_Cossetania_oriental_Tarragona_de_%C3%A9poca_ib%C3%A9rica_al_Bajo_Imperio.

Günther, T., C. Valdiosera, H. Malmström, et al. 2015. 'Ancient genomes link early farmers from Atapuerca in Spain to modern-day Basques'. *Proceedings of the National Academy of Sciences of the United States of America* 112(38): pp. 11917–22. doi:10.1073/pnas.1509851112.

Gurt, J. M. 2000–21. 'Transformaciones en el tejido de las ciudades hispanas durante la antigüedad tardía: dinámicas tardías'. *Zephyrus* 53–4: pp. 443–71.

Gutiérrez González, J. A. and L. Arias Páramo. 2009. 'Novedades sobre el recinto amurallado de Astorga (León)'. *Gladiua Anejos* 13: pp. 757–71.

Gutiérrez Lloret, S. 2004. 'Ilici en la antigüedad tardia'. In *Iberia, Hispania, Spania: Una mirada desde Ilici*, edited by L. Abad Casal and M. S. Hernández Pérez, pp. 95–110. Alicante: Caja de Ahorros del Mediterráneo.

Guzman, F. J. 2016. 'Un siglo aún por descubrir de la Historia de España: El siglo V después de Cristo'. *Cuadernos Medievales* 30: pp. 13–31.

Haak, W., J. Lazaridis, N. Patterson, et al. 2015. 'Massive migration from the steppe was a source for Indo-European languages in Europe'. *Nature* 522(7555): pp. 207–11. doi:10.1038/nature14317.

Hagelberg, E., M. Hofreiter, and C. Keyser, 2015. 'Ancient DNA: The first three decades'. *Philosophical Transactions of the Royal Society B: Biological Sciences* 370(1660): 20130371. doi:10.1098/rstb.2013.0371.

Hagelberg, E., B. Sykes, and R. Hedges. 1989. 'Ancient bone DNA amplified'. *Nature* 342: p. 485. doi:10.1038/342485a0.

Haley, E. W. 1991. *Migration and economy in Roman Imperial Spain*. Barcelona: Universitat de Barcelona.

Hansen, M. H. 2006. *The shotgun method: The demography of the ancient Greek city-state culture*. Columbia and London: University of Missouri Press.

Hanson, J. W. 2016. *An urban geography of the Roman world, 100 BC to AD 300*. Oxford: Archaeopress.

Hanson, J. W. and S. G. Ortman. 2017. 'A systematic method for estimating the population of Greek and Roman settlements'. *Journal of Roman Archaeology* 30: pp. 301–24.

Harper, K. 2019. *El fatal destino de Roma*. Barcelona: Editorial Crítica.

Harris, W. V. 1994. 'Child-exposure in the Roman Empire'. *Journal of Roman Studies*. 84: pp. 1–22.

Haselgrove, C. 1985. 'Inference from ploughsoil artefacts sample'. In *Archaeology from the ploughsoil*, edited by C. Haselgrove, M. Millett, and I. M. Smith, pp. 7–30. Sheffield: University of Sheffield.

Hassan, F. A. 1981. *Demographic archaeology*. New York: Academic Press.

Hauser, G. and G. F. DeStefano. 1989. 'Parámetros del esqueleto postcraneal en la población medieval castellana de "la Olmeda"'. *Boletín de la Sociedad de Antropología Biológica* 12: pp. 61–80.

Hayden, B., G. A. Reinhardt, and R. MacDonald, et al. 1996. 'Space per capita and the optimal size of housepits'. In *People who lived in big houses: Archaeological perspectives on large domestic structures*, edited by G. Coupland and E. B. Banning, pp. 151–63. Madison: Prehistory Press.

Haynes, I. P. 2013. *Blood of the provinces: The Roman auxilia and the making of the provincial society from Augustus to the Severans*. Oxford: Oxford University Press.

Heinzelmann, M. 1998a. 'Beobachtungen zur suburbanen Topographie Ostias. Ein orthogonales Strassensystem im Bereich der Pianabella'. *Römische Mitteilungen* 105: pp. 175–225.

Heinzelmann, M. 1998b. 'Arbeitsbericht zu einer zweiten geophysikalischen Prospektionskampagne in Ostia Antica'. *Römische Mitteilungen* 105: pp. 425–9.

Heinzelmann, M., F. A. Bauer, and A. Martin. 2000. 'Ostia. Ein urbanistisches Forschungsprojekt in den unausgegrabenen Bereichen des Stadtgebiets. Vorbericht zur 2. Grabungskampagne 1999'. *Römische Mitteilungen* 107: pp. 375–416.

Heinzelmann, M., H. Becker, K. Eder, and M. Stephani. 1997. 'Vorbericht zu einer geophysikalischen Prospektionskampagne in Ostia Antica'. *Römische Mitteilungen* 104: pp. 537–48.

Heinzelmann, M. and M. G. Granino Cecere. 2001. 'Ostia, Regio III. Untersuchungen in den unausgegrabenen Bereichen des Stadtgebietes. Vorbericht zur dritten Grabungskampagne 2000'. *Römische Mitteilungen* 108: pp. 313–28.

Heinzelmann, M. and A. Martin. 2002. 'River port, navalia and harbour temple at Ostia: new results of a DAI-AAR project'. *Journal of Roman Archaeology* 15: pp. 5–19.

Hemsley, S. 2008. *The implications of early village architectures: The sensuous geographies and social experience of Near Eastern PPNA and PPNB built environments*. PhD thesis, University of Liverpool.

Henry, L. 1959. 'L'âge au décès d'après les inscriptions funéraires'. *Population* 14(2): pp. 327–9.

Heras, C. and V. Galera. 2016. 'Antropoarqueología en la magdalena. El estudio de restos óseos humanos: Ciencia técnica y método entre la multi y la transdisciplinariedad'. *Revista Otarq* 1: pp. 3–27.

Herce, A. I., M. P. Punter, C. Escriche, et al. 1993. 'Las inscripciones de la "Casa de LIKINE" (Caminreal, Teruel)'. In *Lengua y cultura en Hispania prerromana: Actas del V Coloquio sobre lenguas y culturas de la Península Ibérica (Colonia 25–28 de Noviembre de 1989)*, edited by F. Villar and J. Untermann, pp. 747–72. Salamanca: Universidad de Salamanca.

Herrerín, J., J. Baxarias, E. García-Guixé, et al. 2011. 'Un caso de betatalasemia en un niño de una necrópolis tebana del Imperio Nuevo: La etiopatogenia de la cribra orbitalia a revisión'. In *Paleopatología: Ciencia multidisciplinar*, edited by A. González Martín et al., pp. 265–85. Madrid: Sociedad Española de Paleopatología, Universidad Autónoma de Madrid-Universidad Complutense de Madrid.

Hervella, M., N. Izagirre, S. Alonso, et al. 2012. 'Ancient DNA from hunter-gatherer and farmer groups from Northern Spain supports a random dispersion model for the Neolithic expansion into Europe'. *PLOS One* 7 (4): e34417. doi:10.1371/journal.pone.0034417.

Hidalgo Cuñarro, J. M., and R. Viñas Cué. 1998. 'El Vigo romano y su problemática'. In *Los Orígenes de la ciudad en el Noroeste Hispánico, edited by Antonio Rodríguez Colmenero*, pp. II: 807–838. Lugo: Diputación Provincial de Lugo.

Hill, J. N. 1970. *Broken K Pueblo: Prehistoric social organization in the American Southwest*. Tuscon: University of Arizona.

Hin, S. 2007. 'Family patterns. Economy, culture and biology: Fertility and constraints in Roman Italy'. *Princeton/Stanford Working Papers in Classics* No. 100704. doi:10.2139/ssrn.1426945.

Hin, S. 2013. *The demography of Roman Italy: Population dynamics in an ancient conquest society 201 BCE – 14 CE*. Cambridge: Cambridge University Press.

Hinojo, E. and C. Miró. 2017. 'Intervencions arqueològiques al Mercat de Sant Antoni: Noves dades sobre la xarxa viaria, ocupació i estructuració del pla de Barcelona des d'època romana i de la fortificació abaluardada del segle XVII'. *Tribuna d'Arqueologia* 2014–15: pp. 402–23.

Hipólito Correia, V. 2001. 'O povoamento do Noroeste no I.o millenio a.C'. In *Entre Celtas e Íberos: Las poblaciones protohistóricas de las Galias e Hispania*, edited by

L. Berrocal-Rangel and P. Gardes, pp. 213–26. Madrid: Real Academia de la Historia-Casa de Velázquez.
Hirt, A. M. 2010. *Imperial mines and quarries in the Roman World: Organizational aspects 27 BC–AD 235*. Oxford: Oxford University Press.
Holleran, C. 2016. 'Labour mobility in the Roman world: A case study of mines of Iberia'. In *Migration and mobility in the early Roman Empire*, edited by L. de Ligt and L. E. Tacoma, pp. 95–137. Leiden: Brill.
Holleran, C. and A. Pudsey. 2011. *Demography and the Graeco-Roman world: New insights and approaches*. Cambridge: Cambridge University Press.
Hopkins, K. 1965. 'Contraception in the Roman Empire'. *Comparative Studies in Society and History* 8(1): pp. 124–51.
Hopkins, K. 1966. 'On the probable age structure of the Roman population'. *Population Studies* 20: pp. 245–64.
Hopkins, K. 1983. *Death and renewal*. Cambridge: Cambridge University Press.
Hopkins, K. 2017. 'Graveyards for historians'. In *Sociological studies in Roman history*, edited by C. Kelly, pp. 135–59. Cambridge: Cambridge University Press.
Horai, S., K. Hayasaka, K. Murayama, et al. 1989. 'DNA amplification from ancient human skeletal remains and their sequence analysis'. *Proceedings of the Japan Academy, Series B* 65(10): pp. 229–33. doi:10.2183/pjab.65.229.
Horden, P. and N. Purcell. 2000. *The corrupting sea: A study of Mediterranean history*. Hoboken: Wiley-Blackwell.
Houten, P. H. A. 2021. *Urbanisation in Roman Spain and Portugal: Civitates Hispaniae of the Early Empire*. London: Routledge.
Houten, P. H. A. 2022. 'Small Towns a través de la epigrafía: El caso de la península ibérica'. In *Small Towns; una realidad urbana en la Hispania romana*, MYRTA 10, edited by P. Mateos Cruz, M. Olcina, A. Pizzo, and T. G. Schattner, pp. 71–79. Mérida: IAM - CSIC.
Houten, P. H. A. 2023 'Cities, epigraphies and latinization: A sociolinguistic view on the Hispaniae'. In *Transformations of the Roman West: Social Factors in Latinization*, edited by A. Mullen, pp. 51–77. Oxford: Oxford University Press.
Houten, P. H. A. and S. Panzram, forthcoming. 'In view of the cross: The transformation (or no) of the civitas into sedis episcopalis'. In *Shifting cities in the Iberian peninsula between late antiquity and the early Middle Ages*. Leiden: Brill.
Hug, A. G. 2014. *Fecunditas, sterilitas, and the politics of reproduction at Rome*. PhD thesis, University of York.
Hunt, D. R. 1990. 'Sex determination in the subadult ilia: An indirect test of Weaver's non-metric sexing method'. *Journal of Forensic Sciences* 35(4): pp. 881–5.
Iglésias, J. 1962. 'El fogatge de 1365–1370'. *Memorias de la Real Academia de Ciencias y Artes de Barcelona*.
Iglesias, J. 1979. *El fogatge de 1553*. Barcelona: Fundació Salvador Vives i Casajuana.
Iglesias, J. 1981. *El fogatge de 1553. Estudi i transcripció*. Barcelona: Fundació Salvador Vives i Casajuana.
Iglesias, J. 1991. *El fogatge de 1497. Estudi i transcripció*. Barcelona: Fundació Salvador Vives i Casajuana.
INE Portugal and INE España. 2018. *Península Ibérica en cifras*. https://www.ine.es/prodyser/pubweb/pin/pin2018/.
Isayev, E. 2017. *Migration, mobility and place in ancient Italy*. Cambridge: Cambridge University Press.
Iscan, M. Y. and K. A. R. Kennedy. 1989. *Reconstruction of life from the skeleton*. New York: Alan R. Liss.

Iscan, M. Y. and S. R. Loth. 1985. 'Age estimation from the rib by phase analysis: White females'. *Journal of Forensic Sciences* 30(3): pp. 853–63.

Iscan, M. Y., S. R. Loth, and R. K. Wright. 1984. 'Age estimation from the rib by phase analysis: White males'. *Journal of Forensic Sciences* 29(4): pp. 1094–104.

Iscan, M. Y., S. R. Loth, and R. K. Wright. 1987. 'Racial variation in the sternal extremity of the rib and its effect on age determination'. *Jounal of Forensic Sciences* 32(2): pp. 452–66.

Isidro, A. and A. Malgosa. 2003. *Paleopatología. La enfermedad no escrita*. Barcelona: Masson.

Isoardi, D. 2009. 'L'apport des données démographiques dans une étude de l'organisation de la société préromaine de France méridionale. Une nouvelle lecture des oppida'. In *L'espai domèstic i l'organització de la societat a la protohistòria de la Mediterrània occidental (Ier millenni aC)*, edited by M. C. Belarte, pp. 67–77. Barcelona: Departament de Prehistòria, Història Antiga i Arqueologia de la Universitat de Barcelona.

Isoardi, D. 2012. 'Demographic analysis of the Pre-Roman population near the Greek colony of Massalia (Southern France)'. In *From the Pillars of Hercules to the footsteps of the Argonauts*, edited by A. Hermary and G. R. Tsetskhlazde, pp. 37–60. Leiden: Peeters Press.

Jackes, M. 2000. 'Building the bases for paleodemographic analysis: adult age determination'. In *Biological anthropology of the human skeleton*, edited by M. A Katzenberg and A. L Gauer, pp. 417–66. New York: Wiley-Liss.

Jackson, R. P. J. 1993. 'Roman medicine: The practitioners and their practices'. *ANRW* II 37(1): pp. 79–101.

Janaway, R. C., S. L. Percival, and A. S. Wilson. 2009. 'Decomposition of human remains'. In *Microbiology and aging*, edited by S. L. Percival, pp. 313–34. Totowa: Humana Press.

Jimeno Martínez, A. 2011. 'Las ciudades Celtibéricas de la meseta oriental'. *Complutum* 22.2: pp. 223–76.

Jimeno Martínez, A. and C. Tabernero Galán. 1996. 'Origen de numancia y su evolución urbana'. *Complutum Extra* 6(1): pp. 415–32.

Johnson, P. and M. Millett. 2013 *Archaeological survey and the city*. Oxford: Oxbow Books.

Jongman, W. M., J. P. A. M. Jacobs, and G. M. K. Goldewijk. 2019. 'Health and wealth in the Roman Empire'. *Economics and Human Biology* 34: pp. 138–50.

Jordana, X. and A. Malgosa. 2007. 'Enterraments d'època romana a la plaça de la Vila de Madrid. Barcelona. Resultats de la recerca Antropològica'. *Quarhis* Època II 3: pp. 64–81.

Joshel, S. 2010. *Slavery in the Roman world*. Cambridge: Cambridge University Press.

Kajanto, I. 1965. *The Latin cognomina*. Helsinki: Helsinki Societas Scientiarum Fennica.

Keay, S. J. and G. Earl. 2011. 'Towns and territories in Roman Baetica'. In *Settlement, urbanization, and population*, edited by A. Bowman and A. Wilson, pp. 276–313. Oxford: Oxford University Press.

Keay, S., G. Earl, and F. Felici. 2020. *Uncovering the Harbour Buildings. Excavations at Portus 2007–2012, Volume I. The Surveys, Excavations and Architectural Reconstructions of the "Imperial Palace" and Adjacent Buildings*. Cambridge: Cambridge University Press.

Kennedy, D. 2006. 'Demography, the population of Syria, and the census of Q. Aemilius Secundus'. *Levant* 38: pp. 109–24.

Killgrove, K. and J. Montgomery. 2016. 'All roads lead to Rome: Exploring human migration to the eternal city through biochemistry of skeletons from to Imperial era cemeteries (1st–3rd c. AD)'. *PLOS One* 11(2): e0147585. doi:10.1371/journal.pone.0147585.

King, H. and V. Dasen. 2008. *La médecine dans l'antiquité grecque et romaine*. Lausanne: BHMS.

Kivisild, T. 2017. 'The study of human Y chromosome variation through ancient DNA'. *Human Genetics* 136(5): pp. 529–46. doi:10.1007/s00439-017-1773-z. Erratum in *Human Genetics* 137(10): p. 863.

Klales, A. R., S. D. Ousley, and J. M. Vollner. 2012. 'A revised method of sexing the human innominate using Phenice's nonmetric traits and statistical methods'. *American Journal of Physical Anthropology* 149(1), pp. 104–14. doi:10.1002/ajpa.22102.

Knodell, A. R., T. C. Wilkinson, T. P. Leppard, and H. A. Orengo. 2023. 'Survey archaeology in the Mediterranean world: Regional traditions and contributions to long-term history'. *Journal of Archaeological Research* 31: pp. 263–329. https://doi.org/10.1007/s10814-022-09175-7.

Kocher, A., L. Papac, R. Barquera, et al. 2021. 'Ten millennia of hepatitis B virus evolution'. *Science* 374(6564): pp. 182–8. doi: 10.1126/science.abi5658.

Kolb, A. 2019. *Roman roads: New evidence—new perspectives*. Berlin: De Gruyter.

Koningsberg, L. W. and S. R. Frankenberg. 1992. 'Estimation of age structure in anthropological demography'. *American Journal of Physical Anthropology* 89: pp. 235–56.

Kramer, C. 1979. 'An archaeological view of a contemporary Kurdish village: Domestic architecture, household size, and wealth'. In *Ethnoarchaeology: Implications of ethnography for archaeology*, edited by C. Kramer, pp. 139–63. New York: Columbia University Press.

Krenkel, W. 1965. 'Zu den Tagelöhnen bei der Ernte'. *Romanitas* 6/7: pp. 130–53.

Krogman, W. M. and Y. M. Iscan. 1986. *The human skeleton in forensic medicine*. Springfield, IL: C. C. Thomas.

Kron, G. 2005. 'The Augustan census and the population of Italy'. *Athenaeum* 92: pp. 441–95.

Kron, G. 2017. 'The population of Northern Italy and the debate about the Augustan census figures: Weighting the documentary, literary, and archaeological evidence'. In *Populazione e risorce nell'Italia del nord dalla romanizzaione ai Longobardi*, edited by E. Lo Cascio and M. Maiuro, pp. 49–98. Bari: Edipuglia.

Kulikowski, M. 2006. 'Plague in Spanish late antiquity'. In *Plague and the end of antiquity: The pandemic of 541–750*, edited by L. K. Little, pp. 150–61. Cambridge: Cambridge University Press.

Kulikowski, M. 2010. *Late Roman Spain and its cities*. Baltimore: Johns Hopkins University Press.

Künow, J. 1980. *Negotiator et ventura: Händler und Transport im freiem Germanien*. Marburg: Universität Marburg.

Ladero Quesada, M. A. 2014. 'Población de las ciudades en la baja Edad Media (Castilla, Aragón, Navarra)'. In *I Congresso Histórico Internacional. As cidades na História: Populaçao*, pp. 167–201. Guimarães: Câmera Municipal de Guimarães.

Laes, C. 2011. *Children in the Roman Empire: Outsiders within*. Cambridge: Cambridge University Press.

Lalueza, C. and M. Garcia. 1994. 'La necrópolis romana de la calle Prat de la Riba (Tarragona): Indicadores de estrés ambiental'. *Boletín de la Sociedad Española de Antropología Biológica* 15: pp. 91–100.

Lalueza-Fox, C. 2021. 'Neanderthal assimilation?' *Nature Ecology and Evolution* 5(6): pp. 711–12. doi:10.1038/s41559-021-01421-3.

Lalueza-Fox, C., M. L. Sampietro, C. Caramelli, et al. 2005. 'Neandertal evolutionary genetics: Mitochondrial DNA data from the Iberian peninsula'. *Molecular Biology and Evolution* 22(4): pp. 1077–81. doi:10.1093/molbev/msi094.

Larsen, C. S. 2002. 'Bioarchaeology: The lives and lifestyles of past people'. *Journal of Archaeological Research* 10(2): pp. 119–66.

Larsen, C. S. 2015. *Bioarcheology: Interpreting behavior from the human skeleton*, 2nd edition, Cambridge: Cambridge University Press.

Launaro, A. 2011. *Peasants and slaves: The rural population of Roman Italy (200 BC to AD 100)*. Cambridge: Cambridge University Press.

Laurence, R. 1999. *The roads of Roman Italy: Mobility and cultural change*. London: Routledge.

Laurence, R., S. Esmonde Cleary, and G. Sears. 2011. *The city in the Roman West*. Cambridge: Cambridge University Press.

Lazaridis, I., A. Mittnik, N. Patterson, et al. 2017. 'Genetic origins of the Minoans and Mycenaeans'. *Nature* 548(7666): pp. 214–18. doi:101038/nature23310.

Le Goff, I. 2002. 'Les vestiges de la crémation: Témoins privilégiés des protocoles funéraires'. *Archéopages* 6: pp. 10–17.

Le Roux, P. 1995. 'L'émigration italique en Citérieure et Lusitanie jusqu'a la mort de Néron'. In *Roma y el nacimiento de la cultura epigráfica en Occidente*, edited by F. Beltrán Lloris, pp. 85–95. Zaragoza: Institución Fernando el Católico.

Le Teuff, B. 2012. *Census: Les recensements dans l'empire romain d'Auguste à Diocletien*. Bordeaux: Université Michel de Montaigne—Bordeaux III.

Leblanc, S. 1971. 'An addition to Naroll's suggested floor area and settlement population relationship'. *American Antiquity* 36(2): pp. 210–11.

Ledermann, S. 1969. *Nouvelles tables-types de mortalité*. Paris: Presses Universitaires de Frances.

Lemos, F. S. 2007. *Citânia de Briteiros: Povoado Proto-Histórico*. Guimarães: Sociedade Martins Sarmento.

Lemos, F. S., G. Cruz, J. Fonte, et al. 2011. 'Landscape in the Late Iron Age of Northwest Portugal'. In *Atlantic Europe in the first millenium BC: Crossing the divide*, edited by T. Moore and X. L. Armada, pp. 187–204. Oxford: Oxford University Press.

León, J. C. C. 1996. *Les sources de l'histoire des Bagaudes*. Paris: Annales littéraires de l'Université de Franche-Comté.

Lewis, M. 2007. *The bioarchaeology of children: Perspectives from biological and forensic anthropology*. Cambridge: Cambridge University Press.

Liu, L., S. Oza, D. Hogan, et al. 2015. 'Global, regional, and national causes of child mortality in 2000-13, with projections to inform post-2015 priorities: An updated systematic analysis'. *Lancet* 385(9966): 430–40.

Llanos, O. L. 1990. *Necrópolis del Alto Ebro. In Necrópolis celtibéricas: II Simposio sobre los celtíberos [celebrado en Daroca (Zaragoza), del 28 al 30 de abril de 1988]*, edited by M. Francisco Burillo, pp. 137–48.

Llorens, M. M. 1994. *La Ciudad Romana de Carthago Nova: Las emisiones Romanas*. Murcia: Universidad de Murcia.

Llorens, M. M. and P. P. Ripollès. 1998. *Les encunyacions ibèriques de Lauro*. Granollers: Ajuntament de Granollers.

Lloyd, J. A. and P. R. Lewis. 1977. 'Water supply and urban population in Roman Cyrenaica'. *Libyan Studies* 8: pp. 35–40.

Lo Cascio, E. 2004. 'Considerazioni sulla datazione di *CIL* XIV 375 e sulla cronologia di Gamala *senior*'. In *Ostia, Cicero, Gamala, feasts, & the economy: Papers in memory of John H. D'Arms*, edited by A. Gallina Zevi and J. H. Humphrey, pp. 83–8. Portsmouth: Journal of Roman Archaeology Supplementary Series.

Lo Cascio, E. 2009. 'Urbanization as a proxy of growth'. In *Quantifying the Roman economy: Methods and problems*, edited by A. K. Bowman and A. Wilson, pp. 87–106. Oxford: Oxford University Press.

Lo Cascio, E. 2012. *L'impatto della "Peste Antonina"*. Bari: Edipuglia.

Lo Cascio, E. and L. E. Tacoma. 2017. *The impact of mobility and migration in the Roman Empire*. Leiden: Brill.

Loidi, J. 2017. 'Introduction to the Iberian peninsula, general features: Geography, geology, name, brief history, land use and conservation'. In *The vegetation of the Iberian peninsula*, edited by J. Loidi, pp. 3–27. Cham: Springer.

Longares, L. A., J. L. Peña, F. Escudero, et al. 2018. 'Cartografía histórica y reconstrucción paleotopográfica y geoarqueológica de la ciudad romana de Caesar Augusta (Zaragoza, España)'. *Boletín Geológico y Minero* 129(1/2): pp. 421–35.

López, F. 2012. 'The coinage of Carthago Nova and the Roman fleet of Misenum: Imperial triumphs and local deductiones'. In *The city and the coin in the ancient and early medieval worlds*, edited by F. López, pp. 73–89. Oxford: BAR International Series 2402.

López, M. A. and Fierro, M. J. 1988. 'La época ibérica en Darró, Vilanova i la Geltrú, Barcelona. Evidencias e hipótesis proporcionadas por las últimas excavaciones (1984–1988)'. *Espacio, Tiempo y Forma. Serie II. Historia Antigua* I: pp. 117–41.

López Costas, O. 2012. *Antropología de los restos óseos humanos de Galicia estudio de la población romana y medieval gallega*. PhD thesis, Universidad de Granada.

López Quiroga, J. 2011. *Gentes barbarae. Los bárbaros, entre el mito y la realidad*. Murcia: Universidad de Murcia.

Lorrio, A. J. 1997. *Los Celtíberos*. Alicante/Madrid: Universidad de Alicante/Universidad Complutense de Madrid.

Lorrio Alvarado, A. and Simón García, J. L. 2016. 'El "oppidum" ibérico de El Castellar de Meca y su territorio en la provincia de Albacete'. In *Actas de la I Reunión Científica de Arqueología de Albacete*, edited by B. Gamo Parras and R. Sanz Gamo, pp. 419–38.

Lostal Pros, J. 1992. *Los Miliarios de la provincia Tarraconense (Conventos Tarraconense, Caesarugustano, Cluniense y Cartaginense)*. Zaragoza: Institución Fernando el Católico.

Loth, S. R. and M. Henneberg. 2001. 'Sexually dimorphic mandibular morphology in the first few years of life'. *American Journal of Physical Anthropology* 115(2): pp. 179–86. doi:10.1002/ajpa.1067.

Lovejoy, C. O., R. S. Meindl, T. R. Pryzbeck, et al. 1985. 'Chronological metamorphosis of the auricular surface of the ilium: A new method for the determination of adult skeletal age at death'. *American Journal of Physical Anthropology* 68(1): pp. 15–28. doi:10.1002/ajpa.1330680103.

Lurie, S. 2005. 'The changing motives of cesarean section: From the ancient world to the twenty-first century'. *Archives of Gynecology and Obstetrics* 271: pp. 281–5.

McCormick, M. 2015. 'Tracking mass death during the fall of Rome's empire (I)'. *Journal of Roman Archaeology* 28: pp. 326–57.

McCormick, M. 2016. 'Tracking mass death during the fall of Rome's empire (II): A first inventory'. *Journal of Roman Archaeology* 28: pp. 1008–46.

McCormick, M., U. Büntgen, M. A. Cane, et al. 2012. 'Climate change during and after the Roman Empire: Reconstructing the past from scientific and historical evidence'. *Journal of Interdisciplinary History* 43(2): pp. 169–220.

McEvedy, C. and R. Jones. 1978. *Atlas of world population history*. New York: Penguin.

Macias, J. M. 2000. 'Tarraco en la Antigüedad tardía: un proceos simultáneo de transformación urbana e ideológica'. In *Los orígenes del cristianismo en Valencia y su entorno*, edited by A. Ribera, pp. 259–71. Valencia: Ajuntament València.

Macias, J. M. 2008. 'Vici y articulación del territorium: Segobriga, Ercavica y Valeria'. In *El territorio de las ciudades romanas*, edited by J. Mangas Manjarrés and M. Ángel Novillo, pp. 617–32. Madrid: Sisifo.

Macias, J. M. 2013. 'La medievalización de la ciudad romana'. In *Tarraco christiana ciuitas*, edited by J. M. Macias, and A. Muñoz, pp. 123–47. Tarragona: ICAC.

Macias, J. M., I. Fiz, L. Piñol, et al. 2007. *Planimetria arqueológica de Tarraco*. Tarragona: ICAC.

McIntyre, L. J. 2015. 'Constructing population size in a Romano-British Colonia: The case of Eboracum'. *Journal of Roman Archaeology* 28: pp. 413–29.

MacMullen, R. 1982. 'The epigraphic habit in the Roman Empire'. *The American Journal of Philology* 103: pp. 233–46.

Madrid, M. and A. Sinner. 2019. 'Analysing technical choices: Improving the archaeological classification of Late Republican Black Gloss pottery in north-eastern Hispania consumption centres'. *Archaeological and Anthropological Sciences* 11: pp. 3155–86.

Madrid, M. and A. G. Sinner. 2021. 'La vajilla de barniz negro en Empúries y la Layetania. Origen y técnica de producción a partir de su caracterización arqueométrica'. *Archivo Español de Arqueología* 94: e01.

Magallón, M. A. and M. Navarro. 1992. 'Los desplazamientos humanos en el Conventus Caesaraugustanus'. *Zephyrus* XLIV–XLV: pp. 405–21.

Maiuro, M. 2019. '*Caritas annonae* a Pompeii'. In *Uomini, istituzioni, mercati. Studi di storia per Elio Lo Cascio*, edited by M. Maiuro, G. D. Merola, M. de Nardis, and G. Soricelli, pp. 473–91. Bari: Edipuglia (Pragmateiai 30).

Malgosa, A., R. Montiel, N. Díaz, et al. 2005. 'Ancient DNA: A modern look at the infections of the past'. In *Recent research developments in microbiology*, edited by S. G. Pandalai, pp. 213–36. Trivandrum: Research Signpost.

Maluquer de Motes, J. 1983. *El poblado paleoibérico de La Ferradura, Ulldecona (Tarragona)*. Barcelona: Universitat de Barcelona-CSIC.

Manco, L., J. Albuquerque, M. F. Sousa, et al. 2018. 'The eastern side of the westernmost Europeans: Insights from subclades within Y-chromosome haplogroup J-M304'. *American Journal of Human Biology* 30(2): e23082. doi:10.1002/ajhb.23082.

Mangas, J. 1971. *Esclavos y libertos en la España romana*. Salamanca: Universidad de Salamanca.

Manzaneda Martín, C. 2017. *Los Oretanos: Una visión desde el territorio, la sociedad y la ideología*. PhD thesis, Universitat d'Alacant.

Mar, R. and J. Ruiz de Arbulo. 1987. 'La Basílica de la Colonia Tarraco: Una nueva interpretación del llamado Foro Bajo de Tarragona'. In *Los foros romanos de las provincias occidentales*, pp. 31–44. Madrid: Ministerio de Cultura.

Mar, R. and J. Ruiz de Arbulo. 2011. 'Tarragona romana. República i Alt Imperi (anys 218 aC–265 dC)'. *Història de Tarragona* I: pp. 207–538.

Mar, R., J. Ruiz de Arbulo, D. Vivó, et al. 2012. *Tarraco. Arquitectura y urbanismo de una capital provincial romana. Vol. I: De la Tarragona ibèrica a la construcción del templo de Augusto*. Tarragona: Universitat Rovira i Virgili.

Marín, C. and A. Ribera. 1999. *Las termas Romanas de l'Almoina*. Valencia: Ayuntamiento de Valencia.

Marín Díaz, M. A. 1986. 'La emigración itálica a Hispania en el siglo II a.C.'. *Studia Historica: Historia Antigua* 4–5: pp. 53–63.

Marín Díaz, M. A. 1988. *Emigración, colonización y municipalización en la Hispania Republicana*. Granada: Universidad de Granada.

Maroto Rodríguez, I. D. 2018. 'Los esclavos públicos e imperiales como agentes cultuales en Hispania'. *Revista de Historiografía* 28: pp. 139–66.

Márquez Pérez, J. and J. Pérez Maestro. 2005. 'El primer puticuli documentado en *Augusta Emerita*: Contextualización topográfica y cronológica'. *Mérida Excavaciones Arqueológicas* 8: pp. 533–45.

Márquez Villora, J. C. 1999. *El comercio Romano en el Portus Ilicitanus: El abastecimiento exterior de productos alimentarios (siglos I a. C. – V d. C.)*. Alicante: Publicaciones de la Universidad de Alicante.

Márquez Villora, J. C. and J. Molina Vidal. 2005. *Del Hiberus a Carthago Nova. Comercio de alimentos y epigrafía anfórica grecolatina*. Barcelona: Universitat de Barcelona.

Martín, A. 2017. 'El darrer decenni d'intervencions arqueològiques a Ilturo (Cabrera de Mar, Maresme): Novetats i estat actual de la recerca'. *Tribuna d'Arqueologia* 2014–15: pp. 304–29.

Martín, A. and J. García. 2002. 'La romanización en el territorio de los layetanos y la fundación de la ciudad romana de Iluro (Hispania Tarraconensis)'. In *Valencia y las primeras ciudades romanas de Hispania*, edited by Ajuntament de Valencia, pp. 195–204. Valencia: Ayuntamiento de Valencia.

Martín, A., V. Revilla, and C. Carreras. 2020. 'Economy, viticulture and demography in Laetanian region (Hispania Citerior Tarraconensis) from 1st century BC to 3rd century AD'. In *The resilience of the Roman Empire: Regional case studies on the relationship between population and food. Resources*, edited by D. Van Limbergen, S. Maréchal, and W. De Clercq, pp. 47–70. Oxford: BAR.

Martin, R. and K. Saller. 1957. *Lehrbuch des Anthropologie, in systematischer Darstellung*. Sttutgart: Fischer.

Martínez Jiménez, J. 2014. *Aqueducts and water supply in the towns of post-Roman Spain (AD 400–1000)*. DPhil thesis, University of Oxford.

Martínez Jiménez, J. 2019. 'Tantam pecuniam male perdiderunt: Aqueducts and municipal investment in Hispania'. In *Signs of weakness and crisis in the Western cities of the Roman Empire (c. II–III AD)*, edited by J. Andreu and A. Blanco-Pérez, pp. 59–70. Stuttgart: Franz Steiner Verlag.

Martínez Torrecilla, J. M. and C. Jordán Cólera. 2016. 'Una tésera celtibérica y algunas inscripciones sobre instrumentum procedentes de Graccurris (Alfaro, La Rioja)', *Palaeohispanica* 16: 261–79.

Martínez Jiménez, J., I. Sastre de Diego, and C. Tejerizo García. 2018. *The Iberian peninsula between 300 and 850: An archaeological perspective*. Amsterdam: Amsterdam University Press.

Martínez Vicente, M. J., D. Campillo, J. A. Ginestà, and J. Baxarias. 2007. 'Lesiones de posible origen ocupacional en una población de Tarraco del Bajo Imperio'. In *Enfermedad, muerte y cultura en las sociedades del pasado*, edited by F. J. Barca Durán and J. Jiménez Avila, pp. 217–20. Caceres: Fundación Academia Europea e Iberoamericana de Yuste.

Martínez Vicente, M. J., J. A. Ginesta, J. A. Baxaria, et al. 2005. 'Craneoestenosis y lesiones de probable origen laboral en un individuo de época tardorromana'. In *Nuevas perspectivas del diagnóstico diferencial en Paleopatología*, pp. 168–74. Mahón (Menorca): A. Cañellas.

Martiniano, R., L. M. Cassidy, R. Ó'Maoldúin, et al. 2017. 'The population genomics of archaeological transition in west Iberia: Investigation of ancient substructure using imputation and haplotype-based methods'. *PLoS Genetics* 13(7): e1006852. doi:10.1371/journal.pgen.1006852.

Martins, M. 2004. 'Urbanismo e arquitectura en Bracara Augusta. Balanço dos contributos da Arqueologia urbana'. In *Simulacra romae: Roma y las capitales del Occidente romano*, edited by J. Ruiz de Arbulo, pp. 149–73. Tarragona: Edicions El Mèdol.

Martins, M. and M. Delgado. 1996. '*Bracara Augusta*: Uma cidade na periferia do Império'. In *Los Finisterres Atlánticos en la Antigüedad. Época Prerromana y Romana (Coloquio Internacional)*, edited by C. Fernández Ochoa, pp. 121–7. Madrid: Electa.

Martins, M., J. Ribeiro, F. Magalhâes, et al. 2012. 'Urbanismo e arquitectura de Bracara Augusta. Sociedade, economia e lazer'. In *Evoluçao do paisagem urbana. Sociedade e economia*, edited by M. Do Cardo and A. Sousa, pp. 29–68. Braga: CITCEM–Centro de Investigação Transdisciplinar 'Cultura, Espaço e Memória'.

Marzano, A. 2011. 'Rank-size analysis and the Roman cities of the Iberian peninsula and Britain: Some considerations'. In *Settlement, urbanization, and population*, edited by A. Bowman and A. Wilson, pp. 196–228. Oxford: Oxford University Press.

Masset, C. 1986. 'Estimateurs paléodémographiques'. In *L'Homme, son evolution, sa diversité: Manuel d'anthropologie physique*, edited by M. C. Chamla, D. Ferembach, and C. Susanne, pp. 65–9. Paris: CNRS.

Masset, C. 1990. 'Paléodémographie: Structures et variations de la mortalité'. *Les Nouvelles de l'Archéologie* 40: pp. 33–4.

Mata, C., F. X. Duarte, M. A. Ferrer, J. Garibo, and J. Valor. 2001. 'Kelin (Caudete de las Fuentes, Valencia) y su territorio'. In *Los Íberos en la Comarca de Requena-Utiel*, edited by A. Lorrio, pp. 75–89. Alicante: Publicaciones Universidad de Alicante.

Mateo, D. 2016. *Comercio anfórico y relaciones mercantiles en Hispania Ulterior (s. II aC–s. II dC)*. Barcelona: Universitat de Barcelona.

Mattingly, D. J. 2011. 'Calculating Plough-Zone Demographics'. In *Settlement, Urbanization, and Population*, edited by A. Bowman and A. Wilson, pp. 76–91. Oxford: Oxford University Press.

Maya, J. L. 1998. 'La Campa Torres (Gijón, Asturias) ¿Oppidum Noega? Un Ejemplo de Urbanismo Híbrido'. *In Los Orígenes de La Ciudad En El Noroeste Hispánico, edited by Antonio Rodríguez Colmenero*, II: pp. 945–78. Lugo: Diputación Provincial de Lugo.

Maya González, José Luís, and Francisco Cuesta Toribio. 2001. El castro de La Campa Torres> Período prerromano. Gijón: vtp editorial.

Maya, J. L., S. Rovira, and F. Cuesta. 1993. 'Metalurgia del bronce en el poblado perromano de la Campa Torres (Asturias)'. *Pyrenae* 24: pp. 151–8.

Mayer, M. and O. Olesti. 2001. 'La sortition de Ilici. Del documento epigráfico al paisaje histórico'. *Dialogues d'Histoire Ancienne* 27(1): pp. 109–30.

Mayer, M. and I. Rodà. 1986. 'La epigrafía republicana en Cataluña. Su reflejo en la red viaria'. In *Actas de la reunión sobre epigrafía hispánica de época republicana (Zaragoza, 1983)*, pp. 157–70. Zaragoza: Diputación de Zaragoza.

Mayoral, J., A. Ravotto, C. Carreras, L. Casas, and R. Di Febo, forthcoming. 'Gauloise amphorae at the heart of the Laietania (province Hispania Citerior Tarraconensis)'. *Hommenage to Fannette Laubenheimer.*

Mays, S. and M. Faerman. 2001. 'Sex identification in some putative infanticide victims from Roman Britain using ancient DNA'. *Journal of Archaeological Science* 28(5): pp. 555–9. doi: 10.1006/jasc.2001.0616.

Mays, S., T. Prowse, M. George, and M. Brickley. 2018. 'Latitude, urbanization, age, and sex as risk factors for vitamin D deficiency disease in the Roman Empire'. *American Journal of Physical Anthropology* 167: 484–96.

Meindl, R. S. and C. O. Lovejoy. 1985. 'Ectocranial suture closure: A revised method for the determination of skeletal age at death based on the lateral-anterior sutures'. *American Journal of Physical Anthropology* 68(1): pp. 57–66. doi:10.1002/ajpa.1330680106.

Menchón, J. 2012. 'Necròpolis de l'antiguitat tardana i l'alta edat mitjana a les comarques del Camp de Tarragona, Conca de Barberà i Priorat'. In *Arqueologia funeraria al nord-est peninsular (segles VI–XII)*, edited by N. Molist i Capella and G. Ripoll López, pp. 125–54. Barcelona: Museu d'Arqueologia de Catalunya.

Menéndez Bueyes, L. R. 2013. *Medicina, enfermedad y muerte en la España tardoantigua: Un acercamiento histórico a las patologías de la poblaciones de la época tardorromana y visigótica (siglos IV–VIII)*. Salamanca: Ediciones Universidad de Salamanca.

Menéndez Bueyes, L. R. 2016. 'Condiciones de vida y enfermedad en la tardoantigüedad: Una aproximación desde la parte occidental del antiguo Imperio Romano'. In *Demografía, paleopatologías y desigualdad social en el Noroeste Peninsular en época medieval*, edited by J. A. Quirós, pp. 223–44. Bilbao: Universidad del País Vasco, Servicio Editorial = Euskal Herriko Unibertsitatea, Argitalpen Zerbitzua, D.L.

Menéndez Granda, A. and Á. Villa Valdés. 2013. 'Excavaciones arqueológicas en el Recinto Sacro y puerta de la acrópolis de El Castelón de Coaña'. In *Excavaciones arqueológicas en Asturias 2007–2012*, edited by P. León Gasalla, pp. 197–205. Oviedo: Gobierno del Principado de Asturias.

Menéndez Pidal, R. 1929. *Origenes del español*. Madrid: Editorial Hernando.

Menéndez Pidal, R. 1969. *Dos problemas iniciales relativos a los romances hispánicos*. Madrid: CSIC.

Mennen, I. 2011. *Power and status in the Roman Empire, AD 193–284*. Leiden: Brill.

Meunier, E. 2019. 'El estaño del Noroeste ibérico desde la Edad del Bronce hasta la época romana. Por una primera síntesis'. In *La ruta de las Estrímnides. Navegación y conocimiento del litoral atlántico de Iberia en la Antigüedad*, edited by E. Ferrer Albelda, pp. 179–319. Alcalá de Henares/Sevilla: Universidad de Alcalá de Henares/Universidad de Sevilla.

Meyer, A. 2013. *The creation, composition, service and settlement of Roman auxiliary units raised on the Iberian peninsula*. Oxford: BAR.

Meyer, M., Q. Fu, A. Aximu-Petri, et al. 2014. 'A mitochondrial genome sequence of a hominin from Sima de los Huesos'. *Nature* 505: pp. 403–6. doi:10.1038/nature12788.

Michczyńska, D., A. Michczyński, and A. Pazdur. 2007. 'Frequency distribution of radiocarbon dates as a tool for reconstructing environmental changes'. *Radiocarbon* 49(2): pp. 799–806.

Michczyński, A. and J. Michczyńska. 2006. 'The effect of PDF peaks' height increase during calibration of radiocarbon date sets'. *Journal on Methods and Applications of Absolute Chronology, Geochronometria* 25: pp. 1–4.

Miles, A. E. 1962. 'Assessment of the ages of a population of Anglo-Saxons from their dentitions'. *Proceedings of the Royal Society of Medicine* 55(10): pp. 881–6.

Millett, M. 1990. *The Romanization of Britain*. Cambridge: Cambridge University Press.

Millett, M. 1991. 'Pottery: Population or supply patterns? The Ager Tarraconensis approach'. In *Roman landscapes: Archaeological survey in the Mediterranean region*, edited by G. Barker and J. Lloyd London, pp. 18–26. London: British School at Rome.

Millett, M. and R. Gowland. 2015. 'Infant and child burial rites in Roman Britain: A study from East Yorkshire'. *Britannia* 46: pp. 171–89.

Millett, M., F. Queiroga, K. Strutt, J. Taylor, and S. Willis. 2000. 'The Ave Valley, Northern Portugal: An archaeological survey of Iron Age and Roman settlement'. *Internet Archaeology* 9. https://doi.org/10.11141/ia.9.1.

Mínguez, J. A. and B. Díaz Ariño. 2011. 'Grafitos sobre cerámica—ibéricos, latinos, griegos y signos—procedentes del yacimiento romanorrepublicano de La Cabañeta (El Burgo de Ebro, Zaragoza)'. *Archivo Español de Arqueología* 84: pp. 51–86.

Mínguez, J. A. and B. Díaz Ariño. 2019. 'Dos nuevas inscripciones latinas sobre piedra procedentes de La Cabañeta (El Burgo de Ebro, Zaragoza)'. *Archivo Español de Arqueología* 92: pp. 241–9.

Mínguez, J. A. and A. Ferreruela Gonzalvo. 2012. 'Las ciudades de La Cabañeta y La Corona. Su función en los inicios de la romanización del valle medio del Ebro'. In *Íberos del Ebro*, edited by C. Belarte, J. A. Benavente, L. Fatás, J. Dioli, P. Moret, and J. Noguera, pp. 257–72. Tarragona: Institut Català d'Arqueologia Clàssica.

Moatti, C. 2017. 'Migration et droit dans l'Empire Romain: Catégories, controles et intégration'. In *The impact of mobility and migration in the Roman Empire*, edited by E. Lo Cascio and L. E. Tacoma, pp. 222–46. Leiden: Brill.

Molina Vidal, J. 1997. *La dinámica comercial entre Italia e Hispania Citerior*. Alicante: Universidad de Alicante.

Molina Vidal, J. 2004. 'Comercio y relaciones portuarias en el territorio de Ilici'. In *Iberia, Hispania, Spania: Una mirada desde Ilici*, edited by L. Abad Casal and M. S. Hernández Pérez, pp. 189–96. Alicante: Caja de Ahorros del Mediterráneo.

Molina Vidal, J. 2005. 'La cetaria de Picola y la evolución del Portus Ilicitanus (Santa Pola, Alicante)'. In *III Congreso Internacional de Estudios Históricos: El Mediterráneo: la cultura del mar y la sal*, edited by J. Molina Vidal and M. J. Sánchez Fernández, pp. 95–112. Elche: Ayuntamiento de Santa Pola.

Molleson, T., K. Cruse, and S. Mays. 1998. 'Some sexually dimorphic features of the human juvenile skull and their value in sex determination in immature skeletal remains'. *Journal of Archaeological Science* 25(8): pp. 719–28.

Moncunill, N. and J. Velaza. 2011. 'Abiner, abinericus, abinnericus'. *Sylloge Epigraphica Barcinonensis* 9: pp. 59–62.

Montanini, L. 2009. 'Le donne Romane e la morte'. *Ager Veleias* 4(12): pp. 1–23.

Montero, I. and A. Orejas. 2018. 'Minas, metales reciclados y monedas'. *Mélanges de la Casa de Velázquez* 48(1): pp. 111–35.

Montes Lopéz, R., S. Hevia González, A. Villa Valdés, et al. 2009. 'Monte Castrelo de Pelóu (Grandas de Salime): Avance sobre su secuencia estratigráfica e interpretacion histórica'. In *AAVV Excavaciones arqueológicas en Asturias 2003-2006*, edited by J. Fernández Reyero and C. G. de Castro Valdés, pp. 313–22. Asturias: Consejería de Cultura y Turismo/Ediciones Trabe.

Montes Lopéz, R., S. Hevia González, and A. Villa Valdés. 2010. 'Monte Castrelo de Pelóu: Un asitiamientu prehistóricu de llarga perduración en Grandas de Salime. L'ocasu del paradigma castreñu d'aniciu romanu n'Asturies'. *Asturies: Memoria encesa d'un país* 30: pp. 4–27.

Montes Lopéz, R., S. Hevia González, and A. Villa Valdés. 2012. 'El espacio doméstico como expresión de la aculturación de la comunidad prerromana durante los siglos I y II d.C. En el castro de Chao Samartín (Grandas de Salime, Asturias)'. *Antesteria* 1: pp. 203–18.

Montiel, R., P. Francalacci, and A. Malgosa. 2007. 'Ancient DNA and biological anthropology: Believers vs. skeptics'. In *Recent advances in molecular biology and evolution*, edited by C. Santos and M. Lima, pp. 209–49. Kerala: Research Signpost.

Montiel, R., A. Malgosa, and P. Francalacci. 2001. 'Authenticating ancient human mitochondrial DNA'. *Human Biology* 73(5): pp. 689–713.

Montiel, R., A. Malgosa, and E. Subirà. 1997. 'Overcoming PCR inhibitors in ancient DNA extracts from teeth'. *Ancient Biomolecules* 1: pp. 221–5.

Moore, T. 2017. 'Alternatives to Urbanism? Reconsidering Oppida and the Urban Question in Late Iron Age Europe'. *Journal of World Prehistory* 30: pp. 281–300.

Moorrees, C. F. A., E. A. Fanning, and E. E. Hunt. 1963. 'Formation and resorption of three deciduous teeth in children'. *American Journal of Physical Anthropology* 21(2): pp. 205–13. doi:10.1002/ajpa.1330210212.

Morais, R. 2010. 'Looking towards the north'. In *The Western Roman Atlantic façade: A study of the economy and trade in the Mar Exterior from the Republic to the Principate*, edited by C. Carreras and R. Morais, pp. 91–108. Oxford: Archaeopress.

Morais, R. and C. Carreras. 2004. 'Geografia del consum de les Haltern 70'. In *Culip VIII i les àmfores Haltern 70*, edited by C. Carreras, pp. 93–117. Girona: Museu d'Arqueologia de Catalunya and Centre d'Arqueologia Subaquatica de Catalunya.

Moralejo, J. 2018. *Ubi fuerunt. Soldados y territorios en la Hispania Citerior Alto Imperial. Entre epigrafía y arqueología*. Unpublished thesis, Universitat Autònoma de Barcelona.

Moreda, F. J., S. Vilar, R. Serrano, et al. 2010–11. 'La necrópolis tardorromana de la villa de "El Vergel" (San Pedro de Arroyo, Avila)'. *Oppidum* 6–7: pp. 141–84.

Moreno-Mayar, J. V., B. A. Potter, L. Vinner, et al. 2018. 'Terminal Pleistocene Alaskan genome reveals first founding population of Native Americans'. *Nature* 553: pp. 203–7. doi: 10.1038/nature25173.

Moreno Martín, A. and J. Valor Abad. 2010. Casas, Personas y Comunidades: aproximación al cómputo poblacionalde la ciudad ibérica de Kelin(Caudete de las Fuentes, València)y su territorio, Arqueología Espacial, 28. Arqueología de la Población Teruel, pp. 245–264

Moret, P. 1996. *Les fortificacions ibériques. De la fin de l'Âge du bronze a la conquête romaine*. Madrid: Casa de Velázquez.

Morillo, Á. 2003. 'Los establecimientos militares temporales: Conquista y defensa del territorio en la Hispania republicana'. In *Defensa y territorio en Hispania. De los Escipiones a Augusto (Espacios urbanos y rurales, municipales y provinciales)*, edited by A. Morillo, F. Cadiou, and D. Hourcade, pp. 42–80. León/Madrid: Universidad de León/Casa de Velázquez.

Morillo, Á. 2005. 'Hispania en la estrategia militar del Alto Imperio: Movimientos de tropas en el arco Atlántico a través de los testimonios arqueológicos'. In *Unidad y diversidad en el Arco Atlántico en época romana. I. Hombres, territorios y fronteras*, edited by C. Fernández Ochoa and P. García Diaz, pp. 19–33. Gijón: Archaeopress and Ayuntamiento de Gijón.

Morillo, Á. 2016. 'Campamentos y fortificaciones tardorrepublicanas en Hispania'. In *Fortificaciones y control del territorio en la Hispania republicana*, edited by J. Pera and J. Vidal, pp. 1–52. Barcelona: Libros Pórtico.

Morillo, Á., C. Fernández Ochoa, and J. Salido Dominguez. 2016. 'Hispania and the Atlantic route in Roman times: New approaches to ports and trade'. *Oxford Journal of Archaeology* 35(3): pp. 267–84.

Morín de Pablos, J. 2014. *Los paisajes culturales en el Valle del Cigüela*. Madrid: Audema.

Morín de Pablos, J. and D. Urbina Martínez. 2005. 'El cerro de la Gavia y los recintos amurallados del Hierro II en el centro de la Península'. In *El Cerro de La Gavia: El Madrid que encontraron los romanos*, edited by J. Morín de Pablos and E. Agustí García, pp. 99–124. Madrid: Museo de San Isidro.

Morley, N. 1996. *Metropolis and hinterland: The city of Rome and the Italian economy 200 B.C. - A.D. 200*. Cambridge: Cambridge University Press.

Morley, N. 2011. 'Cities and economic development in the Roman Empire'. In *Settlement, urbanization, and population*, edited by A. Bowman and A. Wilson, pp. 143–60. Oxford: Oxford University Press.

Morris, I. 1992. *Death-ritual and social structure in classical antiquity*. Cambridge: Cambridge University Press.

Moss, M. L. and L. Moss-Salentijn. 1977. 'Analysis of developmental processes possibly related to human dental sexual dimorphism in permanent and deciduous canines'. *American Journal of Physical Anthropology* 46(3): pp. 407–13.

Mullis, K., F. Faloona, S. Scharf, et al. 1986. 'Specific enzymatic amplification of DNA in vitro: The polymerase chain reaction'. *Cold Spring Harbor Symposium on Quantitative Biology* 51: pp. 263–73. doi:10.1101/sqb.1986.051.01.032.

Murcia Muñoz, A. J. 2021. *Análisis del poblamiento rural de época romana en la comarca del Campo de Cartagena: siglos II a.C. - VII d.C.* Doctoral thesis, Universidad de Murcia.

Nadal, J. 1984. *La población española (siglos XVI–XIX)*. Barcelona: Ariel.

Naroll, R. 1962. 'Floor area and settlement population'. *American Antiquity* 27: pp. 287–9.

Navarro, M. 1989–90. 'Una guarnición de la *legio VII Gemina* en *Tritium Magallum*' *Caesaraugusta*. 66–7: pp. 217–25.

Navas, E., A. Garrido, J. Román, et al. 2009. 'Una nueva villa romana en el centro de Granada: Estudio preliminar'. *Antiquitas* 21: pp. 97–113.

Naveiro, J. L. 1991. *El comercio antiguo del NW peninsular*. La Coruña: Ayuntamiento de la Coruña.

Nelson, N. C. 1909. 'Shellmounds of the San Francisco Bay region'. *University of California Publications in American Archaeology and Ethnology* 7: pp. 309–56.

Nelson, S. E. 2009. 'Persephone's seeds: Abortifacients and contraceptives in Ancient Greek medicine and their recent scientific appraisal'. *Pharmacy in History* 51(2): pp. 57–68.

Nesheva, D. 2014. 'Aspects of ancient mitochondrial DNA analysis in different populations for understanding human evolution'. *Balkan Journal of Medical Genetics* 17(1): pp. 5–14. doi:10.2478/bjmg-2014-0019.

Nesta, A., S. Klein, P. Quarati, P. R. Trincherini, C. Rico, and C. Domergue. 2011. 'Sobre el origen de los lingotes de Chipiona. Aportación del método de los isotopos del plomo'. *Habis* 42: pp. 191–207.

Neustupny, E. 1983. 'The demography of prehistoric cemeteries'. *Pamatky Archaeologické* 74: pp. 7–34.

Newfield, T. W., A. T. Duggan, and H. Painer. 2022. 'Smallpox's antiquity in doubt'. *Journal of Roman Archaeology* 35(2). doi:10.1017/S1047759422000290.

Nión-Álvarez, S. 2023. 'A preliminary approach to early Iron Age demography: Testing palaeodemographic methodologies on a microscopal scale: The case of Punta de Muros (NW Iberia)'. *Journal of Archaeological Science: Reports* 48: pp. 1–11.

Nociarová, D. and N. Armentano. 2013. 'Sinusitis fistulizada en la órbita derecha'. In *Vetera corpora morbo afflicta. Actas del XI Congreso Nacional de Paleopatología*, edited by A. Malgosa, A. Isidro, P. Ibáñez, et al., pp. 465–70. Barcelona: Universitat Autònoma de Barcelona.

Noguera, J., J. Sanmartí, M. Belarte, et al. 2020. 'La ciudad ibérica de Masies de Sant Miquel (Banyeres del Penedès, Tarragona) entre los siglos VII-III a. C. Resultados de una investigación con métodos no invasivos'. *Archivo Español De Arqueología* 93: pp. 35–60. https://doi.org/10.3989/aespa.093.020.002.

Noguera Celdrán, J. M. 2010. 'Poblamiento rural romano en el Sureste de Hispania'. In *Poblamiento rural romano en el Sureste de Hispania: 15 años después*, edited by J. M. Noguera Celdrán, pp. 15–24. Murcia: Editum.

Noguera Celdrán, J. M. 2012. 'Carthago Nova: Urbs privilegiada del mediterráneo occidental'. In *Hispaniae Urbes: Investigaciones arqueológicas en ciudades históricas*, edited by J. Beltrán Fortes and O. Rodríguez Gutiérrez, pp. 121–90. Sevilla: Universidad de Sevilla.

Noguera Celdrán, J. M. and M. J. Madrid Balanza (eds.) 2009. *Arx Hasdrubalis. La ciudad reencontrada. Arqueología en el cerro del Molinete*. Cartagena: Tres Fronteras.

Noguera Celdrán, J. M. and M. H. Olcina (eds.) 2020. *Ruptura y continuidad. El callejero de la ciudad clásica en el tránsito del Alto Imperio a la Antigüedad tardía*. Alicante: MARQ Museo Arqueológico de Alicante.

Noguera Giménez, J. F., G. Guimaraens Igual, S. Lara Ortega, et al. 2011–12. 'Teatros romanos de Hispania: Introducción a su estado de conservación y criterios de restauración'. *Arché* 6–7: pp. 383–90.

Nonnis, D. 2015. *Produzione e distribuzione nell'Italia repubblicana. Uno studio prosopografico*. Rome: Roma Edizioni Quasar.

Noonan, J. P., G. Coop, S. Kudaravalli, et al. 2006. 'Sequencing and analysis of Neanderthal genomic DNA'. *Science* 314(5802): pp. 1113–18. doi:10.1126/science.1131412.

Nougier, L. R. 1959. *Géographie humaine préhistorique*. Paris: Gallimard.
Olalde, I., M. E. Allentoft, F. E. Sánchez-Quinto, et al. 2014. 'Derived immune and ancestral pigmentation alleles in a 7,000-year-old Mesolithic European'. *Nature* 507(7491): pp. 225–8. doi:10.1038/nature12960.
Olalde, I., S. Brace, M. E. Allentoft, et al. 2018. 'The Beaker phenomenon and the genomic transformation of northwest Europe'. *Nature* 555: pp. 190–6. doi:10.1038/nature26164.
Olalde, I., S. Mallick, N. Patterson, et al. 2019. 'The genomic history of the Iberian Peninsula over the past 8000 years'. *Science* 363: pp. 1230–4. doi:10.1126/science.aav4040.
Olalde, I., H. Schroeder, M. Sandoval-Velasco, et al. 2015. 'A common genetic origin for early farmers from Mediterranean Cardial and Central European LBK cultures'. *Molecular Biology and Evolution* 32(12): pp. 3132–42. doi:10.1093/molbev/msv181.
Olesti, O. 2010. 'Urbanització, integració i gestió del territori al nord-est de la península Ibèrica en època republicana (segles II–I a.C.)'. In *Time of changes: In the beginning of the Romanization*, edited by J. M. Nolla, pp. 11–59. Girona: Universitat de Girona.
Olesti, O. 2017. 'La génesis de la sociedad provincial y el proceso de urbanización en el Noreste de la Península Ibérica (siglos II-I a.C.)'. *Gerión* 35: pp. 427–59.
Olivier, G. 1960. *Pratique antropologique*. París: Vigot Frères.
Olmo Enciso, L., M. Castro Priego, B. Ruiz Zapata, et al. 2019. 'The construction and dynamics of early medieval landscapes in central Iberia'. In *Mediterranean landscapes in post antiquity: New frontiers and new perspectives*, edited by L. Olmo Enciso and S. Gelichi, pp. 104–28 Oxford: Archaeopress.
Olmo Martín, J. del. 2006. 'Arqueología aérea de las ciudades Romanas en la Meseta Norte'. In *III Congreso de las Obras Públicas Romanas: Nuevos Elementos de Ingeniería Romana*, pp. 313–40. Astorga: Junta de Castilla y León.
OMS. 1948. Constitution of the World Health Service.
Orejas, A. and A. Beltrán. 2010. 'Desplazados e inmigrantes en los metalla hispanorromanos: Epigrafía en contexto'. *Arquelogía Espacial* 28: pp. 399–417.
Orejas, A. and S. F. Ramallo. 2004. '*Carthago Noua*: La ville et le territoire'. In *De la terre au ciel. II Paysages et cadastres antiques*, edited by M. Clavel-Lévêque and G. Tirologos, pp. 87–120. Besançon: Presses Universitaires de Franche-Compté.
Orejas, A. and C. Rico. 2012. *Minería y metalurgia antiguas: Visiones y revisiones*. Madrid: Casa de Velázquez.
Orejas, A. and F. J. Sánchez-Palencia. 2002. 'Mines, territorial organization, and social structure in Roman Iberia, Carthago Noua and the peninsular northwest'. *American Journal of Archaeology* 106: pp. 581–99.
Orlandis, J. 1988. *Historia del Reino visigodo español*. Madrid: Rialp.
Orlando, L., P. Darlu, M. Toussaint, et al. 2006. 'Revisiting Neandertal diversity with a 100,000-year-old mtDNA sequence'. *Current Biology* 16(11): R400–2. doi:10.1016/j.cub.2006.05.019.
Ortego y Frias, T. 1967. *Guia de Numancia. Guia breve historico-arqueologica*. Soria: Dirección General de Bellas Artes.
Ortiz Córdoba, J. 2019a. 'De Gallia a Hispania. La inmigración gala en la Península Ibérica a través de las evidencias epigráficas Hispania'. *Hispania Antiqua Revista de Historia Antigua* XLIII: pp. 155–201.
Ortiz Córdoba, J. 2019b. 'Reclutamiento y unidades militares en las colonias romanas de la Hispania Citerior'. *Gladius* XXXIX: pp. 71–91.
Ortiz Córdoba, J. 2019c. *Las colonias romanas de Hispania y los movimientos de población (siglos I-II dc)*. Doctoral thesis, Universidad de Granada.

Ortner, D. J. 2011. 'Human skeletal paleopathology'. *International Journal of Paleopathology* 1: pp. 4–11.

Osanna, M. 2018. 'Games, banquets, handouts, and the population of Pompeii as deduced from a new tomb inscription'. *Journal of Roman Archaeology* 31: pp. 310–22.

Osborne, D. L., T. L. Simmons, and S. P. Nawrocki. 2004. 'Reconsidering the auricular surface as an indicator of age at death'. *Journal of Forensic Science* 49(5): pp. 905–11.

Osborne, R. 1992. '"Is it a farm?" The definition of agricultural sites and settlements in Ancient Greece'. In *Agriculture in Ancient Greece: Proceedings of the Seventh International Symposium at the Swedish Institute at Athens, 16–17th May*, edited by B. Wells, pp. 21–7. Stockholm: Åströms.

Otiña Hermoso, P. and J. Ruiz de Arbulo. 2000. 'De Cese a Tárraco: Evidencias y reflexiones sobre la Tarragona ibérica y el proceso de romanización'. *Empúries* 52: 107–36.

Oyen, A. van. 2015. 'The moral architecture of villa storage in Italy in the 1st c. B.C.'. *Journal of Roman Archaeology* 28: pp. 97–123.

Ozcáriz, P. 2013. *La administración de la provincia Hispania Citerior durante el Alto Imperio Romano*. Barcelona: Universitat de Barcelona.

Pääbo, S. 1985. 'Molecular cloning of Ancient Egyptian mummy DNA'. *Nature* 314: pp. 644–5. doi:10.1038/314644a0.

Pääbo, S., J. A. Gifford, and A. C. Wilson. 1988. 'Mitochondrial DNA sequences from a 7000-year old brain'. *Nucleic Acids Research* 16(20): pp. 9775–87. doi:10.1093/nar/16.20.9775.

Pääbo, S. and A. C. Wilson. 1988. 'Polymerase chain reaction reveals cloning artifacts'. *Nature* 334: pp. 387–8. doi:10.1038/334387b0.

Padrós, C. 2010. 'Els camins antics i les vies romanes a la Comarca d'Osona. Estat de la qüestió'. *Quaderns de Prehistòria i Arqueologia de Castelló* 28, pp. 233–45.

Padrós, P. 2002. 'El protagonisme de la moneda ibèrica a les ciutats romanes tardo-republicanes: Baetulo i la seca de Baitolo'. In *VI Curs d'Història Monetària d'Hispània. Funció i producció de les seques indígenes*, pp. 105–23. Barcelona: Museu Nacional d'Art de Catalunya.

Padrós, P. 2012. 'Las cecas layetanas. La ceca de Baitolo'. In *La moneda de los íberos. Ilturo y los talleres layetanos*, edited by A. G. Sinner, pp. 44–54. Barcelona: Museu de l'Estampació de Premià de Mar.

Paine, R. R. and G. R. Storey. 2006. 'Epidemics, age at death, and mortality in ancient Rome'. In *Urbanism in the preindustrial world: Cross-cultural approaches*, edited by G. R. Storey, pp. 69–85. Tuscaloosa: University of Alabama Press.

Palao Vicente, J. J. 2009. 'Los asentamientos civiles en los campamentes hispanos durante el alto imperio'. In *Limes XX Congreso International de estudios sobre la frontera romana* (= *Limes XX Roman Frontier Studies* [*Anejos de Gladius*, 13]), edited by A. Morillo Cerdán, N. Hanel. and E. Martín, pp. 525–40. Madrid: Consejo Superior de Investigacions Científicas: Polifemo.

Palol, P. de. 1966. 'Demografía y arqueología hispánicas de los siglos IV al VIII: Ensayo de cartografía'. *BSAA* 32: pp. 5–66.

Palomo-Díez, S., R. Cebrián-Fernández, I. Hortelano-Uceda, et al. 2019. 'Diachronic mtDNA study of the long time occupied archaeological site of Segobriga (Spain) and comparison with nowadays population'. *Forensic Science International: Genetics Supplement Series* 7(1): pp. 859–61. doi:10.1016/j.fsigss.2019.11.001.

Panzram, S. 2002. *Stadtbild und Elite: Tarraco, Corduba und Augusta Emerita Zwischen Republik un Spätantike*. Stuttgart: Franz Steiner Verlag.

Panzram, S. 2019. *The power of cities: The Iberian peninsula from late antiquity to the early modern period*. Leiden: Brill.

Parker, A. J. 1992. *Ancient shipwrecks of the Mediterranean and the Roman provinces*. Oxford: BAR.

Parkin, T. G. 1992. *Demography and Roman society*. Baltimore: Johns Hopkins University Press.

Parodi, J. M. 2001. *Ríos y lagunas de Hispania como vías de comunicación*. Ecija: Gráficas Sol.

Patidar, K. A., R. Parwani, and S. Wanjari. 2010. 'Effects of high temperature on different restorations in forensic identification: Dental samples and mandible'. *Journal of Forensic Dental Sciences* 2(1): pp. 37–43. doi:10.4103/0974-2948.71056.

Patterson, N., A. L. Price, and D. Reich. 2006. 'Population structure and eigenanalysis'. *PLoS Genetics* 2(12): e190. doi:10.1371/journal.pgen.0020190.

Pauling, L. and E. Zuckerkand. 1963. 'Chemical paleogenetics: Molecular restoration studies of extinct forms of life'. *Acta Chemica Scandinavica* 17(suppl.): pp. 9–16. doi:10.3891/acta.chem.scand.17s-0009.

Paz, J. 2015. *Los cubos de las murallas de Zaragoza y del palacio de la Aljafería (1065–1075): Paradigmas de la arquitectura militar en al-Andalus*. Zaragoza: IFC.

Pearce, J. 2008. 'Burial evidence from Roman Britain'. In *Pour une archéologie du rite. Nouvelles perspectives de l'archéologie funéraire*, edited by J. Scheid, pp. 29–42. CEFR 407. Rome: École française de Rome.

Pearce, J., M. Millett, and M. Struck. 2015. *Burial, society and context in the Roman world*. Oxford: Oxbow.

Pelgrom, J. 2012. *Colonial landscapes: Demography, settlement organization and impact of colonies founded by Rome (4th–2nd centuries BC)*. Leiden: University of Leiden.

Pelletier, D. L., E. A. Frongillo, Jr., D. G. Schroeder, et al. 1995. 'The effects of malnutrition on child mortality in developing countries'. *Bulletin of the World Health Organization* 73(4): pp. 443–8.

Pena, M. J. 1986. 'Los magistrados monetales de Valencia'. *Saguntum (PLAV)* 20: pp. 151–64.

Pena, M. J. 2009. 'Plotia Prune (Φρuνη): De Delos a Carthago Nova (*CIL* I/2, 2273 = *CIL* II 3495)'. *Faventia* 31(1–2): pp. 9–23.

Pera, J. 2001. 'Aproximació a la circulació monetària de la ciutat romana de Iesso (Guissona, Lleida)'. In *Moneda i vida urbana, V Curs d'Història Monetària d'Hispània*, pp. 53–63. Barcelona: Museu Nacional d'Art de Catalunya. Gabinet Numismàtic de Catalunya.

Pera, J. 2003. 'Epigrafia ibèrica a la ciutat romana de Iesso (Guissona, La Segarra)'. *Revista d'Arqueologia de Ponent* 13: pp. 237–45.

Pera, J. 2005. 'Pervivencia de la lengua ibérica en el siglo I a.C. El ejemplo de la ciudad romana de Iesso (Guissona)'. *Acta Paleographica IX. Palaeohispanica* 5: pp. 315–32.

Pera, J., C. Carreras, R. Romaní, et al. 2016. 'El proceso de implantación territorial romana en el NE de la Provincia Citerior en el siglo II a.C'. In *Fortificaciones y control del territorio en la Hispania republicana*, edited by J. Pera and J. Vidal, pp. 167–205. Zaragoza: Libros Pórtico.

Pereira Menaut, G. 1982. 'Los castella y las comunidades de Gallaecia'. *Zephyrus* XXXIV–XXXV: pp. 249–67.

Peréx Agorreta, J. and M. Unzu Urmeneta. 1990. 'Emplazamiento de Iturissa, mansio en la vía de Astorga a Burdeos'. In *La red viaria en la Hispania romana*, edited by A. Beltrán Martinez, pp. 373–84. Zaragoza: Institución Fernando el Católico.

Pérez, J. 2010. *Isabel y Fernando: Los reyes Católicos*. Madrid: Editorial Nerea.

Pérez González, C. 1989. *Cerámica romana de Herrera de Pisuerga (Palencia-España): La terra sigillata*. Santiago de Chile: Universidad SEK.

Pérez González, C. and P. Arribas. 2021. 'Epigrafía anfórica romana de Herrera de Pisuerga (Palencia, España)'. *Oppidum* 17: pp. 77–116.

Pérez González, C. and E. Illaguerri. 1992. 'Aproximación al conocimiento del conjunto arqueológico de Herrera de Pisuerga (Palencia)'. *Papeles Herrerenses* I: pp. 15–122.

Pérez Losada, F. 2002. *Entre a cidade e a aldea: Estudio arqueohistórico dos "aglomerados secundarios" romanos en Galicia*. A Coruña: Museo Arqueolóxico e Histórica.

Pérez-Pérez, A. and C. Lazuela. 1992. 'Indicadores de estrés nutricional y patológico en series de Epoca Romana de Catalunya'. *Munibe Suplemento* 8: pp. 145–51.

Pérez Puchal, P. 1972. 'La población del País Valenciano hasta la época estadística'. *Cuadernos de Geografía* 10: pp. 1–30.

Pérez Ruiz, M. 2022. 'Private beliefs, domestic religion, and identity in Hispania'. In *Religious dynamics in a microcontinent: Cult places, identities, and cultural change in Hispania*, edited by A. G. Sinner and V. Revilla, pp. 101–13. Turnhout: Brepols.

Perkins, P. 1999. *Etruscan settlement, society and material culture in central coastal Etruria*. Oxford: J. and E. Hedges.

Pesando, F. and M. P. Guidobaldi. 1989. 'Note di prosopografia minturnense'. In *Minturnae*, edited by F. Coarelli and P. Arthur, pp. 61–73. Rome: Nuova Editrice Romana.

Petr, M., M. Hajdinjak, Q. Fu, et al. 2020. 'The evolutionary history of Neanderthal and Denisovan Y chromosomes'. *Science* 369(6511): pp. 1653–6. doi:10.1126/science.abb6460.

Phenice, T. W. 1969. 'A newly developed visual method of sexing the os pubis'. *American Journal of Physical Anthropology* 30(2): pp. 297–301.

Philpott, R. A. 1991. *Burial practices in Roman Britain: A survey of grave treatement and furnishing, A.D. 43–410*. Oxford: Tempus Reparatum.

Pimenta, J. 2005. *As ânforas romanas do Castelo de São Jorge (Lisboa)*. Lisbon: Instituto Português de Arqueologia.

Pina Polo, F. 2004. 'Deportaciones como castigo e instrumento de colonización durante la República romana. El caso de Hispania'. In *Vivir en tierra extraña: emigración e integración cultural en el mundo antiguo*, edited by F. Marco Simón, F. Pina Polo, and J. Remesal Rodríguez (eds.), pp. 211–246, Barcelona: Universitat de Barcelona.

Pina Polo, F. 2009. 'Deportation of indigenous population as a strategy for Roman dominion in Hispania'. *Añejos Gladius* 13 = Limes XX: pp. 281–8.

Pina Polo, F. 2021. 'Foundations of Provincial Towns as Memorials of imperatores the Case of Hispania'. In *Provinces and provincial command in Republican Rome: genesis, development and governance*, edited by A. Díaz Fernández. Libera res publica, 4. Zaragoza: Prensas de la Universidad de Zaragoza.

Pina Polo, F. 2023. 'The (Non)Integration of Romans and Italians in Hispania during the Republic: Some Reflections'. In *Understanding Integration in the Roman World*, Impact of Empire series, Volume: 47, edited by E. Muñiz and R. Moreno, pp. 84–103. Leiden: Brill.

Pinhasi, R., D. Fernandes, K. Sirak, et al. 2015. 'Optimal ancient DNA yields from the inner ear part of the human petrous bone'. *PLOS One* 10(6): e0129102. doi:10.1371/journal.pone.0129102.

Pitts, M. 2021. 'York's African style Severan pottery reconsidered'. *Britannia* 52: pp. 1–30.

Pitts, M. and M. J. Versluys (eds.) 2015. *Globalisation and the Roman world: World history, connectivity and material culture*. Cambridge: Cambridge University Press.

Pociña, C. A. and J. A. Remolà. 2001. 'Nuevas aportaciones al conocimiento del puerto de Tarraco (Hispania Tarraconensis)'. *Saguntum* 33: pp. 85–96.

Polo-Cerdá, M. and E. García-Prósper. 2001. 'Enterramientos en decúbito prono y un posible preso entre los primeros pobladores de Valencia (siglos II a.C–III d.C)'. In *VI Congreso Nacional de Paleopatología, Madrid*. UAM, pp. 298–316.

Polo-Cerdá, M. and E. García-Prósper. 2002. 'Ritual, violencia y enfermedad. Los enterramientos en decúbito prono de la necrópolis fundacional de Valentia'. *Saguntum* 34: pp. 137–48.

Polo-Cerdá, M. and E. García-Prósper. 2011. 'Pleuritis en la Valencia romana'. In *Paleopatología: Ciencia multidisciplinar Actas del X Congreso Nacional de Paleopatología*, edited by A. González-Martin, O. Cambra-Moo, J. Rascón Pérez, et al., pp. 313–29. Madrid: Congreso Nacional de Paleopatología.

Polo-Cerdá, M., E. García-Prósper, P. Guérin, et al. 2004. 'La fundación de Valentia y sus primeros pobladores primeras evidencias osteoarqueológicas de tuberculosis en Hispania'. In *Miscelánea en homenaje a Emiliano Aguirre*, edited by E. Baquedano Pérez and S. Rubio Jara. *Paleoantropología* 3: pp. 292–305.

Polo-Cerdá, M., E. García-Prósper, and S. Sanchis. 2005. 'Estudio bioarqueológico del monumento funerario romano del Solar de la Moreira de Sagunto'. *ARSE* 39: pp. 229–68.

Polo-Cerdá, M. and J. Villalaín Blanco. 2001. 'Fenomenos porosos en paleopatología: Estado de la cuestión y nuevas aportaciones'. *Actas VI Congreso Nacional de Paleopatología*, pp. 88–101. Madrid: Congreso Nacional de Paleopatología.

Polo López, J. and C. Valenciano Prieto. 2013. 'Phiálemesómphalos del Oppidum carpetano de Titulcia (Madrid)'. *101 obras maestras. Ciencia y arte en los museos y bibliotecas de Madrid, Exotismos, no 17.*

Ponce, A. M. 1975. 'Descripcíon de algunas de las piezas halladas en el yacimiento de Isla Pedrosa'. In *El yacimiento arqueológico submarino ante Isla Pedrosa. Inmersión y Ciencia* 8–9: pp. 95–111.

Posth, C., V. Zaro, M. A. Spyrou, et al. 2021. 'The origin and legacy of the Etruscans through a 2000-year archeogenomic time transect'. *Science Advances* 7(39): eabi7673. doi:10.1126/sciadv.abi7673.

Pounds, N. J. G. 1973. *A historical geography of Europe: 450 BC–AD 1330*. Cambridge: Cambridge University Press.

Prevosti, M. and J. Guitart. 2011. *Ager Tarraconensis 2: El Poblament*. Tarragona: ICAC.

Price, S. 2011. 'Estimating Ancient Greek populations: The evidence of field survey'. In *Settlement, urbanization, and population*, edited by A. Wilson and A. Bowman, pp. 17–35. Oxford: Oxford University Press.

Pudsey, A. 2013. 'Children in Roman Egypt'. In *The Oxford handbook of childhood and education in the classical world*, edited by J. E. Grubbs and T. G. Parkin, pp. 484–509. Oxford: Oxford University Press.

Puerta López, C. and J. Garcia Rosselló. 2012. 'La villa romana de Torre Llauder: Darrers treballs de recerca I restauració, i perspectives de futur (Mataró, El Maresme)'. *Tribuna d'Arqueologia* 2011–12: pp. 189–205.

Purcel, N. 2003. 'The boundless sea of unlikeness? On defining the Mediterranean'. *Mediterranean Historical Review* 18: pp. 9–29.

PXOM. 2012. Plan Xeral de Ordenación Municipal by the Xunta de Galicia. http://siotuga.xunta.gal/siotuga/urb.

Py, M. 1996. 'Les maisons protohistoriques de Lattara (IVe–Ier s. av. n.è.), approche typologique et fonctionnelle'. *Lattara* 9: pp. 141–258.

Quesada, F. 2006. 'Los celtíberos y la guerra: Tácticas, cuerpos, efectivos y bajas. Una análisis a partir de la campaña del 153'. In *Segeda y su contexto histórico. Entre Catón y Nobilior (195 al 153)*, edited by F. Burillo Mozota, pp. 149–67. Mara: Fundación Segeda.

Quesada, F. 2017. 'Los iberos y la cultura ibérica'. In *La protohistoria de la península Ibérica*, edited by S. Celestino Pérez, pp. 439–643. Madrid: Istmo.

Quevedo, A. 2012. 'La ciudad de Carthago Nova (Cartagena, España): Paradigma del cambio y transformación urbana en la Hispania medioimperial. Ensayo para una sintesis'. *Antesteria* 1: pp. 63–77.

Rabanal, M. A. and S. M. García Marínez. 2001. *Epigrafía romana de la provincia de León: revisión y actualización* (= *ERPLeón*). León: Publicaciones Universidad de León.

Ramakrishnan, U. and E. A. Hadly. 2009. 'Using phylochronology to reveal cryptic population histories: Review and synthesis of 29 ancient DNA studies'. *Molecular Ecology* 18(7): pp. 1310–30. doi:10.1111/j.1365-294X.2009.04092.x.

Ramallo, S. 2000. 'Carthago Spartaria, un núcleo bizantino en Hispania'. In *Sedes regiae (ann. 400–800)*, edited by G. Ripoll and J. M. Gurt, pp. 579–611. Barcelona: Reial Academia de Bones Lletres.

Ramallo, S. 2002. 'La arquitectura del espectáculo en Hispania: Teatros, anfiteatros y circos'. In *Ludi Romani: Espectáculos en Hispania Romana*, pp. 92–118. Mérida: Museo Nacional de Arte Romano.

Ramallo, S. F. and M. Martínez Andreu. 2010. 'El puerto de Carthago Nova: Eje de vertebración de la actividad comercial en el sureste de la Península Ibérica'. *Bollettino di Archeologia online I 2010/Volume speciale* B/B8/3: pp. 141–59.

Ramallo, S. and R. Moneo. 2009. *Teatro romano de Cartagena*. Murcia: Fundación Cajamurcia.

Ramallo, S. and E. Ruiz. 1994. 'Un edículo republicano dedicado a Atargatis en Carthago Noua'. *AEspA* 67: pp. 79–102.

Ramallo, S. and J. F. Santiuste de Pablos. 1993. 'Teatro y desarollo monumental urbano en Hispania'. *Cuadernos de Arquitectura Romana* 2: pp. 225–38.

Ramos, M. D., C. Lalueza, E. Girbau, et al. 1995. 'Amplifying dinucleotide microsatellite loci from bone and tooth samples of up to 5000 years of age: More inconsistency than usefulness'. *Human Genetics* 96: pp. 205–12. https://doi.org/10.1007/BF00207380.

Ramos Fernández, R. and A. Ramos Molina. 2004. 'La escultura ibérica de La Alcudia'. In *Iberia, Hispania, Spania: Una mirada desde Ilici*, edited by L. Abad Casal and M. S. Hernández Pérez, pp. 133–44. Alicante: Caja de Ahorros del Mediterráneo.

Rascón, S. 1999. 'La ciudad de Complutum en la tardoantigüedad: Restauración y renovación'. In *Complutum y las ciudades hispanas en la antigüedad tardía: Actas del I Encuentro Hispania en la Antigüedad Tardía*, edited by Luis A. García Moreno and Sebastián Rascón Marqués, pp. 55–72. Alcalá de Henares: Universidad de Alcalá.

Rascón Marqués, S. 2007. 'The so-called house of *Hippolytus*: the foundation of *Anios* as well as the *school* of a collegiate group in the Roman city of *Complutum*'. *Spanish Archeology Archive* 80: pp. 119–152. http://aespa.revistas.csic.es/index.php/aespa/article/view/30/30

Rascón, S. and A. L. Sánchez. 2006. 'Complutum tardoantigua'. *Zona arqueológica* 8(2): pp. 267–92.

Rawson, B. 1986. 'The Roman family'. In *The family in ancient Rome: New perspectives*, edited by B. Rawson, pp. 1–57. Ithaca: Cornell University Press.

Reinhart, W. 1945. 'Sobre el asentamiento de los visigodos en la Península'. *Archivo Español de Arqueología* XVIII: pp. 124–39.

Remesal Rodriguez, J. 2002. Espacios y usos funerarios en el Occidente romano: Actas del Congreso Internacional celebrado en la Facultad de Filosofía y Letras de la Universidad de Córdoba (5–9 junio, 2001), pp. 369–77.

Remolà, J. A. 2000. *Las ánforas tardo-antiguas en Tarraco (Hispania Tarraconensis)*. Barcelona: Universitat de Barcelona.

Reynolds, P. 2010. *Hispania and the Roman Mediterranean, AD 100–700*. London: Duckworth.

Ribera, A. 2001. 'Los pecios con cerámicas calenas de barniz negro: Problemas y solucione'. In *Ceramica calena a vernice nera: Produzione e diffusione*, edited by L. Pedroni, pp. 296–306. Città di Castello: Petruzzi.

Ribera, A. 2007. 'Depositos rituales de Valentia (Hispania): De la primera fundación republicana (138 a.C.) a la segunda auguste'. In *I riti del costruire nelle acque violate*, edited by H. Di Giuseppe and M. Serlorenzi, pp. 269–94. Roma: Scienze e Lettere.

Ribera, A. 2016. 'Valentia (Hispania) en el siglo IV: los inicios de la primera ciudad cristian'. In *Acta Congressus Internationalis XVI Archaeologiae Christianae (22–28.9.2013): Costantino e i costantinidi: l'innovazione costantiniana, le sue radici e i suoi sviluppi*, pp. 1773–92. Città del Vaticano: Pontificio Istituto di archeologia cristiana.

Ribera, A. and J. L. Jiménez. 2012. 'Valentia, ciudad romana: Su evidencia arqueológica'. In *Hispaniae urbes: Investigaciones arqueológicas en ciudades históricas*, edited by J. Beltrán and O. Rodríguez, pp. 77–120. Sevilla: Universidad de Sevilla.

Ribera, A., M. Rosselló, and J. M. Macias. 2020. 'Historia y arqueología de dos ciudades en los siglos VI–VIII dC. Valentia i València la Vell'. *Antigüedad y Cristianismo* 37: pp. 63–106.

Richardson, A. 2000. 'The numerical basis of Roman camps'. *Oxford Journal of Archaeology* 19(4): pp. 425–37.

Rico, C. 2010. 'Sociétés et entrepreneurs miniers Italiques en Hispanie à la fin de l'époque Républicaine: Un comparaison entre les districts de Carthagène et de Sierra Morena'. In *Ab Aquitania in Hispaniam: Mélanges d'histoire et d'archéologie Offerts à Pierre Sillières*, edited by P. Moret and C. Rico, pp. 395–415. Toulouse: Presses Universitaires du Mirail.

Riddle, J. M. 1991. 'Oral contraceptives and early-term abortifacients during classical antiquity and the MiddleAges'. *Past & Present* 132: pp. 3–32.

Riddle, J. M. and J. W. Estes. 1992. 'Oral contraceptives in ancient and medieval times'. *American Scientist* 80(3): pp. 226–33.

Ringrose, D. R. 1972. *Los transportes y el estancamiento económico de España: 1750–1850*. Madrid: Editorial Tecnos.

Río-Miranda Alcón, J. 2011. *La ciudad romana de Cáparra. Municipium Flavium Caparense*. Cáceres: Ulzama.

Ripoll, G. 1989. 'Características generales del poblamiento y la arqueología funeraria visigoda de Hispania'. *Espacio, Tiempo y Forma* 2: pp. 389–418.

Ripoll, G. 2018. 'Aristocratic Residences in Late Antique Hispania'. In The Roman Villa in the Mediterranean basin: Late Republic to Late Antiquity, edited by A. Marzano and G. P. R. Métraux, pp. 426–52. Cambridge: Cambridge University Press.

Ripollès, P. P. 1988. *La Ceca de Valentia*. Valencia: Generalitat Valenciana, Conselleria de Cultura, Educació i Ciència.

Robb, J. 1998. 'The interpretation of skeletal muscle sites: A statistical approach'. *International Journal of Osteoarchaeology* 8: pp. 363–77.

Roberts, C. H. and K. Manchester. 1995. *The archaeology of disease*. Ithaca: Cornell University Press.

Rodríguez Colmenero, A. 1991. '"Aquis Querquennis": Quince anos a carón'. *Larouco* 1: pp. 123–30.

Rodríguez Colmenero, A. 2002. 'El campamento auxiliar de Aquis Querquennis (Naños de Bande, Ourense)'. In *Arqueología militar romana en Hispania*, edited by A. Morillo Cerdán, pp. 227–44. Madrid: CSIC – Polifemo.

Rodríguez Colmenero, A., S. Ferrer Sierra, and F. M. Herves Raigoso. 1998. 'El Complejo arqueológico romano de "Aquis Querquernnis" Porto Quintela (Ourense)'. In *Los Orígenes de la ciudad en el Noroeste Hispánico*, edited by A. Rodríguez Colmenero, pp. 891–910. Lugo: Diputación Provincial de Lugo.

Rodríguez Gutiérrez, O. 2011. *Hispania Arqueológica: Panorama de la cultura material de las provincias hispanorromanas*. Sevilla: Universidad de Sevilla.

Romero and Lorrio. 2011. 'El origen del poblamientoceltibérico en el Alto Duero', *Complutum* 22(2): pp. 95–127. http://dx.doi.org/10.5209/rev_CMPL.2011.v22.n2.37728.

Romero Carnicero, F. and C. Sanz Mínguez. 2010. *De la Región Vaccea a la arqueología Vaccea: Jornadas científicas conmemorativas del 50 aniversario de la publicación de la Región Vaccea*. Valladolid: Centro de Estudios Vacceos 'Federico Wattenberg'.

Ruegg, S. D. 1995. *Underwater investigations at Roman Minturnae: Liris-Garigliano River*. Jonsered: Paul Åströms Förlag.

Ruff, C., B. Holt, and E. Trinkaus. 2006. 'Who's afraid of the big bad Wolff?: "Wolff's law" and bone functional adaptation'. *American Journal of Physical Anthropology* 129(4): 484–98.

Ruiz, A. 1994. 'Una reflexió teòrica sobre l'urbanisme ibèric'. *Cota Zero* 10: pp. 147–56.

Ruiz de Arbulo, J. 2011–12. 'La dedicatoria a Mars Campester del centurión T. Aurelius Decimus y el campus de la guarnición imperial de Tarraco en el siglo II d.C. Algunas reflexiones sobre la topografía militar de la capital provincial'. *CuPAUAM* 37–8: pp. 553–69.

Ruiz Zapatero, G. 2005. *Castro de Ulaca: Solosancho, Ávila*. Ávila: Institución Gran Duque de Alba.

Ruiz Zapatero, G. 2009. 'La segunda edad del Hierro en el centro de la Península Ibérica: Un estado de la situación y una agenda para la acción'. In *Actas de las Terceras Jornadas de Patrimonio Arqueológico de la Comunidad de Madrid*, pp. 187–232. Madrid: Comunidad de Madrid.

Ruiz Zapatero, G. 2011. 'Settlement and landscape in Iron Age Europe: Archaeological mainstreams and minorities'. In *Atlantic Europe in the first millennium BC: Crossing the divide*, edited by T. Moore and X. L. Armada, pp. 81–108. Oxford: Oxford University Press.

Ruiz Zapatero, G. 2018. 'Casas, "hogares" y comunidades: Castros y oppida prerromanos en la meseta'. In *Más allá de las casas: Familias, linajes y comunidades en la protohistoria peninsular*, edited by A. Rodríguez Díaz, I. Pavón Soldevila, and D. M. Duque Espino, pp. 327–62. Cáceres: Universidad de Extremadura.

Ruiz Zapatero, G. and J. R. Álvarez Sanchís. 1995. 'Las Cogotas: Oppida and the roots of urbanism in the Spanish Meseta'. In *Social complexity and the development of towns in Iberia: From the Copper Age to the second century AD*. Proceedings of the British Academy 86, edited by B. Cunliffe and S. J. Keay, pp. 209–36. London: British Academy and Oxford University Press.

Ruiz Zapatero, G. and J. R. Álvarez Sanchís. 2001. 'Cementerios y asentamientos: Bases para una demografía arqueológica de la Meseta en la Edad del Hierro'. In *Entre celtas e íberos: Las poblaciones protohistóricas de las Galias e Hispania*, edited by L. Berrocal Rangel and P. Gardes, pp. 61–75. Madrid: Casa de Velázquez/Real Academia de la Historia.

Ruiz Zapatero, G., J. R. Álvarez Sanchís, and J. Rodríguez-Hernández. 2020. 'Urbanism in Iron Age Iberia: Two worlds in contact'. *Journal of Urban Archaeology* 1: pp. 123–50.

Russell, J. C. 1958. 'Late ancient and medieval population'. *Transactions of the American Philosophical Society* 48(3): pp. 1–152.

Sahakyan, H., A. Margaryan, L. Saag, et al. 2021. 'Origin and diffusion of human Y chromosome haplogroup J1-M267'. *Scientific Reports* 11: p. 6659. https://doi.org/10.1038/s41598-021-85883-2.

Salisbury, J. E. 2015. *Rome's Christian empress: Galla Placidia rules at the twilight of the Empire*. Baltimore: Johns Hopkins University Press.

Sallares, R. 2002. *Malaria and Rome: A history of malaria in ancient Italy*. Oxford: Oxford University Press.

Sallares, R., A. Bouwman, and C. Anderung. 2004. 'The spread of malaria to Southern Europe in antiquity: New approaches to old problems'. *Medical History* 48: pp. 311–28.

Saller, R. P. 1987. 'Men's age at marriage and its consequences in the Roman family'. *Classical Philology* 82(1): pp. 21–34.

Saller, R. P. 1994. *Patriarchy, property and death in the Roman family*. Cambridge: Cambridge University Press.

Saller, R. P. and B. D. Shaw. 1984. 'Tombstones and Roman family relations in the Principate: Civilians, soldiers and slaves'. *Journal of Roman Studies* 74: pp. 124–56.

Salomies, O. 2012. 'The nomina of the Samnites: A checklist'. *Arctos* 46: pp. 137–86.

Salrach, J. M. 1982. *Història dels Països Catalans: Dels orígens a 1714*. Barcelona: Edhasa.

Salvador Conejo, D. 2016. *Tierra de Carpetanos*. Madrid: Ediciones La Librería.

Sampietro, M. L., D. Caramelli, O. Lao, et al. 2005. 'The genetics of the pre-Roman Iberian peninsula: A mtDNA study of ancient Iberians'. *Annals of Human Genetics* 69(5): pp. 535–48.

Sánchez León, J. C. 1996. *Los bagaudas: Rebeldes, demonios, mártires. Revueltas campesinas en Galia e Hispania durante el Bajo Imperio*. Jaén: Universidad de Jaén.

Sánchez Moreno, E. 1998. 'De ganados, movimientos y contactos. Revisando la cuestión trashumante en la protohistoria hispana: La meseta occidenta'. *Studia Historica* 16: pp. 53–84.

Sánchez-Palencia, F. J. and M. D. Fernández-Posse. 1986–1987. "Vivienda y urbanismo en la Asturia interior: La Corona de Corporales", *Zephyrus* 39–40: pp. 375–386.

Sánchez-Palencia, F. J. and M. J. Sáinz Pascual. 2001. 'El Circo de Toletum'. In *El Circo en Hispania Romana*, edited by T. Nogales Basarrate and F. J. Sánchez-Palencia, pp. 97–115. Madrid: Ministerio de educación y ciencia.

Sánchez Priego, J. A. 2015. *Historia de la via Augusta en la Foia de Manuel (La Font de la Figuera, València)*. Valencia: Adif.

Sánchez Ramos, I. and J. Morín. 2015. 'Los paisajes urbanos de la Antigüedad tardía'. *Espacio, Tiempo y Forma* 7: pp. 97–127.

Sancristán de Lama, J. D. 2011. 'Los castros del oeste de la Meseta'. *Complutum* 22(2): pp. 185–222.

Sanmartí, J. 2001. 'La formació i desenvolupament de les societats ibèriques a Catalunya'. *Butlleti Arqueològic* 23: pp. 101–132.

Sanmartí, J. 2004. 'From local groups to early states: The development of complexity in protohistoric Catalonia'. *PYRENAE* 1(35): pp. 7–41.

Sanmartí, J. and C. Belarte. 2001. 'Urbanización y desarrollo de estructuras estatales en la Costa de Cataluña (Siglos VII–III a.C.)'. In *Entre Celtas e Íberos: Las poblaciones protohistóricas de las Galias e Hispania*, edited by L. Berrocal-Rangel and P. Gardes, pp. 161–74. Madrid: Real Academia de la Historia-Casa de Velázquez.

Sanmartí, J. and J. Santacana. 2005. *Els ibers del nord*. Barcelona: Rafael Dalmau.

Santos Yanguas, N. V. 2017. 'Origen y consolidación de los conventus iuridici en el noroeste peninsular'. *Gerión* 35(1): pp. 229–55.

Sanz, A. M. 2012. 'Nuevas reflexiones sobre el régimen jurídico Minero Romano'. In *Minería y metalurgia Antiguas: Visiones y revisionses, Homenaje a Claude Domergue*, edited by A. Orejas and C. Rico, pp. 245–54. Madrid: Casa de Velázquez.

Sanz, V. M. and G. Lázaro. 1995. 'La problemática bagauda (siglo V d.C) en el valle del Ebro: Reflexión historiográfica'. In *Homenaje a don Antonio Durán Gudiol*, pp. 741–62. Huesca: Instituto de Estudios Altoaragonese.

Sanz Mínguez, C. and J. Velasco Vázquez (eds.) 2003. *"Pintia": Un "oppidum" en los confines orientales de la región vaccea*. Valladolid: Universidad de Valladolid.

Sarausa, C. 2006. 'Trabajo y trabajadores en la España del siglo XIX'. In *Historia económica de España, siglos XIX y XX*, edited by A. González and J. M. Matés, pp. 413–33. Barcelona: Ariel – Fundacion Schola.

Sastre Prats, I. 2008. 'Community, identity, and conflict: Iron Age warfare in the Iberian Northwest'. *Current Anthropology* 49(6): pp. 1021–51.

Scheidel, W. 1996. *Measuring sex, age and death in the Roman Empire: Explorations in ancient demography*. Portsmouth: Journal of Roman Archaeology.

Scheidel, W. 2001. *Death on the Nile: Disease and the demography of Roman Egypt*. Leiden: Brill.

Scheidel, W. 2005. 'Human mobility in Roman Italy. II: The slave population'. *Journal of Roman Studies* 95: pp. 64–79.

Scheidel, W. 2007. 'Demography'. In *The Cambridge economic history of the Greco-Roman World*, edited by W. Scheidel, I. Morris, and R. Saller, pp. 38–86. Cambridge: Cambridge University Press.

Scheidel, W. 2014. 'The shape of the Roman world: Modelling imperial connectivity'. *Journal of Roman Archaeology* 27: pp. 7–32.

Scheidel, W. 2017. 'Afterword: On the probable age structure of the Roman population'. In *Sociological studies in Roman history*, edited by C. Kelly, pp. 135–59. Cambridge: Cambridge University Press.

Scheidel, W., I. Morris, and R. Saller (eds.) 2007. *The Cambridge economic history of the Greco-Roman world*. Cambridge: Cambridge University Press.

Scheuer, L. 2002. 'A blind test of mandibular morphology for sexing mandibles in the first few years of life'. *American Journal of Physical Anthropology* 119(2): pp. 189–91.

Scheuer, L. and S. Black. 2000. *Developmental juvenile osteology*. London: Academic Press.

Scheuer, L. and S. Black. 2004. *The juvenile skeleton*. Amsterdam: Elsevier.

Scheuer, L., J. Musgrave, and S. Evans. 1980. 'The estimation of late fetal and perinatal age from limb bone length by linear and logarithmic regressions'. *Annals of Human Biology* 7: pp. 257–65.

Schiffer, M. B. 1996. *Formation processes of the archaeological record*. Salt Lake City: University of Utah Press.

Schmitt, A. 2004. 'Age-at-death assessment using the os pubis and the auricular surface of the ilium: A test on an identified Asian sample'. *International Journal of Osteoarchaeology* 14(1): pp. 1–6.

Schneider, J. 2017. *Ländliche Siedlungsstrukturen im Römischen Spanien. Das Becken von Vera und das Camp de Tarragona—Zwei Microregionen im Vergleich*. Oxford: Archaeopress.

Schour, L. and M. Massler. 1941. 'The development of the human dentition'. *Journal of the American Dental Association* 28: pp. 1153–60.

Schulten, A. 1914. *Numantia I. Die Keltiberer und ihre Kriege mit Rom*. Munich: F. Bruckmann.

Schulten, A. 1945. *Historia de Numancia*. Barcelona: Barna.

Schulten, A. 1952. *Fontes Hispaniae antiquae*. Barcelona: Librería Bosch.

Schulze, W. 1904. *Zur Geschichte Lateinischer Eigennamen*. Berlin: Weidmannsche Verlagsbuchhandlung.

Schutkowski, H. 1993. 'Sex determination of infant and juvenile skeletons: I. Morphognostic features'. *American Journal of Physical Anthropology* 90: pp. 199–205.

Sear, F. 2006. *Roman theatres: An architectural study*. Oxford: Oxford University Press.

Séguy, I. 2019. 'Current trends in Roman demography and empirical approaches to the dynamics of the Limes populations'. In *Finding the limits of the limes: Modelling demography, economy and transport on the edge of the Roman Empire*, edited by P. Verhagen, J. Joyce, and M. Groenhuijzen, pp. 23–41. Cham: Springer International Publishing.

Séguy, I. and L. Buchet. 2013. *Handbook of paleodemography*. Cham: Springer.

Séguy, I., L. Buchet, and A. Bringé. 2008. 'Model life tables for preindustrial populations: First applications in paleodemography'. In *Recent advances in paleodemography: Data, techniques, patterns*, edited by J.-P. Bocquet-Appel, pp. 109–41. Dordrecht: Springer.

Sellier, P. 1995. 'Paléodémographie et archéologie funéraire: Les cimetières de Mehrgarh, Pakistan'. *Paléorient* 21(2): pp. 123–43.

Serrano, J. G., A. C. Ordóñez, and R. Fregel. 2021. 'Paleogenomics of the prehistory of Europe: Human migrations, domestication and disease'. *Annals of Human Biology* 48(3): pp. 179–90. doi:10.1080/03014460.2021.1942205.

Serrano, J. M. 1988. *Status y promoción social de los libertos en Hispania romana*. Sevilla: Universidad de Sevilla.

Sevilla, A. 2014. *Funus Hispaniense. Espacios, usos y costumbres funerarias en la Hispania Romana*. Oxford: BAR International Series.

Shapiro, B. and M. Hofreiter. 2014. 'A paleogenomic perspective on evolution and gene function: New insights from ancient DNA'. *Science* 343(6169): p. 1236573. doi:10.1126/science.1236573.

Shaw, B. D. 1987. 'The age of Roman girls at marriage: Some reconsiderations'. *Journal of Roman Studies* 77: pp. 30–46.

Shaw, B. D. 1991. 'The cultural meaning of death: Age and gender in the Roman family'. In *The family in Italy from antiquity to the present*, edited by D. Kertzer and R. P. Saller, pp. 66–90. New Haven: Yale University Press.

Shaw, B. D. and R. P. Saller. 1984. 'Close-kin marriage in Roman society?' *Man* 19: pp. 432–44.

Shaw, C. N. and J. T. Stock. 2009. 'Intensity, repetitiveness, and directionality of habitual adolescent mobility patterns influence the tibial diaphysis morphology of athletes'. *American Journal of Physical Anthropology* 140: pp. 149–59.

Shennan, S., S. S. Downey, A. Timpson, et al. 2013. 'Regional population collapse followed initial agriculture booms in mid-Holocene Europe'. *Nature Communications* 4: p. 2486. doi:10.1038/ncomms3486.

Shennan, S. and K. Edinborough. 2007. 'Prehistory population history: From the Late Glacial to the Late Neolithic in Central and Northern Europe'. *Journal of Archaeological Science* 34: pp. 1339–45.

Sillières, P. 1999. 'Le camino de Aníbal, principal axe des communications entre l'est et le sud de l'Hispanie'. In *Rutas, ciudades y moneda en Hispania: Actas del II Encuentro Peninsular de Numismática Antigua Porto*, edited by G. Mora, R. M. Sobral Centeno, and M. P. García-Bellido, pp. 239–50. Madrid: CSIC.

Simón, M., X. Jordana, N. Armentano, et al. 2011. 'The presence of nuclear families in prehistoric collective burials revisited: The Bronze Age burial of Montanissell Cave (Spain) in the light of aDNA'. *American Journal of Physical Anthropology* 146(3): pp. 406–13. doi:10.1002/ajpa.21590.

Simón, M. and A. Malgosa. 2016. 'Ancient DNA: From single words to full libraries in 30 years'. In *Anthropology: Current and future developments*, edited by M. Lima, A. Ramos, and C. Santos, pp. 137–58. Sharjah: Bentham Science.

Sinner, A. G. 2013. 'La difusion de las emisiones ibéricas layetanas'. *Sagunto* 45: pp. 171–92.

Sinner, A. G. 2015. 'Cultural contacts and identity construction: A colonial context in NE Spain (2nd – early 1st c. B.C.)'. *Journal of Roman Archaeology* 28: pp. 7–37.

Sinner, A. G. 2017. *La ceca de Ilduro*. Oxford: Archaeopress.

Sinner, A. G. 2021. 'Un nuevo lingote de plomo de Q. Haterius Gallus y la participación de la gens Hateria en la explotación de las minas de Sierra Morena'. *Pyrenae* 52(1): pp. 137–59.

Sinner, A. G. 2024. 'Human mobility between Italy and north-eastern Hispania during the Late Republican period'. In *Connectivity and Mobility in the Ancient Western Mediterranean*, edited by L. Gosner and J. Hayne. Equinox Monographs in Mediterranean Archaeology. Sheffield: Equinox.

Sinner, A. G. and C. Carreras. 2019. 'Methods of palaeodemography: The case of the Iberian oppida and Roman cities in north-east Spain'. *Oxford Journal of Archaeology* 38(3): pp. 302–24.

Sinner, A. G. and J. Ferrer. 2016. 'Del oppidum de Burriac a las termas de Ca l'Arnau: Una aproximación a la lengua y a la identidad de los habitantes de Ilduro (Cabrera de Mar, Barcelona)'. *Archivo Español de Arqueología* 89: pp. 199–223.

Sinner, A.G. and Ferrer, J. 2020. 'Baitolo, a native shipowner's vessel, and the participation of northern Iberians in the Laietanian wine-trade under the Late Republic'. *Journal of Roman Archaeology* 33: pp. 365–382.

Sinner, A. G. and J. Ferrer i Jané. 2018. 'Novedades epigráficas de *Ilduro* (Cabrera de Mar, Barcelona)'. *Palaeohispanica* 18: pp. 203–16.

Sinner, A. G. and C. Martí. 2012. 'La circulación monetaria en el valle de Cabrera de Mar (El Maresme, Barcelona)'. In *La moneda de los íberos: Ilturo y los talleres layetanos*, edited by A. G. Sinner, pp. 55–71. Barcelona: Universitat de Barcelona.

Sinner, A. G. and C. Martí. 2022. 'La moneda griega en la Layetania'. In *La moneda griega en Iberia: Cecas y circulación monetaria. In memoriam Paloma Cabrera Bonet*, edited by X. Aquilué and P. P. Ripollès, pp. 91–109. Barcelona: Museu d'Arqueologia de Catalunya – Centre Iberia Graeca.

Sinner, A. G., A. Nieto-Espinet, and S. Valenzuela-Lamas. 2021. 'Same language, different diet: dynamics and rhythms of change in ancient Ilduro (Cabrera De Mar, Barcelona) based on epigraphic and faunal evidence'. *Journal of Mediterranean Archaeology* 34.2: pp. 193–224. https://doi.org/10.1558/jma.21977.

Sinner, A. G., C. Velasco, and J. Velaza. 2014. 'Una tapadera cerámica con esgrafiado hallada en Cabrera de Mar (El Maresme, Barcelona)'. *Sylloge Epigraphica Barcinonensis* 12: pp. 97–104.

Sinner, A. G. and J. Velaza. 2018. 'Epigraphy: The Palaeohispanic languages'. In *Encyclopedia of Global Archaeology*, edited by C. Smith, pp. 1–13. Cham: Springer.

Sinner, A. G. and J. Velaza (eds.) 2019. *Palaeohispanic languages and epigraphies*. Oxford: Oxford University Press.

Sivan, H. 2011. *Galla Placidia: The last Roman empress*. Oxford: Oxford University Press.

Skoglund, P. and I. Mathieson. 2018. 'Ancient genomics of modern humans: The first decade'. *Annual Review of Genomics and Human Genetics* 19: pp. 381–404. https://doi.org/10.1146/annurev-genom-083117-021749.

Slatkin, M. 2016. 'Statistical methods for analyzing ancient DNA from hominins'. *Current Opinion in Genetics & Development* 41: pp. 72–6. doi:10.1016/j.gde.2016.08.004.

Slatkin, M. and F. Racimo. 2016. 'Ancient DNA and human history'. *Proceedings of the National Academy of Sciences of the United States of America* 113(23): pp. 6380–7. https://doi.org/10.1073/pnas.1524306113.

Slon, V., C. Hopfe, C. L. Weiß, et al. 2017. 'Neandertal and Denisovan DNA from Pleistocene sediments'. *Science* 356(6338): pp. 605–8. doi:10.1126/science.aam9695.

Smith, H. 1991. 'Standards of human tooth formation and dental age assessment'. In *Advances in dental anthropology*, edited by M. A. Kelley and C. S. Larsen, pp. 143–68. New York: Wiley-Liss.

Soares, A. M. 1987. 'O teor em radiocarbono das conchas marinhas: Um indicador paleo-oceanográfico'. *Setúbal Arqueológica* 11–12: pp. 17–25.

Soares Fortes, M. L. 2008. *A xestión da auga na paisaxe romana do occidente peninsular*. Doctoral thesis, Universidad de Santiago de Compostela.

Solana, J. M. 1998. 'Ensayo demográfico de los años 155/133 aC según los datos de las fuentes escritas'. In *Italia e Hispania en la crisis de la república romana: Actas del III Congreso Hispano-Italiano (Toledo, 20–24 de septiembre de 1993)*, edited by J. Mangas Manjárres, pp. 9–32. Madrid: Universidad Complutense de Madrid.

Solin, H. and O. Salomies. 1994. *Repertorium nominum gentilium et cognominum Latinorum*. Hildesheim: Olms-Weidmann.

Speidel, W. 2007. 'Epigraphy and demography: Birth, marriage, family and death'. In *Epigraphy and the historical sciences*, edited by J. Davies and J. Wilkes, pp. 101–29. Oxford: Oxford University Press.

Spradley, M. K. and R. L. Jantz. 2011. 'Sex estimation in forensic anthropology: Skull versus postcranial elements'. *Journal of Forensic Sciences* 56(2): pp. 289–96.

Spyrou, M. A., K. I. Bos, A. Herbig, et al. 2019. 'Ancient pathogen genomics as an emerging tool for infectious disease research'. *Nature Reviews Genetics* 20: pp. 323–40. https://doi.org/10.1038/s41576-019-0119-1.

Stannard, C. and S. Ranucci. 2016. 'Late Cyrenaican bronze coin in central Italy'. In *Le monete di Cirene e della Cirenaica nel Mediterraneo. Problemi e prospettive*, edited by M. Asolati, pp. 157–90. Padua: Esedra.

Stannard, C. and A. G. Sinner. 2014. 'A central Italian 'Dionysus / Panther' coin from Cabrera de Mar (El Maresme, Barcelona), and contacts between Central Italy and Catalonia in the 2nd and 1st centuries BC'. *Saguntum* 46: pp. 159–80.

Stannard, C., A. G. Sinner, and M. Ferrante. 2019. 'Trade between Minturnae and Hispania in the Late Republic: A comparative analysis of the Minturnaean lead issues and the Spanish plomos monetiformes of the Italo-Baetican series, and the numismatic and epigraphic evidence of the trade'. *Numismatic Chronicle* 179: pp. 123–72.

Stefanile, M. 2013. 'Lead ingot cargoes from Carthago Nova to Rome: Some remarks on the presence of people from Campania in the exploitation of Iberian mines'. *Skyllis* 13(1): pp. 24–31.

Stefanile, M. 2015. 'Gentes procedentes de Campania en la explotación de las minas de Carthago Nova'. In *Phicaria: III Encuentros Internaciones del Mediterráneo: Minería y Metalurgia en el Mediterráneo y Su Periferia Oceánica*, edited by J. M. López Ballesta, pp. 170–80. Mazarrón: Universidad Popular de Mazarrón.

Stefanile, M. 2017. *Dalla Campania alle Hispaniae. L'emigrazione dalla Campania romana alle coste mediteranee della Peninsola Iberica in età tardo-repubblicana e proto-imperiale*. Naples: Università degli Studi di Napoli L'Orientale.

Steward, J. 1937. *Ancient caves of the Great Salt Lake region*. Washington: Smithsonian Institution Bureau of American Ethnology Bulletin No. 115.

Storey, G. R. 1997. 'The population of ancient Rome'. *Antiquity* 71: pp. 966–78.

Subirà, E., M. A. Galleg, and A. Malgosa. 2002. 'Dieta i societat a la Tarragona del segles I al VII dC. Anàlisi d'elements traça en les necròpolis de la quinta de Sant Rafael i de l'amfiteatre'. *Empúries: Revista de món clàssic i antiguitat tardana* 53: pp. 303–17.

Summer, W. M. 1979. 'Estimating population by analogy: An example'. In *Ethnoarchaeology: Implications of ethnography for archaeology*, edited by C. Kramer, pp. 164–74. New York: Columbia University Press.

Surovell, T. A., J. Byrd Finley, G. M. Smith, et al. 2009. 'Correcting temporal frequency distributions for taphonomic bias'. *Journal of Archaeological Science* 36: pp. 1715–24.

Susini, A., C. A. Baud, and H. J. Tochon-Danguy. 1988. 'Identification d'un traitement thermique des os Préhistoriques humans'. In *Anthropologie et histoire ou anthropologie historique. Actes des 3èmes journées anthropologiques*, edited by L. Buchet, pp. 43–76. Paris. CNRS.

Swan, V. G. 1992. 'Legio VI and its men: African legionaries in Roman Britain'. *Journal of Roman Pottery Studies* 5: pp. 1–33.

Tacoma, L. E. 2016. *Moving Romans: Migration to Rome in the Principate*. Oxford: Oxford University Press.

Taracena, B. 1941. *Carta Arqueológica de España: Soria*. Madrid: CSIC.

Taracena, B. 1949. 'Las fortificaciones y la población de la España romana'. In *IV Congreso Arqueológico del Sudeste Español. Cartagena (1948)*, pp. 421–42. Cartagena. Imprenta Provincial.

Taylor, L. R. 1961. 'Freedmen and freeborn in the epitaphs of imperial Rome'. *The American Journal of Philology* 82: pp. 113–32.

Tchernia, A. 1986. *Le vin de l'Italie romaine: Essai d' histoire economique d'apres les amphores*. Paris: École Française de Rome.

Tendero Porros, M. 2004. 'Urbanismo'. In *Iberia, Hispania, Spania: Una mirada desde Ilici*, edited by L. Abad Casal and M. S. Hernández Pérez, pp. 125–32. Alicante: Caja de Ahorros del Mediterráneo.

Thompson, E. A. 1982. *Romans and barbarians: The decline of the Western Empire*. Madison: University of Wisconsin Press.

Thompson, E. P. 1979. *Tradición, revuelta y conciencia de clase: Estudio sobre la crisis de la sociedad preindustrial*. Barcelona: Crítica.

Tierney, S. N. and J. M. Bird. 2015. 'Molecular sex identification of juvenile skeletal remains from an Irish medieval population using ancient DNA analysis'. *Journal of Archaeological Science* 62: pp. 27–38. https://doi.org/10.1016/j.jas.2015.06.016.

Tocheri, M. W., T. L. Dupras, T. Sheldrick, et al. 2005. 'Roman period fetal skeletons from Kellis, Egypt'. *International Journal of Osteoarchaeology* 15(5): pp. 326–41.

Todd, T. W. 1921. 'Age changes in the pubic bone'. *American Journal of Physical Anthropology* 4(1): pp. 1–70.

Torra, F. 2009. 'Les inscripcions ibèriques a la ciutat de Baetulo'. *Carrer dels arbres* 20: pp. 7–24.

Torres Martínez, J. F. 2011. *El Cantábrico en el Edad del Hierro*. Madrid: Real Academia de la Historia.

Torres Rodríguez, J. de. 2012. *La tierra sin límites: Territorio, sociedad e identidades en el valle medio del Tajo (S. IX–I a.C.)*. Doctoral thesis, Universidad Complutense de Madrid.

Trancho, G. J. 2010. 'Análsis antropológico de las necrópolis de cremación'. *Revista Española de Antropología Física* 31: pp. 205–32.

Trellisó, L. 2001. 'La acción del fuego sobre el cuerpo humano: La antropología física y el análisis de las cremaciones antiguas'. *Cypsela* 13: pp. 87–98.

Tremoleda, J., M. Santos, and P. Castanyer. 2016. 'Una nova fortificació d'època republicana a Empúries: Una base militar per a la conquista d'Hispània'. *Annals de l'Institut d'Estudis Empordanesos* 47: pp. 47–74.

Trincherini, P. R., P. Barbero, P. Quarati, C. Domergue, and L. Long. 2001. 'Where do the lead ingots of the Saintes-Mariesde-la-Mer wreck come from? Archaeology compared with physics'. *Archaeometry* 43: pp. 393–406.

Trincherini, P. R., C. Domergue, I. Manteca, A. Nesta, and P. Quarati. 2009. 'The identification of lead ingots from the Roman mines of Cartagena (Murcia, Spain): The role of lead isotope analysis'. *Journal of Roman Archaeology* 22(1): pp. 123–45.

Turner, C. G. and L. Lofgren. 1966. 'Household size of prehistoric western Pueblo indians'. *Journal of Anthropological Research* 22: pp. 117–32.

Ubelaker, D. H. 1989. *Human skeletal remains: Excavation, analysis, interpretation.* Washington, DC: Taraxacum.

Ubelaker, D. H. 2009. 'The forensic evaluation of burned skeletal remains: A synthesis'. *Forensic Science International* 183(1): pp. 1–5.

Untermann, J. 1990. *Monumenta Linguarum Hispanicarum III: Die Iberischen Inschriften Aus Spanien* (= *MLH* III). Wiesbaden: Dr. Ludwig Reichert Verlag.

Untermann, J. 2000. *Wörterbuch des Oskisch-Umbrischen.* Heidelberg: Universitätsverlag Winter GmbH Heidelberg.

Urbina Martínez, D. 1997. *Espacio y cultura material del Hierro II en la Mesa de Ocaña.* Doctoral thesis, Universidad Complutense de Madrid.

Urbina Martínez, D. 2000. *La Segunda edad del Hierro en el centro de la Península Ibérica. Un estudio de arqueología espacial en la mesa de Ocaña (Toledo, España).* Oxford: Archaeopress.

Urbina Martínez, D. 2007. 'El espacio y el tiempo. Sistemas de asentamiento de la Edad del Hierro en la Mesa de Ocaña'. *Zona Arqueológica* 10(1): pp. 194–217.

Urbina Martínez, D., C. Urquijo Álvarez de Toledo, and J. Morín de Pablos. 2014a. 'Madrigueras II: Un vicus en el territorio segobricense (Carrascosa del Campo), siglos V a.C. al V d.C.'. In *Los paisajes culturales en el Valle del Cigüela*, edited by J. Morín de Pablos, pp. 123–39. Madrid: Audema.

Urbina Martínez, D., C. Urquijo Álvarez de Toledo, R. de Almeida, et al. 2014b. 'Casas de Luján: Una villae romana en el ager de Segobriga (Saelices, Cuenca) siglos I–III d.C.'. In *Los paisajes culturales en el Valle del Cigüela*, edited by J. Morín de Pablos, pp. 395–423. Madrid: Audema.

Uribe, P. 2015. *La arquitectura doméstica urbana romana en el valle medio del Ebro (siglos II a.C.-III p.C.).* Bordeaux: Aquitania.

Valdiosera, C., T. Günther, J. C. Vera-Rodríguez, et al. 2018. 'Four millennia of Iberian biomolecular prehistory illustrate the impact of prehistoric migrations at the far end of Eurasia'. *Proceedings of the National Academy of Sciences of the United States of America* 115(13): pp. 3428–33. https://doi.org/10.1073/pnas.1717762115.

Valor, J. and J. Garibo. 2002. 'Aroximación al cómputo poblacional de la comarca de Requena-Utiel en época ibérica'. *Saguntum* 34: pp. 105–14.

Vaquerizo, D. 2014. 'Mortes singulares y miedo a los muertos en el mundo romano: Reflexiones, indicios, escatología'. In *Religiosidad, rituales y prácticas mágicas en los mosaicos romanos*, edited by M. L. Neira Jiménez, pp. 211–46. Madrid: Creaciones Vincent Gabrielle.

Vázquez Espinar, A. 2017. *El proceso de salut-enfermedad-atención y muerte en la mujer romana: Estudio antropológico, arqueológico y etnohistórico en la población de Augusta Emerita.* Doctoral thesis, Departament de Psicología y Antropología, Universidad de Extremadura.

Vega Avelaira, T., S. Ferrer Sierra, and A. Rodríguez Colmenero. 2009. 'Los principia del campamento romano de Aquae Querquennae (Portoquintela, Baños de Bande, prov. de Ourense. España)'. In *Limes XX Congreso International de estudios sobre la frontera romana* (= *Limes XX Roman Frontier Studies* [*Anejos de Gladius*, 13]), edited by A. Morillo Cerdán, N. Hanel, and E. Martín, pp. 465–80. Madrid: Consejo Superior de Investigacions Científicas: Polifemo.

Velaza Frías, J. 2009. 'Epigrafía y literacy paleohispánica en territorio vascón: notas para un balance provisional', *Palaeohispanica* 9: 611–22.

Velaza, J. 2017. 'Imagen y texto en la epigrafía ibérica'. *Palaeohispanica* 17: pp. 235–48.

Velaza, J. 2018. 'Epigrafía ibérica sobre soporte pétreo: Origen y evolución'. In *El nacimiento de las culturas epigráficas en el occidente mediterráneo*, edited by F. Beltrán and B. Díaz, pp. 169–83. Madrid: CSIC.

Velaza, J. 2021. '¿Dos iberos en Montecassino?' In *Miscellanea di studi epigrafici per Gianfranco Paci*, edited by S. Antolini and S. M. Marengo, pp. 649–54. Tivoli: Edizioni Tored.

Vergara Quinter, M. C. 2007. 'Disease and illness. Distinctions between professional and popular ideas of sickness'. *Culture Medicine and Psychiatry* 1977: pp. 9–23.

Verhagen, P. 2019. 'Modelling the dynamics of demography in the Dutch Romna Limes zone: A revised model'. In *Finding the limits of the limes: Modelling demography, economy and transport on the edge of the Roman Empire*, edited by P. Verhagen, J. Joyce, and M. Groenhuijzen, pp. 43–59. Cham: Springer International Publishing.

Vetter, E. 1953. *Handbuch der Italischen Dialekte*. Heidelberg: Winter Verlag.

Vidal, J. M. and M. L. González. 2018. 'Asturica Augusta: Actualización de su urbanismo a la luz de las excavaciones recientes'. In *El urbanismo de las ciudades del valle del Duero*, edited by S. Martínez, S. Yaguas, and L. J. Municio, pp. 273–98. Segovia: Asociación de Amigos del Museo de Segovia.

Vigil-Escalera, A. 2007. 'Granjas y aldeas altomedievale al Norte de Toledo (450–800 dC)'. *Archivo Español de Arqueología* 80: pp. 239–84.

Vilaseca, A. and G. Foguet. 1995. 'Els enterraments del carrer Prat de la Riba/Ramon y Cajal: Un nou sector excavat de la necropolis del Francolí'. *Citerior* 1: pp. 151–71.

Villa Valdés, A. 2000. 'Saunas castreñas en Asturias'. In *II Coloquio Internacional de Arqueología en Gijón: Termas romanas en el Occidente del Imperio—Gijón 1999*, edited by F. Ochoa and G. Entero, pp. 97–114. Gijón: VTP Editorial.

Villa Valdés, A. 2007a. 'Mil años de poblados fortificados en Asturias (siglos IX a.C.–II d.C.)'. In *Astures y romanos: nuevas perspectivas*, edited by J. A. Fernández-Tresguerres Velasco, pp. 27–60. Oviedo: Real Instituto de Estudios Asturianos.

Villa Valdés, A. 2007b. 'El Chao Samartín (Grandas de Salime, Asturias) y el paisaje fortificado en la Asturias protohistórica'. In *Paisajes fortificados de la Edad del Hierro*, edited by L. Berrocal-Rangel and P. Moret, pp. 191–212. Madrid: Real Academia de la Historia.

Villa Valdés, A. 2009. '¿De aldea fortificada a Caput Civitatis? Tradición y ruptura en una Comunidad Castreña del siglo I D.C.: El Poblado de Chao Samartín (Grandas de Salime, Asturias)'. *CuPAUAM* 35: pp. 7–26.

Villa Valdés, A. 2013. 'El Castro de Coaña: Un poblado fortificado en los albores de la historia de Asturias'. In *De Neandertales a Albiones: Cuatro lugares esenciales en la prehistoria de Asturias*, edited by P. Arias Cabal, M. de Blas Cortina, M. de la Rasilla Vives, et al., pp. 139–87. Oviedo: Real Instituto de Estudios Asturianos.

Villalaín Blanco, J. 2007. '¿Qué es la paleopatología?' *Jano: Medicina y humanidades* 1646: pp. 45–9.

Villalba-Mouco, V., C. Oliart, C. Rihuete-Herrada, et al. 2021. 'Genomic transformation and social organization during the Copper Age-Bronze Age transition in southern Iberia'. *Science Advances* 7(47): eabi7038. doi:10.1126/sciadv.abi7038.

Villalba-Mouco, V., C. Oliart, C. Rihuete-Herrada, et al. 2022. 'Kinship practices in the early state El Argar society from Bronze Age Iberia'. *Scientific Reports* 12(1): 22415. doi:10.1038/s41598-022-25975-9.

Villalón, J. 2019. *Movilidad y permanencia en época romana en el conventus Cluniensis: Los paradigmas de Clunia Sulpicia, Uxama Argaela, Argenomescon y Vadinia*. Doctoral thesis, Universidad de Cantabria.

Villaronga, L. 2002. 'Troballa del Francolí: Testimoni per a la datació del denari ibèric de Kes'. *Acta Numismàtica* 32: pp. 29–43.

Villotte, S., D. Castex, V. Couallier, et al. 2010. 'Enthesopathies as occupational stress markers: Evidence from the upper limb'. *American Journal of Physical Anthropology* 142: pp. 224–34.

Vivar Lombarte, G. 2016. *Illa Pedrosa: Comerç marítim i xarxes de redistribució en època tardorepublicana al Mediterrani centreoccidental.* Girona: Centre d'Arqueologia Subaquàtica de Catalunya.

Vizcaino, J. 1999. 'Transformaciones del urbanismo tardoantiguo en Cartagena: El caso de los vertederos'. *AnMurcia* 15: pp. 87–98.

Vlak, D., M. Roksandic, and M. A. Schillaci. 2008. 'Greater sciatic notch as a sex indicator in juveniles'. *American Journal of Physical Anthropology* 137(3): pp. 309–15. https://doi.org/10.1002/ajpa.20875.

Voland, E. 1998. 'Evolutionary ecology of human reproduction'. *Annual Review of Anthropology* 27: pp. 347–74.

Voland, E. 2000. 'Contributions of family reconstitution studies to evolutionary reproductive ecology'. *Evolutionary Anthropology* 9: pp. 134–46.

Walker, P. L. 2008. 'Sexing skulls using discriminant function analysis of visually assessed traits'. *American Journal of Physical Anthropology* 136(1): pp. 39–50. https://doi.org/10.1002/ajpa.20776.

Walker, P. L., P. Dean, and P. Shapiro. 1988. 'Age and sex biases in the preservation of human skeletal remains'. *American Journal of Physical Anthropology* 76: pp. 183–8.

Wallace-Hadrill, A. 1988. 'The social structure of the Roman house'. *Papers of the British School at Rome* 56: pp. 43–97.

Wallace-Hadrill, A. 1994. *Houses and society in Pompeii and Herculaneum.* Princeton: Princeton University Press.

Wallace-Hadrill, A. 2019. 'Counting Pompeians'. In *Uomini, istituzioni, mercati: Studi di storia per Elio Lo Cascio*, edited by M. Maiuro, G. D. Merola, M. de Nardis, et al., pp. 173–81. Bari: Edipuglia.

Watson, G. R. 1969. *The Roman soldier.* London: Thames & Hudson.

Watts, W. J. 1973. 'Ovid, the law and Roman society on abortion'. *Acta Classica* 16: pp. 89–101.

Weaver, D. S. 1980. 'Sex differences in the ilia of a known sex and age sample of fetal and infant skeletons'. *American Journal of Physical Anthropology* 52(2): pp. 191–5.

Webb, P. A. O. and J. M. Suchey. 1985. 'Epiphyseal union of the anterior iliac crest and medial clavicle in a modern multiracial sample of American males and females'. *American Journal of Physical Anthropology* 68(4): pp. 457–66. https://doi.org/10.1002/ajpa.1330680402.

Wells, C. 1960. 'A study of cremation'. *Antiquity* 34(133): pp. 29–37.

Wells, C. 1998. 'Celibate soldiers: Augustus and the army'. *American Journal of Ancient History* 41(2): pp. 180–90.

Wells, P. S. 1984. *Farms, villages and cities: Commerce and urban origins in late prehistoric Europe.* Ithaca: Cornell University Press.

Wiedemann, T. 1989. *Adults and children in the Roman Empire.* New Haven: Yale University Press.

Wilk, R. R. and W. L. Rathje. 1981. 'Household archaeology'. *American Behavioral Scientist* 25: pp. 617–39.

Williams, D. F. and C. Carreras. 1995. 'North African amphorae in Roman Britain: A re-appraisal'. *Britannia* 26: pp. 231–52.

Wilson, A. I. 2008. 'Site recovery rates and the ancient population of the Biferno valley'. In *Archaeology and landscape: Central Italy. Papers in Memory of John A. Lloyd*, edited by A. Faustoferri and G. Lock, pp. 233–53. Oxford: Oxford University School of Archaeology.

Wilson, A. I. 2011. 'City sizes and urbanisation in the Roman Empire'. In *Settlement, urbanization, and population*, edited by A. Bowman and A. Wilson, pp. 161–95. Oxford: Oxford University Press.

Wilson, A. J. N. 1966. *Emigration from Italy in the Republican age of Rome*. Manchester: Manchester University Press.

Witcher, R. 2005. 'The extended metropolis: Urbs, suburbium and population'. *Journal of Roman Archaeology* 18: pp. 120–38.

Witcher, R. E. 2008a. 'Regional field survey and the demography of Roman Italy'. In *People, land and politics: Demographic developments and the transformation of Roman Italy, 300 BC–AD 14*, edited by L. de Ligt and S. Northwood, pp. 273–303. Leiden: Brill.

Witcher, R. E. 2008b. '(Re)surveying Mediterranean rural landscapes: GIS and legacy survey data'. *Internet Archaeology* 24. https://doi.org/10.11141/ia.24.2.

Witcher, R. E. 2011. 'Missing persons? Models of Mediterranean survey and ancient populations'. In *Settlement, urbanisation and population*, edited by A. Bowman and A. Wilson, pp. 36–75. Oxford: Oxford University Press.

Woolf, G. 1998. *Becoming Roman: The origins of provincial civilization in Gaul*. Cambridge: Cambridge University Press.

Woolf, G. 2016. 'Movers and stayers'. In *Migration and mobility in the early Roman Empire*, edited by L. de Ligt and L. E. Tacoma, pp. 438–61. Leiden: Brill.

World Health Organization (WHO). 2020. *Stillbirth rate data by WHO Region. Global Health Observatory Data Repository*.

Zamora, D. 2006–7. *L'oppidum de Burriac: Centre del poder polític de la Laietània ibérica*. Mataró: Museu de Mataró.

Zamora López, J. A. 2005. 'La práctica de escribir entre los primeros fenicios peninsulares y la introducción de la escritura entre los pueblos paleohispánicos'. *Palaeohispanica* 5: pp. 155–92.

Zeberg, H. and S. Pääbo. 2021. 'A genomic region associated with protection against severe COVID-19 is inherited from Neandertals'. *Proceedings of the National Academy of Sciences of the United States of America* 118(9): e2026309118. doi:10.1073/pnas.2026309118.

Zevi, F. 1973. 'P. Lucilio Gamala *senior* e i "quattro tempietti" di Ostia'. *MEFRA* 85: pp. 554–81.

Zhang, D., H. Xia, F. Chen, et al. 2020. 'Denisovan DNA in Late Pleistocene sediments from Baishiya Karst Cave on the Tibetan Plateau'. *Science* 370(6516): pp. 584–7. doi:10.1126/science.abb6320.

Zipf, G. K. 1949. *Human behavior and the principle of least effort: An introduction to human ecology*. Cambridge: Addison-Wesley.

Zorn, J. 1994. 'Estimating the population size of ancient settlements: Methods, problems, solutions, and a case study'. *Bulletin of the American Schools of Oriental Research* 295: pp. 31–48.

# Index

*Note*: Tables and figures are indicated by an italic "*t*" and "*f*", respectively, following the page number.

Because the index has been created to work across multiple formats, indexed terms for which a page range is given (e.g. 52–53, 66–70, etc.) may occasionally appear only on some, but not all, of the pages within the range.